THE WINE REGIONS
OF AUSTRALIA

JOHN BEESTON

THE WINE REGIONS
OF AUSTRALIA

ALLEN & UNWIN

To my dear wife Lynn, for her patience and loving support
during the completion of this book

Copyright © John Beeston 1999
Maps by Mapgraphics Pty Ltd

First published in 1999
Allen & Unwin
9 Atchison Street, St Leonards NSW 1590 Australia
Phone: (61 2) 8425 0100
Fax: (61 2) 9906 2218
E-mail: frontdesk@allen-unwin.com.au
Web: http://www.allen-unwin.com.au

National Library of Australia
Cataloguing-in-Publication entry:

Beeston, John.
  Wine regions of Australia.

  Bibliography.
  Includes index.
  ISBN 1 86448 641 4.
  1. Wine and wine making – Australia. 2. Wine industry –
  Australia. 3. Wine and wine making – Australia –
  Directories. I. Title.

641.220994

Set in 10/12 pt Goudy by Midland Typesetters
Printed and bound by Griffin Press

10 9 8 7 6 5 4 3 2 1

❧ CONTENTS

❧ PREFACE

Australia's wine boom, for such it has been since the re-awakening of our export markets in the mid 1980s, has produced a surge of new vineyard areas in addition to our traditional winegrowing areas. For the first time in our vinous history, treaty obligations have made it necessary to define wine zones, regions and sub-regions, converting once vague areas into strictly delineated locations. Such boundary definition, together with the Label Integrity Program instituted some years ago, should ensure the authenticity of origin of our wines and be of great assistance to the discerning consumer of Australian whites and reds.

Over 50 maps of zones, regions, sub-regions and other areas, which will in the course of time achieve regional or sub-regional status, have been included. The maps of zones, regions and sub-regions are based, subject to changes of scale to accommodate the pages of this book, on the official maps used to delineate the boundaries of such areas.

The approach to defining these areas has been interesting. Wine zones have been delineated purely according to 'political' boundaries. Some wine zones in remote parts of Australia presently possess no vines and probably never will. These zones say nothing about the suitability of their vast expanses of territory for vines. The smaller wine regions, however, do make certain statements about Australian wine and the sub-regions even more. It is only natural that all winegrowing areas have sought to encompass and involve all the growers and makers within their 'region'. Thus it is quite understandable that some regional winegrowing associations have adopted a 'political' approach merely following municipal boundaries. Others, however, have looked more deeply into regionality regarding altitude as an important unifying factor. Thus both altitude and municipal limits have been taken into account. None as yet (even Coonawarra, and it has not yet been granted final regional status) has relied solely on uniqueness of soil type as the basis of extent of their region or sub-region. However, even as I write, this consideration is arising in many sub-regions and will surely arise more often in the future.

Thus I have dealt with every wine region and sub-region registered, or in the process of being registered, as at 31 March 1999. I have largely excluded reviews of individual wines, as there is no place for them in a book of this kind, but a very few have been included as being typical of their particular regional style. There are many vineyards and wineries included, both huge and minute, but I can make no claim to be all-inclusive. No writer, however assiduous, ever can. There are winegrowers and makers who wish to keep their activities entirely to themselves, making no response to letters, faxes or phone calls. They are entitled to their privacy, however frustrating it may be to an intrusive author. What I hope I have achieved is not only a valuable vineyard guide for those wine enthusiasts who love to travel to both our new and old vineyard areas to appreciate the great variety of wines found there. I also hope this work will be of some interest to those who may one day, in however large or small a way, become winegrowers themselves and also to those enthusiastic wine and vine explorers who have already become vignerons within the vast and still largely unknown vineland that is Australia.

❦ LIST OF MAPS

🍇 A note on the maps

Wineries and vineyards shown on the maps have cellar door sales outlets open during hours specified or by appointment, or they are vineyards of importance. Wineries or vineyards not shown on the maps either do not have cellar door sales or are very small.

❧ INTRODUCTION: APPELLATION AUSTRALIA AND GEOGRAPHIC INDICATIONS

In the mid-1980s, Australia's wine exports showed the first signs of awakening from a 40-year slumber. As a result, they began to attract the unfavourable attention of European Commission regulators who were keen to protect depressed and oversupplied local markets from foreign competition and to help drain an already flooded European wine lake. They were only too anxious to erect tariff barriers as Australia's winemaking practices differed in a number of technical respects from those of the Europeans.

In 1987, Australia therefore began—at first informally through the sole efforts of Professor Terry Lee, at that time of the Australian Wine Research Institute—what proved to be far-sighted negotiations with the European Commission. They were far-sighted because the European Commission now represents over 350 million people and only the year before (30 June 1986) Australia's wine exports had exceeded 10 million litres for the first time since 1946/7 and were to increase twelvefold in the ensuing eight years. The talks soon became formalised as bilateral Australia–EC negotiations. After nearly six years of complex discussions in both Canberra and Brussels concerning wine and food law, trade practices, trademarks, the Australian Constitution and the Treaty of Rome, the Agreement was initialled in late 1992 and came into effect on 1 March 1994.

The major provisions of the Agreement can be summarised as follows. Australia agreed to protect all European geographical indications and traditional expressions as set out in Annex II of the Agreement except for a few geographic and traditional expressions which Australia either agreed to phase out by certain dates or negotiate a phase-out period by 31 December 1997. This was a very real concession because Australian winemakers and marketers relied quite heavily on generic styles such as 'Chablis' to describe cheap white blends. In return for this concession:

1 The EC provided exemptions from EC wine law for the following winemaking practices for wines originating in Australia:
   a the addition of erythorbate
   b the minimum acidity level
   c botrytised and late harvest wines with a total alcohol content higher than 15%
   d maximum limits for the addition of several specified processing aids
   e the extent to which the initial acidity can be raised by acid addition
   f a five-year exemption on the use of cation exchange
2 The number of analyses required for the VI-1 certificate (a certificate stating that non-EC wines comply with EC wine regulations and which must accompany non-EC wines into the EC) decreased from eight to three—alcohol, titratable acidity and sulfur dioxide—and for red wines malvidin diglucoside.
3 The EC allowed an Australian wine to name up to five grape varieties on one

1

label and to be a blend of wines from up to three geographical indications. (Previously an Australian wine had to come from a single geographical indication and could be described with no more than two varieties on the label from which the wine had to be entirely made.)

4 Australian geographical indications and traditional expressions were to be protected within the EC.

Because of difficulties encountered with the National Food Authority in the revision of the Wine Standards P4 and P6 (winemaking standards and codes of practice), in which the negotiating team had hoped to embody the provisions of the EC Agreement, the team was obliged to suggest to the Government that the *Australian Wine and Brandy Corporation Act 1980* be amended in such a way as to give effect to the provisions of the Agreement.

The amendments which came into force on 1 January 1994:

1 provided for the implementation of the Agreement
2 defined 'wine'
3 established the Register of Protected Names
4 established the Geographical Indications Committee
5 enabled the Australian Wine and Brandy Corporation (AWBC) to write regulations in respect of the labelling of wine and oenological practices and processes.

As a result, Australia's wine law as to the manufacture and labelling of wine in Australia and for export is now embodied in the AWBC Act and Regulations while other relevant sections of wine law are contained in the Food Acts of the states and territories, in particular Standard A16—processing aids, Standard P4—wine, sparkling wine and fortified wine, Standard P5—alcoholic beverages not elsewhere standardised, Standard P6—wine products and Standard S1—miscellaneous foods. Embodied in the Register were all the geographical indications for wine of the European Union as listed in Annex II of the Agreement and as regards Australia the terms 'Australia', 'Australian' and the names of each state and internal territory. In January 1994, as a result of these amendments, the Geographical Indications Committee was constituted and later that year commenced the formulation of the first official wine map of Australia.

Issued on 7 February 1995, the first of the Committee's 'final determinations' consisted of the geographical indication South Eastern Australia (an indication that includes most of the cheaper mass blends of Australian red and white wines) and officially delimited the wine 'zones' of Victoria and New South Wales. Since then the whole of Australia has been divided into wine zones as follows:

1 Victoria: Gippsland; Central Victoria; North East Victoria; North West Victoria; Port Phillip and Western Victoria
2 New South Wales: Big Rivers; Western Plains; Northern Slopes; Northern Rivers; Hunter Valley; South Coast; Central Ranges and Southern New South Wales
3 Tasmania (whole of state)
4 Northern Territory (whole of territory)
5 Queensland (whole of state, though the Granite Belt may at some future stage apply for registration as a region)

AUSTRALIAN WINE ZONES

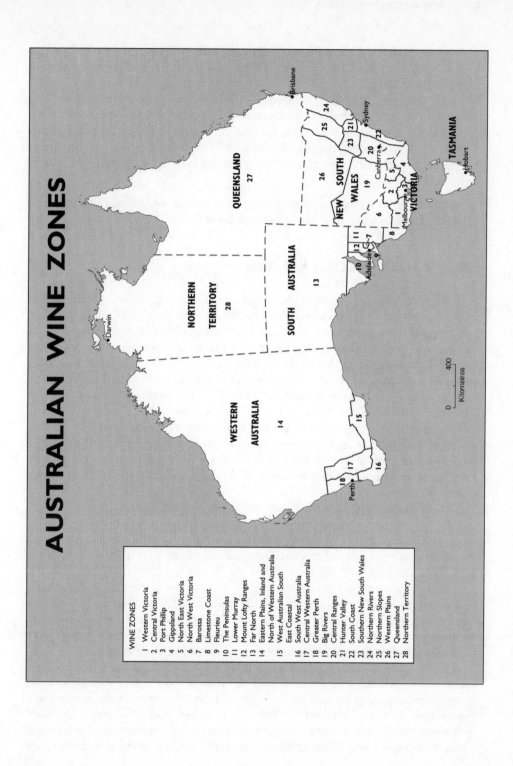

WINE ZONES

1 Western Victoria
2 Central Victoria
3 Port Phillip
4 Gippsland
5 North East Victoria
6 North West Victoria
7 Barossa
8 Limestone Coast
9 Fleurieu
10 The Peninsulas
11 Lower Murray
12 Mount Lofty Ranges
13 Far North
14 Eastern Plains, Inland and
    North of Western Australia
15 West Australian South
    East Coastal
16 South West Australia
17 Central Western Australia
18 Greater Perth
19 Big Rivers
20 Central Ranges
21 Hunter Valley
22 South Coast
23 Southern New South Wales
24 Northern Rivers
25 Northern Slopes
26 Western Plains
27 Queensland
28 Northern Territory

6 Western Australia: Eastern Plains, Inland and North of Western Australia; Western Australia South East Coastal; South Western Australia; Central Western Australia and Greater Perth

7 South Australia: Adelaide, a Superzone which includes the zones Mount Lofty Ranges, Barossa and Fleurieu and suburban Adelaide and the Adelaide Plains: Limestone Coast; Lower Murray; Far North; The Peninsulas (York and Eyre); Mount Lofty Ranges; Barossa; Fleurieu. Winemakers from any of the zones constituting the Superzone may use the name Adelaide instead of their local zonal name, if they so wish.

Regionalisation and sub-regionalisation will continue as Australia discovers and explores its special wine areas in the years to come.

MANDATORY RECORD KEEPING

Soon after the commencement of the negotiations for the EC/Australia Wine Agreement, the Australian wine industry in consultation with the AWBC, introduced its Label Integrity Program to come into force from vintage 1990. LIP, as it became known, was designed to put teeth into wine laws which, though uniform among the Australian states, had been previously left to the individual states to enforce. Importantly, verification of compliance with and enforcement of LIP was to be vested in the AWBC.

The earlier laws had concerned grape variety, area of origin and vintage. In brief, they required that, if the label of a wine included any allusion to grape variety, locality of growth or year of vintage, the wine must contain at least 80% of that variety and must be at least 80% from that locality and 95% of the year of vintage. (From vintage 1994, in line with the EC/Australia Wine Agreement, the percentages for grape varieties and localities were increased to 85% and lowered to 85% in respect of vintage content.)

Thus authorised, the AWBC now insists on the keeping of standard winery records and may audit, at any time, claims made relating to grape variety, area of origin and vintage. It can do this by checking winery records made at four key points in the winemaking and sales process. These are the winery weighbridge where grapes are bought and received; the cellar where the grapes are converted into wine; the sales desk where inter-company sales and purchases take place; and the wholesale desk where finished wine leaves the cellar as a product. The product has either a label stating a grape variety or varieties, the region of origin and year of vintage or an invoice stating those details if the wine has been sold in bulk. Such records must be made within three months of the occurrence of any of these events.

The standard system of record keeping, or 'universal recording system' as it is known by the AWBC, insists that weighbridge records show year of vintage, location of vineyard (origin), grape variety, tonnage and name of grower. In the winery itself, records must indicate the identity of the wine produced from those grapes identified at the weighbridge, the volume of wine made from them, consolidations of identical wines, blendings of non-identical wines, identity of ensuing products and records of release of the finished wine. In this way, the wine retains its official identity acquired at the weighbridge, which it can lose if it is destined to be a generic (such as chablis) or a style (such as dry red). It should be noted that such 'generics' are being phased out because of the EC/Australia Wine Agreement. If the wine is required to be sold in bulk or in unlabelled bottles (cleanskin) in an inter-company transaction, the records must specify the identity, volume and purchaser of such bulk or cleanskin wine and the source, identity and volume of wines brought in from other wineries to form the whole or part of any wine with a vintage, varietal or region of origin claim. Finally, if the wine is destined for the retail market, when bottled, labelled and packaged, its records must show the total production of a wine carrying vintage, variety and region of origin claims, stocks of wine carrying such claims and sales of all such wines.

Thus it has become possible for an auditor not only to check the legitimacy of all vintage, variety and region of origin claims made by winemakers but to go further and check the wines of any company or group of companies, or even the varietal wines of any particular region. Needless to say there are substantial penalties for infraction, not the least of which, in a time of buoyant export sales, is the cancellation of export approvals and the subsequent recall of offending wines.

AUSTRALIAN REGION OF ORIGIN

The Australian wine industry has had few wine scandals. In the past the industry was never important enough in national economic terms. Now, as its economic worth increases, it has realised that it cannot afford them. The occasional infractions of winemaking regulations have been dealt with according to law, the offenders punished and the industry has returned to normality. Though the recent amendments to Australian wine law have considerably extended the control of the Australian Wine and Brandy Corporation, it remains a self-policing industry and takes pride not only in its adherence to existing legal standards but also in its levels of quality, which have always been well above ordinary legal requirements.

This has not always been the case in Europe, where periodic wine scandals led to the scheme Appellation d'Origine Controlée (AOC) being introduced to French law during the first three decades of the twentieth century. This has resulted in governmental control of virtually every aspect of the French industry, from the soil in which the vines are planted, the types of vines that may be planted, the manner of pruning them, maximum grape yields, minimum alcoholic strengths and even the manner in which the finished wines are invoiced to clients. Similar legislation has followed in all the leading wine-producing countries of the European Union. As a result, wine fraud in Europe is now much more difficult, but it has occurred as recently as 1974 in Bordeaux. In some cases, appellation control is therefore equated mistakenly with a guarantee of the quality of a wine, whereas it is often merely a guarantee of origin and of conformity with the standards set out for its appellation. Though tasting does occur in some regions of Europe before a wine can be granted a controlled appellation, what the tasters are seeking is not necessarily quality but typicity—that it has the regional and varietal characters of the other wines of its appellation in that year, be they good or bad. The rules have resulted in a general conservatism pervading the European industry and have accounted in part for the marketing success of Australian and other New World (i.e. non-European) wines in Europe in the past decade.

Not surprisingly, Australian winemakers regard the European system as stultifying and as stifling individual initiative and have been firmly against the introduction of similar schemes to Australia—a view that is now being supported by many younger European winemakers. Due therefore to the quality of New World wines and the strength of their marketing, European wine authorities have been forced to recognise the existence of 'international' grape varieties, such as cabernet sauvignon and chardonnay, and to allow their inclusion on wine labels which were previously blessed only with the name of an obscure village or region. It must, however, be admitted that in most areas of Australia wines are not tasted unless they are intended for export and then only on the basic levels of soundness and marketability. Australian wine legislators have wisely left wine quality to be determined by its winemakers and its acceptance or otherwise to be decided by the wine drinkers of the world.

Definitions of zones, regions and sub-regions

Zone: an area of land that (a) may comprise one or more regions, or (b) may reasonably be regarded as a zone.

Region: an area within a zone or zones consisting of a minimum of five vineyards of at least five hectares each without common ownership and producing at least 500 tonnes.

Sub-region: an area within a region of a minimum of five vineyards of at least five hectares each without common ownership and producing at least 500 tonnes. There must also of course be a factor or factors common to the sub-region which distinguish it from the rest of the region.

These definitions are not intended to encourage over-production, which an average of 20 tonnes per hectare might otherwise suggest, but to ensure 'critical mass' and the economic survival of the region and/or sub-region.

Within the above formulae, the identification of regions and sub-regions has been largely (and wisely) left to the winegrowers themselves. Their various professional organisations have adopted various approaches to these boundaries. Some quite conservatively have adopted municipal boundaries or, in the case of Margaret River, a line of longitude. Others more imaginatively, and relevantly, have used contours of altitude, above or below which the most favoured vine sites for the characteristic wines of their region or sub-region have been proved to exist, for example, the region of Sunbury and the sub-region of Broke-Fordwich. Of course this approach is only possible where there has been historical experience of the quality of certain wines. The more conservative approach is understandable where the wine region is comparatively new and unproved. As for sub-regions, many more common denominators of altitudes and soil types will need to be seen before their existence can be positively justified.

SOME COMPULSORY VITICULTURE

Climate is of course critical to the success or failure of viticulture in any region. Yet prior to the work of RE Smart and PR Dry (*Viticulture*, vol. II), climate as a factor in determining the suitability of a region for viticulture had been defined in little more than degree days which, though useful indicators of heat, do not give a full picture of climate. Smart and Dry chose to paint climate in much greater detail and broader colour, delimiting four important climatic factors: temperature, aridity, relative humidity and sunshine hours. In his own state of Western Australia, John Gladstones, another eminent research scientist, has also made fundamental contributions to viticultural knowledge in the past 35 years. Gladstones' *Viticulture and Environment* is essential reading for any viticultural professional today. In the last decade the whole climatic picture has become much clearer and the whole Australian wine industry owes a considerable debt of gratitude to these researchers.

Throughout this book climatic details of regions are coded as follows. These are basically as defined by Dry and Smart in Chapter 2 of *Viticulture* (edited by Coome and Dry).

MJT (Mean January Temperature) is the mean temperature of Australia's warmest month, which correlates well with degree days.

MAR (Mean Annual Range) is the difference between the Mean January Temperature and the Mean July Temperature (the coldest month). It is a measure of 'continentality' of a region and, if it is higher than another region with the same MJT, means that spring and autumn temperatures will be lower, signifying slower development in spring and ripening in autumn.

HDD (Heat Degree Days) are calculated by taking the mean temperature of months during the growing season in degrees Celsius, subtracting 10°C (below which the vine does not grow) and multiplying by the number of days in the months of the growing season. The growing season is usually October to April in cooler areas, but there seems no good reason why, in warmer areas, that period should not be September to March or—as occasionally happens in benign maritime regions such as Margaret River—July to April.

AR (Annual Rainfall) is given in millimetres and where such data are available the October–April growing season rainfall is listed. If another period applies, that period is specified in the particular regional details given.

RH (Relative Humidity) is the measure of the dryness or dampness of the climate taken (by Smart and Dry) as at 9am approximating the daily mean figure of relative humidity in January or over the growing season. Low humidity accelerates the loss of water from the vine by evapo-transpiration while high humidity slows this process but increases the incidence of some fungal diseases. (Gladstones' relative humidity takes this figure at 3pm, when humidity is likely to be at its lowest for any particular day.)

AI (Aridity Index). It is acknowledged that mature vineyards lose moisture at about half the rate as measured by a Class A pan evaporimeter. Irrigation water requirements can therefore be calculated from month to month by subtracting the millimetres of natural rainfall from half of the millimetres of Class A pan evaporation and totalling the result during the growing season. Dry and Smart specify the season as being from October to March but it can be extended over a longer, slower growing season if necessary.

SH (Sunshine Hours) are the number of bright sunshine hours averaged daily, again from October to March or such longer period of the growing season.

Gladstones (in *Viticulture and Environment* p. 8), however, considers the most important factor in ripening in practice is the mean temperature of the ripening month. He lists three key elements of ripening: (a) loss of malic acid, (b) accumulation of sugar, and (c) the most critical of all, but not necessarily happening at the same time as the preceding two elements—'physiological' or 'flavour' ripening. For high quality table wines, his research points to a mean temperature of just 20°C, as the optimum for 'flavour' ripening, as indeed it seems to be for vine growth, bud formation, flowering and early fruit development.

CLIMATE, SOILS AND VITICULTURE

If local climatic conditions are too cold, too hot, too wet or too arid, the vine will not thrive. So before soil and viticulture are examined, it is necessary to discuss climate. The French use their word *climat* in two senses. They use it to refer to climate as it is understood in English. They also use it as an extension of the word to mean vineyard, which includes the whole raft of factors that influence the growth of the vine and the ripening of its grapes—for they contend that the great difference between the best wines of France and those of the rest of the world, especially the New World, is that their best wines enjoy incomparable *climats*.

Australian viticultural history is short by world standards. Our early settlers often brought grapevines merely to plant as an alternative crop on land they had never even seen. They certainly had little time to study the optimal climate for the varieties planted. They simply learnt day by day, as the vines did or did not flourish. Today the situation is entirely different. There are meteorological records going back many years for many areas. Even a century ago, a Victorian Royal Commission divided that state, then a colony, into three viticultural areas based primarily on climate. About 50 years ago, two eminent Californian viticulturists, Amerine and Winkler, evolved a system of classifying Californian vineyard areas into five regions based on temperature summation through their growing season (April to October). Such summation is measured in degree days and is at best only a general measure of the suitability of an area for any particular grape varieties or indeed wine styles. This system is now considered too simplistic as it neglects many other important meteorological factors which influence a vineyard and the ripening of its fruit, such as frost risk, frequency of rainfall, totality of sunshine hours, prevailing winds at critical times of the season and so on.

Continentality

'Continentality' is often considered a high quality wine factor in that it seems to encourage delicate aromas, fine fruit flavours and the retention of natural acidity, as espoused by Smart and Dry. However, some viticulturists are not convinced, stating that, although continental-type climates have great potential for quality, such potential is often not realised because 'continental' vintages are 'notoriously variable'. As Gladstones points out, Burgundy certainly has a 'continental' climate and its best vintages are characterised by two crucial factors—'a warm, sunny spring' to encourage early development and 'high mid-summer temperatures and sunshine hours'. The next most important factor is sunshine in August and to a lesser extent thereafter. Temperatures during the ripening period, commonly August to September, whether high or low, had virtually no relationship to the quality of the vintage.

Continentality, however, has its advantages. It increases winter dormancy in vines with a correspondingly longer pruning season. In some maritime Australian vineyard sites, such as Margaret River, budburst sometimes occurs in July, resulting in a far longer and therefore more risky development period for the vine and dominance by a cane's terminal shoots with little intermediate budburst. Such canes—often of 'continental' varieties such as traminer, riesling and chardonnay—are very prone to damage by high winds and heavy rain. Continentality on the other hand, with its more sudden onset of warmer weather, results in a more even budburst and subsequent cane development. Continentality and its extreme summer heat can also reduce berry size. This can give a high skin to pulp ratio with attendant better colour extraction and flavour concentration although, as Gladstones suggests, there are maritime viticultural areas which often have summers hot enough to achieve this. Of course, smaller berry size may come at the price of less quantity, though perhaps higher quality, in wine.

Casual temperature variability

If continentality (MAR) is a function of the difference between Mean January Temperature and Mean July Temperature, then, beyond the range of anticipated seasonal fluctuations, casual temperature variability can also cause severe problems. At its coolest, in 'continental' vineyards, it can cause a failure of budburst in spring or a failure to ripen the crop in autumn. It can also cause frosts which, if severe enough in winter (though rarely ever in Australia), can cause the death of vines. Spring frosts can cause havoc in young shoots and their potential crop, whereas frosts in autumn will certainly 'freeze' the ripening. Even in maritime areas where vineyards are within 5 kilometres of the sea, the still, cold nights following a dry spell can cause a damaging frost.

At its warmest and accompanied by high winds and low relative humidity, temperature variability can cause bushfires with attendant severe damage to vineyards. Even if a bushfire does not occur, bunches and berries, especially of red varieties at the time of veraison, may be exposed to sun damage. Wine made from such fruit may suffer from 'off' aromas and flavours. Whether it be heat or cold, the chemistry of the vine prefers equability of temperature.

Sunshine hours

These of course are an index of solar radiation, referring to the number of sunshine hours and not the total of their warmth. Their effects vary according to the season. In spring it is acknowledged that sufficiently warm, still, calm, sunny conditions will aid budburst and later promote growth, pollination and fruit-set. The warming of the soil also promotes cytokinin (see glossary) development in the roots of the vine, while local heating and the spectral quality of direct sunlight may help the bud by reducing its sensitivity to gibberellins (see glossary). During ripening, sunshine will also assist fruit-bearing canes to obtain a more rapid sugar accumulation in the berries. This has been found to be extremely important in the establishment of winegrape quality at or soon after veraison. Gladstones contends that, though numerous— perhaps even unlimited—sunshine hours are desirable for viticulture in theory, in practice the issue is more complex. Very sunny climates tend to be quite variable in temperature and to have low relative humidities, which are usually detrimental to viticulture. He concludes that sunshine hours have a positive benefit for both yield and quality in winegrapes, 'but only if temperature variability and relative humidity remain favourable' (*Viticulture and Environment* p. 21).

The following can be concluded from the relationship between sunshine hours and degree days:

- Vines in warm climates require a greater number of sunshine hours to achieve a given fullness of wine body and style than those in cool climates. This is logical since the consumption of nutrition by the vine increases as temperature increases, whereas nutrition production by photosynthesis stabilises at intermediate temperatures.
- Temperature not sunshine is the primary limiting factor and determinant of wine style in cool climates (no more than 1450 biologically effective degree days). Temperature summation decrees whether particular varieties will ripen at all and, if so, when and on average at what temperatures and total of sunshine hours.
- Differences in sunshine hours over a growing season still influence sugar levels and therefore the formation of aroma and flavour at given physiological ripening stages in cool climates. Flavour development, however, is limited chiefly by the degree of physiological ripeness achieved—as a direct result of temperature. Thus sunshine hours contribute to physiological ripeness but only through their effects on temperature.

Light

Light and its wavelength and colour composition (spectral quality) have recently been shown to be of great viticultural significance. Research has indicated that varying degrees of spectral quality within the vine canopy influence the physiology and perhaps also the fruit quality of the vine. As Gladstones points out (*Viticulture and Environment* p. 26), red wavelengths and sunlight of normal spectral quality are well recognised to cause leafy, stocky growth, vigorous branching, fruitfulness, dark green leaf colour and generous production of pigments, analogous to the supply of ample cytokinins from the roots (see also the comments on red soils on p. 14).

Rainfall

Australia is one of the driest countries in the world. Yet until 30 years ago, except in areas which were the subject of state irrigation schemes, irrigation was a dirty word. Dryland viticulture was de rigueur. It was commonly thought that drought stress was good for vines and even that the ensuing wines, being products of drought years, were somehow superior. Since then, attitudes have undergone a vast change as viticulturists have pointed out the damage that moisture stress, whether too little or too much, can do to vines. These days, drip irrigation is to be seen in virtually all new vineyards. Such irrigation depends on capacious surface dams and is often programmed (by virtue of electronic probes) to cut in when the vineyard shows the merest signs of drought stress. Yet these dams have to be filled and more often than not the only source of good quality water is natural rainfall. Although such rainfall is barely relevant in irrigated areas, except for the direct damage it may cause, it is of utmost importance in vineyards that are non-irrigated or reliant on trickle irrigation from smaller surface dams, which may dry up at critical times during the growing season.

Two of those critical times are flowering and berry-set, when too much or too little moisture can have a tremendous effect on potential crop quantity. Moisture stress in late spring can also affect the differentiation of fruitful buds on new shoots. Equally, too much rain can physically disrupt flowering, upsetting pollination, and the concomitant effects of lack of sunshine and photosynthesis also interfere with fruitful bud differentiation. Heavy rain in spring also promotes heavy vegetative growth, which shades lower leaves and new buds, absorbs excessive amounts of nutrition and produces the vine hormones, auxins (see glossary) and gibberellins, which counteract the fruit-flavouring cytokinins.

After bud differentiation and just before veraison, vines and their young berries seem well able to bear moisture stress. Indeed at this time, in cooler climates, some moisture stress may actually be desirable, (a) to discourage further vegetative growth so that nutrition and cytokinins are diverted to the fruit not the vegetation, and (b) to harden existing vegetative growth so that any consequent stresses during the ripening period are tolerated.

If the period around veraison is subject to moisture stress and to higher temperatures, then the vine will require sufficient moisture for development of full berry size if this is desired. If not, continued (mild) moisture stress at this time will limit berry size but augment berry colour and flavour. A reduction of quantity but increased quality should result. Severe moisture stress at this time is not desirable (if it is ever desirable), as it may interfere with the flow of sugar to the berries.

From the time just after veraison through the weeks to harvest, it is critical that enough moisture is continuously available to maintain the vines in a healthy state and to bring the crop to full maturity. Root growth and the cytokinins ascending through the roots must be uninterrupted to prevent stress and premature ageing. At this stage, healthy vines bearing a full crop need no moisture stress, since the bunches have to be the sole focus of the vine's endeavours to provide nutrients and growth hormones.

Such is the situation in cooler climates. In those that are hotter, moisture stress may cause leaf drop and thereby expose the bunches to direct sunlight. This can be catastrophic if the berries are not fully ripe since they can ripen no further and will only shrivel. Even if leaf drop does not occur, photosynthesis will be reduced with the consequence of reduced sugar supply to the berries and perhaps increased potassium, which can lead to unbalanced musts. Even after maturity and indeed picking, it is necessary to maintain an adequate supply of moisture until normal leaf fall so that the canes mature properly and store sufficient nutrients to ensure a healthy start to budburst in the ensuing spring.

So far this discussion has been concerned with a deficiency of moisture, but what of excess? During winter, the vine is normally dormant, so it has little need for moisture, be it a trickle or a flood. If the former, the subsoil may become excessively dry and will therefore need irrigation on budburst. If the latter, the vigneron must look to the suitability of the natural drainage of the soil to avoid waterlogging and consequent damage to roots. In Mediterranean-type climates, in spring, sufficient rain is necessary if only to fill surface dams for the moisture demands of the ensuing growing season. If the vineyard is unirrigated, it is essential to provide enough subsoil moisture to carry the vine through without stress to the vintage. Important factors here are soil depth and moisture-holding capacity. But whenever excess rain occurs in whatever type of climate, the vigneron will hope that it will not be at flowering. Nor should excess rain occur in the few weeks before ripening as moisture take-up may increase pH and decrease total acidity, even if it does not bloat the berries, making them liable to splitting and thereby susceptible to bunch rot. Nor indeed in any climate should there be hail at this stage. Hail can be devastating at any time during the growing season, but at vintage a year's work can disappear in a flash.

Relative humidity and saturation deficit

What is saturation deficit and how is it relevant to the Australian vineyard? Briefly, it is the difference between the actual water vapour content of a given air body and what it could contain if it were vapour-saturated (100%) at the same temperature. Its value is that it is a direct indicator of the evaporative power of air and therefore very relevant to potential moisture stress in vines. Research has shown that in arid climates, even fully irrigated vines cannot take up water fast enough to meet the evapotranspirational demands of the leaves. The result is that photosynthesis ceases in mid- to late morning as the leaf pores (stomata) close to preserve moisture. The greater the saturation deficit in hot, arid climates, the more moisture is transpired by the leaves per unit of carbon dioxide taken in through the stomata with the consequence that growth and yield per unit of water are reduced (see Gladstones, *Viticulture and Environment* p. 29). Another effect of saturation deficit is an increase in potassium absorption by vines and subsequently by their fruit which leads to a higher potassium content in grape musts. Excess potassium in turn leads to loss of tartaric acid (reduced natural acidity) and an increase in pH through its precipitation as potassium bi-tartrate. The wine consequences of this are detrimental, leading to a loss of flavour freshness and a greater risk of oxidation and perhaps microbial spoilage. As a remedy, the winemaker will add appropriate amounts of tartaric acid or use ion exchange but it is better of course in all cases to start off with a well-balanced must. On the other hand, high relative humidities and high temperatures encourage fungal diseases and rot. The prospective winegrower should therefore find a vineyard site with as high a relative humidity as possible in a cool area, but not so cool as to put at risk the ripening of the grapes. An optimal relative humidity in cool to mild climates seems to be about 55% in early afternoon, a compromise between quality and potential fungal problems. Such sites occur more commonly near our southern and south-western coasts. Coastal or near-coastal climates elsewhere seem either too hot or too wet or both. (Gladstones takes his relative humidities at 3pm as opposed to Smart and Dry who use 9am. Gladstones prefers 3pm because he believes that saturation stress is at its most marked from midday to early afternoon whereas Smart and Dry support 9am as it approximates the daily mean figure.)

Wind

Like rain, wind can be both beneficial and detrimental. Air circulation is important in spring, helping to keep temperatures equable and thereby preventing frosts. Later in the growing season it forestalls excessive humidity and perhaps prevents mildews and rots. Just as importantly it moves the leaves, thereby allowing the entry of sunlight into the canopy to improve photosynthesis.

On the debit side, strong winds may cause direct damage to exposed vineyards at flowering time and later to fruiting canes, sometimes blowing off whole bunches of partially ripe fruit. In maritime areas, strong sea breezes may also carry salt spray, which can seriously interfere with flowering buds. Inland, strong winds are often accompanied by extremely hot weather and such conditions rapidly dehydrate vines, closing down photosynthesis with consequent interruption to the ripening process and perhaps even a reduced yield. Measures to counteract the damaging effects of wind are the planting of quick-growing windbreaks, the use of established forest land, planting on east-facing slopes—usually subject to least wind effect in Australia—or planting on reverse slopes and allowing the brow of the hill to break the force of the prevailing wind, thereby protecting the vines naturally.

Soils

Aspect, soil and climate are all essential ingredients of *climat*. When noble grape types, selected by centuries of winemaking experience and wine history, are added to *climat*, it is easy to see why the French believed their appellation controlée wines to be the best in the world. That many such wines were successfully challenged in the marketplaces of the Old World by the superior technology (and cheaper price) of the wines of the New is now history, but it alters very little. It only underlines the fact that the winemakers of Australia need to know much more about their own *climats*, especially their soils. As Louis Jacquelin and Rene Poulain wrote many years ago in *Wines and Vineyards of France* (p. 39), 'the whole art of the wine grower rests in knowing his [sic] soil, supplementing it wisely, growing only suitable varieties and maintaining a judicious balance between vine and soil in order to achieve the best wine and a reasonable yield'.

So what are the physical properties of soil that will achieve the best wine? Certainly not 'the most fertile and best manured soils' (Busby, *Treatise on the Culture of the Vine*, 1825 p. 7)—although such soils will grow a most luxuriant plant, the resultant wine will probably be unripe and green-tasting. Shallow soils are also unsuitable as the vine roots quickly become waterlogged and, in times of drought, drought-stressed. Nor are thick, clayey soils suitable. Again in Busby's words, 'their firmness prevents the dissemination of the minute fibres of the roots and their coldness is prejudicial to the plant'. As well as this their impermeability prevents the initial absorption of moisture and heat and later the evaporation of any moisture that has managed to penetrate to the roots. Heavy, clay soils therefore conduct heat, air and moisture badly. This leads either to insufficient plant moisture if the surface is impermeable or excessive moisture (waterlogging) if the moisture cannot be evaporated.

Busby recommends soils for the vine that are 'dry, light and free', preferring in general those that are sandy, volcanic in origin, calcareous (limestone) or of a decomposed granite nature which, he says, possess certain wine attributes: '. . . sandy soil will, in general, produce a delicate wine . . . calcareous soil a spirituous wine and decomposed granite a brisk wine'. Another point stressed by Busby and virtually all the French authorities of the nineteenth century is the importance in soil of a 'mixture of stones', even in soils otherwise dry, light and porous. Stony, pebbly soils allow easy root penetration, restrict evaporation of moisture where such stones are on the surface and allow the infiltration of moisture. At the same time they absorb heat which is later re-radiated to the vine canopy and the fruit within it. In the nineteenth century, even the colour of the soil was thought to be important. Reddish soils were thought to increase quality in red wines, while grey or yellow soils were favoured for white. Gladstones (in *Viticulture and Environment* p. 33) points out that the spectral quality of light offers an alternative reason for these widely-held beliefs: reflection of white, yellow or especially orange or reddish light into the lower vine canopy and bunch area might be a factor in raising the ratio of red to far-red wavelengths there and so tip the balance in all grape varieties towards cytokinins and fruitfulness.

Even today, the pragmatic observations of the nineteenth century retain their importance in dry-land viticulture, though most Australian vineyards are now irrigated by one means or another. Yet soil requirements have not changed markedly. What has changed is the capacity to manage water supply, so the extremes of over- and undersupply are avoided and this in turn allows for a wider tolerance of different soils. What is sought in a soil is balance—soils of sufficient organic and inorganic elements and of good enough structure—yet with comparatively poor fertility to allow the vine to develop a successful root system, which will penetrate to sufficient depth to allow use of all available moisture and nutrition.

It is advantageous also to know as much about the chemical properties of a vineyard soil as possible. Is the soil acid, alkaline or neutral? Each type has a varying cation exchange capacity (cec). Soils with low cec have a hydrogen predominance and are acid. Those with a high cec have a predominance of the metal ions calcium, magnesium, potassium and sodium and are alkaline. The cec values for neutral soils lie in between. Thus, in general, when similar soils are compared, acid soils have low nutrient element reserves, neutral soils have adequate reserves and alkaline soils have high reserves.

There are delicate balances in soils of either an acid or alkaline nature. Balances in acid soils can be easily disturbed by overcropping or by continued applications of the same fertiliser and such treatment results in imbalances of other nutrient elements. Alkaline soils containing a great deal of calcium carbonate (such as calcareous earths) may also be upset by heavy phosphate fertiliser applications, causing, for example, a zinc deficiency.

Nutrient elements

Plant growth generally requires a whole larder of nutrient elements. About sixteen are commonly listed: carbon, hydrogen, oxygen, nitrogen, phosphorus, potassium, sulphur, calcium; and the trace elements, boron, chlorine, cobalt, copper, iron, manganese, molybdenum and zinc. The first three are easily found—green plants absorb carbon from the air, while hydrogen and oxygen are obtained from water. The rest are obtained from the soil.

Nitrogen and organic matter in soils are generally provided by decomposing plant remains and soil organisms. Nitrogen can also be fixed by organisms forming nodules on the roots of leguminous plants. Usually all nitrogenous compounds in soil are oxidised by soil organisms to form nitrates, in which form plants will readily accept them. Most Australian grape-growing soil is moderate to low in nitrogen which is a very mobile element in soil and can be readily leached from it. Shallow soils, leached acid soils and sand soils are frequently low in nitrogen. Low soil nitrogen levels also mean low fertility and while vineyard soils need not be highly fertile, soil fertility and with it vine vigour can be improved by the growth of self-regenerating subterranean clover during winter and early spring. The clover can be slashed or turned in before it competes with the budding vines for moisture. Another reason for turning in such crops before budburst is, of course, frost minimisation in frost-prone areas. Production of nitrogen with minimum cultivation has the added advantages of avoiding soil compaction and less destruction of earthworms.

Besides their nitrogen deficit, Australian soils are also deficient in phosphorus. Like nitrogen, phosphorus deficiency in soils can be remedied by legume-rich green-manuring (the growing and turning-in of legumes). As phosphorus is comparatively immobile in soil it is important that it is placed close to the root zone of vines so as to be available. A similar observation applies to the use of superphosphate.

The presence of the metal potassium varies quite widely in our vineyard soils, in both its total and exchangeable forms. (Total potassium includes all potassium present while exchangeable potassium is that part associated with the clay minerals.) In this latter form it is most readily available to plants. Low exchangeable potassium content is usually associated with acid soils, while alkaline soils have higher content and some alkaline soils may indeed be over-supplied.

While sulphur deficiency can exist in acid soils, it is presently rare in vineyard soils. In the past, the widespread use of superphosphate (which contains about 11% sulphur) and the use of sulphur in fungicide sprays have prevented such a deficiency.

Magnesium deficiency is also rare in Australian vineyard soils, though it has been shown to have been induced in Europe by the excessive use of potassium fertiliser.

Iron deficiency is more commonly present, taking the form of chlorosis associated with high pH, and is usually linked with high lime content or with poor soil drainage. In either case iron is made unavailable to the grapevine. Water-induced chlorosis may disappear when the soil dries out. Chlorosis induced by lime is naturally common in high lime soils and other alkaline soils and is particularly evident in spring when the vineyard soils are cold and wet. Again, warmer weather that dries out the soil will reduce the effect of this chlorosis.

Boron deficiency is rare in Australian vineyards and has been recorded only in Stanthorpe in acidic, sandy soils. Excessive boron is more common, existing in Murray River irrigation areas, and can be leached from such soils by irrigation water, provided they are adequately drained.

Deficiency in manganese occurs largely in alkaline soils and soils with thick limestone subsola (calcareous earths). The intake of manganese becomes restricted when soil pH exceeds 6.5. Manganese supply is usually adequate in acid soils, except for highly leached sands and some leached ironstone soils. It has also been shown that the application of lime to acid soils where the resulting pH surpasses 6.5 will induce manganese deficiency.

Of all the trace elements, zinc is most important in its effect on grapevines. Even a mild deficiency can affect yields and zinc deficiency does occur in some of our major irrigation areas where there are alkaline soils. A zinc deficiency has been found in such soils in Riverland, Sunraysia and the Murrumbidgee Irrigation Area. It has also been recorded in acid soils in Western Australia, especially those subject to sub-surface waterlogging.

Copper deficiency, as with sulphur, is rare in Australia, having been recorded only once, over 50 years ago. Applications of copper in various vineyard sprays will ensure that there is no recurrence.

The remaining trace elements—cobalt, molybdenum and chlorine—seem to be required more by legumes than by higher plants, such as grapevines. In any event, deficiencies in trace elements seem fairly easy to remedy with foliar sprays.

Topography and aspect

In addition to soil, topography and aspect are two other crucial but intertwined factors in the appreciation of *climat*. Altitude too may be important. Is the vineyard on flat land? Or hillside? Or on a high plateau? The virtues of stony soils have been discussed and these often occur on lower hillsides and valley slopes. Such soils are usually well-drained and often reasonably deep. If there is also a free movement of air along this hillside or valley slope (thus reducing frost risk) then, subject to its aspect and temperatures, it may make an excellent vineyard site. Based on the European experience, Gladstones (*Viticulture and Enrivonment* p. 41) states that the very best vineyard sites usually have at least two of the following features:

- they are situated on slopes with excellent air drainage above the fog level
- the very best are usually on the slopes of projecting or isolated hills
- even in hot areas, they usually face the sun during some part of the day at least—part-easterly and southerly [for Australian conditions, read northerly] aspects are common
- if the sites are inland, they are usually close to a large body of water (a lake or a major river).

Many French examples readily spring to mind, such as the hill of Hermitage, the hill of Corton, the east and south-east facing slopes of the Côte de Nuits and the Côte de Beaune. Australian examples are more difficult to find, especially those involving large bodies of inland water—Lake George perhaps, and Lake Alexandrina immediately south of the Langhorne Creek Region may also be a case in point, though it could be argued that it is virtually an estuary. We do, however, have significant hills. Over a century ago, Hubert de Castella discoursed on the three notable hills of the Yarra Valley. Other examples of Australian hills influencing local viticulture are Brokenback Range in the lower Hunter Valley, the Strathbogie Ranges in Victoria, the north–south hills forming part of the eastern slope of the Clare Valley and, of course, the Adelaide Hills as a more elevated and very suitable hilly area.

Another important factor is the 'thermal zone', the warm nocturnal air on the middle and lower slopes of hills, sitting above the 'inversion' or fog layer which, in turn, clothes the dense cold air at the valley bottom or on the flats. In the absence of any new chilled air from above, such thermal zones are quite stable in temperature. When temperatures are less variable, the vineyard warms and consequently ripens more quickly. The identification of such sites is critical in very cool climates as it often means the difference in any given grape variety between full and effective ripening on the one hand and incomplete and inferior ripening on the other.

It is a truism that the further north we go towards our tropical areas the warmer the climate becomes and, if table wine grapes are to be grown with any chance of success, then suitable cooler sites must be those that are higher. Several emerging vineyard areas are located over 600 metres in altitude (for example, the South Queensland Granite Belt and Orange in the Central Ranges of New South Wales) and other recently developed areas are only slightly lower at more than 500 metres (such as the Adelaide Hills and the Canberra and District regions). Altitude, however, does have its disadvantages. One is low relative humidity, which has already been discussed. Another is a lower concentration of carbon dioxide.

As Gladstones points out (*Viticulture and Environment*, p. 45) altitude leads to lower concentrations of carbon dioxide in the air, reducing the potential photosynthetic rates of the vine. This may in fact be counteracted by the vine developing more breathing pores (stomata) per unit of leaf area, thus maintaining a normal rate of carbon dioxide intake, but this has its own price—the greater evaporation of water from the leaves for each unit of carbon dioxide absorbed. This in turn may mean a higher rate of potassium accumulation to sugar production in the leaves, then to the berries, then to higher pH in the grapes, musts and wines and a consequent reduction in quality. Moreover, these detrimental effects may be cumulative.

WINE GRAPE VARIETIES: MATURITY AND SUITABILITY FOR VARIOUS REGIONS

It is commonsense to grow grape varieties in regions most suitable for them. Yet in Australia, this has rarely been the case. Our warmer grape-growing areas have mostly happened by happy accident. Grapes were an alternative crop which grew well. There was a market for fresh fruit and wine. Such sites were generally close to inhabited areas (cities, towns or mining regions) or had access to transport to such areas, usually by water and later by rail.

The wine industry, like any other, is subject to fashions. The current preference among consumers for table wines has only really been with us for 25 years and may simply be a longer-lasting fashion, which in time may pass. Consider the trend (though on a much smaller scale of consumption) away from lighter table wines to stronger reds and fortifieds in the late nineteenth century. If certain regions today were restricted to making the wine styles most suitable for their climates, then pity the regions that would be compelled to make only fortified wines. Their economic survival would be gravely imperilled. So in such areas, which are usually very warm, white and red table wines made from varieties not suited to the region will often be found.

What of new areas, where *vitis vinifera* has not previously been attempted in Australia? How are suitable sites selected? It is useful to follow Gladstones' approach. Employing available climatic data, the viticulturist must be able to forecast maturity dates for any given grape variety. Further, as grape varieties mature at different times in any environment, they can be classified into groups with similar maturity times and can be interrelated by being described as ripening a certain number of days before or after another group. Maturity in this context can have differing meanings because of differences in the wine style intended to be made, but it is usually taken to mean the time most suitable for making a dry wine. There may of course be other factors affecting grape maturity. For example, late pruning, leading to correspondingly later budburst, may retard maturity for several weeks or the maturity of a second crop will be delayed after frost damage. Variations in altitude and slight variations in temperature between the site of the weather station and that of the vineyard may mean a hastening or a delaying of maturity by a few days. Soil type also may have an influence.

Having taken all of this into consideration, Gladstones assumes that temperature is the chief element affecting vine phenology. However, he contends that the following three modifications should be made to raw temperature data:

Degree days required for wine grape varieties in commercial use, Australia

Degree days	White/rosé wine variety	Red wine variety**
1050*	—	—
1100	chasselas, pinot gris, pinot noir, meunier, muller-thurgau	—
1150	gewurztraminer, sylvaner, chardonnay, sauvignon blanc, frontignac, melon, verdelho, sultana, pedro ximenes	pinot noir, meunier, gamay, dolcetto, bastardo, tinta amarella
1200	semillon, riesling, cabernet franc	malbec, durif, zinfandel, tinta madeira
1250	chenin blanc, crouchen, marsanne, roussanne, viognier, cabernet sauvignon, taminga, muscadelle***	merlot, cabernet franc, shiraz, cinsaut, barbera, sangiovese, touriga
1300	colombard, palomino, grenache	cabernet sauvignon, mondeuse, ruby cabernet, valdiguie
1350	muscat gordo blanco, trebbiano	mataro, petit verdot, carignan, graciano, grenache
1400	clairette, grenache blanc, doradillo, biancone	tarrango

*   Few areas in Australia have a degree-day maximum that does not exceed 1050. Viticulture in such areas, besides being restricted to a choice of the earliest ripening grape varieties, would probably be precluded for climatic reasons, that is, spring frosts, cold winds, altitude and so on.

**   Most of the early ripening German varieties, such as siegerrebe, and lesser known Italian and Portuguese varieties, such as malvasia bianca (malmsey), have been omitted, as they are not yet grown in Australia on a commercial scale.

***   Gladstones (*Viticulture and Environment*, p. 67) places both semillon and muscadelle in the 1200 degree-day group. He reports that muscadelle is the latest ripening of Bordeaux white varieties, David Morris of Morris Wines, who grows both varieties at Rutherglen, believes that semillon is the earlier ripener. Even though David was ripening muscadelle for fortified wine purposes, it was still at least two weeks behind semillon.

1 A cut-off mean temperature of 19°C for the warmest months, beyond which, he argues, there is 'no further increase in the rate of phenological development'.

2 A day-length/latitude adjustment. This is an additional adjustment for day-length at latitudes over/under 40 degrees for each month of the growing season, where 40 degrees is the approximate mean latitude for world viticulture. Temperatures (less 10°C) in latitudes above 40 degrees were adjusted upwards, temperatures (less 10°C) in latitudes below 40 degrees were adjusted downwards.

3 Adjustment for diurnal temperature range. He suggests that low night temperatures have a retarding effect on budburst and subsequent growth in areas with a widely varying diurnal range of spring temperatures and, consequently, a later than expected maturity. On the other hand, a narrow diurnal range might give rise to earlier than expected maturity. Therefore in sites with a very wide or narrow diurnal range, Gladstones makes an adjustment to raw temperature data in months where the range exceeds 13°C by reducing it by 0.25°C for every 1°C of range over 13°C and increasing it by the same ratio in months where the range is less than 10°C.

The resulting degree-day count, subject to all three adjustments, is in Gladstones' view 'biologically effective'.

Having ascertained the method of calculating biologically effective degree days for prospective grape-growing regions, Gladstones seeks to correlate those particular regions with suitable grape varieties, that is, varieties that will come to full maturity within that region. He does this by formulating a table of degree days commencing at 1050 and dividing this table into eight groups at 50 degree days apart until he reaches 1400 degree days. Red, white and rosé wine styles and the grape varieties from which they are made are set beside the appropriate degree-day group, based on the number of degree days that each variety needs to come to ripeness. The table on p. 19 sets out wine grape varieties in general commercial use in Australia and the number of degree days required for maturity where dry table wines are to be made.

Of grape varieties mentioned in the notes on wine regions, I have included varieties actually grown in any particular region and also mentioned, where possible, varieties suitable for that region that accord with the practical experience of winegrowers within that region.

In general in my description of regions and sub-regions, I have used the following adjectives in relation to various degree-day groups: very cool HDD 1050–1200; cool 1201–1500; warm 1501–1800; hot 1801–2100; very hot above 2101.

Part I

VICTORIA

WINE REGIONS OF VICTORIA

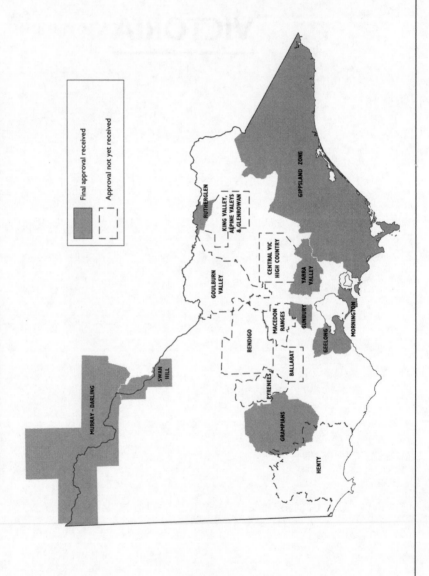

Final approval received

Approval not yet received

MURRAY - DARLING

SWAN HILL

RUTHERGLEN

KING VALLEY, ALPINE VALLEYS & GLENROWAN

GOULBURN VALLEY

CENTRAL VIC HIGH COUNTRY

GIPPSLAND ZONE

YARRA VALLEY

BENDIGO

MACEDON RANGES

SUNBURY

MORNINGTON

GEELONG

PYRENEES

BALLARAT

GRAMPIANS

HENTY

❧ WESTERN VICTORIA ZONE

This is a substantial tract of Victoria, stretching from Ballarat in the east to the South Australian border and the western Victorian coast. It comprises three actual and proposed wine regions at the present—The Grampians, Henty and the Pyrenees.

THE GRAMPIANS REGION

Centred around the village of Great Western and the towns of Stawell to the north-west and Ararat to the south-east, the Grampians wine region is a child of the great Victorian goldrush of the 1850s and 1860s. Its first vineyards were planted by those ever-present miners' suppliers, who usually made much more money providing the miners with the picks and shovels and other necessities of mining than most of their clients ever made by using them. Jean Pierre Trouette and Anne Marie Blampied were two such *providores* who moved to the Great Western region in 1858 after a profitable stay at the north-east Victorian mining town of Beechworth. In the next few years they planted their St Peter's vineyard. The brothers Joseph and Henry Best were two other *providores* who established a profitable butchery in Ararat. They too purchased land at Great Western, Joseph founding his Great Western estate, some say in 1862 or 1865, while Henry planted Concongella virtually across the road in 1866.

The early wines from this region were table wines, matured at Great Western in 'drives' which were tunnels beneath the winery excavated by former miners. Later that century and in the twentieth, they were extended and put to even better use as the wine fame of the region came to be based firmly on *methode champenoise* sparkling wines, made there by a Frenchman, Charles Pierlot. He had been brought to Great Western by Hans Irvine, the purchaser of Great Western after Joseph's death in 1887. Its reputation as a sparkling wine producer soared during the first half of the twentieth century, especially after Seppelt purchased Great Western from Hans Irvine in 1918 and popularised sparkling wine nationally. The production of table wines, however, though much smaller, never ceased. Colin Preece, Seppelt Great Western winemaker from 1932 to 1963, made some superb reds during that time.

Great Western today, and the Grampians region generally, specialise once more in table wines, though its local sparkling wines—now chiefly made of the classic Champagne grape varieties, pinot noir, meunier and chardonnay—remain of high quality.

Location: latitude 37°09'S, longitude 142°50'E, about 220 km west-north-west of Melbourne
Altitude: 330 m
Topography and soils: Moderately undulating with vineyards planted both on slopes

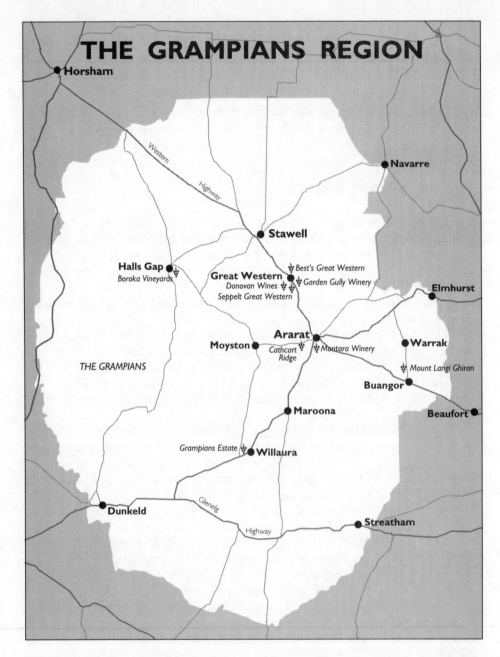

THE GRAMPIANS REGION

● Horsham

● Navarre

Western
Highway

● Stawell

Halls Gap ●
Boroka Vineyards

🍇 *Best's Great Western*

Great Western 🍇 *Garden Gully Winery*
Donovan Wines 🍇
Seppelt Great Western

● Elmhurst

THE GRAMPIANS

Ararat ●
Moyston ● 🍇 *Montara Winery*
Cathcart Ridge

● Warrak

🍇 *Mount Langi Ghiran*

● Buangor

● Beaufort

● Maroona

Grampians Estate 🍇 ● Willaura

● Dunkeld

Glenelg
Highway

● Streatham

and flats. Hard, mottled yellow duplex soils with yellow, clayey subsoils (flats) (Dy 3.41, Dy 3.42) and hard red duplex soils with red-brown, clayey subsoils (slopes) (Dr 2.21, Dr 2.22). Subsoils drain only moderately well. Soil types are only moderately fertile. pH: acid to neutral.

Climate: MJT 20.2°C, MAR 12.2°C, HDD (raw) 1464, AR 591 mm (Oct–Mar

238 mm), RH 59% (9am), AI 362 mm, SH 8.3. Warm and dry with risk of spring frosts on flatter areas. Moderate evaporation, radiation and relative humidity. A 'continental' climate—cool nights, warm days. Annual rainfall is slightly winter-dominant. Other water resources: drip irrigation from surface storage dams only, as creeks and bores are sometimes saline.

Harvest time: Mid-March to mid-May

Principal grape varieties: Red—shiraz, cabernet sauvignon, pinot noir*, meunier*; White—riesling, chardonnay*, ondenc* (*also used for sparkling wine base)

Total area as at March 1996: 240 ha, further plantings anticipated: 150 ha

Major wine styles: Shiraz, Sparkling, Chardonnay, Riesling

Best's Great Western   R8.5

Concongella, Great Western, Victoria 3377
Ph 03 5356 2250, Fax 03 5356 2430

Owner: Best's Wines Pty Ltd (the Thomson family)
Chief winemaker: Viv Thomson
Year of foundation: 1866
Tonnes crushed on average each year: 157
Location: Great Western
Area: 21 ha
Soils: Powdery sandy loams overlying a deep clay subsoil. Newer plantings sited on a gravelly quartz hill
Varieties planted: White—chardonnay, gewurztraminer, ondenc, riesling; Red—cabernet sauvignon, cabernet franc, dolcetto, merlot, meunier, pinot noir, shiraz
Leading wines: Thomson Family Shiraz, Bin 0 Shiraz, Cabernet Sauvignon, Chardonnay, Riesling
Notes: This is the original vineyard site of Henry Best and there are still four hectares of vines existing from his first plantings over 130 years ago. The Thomson family itself can look back on a century of involvement with Great Western viticulture and three-quarters of a century of involvement with Concongella. Its wines, especially Shiraz, consistently rank among the best of the region. Cellar door sales: Mon–Fri 9am–5pm, Sat 9am–4pm, Sun and hols, noon–4pm.

Boroka Vineyards   NR

Lake Fyans Tourist Road, Halls Gap, Vic 3381
Ph 03 5356 4252

Owners: Bernard and Cordelia Breen
Chief winemaker: Bernard Breen
Year of foundation: 1970
Tonnes crushed on average each year: 25, of which 8–9 tonnes are used for Boroka's own label
Location: Hall's Gap
Area: 9 ha
Soils: poor sandy soils now being improved
Varieties planted: White—colombard, riesling, sauvignon blanc; Red—cabernet sauvignon, shiraz
Leading wines: Boroka Vineyards Shiraz
Notes: Because of poor soils and correspondingly poor yields, Bernard Breen has been using fertigation techniques to increase yields. Cellar door sales: Mon–Sat 10am–5pm, Sun 10am–4pm.

Cathcart Ridge   NR

Moyston Road, Cathcart via Ararat, Vic 3377
Ph 03 5352 1997, Fax 03 5352 1558

Owner: Farnhill family
Chief winemaker: David Farnhill
Year of foundation: 1977
Tonnes crushed on average each year: 120

Location: Ararat
Area: 10 ha plus 160 ha at Great Western
which commenced in 1998.
Soils: shale underlying gravelly loam, not overly
fertile
Varieties planted: White—chardonnay, riesling;
Red—cabernet franc, cabernet sauvignon,
merlot, shiraz
Leading wines: Cathcart Ridge Cabernet
Sauvignon, Merlot, Shiraz
Notes: Winner of a gold award for Cabernet
Sauvignon at the recent World Wine
Championships in Chicago, David Farnhill has
commenced the establishment of a very large
vineyard at Great Western which will, when
bearing, considerably increase production at
Cathcart Ridge. Cellar door sales: 7 days
10am–5pm, barbecue area.

Donovan Wines R6

Main Street, Great Western, Vic 3377
(cellar door)
Ph 03 5356 2288, 03 5358 2727

Owner: Donovan Family
Chief winemaker: Peter Donovan
Year of foundation: 1977
Tonnes crushed on average each year: 20
Location: winery and vineyard, Pomona Road,
Stawell
Area: 7 ha
Soils: sandy loam over clay
Varieties planted: White—chardonnay;
Red—cabernet sauvignon, merlot, pinot noir,
shiraz
Leading wines: Donovan Wines Shiraz
Notes: Like most of the makers in the
Grampians region, Peter Donovan makes sturdy
Shiraz reds of great character. (In 1985 he won
a trophy at Ballarat for the best Shiraz in the
Western Districts.) Cellar door sales: Mon–Sat
10am–5pm, Sun noon–5pm.

Garden Gully Winery R8

Western Highway, Great Western,
Vic 3377
(east of the village)
Ph/Fax 03 5356 2400

Owners: Brian Fletcher, Warren Randall and a
syndicate of business people
Chief winemakers: Brian Fletcher, Warren
Randall
Year of foundation: 1987
Tonnes crushed on average each year: 30
Location: Great Western
Area: 6 ha
Soils: brown loam over clay
Varieties planted: White—riesling;
Red—shiraz
Leading wines: Garden Gully Shiraz, Sparkling
Shiraz
Notes: Garden Gully is the creation of two
former winemakers at Seppelt Great Western,
Brian Fletcher and Warren Randall, and the
leading wines reflect the expertise learnt there.
When you add to that expertise a 6 ha
vineyard with old shiraz vines, you have a
formula for successful Shiraz. Cellar door sales:
7 days 10.30am–5.30pm.

Grampians Estate NR

'Thermopylae', Willaura, Vic 3379
Ph 03 5354 6245

Owner: Grampians Estate Wine Co Pty Ltd
Chief winemaker: contract
Year of foundation: 1989
Tonnes crushed on average each year: 5,
increasing to 20 when the vineyard is in full
bearing
Location: Willaura
Area: 3.2 ha including new plantings
Soils: granite sand
Varieties planted: White—chardonnay;
Red—shiraz
Leading wines: Mafeking Gold Chardonnay,
Mafeking Shiraz

Notes: Grampians Estate is yet another vineyard established close to the site of an old gold area, in this case the Mafeking mine discovered near Willaura in 1900. Cellar door sales by appointment.

Montara Winery **R6.5**

Chalambar Road, Ararat, Vic 3377
Ph/Fax 03 5352 3868

Owner: McRae family
Chief winemaker: Mike McRae
Year of foundation: 1970
Tonnes crushed on average each year: 150
Location: Ararat
Area: 17 ha
Soils: rich red loam
Varieties planted: White—chardonnay, chasselas, riesling; Red—cabernet sauvignon, pinot noir, shiraz
Leading wines: Montara Pinot Noir, Shiraz
Notes: A maker of good Shiraz in the manner of the region and, less frequently, very good Pinot Noir. Cellar door sales: Mon–Sat 9.30am–5pm, Sun noon–4pm.

Mt Langi Ghiran **R10**

Warrak-Buangor Road, Buangor via Ararat, Vic 3375
Ph 03 5354 3207, Fax 03 5354 3277

Owners: Trevor Mast and Riquet Hess
Chief winemaker: Trevor Mast
Year of foundation: 1966
Tonnes crushed on average each year: 350, but will increase substantially as new plantings come into bearing
Location: Buangor
Area: 98 ha, including 23 ha of non-bearing vines
Soils: deep granite sand over clay and also sandy loam over red-brown clay loam with 'buckshot'
Varieties planted: White—pinot grigio, riesling; Red—cabernet franc, cabernet sauvignon, merlot, sangiovese, shiraz
Leading wines: Mount Langi Ghiran Shiraz, Riesling, Cabernet Sauvignon
Notes: Mount Langi Ghiran is located in the Central Victorian crescent which produces some of the most intense Shiraz in Australia. Black pepper with the occasional whiff of eucalyptus on nose and deep meaningful berry, pepper and tannin palates. These wines are the essence of great Shiraz and establish the Grampians as a specialist region. Mount Langi Ghiran Riesling can also be rather special. Trevor Mast also owns the 4 ha Mount Chalambar vineyard which was planted to chardonnay and produced sparkling wines for several years. It has now been grafted over to riesling. How the pendulum of fashion swings! Cellar door sales: Mon–Fri 9am–5pm, weekends noon–5pm.

St Gregory's **NR**

Bringalbert South Road, Bringalbert South via Apsley, Vic 3319
Ph 03 5586 5225

Owner/chief winemaker: Gregory Flynn
Year of foundation: 1983
Tonnes crushed on average each year: not disclosed but est. at 10
Location: Bringalbert South
Area: 2.4 ha
Soils: not known
Varieties planted: White—none; Red—cabernet sauvignon, shiraz, touriga
Leading wine: St Gregory's Port
Notes: A very small vineyard, devoted entirely to port style. Cellar door sales by appointment.

Seppelt Great Western **R10**

Western Highway, Great Western, Vic 3377
Ph 03 5361 2222, Fax 03 5361 2200

Owner: Southcorp Wines
Chief winemaker: Ian McKenzie
Year of foundation: 1865
Tonnes crushed on average each year: (from the region) not disclosed but estimated at 1100
Location: Great Western
Area: 108.6 ha
Soils: infertile yellow duplex soils on flats, a better red duplex soil on hillsides; soils incline to acidity
Varieties planted: White—chardonnay, chenin blanc, ondenc, sauvignon blanc, viognier; Red—cabernet sauvignon, pinot noir, shiraz
Leading wines: Salinger (superb sparkling white made from pinot noir and chardonnay, which often includes a small portion of meunier), Seppelt Great Western Shiraz, Seppelt Victorian portfolio
Notes: This is the vineyard founded by Joseph Best which was purchased after his death in 1887 by Hans Irvine, a leading figure in the business and political life of Victoria from 1880 onwards. Irvine's passion in wine was champagne, which was one of his chief objectives in making the purchase and for which in 1890 he brought Charles Pierlot to Australia from Champagne to make the wine. Champagne making and the popularisation of this Australian sparkling wine style was his lasting contribution to Australian wine. At Great Western he expanded the cellars substantially and also much enlarged the vineyards by planting a white grape variety, which he understood to be 'white pinot'. Irvine's White, as it came to be called, turned out to be ondenc, a fairly ordinary white variety from the south of France. On Irvine's retirement in 1918, the estate was purchased by Seppelt, which is now part of Southcorp Wines. The cellars are famous for their 'drives', about 1.6 km of tunnels dug by miners in the late nineteenth century for the purpose of maturing sparkling wine. Its most outstanding winemaker during the middle of the twentieth century was Colin Preece (1932–1963), destined to be remembered more for his red wines than his sparklings which, during the last 20 years, because of the introduction of the classic champagne varieties—chardonnay, meunier and pinot noir—have improved tremendously in quality. Today Seppelt Great Western is vast and dedicated to making sparkling wine from sources all over Australia. There are, however, small parcels of Great Western Shiraz still made. Cellar door sales: 7 days 10am–5pm.

THE PYRENEES REGION (PROPOSED)

It is said that there were vines at Avoca even before the goldrushes of the 1850s, which is not unremarkable considering the usual pattern of south-east Australian rural settlement. First came the explorers, in Avoca's case the ubiquitous Major Thomas Mitchell, Surveyor-General of New South Wales, in 1836. Then the graziers began arriving in the mid-1840s with their cattle and sheep and often with a few vines, looking for permanent water. Then came the prospectors with their picks and gold pans in 1853. Avoca saw them all. As for the vineyards, they expanded. Near Avoca, the Mackereth family worked a vineyard of 40 acres (16 ha) in the early years of the twentieth century. Like those of the Yarra Valley, this vineyard eventually fell to the dairy cow. About the same time Kofoed had a vineyard of 20 acres (8 ha) at Mountain Creek which went out of production soon after the Second World War.

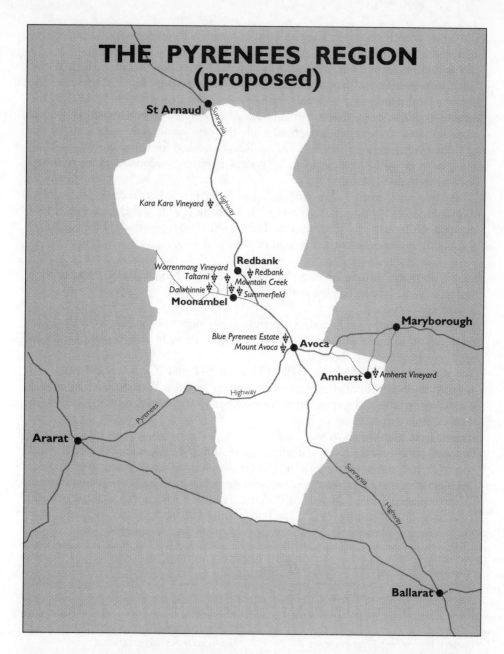

THE PYRENEES REGION
(proposed)

St Arnaud

Sunraysia Highway

Kara Kara Vineyard

Redbank

Worrenmang Vineyard
Taltarni
Redbank
Mountain Creek
Dalwhinnie
Summerfield
Moonambel

Maryborough

Blue Pyrenees Estate
Mount Avoca
Avoca

Amherst   Amherst Vineyard

Highway

Pyrenees

Ararat

Sunraysia Highway

Ballarat

But at no time was Avoca's wine industry the *raison d'etre* of the region. By 1950, it had become the land of wool and mutton.

During all this time, table wine was in the doldrums and the only expanding vineyards were those devoted to the production of brandy. So it was that Nathan and Wyeth, important wine and spirit distributors, formed a joint venture in 1960 with their French principal, Remy Martin of Cognac, to produce Australian brandy at a site 7 kilometres west of Avoca, at the foot of the Pyrenees range. On the 80 hectares purchased, they planted ugni blanc and doradillo, two varieties then very much in vogue for distillation and the production of brandy. By 1970, the taxation rates on local brandy and the public taste in wine had changed entirely. Back to the drawing board, Chateau Remy virtually ceased production of brandy and grafted its doradillo vines to cabernet sauvignon, while the ugni blanc vines were used for the production of sparkling wine. By 1982, as Remy searched for better quality sparkling wine, areas of ugni blanc began to be grafted over to chardonnay. Pinot noir and meunier were also planted.

By this time, many other vineyards had been planted in the region. Taltarni (beginning in 1969), Mount Avoca (1970), Redbank (1973) and Dalwhinnie (1976) are some of the wineries in operation. The region is now proud of its wine industry and rightly insists on its title 'the land of wool and wine'.

Location: Avoca latitude 37°05'S, longitude 143°29'E; Moonambel is about 12 km north of Avoca, about 175 km north-west of Melbourne
Altitude: 250–600 m
Topography and soils: Undulating vineyards on the slopes of the Victorian Pyrenees. Soils similar to those of Great Western but often gravelly with a quartz and clay content. pH: tending to be acid.
Climate: MJT 20°C, MAR na, HDD 1532, AR 542 mm (Oct–Apr 258 mm), RH 45%, AI na, SH 8.75. Slightly warmer but similar to Great Western. Annual rainfall is chiefly in winter and spring. Other water resources are limited, drip irrigation being supplied from surface dams or bores.
Harvest time: Mid-March to mid-May
Principal grape varieties: Red—cabernet sauvignon (69 ha), shiraz (64 ha), pinot noir* (29 ha); other red varieties (5–15 ha planted): cabernet franc, merlot, pinot meunier; White—chardonnay* (92 ha), sauvignon blanc (47 ha); other white varieties (5–15 ha planted): semillon, riesling (* denotes those also used for sparkling wine base)
Total area: (1996) bearing 297.32 ha, non-bearing 165 ha
Major wine styles: Shiraz, Chardonnay, Sauvignon Blanc, Sparkling

Amherst Vineyard NR

Talbot Avoca Road, Amherst, Vic 3467
Ph 03 5463 2105, Fax 03 9388 9148

Owners: Norman and Elizabeth Jones
Chief winemaker: Rod Stott (contract)
Year of foundation: 1990
Tonnes crushed on average each year: 4 but should increase in 2–3 years as recent plantings come into bearing
Location: Amherst

Area: 4 ha
Soils: clayey loam
Varieties planted: White—chardonnay; Red—cabernet sauvignon, shiraz
Leading wines: Amherst Shiraz
Notes: Norman Jones decided to start slowly and build solidly. That is why Amherst is quite small but it is growing. Like many in the region, Norman is proud of his Shiraz. No cellar door sales.

Blue Pyrenees Estate   R7.5

Vinoca Road, Avoca, Vic 3467
Ph 03 5465 3202, Fax 03 5465 3529

Owner: Remy Australie (Australian subsidiary of
Remy Martin France)
Chief winemaker: Kim Hart
Year of foundation: 1963
Tonnes crushed on average each year: not
disclosed but estimated at 1500
Location: Avoca
Area: 153 ha
Soils: red duplex clay with chalky limestone
country
Varieties planted: White—chardonnay,
sauvignon blanc, semillon, viognier;
Red—cabernet franc, cabernet sauvignon,
merlot, meunier, pinot noir, shiraz
Leading wines: Blue Pyrenees Estate (red,
a blend of cabernet, shiraz and merlot),
Chardonnay, Brut, Leydens Vale (mid-range
table wines), Fiddlers Creek (lower priced table
wines)
Notes: Blue Pyrenees Estate is the former
Chateau Remy which, from 1960, specialised in
brandy, then in sparkling wine of modest
quality (made primarily from ugni blanc until it
had finalised the planting of specialised
sparkling varieties), then in much improved
sparkling wine (but not usually of a quality to
rival Australia's best brands). It now specialises
in both sparkling and table wines, the Estate
red and the Chardonnay being the best. Cellar
door sales: Mon–Fri 10am–4.30pm, weekends
and public holidays 10am–5pm.

Dalwhinnie   R9

Taltarni Road, Moonambel, Vic 3478
Ph 03 5467 2388, Fax 03 5467 2237

Owner: Dalwhinnie Wines Pty Ltd
Chief winemakers: David Jones for Special
Shiraz, otherwise Mitchelton Wines (contract)
Year of foundation: 1976
Tonnes crushed on average each year: 100, of

which 60 are used for the Dalwhinnie labels
Location: Moonambel
Area: 18.42 ha at two vineyards, Dalwhinnie
(16 ha) and Forest Hut (2.42 ha)
Soils: gravel, quartz, clay
Varieties planted: White—chardonnay;
Red—cabernet franc, cabernet sauvignon,
merlot, pinot noir, shiraz
Leading wines: Dalwhinnie Eagle Series Special
Shiraz, Chardonnay, Moonambel Shiraz,
Moonambel Cabernet Sauvignon
Notes: For consistency and quality across the
whole range of its wines, Dalwhinnie is
arguably the best vineyard of the region. Its
Chardonnay is always outstanding, and its
Shiraz, both the Eagle Series and the
Moonambel, is superb. Cellar door sales:
7 days 10am–5pm.

Glenlofty (vineyard only)   NR

Warrenmang Road, Elmhurst, Vic 3469

Owner: Southcorp Wines
Chief winemaker: Ian McKenzie
Year of foundation: 1995
Tonnes crushed on average each year: vineyard
not yet in full bearing
Location: Elmhurst
Area: 78.6 ha
Soils: red to yellow friable clay loams
Varieties planted: White—chardonnay,
roussanne, sauvignon blanc; Red—shiraz
Leading wines: none yet
Notes: Little has yet been picked from
Glenlofty, but the wines will ultimately form
part of Seppelt Victorian portfolio. No local
cellar door sales.

Kara Kara Vineyard   NR

Sunraysia Highway, St Arnaud Vic 3478
(10 km south of town)
Ph/Fax 03 5496 3294

Owner: S. & M. Zsigmond Pty Ltd
Chief winemaker: John Ellis (contract), Steve Zsigmond (viticulturist)
Year of foundation: 1977
Tonnes crushed on average each year: 40, all used for Kara Kara labels
Location: Kara Kara
Area: 8 ha
Soils: gravelly, quartz over clay base
Varieties planted: White—chardonnay, sauvignon blanc, semillon; Red—cabernet sauvignon, shiraz
Leading wines: Kara Kara Vineyard Chardonnay, Sauvignon Blanc, Semillon, Cabernet-Shiraz
Notes: The most northerly of the Pyrenees wineries, Kara Kara is a true wine estate, utilising only its own grapes for its own wines. The estate concentrates on white wines, unusual for the Pyrenees area which is more renowned for reds. The Sauvignon Blanc and Semillon are sometimes blended, sometimes oaked. Cellar door sales: daily 9am–6pm.

Mount Avoca R7

Moates Lane, Avoca, Vic 3467
Ph 03 5465 3282, Fax 03 5465 3544

Owners: John, Arda and Matthew Barry
Chief winemakers: John and Matthew Barry
Year of foundation: 1970
Tonnes crushed on average each year: 160, all used for Mount Avoca labels
Location: Avoca
Area: 25 ha
Soils: clay and gravel
Varieties planted: White—chardonnay, sauvignon blanc, semillon, trebbiano; Red—cabernet franc, cabernet sauvignon, merlot, shiraz
Leading wines: Mount Avoca Sauvignon Blanc, Shiraz, Chardonnay, Cabernets, Classic Dry White
Notes: Mount Avoca is a true wine estate, growing and vinifying its entire production in

its own winery. It is also a consistent medal winner at local and national wine shows. Mount Avoca Sauvignon Blanc is typically lively and herbaceous and its reds are well in the mainstream of Pyrenees quality. Cellar door sales: Mon–Fri 9am–5pm, weekends and public holidays 10am–5pm, closed Christmas Day.

Mountain Creek NR

Mountain Creek Road, Moonambel, Vic 3478
Ph/Fax 03 5467 2230

Owner: Brian Cherry
Chief winemaker: contract
Year of foundation: 1973
Tonnes produced on average each year: 28, of which about one-third is used for Mountain Creek labels, but only in good years
Location: Moonambel
Area: 6.25 ha
Soils: red loamy clay over schist with occasional quartz intrusions
Varieties planted: White—sauvignon blanc; Red—cabernet sauvignon, shiraz
Leading wines: Mountain Creek Sauvignon Blanc, Cabernet-Shiraz
Notes: Now an established vineyard, its wines are typical of the region. Cellar door sales: weekends and public holidays 10am–7pm.

Redbank R8

Sunraysia Highway, Redbank, Vic 3467
Ph 03 5467 7255, Fax 03 5467 7248

Owners: Neill and Sally Robb
Chief winemaker: Neill Robb
Year of foundation: 1973
Tonnes crushed on average each year: 520 from its own vineyard sources and from growers, all used for Redbank's own labels
Location: Redbank
Area: 20 ha
Soils: quartz gravel over red clay
Varieties planted: White—none; Red—cabernet

franc, cabernet sauvignon, malbec, merlot, pinot noir, shiraz
Leading wines: Redbank Sally's Paddock (a red blend from a single vineyard), Long Paddock Shiraz, Chardonnay, Hundred Tree Hill Series (Shiraz, Cabernets, Pinot Noir)
Notes: Now well established (having celebrated its 25th anniversary in 1998), Redbank concentrates on the red wines which are the forte of the region. Its Sally's Paddock blend is usually excellent. Cellar door sales: Mon–Sat 9am–5pm, Sun 10am–5pm.

Summerfield R7.5

Main Road, Moonambel, Vic 3478
Ph 03 5467 2264, Fax 03 5467 2380

Owner: Ian Summerfield
Chief winemaker: Ian Summerfield, assisted by Mark Summerfield
Year of foundation: 1970
Tonnes crushed on average each year: 40 but will increase as new plantings come into bearing
Location: Moonambel
Area: 7.2 ha of which 3.26 ha are new plantings
Soils: quartz clay
Varieties planted: White—chardonnay, sauvignon blanc, trebbiano; Red—cabernet sauvignon, shiraz
Leading wines: Summerfield Shiraz, Cabernet Sauvignon
Notes: Ian Summerfield is a maker of consistently good Shiraz in the robust tradition of the Pyrenees region. He has also been showing his wines since 1988. Since then, he has won more than 80 awards, including several trophies at the Ballarat Wine Show. Cellar door sales: Mon–Sat 9am–6pm, Sun 10am–6pm. There are five self-contained accommodation units and a one-kilometre grass airstrip, if you wish to arrive in style.

Taltarni R9

Taltarni Road, Moonambel, Vic 3478
Ph 03 5467 2218, Fax 03 5467 2306

Owner: a private company
Chief winemaker: Chris Markell
Year of foundation: 1972
Tonnes crushed on average each year: 800
Location: Moonambel
Area: 130 ha
Soils: well drained schist, red clay over quartz
Varieties planted: White—chardonnay, riesling, sauvignon blanc; Red—cabernet franc, cabernet sauvignon, malbec, merlot, meunier, pinot noir, shiraz
Leading wines: Taltarni Sauvignon Blanc, Shiraz, Cabernet Sauvignon, Merlot, Cuvee Brut, Brut Tache
Notes: One of the pioneers of the Moonambel area of the Pyrenees region, for a long time Taltarni was renowned for the tannic 'size' of its reds, some of which never quite rewarded the patience required for them to soften into balance. Nowadays, more emphasis is laid on fruit and the reds are not so big but still need cellaring and the patience to go with it. Taltarni Sauvignon Blanc is usually suitably herbaceous and refreshingly acid. Taltarni also owns Clover Hill at Lebrina in Tasmania, some of whose sparkling wine is now used to lift the quality of the Pyrenees sparkling material. Cellar door sales: 7 days 10am–5pm.

Warrenmang Vineyard Resort R7

Mountain Creek Road, Moonambel, Vic 3478
Ph 03 5467 2233, Fax 03 5467 2309

Owners: Luigi and Athalie Bazzani
Chief winemaker: to be appointed
Year of foundation: 1974
Tonnes crushed on average each year: 30
Location: Moonambel
Area: 12.5 ha

Soils: red clay which holds moisture well below a sandy topsoil
Varieties planted: White—chardonnay, sauvignon blanc, traminer; Red—cabernet franc, cabernet sauvignon, dolcetto, merlot, nebbiolo, sangiovese, shiraz
Leading wines: Warrenmang Estate Shiraz, Grand Pyrenees (a red blend of merlot, cabernet sauvignon, cabernet franc and shiraz), Chardonnay Bazzani Cabernet-Shiraz-Dolcetto

Notes: Warrenmang Estate is more than a run-of-the-mill winery. It is a resort and a very plush one at that. Its Estate reds are very much in the midstream of big Pyrenees style and its result card at wine shows has been consistent and good. There is also an excellent restaurant. House guests receive 20% discount for wine purchases. Cellar door sales: 7 days 10am–5pm.

THE BALLARAT AREA

Ballarat is one of the larger urban centres of Western Victoria and, like Bendigo to its north, founded on the gold winnings of the 1850s. The Eureka Stockade, a revolt of volatile miners against an equally hot-tempered government, is legendary and very much an integral part of Ballarat's and Australia's history. Here once more, the vine followed the mine.

Australia's first roving wine reporter, Ebenezer Ward, records a vineyard at Dead Horse Gully in 1864, planted some five years previously by a Frenchman. Hopefully it was not his wine that killed the horse. Undoubtedly there were other local vineyards—miners are ever a thirsty lot—but recorded history is absent.

Ballarat's modern wine era commenced in 1971 with the planting, by Melbourne businessman Ian Home, of the Yellowglen Vineyard near Smythesdale initially to cabernet sauvignon and shiraz. Other plantings (chardonnay and pinot noir) took place in 1979. Home was convinced that his vineyard was suitable for the production of sparkling wines and in 1982 Dominique Landragin, then employed by Seppelt at Great Western, joined Home at Yellowglen. What followed was the meteoric rise of Yellowglen 'Champagne' and the merger with Mildara Wines in 1984. Since then, the vineyards and wineries of Ballarat have grown steadily but not spectacularly, which may be illustrative of the difficulties of viticulture in this very cool part of Australia.

Location: latitude 37°35'S, longitude 143°50'E, about 110 km west-north-west of Melbourne
Altitude: 437 m
Topography and soils: One of the lower parts of the western section of the Great Dividing Range, it is undulating country with a northerly aspect, one of the few factors favouring viticulture here. For soil information, see individual vineyard entries.
Climate: MJT 17.3°C, MAR na, HDD (raw) 1072, 1154 adjusted for vine sites, AR 719 mm (Oct–Apr 367 mm), RH 37% (G), AI na, SH 7.6. Ballarat is extremely cool with a high degree of frost risk. Careful site selection is imperative and then only early ripening varieties such as chardonnay and pinot noir should be planted.
Harvest time: Chardonnay early to mid-April, pinot noir late April to early May.

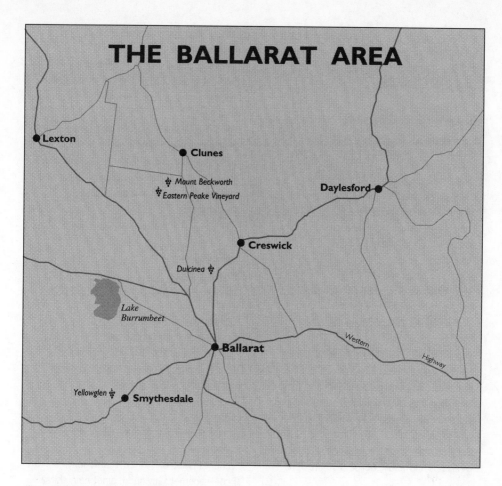

THE BALLARAT AREA

- Lexton
- Clunes
- Mount Beckworth
- Eastern Peake Vineyard
- Daylesford
- Creswick
- Dulcinea
- Lake Burrumbeet
- Ballarat
- Western Highway
- Yellowglen
- Smythesdale

Principal grape varieties: White—chardonnay; Red—pinot noir
Total area: na
Major wine styles: Sparkling, Chardonnay, Pinot Noir

Dulcinea NR

Jubilee Road, Sulky, Ballarat, Vic 3352
Ph 03 5334 6440, Ph/Fax 03 5334 6828

Owners: Rod and Veronica Stott
Chief winemaker: Rod Stott
Year of foundation: 1983
Tonnes crushed on average each year: 18
Location: Sulky
Area: 2 ha but will increase
Soils: shallow, clayey soil needing mulching and feeding

Varieties planted: White—chardonnay, sauvignon blanc; Red—cabernet sauvignon, pinot noir, shiraz
Leading wines: Dulcinea Chardonnay, Pinot Noir
Notes: Dulcinea is a pretty name with even prettier wine show results. The Stotts are limited in the quantities of wine that they make and therefore limited to wine shows with smaller qualifying quantities but gold awards at

Ballarat and Stanthorpe, a silver at Hobart for Chardonnay and silvers for Pinot at Ballarat and Stanthorpe are impressive. Cellar door sales: 7 days 10am–6pm.

Eastern Peake Vineyard NR

Clunes Road, Coghills Creek, Vic 3364
Ph 03 5343 4245, Fax 03 5343 4365

Owners: Norman Latta and Di Pym
Chief winemaker: Norman Latta
Year of foundation: 1983
Tonnes crushed on average each year: 15
Location: Coghills Creek
Area: 5 ha
Soils: grey basalt
Varieties planted: White—chardonnay;
Red—pinot noir
Leading wines: Eastern Peake Pinot Noir,
Chardonnay
Notes: Establishing Eastern Peake was a 12-year labour of love for Norman Latta and Di Pym. Their first vintage was 1995 and their Pinot Noir was rewarded with bronze medals at Rutherglen and Ballarat in 1997. So the varietal selection certainly corresponded with the requirements of the area. Cellar door sales: weekends and public holidays 10am–5pm.

Mount Beckworth

Learmonth Road, Tourello via Ballarat, Vic 3363
Ph/Fax 03 5343 4207

Owners: Paul and Jane Lesock
Chief winemaker: Paul Lesock, Simon Clayfield, consultant
Year of foundation: 1984
Tonnes crushed on average each year: 15
Location: Tourello, near Ballarat
Area: 4 ha

Soils: a slope on which red loamy clay runs down to black clay
Varieties planted: White—chardonnay; Red—cabernet sauvignon, pinot noir, merlot shiraz
Leading wines: Mount Beckworth Chardonnay, Pinot Noir
Notes: Paul Lesock believes that Ballarat is a chardonnay and pinot noir area, his own wines being consistent award winners at the Ballarat, Hobart and Victorian wine shows. Cellar door sales: weekends 10am–6pm and by appointment.

Yellowglen R8

Whytes Road, Smythesdale, Vic 3351
Ph 03 5342 8617, Fax 03 5333 7102

Owner: Mildara Blass Ltd
Chief winemaker: Nick Walker
Year of foundation: 1971
Tonnes produced on average each year: 45 (total crush of 4500 tonnes)
Location: Smythesdale
Area: 10 ha
Soils: quartz, gravelly duplex soils on a clay base
Varieties planted: White—chardonnay; Red—cabernet sauvignon, pinot noir, shiraz
Leading wines: Cuvee Victoria and the Yellowglen Sparkling range though, as with most major sparkling wine brands, a great deal of fruit is purchased from outside the district and even Cuvee Victoria may have ceased to be totally from Victorian sources
Notes: Founded in 1971, Yellowglen is the pioneer winery and vineyard in the modern era. It is now and has for many years been totally devoted to the making of sparkling wine base, for which the area seems quite suited. Cellar door sales: 7 days 9am–5pm.

FAR SOUTH WEST VICTORIA (PROPOSED HENTY REGION)

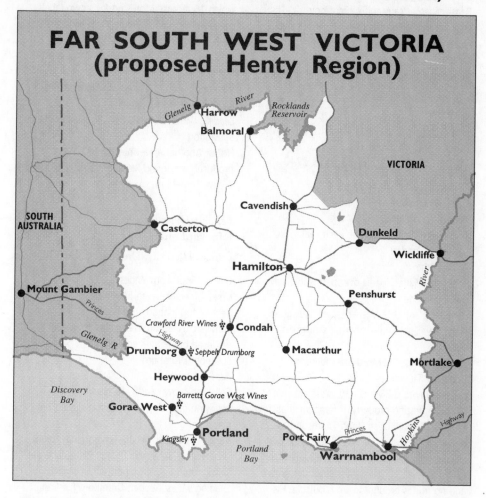

Pioneered by Seppelt in 1964, the Far South West of Victoria is well suited to riesling and possibly would be one of Australia's premium riesling areas if its climate was not so unpredictable. At the time of writing, this area was proposed as the Henty Region. It is distinguished by its vivid red basaltic soils of volcanic origin.

Barretts Gorae West Wines **NR**

Nelson Highway, Gorae West, Vic 3305
(about 20 km north-west of Portland)
Ph 03 5526 5251

Owners: Rod and Sandra Barrett
Chief winemaker: Rod Barrett

Year of foundation: 1983
Tonnes crushed on average each year: 15
Location: Gorae West
Area: 4.5 ha
Soils: basaltic red soils of volcanic origin

Varieties planted: White—riesling, traminer; Red—cabernet sauvignon, pinot noir
Leading wines: Barretts Riesling, Pinot Noir
Notes: In an area very suited to riesling, the Barretts wisely planted this variety and traminer. Cellar door sales: 7 days 11am–5pm.

Crawford River R8

Upper Hotspur Road, Condah, Vic 3305
(about 8 km west of the town)
Ph 03 5578 2267, Fax 03 5578 2240

Owner: Crawford River Wines
Chief winemaker: John Thomson
Year of foundation: 1975
Tonnes crushed on average each year: 50
Location: Condah
Area: 10 ha
Soils: gravelly red loams over permeable clay over limestone
Varieties planted: White—riesling, sauvignon blanc, semillon; Red—cabernet sauvignon, merlot
Leading wines: Crawford River Riesling, Cabernet Sauvignon
Notes: Crawford River is a working western Victorian grazing property. It happens that, for the last 20 years or so, John Thomson has been broadening his pastoral experience by viticulture and winemaking and it has worked extremely well. All his wines are estate grown and no fruit is brought in from outside. His Rieslings (usually dry but accompanied by an occasional botrytised) are exceptionally good and his Cabernet Sauvignon is full-flavoured with ripe berry and cassis characters. Cellar door sales: 7 days 9am–5pm.

Kingsley NR

6 Kingsley Court, Portland, Vic 3305
Ph 03 5523 1864

Owner: Tom Beauglehole
Chief winemaker: contract
Year of foundation: 1983

Tonnes produced on average each year: 20, of which 15 are used for Kingsley's own labels
Location: (vineyards) Gorae West and Portland
Area: 7.5 ha
Soils: very fertile deep red gravelly 'buckshot', rich in iron
Varieties planted: White—chardonnay, riesling; Red—cabernet sauvignon
Leading wines: Kingsley Riesling, Cabernet Sauvignon
Notes: Another area vineyard which has produced very good Riesling. Cellar door sales: 7 days 1pm–4pm.

Seppelt Drumborg (vineyard only) R9

Princes Highway, Drumborg, Vic 3305

Owner: Southcorp Wines
Chief winemaker: Ian McKenzie
Year of foundation: 1964
Tonnes crushed on average each year: not disclosed but estimated at 400
Location: Drumborg
Area: 58.1 ha
Soils: red-brown earths to black loams overlying grey clay; grey loam overlying red clay
Varieties planted: White—chardonnay, pinot gris, riesling, sauvignon blanc; Red—cabernet sauvignon, meunier, pinot noir, rose cross
Leading wines: Seppelt Drumborg Riesling
Notes: An important, if somewhat intermittent, jewel in the Seppelt crown, Drumborg has been renowned for producing a distinctly Germanic style of riesling, supremely elegant and very stylish. In some years in the past it produced none at all, but these days the riesling is still superb and production is in reasonable but not exciting quantity. The vineyard also contributes much to the quality of Seppelt sparkling wines, Salinger and Fleur de Lys, and to other Victorian table wines in its range. There are no cellar door sales here.

❧ CENTRAL VICTORIA ZONE

Like most of Victoria, this is a broad area nurtured first by grazing and later exalted by gold. It is surprisingly diverse with terrain varying from the cooler uplands of midland Victoria northwards to the warmer dunes of the central Murray Valley.

It encompasses the proposed wine regions of Goulburn Valley, Bendigo and Heathcote. Its wine speciality is red, with robust Shiraz predominant.

BENDIGO REGION (PROPOSED)

Bendigo followed a fairly typical pattern of New South Wales colonial settlement. It was settled by graziers in the 1840s and, after the creation of Victoria in 1851, became the focus of a huge goldrush and the 'golden' years that followed. At its greatest extent, its gold-bearing area encompassed about 370 square kilometres.

Typically once again, vines are said to have followed the miners, arriving in the area about 1855. However, Ebenezer Ward, the peripatetic wine correspondent, noted vines in the area that appeared to be 15 years old when he passed through in 1864. He also noted several younger vineyards so it would seem that most if not all of the first flush of viticulture in Bendigo was gold-inspired.

By 1880, vineyards in the region covered over 200 hectares and it is said that there were more than 100 wineries in production. Its wines were quite famous. One in particular, when shown at the Vienna Exhibition in 1873, caused a walkout by the French judges who alleged that it was so good, it just had to be French. The range of wines produced was also quite broad, ranging from light dry red and white types, through bigger Shiraz to quite sweet dessert wines. As a wine region, Bendigo began to decline in 1893 when phylloxera was discovered and thereafter its fall was swift, the Victorian government ordering the wholesale uprooting of vineyards as it had done in Geelong's case some years earlier.

The modern era of Bendigo wine began in 1969 when Bendigo pharmacist Stuart Anderson planted Balgownie. Though other vineyards were planted in the early to mid-1970s, the eclat created by his dense-coloured reds made Victoria very aware of the area's potential. Today the region is well-established and equally well-respected as one of Victoria's premium areas.

The Heathcote area decided late in 1998 to become a separate region. Its application for such status is pending. Wineries and vineyards that fall within this region are marked * on the following listing.

Location: Bendigo (city) latitude 36°46'S, longitude 144°17'E, about 130 km north-west of Melbourne. As proposed, the region is roughly egg-shaped, its boundaries encompassing the country from the Pyrenees region of Western Victoria in the west to the boundary of the Goulburn River region in the east. At the circle's western edge, it encompasses the towns of Maryborough, Bridgewater and Bendigo, then south-easterly

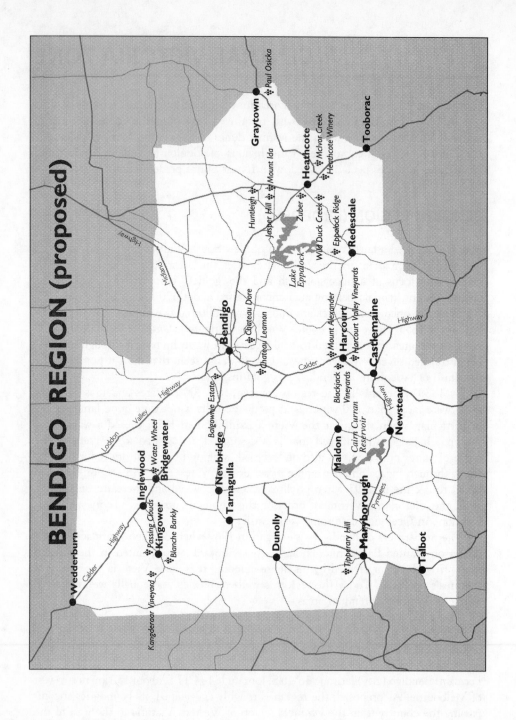

BENDIGO REGION (proposed)

Paul Osicka

Graytown

McIvor Creek
Heathcote
Heathcote Winery
Mount Ida
Tooborac

Huntleigh
Jasper Hill
Zuber
Eppalock Ridge
Wild Duck Creek
Redesdale

Lake
Eppalock

Chateau Dore
Chateau Leamon
Bendigo

Mount Alexander
Harcourt
Harcourt Valley Vineyards
Castlemaine

Calder

Highway

Blackjack
Vineyards
Cairn Curran
Reservoir

Newstead

Highway

Balgownie Estate

Water Wheel
Bridgewater
Inglewood

Newbridge

Tarnagulla

Maldon

Maryborough

Pyrenees

Highway

Valley
Loddon

Passing Clouds
Kingower
Blanche Barkly

Dunolly

Tipperary Hill

Talbot

Calder
Highway
Wedderburn

Kangderaar Vineyard

Midland

Highway

to Heathcote, travelling as far east as Graytown. The southern boundary passes north of Kyneton (itself in Port Phillip zone) and encloses Redesdale and Castlemaine.

Altitude: 230–400 m

Topography and soils: Flat in the north-west, becoming more undulating to the east and quite hilly in the south of the region with deeper valleys. In soil terms, the region falls naturally into three sub-regions, the Loddon (Bendigo-Kingower-Bridgewater), the Castlemaine-Harcourt and the Heathcote*. As befits a gold-mining area and as the individual vineyard notes illustrate, its Loddon soils in the west and north-west are alluvial sands and clay loams over silty clays, quartz and ironstone subsoils, with mostly good moisture retention during the dry summer periods. Castlemaine-Harcourt has grey sandy loams over sandy clay loams while Heathcote is quite distinctive with its red Cambrian soils. Such soils seem to give an added dimension to Shiraz. Bendigo is certain to achieve sub-regional status in time.

Climate: (Bendigo) MJT 21.7°C, MAR na, HDD 1571 (not for vine sites), AR 546 mm (Oct–Apr 267 mm), RH 36%, AI na, SH 8.9. The region slopes down from the Great Dividing Range to the north and north-west. In its northern parts it has a typically warm but not extreme inland Australian climate. In its southern higher areas it is slightly cooler. The climate as a whole favours robust red table wines. Its rainfall is generally low but evenly spread from month to month between November and March, though supplementary irrigation is sometimes necessary on shallower soils. Its low relative humidity assists in the prevention of mildews and rots. Weather is even during ripening with clear sunny days. Birds can be a nuisance and Ron Laughton has noticed an increasing colonisation of his area by Indian mynahs.

Harvest time: As befits a large region with varying mesoclimates, shiraz ripening is quite diverse. In the Bendigo area and north-west, late March. At Heathcote, early April and at Castlemaine-Harcourt fractionally later.

Principal grape varieties: shiraz, cabernet sauvignon, chardonnay

Total area: not known but certainly not less than 250 ha and increasing

Major wine styles: Shiraz—deeply coloured wines showing distinct black pepper characters on nose and palate. Sometimes a eucalyptus nuance can be discerned. Such wines are rich and long-lasting (8+ years in good years). Cabernet Sauvignon—as with Shiraz, these are wines of deep red-purple hues, built usually for long-term 8–10 years maturation. Complex and richly structured wines with an emphasis on ripe berry fruit.

Balgownie Estate   **R8**

Hermitage Road, Maiden Gully, Vic 3551
Ph 03 5449 6222, Fax 03 5449 6506

Owner: Mildara Blass Ltd
Chief winemaker: Lindsay Ross
Year of foundation: 1969
Tonnes crushed on average each year: 110
Location: Maiden Gully
Area: 17 ha

Soils: alluvial clay loam over silty clays
Varieties planted: White—chardonnay;
Red—cabernet sauvignon, pinot noir, shiraz
Leading wines: Balgownie Estate Shiraz,
Cabernet Sauvignon
Notes: Founded by master-winemaker Stuart
Anderson in 1969, Balgownie was purchased
by Mildara Blass in 1985. Its lights were

dimmed for a while but these days are tending to glow a little brighter, as the vineyard's inherent quality shines through. Balgownie's show results are consistently good, with silver and bronze medals in capital city wine shows for the Estate Cabernet Sauvignon and Estate Shiraz and golds for the 1995 versions of these wines. Cellar door sales: Mon–Sat 9am–5pm.

Blackjack Vineyards NR

Just off Blackjack Road on Calder Highway, Harcourt, Vic 3453
Ph/Fax 03 5474 2355

Owners: McKenzie and Pollock families
Chief winemaker: Ken Pollock and Ian McKenzie
Year of foundation: 1988
Tonnes crushed on average each year: 40 and increasing as new vineyard plantings come into bearing
Location: Harcourt
Area: 4 ha
Soils: granitic sand with quartz and granite 'floaters'
Varieties planted: White—none; Red—cabernet sauvignon, merlot, pinot noir, shiraz
Leading wines: Blackjack Vineyards Shiraz
Notes: Like many Australian vineyards, Blackjack is located on the site of an old orchard. It has a rising reputation, not diminished by the trophy won for best 1994 Shiraz at the Royal Melbourne wine show. Its owner, Ian McKenzie, is not to be confused with Ian McKenzie of Seppelt.
Cellar door sales: weekends and public holidays 11am–5pm.

Blanche Barkly NR

Rheola Road, Kingower, Vic 3517
Ph 03 5438 8223, 03 5443 3664

Owners/chief winemakers: Alvin and David Reimers
Year of foundation: 1972

Tonnes crushed on average each year: 25
Location: Kingower
Area: 3.2 ha
Soils: ironstone, quartz, black loamy clay, auriferous country
Varieties planted: White—none; Red—cabernet franc, cabernet sauvignon, mondeuse, shiraz
Leading wines: Blanche Barkly Alexander Cabernet Sauvignon, George Henry Cabernet Sauvignon, Mary Eileen Shiraz
Notes: This is an old established Bendigo winery, well respected for its reds. Cellar door sales: weekends and public holidays 10am–5pm.

Charlotte Plains NR

Dooleys Road, Simpson, Maryborough, Vic 3465
Ph 03 5461 3137

Owners: Ian and Vera Kemp
Chief winemaker: Roland Kaval (contract)
Year of foundation: 1990
Tonnes crushed on average each year: 2
Location: Simpson near Maryborough
Area: 1.6 ha
Soils: thin alluvial soils and sandy clay loam, which hold moisture quite well during dry summers
Varieties planted: White—sauvignon blanc; Red—shiraz
Leading wines: Charlotte Plains Shiraz
Notes: A small vineyard (close planted, 25 rows each 100 m long, 1.5 m apart). Charlotte Plains has not entered wine shows because of its tiny production, but a Winestate tasting in 1997 produced an encouraging 4-star rating for its 1996 Shiraz. Sales by mailing list only.

Chateau Dore NR

303 Mandurang Road, Mandurang, Vic 3551
Ph 03 5439 5278

Owners: Ivan and Jan Gross
Chief winemaker: Ivan Gross
Year of foundation: 1860 (ceased original
operation about 1900, re-established 1969)
Tonnes crushed on average each year: 10
Location: Mandurang
Area: 3 ha
Soils: slate country, sandy loams and ironstone
over red clay, loam with gravel beds
Varieties planted: White—chardonnay, riesling;
Red—cabernet sauvignon, shiraz
Leading wines: Chateau Dore Shiraz
Notes: The ancestral winery was built by Ivan's
great-grandfather in the 1860s and was put to
work again when winemaking recommenced.
Cellar door sales: Tues–Sun 10.30am–5pm,
closed Sat from 1pm.

Chateau Leamon NR

Calder Highway, Bendigo, Vic 3550
Ph 03 5447 7995, Fax 03 5447 0855

Owner: Alma Leamon
Chief winemaker: Ian Leamon
Year of foundation: 1973
Tonnes crushed on average each year: 40
Location: Bendigo
Area: 5.6 ha
Soils: clayey loams
Varieties planted: White—riesling, semillon;
Red—cabernet sauvignon, merlot, shiraz
Leading wines: Chateau Leamon Shiraz
Notes: Bendigo is of course a very good Shiraz
area, Chateau Leamon's Shiraz being typical of
the region. Cellar door sales: 6 days (closed
Tuesdays).

Eppalock Ridge NR

Metcalfe Pool Road, Redesdale, Vic 3444
Ph 03 5425 3135, Fax 03 5425 3135

Owners: Rod and Sue Hourigan
Chief winemaker: Rod Hourigan
Year of foundation: 1979

Tonnes crushed on average each year: 30
including some purchased fruit
Location: Redesdale
Area: 2.4 ha
Soils: young volcanic basalt
Varieties planted: White—none;
Red—grenache, malbec, merlot, shiraz
Leading wines: Eppalock Ridge Shiraz,
Cabernet Merlot
Notes: Rod Hourigan does not show his wines
as often now but he has won golds at the
Victorian wine show. As is typical for the
region, Shiraz is his pick of his wines but he
has more than a sneaking regard for his
Cabernet Merlot. Cellar door sales: 10am–6pm
daily, but phone first.

Harcourt Valley Vineyards NR

Calder Highway, Harcourt, Vic 3453
Ph 03 5474 2223, Fax 03 5474 2293

Owners: John and Barbara Livingstone
Chief winemaker: John Livingstone
Year of foundation: 1982
Tonnes crushed on average each year: 20
Location: Harcourt
Area: 4.5 ha
Soils: granitic
Varieties planted: White—chardonnay, riesling;
Red—cabernet sauvignon, shiraz
Leading wines: Harcourt Valley Shiraz,
Cabernet Sauvignon
Notes: Robust reds typical of the region. Cellar
door sales: 11am–6pm daily.

*Heathcote Winery NR

185 High Street, Heathcote, Vic 3523
Ph 03 5433 2595, Fax 03 5433 3081

Owner: Heathcote Winery and Vineyard Pty Ltd
Chief winemaker: Mark Kelly
Year of foundation: 1979
Tonnes crushed on average each year: 175
Location: Heathcote
Area: 12 ha

Soils: 'Heathcote' Cambrian red soil, which is a decomposition of Heathcote 'Greenstone', a metamorphosed igneous intrusion rock and adjoining sedimentary layers
Varieties planted: White—chardonnay, roussanne, verdelho, viognier; Red—shiraz
Leading wines: Heathcote Winery Cambrian Viognier, Mail Coach Shiraz, Chardonnay
Notes: Heathcote Winery changed hands recently. The region has a spectacular reputation for Shiraz and, as the French experience in the northern Rhone shows, terrain that is good for shiraz may also be very suitable for viognier. Cellar door sales: daily during summer 10am–6pm, at other times of year Thurs–Sun.

*Huntleigh NR

Tunnicliffe's Lane, Heathcote, Vic 3523
Ph 03 5433 2795

Owners: Leigh and Johanne Hunt
Chief winemaker: Leigh Hunt
Year of foundation: 1975
Tonnes crushed on average each year: 7
Location: Heathcote
Area: 5 ha
Soils: from lighter, sandy, quartzy soils through red to heavy black loam
Varieties planted: White—gewurztraminer, riesling; Red—cabernet franc, cabernet sauvignon, merlot, shiraz
Leading wines: Huntleigh Cabernet Sauvignon
Notes: In an area where shiraz is king, Leigh Hunt prefers his Cabernet Sauvignon because of its complexity. Cellar door sales: most days, always on weekends and public holidays 10am–5.30pm.

*Jasper Hill R9.5

Drummonds Lane, Heathcote, Vic 3523
Ph 03 5433 2528, Fax 03 5433 3143

Owners: Ron and Elva Laughton
Chief winemaker: Ron Laughton

Year of foundation: 1975
Tonnes crushed on average each year: 50
Location: Heathcote
Area: 24 ha (some not bearing)
Soils: red Cambrian soil about 4 m deep; this dryland vineyard's soils have good moisture retention
Varieties planted: White—riesling; Red—cabernet franc, nebbiolo, shiraz
Leading wines: Jasper Hill Georgia's Paddock Shiraz, Riesling, Emily's Paddock Shiraz (which usually has a 5% addition of cabernet franc)
Notes: The overwhelming influence of soil is shown by this vineyard and the adjoining Mount Ida (both on red Cambrian soils). Both produce magnificent Shiraz. Apart from invitations to the occasional international exhibition, Jasper Hill does not enter its wines in wine shows. It does not need to. It has such renown that its wines sell out automatically to a hungry mailing list in a very short time after release, which usually takes place on 1 September each year. Accordingly Jasper Hill is rarely open for cellar door sales.

Kangderaar Vineyard NR

Melvilles Caves Road, Rheola, Vic 3517
Ph/Fax 03 5438 8292

Owners: James and Christine Nealy
Chief winemaker: James Nealy
Year of foundation: 1980
Tonnes crushed on average each year: 10
Location: Rheola
Area: 4.5 ha
Soils: granitic sand, very dry and 'thirsty' in Christine Nealy's own words
Varieties planted: White—chardonnay, gewurztraminer, riesling; Red—cabernet sauvignon, merlot, touriga
Leading wines: Kangderaar Chardonnay, Cabernet-Merlot
Notes: Another small regional vineyard with consistent standards. Its 1996 Cabernet Sauvignon won bronzes at Ballarat and the

Victorian wine show. Cellar door sales: Mon–Sat 9am–5pm, Sun 10am–5pm.

Laanecoorie R7

Bendigo Road, Betley, Vic 3472
Ph 03 5468 7260, Fax 03 5468 7388

Owners: John and Rosa McQuilten
Chief winemaker: John Ellis (contract)
Year of foundation: 1982
Tonnes produced on average each year: 14
Location: Betley
Area: 6 ha
Soils: alluvial with sandy clay loam
Varieties planted: White—none; Red—cabernet franc, cabernet sauvignon, merlot
Leading wines: Laanecoorie (a blend of the three varieties mentioned)
Notes: No cellar door sales.

**McIvor Creek* NR

Costerfield Road, Heathcote, Vic 3523
Ph 03 5433 3000, Fax 03 5433 3456

Owners: Peter and Robyn Turley
Chief winemaker: Peter Turley
Year of foundation: 1973
Tonnes crushed on average each year: 45
Location: Heathcote
Area: 7.5 ha
Soils: Robyn Turley describes the soil as 'clay and rocks'
Varieties planted: Whites—none;
Red—cabernet franc, cabernet sauvignon
Leading wines: McIvor Creek Cabernet-Shiraz 1991
Notes: An interesting Heathcote winery with some well-aged wines in stock. Peter Turley, who buys in fruit from other regions, also makes a good botrytised Auslese Riesling.
Cellar door sales: 7 days 10am–5.30pm.

Mount Alexander NR

Calder Highway, North Harcourt, Vic 3453
Ph 03 5474 2262, Fax 03 5474 2553

Owner/chief winemaker: Keith Walkden
Year of foundation: 1983
Tonnes crushed on average each year: 65
Location: North Harcourt
Area: 10 ha expanded to 16 ha in 1998
Soils: granitic loam
Varieties planted: White—chardonnay, muller-thurgau, muscadelle, riesling, sauvignon blanc, semillon; Red—cabernet franc, cabernet sauvignon, meunier, muscat a petits grains rouge, pinot noir, shiraz touriga tinta cao
Leading wines: Mount Alexander Vintage Port, Cabernet Sauvignon, Chardonnay, Semillon
Notes: For the Bendigo region, Mount Alexander is quite a large maker with a diverse range of wines and fruit brandies. There is also a cider. Cellar door sales: Mon–Sat 9.30am–5.30pm. Picnic and barbecue facilities.

**Mount Ida (vineyard only)* R9.5

Northern Highway, Heathcote, Vic 3523

Owner: Mildara Blass Ltd
Chief winemaker: Toni Stockhausen
Year of foundation: 1978
Tonnes crushed on average each year: 30
Location: Heathcote
Area: 6 ha
Soils: red Cambrian loam
Varieties planted: White—none; Red—cabernet sauvignon, shiraz
Leading wines: Mount Ida Shiraz
Notes: A very famous Shiraz which usually contains about 10% cabernet. The 1996 has been a consistent trophy winner. Winemaker Toni Stockhausen modestly attributes its quality to the vineyard soils. There are no local cellar door sales.

Paul Osicka **R7**

Graytown, Vic 3608
Ph 03 5794 9235, Fax 03 5794 0288

Owner: Paul Osicka Wines Pty Ltd
Chief winemaker: Paul Osicka
Year of foundation: 1955
Tonnes crushed on average each year: 100
Location: Graytown (in the east of the region)
Area: 13 ha
Soils: sandy soils on ironstone and quartz
gravel subsoil
Varieties planted: White—chardonnay, riesling,
roussanne; Red—cabernet franc, cabernet
sauvignon, shiraz
Leading wines: Paul Osicka Shiraz, Cabernet
Sauvignon, Chardonnay
Notes: This consistent winery, now established
over 40 years—long before table wine became
fashionable—deserves to be better known
because of its very good reds. Cellar door
sales: Mon–Sat 10am–5pm, Sun noon–5pm.

Passing Clouds **R8.5**

RMB 440 Kurting Road, Kingower,
Vic 3517
Ph 03 5438 8257, Fax 03 5438 8246

Owners: Graeme Leith and Sue Mackinnon
Chief winemaker: Graeme Leith, Greg Bennett
(winemaker)
Year of foundation: 1974
Tonnes crushed on average each year: 65
(includes local fruit purchases)
Location: Kingower
Area: 6 ha
Soils: Passing Clouds is on old creek flats and
its vines are well established on non-irrigated
deep sandy loam
Varieties planted: White—chardonnay,
sauvignon blanc; Red—cabernet sauvignon,
shiraz
Leading wines: Passing Clouds Graeme's Blend
Shiraz-Cabernet, Angel Cabernets, Pinot Noir,
Shiraz

Notes: After a quarter of a century, Graeme
Leith and Sue Mackinnon have a wealth of
experience of the Kingower area. Their wines
are often shown at the Victorian wine show
and at Melbourne where the 1994 Angel
Cabernet struck gold in 1996. Cellar door sales
by appointment.

Tipperary Hill **NR**

Alma-Bowenvale Road, Alma,
Maryborough, Vic 3465
Ph/Fax 03 5461 3312

Owner/chief winemaker: Paul Flowers
Year of foundation: 1986
Tonnes crushed on average each year: 7
Location: Alma
Area: 2 ha
Soils: alluvial soils on a sandstone, quartz and
ironstone reef
Varieties planted: White—none; Red—cabernet
franc, cabernet sauvignon, merlot, pinot noir,
shiraz
Leading wines: Tipperary Hill Shiraz, Pinot Noir,
Pinot-Shiraz
Notes: A pretty spot close to a state forest
near an old gold-mining area. There is a
restaurant and a picnic ground. Cellar door
sales: weekends 10am–5pm or by
appointment.

Water Wheel **R8**

Bridgewater on Loddon, Bridgewater,
Vic 3516
Ph 03 5437 3060, Fax 03 5437 3082

Owner: Peter Cumming
Chief winemakers: Peter Cumming and
Bill Trevaskis
Year of foundation: 1972
Tonnes crushed on average each year: 500
Location: Bridgewater on Loddon
Area: 50 ha
Soils: white light loam for the whites; red

sticky clay with small pieces of limestone for the reds

Varieties planted: White—chardonnay, sauvignon blanc; Red—cabernet franc, cabernet sauvignon, malbec, merlot, petit verdot, shiraz

Leading wines: Water Wheel Chardonnay, Sauvignon Blanc, Cabernet Sauvignon, Shiraz

Notes: Water Wheel is the region's largest producer and maintains consistent standards for both whites and reds. It gained a silver award for its 1996 Shiraz at the National Wine Show in Canberra in 1997. Cellar door sales: Mon–Sat 10am–5pm, Sundays and public holidays noon–5pm.

Wild Duck Creek R7.5

Spring Flat Road, Heathcote, Vic 3523
Ph/Fax 03 5433 3133

Owners: David and Diana Anderson
Chief winemaker: David Anderson
Year of foundation: 1980
Tonnes crushed on average each year: 10
Location: Heathcote
Area: 3 ha
Soils: shales and mudstones, 'buckshot' and quartz and some Cambrian red

Varieties planted: White—none; Red—cabernet franc, cabernet sauvignon, malbec, merlot, petit verdot, shiraz

Leading wines: Wild Duck Creek Estate Alans Cabernet, Spring Flat Shiraz

Notes: David Anderson is a committed red winemaker, devoted to quality and complexity in his wines. His favourite wine show is the Victorian where in several years of exhibiting, he has won 45 awards. Cellar door sales, by appointment.

Zuber NR

Northern Highway, Heathcote, Vic 3523
Ph 03 5433 2142

Owner/chief winemaker: Albino Zuber
Year of foundation: 1971
Tonnes crushed on average each year: 23
Location: Heathcote
Area: 7 ha
Soils: red Cambrian
Varieties planted: White—chardonnay; Red—cabernet sauvignon, pinot noir, shiraz
Leading wines: Zuber Shiraz
Notes: A low profile Heathcote winery whose leading wine is its Shiraz. Cellar door sales: 7 days 9am–6pm.

GOULBURN VALLEY REGION (PROPOSED)

The Goulburn Valley owes its existence as a vineyard area to the massive contribution of Chateau Tahbilk, without which it may long ago have been returned to pastoral pursuits. Founded in 1860 by a group of investors led by a poet (R. H. Horne), Tabilk Vineyard Proprietary with its capital of $50 000 purchased 259 hectares of land adjoining the right bank of the Goulburn River, north of Seymour, and by the end of 1861 had 87 hectares under vine. Substantial cellars were constructed and by 1877 Tabilk's production reached 17 500 cases a year. By this time, Chateau Tahbilk (the name was first used in 1879) was owned and capably managed by John Pinney Bear in whose family it remained until 1926. It was then purchased by the Purbrick family and shortly afterwards was occupied by Eric Purbrick. The Purbrick family has owned Chateau Tahbilk ever since.

Mitchelton, the vision of the late Ross Shelmerdine and the region's other major

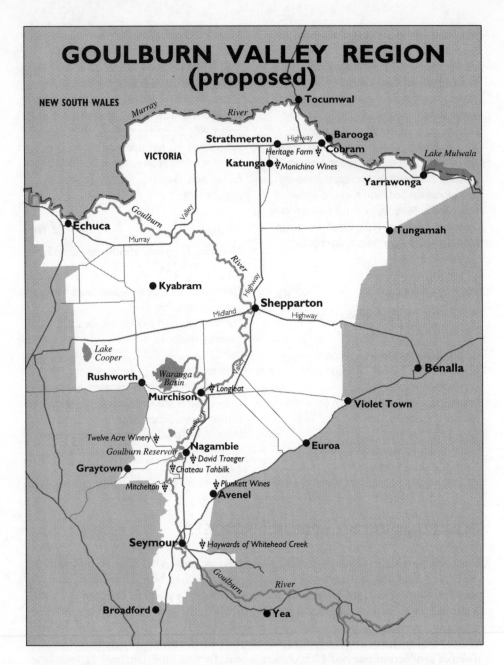

GOULBURN VALLEY REGION
(proposed)

NEW SOUTH WALES

VICTORIA

Murray   River   Tocumwal

Strathmerton   Highway   Barooga
Heritage Farm 🍇   Cobram

Katunga 🍇 Monichino Wines

Lake Mulwala

Yarrawonga

Goulburn   Valley

Echuca

Murray

Tungamah

Kyabram

River   Highway

Shepparton

Midland   Highway

Lake
Cooper

Bénalla

Rushworth

Waranga
Basin
🍇 Longleat

Murchison

Violet Town

Twelve Acre Winery 🍇

Goulburn Reservoir   Nagambie
🍇 David Traeger
🍇 Chateau Tahbilk

Euroa

Graytown

Mitchelton 🍇

🍇 Plunkett Wines
🍇 Avenel

Seymour   🍇 Haywards of Whitehead Creek

Goulburn   River

Broadford   Yea

winery, is of much more recent origin. Lying about 5 km from Chateau Tahbilk and abutting the left bank of the Goulburn River, it became part of Victoria's wine resurgence in the late 1960s. Its vines were established in sandy country on their own rootstocks in the belief that phylloxera had ceased to be a hazard and anyhow would not present a danger in such soil. They were first planted in 1969. Its modern winery with its distinctive 'witch's hat' tower was completed in 1974. Mitchelton was purchased by Petaluma Limited in 1994. Sadly, phylloxera has now appeared in the Mitchelton vineyard and replacement vines are now planted on resistant rootstocks.

The Goulburn Valley is by no means Australia's premier vineyard area but has deservedly built a reputation for sturdy, reliable Cabernet and Shiraz reds and, considering its generally warm climate, distinctive Marsannes and surprisingly delicate Rieslings.

Location: latitude 36°23' to 37°02'S, longitude 145°19'E, the region begins at Tallarook, about 70 km north of Melbourne on the Hume Highway and proceeds about 20 km to the south-east along the Goulburn Valley Highway. It then turns north to meet the Hume Highway once more near Avenel, travelling 50 km north-east along or close to that highway as far as Violet Town. It then veers north to take in the Dookie area, then west to encompass the fruit-growing areas of Shepparton and neighbouring Mooroopna. It proceeds to the River Murray before turning south-west as far as Rushworth then returning roughly south about 70 km to Tallarook. Its principal towns are Seymour, Nagambie, Euroa, Violet Town, Shepparton and Tatura.
Altitude: 140 m
Topography and soils: The region generally follows the west–north course of the Goulburn River. Rising near Mount Buller in the Victorian Alps, the river flows swiftly through Lake Eildon and the surrounding steeply mountainous country to reach its wine region south-east of Tallarook. From there, the country is flat and the river's flow is slower, though it is subject to flooding in many places in times of heavy rain. Its sandy, gravelly soils, mainly alluvial in origin, accordingly reflect the history of their river. Further away from the river beds, both current and ancient, there are the typical moderately fertile, hard, red duplex soils, found in many vineyard areas of south-eastern Australia. Water resources of the Goulburn Valley are regarded as very good as there are aquifers at 30 metres.
Climate: Seymour MJT 20.9°C, MAR na, HDD (raw) 1694, 1485 (cut off and adjusted for latitude, daily temperature range but not adjusted for vine sites), AR 596 mm (Oct–Apr 293 mm), RH 41%, AI na, SH 8.7. Euroa MJT 21.8°C, MAR na, HDD (raw) 1898, 1460 (cut off and adjusted for latitude, daily temperature range and vine sites Gladstones), AR 649 mm (Oct–Apr 308 mm), RH 46% (both Gladstones). Goulburn Valley MJT 21.2°C, MAR 13.7°C, HDD (raw) 1681, AR 597 mm (Oct–Mar 248 mm), RH 52% (9am), AI 309 mm, SH 9 (D&S). Quite warm in summer, though not as warm as Rutherglen and the north-east, the Goulburn Valley has a reputation for table wines of good quality. Slightly less than half the average annual rainfall occurs between October and March and drip-irrigation is now becoming more common. The region also experiences spring frosts and is phylloxerated, new plantings requiring phylloxera-resistant rootstocks.
Harvest time: chardonnay, sauvignon blanc in March; marsanne and riesling in mid-March to mid-April; shiraz in late March to late April; cabernet sauvignon mid-April to mid-May.
Principal grape varieties: Red—shiraz, cabernet sauvignon, merlot, cabernet franc; White—chardonnay, marsanne, riesling, sauvignon blanc, semillon, viognier, verdelho.

Total area: 375 ha
Major wine styles: White—Marsanne, Chardonnay, Riesling; Red—Shiraz, Cabernet Sauvignon

Chateau Tahbilk   R8.5

Tabilk, Vic 3608 (8 km south-west of Nagambie)
Ph 03 5794 2555, Fax 03 5794 2350

Owners: Purbrick family
Chief winemaker: Alister Purbrick
Year of foundation: 1860
Tonnes crushed on average each year: 2000, about 1400 of which are used for Chateau Tahbilk's own labels
Location: Tabilk
Area: 155 ha; there are also two other vineyards, AHN of 81 ha and Pogue of 55 ha
Soils: Chateau Tahbilk—fine sand, sandy loam and red loam; AHN—red loam; Pogue—fine sand
Varieties planted: Chateau Tahbilk Vineyard, White—chardonnay, chenin blanc, marsanne, riesling, roussanne, sauvignon blanc, semillon, viognier; Red—cabernet franc, cabernet sauvignon, malbec, merlot, shiraz. AHN, White—chardonnay; Red—shiraz. Pogue, White—chardonnay, sauvignon blanc, verdelho; Red—cabernet sauvignon, merlot, shiraz
Leading wines: Chateau Tahbilk 1860 Vines Shiraz, Reserve Cabernet Sauvignon
Notes: Chateau Tahbilk is one of the historical showplaces of Australian wine. Though it deserves reverence, it is a veteran that is still very much alive. With one exception, reds are Tahbilk's forte—the 1962 Reserve Cabernet Sauvignon was a show wine that was still remarkably resilient 25 years later. Of course there are the few rows of the original plantings of shiraz which somehow escaped the march of phylloxera a century ago. These too now receive the respect and identity due to worthy veterans. The exception to the reds is the Marsanne which, in good years and given due cellaring, develops a marvellous honeysuckle character on nose and palate. Cellar door sales: Mon–Sat

9am–5pm. Sun and public holidays 11am–5pm. Closed Christmas Day.

David Traeger   R7.5

139 High Street, Nagambie, Vic, 3608
Ph/Fax 03 5794 2514

Owner/chief winemaker: David Traeger
Year of foundation: 1986
Tonnes crushed on average each year: 300
Locations: Avenel (18 ha and expanding), Graytown 12.8 ha (Bendigo region)
Area: 30.8 ha
Soils: Avenel—red clay loam with good fertility and water-holding capacity; Graytown—red sandy loam, well-drained, friable
Varieties planted: White—verdelho; Red—cabernet sauvignon, merlot, shiraz
Leading wines: David Traeger Verdelho, Shiraz, Old Vine Shiraz, Cabernet Sauvignon
Notes: David Traeger is a former assistant winemaker at Mitchelton and well-versed in the Goulburn Valley and its wines. There have been consistent show results for Verdelho and Shiraz, as one would expect from an experienced Goulburn Valley hand. Cellar door sales: daily 10am–5pm.

Haywards of Whitehead Creek   NR

Hall Lane, Seymour, Vic 3660
Ph 03 5792 3050

Owners: Mr and Mrs B Hayward
Chief winemakers: Sid and David Hayward
Year of foundation: 1975
Tonnes crushed on average each year: 10
Location: Whitehead Creek
Area: 5 ha
Soils: clay loam over mottled clay

Varieties planted: White—riesling;
Red—cabernet sauvignon, malbec, pinot noir,
shiraz
Leading wines: Haywards of Whitehead Creek
Shiraz, Cabernet Sauvignon
Notes: Cellar door sales: Mon–Sat 9am–6pm,
Sun 10am–6pm, closed Good Friday and
Christmas Day.

Heritage Farm NR

Murray Valley Highway, Cobram,
Vic 3644
Ph 03 5872 2376

Owner/chief winemaker: Kevin Tyrrell
Year of foundation: 1987
Tonnes crushed on average each year: 50
Location: Cobram
Area: 6 ha
Soils: old river flood plain consisting of light
alluvial brown loam
Varieties planted: White—chardonnay, riesling,
sauvignon blanc, trebbiano; Red—cabernet
franc, cabernet sauvignon, mourvedre, muscat
a petits grains rouge, shiraz, zinfandel
Leading wines: Heritage Farm Workhorse Red
(a red blend), Traminer Riesling, Liqueur
Muscat, Ploughman's Port, Clydesdale Port
Notes: A small family-operated vineyard. Cellar
door sales: 7 days 9am–5pm.

Longleat NR

Old Weir Road, Murchison, Vic 3610
Ph 03 5826 2294, Fax 03 5826 2510

Owner: Longleat Estate Pty Ltd
Chief winemaker: Alister Purbrick (contract)
Year of foundation: 1975
Tonnes crushed on average each year: 59, of
which about 18 tonnes are used for the
Longleat labels
Location: Murchison
Area: 9 ha
Soils: sandy loam on a clay base

Varieties planted: White—riesling, semillon;
Red—cabernet sauvignon, shiraz
Leading wines: Longleat Shiraz, Cabernet
Sauvignon, Riesling
Notes: The vineyard and winery changed hands
in February 1998, but Longleat will no doubt
continue to make full-flavoured whites and
reds typical of the Goulburn Valley. Cellar door
sales: daily 10am–5pm.

Mitchelton R9

Mitchellstown, Nagambie, Vic 3608
Ph 03 5794 2710, Fax 03 5794 2615

Owner: Petaluma Ltd
Chief winemaker: Don Lewis
Year of foundation: 1969
Tonnes crushed on average each year: 3000
(including fruit purchases from growers)
Location: Mitchellstown
Area: 142.2 ha, of which 21.2 ha are yet to
come into bearing
Soils: typically alluvial, with soils varying from
sandy loams to fine clay loams; red-brown
earths predominantly overlying lighter clay
dominant soils; pH 5.5–6.5 (very slightly acidic)
Varieties planted: White—chardonnay,
marsanne, riesling, roussanne, semillon,
viognier; Red—cabernet franc, cabernet
sauvignon, merlot, shiraz
Leading wines: Mitchelton Print Shiraz,
Blackwood Park Riesling, Blackwood Park
Botrytised Riesling, Goulburn Valley Marsanne,
Goulburn Valley Shiraz, Chardonnay,
Marsanne, Cabernet Sauvignon, Preece,
Thomas Mitchell
Notes: Like its near neighbour Chateau Tahbilk,
5 km away, Mitchelton is typically riverine, light
sandy loam soils from ancient Goulburn River
beds and a warm but not scorching climate
with cooling river breezes. All of this produces
stable fruit, from which Don Lewis makes
superb award winning Rieslings, Marsannes
and Shiraz. Cellar door sales: daily 10am–5pm.
There is also a restaurant open daily for lunch.

Monichino Wines R6.5

Berry's Road, Katunga, Vic 3644
Ph 03 5864 6452, Fax 03 5864 6538

Owners: Carlo and Terry Monichino and Ann Sergi (nee Monichino)
Chief winemakers: Terry and Carlo Monichino
Year of foundation: 1962
Tonnes crushed on average each year: 200
Location: Katunga
Area: 25 ha
Soils: heavy clay loam with underlying sand
Varieties planted: White—chardonnay, orange muscat, riesling, sauvignon blanc, semillon, white frontignac; Red—cabernet franc, cabernet sauvignon, merlot, shiraz
Leading wines: Monichino Chardonnay, Botrytis Semillon, Shiraz, Merlot, Cabernet Sauvignon
Notes: A winery and vineyard little known north of the Murray but with a consistent record of silver and bronze awards at Victorian and other wine shows. Cellar door sales: Mon–Sat 9am–5pm, Sun 10am–5pm.

Plunkett Wines R7.5

Lambing Gully Road, Avenel, Vic 3147.
Cellar door sales: Hume Highway, Avenel.
Ph 03 5796 2150, Fax 03 5796 2147

Owner: Plunkett family
Chief winemaker: Sam Plunkett
Year of foundation: 1968
Tonnes crushed on average each year: 160 (most fruit is sold to other winemakers)
Locations: 3 vineyards—Strathbogie Ranges (100 ha), Avenel (2.8 ha) and Mulwala (20 ha)
Area: 122.8 ha
Soils: Strathbogie Ranges—granite top soil over granite and granodiorite; Avenel—ironstone with an abundance of surface rock; Mulwala—red clay loam with some sand ridges
Varieties planted: White—chardonnay, gewurztraminer, riesling, sauvignon blanc, semillon; Red—cabernet franc, cabernet sauvignon, merlot, pinot noir, shiraz
Leading wines: Plunkett Unwooded Chardonnay, Chardonnay
Notes: Though they make no such claim, the Plunketts, with their vineyard high in the Strathbogie Ranges yielding almost perfect fruit, are in fact Chardonnay specialists. Their complex, long-flavoured wines are a pleasure to drink when young. Cellar door sales: daily 11am–5pm.

Twelve Acre Winery NR

RMB 1628 Nagambie-Rushworth Road, Bailieston, Vic 3608
Ph/Fax 03 5794 2020

Owners/chief winemakers: Peter and Jana Prygodicz
Year of foundation: 1990
Tonnes crushed on average each year: 13
Location: Bailieston
Area: no vineyard—all fruit presently purchased from growers
Leading wines: Twelve Acres Shiraz, Merlot, Cabernet Sauvignon
Notes: A promising winery whose Shiraz has won a trophy at the excellent Victorian wine show. Cellar door sales: weekends and public holidays 10am–6pm.

CENTRAL VICTORIAN HIGH COUNTRY AREA

This area consists of what might be called the catchment area of the Goulburn River. It is high and cool and stretches from the upper Goulburn Valley, including the Strathbogie Ranges and Mansfield, east to the foothills of Mount Buller. Perhaps it will become a sub-region of the Goulburn Valley but local opinion suggests that it should be a region in its own right. Its tentative boundaries commence at Avenel on the eastern side of the Hume Highway, run north along the highway to Violet Town, then turn south to Lake Nillahcootie. It then runs east to Tolmie (west of Whitlands), to Mount Buller and Jamieson, then to Buxton adjoining the Yarra Valley then west above the Yarra Valley to Flowerdale, then to Strath Creek and finally north to Avenel. There is little climatic information except a heat summation of 308 DD for the month of January 1996 for the Mount Helen vineyard. The Delatite vineyards ripen about a week later than Mount Helen.

Antcliffs Chase   **NR**

Caveat, via Seymour, Vic 3660
Ph/Fax 03 5790 4333

Owners: Chris Antcliff Bennett and Nonie Bennett
Chief winemakers: Chris Antcliff Bennett and Ian Leamon
Year of foundation: 1982
Tonnes crushed on average each year: 30
Location: Caveat, Strathbogie Ranges
Area: 4.4 ha
Soils: a well-drained slope with volcanic loam
Varieties planted: White—chardonnay, riesling;
Red—cabernet franc, cabernet sauvignon, merlot, pinot noir
Leading wines: Antcliffs Chase Riesling, Pinot Noir
Notes: At 600 m in altitude, Antcliffs Chase is high and cool in the Strathbogie Ranges—a location that seems suitable for riesling and perhaps pinot noir. Cellar door sales: weekends 10am–5pm.

Delatite   **R8**

Stoneys Road, Mansfield, Vic 3722
Ph 03 5775 2922, Fax 03 5775 2911

Owners: Ritchie family
Chief winemaker: Ros Ritchie; Viticulturist: David Ritchie

Year of foundation: 1968
Tonnes crushed on average each year: 210, of which 180 are used for Delatite's own labels
Location: Mansfield
Area: 25 ha
Soils: striated ironstone rock; the vineyard has minimum drip irrigation
Varieties planted: White—chardonnay, gewurztraminer, riesling, sauvignon blanc;
Red—cabernet sauvignon, malbec, merlot, pinot noir, shiraz
Leading wines: Delatite Demelza NV (sparkling), Riesling, Gewurztraminer, Sauvignon Blanc, Unoaked Chardonnay, Chardonnay, Devils River (a red blend), Pinot Noir, Merlot, Cabernet Sauvignon, Shiraz
Notes: A vineyard with an excellent reputation for delicate aromatic whites and fruit-driven reds which are always worth drinking. Cellar door sales: daily 10am–4pm.

Henke   **NR**

175 Henke Lane, Yarck, Vic 3719
Ph/Fax 03 5797 6277

Owners/chief winemaker: Tim and Caroline Miller
Year of foundation: 1970
Tonnes crushed on average each year: 5
Location: Yarck

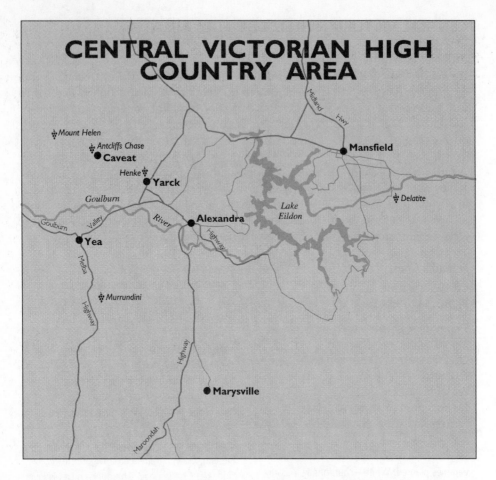

CENTRAL VICTORIAN HIGH COUNTRY AREA

Area: 2.4 ha
Soils: porous clayey soil, not high in fertility, which has been much improved by mulching
Varieties planted: White—none; Red—cabernet sauvignon, shiraz
Leading wines: Henke Shiraz, Shiraz Cabernet
Notes: Good blends of Shiraz and Cabernet. Cellar door sales by appointment and mail order.

Mount Helen (vineyard only)   R7.5

Upton Road, Avenel, Vic 3664

Owner: Normans
Chief winemaker: Toni Stockhausen
Year of foundation: 1975

Tonnes crushed on average each year: 419
Location: Strathbogie Ranges
Area: 78 ha
Soils: granitic topsoil over granite and granodiorite, sandy loam
Varieties planted: White—chardonnay, riesling, sauvignon blanc, semillon; Red—cabernet franc, cabernet sauvignon, merlot, meunier, pinot noir, shiraz
Leading wines: Mount Helen Cabernet-Merlot
Notes: One of the first high country Victorian vineyards, Mount Helen was a high-profile brand of the 1980s, when owned by Dr Peter Tisdall, and very much sought after for its Chardonnay and Cabernet Merlot. There are no local cellar door sales.

Murrundindi **R7**

RMB 6070 Cummins Lane, Murrundindi, Vic 3717
Ph 03 5797 8217, Fax 03 5797 8422

Owners: Alan and Janet Cuthbertson
Chief winemakers: Hugh Cuthbertson and Alan Cuthbertson
Year of foundation: 1977
Tonnes crushed on average each year: 45, of which about 30 are used for the Murrundindi labels
Location: Murrundindi
Area: 15 ha

Soils: gravel, mudstone, quartz
Varieties planted: White—chardonnay; Red—cabernet sauvignon, merlot, shiraz
Leading wines: Murrundindi Chardonnay, Cabernets
Notes: Murrundindi is located near Yea in a very cool area and, as one would expect, it makes unmistakeably cool-area wines, producing very good Chardonnay and an excellent Cabernet. The wines, however, are not 'big' in any warm-area sense of the word, but fruit-driven and elegant in the best high country style. No cellar door sales.

❦ Pinot Noir

Great Pinot Noir has been said to be the result not only of great winemaking but also of the art of barrel selection. This may be true as far as treatment goes, but it omits one crucial factor. Premium grape varieties are like thoroughbred horses. They are highly sensitive not only to their treatment but also to their environment. This applies particularly to pinot noir, which is the most pernickety of all noble red cultivars.

It is generally agreed that the style of pinot that most fulfils the red wine lover's expectations of the variety is Burgundy, that is, reds of medium to full colour, of fragrant but complex 'berry', violet and gamey-earthy aromas and soft yet full savoury-sweet berry flavours without any jarring or astringent tannins on finish. If our putative Pinot, when made, results in any other style of red, it seems plain and unworthy of recognition as a good Pinot. It must also be capable of developing well in bottle. This would seem to suggest that climatic and soil (terroir) characteristics similar to those of Burgundy are required. Given that we will never be able or indeed want to duplicate exactly the Burgundian climate and terroir, the search must focus on an Australian terroir that approximates the conditions in which pinot noir is recognised to produce a noble wine. If, therefore, it is to succeed in Australia, it positively demands a long, cool growing season which points to southern Victoria, Tasmania, the Adelaide Hills of South Australia and the southern regions of Western Australia.

Within southern Victoria, several areas have already proved themselves suitable for pinot noir: the Yarra Valley, south-western Gippsland, the Mornington Peninsula and Geelong. Within Tasmania, there are three sites which produce excellent pinot noir: Bicheno on the east coast, Pipers Brook and Hobart. South Australia's Adelaide Hills is also gaining a reputation for pinot quality and areas in the south of Western Australia, such as Albany, Denmark and Pemberton, are showing much promise. These are of course generalisations—not every part of the Yarra Valley or any of the others is totally suitable and there are probably others quite suitable that have yet to see even one pinot vine.

Pinot noir is not only very site- and climate-specific but also maker-specific—it requires the experience of the makers of great pinot. What are the parameters of site, climate and viticultural and winemaking techniques for these sites? To help answer this, the advice was sought of eight makers of Australian pinot noir who most certainly have achieved eminence in this field.

At Freycinet near Bicheno on Tasmania's east coast, Geoff Bull, his daughter Lindy and winemaker Claudio Radenti make a phenomenal Pinot Noir that absolutely radiates fruit aromas and flavours, being at the same time robust, complex and subtle and capable of ageing well. Freycinet is set in an amphitheatre facing north-east. It is a natural suntrap and rain shadow in an otherwise extremely cool area. It has good cold-air drainage so it suffers little frost damage and is protected from the worst of Tasmania's often howling winds. Its soil is podsolic over red clay and well-drained. Its rainfall is about 750 mm annually and it has supplementary irrigation to relieve extreme drought stress. As for technique in viticulture, Freycinet's chief purpose is to expose the ripening fruit to sunlight and to achieve ripeness between 13° and 14° Baume. In winemaking, the grapes are fermented up to 32°C in a roto-fermenter and the wine allowed to reach dryness. It is then transferred to barrel to undergo malolactic fermentation. Only about one-quarter new oak is used each year in barrel maturation. The rest of the barrels are from one to four years old. After 10 months it is bottled. Claudio states his purpose, quite simply as 'to let the fruit express itself'.

In north-east Tasmania at Pipers Brook, pinot noir has become Andrew Pirie's favoured red variety as in most years it suits local conditions much more than cabernet sauvignon. 'Pellion', his premium pinot, is grown on red basalt soil, high in iron. It is well-drained but has a sufficient clay content to ensure retention of some moisture. Its climate is very cool and has appropriate humidity that Pirie believes gives pinot the fleshiness it requires to become a top wine. Rainfall is about 750 mm annually, falling mainly in winter, though the growing season does account for slightly less than half.

As for viticulture, Pirie uses vertical shoot positioning (VSP), Lyre and Scott Henry trellissing. Hedging and leaf-plucking are carried out when necessary. Andrew believes that pinot crops optimally at about 5 tonnes per hectare. In the winery, he uses open fermentation and ferments on wild yeasts to about 32°C, using 'pigeage' to cool 'hotspots' in the ferment, which takes on average 11 days to carry through to dryness. The wine is then transferred to casks to undergo its malolactic fermentation. He has no particular French oak preferences, but relies on Burgundian coopers to provide an oak that he has tasted and liked in red Burgundies.

Across Bass Strait, south of Leongatha in Gippsland lies the Bass Phillip vineyard, home of what is arguably Australia's finest pinot noir. There are other varieties of course, a fraction of chardonnay and a skerrick of gamay. Both are fascinating in their own ways, especially the gamay, but pinot noir is Phillip Jones' all-conquering passion. To Jones, the soil of a vineyard is the soul of pinot noir excellence, affecting not only the basic structure of the wine but also its aromatic characters, though these complexities are not noticed until some years after bottling. His soils at Bass Phillip are very old and he has identified five different types in that 4-hectare vineyard. Although there is little limestone (a favourite moisture-holding soil constituent of the Burgundians), the vineyard does have adequate clay content for water retention and sufficient numbers of small stones which trap capillary water. He knows that in every vintage his Premium wine (and that is its name) will come from exactly the same patch of soil, as it develops more layers of flavour than other wines that may be made from soils a mere 50 metres away. To Phillip, soils suitable for the best pinot must have a constant water regime in the root zones of the vine, that is, a clayey, rubbly, pebbly texture to hold water, but not excessive water. Within those soil parameters, the climate requirements of pinot noir are fairly simple, though critical— a long, slow, cool summer and autumn and an ambient humidity at those times to preserve root moisture and canopy humidity. Pinot noir must never be allowed to 'dry out'.

In Gippsland's extremely cool climate, proper canopy management is essential. The canopy must allow bunches to be exposed to sunlight for development and ripening and, importantly, to avoid vegetal flavour. Phillip Jones believes that pinot noir is more representative of its site of origin than any other variety, because it is less primary-fruit dominated. It is also important to have 'balanced' fruit on the vine (i.e. fruit that does not produce excessive malic acid, which will in turn, after malolactic fermentation, produce excessive lactic characters). Above all, for premium pinot, overcropping must be avoided at all costs. Jones suggests no more than five tonnes to the hectare.

As for winemaking, Phillip Jones favours warm to hot ferments (30–32°C) on wild yeasts, using only a small percentage of stalks. For oak, he uses light toast Allier and, depending on vintage, 30–50% of new wood. As Phillip says, 'oak should be a balancing medium in pinot noir, never a flavour component'.

Due to winemaker Gary Farr's experience at Domaine Dujac over the years, Bannockburn has built a reputation for the excellence of its Pinot. Farr believes that we in Australia are beginning to learn about suitable soils for pinot noir, having discovered that the right climate is also crucially important. He too believes that soil drainage is a vital factor in succeeding with pinot noir which, he says, prefers a cool and damp climate. Gary has both close-planted and standard-row vineyards and hedges—the close-planted vines for exposure to sunlight and for spray access. The standard row vines are not vigorous and usually do not need hedging.

In winemaking, he ferments his pinot fruit on natural (wild) yeasts to about 32°C and it rarely needs cooling. The classic Burgundian 'pigeage' technique is used when necessary to control 'hotspots' in the ferment and the whole process, to the total dryness of the wine, usually lasts from 14 to 20 days. The wine is then transferred to barrel and proceeds naturally to malolactic fermentation. As for oak, Gary prefers Allier or Vosges, but normally the percentage of new oak used does not exceed one-third.

The Yarra Valley is perhaps the northernmost latitude for successful pinot making, that is, at normal altitudes. As one goes north, so the Australian climate warms and it is necessary to seek a suitable pinot site at higher altitudes to obtain the necessary coolness of climate for the variety. In the Yarra, one of its most successful pinot makers has been David Lance at Diamond Valley Vineyards. His pinot vineyard is located on a hillside with soils of clay over mudstone. Because of the hillside, they are well-drained and they are low enough in fertility to discourage excessive vigour in the pinot vines. Diamond Valley usually has a long, slow, ripening season and David Lance prefers autumns to be dry and cool to stop vegetative growth and to cause his pinot vines to drop their basal leaves. He feels that the vines should be subjected to a 'drought' stress at this time, so that the fruit is ripened.

As for viticultural techniques, his trellising is designed to expose his pinot fruit to light. Leaf-plucking is also carried out when necessary. In the winery, he ferments his pinot between 30°C and 32°C on cultured yeasts for five to six days and does not favour stem return to the must. For maturation, he uses new Nevers oak, but never more than 20% in any one vintage.

During the past decade, a friendly rivalry has arisen between Diamond Valley and that other producer of premium Yarra Valley Pinot Noir, Coldstream Hills. Coldstream, on the southern side of the valley, produces its Reserve Pinot Noir from estate-grown fruit sourced primarily from the mature, 12-year-old pinot vines on its steep, north-facing Amphitheatre vineyard. Winemaker James Halliday believes that the Amphitheatre soils, which consist of a sandy, clay loam over broken sandstone, are well-drained and sufficiently moisture-retentive to favour the production of high-quality pinot fruit. He accepts that for premium pinot, the soil must never be allowed to dry out. As in Diamond Valley, the growth and ripening season is long and slow and spring rainfall is usually reliable. Irrigation to preserve optimal humidity is necessary in some years.

In its viticulture, Coldstream cultivates about 3200 vines to the hectare. Its rows are 2.1 m apart and the separation between vines is 1.5 m. It employs vertical shoot positioning with movable foliage wires. Spring growth is usually very vigorous and trimming is usually carried out two to three times during the growing season. Leaf-plucking is also used. As for winemaking, Halliday cold-soaks (i.e. macerates) part of the crushed pinot must prior to fermentation and follows basic Burgundian practice, though normally cultured yeasts are used to begin fermentation. (Since 1993, however, Coldstream has experimented with wild yeasts for this purpose.) Whole bunches are added to the ferment, which runs hot (up to 32°C). The must is foot-stamped (pigeage) to remove hotspots. About halfway through fermentation, the must is inoculated for malolactic fermentation and when it has reached 2° Baume, both free-run juice and pressings are combined and run off into barrel to complete primary ferment and the subsequent malo. For maturation, he believes that a tight-grained French oak is most suitable for premium pinot and uses new Dargaud and Jaegli barrels of Troncais and 'Bourgogne' oak up to a level of 60% in Coldstream Hills Reserve Pinot.

In the Adelaide Hills, a region where it might be contended that pinot noir has not yet proved itself, Lenswood seems to hold out most promise for the variety. Tim Knappstein at Lenswood Vineyard grows his pinot noir on a shallow, red-grey loam over a subsoil of crumbly clay and gravelly ironstone. It is well-drained and its climate is cool and slow-ripening. In his pinot viticulture, Tim believes that it is important to allow sunlight into the canopy to encourage ripening. As a consequence, he practises shoot-thinning and leaf-plucking. In his winemaking, after a pre-ferment maceration (chilled for up to four days), he ferments his must of wholly destemmed berries (sometimes with up to 20% whole bunches) at temperatures up to 32°C with a post-fermentation maceration, with the result that the total 'fermentation' time (including pre- and post-) is 13 to 15 days. Tim matures his pinot in new and one-year-old oak, using up to 50% new oak. His oak preferences are Allier, Troncais and Vosges and he is increasingly favouring the 'pinot' barrel made by the Seguin Moreau cooperage at Chagny in Burgundy. This is a mixed stave barrel of high toast, utilising wood from the forests of central France.

As a wine-growing area, Pemberton is a cool, slow-ripening region, less than 20 years old. Picardy, the estate of Bill Pannell, founder of Moss Wood in Margaret River (which is now owned by Keith and Claire Mugford) is younger still, completing only its third vintage in 1998. Bill has always been a Burgundy enthusiast, so it was only natural that pinot noir would be planted on the loamy, gravelly, clay 'karri' soils of Picardy. Pinot must be in the Pannell genes, as winemaker son Dan shares his father's enthusiasm. Pemberton's 'karri' soils can be a little heavy in places, but not at Picardy. There, Dan feels they are ideal for pinot, draining freely enough yet holding sufficient moisture to prevent excessive drought stress, which is extremely important at Picardy as it is not irrigated.

In his viticultural techniques, Dan uses vertical shoot positioning, leaf-plucks and hedges the rows when necessary. In the winery, Dan utilises the whole range of Burgundian winemaking practice: pre-fermentation maceration, fermentation up to 32°C, pigeage, addition of whole bunches and post-fermentation maceration. His fermentation process takes up to two weeks to complete. In maturation, Dan favours tight-grained French oak, preferably Allier and Troncais, and only 25% new, the balance being similar oak up to three years old. Dan shares the author's opinion that Pemberton pinot often has a naturally smoky nose and flavour (which is certainly not mercaptan nor the result of excessive maturation in high-toast new oak). This appears to be a genuine *goût de terroir*.

Pinot noir growing and making practice in the cooler areas of Australia seems to be becoming standardised, which is no bad thing. What is needed is a cool, slow-ripening climate and suitable gravelly soils with a degree of clay—a growth regime which permits retention of some humidity both above and below ground (never letting the vine 'dry out'), but permitting good drainage and ripening of fruit slowly but surely. Certainly hedging and leaf-plucking may at times be necessary to assist ripening. Its wines should be fermented quickly up to 32°C. 'Pigeage' may be employed to remove hotspots in the fermenting must; some whole bunch fermentation may be employed and both pre- and post-fermentation maceration can be very effective, provided that care is taken at all times to avoid oxidation. As for oak maturation, there are, as we have seen, differing approaches. The result of such site selection, growth regime and winemaking technique should at least be a recognisable Pinot Noir of decent quality.

❦ PORT PHILLIP ZONE

This is the heartland of Victorian table wine and all that cool area Victorian viticulture is about. The Port Phillip Zone is dominated by and within easy reach of metropolitan Melbourne to the north east of the Bay and encompasses the wine regions of Mornington Peninsula, Yarra Valley and Geelong and the proposed regions of Sunbury and Macedon Ranges.

YARRA VALLEY REGION

The Yarra Valley is Victoria's oldest vineyard area, dating from 1837 when William Ryrie travelled overland with his cattle from the Monaro region of southern New South Wales to squat at Yering in what is now the Yarra Valley. By 1840, he had planted an acre (0.4 ha) of vines. From its first settlement in 1835, Victoria grew rapidly, being particularly fortunate in that many of its immigrants, chiefly those from Switzerland and Germany, were wine-conscious if not actually skilled in viticulture and wine production.

Commencing in 1849 with the arrival of Paul de Castella, Swiss settlers were particularly active in the development of the Yarra vine. Paul purchased part of Ryrie's run at Yering including the vineyard and expanded it rapidly until, by 1857, it comprised nearly 100 acres (40 ha). It included 20 000 cabernet sauvignon cuttings imported from Chateau Lafite in Pauillac. Also during the 1850s, the Deschamps brothers planted vineyards near Lilydale. In 1862, Hubert de Castella began to plant St Hubert's, a few kilometres to the south-east of Yering, and other Swiss settlers such as Guillaume de Pury of Yeringberg also planted vineyards about this time.

Yarra wine, especially from Yering and St Hubert's, was to win many international prizes over the next 30 years and became much sought-after in Melbourne, Australia's largest and most prosperous city at that time. Indeed, by 1890, the Yarra was at the height of its reputation. Its decline and fall over the next 30 years was due to two quite diverse causes: a general lack of interest in table wines and the preference of wine drinkers for stronger fortified wines, for which Yarra wine was not suited; and the election of a Victorian government that wished to encourage teetotalism and the consumption of more milk. By the 1920s, viticulture in the Yarra Valley had succumbed, not to phylloxera as in other places but to the dairy cow.

The Yarra Valley's rebirth coincided with the general rise of interest in Australian wine in the 1960s. Quite close to its original site, St Hubert's was re-established on a former chicken farm in 1968. In the following year, a minute portion of the original Yeringberg was replanted by the founder's grandson, also Guillaume de Pury, there being no need for a winery as the 'new' winery of 1885 did quite nicely. The medical profession lent a hand as usual—Mount Mary near Lilydale was planted in 1971 by Dr John Middleton and Seville Estate near Seville was established the following year

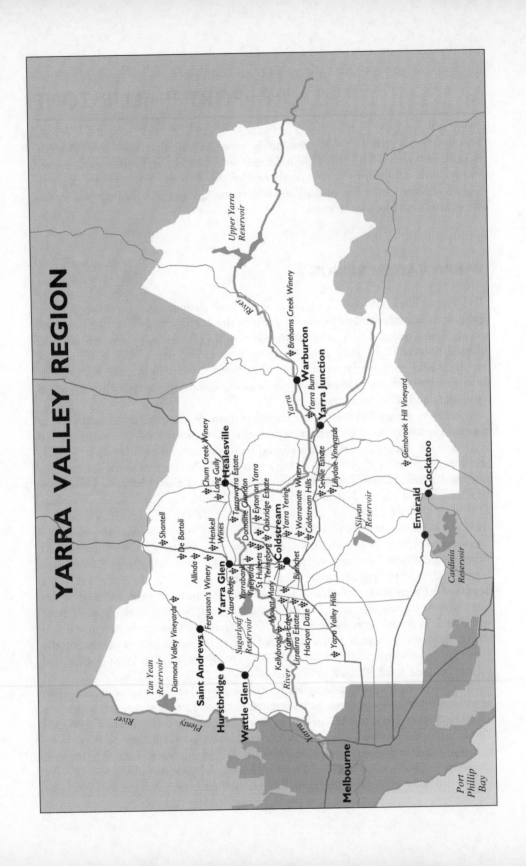

YARRA VALLEY REGION

Upper Yarra Reservoir

River

Brahams Creek Winery

Warburton

Yarra Burn

Yarra Junction

Yarra

Lillydale Vineyards

Gembrook Hill Vineyard

Seville Estate

Cockatoo

Chum Creek Winery

Healesville

Warramate Winery

Emerald

Long Gully

Tarrawarra Estate

Eyton on Yarra

Coldstream Hills

Silvan Reservoir

Shantell

Henkell Wines

Domaine Chandon

Oakridge Estate

Yarra Yering

Cardinia Reservoir

De Bortoli

Allinda

Fergusson's Winery

Yarra Glen

Yarra Ridge

Yarrabank Vineyards

St Huberts

Coldstream

Burchet

De Bortoli

Sugarloaf Reservoir

Mount Mary Yeringberg

Diamond Valley Vineyards

Saint Andrews

Kellybrook

Yarra Edge

Lirralirra Estate

Halcyon Daze

Yarra Valley Hills

Yan Yean Reservoir

Hurstbridge

Wattle Glen

River

Plenty

Yarra

River

Melbourne

Port Phillip Bay

by Middleton's medical partner, Peter McMahon. During the 1980s, retired lawyers such as James Halliday and Louis Bialkower also contributed to its phoenix-like revival. Coldstream Hills and Yarra Ridge bear witness to their efforts.

The Yarra has grown apace and over 30 wineries are now scattered about the Valley, including the important Domaine Chandon, offshoot of Moet & Chandon of Epernay. More importantly—or perhaps alarmingly for some—the 'big battalions' of the Australian wine industry now have a Yarra address, either by way of vineyard ownership or by having purchased an existing winery and continuing to trade under the original name. For example, Mildara Wines purchased the remaining 50% of Yarra Ridge in 1995, having owned half for several years; McWilliam's wines bought Lillydale Vineyards in 1994; BRL Hardy purchased Yarra Burn in 1996; and Southcorp Wines acquired Coldstream Hills in the same year. Certainly their presence should ensure a consistency of quality and national distribution for many more Yarra wines but, it is hoped, at no cost to their regional origin. It seems unlikely that the dairy cow will cause upheaval ever again in the Yarra vignoble. A more pressing and present danger is the ever-expanding eastern suburbia of Melbourne.

Location: latitude 37°45'S, longitude 145°21'E. Situated about 35 km north-east of Melbourne, around and to the north, east and south of Lilydale, and around Coldstream, Yarra Glen, Dixons Creek, Healesville, St Andrews and Seville.
Elevation: 50–400 m
Topography and soils: Vineyards on both flat and undulating country, quite steep in parts. Soils are of two principal types. One is the hard red duplex soils (Dr 2.21, Dr 2.22) which appear grey-brown in colour with a subsoil of red-brown clay. The other major soil type is a very vigorous, deep red loam (Dr 2.42), common around the Seville area and other areas in the southern part of the Valley. Good but not excessive drainage is important and this depends on the clay content of the subsoils, which varies from place to place within the Valley. Both major soil types are acidic.
Climate: (local) MJT 18.8°C, MAR na, HDD 1250, AR 1008 mm, RH 57%, AI na, SH na; (Healesville) MJT 17.9°C, MAR na, HDD (raw) 1251, 1352 adjusted for vine sites, AR 1008 mm (Oct–Apr 597 mm), RH na, AI na, SH 7; (Gladstones) MJT 19.4°C, MAR 11°C, HDD 1489, AR 911 mm (Oct–Mar 404 mm), RH 63% (9am), AI 52 mm, SH 7.4 (Dry and Smart). Generally cool, even in its 'warmest' areas, with higher and more exposed areas downright cold. Northerly aspects are most favoured because of their warmth, but these are most exposed to wind and rain which, if combined at critical flowering times (December), can be devastating, as they also may be during ripening (March–April). For this reason too, fungal diseases can present difficulties. In addition, spring frosts can be a problem in low-lying vineyards. During ripening, birds are another hazard. Annual rainfall (750 mm in the northern Yarra Valley (Yarra Glen) and 1150 mm on the southern side of the Valley) does not preclude water stress in the January–March period and the consequent need for drip irrigation from surface dams. Another problem is excessive vine vigour on the deep red loam country.
Harvest time: late March (for sparkling wine base) to late May
Principal grape varieties: Red—pinot noir*, cabernet sauvignon, shiraz, merlot, cabernet

franc, malbec; White—chardonnay*, sauvignon blanc, semillon, riesling (*indicates use for sparkling wine base)

Total area (1996): 850 ha planted, about 12% non-bearing

Major wine styles: Chardonnay, Pinot Noir, Cabernet Sauvignon

Allinda NR

119 Lorimers Lane, Dixons Creek, Vic 3775

Ph/Fax 03 5965 2467

Owners: Al and Linda Fencaros
Chief winemaker: Al Fencaros
Year of foundation: 1991
Tonnes crushed on average each year: 40
Location: Dixons Creek
Area: 3 ha
Soils: shallow grey loam over mudstone clay subsoil
Varieties planted: White—chardonnay, riesling, sauvignon blanc; Red—cabernet franc, cabernet sauvignon, merlot
Leading wines: Allinda Cabernets, Chardonnay
Notes: With a view to contract winemaking work, Allinda completed its new winery in 1997 in time for a vintage, high in quality but low in quantity. Cellar door sales: 10am–6pm weekends and public holidays.

Arthurs Creek Estate R9

'Kurnalpi', Strathewen Road, Arthurs Creek, Vic 3099

Ph/Fax 03 9714 8202

Owner: The Arthurs Creek Estate Pty Ltd
Chief winemaker: contract, Gary Baldwin (consultant)
Year of foundation: 1975
Tonnes produced on average each year: 18.2
Location: Arthurs Creek
Area: 7.6 ha (3.15 ha of which was not bearing in 1997)
Soils: grey loam
Varieties planted: White—chardonnay; Red—cabernet sauvignon

Leading wines: Arthurs Creek Cabernet Sauvignon, Chardonnay
Notes: Arthurs Creek lies on the western edge of the Yarra and seems ideally suited for cabernet sauvignon. Its owner, S. E. K. Hulme, is a leading Melbourne QC with not only a passion for great Cabernet but also a great deal of patience. Why? He first began trial plantings at Arthurs Creek in 1975. In 1976 he planted cabernet sauvignon and the first wine from this vineyard was made in 1979. From then on, vintages came and went but no wine was released until 1992. By that time the Arthurs Creek cellars must have resembled Aladdin's cave, as Melbourne wine consultant Joe Sullivan went about the arduous but immensely pleasurable task of assessing the quality of 13 vintages of Cabernet Sauvignon. The pick of the 13 crops proved to be 1982, unfortunately no longer available. Since 1992 the wines have been exhibited regularly. The 1992, 1994 and 1995 have won gold medals and trophies at various Victorian wine shows. The Cabernets are usually concentrated and very powerful (the 1991 which I tasted early in 1996 is particularly so) and often need 10 years maturation, but that is the way of great Cabernet. The Chardonnay too has proved worthy of gold. There are no cellar door sales.

Barkala Ridge (vineyard only)

Parker Road, Wandin East, Vic 3139

Owners: Harry and Pauline Jones
Chief winemaker: none
Year of foundation: 1990
Tonnes produced on average each year: 30
Location: Wandin East
Area: 3.1 ha
Soils: red clay loam

Varieties planted: White—chardonnay; Red—cabernet sauvignon
Leading wines: none
Notes: All grapes are sold. There are no cellar door sales.

Bianchet R6

Lot 3 Victoria Road, Lilydale, Vic 3140
Ph 03 9739 1779, Fax 03 9739 1277

Owner: Keith and Greg Tribe
Chief winemaker: Martin Williams with Keith Salter
Year of foundation: 1976
Tonnes crushed on average each year: not disclosed but estimated at 30
Location: Lilydale
Area: 4 ha
Soils: grey loam with gravelly shale subsoil over yellow clay.
Varieties planted: White—chardonnay, riesling, semillon, traminer, verduzzo; Red—cabernet franc, cabernet sauvignon, merlot, pinot noir, shiraz
Leading wine: Bianchet Verduzzo
Notes: For many years owned by the late Lou Bianchet and now under new ownership, Bianchet is an established Yarra Valley winery. Its wines are made in a simple, straightforward way, a point of interest being the unusual Verduzzo variety. Cellar door sales: weekends 10am–6pm, other times by appointment.

Brahams Creek Winery NR

Woods Point Road, East Warburton, Vic 3799
Ph 03 9560 0016, Fax 03 9574 9630

Owners: Gordon Valentine, Geoffrey Richardson and Don Valentine
Chief winemaker: Geoffrey Richardson (B. Wilson—consultant)
Year of foundation: 1990
Tonnes crushed on average each year: 11
Location: East Warburton

Area: 4.6 ha (including 2.2 ha newly planted and not yet bearing)
Soils: a north facing vineyard with grey loam on a clay base
Varieties planted: White—chardonnay, sauvignon blanc; Red—cabernet sauvignon, merlot, pinot noir
Leading wines: Brahams Creek Chardonnay, Pinot Noir
Notes: Cellar door sales: 11am–5pm weekends and public holidays.

Chum Creek Winery NR

28 Cunningham Road, Healesville, Vic 3777
Ph 03 5962 5551

Owner: James Broussard
Chief winemaker: wines are contract-made
Year of foundation: 1977
Tonnes produced each year on average: 20
Location: Healesville
Area: 3 ha
Soils: grey loam
Varieties planted: White—chardonnay; Red—cabernet sauvignon, pinot noir
Leading wines: Chum Creek, Chardonnay, Cabernet Sauvignon, Pinot Noir
Notes: This small Yarra winery sells most of its fruit, retaining only 3 tonnes for its own winemaking purposes. Cellar door sales: weekends and public holidays 10am–6pm.

Coldstream Hills R10

31 Maddens Lane, Coldstream, Vic 3770
Ph 03 5964 9388, Fax 03 5964 9389

Owner: Southcorp Wines
Chief winemakers: James Halliday and Paul Lapsley
Year of foundation: 1985
Tonnes crushed on average each year: not disclosed but estimated at 400
Location: Coldstream (three vineyards, Coldstream Hills, Briarston and Fernhill)

Area: 41.2 ha

Soils: grey loam

Varieties planted: White—chardonnay, sauvignon blanc, viognier; Red—cabernet franc, cabernet sauvignon, malbec, merlot, shiraz, pinot noir

Leading wines: Coldstream Hills Reserve Pinot Noir, Reserve Chardonnay, Reserve Cabernet Sauvignon

Notes: Taken over by Southcorp Wines in 1996, the premium Yarra Valley winery, Coldstream Hills, was formerly the property of a publicly listed company, founded by eminent wine writer, judge and maker, James Halliday. While Halliday remains in charge at Coldstream Hills there is little doubt that it will retain its premier position. Its Reserve Pinot Noirs are arguably Australia's best and its Reserve Chardonnays are never less than top class. Its Reserve Cabernet Sauvignon is always classically elegant and the epitome of Yarra Cabernet style. Cellar door sales: Mon–Fri 12 noon–2pm, public holidays and weekends 10am–5pm.

De Bortoli Yarra Valley **R10**

Pinnacle Lane, Dixons Creek, Vic 3775
Ph 03 5965 2271, Fax 03 5965 2442

Owner: De Bortoli Wines Pty Ltd

Chief winemaker: Stephen Webber

(Winemakers: David Slingsby Smith, David Bicknell)

Year of foundation: 1971 (as Chateau Yarrinya)

Tonnes crushed on average each year: 1500

Location: Dixons Creek

Area: 140 ha

Soils: grey loam over clay base

Varieties planted: White—chardonnay, gewurztraminer, riesling, sauvignon blanc, semillon; Red—cabernet franc, cabernet sauvignon, merlot, pinot noir, shiraz

Leading wines: De Bortoli Melba (a super-premium red blend from the pick of the red varieties mentioned above except pinot noir);

Yarra Valley Chardonnay, Pinot Noir, Cabernet Sauvignon, Cabernet Merlot, Shiraz (from the pick of the Yarra Valley wines, after the selection of the wines for Melba); Gulf Station Semillon-Sauvignon Blanc, Riesling, Chardonnay, Cabernet Sauvignon (all from the Yarra Valley); Windy Peak Prestige (a sparkling Rose Brut made from pinot noir), Riesling, Sauvignon Blanc, Chardonnay, Pinot Noir, Cabernet-Shiraz-Merlot

Notes: The De Bortoli purchase of Graeme Miller's Chateau Yarrinya in 1987 has been a great success and the De Bortoli family, in the years since, have proved to some sceptical wine critics that its Yarra wines are as good as any in the Valley and a lot better than most. Many trophies have been won in the past decade, especially by the Chardonnay and Cabernet Sauvignon (more recently a Jimmy Watson Trophy in 1997 for a 1996 Reserve Shiraz) and the wines in the Yarra Valley range are never less than very good. Melba (named after the opera diva, Nelly Mitchell, who was raised a century ago on nearby St Huberts) is of course unimpeachable. The Windy Ridge range usually includes Victorian fruit from outside the Yarra Valley. De Bortoli also conducts a fine restaurant specialising in northern Italian cucina, open every day for lunch and on Saturday night only for dinner. Cellar door sales: 7 days 10am–5pm.

Diamond Valley Vineyards **R10**

Kinglake Road, St Andrews, Vic 3761
Ph 03 9710 1484, Fax 03 9710 1369

Owners: David and Katherine Lance

Chief winemaker: David Lance

Year of foundation: 1976

Tonnes crushed on average each year: 75

Location: St Andrews

Area: 3.6 ha

Soils: clay over mudstone, 'mean and lean', as Kathy Lance says

Varieties planted: White—chardonnay,

sauvignon blanc; Red—cabernet franc, cabernet sauvignon, malbec, merlot, pinot noir (close planted)

Leading wines: Diamond Valley White Label Pinot Noir, Chardonnay, Cabernet (all estate grown and made); and the excellent Blue Label wines which are made from non-estate fruit, but all purchased from the Yarra Valley

Notes: With numerous trophies (30 at the time of writing) and gold medals to its credit, Diamond Valley has built a well-justified reputation for excellence, especially in its Pinot Noir, both the estate grown and the Blue Label. Its Chardonnay can also be relied on to give a great deal of pleasure. There are no cellar door sales. Tasting and sales are strictly by appointment or by mailing list. The Lances also own the Phillip Island vineyard and winery in the Gippsland wine zone.

Domaine Chandon R10

'Green Point', Maroondah Highway, Coldstream, Vic 3770
Ph 03 9739 1110, Fax 03 9739 1095

Owner: Moet & Chandon (Epernay, France)
Chief winemaker: Dr Tony Jordan (Managing Director/Winemaker), Wayne Donaldson (Operations Manager/Winemaker)
Year of foundation: 1985
Tonnes crushed on average each year: 1500
Location: Coldstream
Area: 50 ha
Soils: fine sandy clay loam, grey in colour over silty clay subsoil
Varieties planted: White—chardonnay; Red—meunier, pinot noir
Leading wines: Domaine Chandon Vintage Brut, Vintage Brut Rose, Blanc de Blancs, Blanc de Noirs, Green Point Chardonnay
Notes: Domaine Chandon's name is synonymous with sparkling excellence. Each year its wines improve from best to even better. The sparkling wines are blended from superb fruit purchased from virtually all the

cooler regions of Australia. The Green Point Chardonnay is 100 per cent estate grown, made and bottled and of superb quality. Sales are made in the Green Point Room by the glass or bottle, open daily 10.30am–4.30pm. Food and guided tours available.

Eltham Vineyards NR

225 Shaws Road, Arthurs Creek, Vic 3099
Ph 03 9439 4688, Fax 03 9439 5121

Owner/chief winemaker: George Apted
Year of foundation: 1986
Tonnes crushed on average each year: 5
Location: Arthurs Creek
Area: 4 ha (most not yet bearing)
Soils: grey loam
Varieties planted: White—chardonnay; Red—cabernet franc, cabernet sauvignon, merlot, pinot noir
Leading wine: Eltham Vineyards Cabernet Sauvignon
Notes: A very small vineyard with local distribution but no cellar door sales.

Eyton on Yarra R8

Cnr Maroondah Highway and Hill Road, Coldstream, Vic 3770
Ph 03 5962 2119, Fax 03 5962 5319

Owner: Deidre Cowan
Chief winemaker: Matt Aldridge
Year of foundation: 1989 (as Yarra Vale)
Tonnes crushed on average each year: 300
Location: Coldstream
Area: 56 ha (two vineyards: Eyton 11 ha and Dalry Road 45 ha)
Soils: yellow grey loam over clay base
Varieties planted: White—chardonnay, riesling, sauvignon blanc, traminer; Red—cabernet franc, cabernet sauvignon, merlot, pinot noir
Leading wines: Eyton Pinot Noir, NDC Reserve Merlot
Notes: Purchased by the late Newell Cowan in

1994 and extensively refurbished in the years since, Eyton on Yarra is one of the showplaces of the Valley, boasting a modern winery, cellar door and restaurant complex and some very good whites and reds, the standard of which will be raised to premium now that Matt Aldridge has become chief winemaker. Cellar door sales and restaurant: 7 days 10am–5pm.

Fergusson's Winery **R7.5**

Wills Road, Yarra Glen, Vic 3793
Ph 03 5965 2237, Fax 03 5961 2401

Owners: Peter and Louise Fergusson
Chief winemaker: Christopher Keyes
Year of foundation: 1968
Tonnes crushed on average each year: 100
Location: Yarra Glen
Area: 16 ha
Soils: grey brown sandy clay loam over a heavy orange clay subsoil interspersed with schist
Varieties planted: White—chardonnay, sauvignon blanc; Red—cabernet franc, cabernet sauvignon, pinot noir, shiraz
Leading Wines: Fergusson's, Victoria Chardonnay, Jeremy Shiraz, Benjamin Cabernet
Notes: A typically good Yarra winery with excellent Chardonnay and Cabernet and—still quite rare in the Yarra—a very good white peppery Shiraz. All the wines are estate grown and made and named after the Fergusson children. There is a restaurant and cellar door sales: 11am–5pm each day.

Gembrook Hill Vineyard **R8**

Launching Place Road, Gembrook, Vic 3783
Ph 03 5968 1622, Fax 03 5968 1699

Owners: June and Ian Marks
Chief winemakers: Ian Marks and David Lance (contract)
Year of foundation: 1983
Tonnes crushed on average each year: 18
Location: Gembrook

Area: 6 ha
Soils: red volcanic loam, well drained, of low fertility and pH
Varieties planted: White—chardonnay, sauvignon blanc, semillon; Red—pinot noir
Leading wines: Gembrook Hill Sauvignon Blanc, Chardonnay, Pinot Noir
Notes: A very cool site, located in the south-west of the Yarra Valley region, on those rich red volcanic loams that look so spectacular but generally have to be tamed because of excessive vigour. The taming in this case is by non-irrigation. Hence the low yields, which are of course a great quality factor but never please the accountants and bank managers, but the Marks are fortunate in not having to. The Sauvignon Blanc is excellent, showing concentrated tropical-passionfruit aromas and a complex, fruit-driven gooseberry-passionfruit palate. Cellar door sales by appointment only.

Halcyon Daze **R6.5**

19 Uplands Road, Chirnside Park, Vic 3116
Ph/Fax 03 9726 7111

Owners: Richard and Cheryl Rackley
Chief winemaker: Richard Rackley
Year of foundation: 1982
Tonnes crushed on average each year: 40
Location: Chirnside Park
Area: 6.25ha
Soils: grey loam over a clay base
Varieties planted: White—chardonnay, riesling; Red—cabernet franc, cabernet sauvignon, merlot, pinot noir
Leading wines: Halcyon Daze Cabernet Blend, Pinot Noir, 'Halcyon' (a methode champenoise sparkling wine), Riesling
Notes: A smaller winery which utilises about a quarter of its own fruit for winemaking, while the rest is sold to other winemakers. Cellar door sales by appointment only.

Hanson
(see Tarrahill Vineyard entry)

Henkell Wines **NR**
Melba Highway, Yarra Glen, Vic 3755
Ph 03 5965 2016

Owner: Hans A. Henkell
Chief winemaker: Yarra Ridge (contract)
Year of foundation: 1988
Tonnes produced on average each year: 200
(a minimal amount is used for the Henkell
label—most grapes go to Yarra Ridge)
Location: Dixons Creek
Area: 17.7 ha
Soils: grey clay loam over a clay base with
some stones
Varieties planted: White—chardonnay,
sauvignon blanc; Red—cabernet sauvignon,
pinot noir
Leading wines: Henkell Chardonnay, Cabernet
Sauvignon
Notes: Hans Henkell is a member of the
famous Henkell winemaking family in
Germany. Although not a professional
winemaker himself, his family roots are deep in
winemaking—hence, Henkell Yarra Valley. Rob
Dolan of Yarra Ridge always does an excellent
job. Cellar door sales: weekends and public
holidays 11am–5pm.

Hillcrest Vineyard (vineyard only)
Philip Road, Woori Yallock, Vic 3139

Owners: Joy and Graham Sweet
Chief winemaker: no wine made commercially
Year of foundation: 1984
Tonnes produced on average each year: 9
Location: Woori Yallock
Area: 3 ha
Soils: grey clay loam
Varieties planted: White—chardonnay,
semillon; Red—cabernet sauvignon, malbec,
pinot noir, shiraz

Leading wines: none
Notes: Graham Sweet makes a little wine from
the family vineyard for his own amusement
and doubtless for family consumption, but
otherwise all fruit is purchased by Coldstream
Hills. No cellar door sales.

Hoddles Creek (vineyard only) **R9**
Gladysdale, Vic 3797

Owner: BRL Hardy Ltd
Year of foundation: 1986
Tonnes crushed on average each year: 600
Location: Gladysdale
Area: 87.25 ha (two vineyards: Beenak Road
57.25 ha; Prices Road 30 ha)
Soils: deep, rich red loam
Varieties planted: White—chardonnay,
sauvignon blanc; Red—cabernet sauvignon,
meunier, pinot noir
Leading wines: By any standards, the severely
undulating Hoddles Creek estate is an
imposing pair of vineyards whose crop finds its
way into many of the BRL Hardy sparkling
wines, although Bastard Hill Pinot Noir and
Chardonnay are two still products that have
sprung into the spotlight in recent years.
Notes: Cellar door sales facilities are at Yarra
Burn (see entry).

Kellybrook **R7**
Fulford Road, Wonga Park, Vic 3115
Ph 03 9722 1304, Fax 03 9722 2092

Owners: Darren and Farley Kelly
Chief winemaker: Darren Kelly
Year of foundation: 1970
Tonnes crushed on average each year: 40
Location: Wonga Park
Area: 8 ha
Soils: grey topsoil over clay over mudstone
Varieties planted: White—chardonnay, riesling,
traminer; Red—cabernet sauvignon, merlot,
pinot noir, shiraz
Leading wines: Kellybrook Pinot Noir,

Chardonnay, Cabernet, Shiraz, Sparkling
Pinot-Chardonnay
Notes: Kellybrook is one of the older
established Yarra wineries with a good
reputation for Chardonnay. It also makes a
range of ciders including an apple brandy in
the Calvados style. Cellar door sales: Mon–Sat
9am–6pm, Sun 11am–6pm.

Lillydale Vineyards **R8**

10 Davross Court, Seville, Victoria 3139
Ph 03 5964 2016, Fax 03 5964 3009

Owner: McWilliam's Wines Pty Limited
Winemakers: Max McWilliam and Jim Brayne
Year of foundation: 1976
Tonnes crushed on average each year: 120
Location: Seville
Area: 12.85 ha
Soils: grey loam over a clay base
Varieties planted: White—chardonnay,
gewurztraminer, sauvignon blanc;
Red—cabernet sauvignon, pinot noir
Leading wines: Lillydale Yarra Sauvignon Blanc,
Yarra Chardonnay, Yarra Pinot Noir, Yarra
Cabernet Merlot
Notes: Founded in 1976 by Alex White and
Martin Grinbergs, Lillydale Vineyards performed
the enviable feat of winning three gold awards
and one silver from four entries at the 1988
Royal Sydney Wine Show, a remarkable
achievement for a small producer. The vineyard
and winery were purchased by McWilliam's in
1994. Cellar door sales: 7 days 11am–5pm.

Lirralirra Estate **R7**

15 Paynes Road, Chirnside Park,
Vic 3116
Ph/Fax 03 9735 0224

Owners: Alan and Joycelin Smith
Chief winemaker: Alan Smith
Year of foundation: 1981
Tonnes produced on average each year: 12
(about half is sold to other winemakers)

Location: Chirnside Park
Area: 2.1 ha
Soils: grey sandy loam over heavy clay over
extremely weathered silt stone
Varieties planted: White—sauvignon blanc,
semillon; Red—cabernet franc, cabernet
sauvignon merlot, pinot noir
Leading wines: Lirralirra Estate Semillon, Pinot
Noir, Cabernets, Sauvignon Blanc
Notes: This is a small family-owned vineyard
and winery located in the western end of the
Valley in one of its warmer and lower
(80 metres altitude) parts. In an area with an
abundance of chardonnay, here there is none,
just a wooded Semillon and a crisp Sauvignon
Blanc. Cellar door sales: 10am–6pm each day
during January. At other times, weekends and
public holidays, 10am–6pm.

Lusatia Park Vineyards (vineyard only)

Woori Yallock, Vic 3139
Ph 03 5964 6070

Owner: Shelmerdine Vineyards Pty Ltd
Chief winemaker: no wine made commercially
Year of foundation: 1987
Tonnes produced on average each year: 150
Location: Woori Yallock
Area: 18 ha
Soils: rich red loam
Varieties planted: White—chardonnay,
sauvignon blanc; Red—cabernet sauvignon,
pinot noir
Leading wines: None. All fruit is sold.
Notes: No cellar door sales.

Mount Mary **R10**

Coldstream West Road, Lilydale,
Vic 3140
Ph 03 9739 1761, Fax 03 9739 0137

Owners: John and Marli Middleton
Chief winemakers: John Middleton, Mario
Marson and Peter Draper

Year of foundation: 1971
Tonnes crushed on average each year: 50
Location: Lilydale
Area: 15 ha (including new plantings which
have not yet come into bearing)
Soils: grey silurian over mudstone on sandy clay
loam—duplex podsols
Varieties planted: White—chardonnay,
muscadelle, sauvignon blanc, semillon;
Red—cabernet franc, cabernet sauvignon,
malbec, merlot, petit verdot, pinot noir
Leading wines: Quintet (a red blend of the
'Bordeaux' varieties listed above), Triolet
(a white blend of sauvignon blanc, semillon
and muscadelle a la Graves), Chardonnay,
Pinot Noir

hough he was not quite the first to replant
vines commercially in the Yarra Valley, Dr
John Middleton is certainly one of its
veterans, a winemaker with over 40 years'
experience of the Valley and an energetic
proponent of its elegant wines, many of
which are his own. Hectare for hectare, his
production is quite small, but his quality is
extremely high. Every wine lover should taste
a Mount Mary Quintet or Pinot Noir at least
once in a lifetime. No cellar door sales.

Oakridge Estate R8

864 Maroondah Highway, Coldstream,
Vic 3770
Ph 03 9739 1920, Fax 03 9739 1923

Owner: Oakridge Vineyards Ltd
Chief winemaker: Michael Zitzlaff
Year of foundation: 1978
Tonnes crushed on average each year: 100
Location: Seville and Coldstream
Area: 15 ha
Soils: Seville—rich red loam; Coldstream—grey
loam over yellow clay
Varieties planted: White—chardonnay,
sauvignon blanc; Red—cabernet sauvignon,
merlot, pinot noir, shiraz
Leading wines: Oakridge Reserve Cabernet,

Merlot, Chardonnay; Oakridge Cabernet
Merlot, Chardonnay
Notes: Located on the red volcanic loam of the
Seville district, Oakridge Estate has built an
excellent reputation due to its consistently
good Cabernet Sauvignon. Cellar door sales:
daily 11am–5pm. There is also a restaurant
open for lunch from Wednesday to Sunday
and for dinner on Saturdays.

Seville Estate NR

Linwood Road, Seville, Vic 3139
Ph 03 5964 2622, Fax 03 5964 2633

Owner: Brokenwood Wines Pty Ltd and the
partners of Brokenwood Wines
Chief winemaker: Iain Riggs
Year of foundation: 1972
Tonnes crushed on average each year: 25
Location: Seville
Area: 8 ha (4 ha planted 1997)
Soils: red volcanic Kraznozem; grey loams also
Varieties planted: White—chardonnay;
Red—cabernet franc, cabernet sauvignon,
merlot, pinot noir, shiraz
Leading wines: Seville Estate Cabernet
Sauvignon, Shiraz, Pinot Noir; GP range
Notes: Established in 1972 on the rich red
loams of Seville as one of the first of the
reborn Yarra Valley vineyards by former
proprietors Peter and Margaret McMahon,
Seville Estate has always been one of the
region's leading vineyards. It is famouⁱ for its
Cabernet Sauvignon and more recently for a
superb Shiraz, very much in the 'white pepper'
mould of the Yarra Valley. In 1997, Seville
Estate was purchased by Brokenwood Wines of
the Hunter Valley. Suffice it to say that Seville
had a very good 1997 and 1998 vintage in
quality. No cellar door sales.

Shantell R9

Off Melba Highway, Dixons Creek,
Vic 3775
Ph 03 5965 2264, Fax 03 5965 2331

Owners: Shan and Turid Shanmugam
Chief winemaker: Shan Shanmugam
Year of foundation: 1981
Tonnes crushed on average each year: 60
Location: Dixons Creek
Area: 10 ha
Soils: light grey clay loam over yellow
clay sub-soil
Varieties planted: White—chardonnay, riesling,
semillon; Red—cabernet franc, cabernet
sauvignon, merlot, pinot noir, shiraz
Leading wines: Shantell Chardonnay, Cabernet
Sauvignon, Semillon, Pinot Noir
Notes: The wine styles of Shantell are
restrained and elegant, typical of the higher
levels of Yarra winemaking, and its Cabernet
Sauvignon is always worth cellaring. Yet it
continues to sell more than half its grapes to
outside wineries, retaining only about
25 tonnes for its own winemaking purposes.
Its wines are surely worth a lot more attention
and recognition than they seem presently to be
receiving. Cellar door sales: weekends and
public holidays 10am–5pm.

St Huberts R8

St Huberts Road, Coldstream, Vic 3770
Ph 03 9739 1118, Fax 03 9739 1015

Owner: Mildara Blass
Chief winemaker: Rob Dolan
Year of foundation: 1966 (originally in a
slightly different spot, 1862)
Tonnes crushed on average each year: 170
Location: Coldstream
Area: 29 ha
Soils: grey loams over clay
Varieties planted: White—chardonnay,
roussanne; Red—cabernet sauvignon, merlot,
pinot noir

Leading wine: St Huberts Chardonnay
Notes: For St Huberts, ownership has been a
roller-coaster ride during the past 30 years. In
the modern era, that is since 1966, it has been
through five sets of proprietors, the longest
ownership being that of the Cester Family to
whom it owes its renaissance. Chardonnay is
the leading variety here, though at times there
is a most interesting Roussanne. Frost in late
1997 had a severe impact on the quantity of
1998 vintage. Cellar door sales: weekdays
9am–5pm, weekends and public holidays
10.30am–5.30pm.

Steels Creek Vineyard (vineyard only)

Steels Creek, Vic 3775

Owner: Cynthia Staley
Chief winemaker: none
Year of foundation: 1978
Tonnes produced on average each year: 17
Location: Steels Creek
Area: 2.4 ha
Soils: grey loams
Varieties planted: White—chardonnay;
Red—pinot noir
Leading wines: none
Notes: All grapes are sold. No cellar door sales.

Strathewen Hills (vineyard only)

1090 Strathewen Road, Strathewen,
Vic 3099
Ph/Fax 03 9714 8464

Owners: William and Joan Christopherson
Chief winemaker: no-one as yet, but it is
certain to be Bill Christopherson in the near
future
Year of foundation: 1990
Tonnes produced on average each year: 3 (due
to major frost problems, now being resolved by
the installation of a sprinkler system)
Location: Strathewen
Area: 3.04 ha

Soils: Shallow clay-gravel with 'buckshot'; a duplex soil of low fertility
Varieties planted: White—chardonnay, sauvignon blanc, semillon; Red—cabernet sauvignon, merlot, pinot noir
Leading wines: none yet, but they will be Strathewen Merlot, Pinot Noir, Sparkling Brut
Notes: Bill Christopherson is not only a viticultural consultant but also a keen wine judge at local wine shows and equally keen to make wine only of a very high standard. He is establishing only the best clones on the close-planted Strathewen Hills vineyard which is very cold and frost-prone. Bill believes his pinot noir, presently sold for winemaking elsewhere, will be exceptional. No cellar door sales, but there is bed and breakfast accommodation.

Tarraford Vineyard (vineyard only)
440 Healesville Road, Yarra Glen, Vic 3775

Owners: Chris and Anna Long and Pauline and Graham Williams
Chief winemaker: none (no wine made in commercial quantities)
Year of foundation: 1989
Tonnes produced on average each year: 20, increasing to 80 by 2000
Location: Yarra Glen
Area: 8.3 ha (5.4 ha not bearing in 1997)
Soils: grey loam over clay
Varieties planted: White—chardonnay; Red—pinot noir
Leading wines: none
Notes: No cellar door sales.

Tarrahill Vineyard   🍇 **R7**
340 Old Healesville Road, Yarra Glen, Vic 3775
Sales office: 49 Cleveland Ave, Lower Plenty, Vic 3093
Ph 03 9439 7425, Fax 03 9435 9183

Owner and chief winemaker: Dr Ian Hanson
Year of foundation: 1983
Tonnes crushed on average each year: 12
Location: Two vineyards, Yarra Glen and Lower Plenty
Area: 4 ha
Soils: brown clay loam over mostly a sandy clay base; elsewhere the base is gravel
Varieties planted: White—sauvignon blanc; Red—cabernet franc, cabernet sauvignon, merlot, pinot noir
Leading wines: Hanson Cabernets (a blend of the two cabernets mentioned and merlot), Cabernet Franc, Pinot Noir
Notes: Ian Hanson is a dental surgeon and keen winemaker who, in an extremely busy life, manages to combine both professions successfully. His 'dusty' Cabernet Franc is typical of the variety and always very interesting. No cellar door sales. Sales by mailing list to the above address.

Tarrawarra Estate   **R9**
Healesville Road, Yarra Glen, Vic 3775
Ph 03 5962 3311, Fax 03 5962 3887

Owner: Tarrawarra Estate Pty Ltd
Chief winemaker: Clare Halloron
Year of foundation: 1983
Tonnes crushed on average each year: 125
Location: Tarrawarra (just over halfway between Yarra Glen and Healesville)
Area: Tarrawarra Estate has two vineyards: 19.66 ha on Healesville Road, 8.46 ha of which is not yet bearing; and 45.5 ha (the Tarrawarra Grange Vineyard) on Maroondah Highway, Coldstream, planted in 1996 and not yet bearing, the fruit to be shared between Tarrawarra and BRL Hardy Ltd
Soils: light well-drained grey soils over clay
Varieties planted: White—chardonnay at each vineyard, sauvignon blanc at Tarrawarra Grange Vineyard; Red—cabernet sauvignon, merlot and shiraz at Tarrawarra Grange Vineyard, pinot noir at each vineyard

Leading wines: Tarrawarra Pinot Noir, Chardonnay; Tunnel Hill Pinot Noir, Chardonnay

Notes: Tarrawarra, formerly a specialist producer of Pinots and Chardonnays, is one of the established estates of the Yarra Valley. It is now rapidly increasing in size and branching out into other wines, its share of fruit from the Tarrawarra Grange Vineyard having the potential virtually to double its production. It has produced some excellent Pinots in recent years, especially the 1995 which won the Pinot Noir/Burgundy trophy (equivalent to world's best Pinot) at the International Wine Challenge in London. Its 1996 may be even better. Cellar door sales: 7 days 10.30am–4.30pm.

Wantirna Estate   **R7**

Bushy Park Lane, Wantirna South, Vic 3152
Ph 03 9801 2367, Fax 03 9887 0225

Owners: Reg, Bertina and Maryann Egan
Chief winemakers: Reg and Maryann Egan
Year of foundation: 1963
Tonnes crushed on average each year: 17
Location: Wantirna South
Area: 4 ha
Soils: light grey clay topsoil over a 'porridgey' marl subsoil
Varieties planted: White—chardonnay; Red—cabernet franc, cabernet sauvignon, merlot, petit verdot, pinot noir
Leading wines: Wantirna Estate Cabernet Merlot (a blend of the Bordeaux red varieties mentioned above), Pinot Noir, Chardonnay
Notes: Wantirna Estate is one of the older and more established vineyards of the Yarra Valley, old enough in fact to have totally confused the author at his first tasting of its wine (blind) at a 1975 interstate wine options game. Over the years Reg Egan has tried many different vine varieties on the duplex podsolic soil of the estate and has settled on the classic French red varieties as being most suitable. Mailing list

sales only, except for a very few retail outlets and some restaurants.

Warramate Winery   **R7**

27 Maddens Lane, Gruyere, Vic, 3770
Ph/Fax 03 5964 9219

Owners: Jack and June Church
Chief winemakers: Jack and David Church
Year of foundation: 1969
Tonnes crushed on average each year: 12
Location: Gruyere
Area: 2 ha
Soils: grey loam soils over clay and rocks, similar to its neighbours, Coldstream Hills and Yarra Yering
Varieties planted: White—riesling; Red—cabernet franc, cabernet sauvignon, merlot, shiraz
Leading wines: Warramate Cabernet, Shiraz, Riesling
Notes: A family-run estate utilising only its own fruit, Jack Church planted the Warramate vineyard in 1969. It is unirrigated and low-yielding at 6 tonnes to the hectare. Jack is now one of the veterans of the reborn Yarra Valley, planting his vineyard in the pre-chardonnay era. Instead, a typically elegant Yarra Riesling is made and these days his son David, yet another medical man but also a qualified winemaker, is in the thick of things at vintage. Warramate Shiraz is also excellent. Cellar door sales: weekends and public holidays 10am–6pm, at other times by appointment only.

Wombat Creek Vineyards (vineyard only)

Hazledene Road, Gladysdale, Vic 3797

Owners: David and Faye Griffith and Andrew Griffith
Chief winemaker: no wine made
Year of foundation: 1988
Tonnes produced on average each year: 150
Location: Gladysdale

Area: 11 ha
Soils: volcanic red loam
Varieties planted: White—chardonnay;
Red—pinot noir
Leading wines: none produced
Notes: At 500 metres altitude, Wombat Creek
is one of the highest vineyards in the Yarra
Valley. As befits its height, coolness and the
varieties planted, the vineyard produces fruit
for premium sparkling styles. There are no
cellar door sales.

Yarrabank Vineyards, Thibaut & Gillet (see also entry for Yering Station) R8

42 Melba Highway, Yarra Glen, Vic 3775
Ph 03 9730 2188, Fax 03 9730 2189

Owners: Yering Station and Champagne
Devaux
Chief winemaker: Claude Thibaut
Year of foundation: 1993
Tonnes crushed on average each year: 48 but
increasing to 80 in future years
Locations: Yarra Valley, Mornington Peninsula
and Macedon
Soils: see note on Yering Station
Varieties planted: White—chardonnay;
Red—pinot noir
Leading wines: Yarrabank Cuvee No 1
Notes: Yarrabank Vineyards is a joint venture
between Yering Station and Champagne
Devaux, specialising in premium sparkling
wines.

Yarra Burn R8

Settlement Road, Yarra Junction,
Vic 3797
Ph 03 5967 1428, Fax 03 5967 1146

Owner: BRL Hardy Ltd
Chief winemakers: Steve Pannell (red), Ed Carr
(sparkling), Tom Newton (white)
Year of foundation: 1976
Tonnes crushed on average each year: 75

Location: Yarra Junction
Area: 9.5 ha
Soils: grey-brown sandy loam, and grey clay
Varieties planted: White—chardonnay,
semillon; Red—cabernet franc, cabernet
sauvignon, merlot, pinot noir
Leading wines: Yarra Burn Bastard Hill Pinot
Noir (appears in good years), Yarra Burn
Cabernet Sauvignon, Yarra Burn Chardonnay
Notes: Yarra Burn was purchased by BRL Hardy
in 1995. Prior to that it had been owned by its
founders, David and Christine Fyffe. Currently
its 200-tonne winery is being increased tenfold
to accommodate the Hoddles Creek crop and
other fruit purchases. By 2000, the conversion
should be complete and BRL Hardy will be the
largest producer in the Yarra Valley. In the
meantime the consumer should look forward
to special releases of Bastard Hill Pinot Noir
(a Hoddles Creek product). Cellar door sales:
7 days 10am–5pm. There is also very pleasant
bed and breakfast accommodation available.

Yarra Edge R7

Lot 3 Edward Road, Lilydale, Vic 3140
Ph 03 9735 3473, Fax 03 9735 4853

Owner: Bingeman family
Chief winemaker: Martin Williams (contract)
Year of foundation: 1984
Tonnes crushed on average each year: 30 (but
set to increase substantially in vintage 2000
when new plantings come into bearing)
Location: Lilydale
Area: 13 ha (5 ha of which was planted in
1997 and is not yet bearing)
Soils: grey loam clay over shale base
Varieties planted: White—chardonnay;
Red—cabernet franc, cabernet sauvignon,
malbec, merlot, pinot noir
Leading wines: Yarra Edge Chardonnay,
Cabernets
Notes: Yarra Edge is a consistent medal winner
at various wine shows in Victoria and
elsewhere, including a top silver at the Lilydale

Wine Show. Cellar door sales: Sundays and public holidays 10am–5pm, at other times by appointment.

Yarra Ridge R9

Glenview Road, Yarra Glen, Vic 3755
Ph 03 9730 1022, Fax 03 9730 1131

Owner: Mildara-Blass
Chief winemaker: Rob Dolan
Tonnes crushed on average each year: 900
Location: Yarra Glen
Area: 91.6 ha
Soils: grey loam over grey clay base
Varieties planted: White—chardonnay, sauvignon blanc; Red—cabernet sauvignon, merlot, pinot noir
Leading wines: Yarra Ridge Chardonnay, Pinot Noir, Reserve Pinot Noir
Notes: From its outset, under the ownership of its founder, Louis Bialkower, Yarra Ridge became one of the high fliers of the region and worthily so. Consistently good Chardonnays, Sauvignon Blancs and Pinot Noirs poured from Yarra Ridge, vintage after vintage. These days perhaps the Sauvignon Blanc has slipped a little from its pungent best, but the Chardonnays and Pinots remain excellent in quality and, in times of ever-rising wine prices, in value also. Cellar door sales: 7 days 10am–5pm.

Yarra Vale R7

Paynes Road, Seville, Vic 3139
Ph/Fax 03 9735 1819

Owner: Morwood Grange Pty Ltd
Chief winemaker: Domenic Bucci
Year of foundation: 1991
Tonnes crushed on average each year: 25
Location: Seville
Area: 6 ha
Soils: red loam
Varieties planted: White: none; Red—cabernet sauvignon

Leading wines: Yarra Vale Cabernet Sauvignon
Notes: No cellar door sales. The wines are mostly sold through restaurants and wine retailers.

Yarra Valley Hills R9

Delaneys Road, Warrandyte South, Vic 3134
Ph 03 5962 4173, Fax 03 5962 4059

Owners: Terry and Leah Hill
Chief winemaker: Martin Williams
Year of foundation: 1993
Tonnes crushed on average each year: 160
Locations: Warrandyte South, Gruyere, Healesville
Area: 16 ha, encompassing three separate vineyards: Warranwood (Warrandyte South), Log Creek (Gruyere) and Kish Yallambee (Healesville)
Soils: grey loams over a clay base
Varieties planted: White—chardonnay, riesling, sauvignon blanc; Red—cabernet sauvignon, pinot noir
Leading wines: Yarra Valley Hills Chardonnay, Pinot Noir, Sauvignon Blanc, Cabernet Sauvignon
Notes: Terry Hill is a vigneron in a hurry. Yarra Valley Hills is not only an amusing play on words, based on location and the name of the proprietors, but also the newest star in the Yarra constellation. Trophies, medals and media recognition have come from virtually everywhere in a short period of time, to the extent that it would be difficult to find a Yarra Valley Hills wine that has not been awarded something somewhere. Its pinot noirs are very good and its Chardonnays exceptional (1995 best dry white current vintage at the National Wine Show), nor is its Sauvignon Blanc to be ignored, being served in first class on Qantas international flights. Cellar door sales: Warrandyte South open weekends and public holidays during summer 10am–6pm, winter by appointment. Restaurant 'La Fontana' open

Thursday to Sunday nights and Sunday for lunch.

Yarra Yering R10

Briarty Road, Gruyere, Vic 3770
Ph 03 5964 9267, Fax 03 5964 9239

Owner/chief winemaker: Dr Bailey Carrodus
Year of foundation: 1969
Tonnes crushed on average each year: 90
Location: Gruyere
Area: 20 ha
Soils: grey silty clay loams over deep clay
Varieties planted: White—chardonnay, marsanne, sauvignon blanc, semillon, viognier; Red—alvarelhao, bastardo, cabernet sauvignon, malbec, merlot, nebbiolo, pinot noir, roriz, sangiovese, shiraz, souzao, tinta amarello, tinta cao, touriga
Leading wines: Yarra Yering No 1 Dry Red (Cabernet Malbec Merlot), No 2 Dry Red (Shiraz Marsanne Viognier), Pinot Noir, Merlot, Chardonnay, No 1 Dry White (Semillon Sauvignon Blanc), Underhill Shiraz, Portsorts (a blend of the port varieties mentioned above)
Notes: What can one say about Dr Bailey Carrodus? He has certainly been a pioneer of modern Yarra winemaking and viticulture and often controversial in his winemaking methods. And Yarra Yering? A whole catalogue of grape varieties is grown but it has never been a mishmash, only order and superb quality. The No 1 Dry Red (the Bordeaux blend) is never less than excellent, nor is the Pinot Noir. And the Underhill Shiraz is a benchmark for cool-area winemakers everywhere. Cellar door sales: Open May and November ('for as long as we have stock'), Sat, public holidays 10am–5pm, Sun 12 noon–5pm.

Yeringberg R10

Maroondah Highway, Coldstream, Vic 3770
Ph 03 9739 1453, Fax 03 9739 0048

Owner: Yeringberg Pty Ltd
Chief winemaker: Guill de Pury
Year of foundation: 1863 to 1921, ceasing at that time for economic reasons, and 1969
Tonnes crushed on average each year: 16
Location: Coldstream
Area: 2 ha
Soils: grey loams on heavy grey clay subsoil with interspersed 'buckshot' gravel
Varieties planted: White—chardonnay, marsanne, roussanne; Red—cabernet franc, cabernet sauvignon, malbec, merlot, pinot noir
Leading wines: Yeringberg Chardonnay, Yeringberg (a white blend of marsanne and roussanne), Yeringberg Pinot Noir, Yeringberg (a red blend of the 'Bordeaux' varieties, cabernet sauvignon, cabernet franc, malbec and merlot)
Notes: Yeringberg has belonged to the de Pury family for over 130 years and, as a vineyard, is tiny. Yet Guill de Pury's leading wines lead in every sense of the word—elegance, balance, style, length of palate, regional typicity and ageing potential. The pity of it is that production is so small, but as well as excelling in winemaking, Guill is a farmer and always aware that Yeringberg wine is part of a bigger scheme of things. So for me Yeringberg is rare wine of rare quality. Cellar door sales: usually only one weekend late in May (which should be ascertained by telephone inquiry). Otherwise strictly by appointment.

Yering Station R8

Melba Highway, Yarra Glen, Vic 3775
Ph 03 9730 2188, Fax 03 9730 2189

Owners: Rathbone family
Chief winemaker: Tom Carson
Year of foundation: Originally established 1838 by William Ryrie as the first Yarra vineyard, then owned from 1849 onwards by Paul de Castella, under whom it reached the zenith of its nineteenth-century fame. After ceasing to be a vineyard in the early years of the

twentieth century, it was re-established in 1988 by the Dominguez family, who subsequently resold in 1996 to the present proprietors.

Tonnes crushed on average each year: 110, but increasing substantially as recently planted vineyard areas come into bearing

Location: Yering

Area: 68 ha (only 8 ha of which was bearing at the time of writing)

Soils: grey loams over aging mudstones

Varieties planted: White—chardonnay, sauvignon blanc, semillon; Red—cabernet franc, cabernet sauvignon, merlot, pinot noir, shiraz

Leading wines: Yering Station Yarra Valley Chardonnay, Pinot Noir, Cabernet Sauvignon Merlot, Yarrabank Sparkling Wines

Notes: No expense has been spared since the present proprietors assumed ownership in 1996. Sixty hectares of vineyard have been planted and a brand new winery erected for 1997 vintage. When the vines, planted in 1996–7, come into bearing, there will be some exciting table wines. Cellar door sales: 7 days 10am–5pm. There is also a restaurant at which the wines, including the new Yarrabank Vineyards sparkling wines, may be tasted with appropriate food.

MORNINGTON PENINSULA REGION

It could be argued that the Mornington Peninsula is yet another born-again Victorian viticultural area. In 1891, about 8 hectares of vineyard were listed in a Victorian government report on fruit and vegetables as existing in the region around Somerville, but they were not noteworthy and, as in the Yarra Valley, died out for economic reasons in the 1920s. Its next flirtation with the vine occurred in the early 1950s, when the late Douglas Seabrook (of the famous Melbourne wine merchant family) planted riesling vines on a relative's holiday property at Arthur's Seat near Dromana. This small and very private vineyard flourished until the mid-1960s when it was burnt out in a bushfire and never replanted. The Mornington vine came to stay in the early 1970s when Baillieu Myer planted cabernet and riesling vines on his Elgee Park property at Merricks North. Shortly afterwards (1975), Nat White commenced planting his small property at Main Ridge, the Keffords began to establish their Merricks Estate in 1976 and by 1980 the permanence of Mornington Peninsula wine seemed assured. During the 1980s and 1990s, an explosion of viticultural enthusiasm on the peninsula saw new vineyards springing up everywhere. In some respects it is like Burgundy—many small vineyards, fewer larger ones, with pinot noir and chardonnay the dominant varieties and complex wine styles to match.

Location: latitude 38°20'S, longitude 144°58'E, about 60 km south and south-east of Melbourne, along the Nepean Highway. The region extends from Mount Eliza south of Frankston on Port Phillip Bay, south-easterly to Somerville on Western Port Bay then along the western shore of the bay south until the bay joins Bass Strait. It then extends south-westerly and westerly along the Bass Strait coast to Point Nepean, then south-east and east along the southern shore of Port Phillip and north-east along that shore to Mount Eliza (the starting point).

MORNINGTON PENINSULA REGION

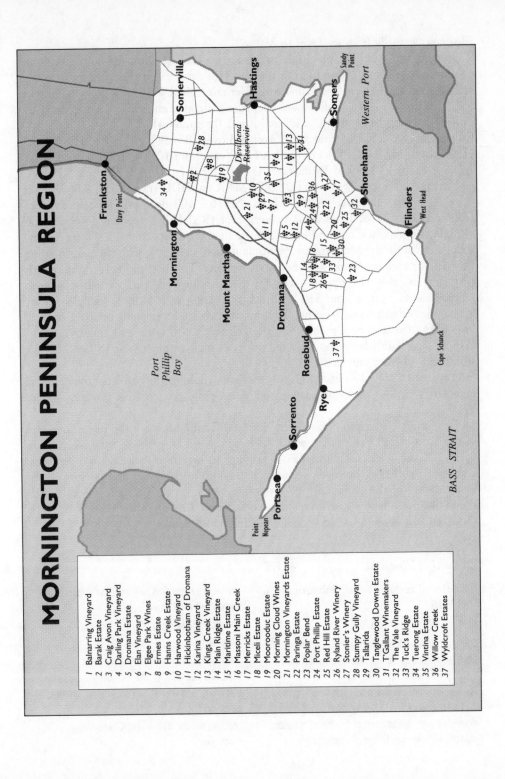

1   Balnarring Vineyard
2   Barak Estate
3   Craig Avon Vineyard
4   Darling Park Vineyard
5   Dromana Estate
6   Elan Vineyard
7   Elgee Park Wines
8   Ermes Estate
9   Hanns Creek Estate
10 Harwood Vineyard
11 Hickinbotham of Dromana
12 Karina Vineyard
13 Kings Creek Vineyard
14 Main Ridge Estate
15 Maritime Estate
16 Massoni Main Creek
17 Merricks Estate
18 Miceli Estate
19 Moorooduc Estate
20 Morning Cloud Wines
21 Mornington Vineyards Estate
22 Paringa Estate
23 Poplar Bend
24 Port Phillip Estate
25 Red Hill Estate
26 Ryland River Winery
27 Stonier's Winery
28 Stumpy Gully Vineyard
29 Tallarida
30 Tanglewood Downs Estate
31 T'Gallant Winemakers
32 The Vale Vineyard
33 Tuck's Ridge
34 Tuerong Estate
35 Vintina Estate
36 Willow Creek
37 Wyldcroft Estates

Elevation: virtually from sea-level to 250 m

Topography and soils: The peninsula rises from sea-level at Dromana quite steeply to a central ridge about 250 m high in the Red Hill district and then falls away to the coastal strip at Merricks and Balnarring. The most usual soil is a yellow podsol, but soil types do vary—around Dromana there are skeletal acidic soils, while around Red Hill in the region's centre there are red loams (kraznozems).

Climate: MJT 18.8°C (Mornington) (averaged over 20 years), 20°C (Red Hill South) (1995 only), MAR 11.4°C (1995 only), HDD vary from 1050 to 1600 depending on site (for example, 1240 at Dromana, 1431 at Mornington), AR 736 mm, RH 55% at Mornington. Mornington MJT 18.8°C, MAR na, HDD (raw) 1427, AR 736 mm (Oct–Apr 386 mm), RH 48%, AI na, SH 6.7 (Gladstones). Moderately cool (Moorooduc) to cool (Dromana) to very cool (Red Hill), ripening depending on altitude and exposure to wind chill. Similar in certain aspects to the Yarra Valley, though of course the Mornington Peninsula is more maritime, with the neighbouring Bass Strait providing bleak, wet and windy weather. This may seriously interfere with flowering and also with ripening, but has the advantage of being virtually frost-free. Annual rainfall varies from 730–950 mm, increasing with altitude. Supplementary irrigation is often necessary during the summer and autumn ripening period. Excessive vine vigour can also be a problem on the volcanic soil (kraznozem) country.

Harvest time: late March for early red varieties such as pinot noir to late May for shiraz and cabernet sauvignon

Principal varieties: Red—pinot noir, cabernet sauvignon, merlot, cabernet franc, shiraz, meunier; White—chardonnay, sauvignon blanc, pinot gris, riesling, gewurztraminer.

Total area: na

Major wine styles: Undoubtedly Pinot Noir and Chardonnay are the major successes of the Mornington Peninsula, both as table wines and as sparkling wine when made by the classic method. Shiraz too is proving its worth in selected warmer sites. Cabernet Sauvignon, however, seems to be limited to the lower and warmer north-eastern areas of the peninsula and sometimes when grown on more vigorous soils shows distinctly 'green' methoxypyrazine characters. Among other wines, Pinot Gris shows great promise as an unwooded fresh fruit-driven style.

Balnarring Vineyard   **NR**

62 Bittern-Dromana Road, Balnarring,
Vic 3926
Ph/Fax 03 9787 7191

Owners: Julie and Lee Scholte
Chief winemaker: Tod Dexter (contract)
Year of foundation: 1982
Tonnes crushed on average each year: formerly 28 but the vineyard is being rehabilitated and extended with an additional 3.6 ha of vineyard planted but not yet bearing. Accordingly,

vineyard production will increase substantially within the next three years.
Location: Balnarring
Area: 8 ha
Soils: shallow loam over a clay base
Varieties planted: White—chardonnay, riesling, traminer; Red—cabernet sauvignon, merlot, pinot noir
Leading wines: Balnarring Chardonnay, Pinot Noir

Notes: Balnarring Estate underwent a change of ownership recently. As a result, the vineyard is being refurbished and Balnarring's philosophy reassessed. Balnarring's previous wines were some of the more sturdy of the peninsula and hopefully will not stray too far in the opposite direction. No cellar door sales at present.

Barak Estate NR

Barak Road, Moorooduc, Vic 3933
Ph/Fax 03 5978 8439

Owner/chief winemaker: James Williamson
Year of foundation: 1990
Tonnes crushed on average each year: 3
Location: Moorooduc
Area: 1.5 ha
Soils: grey loam over shale over clay
Varieties planted: White—chardonnay;
Red—cabernet sauvignon, pinot noir, shiraz
Leading wines: Barak Estate Chardonnay, Cabernet
Notes: A small family vineyard with a rustic winery, hand-built by owner/maker James Williamson. Cellar door sales: open every weekend.

Brickenden Vineyard (vineyard only)

Patterson Road, Fingal, Vic 3939

Owner: Michael Hamson
Chief winemaker: no wine made
Year of foundation: 1994
Tonnes produced on average each year: first crop was in 1997, but when the vineyard is in full bearing, about 90 tonnes are anticipated
Location: Fingal
Area: 9.4 ha
Soils: deep sand
Varieties planted: White—chardonnay, sauvignon blanc; Red—pinot noir
Leading wines: no wine presently made
Notes: There are no cellar door facilities.

Brinalon Vineyard (vineyard only)

18 Paringa Road, Red Hill South, Vic 3937
Ph 03 5989 2105

Owners: Jeff and Robin Seager
Chief winemaker: not yet appointed
Year of foundation: 1996
Tonnes crushed on average each year: vineyard not yet in bearing, but anticipated that it will produce 30–40 tonnes
Location: Red Hill South
Area: 4 ha
Soils: rich red basaltic loam over red gravel
Varieties planted: White—chardonnay;
Red—pinot noir, shiraz
Leading wines: no wine yet made
Notes: Jeff Seager intends to concentrate on pinot noir and shiraz, but no grapes are expected before 1999. No cellar door sales.

Coronel Vineyard NR

19 Hillcrest Road, Shoreham, Vic 3937
Ph 03 5989 8050

Owners: Paul and Louise Coronel
Chief winemaker: none yet
Year of foundation: 1995
Tonnes produced on average each year: vineyard not yet in bearing
Location: Shoreham
Area: 1.5 ha (it is planned to increase this to 5 ha)
Soils: sandy loam of basalt origin over a clay base
Varieties planted: White—chardonnay;
Red—pinot noir
Leading wines: no wine is yet produced
Notes: This vineyard yielded its first crop in 1998. Wine sales accordingly are a future objective, but certainly the grape varieties should be suitable.

Craig Avon Vineyard R7

Craig Avon Lane, Merricks North,
Vic 3825
Ph 03 5989 7465

Owners: Ken and Helen Lang
Chief winemaker: Ken Lang
Year of foundation: 1986
Tonnes crushed on average each year: 18
Location: Merricks North
Area: 2.6 ha
Soils: red clay loam
Varieties planted: White—chardonnay;
Red—cabernet franc, cabernet sauvignon,
merlot, pinot noir
Leading wines: Chardonnay
Notes: This is one of the best sites on the
peninsula, protected from the south and the
west. Soil is deep red clay loam with good
retention of moisture yet good drainage.
Cellar door sales: 12–5pm weekends and
public holidays.

Darling Park Vineyard R8.5

Red Hill Road, Red Hill, Vic 3937
Ph 03 5989 2324, Fax 03 5989 2254/
03 5989 2732

Owners: John and Delys Sargeant
Chief winemakers: Kevin McCarthy (contract),
rosé and white; John Sargeant with
consultancy assistance, red
Year of foundation: 1986
Tonnes crushed on average each year: 18
Location: Red Hill
Area: 2.8 ha
Soils: Main Vineyard—deep red volcanic loam;
Home block—colourfully described by Delys
Sargeant as pulverised dinosaur bones over
split rock
Varieties planted: White—chardonnay, pinot
gris; Red—pinot noir, cabernet franc, cabernet
sauvignon, merlot
Leading wines: Darling Park Querida (a rosé
style made from the Bordeaux varietals

mentioned above), Pinot Gris, Pinot Noir,
Chardonnay
Notes: At Darling Park, there is an unusual rosé
style and excellent Chardonnay. Cellar door
sales and restaurant open weekends and public
holidays.

Dexter Vineyard (vineyard only)

Ellerina Road, Merricks North, Vic 3926

Owners: Tod and Debbie Dexter
Chief winemaker: none
Year of foundation: 1987
Tonnes produced on average each year: 55
Location: Merricks North
Area: 6.9 ha
Soils: shallow grey sandy loam over yellow clay
Varieties planted: White—chardonnay;
Red—cabernet sauvignon, pinot noir
Leading wines: all fruit is sold
Notes: This is the vineyard of Tod Dexter, chief
winemaker of Stoniers. There are no cellar
door sales.

Dromana Estate R8.5

Harrisons Road, Dromana, Vic 3936
Ph 03 5987 3800, Fax 03 5981 0714

Owners: Garry and Margaret Crittenden
Chief winemaker: Garry Crittenden
Year of foundation: 1982
Tonnes crushed on average each year: 50
Location: Dromana
Area: 5 ha
Soils: sandy loam over a clay base
Varieties planted: White—arneis, chardonnay;
Red—cabernet sauvignon, merlot, pinot noir
Leading wines: Dromana Estate Pinot Noir
Notes: Garry Crittenden is the tremendously
energetic force behind three ranges of wine.
First there is Dromana Estate, whose
Chardonnays and Pinots over the years have
placed the Mornington Peninsula region firmly
in the quality spotlight. Then there is the
Schinus range of quality wines made from fruit

purchased from various quality regions in Australia. Finally there is the extremely popular 'I', a range of Italian varietals, such as Barbera, Nebbiolo and Dolcetto and shortly Arneis. I suspect, however, that Gary Crittenden's first wine love will remain Dromana Estate Chardonnay and Pinot Noir. Cellar door sales: 11am–4pm each day except Christmas Day, Boxing Day and Good Friday.

Elan Vineyard & Winery NR

17 Turners Road, Bittern, Vic 3918
Ph 03 5983 1858, Fax 03 5983 2321

Owners: Selma and Jonathan Lowther
Chief winemaker: Selma Lowther
Year of foundation:1990
Tonnes crushed on average each year: 8
Location: Bittern
Area: 2.4 ha
Soils: grey sandy loam over clay subsoil
Varieties planted: White—chardonnay, riesling; Red—cabernet sauvignon, gamay, merlot, shiraz
Leading wines: Elan Cabernet Merlot
Notes: This is a typically small Mornington Peninsula vineyard with a selection of estate-made wines. Cellar door sales: first weekend of the month, public holidays or by appointment.

Elgee Park Wines R7

Junction Road, Merricks North, Vic 3926
Ph 03 5989 7338, Fax 03 5989 7553

Owner: Baillieu Myer family
Chief winemakers: Tod Dexter (contract); Kevin McCarthy (contract, viognier); Gordon Cope Williams (contract, sparkling)
Year of foundation: 1972
Tonnes crushed on average each year: 22
Location: Merricks North
Area: 4 ha
Soils: grey loam clay subsoil
Varieties planted: White—chardonnay, riesling, viognier; Red—cabernet franc, cabernet sauvignon, merlot, pinot noir
Leading wines: Elgee Park Chardonnay, Viognier, Cabernet Merlot
Notes: This was arguably the first vineyard and winery on the Mornington Peninsula in its twentieth century renaissance. The winery no longer operates, most wines being made under contract by Tod Dexter who, as one would expect, makes excellent Elgee Park Chardonnay. No cellar door sales.

Ermes Estate NR

2 Godings Road, Moorooduc, Vic 3933
Ph/Fax 03 5978 8376

Owners: Ermes and Denise Zucchet
Chief winemaker: Ermes Zucchet
Year of foundation: 1989
Tonnes crushed on average each year: 8
Location: Moorooduc
Area: 2.2 ha
Soils: light sandy clay loam
Varieties planted: White—chardonnay, malvasia, pinot gris, riesling; Red—cabernet sauvignon, merlot
Leading wines: Ermes Estate Cabernet Sauvignon
Notes: A consistent bronze medallist at the Royal Melbourne Wine Show, Ermes Estate is run enthusiastically as a family vineyard by Ermes and Denise Zucchet. With its northerly aspect and its location in one of the warmer parts of the peninsula, it ripens cabernet sauvignon quite satifactorily. Cellar door sales: weekends and public holidays, 11am–5pm.

Frogs Pond (vineyard only)

Arthurs Seat Road, Red Hill, Vic 3937

Owners: Marian and Dean Nelson
Chief winemaker: contract
Year of foundation: 1994
Tonnes crushed on average each year: 12.5

(1st vintage 1997) but will increase as vineyard comes into full bearing
Location: Red Hill
Area: 2 ha
Soils: red Kraznozem
Varieties planted: White—chardonnay; Red—pinot noir
Leading wines: no wine yet made
Notes: Frogs Pond is a well sheltered vineyard overlooking Port Phillip Bay, an area often subject to strong winds. No wines are yet made, but in a region of quality such as Mornington Peninsula, it may well happen. No cellar door sales.

Hanns Creek Estate NR

Kentucky Road, Merricks North, Vic 3926
Ph 03 5989 7266, Fax 03 5989 7500

Owner and chief winemaker: Tony Aubrey-Slocock
Year of foundation: 1987
Tonnes crushed on average each year: 25
Location: Merricks North
Area: 5.3 ha
Soils: red clay
Varieties planted: White—chardonnay; Red—cabernet sauvignon, pinot noir, shiraz
Leading wines: Hanns Creek Estate Chardonnay, Cabernet Sauvignon
Notes: Hanns Creek Estate is a small Mornington Peninsula winery. Cellar door sales: 11am–5pm each day.

Harwood Vineyard NR

Ellerina Road, Merricks North, Vic 3926
Ph 03 5989 7417, Fax 03 5989 7510

Owners: Frank and Pam Osborn
Chief winemaker: Richard McIntyre (contract)
Year of foundation: 1988
Tonnes crushed on average each year: 60
Location: Merricks North
Area: 6 ha
Soils: clay loam on clay
Varieties planted: White—chardonnay; Red—cabernet sauvignon, merlot, pinot noir, shiraz
Leading wines: Harwood Vineyard Pinot Noir, Chardonnay, Cabernet Merlot
Notes: With its vineyard sited on grey, clay-loam soils, Harwood is located on a north-facing slope protected from adverse southerly and westerly winds. Cellar door sales by appointment.

Hickinbotham of Dromana R7

Wallaces Road, Dromana, Vic 3936
Ph/Fax 03 5981 0355

Owners: Hickinbotham family
Chief winemaker: Andrew Hickinbotham
Year of foundation: 1988
Tonnes crushed on average each year: 60
Location: Dromana
Area: 6 ha
Soils: sandy loam over 'coffee' rock
Varieties planted: White—chardonnay, taminga; Red—cabernet sauvignon, merlot, pinot noir, shiraz
Leading wines: Hickinbotham of Dromana Chardonnay, Pinot, Merlot
Notes: Andrew Hickinbotham is the third generation of the wine-involved Hickinbotham family. His grandfather, Alan, was the mainspring in the introduction of the oenology course at Roseworthy in the 1930s. His father, Ian, is still very much engaged in wine-writing and education after many years of winemaking in Coonawarra, the Barossa Valley and Geelong. Now it is Andrew's turn to make premium wines in the excellent Dromana area. In the past decade, the Hickinbothams have built up a strong reputation for pinot noir and doubtless this will continue. Cellar door sales: 11am–6pm weekends, public holidays and most weekdays.

Jack (vineyard only)

Cnr Junction Road and Bittern-Dromana Road, Merricks North, Vic 3926

Owners: Graeme and Susan Jack
Chief winemaker: no wine yet made
Year of foundation: 1996
Tonnes crushed on average each year: none yet, but about 40–50 when the vineyard is fully planted and the vines are bearing
Location: Merricks North
Area: 5 ha
Soils: red volcanic loam at the top of the hill; greyish loam at the base
Varieties planted: White—chardonnay; Red—pinot noir
Leading wines: none yet
Notes: This small family vineyard is wisely planted to the region's premium varieties. No cellar door sales.

Karina Vineyard R7

Harrison's Road, Dromana, Vic 3936
Ph/Fax 03 5981 0137

Owners: Graeme and Janice Pinney
Chief winemaker: Graeme Pinney
Year of foundation: 1984
Tonnes crushed on average each year: 20
Location: Dromana
Area: 3.5 ha
Soils: grey sandy loam over a clay subsoil
Varieties planted: White—chardonnay, riesling, sauvignon blanc; Red—cabernet sauvignon, merlot
Leading wines: Karina Vineyard Chardonnay, Sauvignon Blanc
Notes: One of the more senior vineyards in the Mornington Peninsula region with mature vines, Karina is highly respected for its Sauvignon Blanc. All wines are estate grown and made. Cellar door sales: weekends and public holidays 11am–5pm; from 26 Dec to 31 Jan cellar door is open daily, same hours.

Kewleys NR

Whitehall Road, Flinders, Vic 3939

Owners: Brian and Gretchen Kewley
Chief winemaker: Brian Kewley
Year of foundation: 1975
Tonnes crushed on average each year: 1.5 (about 1000 litres)
Location: Flinders
Area: 0.4 ha
Soils: reddish-brown loam
Varieties planted: White—chardonnay; Red—cabernet franc, cabernet sauvignon, merlot, pinot noir, shiraz
Leading wines: Kewleys Chardonnay, Pinot Noir
Notes: The Kewley vineyard has 525 vines and some might say that Brian Kewley, who celebrated his twentieth vintage in 1997, knows them all by name. Brian is one of the veteran winemakers of the Mornington Peninsula region and, as a winemaker with such a wealth of experience, he can state without fear of contradiction that 'chardonnay and pinot always ripen well'. There are no cellar door sales. It is a family vineyard and, as he says, he does it 'just for our pleasure'.

Kings Creek Vineyard R9

237 Myers Road, Bittern, Vic 3918
Ph/Fax 03 5983 2102

Owners: Bill Glover and the Bell and Perraton families
Chief winemakers: Kathleen Quealy and Kevin McCarthy (contract)
Year of foundation: 1981
Tonnes crushed on average each year: 25
Location: Bittern
Area: 4 ha (plus the crops from two contract-grown vineyards from 1999)
Soils: sandy topsoil over a clay base; well-drained
Varieties planted: White—chardonnay; Red—cabernet sauvignon, merlot, pinot noir

Leading wines: Kings Creek Chardonnay, Pinot Noir

Notes: Kings Creek first came to prominence winning a trophy for its 1990 Pinot Noir at the Royal Melbourne Wine Show. It is located on flat country at Bittern on grey loam soil and, being scarcely 2 kilometres from the sea, is subject to a moderate maritime climate. Its forte is definitely Pinot Noir and Chardonnay and I remember with great pleasure the 1994 Pinot Noir. Cellar door sales: weekends, public holidays and the first two weeks of January.

Lavender Bay Vineyard NR

39 Paringa Road, Red Hill South, Vic 3937

Owners: Kevin and Barbara Luscombe
Chief winemaker: Gary Crittenden (contract)
Year of foundation: 1988
Tonnes crushed on average each year: 5, but will increase as newly planted chardonnay comes into bearing
Location: Red Hill South
Area: 2 ha
Soils: deep red volcanic loam
Varieties planted: White—chardonnay;
Red—pinot noir
Leading wines: Lavender Bay Pinot Noir
Notes: Gary Crittenden can make an elegant pinot noir that is always worth tasting. No cellar door sales. All wines are sold through distributors and mostly to local restaurants.

McCabe Vineyard (Vineyard only)

38 Kentucky Road, Merricks North, Vic 3926

Owners: Madeleine and Patrick McCabe
Chief winemakers: Kathleen Quealy and Kevin McCarthy (T'Gallant contract)
Year of foundation: 1990
Tonnes produced on average each year: 5.7
Location: Merricks North
Area: 1.5 ha

Soils: a hillside vineyard with red volcanic loam on its upper parts, grey loam at its base
Varieties planted: White—pinot gris, viognier;
Red—none
Notes: Madeleine and Patrick McCabe are grape-growing partners in T'Gallant Winemakers. Their grapes are separately made into wine, and bottled under the T'Gallant label with their name on the bottle as growers. No cellar door sales.

Main Ridge Estate R8.5

William Road, Red Hill, Vic 3937
Ph/Fax 03 5989 2686

Owners: Nat and Rosalie White
Chief winemaker: Nat White
Year of foundation: 1975
Tonnes crushed on average each year: 12
Location: Red Hill
Area: 2.8 ha
Soils: deep red volcanic loam
Varieties planted: White—chardonnay;
Red—cabernet sauvignon, merlot, pinot noir
Leading wines: Main Ridge Chardonnay, Half Acre Pinot Noir
Notes: Nat White is the senior winemaker of the Mornington Peninsula region, having erected his winery in 1980. Since then, there has been a progression of very fine Chardonnays and Pinots from Main Ridge. Elegance is Nat White's hallmark. Cellar door sales: weekdays 12 noon–4pm, weekends 12 noon–5pm.

Maraquita (vineyard only)

Baynes Road, Red Hill South, Vic 3937

Owner: Maraquita Pty Ltd
Chief winemaker: none, all grapes sold
Year of foundation: 1990
Tonnes crushed on average each year: 6.5
Location: Red Hill South
Area: 1.7 ha
Soils: red clay

Varieties planted: White—chardonnay;
Red—none
Leading wine: no wine made
Notes: No cellar door sales.

Maritime Estate NR
Tuck's Road, Red Hill, Vic 3937
Ph 03 5989 2735

Owners: John and Kevin Ruljancich
Chief winemaker: Kevin McCarthy
Year of foundation: 1993
Tonnes crushed on average each year: 9, but
will increase as new planting comes into
bearing
Location: Red Hill
Area: 4.8 ha (2.4 ha of which were planted
in 1995)
Soils: red volcanic loam on basalt
Varieties planted: White—chardonnay (1.6 ha),
pinot gris (0.8 ha); Red—cabernet sauvignon
(0.2 ha), pinot noir (2.2 ha).
Leading wines: Maritime Estate Chardonnay,
Pinot Noir
Notes: Maritime Estate is yet another
Mornington vineyard, which shows just how
suited the region is to chardonnay, wooded or
unwooded. Maritime Estate Chardonnay 1995,
tasted in wood at T'Gallant in early 1996, was
excellent and later went on to win a gold
award at the French-Australian Chamber of
Commerce Les Concours des Vins de Victoria.
The pinot was also good, winning a silver at
the 1996 Royal Melbourne Wine Show. Cellar
door sales: first weekend of each month,
public holiday weekends and during January,
11am–5pm.

Massoni Main Creek R7.5
Main Creek Vineyard, Mornington-
Flinders Road, Red Hill South, Vic 3937
Ph 03 5989 2352, Fax 03 5989 2014

Owners: Ian and Sue Home
Chief winemakers: Ian Home and Daniel
Greene

Year of foundation: 1984
Tonnes crushed on average each year: 40
Location: Red Hill South
Area: 2 ha
Soils: brown clay loam
Varieties planted: White—chardonnay;
Red—none
Leading wines: Massoni Main Creek
Chardonnay, Pinot Noir, Lectus Cuvee
Notes: I have always been impressed by the
size of Massoni Main Creek Pinot. It has never
been a wishy-washy rosé style, as some tend
to be. The pinot grapes are all bought in from
local vineyards. The Chardonnay too is often
on the bigger, more flavoursome side and
certainly none the worse for that. As Ian Home
is the founder of Yellowglen, it is only natural
that there should be a sparkling wine and that
is Lectus. Cellar door sales: Queens Birthday
weekend, at other times by appointment.

Merricks Estate R7
Thompsons Lane, Merricks, Vic 3916
Ph 03 5989 8416

Owners: George and Jacqui Kefford
Chief winemaker: Mike Zitzlaff (contract)
Year of foundation: 1977
Tonnes crushed on average each year: 20
Location: Merricks
Area: 3 ha
Soils: brown clay loam over red clay with some
'buckshot'
Varieties planted: White—chardonnay;
Red—cabernet sauvignon, merlot, pinot noir,
shiraz
Leading wines: Merricks Estate Shiraz
Notes: Merricks Estate is now one of the senior
Mornington vineyards, producing a well
respected and award winning Shiraz. Cellar
door sales: first weekend of each month
12 noon–5pm, public holiday weekends and
every weekend in January.

Miceli Winery **R7**

Main Creek Road, Main Ridge, Vic 3928
Ph 03 5979 2930, Fax 03 5989 2755

Owners: Anthony and Pauline Miceli
Chief winemaker: Anthony Miceli
Year of foundation: 1991
Tonnes crushed on average each year: 10, but
increasing as new plantings of pinot gris come
into bearing
Location: Main Ridge
Area: 3 ha
Soils: deep red basalt soil
Varieties planted: White—chardonnay, pinot
gris; Red—pinot noir
Leading wines: Miceli Chardonnay, Pinot Noir
Notes: Miceli is a small family winery in the
heart of the Mornington Peninsula.
Cellar door sales: first weekend of each month
and for special events.

Moorooduc Estate **R8**

501 Derril Road, Moorooduc, Vic 3933
Ph 03 9696 4130/03 5978 8585,
Fax 03 9696 2841

Owners: Richard and Jill McIntyre
Chief winemaker: Richard McIntyre
Year of foundation: 1983
Tonnes crushed on average each year: 48
Location: Moorooduc
Area: 5 ha
Soils: duplex light sandy loam on a yellow clay
subsoil
Varieties planted: White—chardonnay,
sauvignon blanc, semillon; Red—cabernet
franc, cabernet sauvignon, merlot, pinot noir,
shiraz
Leading wines: Moorooduc Estate Chardonnay,
Pinot Noir, Cabernet Sauvignon
Notes: Richard McIntyre is another of
Australia's medical men in the grip of the
grape. His Moorooduc vines are now quite
mature and produce a most appealing, fuller
(for the Mornington region) Chardonnay style,

due no doubt to their age and the area's
relative warmth compared with some of the
higher, cooler sites of Mornington. Shiraz has
just been planted and, in Moorooduc Estate's
favourable location, should be a success. Cellar
door sales: first weekend of each month
12 noon–5pm.

Morning Cloud Wines **NR**

15 Ocean View Avenue, Red Hill South,
Vic 3937
Ph 03 5989 2044, Fax 03 5989 2700

Owners: Bill and Kathy Allen, Peter and Judy
Maxwell
Chief winemakers: Tod Dexter, Ken Lang (Red);
Lindsay McCall (White)
Year of foundation:1984
Tonnes crushed on average each year: 5
Location: Red Hill
Area: 0.5 ha
Soils: red volcanic clay loam
Varieties planted: White—chardonnay;
Red—cabernet sauvignon
Leading wines: Morning Cloud Chardonnay
Notes: Morning Cloud is yet another small
Mornington Peninsula vineyard and is
enthusiastically run by the Allen and Maxwell
families, with a very successful Chardonnay.
The vineyard is fully and permanently netted to
protect against birds which often enjoy their
chardonnay straight off the vine. No cellar door
sales. All sales are made by mailing list or to
local restaurants, which is understandable in
view of the small production.

Mornington Vineyards Estate **NR**

Moorooduc Road, Moorooduc South,
Vic 3933
Ph/Fax 03 5974 2097

Owners: Hugh and Isabelle Robinson
Chief winemaker: Vincent Gere (contract)
Year of foundation: 1988
Tonnes crushed on average each year: 60

Location: Moorooduc
Area: 11 ha, but it is intended to expand the vineyard to 60 ha in the future
Soils: sandy loam over red clay
Varieties planted: White—chardonnay, sauvignon blanc, semillon; Red—pinot noir, shiraz
Leading wines: Mornington Vineyards Estate Pinot Noir, Chardonnay, Sauvignon Blanc
Notes: Mornington Vineyards Estate is already, by Mornington standards, a medium to large estate and it harbours ambitions to become much larger. About half of its crop is sold to other makers. Its Pinot Noir has an excellent reputation. Cellar door sales: every day in January 11am–5pm and every weekend during the rest of the year at the same times.

Osborn's Harwood Vineyard (see Harwood Vineyard entry)

Paringa Estate R10

Paringa Road, Red Hill South, Vic 3937
Ph/Fax 03 5989 2669

Owners: Lindsay and Margaret McCall
Chief winemaker: Lindsay McCall
Year of foundation: 1985
Tonnes crushed on average each year: 30
Location: Red Hill South
Area: 4.2 ha (part of the vineyard has been recently replanted and is not yet in bearing)
Soils: deep red volcanic clay
Varieties planted: White—chardonnay, pinot gris; Red—cabernet sauvignon, pinot noir, shiraz
Leading wines: Paringa Estate Chardonnay, Pinot Noir, Shiraz
Notes: After some years of growing fame, Paringa Estate is now established as one of the outstanding wineries of the Mornington Peninsula. Its wines are produced only from fruit grown on the estate. Its Pinot Noir and

Shiraz are outstanding cool-area examples of their cultivars and must be tasted. Like many of his Mornington colleagues, Lindsay McCall is seriously thinking of discontinuing his Cabernet Sauvignon. Cellar door sales: each weekday except Tuesday 12 noon–5pm, weekends and public holidays 11am–5pm.

Peninsula Ridge Vineyards (vineyard only)

Cnr Shands and Roberts Roads, Main Ridge, Vic 3928

Owners: McCutcheon family, Hogg family, Virginia Swanton and William Power
Chief winemaker: none appointed
Year of foundation: 1994
Tonnes crushed on average each year: 1997 was the first vintage and 12 tonnes were produced; when the vineyard is fully bearing, about 50 tonnes could be produced
Location: Main Ridge
Area: 5.7 ha
Soils: grey loam over a clay base
Varieties planted: White—chardonnay; Red—pinot noir
Leading wines: no wine is produced commercially, only sufficient for partners' needs
Notes: No cellar door sales.

Pen-y-Bryn Estate (vineyard only)

Lot 13 Whitehall Road, Flinders, Vic 3929

Owners: Les and Bets Plumridge
Chief winemaker: no wine made
Year of foundation: 1993
Tonnes produced on average each year: vineyard not yet fully in bearing
Location: Flinders
Area: 0.4 ha.
Soils: red volcanic loam
Varieties planted: White—chardonnay; Red—shiraz

Leading wines: no wines made as yet
Notes: No cellar door sales.

Poplar Bend **NR**

Main Creek Road, Main Ridge, Vic 3928
Ph/Fax 03 5989 6046

Owner/chief winemaker: David Briggs
Year of foundation: 1988
Tonnes crushed on average each year: 8
Location: Main Ridge
Area: 1 ha
Soils: rich red clay volcanic loams
Varieties planted: White—none; Red—pinot
noir (Mariafeld clone)
Leading wines: Sparkling Chloe, Pineau Chloe,
Cabernet Chloe
Notes: Poplar Bend is the small winery formerly
owned by Keith and Marie Dunstan and since
purchased by David Briggs, who fully intends
to maintain Keith's wine styles. Cellar door
sales: first weekend each month and public
holidays.

Port Phillip Estate **R9**

261 Red Hill Road, Red Hill, Vic 3937
Ph 03 5989 2703, Fax 03 5989 2891

Owner: Jeffrey Sher
Chief winemaker: Lindsay McCall (contract)
Year of foundation: 1987
Tonnes crushed on average each year: 50
Location: Red Hill
Area: 6 ha
Soils: red and grey basalt loam
Varieties planted: White—chardonnay,
sauvignon blanc; Red—pinot noir, shiraz
Leading wines: Port Phillip Estate Pinot Noir
Notes: Jeffrey Sher's Port Phillip Estate is one
of the high-flyers of Mornington Peninsula, its
Pinots receiving great acclaim in the few years
that they have been on the market. The 1994
Reserve was judged 'Best Pinot' at the
prestigious Victorian Wines Show in 1995.
Cellar door sales: each weekend except in July

and August from 12 noon–5pm, at the same
times all public holidays and from
mid-December to mid-January.

Red Hill Estate **R8**

53 Red Hill Shoreham Road, Red Hill
South, Vic 3937
Ph 03 5989 2838, Fax 03 5989 2855

Owners: Sir Peter and Lady Derham
Chief winemaker: Jenny Bright
Year of foundation: 1989
Tonnes crushed on average each year: 150
Location: Red Hill South
Area: 16.8 ha, consisting of three peninsula
vineyards, Red Hill Estate (9.6 ha), Lindenberry
(3.6 ha) and Briars (3.6 ha)
Soils: deep red volcanic clay
Varieties planted: White—chardonnay,
sauvignon blanc; Red—cabernet sauvignon,
meunier, pinot noir, merlot
Leading wines: Red Hill Estate Methode
Champenoise Brut (vintage), Chardonnay, Pinot
Noir
Notes: Red Hill Estate and its modern winery
are the fulfilment of Sir Peter Derham's dream,
but it is a dream based on realistic planning
and wine quality. In a region where there are
so many Chardonnays and Pinots of excellence,
the priority here is top Methode Champenoise.
There is a splendid restaurant at which to try
it, open for lunch throughout the year and for
dinner during summer, Thursdays to Saturdays.
Cellar door sales: 11am–5pm each day.

Red Ridge Vineyard (vineyard only)

Lot 7 Red Hill Shoreham Road, Red Hill
South, Vic 3937

Owners: Ian and Anne Thomson
Chief winemaker: none yet
Year of foundation: 1988
Tonnes produced on average each year: 4
Location: Red Hill South
Area: 1.1 ha

Soils: deep red volcanic loam
Varieties planted: White—chardonnay;
Red—cabernet sauvignon, merlot, pinot noir,
shiraz
Leading wines: none yet
Notes: Red Ridge is a small vineyard with a
fairly typical Mornington Peninsula planting.
A small winery is planned for the future.
No cellar door sales.

Ryland River Winery NR

Main Creek Road, Main Ridge, Vic 3928
Ph 03 5989 6098

Owners: John and Valerie Bray
Chief winemaker: John Bray
Year of foundation: 1986
Tonnes crushed on average each year: 40
Location: Main Ridge
Area: 2.5 ha
Soils: red volcanic loam
Varieties planted: White—chardonnay,
sauvignon blanc, semillon; Red—cabernet
sauvignon, merlot, shiraz
Leading wines: Ryland River Chardonnay,
Cabernet Sauvignon
Notes: By Mornington Peninsula standards,
Ryland River is a small- to medium-sized
winery. There is also a herb garden and trout
fishing. Cellar door sales: 10am–5pm
weekends and public holidays, other times by
appointment.

Seawinds NR

Main Creek Road, Main Ridge, Vic 3928
Ph/Fax 03 5989 6204

Owner: Ron Matson
Chief winemaker: T'Gallant Winemakers
(contract)
Year of foundation: 1989
Tonnes crushed on average each year: 18
Location: Main Ridge
Area: 3 ha
Soils: red volcanic loam

Varieties planted: White—chardonnay,
sauvignon blanc; Red—pinot noir
Leading wine: Seawinds Sauvignon Blanc
Notes: No cellar door sales.

Shergold Park (vineyard only)

Shergolds Lane, Dromana, Vic 3936
Ph 03 9819 1393, Fax 03 9819 3276

Owners: Kevin and Judith Burt
Chief winemaker: Daniel Green (contract)
Year of foundation: 1988
Tonnes crushed each year on average: 22, but
may increase slightly as the vineyard was
'rejuvenated' during 1997
Location: Dromana
Area: 3.2 ha
Soils: organic loam over clay
Varieties planted: White—sauvignon blanc;
Red—cabernet franc, cabernet sauvignon,
merlot, petit verdot, shiraz
Leading wine: Merlot (all grapes are sold with
the exception of a small parcel of merlot,
which is retained by the owners)
Notes: Shergold Park's 'rejuvenation' involved
the removal of two out of three cabernet franc
vines (formerly closely planted in the hope—in
vain, as it turned out—of restricting excess vine
vigour). The new planting configuration could
restrict such vigour without affecting crop
quantity and might even improve it. Kevin Burt
is waiting and hoping. No cellar door sales.

Stonier's Winery R10

362 Frankston-Flinders Road, Merricks,
Vic 3916
Ph 03 5989 8300, Fax 03 5989 8709

Owner: Stonier Yuill Hamson and Limb Pty Ltd
Chief winemaker: Tod Dexter
Year of foundation: 1978
Tonnes crushed on average each year: 200
Location: Merricks
Area: 45 ha (including 20 ha not yet bearing)

Soils: chocolate brown deep clay loam over red clay
Varieties planted: White—chardonnay, sauvignon blanc; Red—cabernet franc, cabernet sauvignon, merlot, pinot noir
Leading wines: Stonier's Reserve Chardonnay, Reserve Pinot Noir, Reserve Cabernet
Notes: Without doubt the outstanding winery of the Mornington Peninsula region, Stonier's has won many trophies for its Reserve Pinot. Its Reserve Chardonnay is also excellent. Cellar door sales: weekends and public holidays, otherwise by appointment.

Stony Creek Estate Vineyard (vineyard only)

Tucks Road, Red Hill, Vic 3937

Owners: Meran and Brian Jennings
Chief winemaker: no wine is made
Year of foundation: 1990
Tonnes produced on average each year: 35
Location: Red Hill
Area: 4.5 ha
Soils: a hillside vineyard with rich red volcanic loam at its crest and grey loam as it descends
Varieties planted: White—chardonnay; Red—pinot noir
Leading wines: no wine produced, all fruit is sold
Notes: No cellar door sales.

Stumpy Gully Vineyard   NR

1247 Stumpy Gully Road, Moorooduc, Vic 3933
Ph/Fax 03 5978 8429

Owners: Frank and Wendy Zantwoort
Chief winemaker: Wendy Zantwoort
Year of foundation: 1989
Tonnes crushed on average each year: 105
Location: Moorooduc
Area: 10.4 ha
Soils: rich black topsoil up to 60 cm in depth over red gritty clay

Varieties planted: White—chardonnay, marsanne, pinot gris, riesling, sauvignon blanc; Red—cabernet sauvignon, merlot, pinot noir, sangiovese, shiraz
Leading wines: Stumpy Gully Sauvignon Blanc, Marsanne, Cabernet Sauvignon
Notes: With a crush in excess of 100 tonnes, Stumpy Gully is one of the larger producers of the Mornington Peninsula and Moorooduc is one of the slightly warmer places here. As a result, cabernet sauvignon, merlot and shiraz should thrive. Cellar door sales: first weekend each month, 11am–5pm.

Tallarida Winery Boneo   NR

Browns Road, South Rosebud, Vic 3939
Ph 03 5988 6208

Owner: Rocco Tallarida
Chief winemaker: Larry Keach (contract)
Year of foundation: 1988
Tonnes crushed on average each year: 10
Location: South Rosebud
Area: 7 ha
Soils: deep sandy soils
Varieties planted: White—chardonnay; Red—cabernet sauvignon, merlot, pinot noir
Leading wines: Tallarida Cabernet, Chardonnay
Notes: The small tonnage in recent years was due to problems in the vineyard and to the fact that new plantings have not yet come into bearing. No cellar door sales.

Tanglewood Downs Estate   NR

Bulldog Creek Road, Merricks North, Vic 3926
Ph 03 5974 3325, Fax 03 5974 4170

Owners: Ken and Wendy Bilham
Chief winemaker: Ken Bilham
Year of foundation: 1984
Tonnes crushed on average each year: 16
Location: Merricks North
Area: 3 ha
Soils: grey clay loam with patches of quartz

Varieties planted: White—chardonnay, gewurztraminer, riesling; Red—pinot noir (4 clones—mv6, d5v12, mariafeld and a newer burgundy clone), cabernet franc, cabernet sauvignon, merlot

Leading wines: Tanglewood Downs Pinot Noir

Notes: Tanglewood Downs is a well sheltered vineyard with extensive views over Port Phillip Bay. Its soil is not fertile, but its structure and water-holding capacity have been much improved by extensive mulching and Scott-Henry trellising has maximised sunlight exposure. As can easily be seen from the list of varieties, Ken Bilham tends to specialise in Pinot and is justifiably pleased with this red which is usually worth an award at the Victorian Wines Show (he won a Gold in 1991). He also makes a little Shiraz, a variety which is still quite rare on the peninsula. Cellar door sales: daily 12 noon–5pm. There is also a function facility for special parties.

Tannematt **NR**

Cape Schank, Vic
Ph 03 9899 7677, Fax 03 9899 7466

Owner: P Spring
Chief winemaker: Kevin McCarthy (contract)
Year of Foundation: 1989
Tonnes crushed on average each year: 3
Location: Cape Schank
Area: 1.25 ha
Soils: sandy soils over clay
Varieties planted: White—chardonnay; Red—pinot noir
Leading wines: Tannematt Chardonnay Pinot Blend (a white)
Notes: No cellar door sales. The wine is distributed locally by the owner.

T'Gallant Winemakers **R9**

Mornington-Flinders Road, Main Ridge, Vic 3928
Ph 03 5989 6565, Fax 03 5989 6577

Owners/chief winemakers: Kathleen Quealy and Kevin McCarthy
Year of foundation: 1990
Tonnes crushed on average each year: 250
Location: Main Ridge
Area: 16 ha
Soils: deep red volcanic loam
Varieties planted: White—chardonnay, gewurztraminer, pinot gris; Red—muscat, pinot noir
Leading wines: T'Gallant Lot 2 Chardonnay, Celia's White Pinot, Tribute Pinot Gris, and Pinot Grigio
Notes: Kathleen Quealy and Kevin McCarthy selected Mornington Peninsula as Australia's premium region for unwooded whites and buy in quite a lot of Mornington Peninsula fruit for winemaking purposes. As well, they are extremely busy contract winemakers. T'Gallant is one of the originators of the unwooded Chardonnay style in Australia and also the pioneer of Pinot Gris and Pinot Grigio in Australia. Yes, it is the same variety, but Kathleen Quealy says that she makes the Grigio in the Italian manner. In addition, there may in future years be variations on a muscat theme, such as a 'Moscato Frizzante' or a 'Muscat Ottonel'. Cellar door sales: daily 11am–5pm.

The Garden Vineyard *(vineyard only)*

174 Graydens Road, Moorooduc, Vic 3933

Owners: Doug and Diane Johnson
Chief winemaker: Kevin McCarthy (contract)
Year of foundation: 1994 (as The Garden Vineyard), previously known as Devil Bend Vineyard
Tonnes crushed on average each year: 4, but this will increase as vines recently planted come into bearing
Location: Moorooduc
Area: 2 ha

Soils: deep grey sandy loam
Varieties planted: White—pinot gris;
Red—pinot noir
Leading wines: The Garden Vineyard Pinot Noir
Notes: The Johnsons have their own label and
their own wine but are presently not licensed
to sell. Cellar door sales may be available some
time in 1999.

The Vale Vineyard NR

'Gannawarra', 2914 Frankston-Flinders
Road, Balnarring, Vic 3926
Ph/Fax 03 5983 1521

Owners: John and Susan Vale
Chief winemaker: John Vale
Year of foundation: 1991
Tonnes crushed on average each year: 2
Location: Balnarring
Area: 1.6 ha
Soils: grey loam up to 30 cm deep over yellow
clay
Varieties planted: White—chardonnay,
marsanne; Red—cabernet sauvignon, merlot,
shiraz
Leading wines: The Vale Vineyard Cabernet
Sauvignon-Merlot, Chardonnay
Notes: The Vale Vineyard at 1.6 ha in area is
still very small, but it has recently been
quadrupled in size. A one-person winery has
been commissioned and will be open by
appointment for cellar door sales when a
licence is obtained.

Tuck's Ridge at Red Hill R8

37 Red Hill Shoreham Road, Red Hill
South, Vic 3937
Ph 03 5989 8660, Fax 03 5989 8579

Owner: Peter Hollick
Chief winemaker: Daniel Greene
Year of foundation: 1986
Tonnes crushed on average each year: 150
Location: Red Hill South
Area: There are two vineyards both at Red Hill

South, the first at 37 Red Hill Shoreham Road
is 12.8 ha, the second at Callanan's Road is
13.1 ha.
Soils: rich red volcanic loam
Varieties planted: White—chardonnay, riesling,
semillon; Red—meunier, pinot noir
Leading wines: Tuck's Ridge Pinot Noir, VUES
(a champagne method sparkling wine),
Chardonnay
Notes: One of the bigger estates of the region,
Tuck's Ridge is another exciting young winery
whose wines were first enthusiastically received
in 1993. Since then, if anything, its standards
have improved and will continue to do so as its
vines come to maturity. Look out for the Pinot
Noir. Cellar door sales: weekends and public
holidays 12 noon–5pm.

Tuerong Estate Vineyard NR

Mornington-Flinders Road, Red Hill,
Vic 3937
Ph 03 5989 2129

Owner: Gennaro Mazzella
Chief winemaker: Peter Cumming (contract)
Year of foundation: 1984
Tonnes crushed on average each year: 6
Location: Red Hill
Area: 2 ha (with 4 ha remaining to be planted)
Soils: deep red volcanic loam
Varieties planted: White—chardonnay;
Red—cabernet franc, cabernet sauvignon,
malbec, merlot, pinot noir
Leading wines: Tuerong Estate Methode
Champenoise, Chardonnay, Cabernet
Sauvignon
Notes: A family-run Italian-style restaurant on
site provides a perfect opportunity to try the
wines with food. Restaurant and cellar door
sales: weekends and public holidays
11am–5pm and during January.

Two Bays Estate (vineyard only)

Mornington-Flinders Road, Red Hill,
Vic 3937
Ph 03 5989 2536

Owners: Graham and Carol Rutter
Chief winemaker: none yet appointed, first
vintage due this year
Year of foundation: 1995
Tonnes produced on average each year: first
vintage was in 1998, vineyard not yet fully
bearing
Location: Red Hill
Area: 2 ha (with 2 ha to be planted in 1998)
Soils: heavy red clay loam
Varieties planted: White—chardonnay;
Red—pinot noir
Leading wines: no wines yet made
Notes: Two Bays is a very young vineyard
whose owners sell its fruit to a local winery,
which in turn makes wine for them off-site.
No cellar door sales. It is still too early.

Vintina Estate   NR

1282 Nepean Highway, Mount Eliza,
Vic 3930
Ph 03 9787 8166, Fax 03 9775 2935

Owners: Jim and Tina Filippone
Chief winemaker: Jim Filippone
Year of foundation: 1985
Tonnes crushed on average each year: 4
Location: Mount Eliza
Area: 1.6 ha
Soils: grey sandy loam over a clay subsoil
Varieties planted: White—chardonnay, pinot
gris; Red—cabernet sauvignon, pinot noir
Leading wines: Vintina Estate Louisa
Chardonnay, Mitchel James Cabernet
Sauvignon
Notes: Vintina Estate Chardonnays have won
some critical support from time to time.
Cellar door sales: 7 days 11am–5pm.

Willow Creek   NR

166 Balnarring Road, Merricks North,
Vic 3926
Ph 03 5989 7448, Fax 03 5989 7584

Owners: Harris, Ball and Knowles families
Chief winemaker: Kim Hart (contract)
Year of foundation: 1989
Tonnes crushed on average each year: 150
Location: Merricks North
Area: 13 ha
Soils: red chocolate grey and black loam with
limestone deposits
Varieties planted: White—chardonnay;
Red—cabernet sauvignon, pinot noir
Leading wines: Willow Creek Pinot Noir
Notes: Willow Creek is one of the largest
vineyards in Mornington Peninsula and already
it is proving eminently suited to pinot noir with
Willow Creek Pinot Noir 1995 winning two
trophies at the Perth and Lilydale wine shows.
Its Chardonnay, both wooded and unwooded,
is also enjoying considerable show success.
Cellar door sales: Thurs–Mon 11am–5pm.

Wyldcroft Estates   NR

Stanleys Road, Red Hill South, Vic 3937
Ph/Fax 03 5989 2646

Owners: Richard Condon and Sharon Stone
Chief winemaker: Kevin McCarthy
Year of foundation: 1987
Tonnes crushed on average each year: 20
Location: Red Hill South
Area: 3 ha
Soils: deep red volcanic loam
Varieties planted: White—chardonnay;
Red—cabernet sauvignon, pinot noir, shiraz
Leading wines: Wyldcroft Estate Pinot Noir,
Chardonnay
Notes: At Red Hill South, Wyldcroft Estate is at
the centre of the Mornington action. Like other
vineyards in its vicinity it makes good pinot
noir, though Richard Condon is encouraged by
his Cabernet Sauvignon. A Wyldcroft Estate

Shiraz 1997 will be released in 2000. Cellar door sales: weekends and public holidays.

Yal Yal Estate (vineyard only)
21 Yal Yal Road, Merricks North, Vic 3937

Owners: Lou and Elisabeth Butterfield
Chief winemaker: no wine yet made
Year of foundation: 1995
Tonnes crushed on average each year: vineyard not yet in bearing
Location: Merricks North
Area: 2.6 ha
Varieties planted: White—chardonnay; Red—pinot noir
Leading wines: no wines are presently made
Notes: Yal Yal Estate is another small Mornington Peninsula vineyard in its early days. No cellar door sales.

Yrsa's Vineyard (Vineyard only)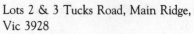
Lots 2 & 3 Tucks Road, Main Ridge, Vic 3928

Owner: Zug Investments Pty Ltd
Chief winemaker: none yet appointed
Year of foundation: 1994
Tonnes crushed on average each year: vineyard not yet fully bearing
Location: Main Ridge
Area: 6.5 ha
Soils: rich red volcanic loam at the top of the hill, becoming a grey loam as the vineyard descends
Varieties planted: White—chardonnay; Red—pinot noir
Leading wines: First vintage 1998
Notes: Though some wine was produced off-site in 1998, there are no present plans for a winery or cellar door facilities.

GEELONG REGION

Geelong is at once one of the oldest and youngest Australian wine regions. Its vineyards were founded 150 years ago by Swiss and German immigrants, encouraged by Sophie de Montmollin, wife of the Superintendent of Melbourne Charles La Trobe. They soon prospered and by 1860 there were over 200 hectares under vine. But it was a fleeting prosperity. Fifteen years later, phylloxera chose Geelong as its point of entry and began its devastation of Australia. The Victorian government, anxious to localise the outbreak, offered a bounty for the uprooting of its vineyards. Despite this, the spread of the louse was inexorable. By the turn of the century there were few, if any, vineyards remaining in Geelong and phylloxera was well established in Victoria.

Nearly 70 years later, in 1966, came the renaissance of Geelong wine when Daryl and Nini Sefton planted their Idyll vineyard. Two years later, Tom Maltby established the Anakie vineyard (now called Zambelli) and the Geelong region was set for steady growth in the 1970s (Mount Duneed 1970, Tarcoola 1971, The Minya 1974, Bannockburn 1974, Asher 1975, Prince Albert 1975) and further growth still in the 1980s (Innisfail 1980, Waybourne 1980, the Hickinbotham family lease of Anakie in 1981, Scotchman's Hill 1982, Staughton Vale 1986). Though pinot noir has certainly been extremely successful in the region (witness Bannockburn, Scotchman's Hill and, in some years, Prince Albert) and Geelong is growing rapidly, it is not yet a name that hangs from every winelover's lips.

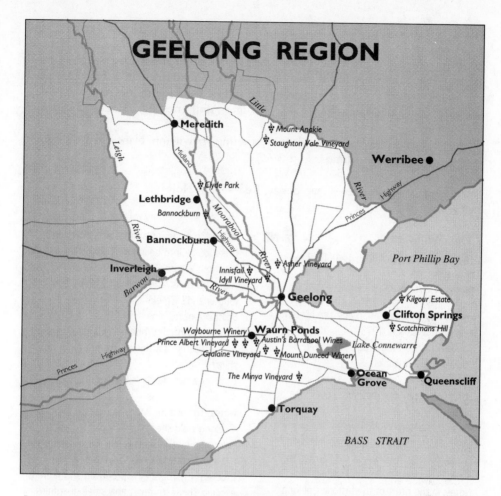

Location: latitude 38°7'S, longitude 144°22'E, about 70 km south-west of Melbourne along the Princes Highway. Though reasonably small in its area of vines under cultivation, Geelong is quite widespread with vineyards to the east, north, north-west and south-west of the centre of the city up to 30 km away.

Elevation: 20–300 m

Topography and soils: quite steep and undulating country especially to the north and north-west of Geelong (around Anakie, to about 350 m). Lower hills to the east and south. There are two basic soils: (i) heavy grey soils on basalt, found north of the Barwon River, these are brownish-grey in colour and overlie grey and yellow-grey clay subsoils, being slightly acid in nature; (ii) red duplex soils (podsolic, sandy loams overlying yellow-grey heavy clay subsoils), quite acid in nature. Other soils in the region are limestone-based rendzinas and terra rossas.

Climate: MJT 18.8°C, MAR na, HDD (raw) 1457 (cut off and as adjusted for latitude daily temperature range and vine sites 1354), AR 541 mm (Oct–Apr 301 mm), RH 52% (Gladstones). MJT 19°C MAR 9.4°C, HDD (raw) 1471, AR 538 mm

(Oct–Mar 311 mm), RH 62% (9am), AI 266 mm, SH 7.8. (Dry & Smart). Quite cool and dry with low radiation. Wind chill and frosts sometimes a problem at flowering. Maritime influences (Bass Strait) in its eastern and southern parts. Annual rainfall figures are very low at 538 mm and 541 mm and certainly indicate a need for supplementation by drip irrigation from surface dams during ripening.

Harvest time: mid-March (pinot noir) to late April (riesling, shiraz and cabernet sauvignon)

Principal varieties: White—chardonnay, riesling, sauvignon blanc; Red—cabernet sauvignon, pinot noir, shiraz

Total area: 221 ha (1996)

Major wine styles: White—Chardonnay; Red—Pinot Noir

Asher Vineyard NR

360 Goldsworthy Road, Lovely Banks, Vic 3221
Ph 03 5276 1365

Owners/winemakers: Brian and Lee Moten
Year of foundation: 1975
Tonnes crushed on average each year: 8
Location: Lovely Banks
Area: 1.6 ha
Soils: heavy clay over limestone over weathered rock
Varieties planted: White—chasselas, sauvignon blanc; Red—cabernet sauvignon, malbec
Leading wines: Asher Vineyard Sauvignon Blanc, Cabernet Sauvignon Malbec
Notes: In the heart of the historic Geelong wine area, which was originally planted last century and these days virtually in the suburbs of Geelong, Asher is a small family vineyard. Cellar door sales: Saturdays and public holidays 10am–5pm, Sundays 12 noon–5pm, other times by appointment.

Austin's Barrabool Wines R8

50 Lemins Road, Waurn Ponds, Vic 3221
Ph 03 5241 8114, Fax 03 5241 8122

Owners: Richard and Pamela Austin
Chief winemaker: John Ellis (contract)
Year of foundation: 1982
Tonnes crushed on average each year: 10, but increasing as new plantings at Sutherland's Creek come into bearing
Location: Waurn Ponds and Sutherland's Creek
Area: 1.5 ha (Waurn Ponds), 11 ha (Sutherland's Creek)
Soils: see notes
Varieties planted: White—chardonnay, riesling; Red—cabernet sauvignon, merlot, pinot noir, shiraz
Leading wines: Austin's Barrabool Chardonnay, Shiraz
Notes: The Waurn Ponds vineyard is another of Geelong's old sites originally planted about 150 years ago by the Swiss family Triboulet. Its soil is a rich terra rossa over a limestone base. Excellent Chardonnay is produced and there is exciting Shiraz in regrettably small quantities. Tasting by appointment only.

Backwell (vineyard only)

145 Lemins Road, Waurn Ponds, Vic 3221
Ph 03 5241 8311

Owner: Ian Backwell
Year of foundation: 1989
Tonnes produced on average each year: 8, but increasing as more vineyard area is coming into bearing
Location: Waurn Ponds
Area: 2 ha

Soils: 30–50 cm of reddish-brown heavy loam over limestone
Varieties planted: White—semillon; Red—pinot noir
Notes: A small vineyard with Scott Henry trellising and supplementary drip irrigation. No wine is made. No cellar door sales.

Bannockburn R10

Midland Highway, Bannockburn, Vic 3331
Ph 03 5281 1363, Fax 03 5281 1349

Owner: Bannockburn Vineyard Pty Ltd
Chief winemaker: Gary Farr
Year of foundation: 1974
Tonnes crushed on average each year: 100
Location: Bannockburn
Area: 17.5 ha
Soils: heavy clay loam over limestone and over 'buckshot' clay
Varieties planted: White—chardonnay, sauvignon blanc; Red—cabernet sauvignon, malbec, merlot, pinot noir, shiraz
Leading wines: Bannockburn Pinot Noir, Chardonnay, Shiraz
Notes: Averaging less than six tonnes to the hectare, Bannockburn is a very low-yielding vineyard, usually giving fruit of marvellously concentrated flavour. Gary Farr is a frequent traveller to Burgundy during the European vintage and has become one of Australia's most experienced and talented makers of chardonnay and pinot noir. When these two factors are put together, it is easy to understand why Bannockburn's reputation of excellence for its complex Pinot Noirs and Chardonnays is totally deserved. Due to his Burgundian experience, Bannockburn Pinot Noir is one of the longest lived of all Australian pinots with the possible exception of Bass Phillip. Bannockburn Shiraz can also be outstanding. No cellar door sales.

Clyde Park NR

Midland Highway, Bannockburn, Vic 3331
Ph/Fax 03 5281 7274

Owner: Donlevy Fitzpatrick
Chief winemaker: Scott Ireland
Year of foundation: 1980
Tonnes crushed on average each year: 50, but will increase as new plantings come into bearing
Location: Bannockburn
Area: originally 1.2 ha, but recently extended to 10.7 ha
Soils: black volcanic loam over a limestone base
Varieties planted: White—chardonnay, pinot gris, sauvignon blanc; Red—cabernet sauvignon, pinot noir, shiraz
Leading wines: Clyde Park Pinot Noir, Chardonnay
Notes: Owned by Bannockburn winemaker Gary Farr until 1994, and now by Melbourne restaurateur, Donlevy Fitzpatrick, Clyde Park under Farr's winemaking had built up a solid quality reputation for Chardonnay and Pinot Noir. Under Scott Ireland, there should certainly be no diminution of quality. No cellar door sales.

Gralaine Vineyard NR

65 Feehan's Road, Mount Duneed, Vic 3216
Ph 019 969 813, Fax 03 9877 7258

Owners: Graeme and Elaine Carroll
Chief winemaker: John Ellis (contract)
Year of foundation: 1983
Tonnes crushed on average each year: 5
Location: Mount Duneed
Area: 2 ha (planned to double by the year 2000)
Soils: light sandy loam over reactive clay over yellow clay

Varieties planted: White—none; Red—cabernet sauvignon, merlot
Leading wine: Gralaine Merlot
Notes: Gralaine is almost a merlot monoculture. However, there are a few cabernet vines. John Ellis is an excellent winemaker. There are no cellar door sales at the vineyard, but the wine may be tasted at the Hanging Rock Winery, Newham, Victoria.

Idyll Vineyard R6.5

265 Ballan Road, Moorabool, Vic 3221
Ph 03 5276 1280, Fax 03 5276 1537

Owners: Daryl and Nini Sefton
Chief winemaker: Daryl Sefton
Year of foundation: 1966
Tonnes crushed on average each year: 80
Location: Moorabool
Area: 15 ha
Soils: dark brown soil over clay and limestone
Varieties planted: White—chardonnay, gewurztraminer; Red—cabernet sauvignon, shiraz
Leading wines: Idyll Blush (rosé), Bone Idyll (an unoaked light-bodied Shiraz), Idyll Gewurztraminer, Chardonnay, Cabernet-Shiraz, Oak-Aged Shiraz
Notes: Daryl and Nini Sefton re-established viticulture in Geelong in 1966 on a site at the centre of the nineteenth century vinegrowing area. All wines are grown, made and bottled on the estate. No fruit is bought in from outside. In the years since its establishment, Idyll has earned a reputation for very reliable wines. Among smaller winemakers, it has also been extremely effective in exporting wine to Europe and local and overseas awards for wine quality have been numerous. Cellar door sales: Tues–Sun 10am–5pm, Mondays only on public holidays between the same hours.

Innisfail NR

Cross Street, Batesford, Vic 3221
Ph 03 5276 1258, Fax 03 5221 8442

Owner: Shaaron Griffiths
Chief winemaker: Ron Griffiths
Year of foundation: 1980
Tonnes crushed on average each year: 35
Location: Batesford
Area: 6 ha
Soils: heavy volcanic loam over a limestone base
Varieties planted: White—chardonnay, riesling; Red—cabernet sauvignon, merlot, pinot noir.
Leading wines: Innisfail Chardonnay
Notes: The Griffiths have a small but mature vineyard, make their own wine and have a good reputation for their Chardonnay. No cellar door sales.

Kilgour Estate NR

85 McAdams Lane, Bellarine, Vic 3223
Ph/Fax 03 5251 2223

Owner: Anne Timms
Chief winemaker: Kevin McCarthy (contract)
Year of foundation: 1989
Tonnes crushed on average each year: 25, increasing to 60 in the next few years as new plantings come into bearing
Location: Bellarine
Area: 10 ha
Soils: heavy sandy loam leading to sand over a limestone base
Varieties planted: White—chardonnay, pinot gris; Red—cabernet franc, cabernet sauvignon, merlot, pinot noir, brown muscat
Leading wines: Kilgour Estate Pinot Noir, Cabernet Sauvignon, Chardonnay
Notes: Kilgour Estate is beautifully situated with panoramic views over Port Phillip, Corio Bay and Bass Strait. There is a restaurant and outdoor barbecue facilities. Cellar door sales: 7 days 11am–6pm.

McGlashan Estate Wallington (vineyard only)

225 Swan Bay Road, Wallington,
Vic 3221
Ph/Fax 03 5255 2916

Owners: Russell and Jan McGlashan
Chief winemaker: no wine yet made
Year of foundation: 1995
Tonnes crushed/produced on average each
year: vineyard yet to come into bearing,
anticipated first vintage 1998
Location: Wallington
Area: 7 ha
Soils: sandy loam over 'buckshot' and clay
Varieties planted: White—chardonnay;
Red—pinot noir
Leading wines: no wine yet produced
Notes: It is still early days for McGlashan
Estate.

Moorabool Vineyard   **NR**

40 Dog Rocks Road, Batesford, Vic 3221
Ph/Fax 03 5243 6766

Owners: Graham and Ruth Bonney
Winemaker: John Darling (contract)
Tonnes crushed on average each year: 0.5
from a trial block, but will increase as new
plantings come into bearing
Location: Batesford
Area: 2 ha
Soils: grey loam over broken limestone marl
Varieties planted: White—chardonnay;
Red—cabernet franc, cabernet sauvignon,
merlot, shiraz
Leading wine: the blend of the four red
varieties
Notes: Planted on a north-easterly slope above
the Moorabool River, Moorabool Vineyard is
very small but has history on its side, as it
forms part of the site of the original Paradise
Vineyard planted in 1848 by James Henry
Dardell. No cellar door sales.

Mount Anakie Wines   **NR**

Staughton Vale Road, Anakie, Vic 3221
Ph 03 5284 1452, Fax 03 5284 1405

Owner: O Zambelli
Chief winemaker: O Zambelli
Year of foundation: 1969
Tonnes crushed on average each year: 120
Location: Anakie
Area: 18 ha
Soils: black volcanic soils over 'scoria'—broken
lava rock, part of an old volcanic cone
Varieties planted: White—biancone,
chardonnay, riesling, semillon; Red—cabernet
franc, cabernet sauvignon, shiraz
Leading wines: Mount Anakie Shiraz,
Chardonnay
Notes: Founded by Tom Maltby in 1969 and
for several years leased to Hickinbotham
Winemakers, this is another longstanding
Geelong vineyard. Cellar door sales: Tues–Sun
11am–6pm.

Mount Duneed Winery   **NR**

70 Feehan's Road, Mount Duneed,
Vic 3216
Ph/Fax 03 5264 1281

Owner: Ken and Joy Campbell
Chief winemaker: Ken Campbell
Year of foundation: 1970
Tonnes crushed on average each year: 15, but
will increase as newly planted vines come into
bearing
Location: Mount Duneed
Area: 4.3 ha
Soils: sandy loam over basaltic clay
Varieties planted: White—muscadelle,
sauvignon blanc, semillon; Red—cabernet
franc, cabernet sauvignon, malbec, merlot,
pinot noir, shiraz
Leading wines: Mount Duneed Cabernet-
Merlot-Malbec (blend), Semillon-Sauvignon
Blanc (blend)
Notes: This vineyard is in a very cool area close

to Bass Strait only 6 km from the sea with 'Bordeaux' blends, both red and white. Cellar door sales: weekends and public holidays 10am–5pm, other times by appointment only.

Prince Albert Vineyard R8

100 Lemins Road, Waurn Ponds, Vic 3216
Ph/Fax 03 5241 8091

Owners: Susan and Bruce Hyett
Chief winemaker: Bruce Hyett
Year of foundation: 1975
Tonnes crushed on average each year: 11
Location: Waurn Ponds
Area: 2 ha
Soils: red terra rossa over limestone base
Varieties planted: White—none;
Red—pinot noir
Leading wine: Prince Albert Pinot Noir
Notes: Prince Albert is a monoculture, producing a single vineyard Pinot Noir and nothing else. Its early Pinots were exciting, if only because there was little other cool area pinot noir in Australia at the time. The vineyard and its winemaking then went through an uncertain stage for several years, but recently it has become very good once more. Cellar door sales by appointment.

Rothwell Estate (vineyard only)

675 Old Melbourne Road, Little River, Vic 3211
Ph 03 5283 1249

Owner: N Karakasch
Chief winemaker: none appointed
Year of foundation: 1995
Tonnes crushed on average each year: vineyard not yet in bearing, but 20 tonnes are anticipated when the vineyard is in full bearing
Location: Little River
Area: 2 ha
Soils: grey loam over limestone
Varieties planted: White—chardonnay;

Red—shiraz
Leading wines: none yet
Notes: It is early days for Rothwell Estate. First vintage is due in 1998 and a contract winemaker will be employed. No cellar door sales.

Scotchman's Hill R9

190 Scotchman's Road, Drysdale, Vic 3222
Ph 03 5251 3176, Fax 03 5253 1743

Owners: Browne family
Chief winemaker: Robin Brockett
Year of foundation: 1982
Tonnes crushed on average each year: 400
Location: Drysdale
Area: 40.5 ha
Soils: black, heavy volcanic clay over broken basalt
Varieties planted: White—chardonnay, riesling, sauvignon blanc; Red—cabernet franc, cabernet sauvignon, merlot, pinot noir
Leading wines: Scotchman's Hill Chardonnay, Pinot Noir
Notes: Located east of Geelong on the Bellarine Peninsula and with a cool, maritime climate, Scotchman's Hill has rapidly built up an excellent reputation for its Pinot Noir and Chardonnay. Cellar door sales: 7 days 10.30am–4.30pm.

Staughton Vale Vineyard NR

20 Staughton Vale Road (cnr Ballan Road), Anakie, Vic 3221
Ph 03 5284 1477, Fax 03 5284 1229

Owners: Paul and Lyn Chambers
Chief winemaker: Paul Chambers
Year of foundation: 1986
Tonnes crushed on average each year: 20
Location: Anakie
Area: 6 ha (including 1 ha not yet bearing)
Soils: part of an old volcanic cone—black basalt soils over 'scoria'

Varieties planted: White—chardonnay, riesling, semillon; Red—cabernet franc, cabernet sauvignon, malbec, merlot, petit verdot, pinot noir

Leading wines: Staughton (a blend of the Bordeaux red varieties listed above), Staughton Riesling

Notes: Staughton Vale is a close-planted vineyard with a vine density of 3200 vines to the hectare. Cellar door sales: Fri–Mon and public holidays 10am–5pm, other times by appointment. A restaurant, open for lunch and morning and afternoon tea, is located in the vineyard.

The Minya Vineyard and Winery NR

Minya Lane, Connewarre, Vic 3227
Ph 03 5264 1397

Owners: Jeff and Sue Dans
Chief winemaker: Sue Dans
Year of foundation: 1974
Tonnes crushed on average each year: 20
Location: Connewarre
Area: 4 ha
Soils: light sandy loam
Varieties planted: White—chardonnay; Red—cabernet sauvignon, grenache, merlot, shiraz
Leading wines: The Minya Grenache, Cabernet Sauvignon-Shiraz-Merlot
Notes: This small vineyard is within sea-spray of Bass Strait and requires wind breaks and also

netting protection from the many birds in the area. Unusually for the region, The Minya cultivates grenache. Cabin accommodation is available. Cellar door sales: weekends after Christmas until Easter, most public holidays and by appointment.

Waybourne Winery NR

60 Lemins Road, Waurn Ponds, Vic 3221
Ph/Fax 03 5241 8477

Owners: Tony and Kaye Volpato
Chief winemaker: Tony Volpato
Year of foundation: 1978
Tonnes crushed on average each year: 10
Location: Waurn Ponds
Area: 1.6 ha
Soils: red terra rossa over limestone base
Varieties planted: White—chardonnay, frontignac, pinot gris, riesling; Red—cabernet sauvignon
Leading wines: Waybourne Cabernet Sauvignon, Riesling
Notes: Adjoining Prince Albert Vineyard and sharing a rich basaltic soil over a limestone base, Waybourne is another vineyard planted in the centre of the historic Geelong wine-growing district. Perhaps the soil here is too rich as it promotes vigorous vine growth at the expense of fruit, making cultivation and sulfur spraying extremely difficult and yielding only a small crop. Tasting and cellar door sales by appointment only.

SUNBURY REGION

The region was first crossed by Hume and Hovell in 1824 on their mistaken way to Western Port Bay, a journey which ended at Corio Bay off Port Phillip. But it was not a journey in vain, though it may have seemed so at the time. They found valuable pastoral land, needing little clearance, natural grassland virtually devoid of eucalypts. This was later to encourage John Batman, a free settler in Van Diemens Land, in 1835 to make the initial barterings with Aboriginal tribes that led to the settlement

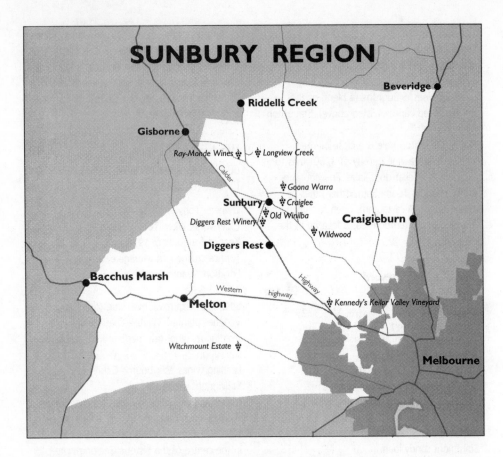

of what was ultimately to be called Melbourne. Batman did not plan a future metropolis—what initially interested him and his immediate circle, the Port Phillip Association, were its grazing prospects. Shortly after, these were exploited by members of that Association, who moved their flocks to what is today the Sunbury area, so named by Jackson Brothers after Sunbury on Thames in England. Discoveries of gold at Bendigo in the 1850s also created a demand for overnight accommodation in the area and in 1859 the area received its first railway service.

The first vineyards appeared there during the late 1850s. James Goodall Francis, later to be a premier of Victoria, erected his Goona Warra homestead and winery in 1858, at the same time employing European vignerons to plant a terraced vineyard. In 1865 James Johnston, a man of varying business interests—hotel-keeper, grazier, newspaper proprietor and politician—erected Craiglee, having the year before planted 16 acres of vines, including riesling and hermitage. Those two varieties later proved the most successful on the site. His 1872 Craiglee Hermitage, an award-winner at the Vienna Exposition in 1875, is the oldest Australian wine I have ever tasted and quite remarkable for its 102 years of age at the time of tasting. By 1870, there were over 300 acres of vines in and around Sunbury. Later the region miraculously avoided phylloxera, which devastated both Geelong and later Bendigo. Although the region continued to produce wine until the late 1920s, the nineteenth century was its golden age. By the time of the Great Depression, sheer economics forced the grubbing out of the vines and, as in most former vineyards, the substitution of more viable sheep and wool.

The Carmody family came to Craiglee in 1961 and, in 1976, Patrick Carmody planted the first vines it had seen in virtually 50 years. In 1979 came the first vintage of reborn Craiglee. Since then the Sunbury region has grown steadily. Goona Warra was re-established in 1983 and several more old Sunbury names, such as Old Winilba, are with us once more. In 1997, the region produced 150 tonnes of fruit from 82.5 ha of mostly young vines. Plantings in 1998 were anticipated to be a further 150 hectares with the 500-tonne criterion being reached by 2000.

Location: latitude 37°35'S, longitude 144°44'E about 30 km north-west of Melbourne
Elevation: 50–400 m (contour boundary)
Topography and soils: The region is flat to undulating, rising to the north and north-west to a 400-metre contour line, forming the boundary between it and the Macedon Ranges region. It is a mixture of igneous and sedimentary rocks, the igneous rocks being chiefly new basalt formed during the Pleistocene period with small areas of older basalt from the Lower Tertiary period. There are also areas of Upper Palaeozoic granite and granodiorite. The sedimentary rocks are formed from small areas of Tertiary sand, clay and lignite and shale, sandstone, mudstone and limestone, Silurian, slate and sandstone from the Ordovician age.

Its major soil is hard alkaline red duplex (Dr 2.23 Northcote), quite common in vineyard areas of south-eastern Australia with some areas of cracking clays and others of hard acidic duplex soils. There are also free-draining sandy loams (alluvial) along creek valleys, which are acidic (pH 5.5).
Climate: (local) Sunbury (Weather Station Melbourne Airport) MJT 19.6°C, MAR 10.5°C, HDD (raw) 1400, AR 562 mm (Oct–Apr 292.3 mm), RH 73% (av % Oct–March) (3pm). AI na, SH na. Cf Melbourne: MJT 19.6°C, MAR na, HDD (raw) 1554, 1501 (cut off and adjusted for altitude daily temperature range and vine sites), AR 658 (Oct–Apr 394 mm), RH 48% (Jan 3pm), AI na, SH 6.7 (Gladstones). Additional local data: Sunbury AR 592 mm (Oct–Apr 301.2 mm).

Sunbury is undoubtedly much warmer and drier than Macedon Ranges to its north and north-west, but can share heavy damaging winds. By comparison, Melbourne to the south-east is warmer, possibly due to an urban warming factor, and wetter (possibly due to closer proximity to Port Phillip and its maritime effect). Practical experience (Pat Carmody carried out his twentieth vintage at Craiglee in 1998) has shown that the region is climatically suited to all but the latest ripening grape-types, that is, only late Southern French varieties such as grenache and mourvedre and Italians such as sangiovese may fail to ripen. As in most parts of vinous Australia, irrigation is necessary and is effected through surface catchment in private dams, through town water supplies and by pumping from some creeks. Bore water is likely to be salty. Frost is a slight risk. At Craiglee, situated on fairly flat ground, it has affected the vineyard only twice in 20 years (1982 and 1997). Birds account for about 1% crop loss at Craiglee which is not netted. This is due to a natural absence of trees in the region and such a loss is much lower than in other regions, such as the Yarra Valley and Mornington Peninsula.

Harvest time: chardonnay early to mid-April, shiraz mid-April to early May

Principal varieties: White—chardonnay, sauvignon blanc; Red—cabernet sauvignon, shiraz, pinot noir

Total area: 82.5 ha (1997)

Major wine styles: *Chardonnay* Young Chardonnay from this region generally shows melony aromas, which are made more complex by barrel and malolactic fermentation. In good years the wine is well balanced with good acidity, causing it to age well over 5 years. If a French comparison is needed, Sunbury Chardonnays tend to 'Chablis' style in youth, filling out on palate with 3+ years bottle age. *Shiraz* In good years, the Shiraz of the region is medium-bodied and fruit-driven, accepting subtle French oak extremely well. On nose it is typically but not heavily peppery, inclining more to white than black pepper, and this coupled with cherry fruit aromas causes great aromatic complexity. Its palate is medium bodied, of berry and spice flavours with well integrated, lightly peppery tannins. In all, these are wines of excellent vinosity and quite long in the mouth. In poor years, the wines can be thin, ungenerous and a trifle green.

Craiglee R10

Sunbury Road, Sunbury, Vic 3429
Ph 03 9744 4489, Fax 03 9744 7905

Owners: Carmody family
Chief winemaker: Pat Carmody.
Year of foundation: 1976
Tonnes crushed on average each year: 40, but will increase to 60 as new vineyards come into bearing
Location: Sunbury
Area: 10 ha
Soils: sandy loams, clay loams
Varieties planted: White—chardonnay, sauvignon blanc; Red—cabernet sauvignon, pinot noir, shiraz
Leading wines: Craiglee Shiraz, Chardonnay
Notes: Modern Craiglee is a vineyard of nostalgia for me as its nineteenth century incarnation produced the oldest Australian wine I have ever tasted—1872 Craiglee Hermitage. Though its modern style is consistently excellent, it pales a little in comparison with the current plethora of hyper-American-oaked Shiraz from warmer regions.

When tasting Craiglee Shiraz, expect subtlety, not super-charge, on the palate. Cellar door sales: Sundays and Public Holidays 10am–5pm, other times by appointment.

Diggers Rest Winery NR

205 Old Vineyard Road, Sunbury,
Vic 3429
Ph/Fax 03 9740 1660

Owners: Frank and Judy Hogan
Chief winemaker: Peter Dredge
Year of foundation: 1987
Tonnes crushed on average each year: 15, and increasing
Location: Sunbury
Area: 6 ha
Soils: black basaltic and quartzite clay gravel
Varieties planted: White—Chardonnay; Red—cabernet sauvignon, pinot noir, shiraz
Leading wines: Diggers Rest Chardonnay
Notes: Cellar door sales: daily 10am–5pm.

Goona Warra R7

Sunbury Road, Sunbury, Vic 3429
Ph 03 9740 7766, Fax 03 9744 7648

Owners: John and Elizabeth Barnier
Chief winemaker: John Barnier
Year of foundation: 1863, re-established 1983
Tonnes crushed on average each year: 35
Location: Sunbury
Area: 5 ha
Soils: black basaltic clays on hills varying to
sandy loams on river flats
Varieties planted: White—chardonnay,
roussanne, semillon; Red—cabernet franc,
cabernet sauvignon, merlot, pinot noir
Leading wines: Goona Warra Cabernet Franc,
Chardonnay, Semillon
Notes: Goona Warra, like Craiglee, is a
reincarnation of another nineteenth century
Victorian vineyard. Cabernet Franc is its forte
and is very good. Cellar door sales: daily
10am–5pm except Good Friday and Boxing
Day.

Kennedy's Keilor Valley Vineyard NR

Overnewton Road, Keilor, Vic 3036
Ph/Fax 03 9331 6246

Owners: Colin and Denise Kennedy
Chief winemaker: Peter Dredge (contract)
Year of foundation: 1989
Tonnes crushed on average each year: 6
Location: Keilor
Area: 1.8 ha
Soils: rich red soil, clay subsoil
Varieties planted: White—chardonnay
Leading wines: Kennedy's Keilor Valley
Chardonnay (lightly wooded)
Notes: There are no cellar door sales. Sales
by personal contact and through a local
distributor.

Longview Creek NR

150 Palmers Road, Sunbury, Vic 3429
Ph/Fax 03 9744 1050

Owners: Sten Bergmann and Philippa
Bergmann-Hill
Winemaker: David Hodgson
Year of foundation: 1987
Tonnes crushed on average each year: 5.5
Location: Sunbury
Area: 6.5 ha
Soils: volcanic black clay
Varieties planted: White—chardonnay, chenin
blanc; Red—pinot noir, shiraz
Leading wines: Longview Creek Chardonnay,
Pinot Noir
Notes: At about 450 metres in altitude, the
vineyard is quite high for the region. Sunbury
has an ancient and honourable tradition for
good shiraz. Cellar door sales: 7 days
11am–5pm.

Old Winilba NR

150 Vineyard Road, Sunbury, Vic 3429
Ph/Fax 03 9740 9703

Owners: Fred and Sam Andraos
Chief winemaker: Mario Marson
Year of foundation: originally 1864, closed
1912, re-established 1989
Tonnes crushed on average each year: 25
Location: Sunbury
Area: 5 ha
Soils: volcanic ash of a light to dark brown
colour; between 220 and 250 metres in altitude,
the vineyard is sited on an east-facing slope
Varieties planted: White—chardonnay, riesling,
sauvignon blanc, semillon; Red—cabernet
sauvignon, pinot noir, shiraz
Leading wines: Old Winilba Cabernet
Sauvignon, Chardonnay, Pinot Noir
Notes: Old Winilba has a consistent show
record, winning silver and bronze awards at
local wineshows. Cellar door sales: ring the
winery for times.

Ray-Monde Wines NR

250 Dalrymple Road, Sunbury, Vic 3429
Ph 03 5427 2777, Fax 03 5428 3390

Owners: Lakey Family
Chief winemaker: John Lakey
Year of foundation: 1989
Tonnes crushed on average each year: 10, but
increasing
Location: Sunbury
Area: 6 ha
Soils: basaltic clay, problems with drainage in
wet weather
Varieties planted: White—none; Red—pinot
noir
Leading wines: Ray-Monde Pinot Noir
Notes: Cellar door sales by appointment.

Wildwood NR

St Johns Lane, Wildwood, Bulla,
Vic 3428
Ph 03 9307 1118, Fax 03 9331 1590

Owner: Dr Wayne G Stott
Chief winemakers: Wayne Stott and Peter
Dredge
Year of foundation: 1983
Tonnes crushed on average each year: 25
Location: Bulla
Area: 8 ha
Soils: heavy black basalt for the 'Bordeaux'
varieties, lighter terra rossa for the white
varieties and pinot noir
Varieties planted: White—chardonnay, viognier;
Red—cabernet franc, cabernet sauvignon,
merlot, pinot noir, shiraz

Leading wines: Wildwood Chardonnay,
Cabernets, Viognier, Shiraz
Notes: If you miss a flight and have a long wait
at Melbourne Airport, go a further 4 km and
visit Wildwood—it's just about the closest
winery to the airport and, at 132 metres above
sea-level, you can enjoy the view back to
Melbourne. At least that is what the brochure
advises. The owner/winemaker Wayne Stott
and winemaker Peter Dredge are both
graduates of Charles Sturt University's
viticulture and oenology courses. Cellar door
sales: 7 days 10am–6pm.

Witchmount Estate NR

Leakes Road, Rockbank, Vic 3335
Ph 03 9747 1155, Fax 03 9747 1744

Owners: M. and G. Ramunno
Chief winemaker: Peter Dredge (contract)
Year of foundation: 1991
Tonnes crushed on average each year: 7, but
the vineyard is not yet in full bearing
Location: Rockbank
Area: 5.6 ha
Soils: red loam
Varieties planted: White—chardonnay,
sauvignon blanc; Red—cabernet franc,
cabernet sauvignon, merlot, nebbiolo, shiraz
Leading wines: Witchmount Chardonnay,
Cabernet Sauvignon-Shiraz
Notes: This Sunbury name is quite new to me
but a gold at the Victorian Wine Show for a
1996 Chardonnay is a very good result,
indicating a promising future. Cellar door sales:
Wed–Sun all day. There is also a restaurant.

MACEDON RANGES REGION (PROPOSED)

First traversed in 1824 by Hume and Hovell during their mistaken journey to Port
Phillip (they were heading for Westernport), the Macedon Ranges were crossed and
reported on by the energetic Surveyor General of New South Wales, Major Thomas
Mitchell in 1836. There were earlier attempts at settlement in Southern Victoria

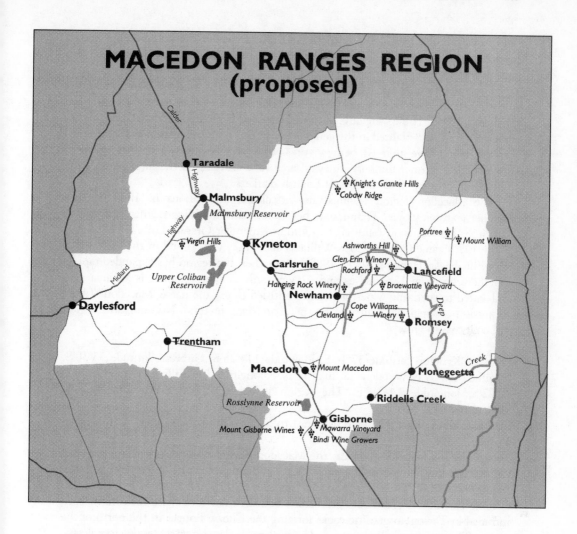

MACEDON RANGES REGION
(proposed)

Taradale

Malmsbury

Malmsbury Reservoir

Knight's Granite Hills

Cobaw Ridge

Virgin Hills

Kyneton

Ashworths Hill

Portree

Mount William

Upper Coliban Reservoir

Carlsruhe

Glen Erin Winery

Rochford

Lancefield

Hanging Rock Winery

Braewattie Vineyard

Newham

Daylesford

Cope Williams Winery

Cleveland

Romsey

Trentham

Macedon

Mount Macedon

Monegeetta

Creek

Deep

Rosslynne Reservoir

Riddells Creek

Mount Gisborne Wines

Gisborne

Mawarra Vineyard

Bindi Wine Growers

soon after Hume and Hovell, for example, the failed attempt from Tasmania in 1827 by Hume's old school friend, John Batman, who finally succeeded by surreptitiously settling in Melbourne in May 1835. He was followed in August of the same year by John Pascoe Fawkner, who took up land at Monegeeta west of Romsey but did not settle there. In 1837, the New South Wales government recognised Batman's *fait accompli* and the area was officially opened for settlement, but by then there were over 200 squatters in the area stretching from Melbourne to Mount Macedon. Like much of rural Australia at that time, grazing was the chief pursuit, the towns in the general area beginning to develop in the 1840s. In the 1850s, the goldrushes to the north-west (Castlemaine and Bendigo) furthered their development. By the time Burke and Wills pushed north through the region in 1860 on their ill-fated north–south traverse of the continent, the Macedon Ranges were well settled, both legally by the station owners and rather more irregularly by bushrangers. From this time also and well into the twentieth century, the cool heights of the area became known as a refuge from the heat of the Australian summer and so became a holiday and health resort.

The viticultural history of the region began as usual with early graziers and farmers planting small vineyards in the 1840s and 1850s (see David Dunstan's *Better than Pommard*, 1994). These were at Carlsruhe, Darraweit Guim and Riddells Creek. Other vineyards were also planted in the general area at this time and later in the nineteenth century. None have survived, being victims of the 1890s eastern Australian recession, the adjoining warmer Sunbury vineyard area (also thriving in the later years of the nineteenth century) and the loss of English markets.

The Macedon region resumed its viticultural associations in 1968 when a Melbourne restaurateur, Tom Lazar, began to plant his Virgin Hills vineyard at Lauriston. He was soon followed by Gordon Knight at Granite Hills (1970). Later in the 1970s came Gordon Cope-Williams at Romsey (1977) and in the early 1980s John Ellis began Hanging Rock (1982). Since then the region has expanded rapidly and there are now 17 wineries and 42 vineyards in the region. It is an area very well-suited to sparkling wines, which are entitled to use the name 'Macedon' if they are made from regional fruit and by the champagne method. No doubt the region will continue to grow.

Location: Kyneton latitude 37°16'S, longitude 144°25'E; Gisborne latitude 33°30'S, longitude 144°37'E; Woodend latitude 37°22'S, longitude 144°33'E; Lancefield latitude 37°22'S, longitude 144°48'E. The region is about 65 km north-north-west of Melbourne.
Elevation: from about 400 m (Gisborne) to about 600 m (Woodend) with a mean altitude of 492 m.
Topography and soils: Geologically the Macedon Ranges region lies within an area of Ordovician and Silurian sedimentary rocks extending from east of Ballarat to east of Mount Macedon. These are bounded on the east by the Cambrian greenstones forming part of the Heathcote greenstone belt. In their turn these rocks have been intruded by Devonian granitic rocks forming the Cobaw Ranges in the north of the region. These also have been intruded by tertiary basalts and trachytes due to volcanic activity. The results of this are gently rounded hills punctuated by the granitic Cobaw Ranges to the north and the extinct volcanoes Mount Macedon, Mount Gisborne and Bullengarook in the south.

The soils resulting from the Ordovician and Silurian sandstones and shales are acidic duplex shallow brown-yellow clay loams of low fertility occurring in the west and south-west of the region, but also extending to the base of Mount Macedon, Macedon and Bullengarook and also to the Cobaw Ranges in parts. The soils derived from the granites of the Cobaw Ranges and parts of Mount Macedon on the steeper slopes are mostly free-draining uniform or gradational sandy to stony shallow loams. The soils around Romsey, to the south and east of Gisborne and around Woodend are rich gradational sometimes red friable clayey soils. They are volcanic in origin and are frequently found in contact with the Ordovician and Silurian duplex soils along old stream valleys.

Climate: Kyneton MJT 18.4, MAR 12.6°C, HDD 1041, AR 828 mm, RH 61.9% (3pm); Macedon MJT 17.4, MAR 12.2°C, HDD 1005, AR 853 mm, RH 59.8% (3pm) (both local); Cf Macedon MJT 17.7°C, MAR 12.8°C, HDD (raw) 1035, AR 753 mm (Oct–Mar 294 mm), RH 64% (9am), AI 168 mm, SH 8 (Dry & Smart). The Macedon Ranges region is undoubtedly cold. By way of comparison, the statistics for Reims in Champagne are MJT 18.3, MAR 16.3, HDD 1031, AR 700 mm, RH 58% (1pm July), SH 6.2 (Gladstones). The heat summations are some of the lowest in Australia and are very similar to those in Reims. No wonder then that the region has shown itself to be very suitable for sparkling wine style and early ripening still whites. The heat summations are also much lower than the neighbouring region to the north, Bendigo, where medium- to full-bodied red wines of good to excellent quality are made from cabernet sauvignon and shiraz grapes. This suggests that such varieties are generally unsuitable for the Macedon Ranges region, except in extremely favourable locations. Virgin Hills, which makes a classic Australian cool-area red, is such an exception. It is predominantly cabernet sauvignon, which as a general rule in this region ripens late in May and on some occasions early in June. The cause of this apparent anomaly is its sheltered north-facing microclimate and the very small crops that the Virgin Hills vines carry. Even earlier ripening red cultivars, such as pinot noir, must be regarded as marginal for table wines in this region. As a comparison, the HDD of Dijon in the north of the Cote d'Or is 1223, much warmer than Kyneton. Leongatha in Gippsland at about 1300 is similarly better placed. It would seem that there needs to be quite favourable lengthy ripening conditions or a warm and sheltered location for a Macedon Ranges site to obtain medium- to full-body in Pinot Noir in most years. In Macedon Ranges, therefore, microclimate is all-important in the production of even medium-bodied reds.

Strong, cold winds at flowering may also present serious problems unless vineyards are naturally sheltered or have wind breaks and sometimes even these are not enough to prevent loss. Frosts too can present problems, so sites with good air drainage should be chosen. Other problems may include birds, both native and imported, but these may be alleviated if there are alternative food supplies or if vineyards are netted.

The district is a substantial catchment area. Irrigation water is of good quality and, if used, is supplied to vineyards from surface dams and bores.

Harvest time: for chardonnay and pinot noir, late April to May, for other varieties, ripening may extend as late as mid-June, subject to favourable conditions at this difficult time of the year

Principal varieties: White—chardonnay; Red—pinot noir; other varieties often found in the region include sauvignon blanc, semillon, riesling and traminer, as well as cabernet sauvignon, merlot, cabernet franc and shiraz

Total area: 200 ha approx.

Major wine styles: Sparkling Macedon, Chardonnay, Pinot Noir, Sauvignon Blanc

Ashworths Hill **NR**

Ashworths Road off Burke and Wills
Track, Lancefield, Vic 3435
Ph/Fax 03 5429 1689

Owners: Peg and Ken Reaburn
Chief winemakers: (contract) John Ellis (whites),
Ann Manning (reds)
Year of foundation: 1982
Tonnes crushed on average each year: 2
Location: Lancefield
Area: 3.2 ha
Soils: volcanic red loam and 'buckshot' (a stony
clay)
Varieties planted: White—chardonnay, riesling;
Red—cabernet sauvignon, meunier, pinot noir
Leading wine: Ashworths Hill Cabernet
Notes: This is a small vineyard indicative of the
widespread interest shown in vines by farmers
throughout Australia. The Reaburns have a
silver medal for Riesling to their credit at
Ballarat and bronzes at other Victorian shows.
Cellar door sales: daily 10am–6pm.

Bindi Wine Growers **NR**

145 Melton Road, Gisborne, Vic 3437
Ph/Fax 03 5428 2564

Owner: Dhillon family
Chief winemakers: Michael Dhillon, Stuart
Anderson (consultant)
Year of foundation: 1988
Tonnes crushed on average each year: 20
Location: Gisborne
Area: 4.5 ha
Soils: quartz-laden siltstone clay; strict canopy
management in the vineyard
Varieties planted: White—chardonnay;
Red—pinot noir
Leading wines: Bindi Chardonnay, Pinot Noir,
'Macedon' (a champagne method sparkling
wine)
Notes: Making its first wine only in 1991, Bindi
is very much quality-oriented and has come a
long way in a very short time. There have been

consistently good reports of its very complex
Chardonnay. Mail orders. No cellar door sales.

Braewattie Vineyard **NR**

Woodend Road, Rochford, Vic 3442
Ph 03 5429 1266, Fax 03 5429 1015

Owner: Emu Hill Pty Ltd
Chief winemakers: John Flynn (pinot—
contract), Murray Cousins (chardonnay—
contract)
Year of foundation: 1993
Tonnes produced on average each year:
estimates 20 by 1999 vintage
Location: Rochford
Area: 4 ha
Soils: free-draining red volcanic soil. The
vineyard is situated at 560–600 metres in
altitude on the middle reaches of a north-
easterly slope giving maximum sunlight
exposure and has good air drainage, which
should minimise frost risks.
Varieties planted: White—chardonnay;
Red—pinot noir
Leading wines: yet to be released, but labels
will be 'Braewattie', 'Rochford Hill' and
'Millennium'
Notes: Braewattie is planted to the region's
most suitable varieties and there is no reason
why its wines should not be of top quality.
Wine sales by appointment only.

Cleveland **NR**

Shannons Road, Lancefield, Vic 3435
Ph 03 5429 1449, Fax 03 5429 2017

Owners: Keith and Lynette Brien
Chief winemaker: Keith Brien
Year of foundation: 1984
Tonnes crushed on average each year: 45, of
which 30 are grown at Cleveland, the rest
purchased from other areas and blended with
estate fruit for the 'Brien' label
Location: Lancefield
Area: 4 ha

Soils: podsolic with varying depths of grey sandy loam over ironstone gravel and well-drained
Varieties planted: White—chardonnay; Red—cabernet sauvignon (being grafted over progressively to pinot noir), pinot noir
Leading wines: Cleveland Sparkling 'Macedon' Brut, Reserve Pinot Noir, Chardonnay (made only in exceptional years)
Notes: Keith Brien is now one of the veterans of the Lancefield area of the Macedon Ranges. He has studied his area carefully and likens it to the Champagne region of France. Thus, just as the Champenois do not grow cabernet sauvignon in their region, so cabernet sauvignon, which often ripens in Lancefield in June, is not really suited to the area. There are two bed and breakfast rooms, a restaurant open every Sunday for lunch and cellar door sales available 7 days.

Cobaw Ridge   R7.5

Perc Boyers Lane, East Pastoria, via Kyneton, Vic 3444
Ph/Fax 03 5423 5227

Owners: Nelly and Alan Cooper
Chief winemaker: Alan Cooper
Year of foundation: 1985
Tonnes crushed on average each year: 20
Location: East Pastoria
Area: 4 ha
Soils: granite sand
Varieties planted: White—chardonnay, viognier; Red—lagrein dunkel, pinot noir, shiraz
Leading wines: Cobaw Ridge Chardonnay, Shiraz
Notes: Cobaw Ridge is high in the Great Dividing Range on a sandy, well-drained site close to Cobaw National Park. The vineyard is now well established and at 610 m in altitude has some of the highest shiraz vines in Australia. Fortunately in a cool area, Cobaw Ridge has a warmer northerly aspect which enables the shiraz to ripen well. Alan Cooper's

Chardonnay is also a great success, being very fine, elegant and long keeping, and the Lagrein Dunkel, an Italo-Austrian alpine cultivar, must be one of the rarest grape varieties in Australia. When quantities allow, Alan also shows his wines and has won over 30 medals, including two gold at the last count. Cellar door sales: weekends 10am–5.30pm, at other times telephone first.

Cope Williams Winery   R7.5

Glenfern Road, Romsey, Vic 3434
Ph 03 5429 5428, Fax 03 5429 5655

Owner: Cope-Williams family
Chief winemaker: Michael Cope-Williams
Year of foundation: 1977
Tonnes crushed on average each year: 100
Location: Romsey
Area: 13 ha
Soils: deep Romsey red loam, basically volcanic
Varieties planted: White—chardonnay; Red—cabernet franc, cabernet sauvignon, merlot, pinot noir
Leading wines: Romsey Brut, Chardonnay, Pinot Noir, Cabernet-Merlot, Willow (a fortified wine made of pinot noir and chardonnay base wines which results in a golden coloured dessert wine)
Notes: Cricket is a popular game in Australia, but Gordon Cope-Williams has enshrined it at Romsey, where sparkling wine and cricket are integral parts of the local ethos. Here the only 'fine legs' you will encounter are on the field or in the wine glasses. The sparkling wines are well flavoured but with a delicacy imposed by the region and 'Willow' will certainly cause no tears. The Chardonnay, Pinot Noir and Cabernet-Merlot are also very well made. Cellar door sales: daily 10am–5.30pm.

Glen Erin Winery and the Grange Restaurant NR

Woodend Road, Lancefield, Vic 3435
(4 km west of the town)
Ph 03 5429 1041, Fax 03 5429 2053

Owners: Brian and Kim Scales
Chief winemakers: Brian Scales, John Ellis
(contract)
Year of foundation: 1993
Tonnes crushed on average each year: 10
Location: Lancefield
Area: 4.8 ha
Soils: volcanic loam on a clay base
Varieties planted: White—chardonnay,
gewurztraminer; Red—merlot, pinot noir
Leading wines: Glen Erin Chardonnay, Pinot
Noir, Merlot, Gewurztraminer
Notes: Cellar door sales: weekends and public
holidays 10am–6pm, weekdays by
appointment. There is also a restaurant open
Friday night for dinner, Saturday lunch and
dinner and Sunday lunch.

Hanging Rock Winery R9

The Jim Jim, Jim Road, Newham,
Vic 3442
Ph 03 5427 0542, Fax 03 5427 0310

Owner: The Hanging Rock Winery Pty Ltd
Chief winemaker: John Ellis
Year of foundation: 1982
Tonnes crushed on average each year: 60
Location: Newham
Area: 6 ha
Soils: volcanic decomposing basalt
Varieties planted: White—chardonnay,
sauvignon blanc, semillon; Red—pinot noir
Leading wines: Hanging Rock 'Macedon' (a
champagne method sparkling wine), The Jim
Jim Sauvignon Blanc
Notes: Hanging Rock is planted on one of the
old lava flows of the 'Jim Jim', an extinct
volcano. At 650 m in altitude, it is a very cool
if not cold site and as such has proved itself

for early ripening and sparkling wine varieties.
John Ellis' 'Macedon', of rich autolysed nose
and palate characters, is a very fine sparkling
wine. The Jim Jim Sauvignon Blanc is also
excellent. Cellar door sales: 7 days 10am–5pm.

Knight's Granite Hills R7.5

Burke and Wills Track, Bayneton, via
Lancefield, Vic 3444
Ph 03 5423 7264, Fax 03 5423 7288

Owner: Knight family
Chief winemaker: Llew Knight
Year of foundation: 1970
Tonnes crushed on average each year: 85
Location: Bayneton
Area: 9 ha
Soils: coarse sandy decomposed granite loam
Varieties planted: White—chardonnay, riesling;
Red—cabernet franc, cabernet sauvignon,
merlot, shiraz
Leading wines: Knight's Granite Hills Shiraz,
Riesling, Chardonnay
Notes: Located on the northern side of the
Great Dividing Range, where the climate is
generous enough to ripen shiraz, Knight's can
be counted as one of the veterans of the
region, having planted its first vineyard in
1970. Its Riesling is still one of its best wines
and recently at the local Macedon Exhibition
was voted 'Wine of the Region'. Its
Chardonnay also won gold at Rutherglen, as
did its Shiraz at Ballarat. Cellar door sales:
Mon–Sat 10am–6pm, Sun 12 noon–6pm.

Mawarra Vineyard NR

Short Road, Gisborne, Vic 3437
Ph 03 5428 2228, Fax 03 5428 4816

Owner: Bob Nixon and Associates Pty Ltd
Chief winemaker: John Ellis (contract)
Year of foundation: 1978
Tonnes crushed on average each year: 10, but
will increase as further plantings are made and
come into bearing

Location: Gisborne
Area: 4 ha
Soils: volcanic grey loam over a clay base
Varieties planted: White—chardonnay,
semillon; Red—pinot noir
Leading wines: Mawarra Pinot Noir
Notes: Though first plantings took place as
long ago as 1978, it has been a long road for
Bob Nixon and Mawarra but, according to Bob,
Mawarra Pinot Noir makes it seem that it has
all been worthwhile. Cellar door sales.

Mount Charlie Winery **NR**

Lot 52 Mount Charlie Road, Riddells
Creek, Vic 3431
Ph/Fax 03 5428 6946

Owner/chief winemaker: Professor Trefor
Morgan
Year of foundation: 1988
Tonnes crushed on average each year: 5
Location: Riddells Creek
Area: 2.5 ha
Soils: granitic
Varieties planted: White—chardonnay,
sauvignon blanc; Red—cabernet sauvignon,
merlot, shiraz
Leading wines: Mount Charlie Chardonnay,
Sauvignon Blanc, Red (a blend of the red
varieties mentioned)
Notes: Trefor Morgan is a graduate in Wine
Science from Charles Sturt University. His
vineyard is on the southern side of the
Macedon spur and the most southerly in the
region. Despite this general aspect, the
vineyard is situated on a north-facing knoll
which provides protection from cold southerly
winds, giving the vines a favourable
microclimate in which to ripen red varieties,
which can be difficult in less favourable parts
of the Macedon Ranges. Wine sales are made
by mail order. There are no cellar door sales
and the vineyard is open only by appointment
at weekends.

Mount Gisborne Wines **NR**

5 Waterson Road, Gisborne, Vic 3437
Ph/Fax 03 5428 2834

Owner: David Ell
Chief winemakers: David Ell, Stuart Anderson
(consultant)
Year of foundation: 1986
Tonnes crushed on average each year: 11
Location: Gisborne
Area: 3 ha
Soils: volcanic decomposing basalt
Varieties planted: White—chardonnay;
Red—pinot noir
Leading wines: Mount Gisborne Chardonnay,
Pinot Noir
Notes: A specialist vineyard under consultancy
from Stuart Anderson, a specialist winemaker.
Cellar door sales by appointment.

Mount Macedon **NR**

off Bawden Road, midway between
Mount Macedon and Woodend,
Vic 3441
Ph 03 5427 2735, Fax 03 5427 1071

Owners: Pam and Don Ludbey
Chief winemaker: Peter Dredge (contract)
Year of foundation: 1989
Tonnes crushed on average each year: 40
Locations: Mount Macedon and Hay Hill
Area: 8 ha (Mount Macedon 5 ha, Hay Hill
3 ha)
Soils: volcanic with brown clay loams and
friable red clay loams
Varieties planted: White—chardonnay;
Red—cabernet sauvignon, merlot, pinot noir,
shiraz
Leading wines: Mount Macedon Chardonnay,
Pinot Noir, Shiraz, Cabernet Sauvignon,
Sparkling Wines
Notes: At 680 m above sea-level in such an
area, Mount Macedon is obviously a very cool,
even cold site. Hay Hill is to the south-east and

somewhat lower in altitude near Riddells Creek. Cellar door sales: 7 days 10am–6pm.

Mount William R6.5

Mount William Road, Tantaraboo, via Kilmore, Vic 3764
Ph 03 5429 1595, Fax 03 5429 1998

Owners: Murray and Adrienne Cousins
Chief winemakers: Murray Cousins, Michael Cope-Williams (contract) (sparkling)
Year of foundation: 1987
Tonnes crushed on average each year: 10
Location: Tantaraboo
Area: 6 ha
Soils: stony grey loam
Varieties planted: White—chardonnay, semillon; Red—cabernet franc, pinot noir
Leading wines: Mount William Chardonnay, Pinot Noir, Sparkling Pinot Noir
Notes: At 600 m in altitude and with snow quite often in winter, Mount William has a climate that can only be described as cold. No wonder then that there is low flavour-developing ripening and that vintage extends from mid-April (chardonnay) to early June (semillon). Cellar door sales: 7 days 11am–5pm.

Portree R6.5

Powell's Track via Mount William Road, Lancefield, Vic 3455
Ph 03 5429 1422, Fax 03 5429 2205

Owners: Ken and Lyn Murchison
Chief winemaker: Ken Murchison
Year of foundation: 1983
Tonnes crushed on average each year: 25
Location: Lancefield
Area: 5 ha
Soils: red basalt (chardonnay), grey loam (cabernet franc)
Varieties planted: White—chardonnay; Red—cabernet franc, pinot noir
Leading wines: Portree Chardonnay

Notes: Portree makes a full round early drinking style of Cabernet Franc and also a pleasant Chardonnay. Cellar door sales: weekends and public holidays 11am–5pm.

Rochford R7

Romsey Park, Rochford, Vic 3442
Ph 03 5429 1428, Fax 03 5429 1066

Owner: Helmut Konecsny
Chief winemaker: David Creed
Year of foundation: 1983
Tonnes crushed on average each year: 50
Location: Rochford
Area: 7.2 ha (with recent plantings to come into bearing in 1999)
Soils: red volcanic loam
Varieties planted: White—chardonnay, riesling; Red—cabernet sauvignon, merlot, pinot noir
Leading wines: Rochford Premier Pinot Noir, Cabernet
Notes: Rochford changed hands early in 1998, but the quality of the Premier range remains in the same hands. Cellar door sales by appointment or mail order.

Virgin Hills R9

Salisbury Road, Lauriston West, via Kyneton, Vic 3444
Ph 03 5423 9169, Fax 03 5423 9324

Owner: Marcel Gilbert
Chief winemaker: Martin Williams
Year of foundation: 1968
Tonnes crushed on average each year: 70
Location: Lauriston West
Area: 16 ha (two vineyards at 600 m and 580 m respectively)
Soils: sandy loam of weathered granite over clay, well drained
Varieties planted: White—chardonnay (not yet bearing); Red—cabernet sauvignon, malbec, merlot, pinot noir, shiraz
Leading Wines: Virgin Hills (a blend of the red varieties mentioned above)

Notes: In an isolated, very high and cool area, not always ideal for the varieties grown, Virgin Hills makes one of Australia's most notable and long-living reds. There will be a Chardonnay also in a few years. No cellar door sales. Sales only to retailers and restaurants.

EMERALD

Paternoster NR

17 Paternoster Road, Emerald, Vic 3782
Ph 03 5968 3197

Owner/chief winemaker: Philip Hession
Year of foundation: 1985
Tonnes crushed on average each year: 10
Location: Emerald
Area: 1.6 ha
Soils: reddish mountain loam
Varieties planted: White—chardonnay; Red—cabernet sauvignon, pinot noir
Leading wines: Paternoster Chardonnay, Pinot Noir
Notes: A small vineyard just beyond the southern boundary of the Yarra Valley and sharing many of its characteristics, Paternoster is 330 m in altitude, close planted and organically grown. Its wines are unfiltered and treated with minimal amounts of sulfur. Cellar door sales: weekends 11am–6pm.

Like most Victorian agricultural regions, Gippsland had its viticultural origins in the nineteenth century and met a similar economic fate in the early years of the twentieth. Its rebirth also began about 1970, but it has had a slow growth since then. Apart from Chardonnay in the hands of makers like Ken Eckersley at Nicholson River, and Pinot Noir made by that master of Pinot, Phillip Jones at Bass Phillip, Gippsland wines await a final verdict. Certainly in ripe warm years such as 1983 and 1991, the Chardonnays and Pinots of Gippsland can be magnificently full-flavoured and even Cabernet Sauvignon ripens well, but Gippsland's problem is that such years are atypical. In cooler years, later ripening reds and whites, though delightful in their fruit character, seem to gain insufficient weight to interest the normal consumer of Australian wines. Cool areas, however, do not need such wines and Gippsland, which is most definitely cool, needs only to point to its Chardonnays and Pinots as wines deserving of the greatest respect.

Location: that part of Victoria approximately between latitude 145°30'E and 150°E and longitude 37°30'S and 39°S, a vast area stretching virtually from the south-eastern suburbs of Melbourne, south to the south-east coast of Victoria then east to the New South Wales border at Cape Howe. It stretches north-west from there into the Snowy Mountains, returning westerly mainly through the alpine country to its starting point. There are no official wine regions or sub-regions at the present time as the area, in terms of wine production, is too small. It would seem logical for the future, however, in view of the present viticultural sites, to divide Gippsland into three regions, West, South and East, which is the way I have classified the wineries.
Topography and soils: as must be expected in an area so large, these are very variable, from the lush green hills of western Gippsland, via the flood plains, lakes and coastal sands of central and eastern Gippsland to the temperate rainforests, alpine country and snowfields of the north and east.
Climate: Bairnsdale (East Gippsland): MJT 18°C, MAR na, HDD 1331, AR 696 mm (Oct–Apr 428 mm), RH 53%, AI na, SH 8; Leongatha (South-West Gippsland): MJT 18.1°C, MAR na, HDD 1301, AR 998 mm (Oct–Apr 530 mm), RH na, AI na, SH 6.5 (Gladstones). Windy and often wet along the Bass Strait coast in spring and early summer. In some years also, except for grape varieties such as pinot noir and chardonnay, autumn rain and cold bring the ripening season to an end too soon for the full maturation of most popular Australian wine grape varieties, a problem that Gippsland shares with northern Tasmania. In higher areas, it is sometimes frosty with snow in winter at altitudes above 1000 m.
Harvest time: late March to May
Principal varieties: Red—pinot noir, cabernet sauvignon, merlot; White—chardonnay, riesling, sauvignon blanc
Total area: na
Major wine styles: Chardonnay, Pinot Noir

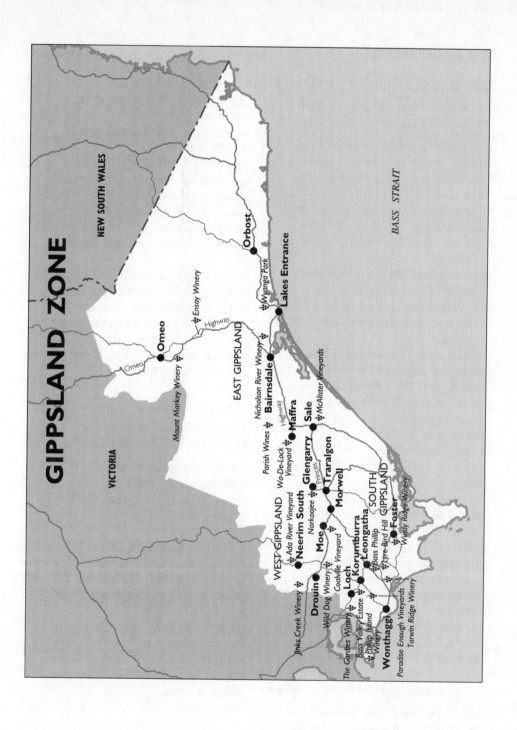

GIPPSLAND ZONE

NEW SOUTH WALES

VICTORIA

Omeo

Omeo

Mount Markey Winery

Ensay Winery

Highway

EAST GIPPSLAND

Orbost

Wyanga Park

Lakes Entrance

Nicholson River Winery

Parish Wines

Bairnsdale

Highway

Maffra

McAlister Vineyards

Sale

Wa-De-Lock Vineyard

Glengarry

Princes

Traralgon

Narkoojee

Morwell

WEST GIPPSLAND

Ada River Vineyard

Neerim South

Moe

SOUTH GIPPSLAND

Coalville Vineyard

Korumburra

Leongatha

Foster

Windy Ridge Winery

Loch

Eye-Bird Hill

Bass Phillip

Jinks Creek Winery

Drouin

Wild Dog Winery

Bass Valley Estate

Phillip Island

Wonthaggi

Paradise Enough Vineyards

Tarwin Ridge Winery

The Gurdies Winery

BASS STRAIT

WEST GIPPSLAND

Ada River Vineyard R6.5

Main Road, Neerim South, Vic 3831
Ph 03 5628 1221, Fax 03 5623 6723

Owners/chief winemakers: Peter and Chris
Kelliher
Year of foundation: 1983 (vineyard), 1995
(wine sales)
Tonnes produced on average each year: 15,
but increasing
Locations: Neerim South (West Gippsland) and
Yarra Valley
Area: 14.3 ha consisting of 9.3 ha (Neerim
South) and 5 ha (Yarra Valley, leased)
Soils: Neerim South: rich red volcanic soil; Yarra
Valley: typical grey clay loam (neither vineyard
is irrigated)
Varieties planted: Neerim South: White—
chardonnay, gewurztraminer, pinot gris;
Red—cabernet franc, cabernet sauvignon,
merlot, pinot noir. Yarra Valley: White—
chardonnay, gewurztraminer; Red—pinot noir
Leading wines: Ada River Neerim South
Chardonnay, Neerim South Pinot Noir, Ada
River Yarra Valley Chardonnay, Yarra Valley
Pinot Noir
Notes: Ada River vineyard is situated in the
heart of Gippsland's cheese country (the
homes of Gippsland Blue and Jindi Brie are
within 5 km of the vineyard. The Ada River
reds, especially the Cabernet blend (very good
in warmer years) make very interesting
companions to these premium cheeses.
Production at Ada River will increase as new
plantings of pinot gris and traminer come into
bearing. Cellar door sales: weekends and
public holidays 10am–6pm.

Coalville Vineyard R6

Moe South Road, Moe, Vic 3825
Ph 03 5127 4229, Fax 03 5127 2148

Owners: Peter and Libby Beasley
Chief winemaker: Peter Beasley
Year of foundation: 1972
Tonnes crushed on average each year: 25
Location: Moe
Area: 4.6 ha
Soils: sandy loam over red clay not far above
seams of brown coal
Varieties planted: White—chardonnay;
Red—cabernet franc, cabernet sauvignon,
malbec, merlot, pinot noir, ruby cabernet,
shiraz
Leading wines: Coalville Cabernet Sauvignon
Notes: Coalville Vineyard is the workaday life
of vintage car enthusiast, Peter Beasley.
In warm years, it ripens cabernet very well.
I remember its 1991 well. Coalville has a
restaurant overlooking its vineyard. Cellar door
sales: 7 days 10am–5pm.

Jinks Creek Winery NR

Tonimbuk Road, Tonimbuk, Vic 3815
Ph 03 5629 8502, Fax 03 5629 2342

Owner/chief winemaker: Andrew Clarke
Year of foundation: 1981
Tonnes crushed on average each year: 3
Location: Tonimbuk, West Gippsland
Area: 2.4 ha
Soils: granitic free-draining loam
Varieties planted: White—chardonnay,
sauvignon blanc; Red—pinot noir
Leading wines: Jinks Creek Sauvignon Blanc,
Pinot Noir, Chardonnay
Notes: A small estate in West Gippsland on the
road from Bunyip to Gembrook in the Yarra
Valley. It has a very small but much sought-
after production. Cellar door sales by
appointment only.

Narkoojee **R6**

Francis Road, Glengarry, Vic 3854
Ph/Fax 03 5192 4257

Owners: Harry and Val Friend
Chief winemaker: Harry Friend
Year of foundation: 1980
Tonnes crushed on average each year: 15
Location: Glengarry, West Gippsland
Area: 2.2 ha
Soils: alluvial, deep gravelly, clayey, sandy, well-drained soils; a lyre trellis is used to minimise mildews and maximise fruit exposure
Varieties planted: White—chardonnay; Red—cabernet franc, cabernet sauvignon, merlot
Leading wines: Narkoojee Chardonnay, Cabernets-Merlot
Notes: Narkoojee makes a big and flavoursome malo-influenced Chardonnay, which is good drinking. Cellar door sales: most days, but telephone first.

Wild Dog Winery **R6**

Warragul-Korumburra Road, Warragul, Vic 3820
Ph 03 5623 1117, Fax 03 5623 6402

Owner: John and Helen Farrington
Chief winemaker: John Farrington
Year of foundation: 1981 (wine made from 1988)
Tonnes crushed on average each year: 35
Location: Warragul, West Gippsland
Area: 10 ha and growing
Soils: deep red Gippsland loam (kraznozem) about 3 m deep with poor moisture retention; drip irrigation available but rarely used
Varieties planted: White—chardonnay, riesling, semillon; Red—cabernet franc, cabernet sauvignon, merlot, pinot noir, shiraz
Leading wines: Wild Dog Shiraz, Riesling, Chardonnay, Cabernet
Notes: John Farrington finds his seasons very variable and this causes a similarly variable performance in his vineyard. As he says, 'The '97 vintage is looking like McLaren Vale material, while '96 looks more like Tasmania in a poor year'. Nonetheless he is happy with his reds and his Riesling. I have found quite good Shiraz there. Cellar door sales: every day 9am–5pm.

SOUTH GIPPSLAND

Bass Phillip **R10**

cnr Hunt and Tosch's Road, Leongatha South, Vic 3953
Ph 03 5664 3341, Fax 03 5664 3209

Owners: Phillip and Sairung Jones
Chief winemaker: Phillip Jones
Year of foundation: 1979
Tonnes crushed on average each year: 8
Location: Leongatha South, South Gippsland
Area: 4 ha, but the vineyard is being extended to 16 ha and it is hoped that production might increase to 50 tonnes by the year 2000
Soils: deep silty loams, rich in minerals of ancient volcanic origin, with some areas of raised sea-bed
Varieties planted: White—chardonnay; Red—gamay, pinot noir
Leading wines: Bass Phillip Pinot Noir, Premium Pinot Noir, Reserve Pinot Noir, Chardonnay, Gamay

Notes: Bass Phillip is very much the holy water of Australian Pinot Noir and, like holy water, it is dispensed unfortunately in tiny quantities. Carrying the ecclesiastical analogy further, its proprietor-winemaker, Phillip Jones, who controls one of the very few Australian vineyards that can aptly be called a 'domaine', is most certainly the Apostle of Pinot, totally devoted to pinot noir and its propagation. This religious fervour is tempered by Phillip's vast knowledge of his vineyard's climate and soil parameters. Pinot must certainly not be grown everywhere. It is, as Phillip says, very fussy about its microclimates, but he has found his own little spot in Leongatha South to be, if not infallible, as close as it is possible to be to that sublime state. The Bass Phillip Chardonnay and Gamay, each made in minute quantity, are also excellent. Visits by appointment only.

Bass Valley Estate NR

St Helier Road, Loch, Vic 3945
Ph 03 5659 6306/03 5659 6321

Owner: Robert Cutler
Chief winemaker: Roger Cutler
Year of foundation: 1989
Tonnes crushed on average each year: 5, and increasing as the vines come into full bearing
Location: Loch, South Gippsland
Area: 2.8 ha
Soils: grey loam with slight clay content, sandstone subsoil
Varieties planted: White—riesling; Red—cabernet sauvignon, pinot noir, shiraz
Leading wines: Bass Valley Estate Cabernet Sauvignon
Notes: Like many Gippsland vineyards, Bass Valley Estate is a small family-operated winery with a very cool climate, its cabernet sauvignon not ripening until late in May. Cellar door sales: 7 days 10am–6pm.

Lyre Bird Hill R6.5

Inverloch Road, Koonwarra, Vic 3954
Ph 03 5664 3204, Fax 03 5664 3206

Owners: Owen and Robyn Schmidt
Chief winemaker: Owen Schmidt
Year of foundation: 1987
Tonnes crushed on average each year: 15
Location: Koonwarra, South Gippsland
Area: 2.4 ha
Soils: sandy, gravelly, acidic duplex soils
Varieties planted: White—chardonnay, riesling, traminer; Red—cabernet sauvignon, pinot noir, shiraz
Leading wines: Lyre Bird Hill Pinot Noir, Shiraz
Notes: Lyre Bird Hill is a pleasant wine estate and, like its general area, favours pinot noir, although Owen Schmidt has a soft spot for his Shiraz. Robyn Schmidt provides excellent bed and breakfast accommodation and there are dinners by arrangement. Cellar door sales: weekends and public holidays 10am–5pm.

Paradise Enough Vineyards NR

Stewarts Road, Kongwak, Vic 3951
Ph 03 5657 4241, Fax 03 5657 4229

Owners: John Bell and Sue Armstrong
Chief winemaker: John Bell
Year of foundation: 1987
Tonnes crushed on average each year: 10
Location: Kongwak, South Gippsland
Area: 4 ha, but not all bearing; the vineyard will double in size in the next few years
Soils: fine sandy loam over fine sandy clay, average drainage, over sandstone rock; a sheltered microclimate
Varieties planted: White—chardonnay; Red—cabernet franc, cabernet sauvignon, merlot, pinot noir, shiraz
Leading wines: Paradise Enough Reserve Chardonnay
Notes: John Bell is very Burgundian in his viticultural and winemaking approach, regarding his dry-land chardonnay and pinot

noir as his two premium varieties. His wines are also non-interventionist, low sulfur and unfiltered. He is very much a disciple of Phillip Jones and it seems that is the way things in South Gippsland should be. Cellar door sales: weekends and public holidays noon–5pm, other times by appointment.

Phillip Island Winery R9
Berry's Beach Road, Phillip Island,
Vic 3922
Ph/Fax 03 5956 8465

Owners: David and Catherine Lance
Chief winemaker: Dr David Lance
Year of foundation: 1994
Tonnes produced on average each year: 10
(though more local and Yarra Valley fruit is purchased and about 30 tonnes in all crushed for winery purposes)
Location: Phillip Island
Area: 2 ha
Soils: rich volcanically derived soil with some pebbles and small stones over a well drained clay subsoil
Varieties planted: White—chardonnay, sauvignon blanc; Red—cabernet sauvignon, merlot, pinot noir
Leading wines: Phillip Island Sauvignon Blanc, Nobbies Pinot Noir
Notes: David and Catherine Lance are the proprietors of the renowned Diamond Valley Vineyards in the Yarra Valley. Phillip Island Winery can thus be described as 'winery away from winery'. However, despite its seaside location (only one kilometre from Bass Strait), Phillip Island Winery is certainly no holiday retreat for the Lance family. Its vineyard is double-planted and totally netted as a protection against the strong Bass Strait winds. At the present time the winery makes only reds, its whites being made at Diamond Valley where there are better facilities for this purpose. From its first crop (1997), its Sauvignon Blanc won a gold medal and trophy

for Best White Wine at the Southern Victorian (formerly Lilydale) Wine Show. The cellar door sales area features light food and is open every day in summer (November–March) 11am–7pm, in winter (April–October) 11am–5pm.

Tarwin Ridge Wines NR
Wintles Road, Leongatha South,
Vic 3953
Ph/Fax 03 5664 3211

Owners: Brian Anstee and Rhonda Givoni
Chief winemaker: Brian Anstee
Year of foundation: 1983
Tonnes crushed on average each year: 11
Location: Leongatha South, South Gippsland
Area: 2.8 ha
Soils: light grey sandy loam over clay
Varieties planted: White—chardonnay, riesling, sauvignon blanc, semillon; Red—cabernet franc, cabernet sauvignon, merlot, pinot noir
Leading wines: Tarwin Ridge Pinot Noir, Sauvignon Blanc, Cabernet-Merlot, White Merlot
Notes: Brian Anstee is somewhat of a Pinot specialist in an area that specialises in excellent Pinot. Cellar door sales: weekends and holidays 10am–5pm.

The Gurdies Winery NR
St Helier Road, The Gurdies, Vic 3984
Ph 03 5997 6208, Fax 03 5997 6511

Owners: Peter Kozik and Peter Svans
Chief winemaker: Peter Kozik
Year of foundation: 1982
Tonnes crushed on average each year: 8
Location: The Gurdies, South Gippsland
Area: 4 ha
Soils: sandy loam
Varieties planted: White—chardonnay, riesling; Red—cabernet sauvignon, merlot, pinot noir, shiraz
Leading wines: The Gurdies Cabernet Sauvignon
Notes: Though established in 1982,

The Gurdies vineyards were badly pruned and neglected. Under the present ownership, the long road to rehabilitation has begun. Cellar door sales: 7 days 10am–5pm.

Windy Ridge Winery **NR**

Fish Creek Road, Foster, Vic 3960
Ph 03 5682 2035

Owners: Graeme and Georgia Wilson
Chief winemaker: Graeme Wilson
Year of foundation: 1978
Tonnes crushed on average each year: 4
Location: Foster, South Gippsland

Area: 2.65 ha
Soils: duplex black loams, 20–30 cm deep, over clay subsoil
Varieties planted: White—traminer; Red—cabernet sauvignon, malbec, pinot noir
Leading wines: Windy Ridge Cabernet Sauvignon and Malbec, Pinot Noir
Notes: A small family-operated winery, whose winemaking policy appears to favour late release of reds, which at the time of writing were a 1991 Cabernet Sauvignon and Malbec and a 1994 Pinot Noir. Cellar door sales: holiday weekends and other summer weekends 10am–5pm, telephone to check.

EAST GIPPSLAND

Ensay Winery **NR**

Great Alpine Road (formerly Omeo Highway), Ensay, Vic 3895
Ph 03 5157 3203

Owners: Peter, Helen and David Coy
Chief winemaker: David Coy
Year of foundation: 1992
Tonnes crushed on average each year: 10, increasing to 20 as vineyard comes into full bearing
Location: Ensay
Area: 3 ha
Soils: granitic clay loam, free-draining
Varieties planted: White—chardonnay; Red—cabernet sauvignon, merlot, pinot noir, shiraz
Leading wines: Ensay Winery Chardonnay, Shiraz
Notes: Situated about 220 m in altitude in an isolated area and in a rain shadow, the Ensay Winery is about an hour's drive from Mount Hotham on Lakes Entrance watershed. The vineyard is drip irrigated. Vertical shoot positioning is employed. Cellar door sales: public and school holidays 9am–5pm, other times by appointment.

McAlister Vineyards **NR**

Golden Beach Road, Longford, Vic 3851
Ph/Fax 03 5149 7229

Owners: Maureen and Peter Edwards
Chief winemaker: Peter Edwards
Year of foundation: 1975
Tonnes crushed on average each year: 11
Location: Longford, south-east Gippsland
Area: 2 ha
Soils: silicate in nature with clay and ironstone protrusion on a limestone base
Varieties planted: White—none; Red—cabernet franc, cabernet sauvignon, merlot, petit verdot
Leading wine: The McAlister (a blend of the 'Bordeaux' varieties listed above)
Notes: Though McAlister Vineyards may not be called a monoculture, it is certainly a 'Bordeaux' culture, one wine only being produced. Cellar door sales by appointment only.

Mount Markey Winery   **NR**

Swifts Creek-Omeo Road, Cassilis,
Vic 3896
Ph 03 5159 4328, Fax 03 5159 4599

Owners: Howard and Christine Reddish
Chief winemaker: Howard Reddish
Year of foundation: 1991
Tonnes crushed on average each year: 5
Location: Cassilis, East Gippsland
Area: 1.8 ha close planted
Soils: Mount Markey adjoins an old gold-mining site. As a result, the 'top soil' is gold-mining schist, but it is not too disturbed and very free-draining. In the vineyard, vertical shoot positioning is employed as is leaf-plucking and the removal of unfruitful canopy shoots early in the season. Basic organic fertilisers and organic foliar spray are also employed.
Varieties planted: White—chardonnay, kerner, pinot gris, sauvignon blanc, traminer; Red—cabernet sauvignon, meunier, pinot noir, shiraz
Leading wines: Mount Markey Chardonnay, Lone Hand Cabernet, Rose of Australia Honey Mead
Notes: At nearly 500 m in altitude, Mount Markey is on the Lakes Entrance catchment of the Carriage Range and during summer is about 20% warmer than Melbourne. It is a dry area, which means that drip irrigation is needed in times of moisture stress. Cellar door sales: 6 days 10am–5pm except Tuesday unless it is a public holiday. There is also a potters' gallery.

Nicholson River Winery   **R8.5**

Nicholson, Vic 3882 (about 3 km north of Princes Highway, between Bairnsdale and Lakes Entrance)
Ph 03 5156 8241, Fax 03 5156 8433

Owners: K and J Eckersley
Chief winemaker: Ken Eckersley
Year of foundation: 1978
Tonnes crushed on average each year: 20, but will increase as young, recently planted vines come into bearing
Location: Nicholson
Area: 8 ha, including many young vines
Soils: gravelly to sandy loams
Varieties planted: White—chardonnay, riesling, sauvignon blanc, semillon; Red—cabernet sauvignon, merlot, pinot noir
Leading wines: Nicholson River Chardonnay, Semillon, Cabernet-Merlot, Pinot Noir, Sur-lie Riesling
Notes: Ken Eckersley is one of the pioneers of modern Gippsland viticulture. He is quite famous for his full-bodied chardonnays, usually wines of immense depth of flavour and complexity. Unfortunately, the elements often conspire to produce a rather small crop, but the devotion to quality is undoubted. Unusually, there is also a barrel-fermented riesling. Cellar door sales: 7 days 10am–4pm.

Parish Wines (Briagolong Estate)   **NR**

Valencia Creek, Briagolong Road, Briagolong, Vic 3860
Ph 03 5147 2322, Fax 03 5147 2400

Owners: Gordon and Christine McIntosh
Chief winemaker: Gordon McIntosh
Year of foundation: 1975
Tonnes crushed on average each year: 5, but will increase as newly planted vines come into bearing
Location: Briagolong, East Central Gippsland (north of Maffra)
Area: 3 ha
Soils: highly leached Tanjil series, a thin layer of sandy loam over very sticky clay
Varieties planted: White—chardonnay; Red—pinot noir
Leading wines: Parish Wines Pinot Noir, Chardonnay
Notes: A small wine estate with a very low

rainfall and without irrigation, only making wine from its own fruit, which accounts for a very small production. No cellar door sales.

Wa-De-Lock Vineyard NR

Stratford Road, Maffra, Vic 3860 (4.5 km from the Princes Highway on the Maffra–Stratford Road, 3.2 km from Maffra)
Ph 03 5147 3244, Fax 03 5147 3132

Owners: Graeme and Astrid Little
Chief winemaker: Graeme Little
Year of foundation: 1987
Tonnes crushed on average each year: 17, but will increase as new plantings come into bearing
Location: Maffra
Area: 5.64 ha not all yet bearing
Soils: the vineyard is established on an elevated north-east facing slope with good air drainage. Soils are sandy loam with porous clay and broken sedimentary sandstone throughout. Good drainage
Varieties planted: White—chardonnay (clone I10V5), sauvignon blanc (H5V10); Red—cabernet sauvignon (G9V3), nebbiolo (vars), pinor noir (MV6), shiraz (PT23)
Leading wines: Wa-de-Lock Pinot Noir, Sauvignon Blanc, Chardonnay
Notes: Wa-de-Lock is a consistent winner of silver and bronze awards at Victorian regional wine shows. Cellar door sales: Fri–Mon 10am–5pm.

Wyanga Park NR

Baades Road, Lakes Entrance, Vic 3909
Ph 03 5155 1508, Fax 03 5155 1443

Owners: Andrew Smith, Geoff Mahlook and Lindel Mahlook
Chief winemaker: Andrew Smith
Year of foundation: vineyard 1970, winery 1980
Tonnes crushed on average each year: 70
Location: Lakes Entrance
Area: 6.4 ha (some fruit is bought in from local growers)
Soils: gravel through to sandy loam, well drained, 60 m in altitude abutting north arm of lake
Varieties planted: White—chardonnay, riesling, sauvignon, traminer; Red—cabernet sauvignon, pinor noir
Leading wines: Wyanga Park Sauvignon Blanc, Cabernet Sauvignon
Notes: Wyanga Park is an unusual Australian vineyard site for two reasons: it sometimes experiences a California-like sea mist coming off Bass Strait and it also offers a lake cruise as a means of access to its restaurant and cellar-door facility. It serves morning tea and lunch and dinner on Thursday to Saturday nights and is open 7 days.

❦ NORTH EAST VICTORIA ZONE

This is yet another Victorian zone whose future was firmly founded upon the gold discoveries of the Beechworth and Rutherglen fields in the second half of the 19th century. It is a zone of extremes, both in climate and terrain, varying from the snowy alpine peaks of Mount Buller and Mount Hotham to the hot plains of the eastern Murray Valley. Currently Rutherglen is the only wine region, famous for its unique muscat and rich reds. There are, however, several other mooted wine regions, but only one of these, King Valley, has reached interim status and its boundaries have as yet to be determined. Others will certainly be created.

RUTHERGLEN REGION

By the 1820s, the exploration and settlement of New South Wales was expanding not only to the north and the west but rather more accessibly to the south and south-west. In 1824 the explorers Hume and Hovell crossed what they called the Hume River near present-day Albury. The River was renamed the Murray five years later by Charles Sturt, who discovered it much further west, at its junction with the Murrumbidgee. Hume and Hovell went on to discover Corio Bay (part of Port Phillip) which they mistakenly thought was Westernport, the objective of their expedition. The peripatetic Sir Thomas Mitchell also passed close to the area in 1836 on his return journey from Portland.

The Rutherglen story really begins in 1837 when E. P. S. Sturt, a Commissioner for Crown Lands, toured the area to extract fees from squatters. Official records of the area began in 1841 when the New South Wales Lands Department noted a cattle run at Wahgunyah being held by two licensees. By 1845, there were many squatters' runs and over 800 settlers were recorded as living between the Murray and Goulburn Rivers. Within a decade, Victoria had achieved its independence from New South Wales and the river-boat trade on the Murray originating in South Australia, and inspired by the gold rush to Beechworth in 1852, had also begun to develop. By 1860 further gold discoveries in the region had consolidated Wahgunyah's status as a thriving river-port and when in 1860 a further gold discovery was made only 10 km away, it seemed that the prosperity of the area was established. Within a few months a town sprang up, and was soon named Rutherglen by one John Wallace, a Scot and a successful former 'digger', who called it after his birthplace. Gold, however, was a fickle ally and soon, due to difficult 'leads', production began to fall and the population of the town dwindled. By 1870, the area's economy was agricultural, but the romance of gold was not forgotten. It was a love affair to be renewed in the 1890s.

It has often been said that the vine marched arm in arm with the gold seekers, but perhaps in Rutherglen's case it preceded the discoveries that were to be so important to the development of Australia in 1850s. The story has it that in 1851

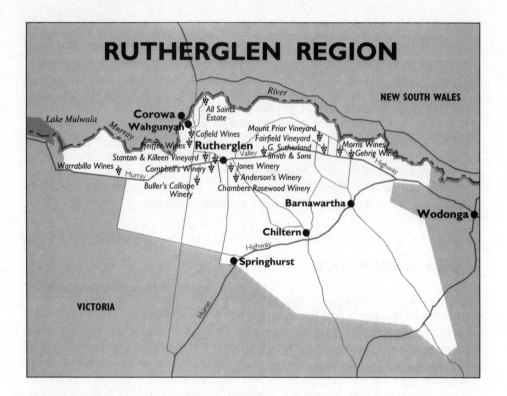

three German settlers, Frauenfelder, Schumbach and Rau (who were perhaps former indentured agricultural labourers from New South Wales, brought to that Colony in the 1840s for their vinuous expertise) persuaded the squatter Lindsay Brown of the Gooramadda run to be allowed to plant some vines there. The vines flourished and were quickly followed by more plantings. Former gold miners such as George Morris and John Campbell also took up the vine. By 1865, Morris, Campbell, Sutherland Smith and Gehrig were all vignerons of the Rutherglen district. By 1881, there were over 800 hectares of vines in the area.

The coming of the railway in 1879 also spurred on vinous expansion. Winemakers could now ship their produce to Melbourne and, indeed, overseas to London, where tastes were growing for the sturdy reds and fortifieds that the Rutherglen district, with its abundance of sun, made so well. And when, with the fall of wool and wheat prices in the late 1880s, the Victorian Government stepped in with cash bounties for vinegrowing, six-and-a-half million litres of wine poured from the local wine presses. Within a few years, Rutherglen was the showplace of the north-east.

By 1900, the Rutherglen wine boom had abated. There were three causes: the election of a teetotal Government that abolished the vine bounty; the financial malaise that afflicted all of eastern Australia in the mid-1890s; and, much more serious, the onset of phylloxera. Phylloxera had wiped out the Geelong vineyards over 20 years earlier and had seriously set back Bendigo and the Goulburn Valley in the 1890s. Now it was Rutherglen's turn. Even though its march was inexorable, the industry was not wiped out. In 1908, in a sensible effort to combat phylloxera, Francois de Castella, son of Hubert of Yarra Valley fame, was sent to Europe to investigate new grape varieties as well as new techniques that allowed new vines to be grafted onto phylloxera-resistant root stock. His collection of new varieties was established in the Rutherglen Viticultural College, which later became the Rutherglen Research Institute.

While Rutherglen recovered from phylloxera, it never regained its former glory. Although wine tastes, such as they were in the early 20th century, favoured its products (many millions of litres of strong reds and fortifieds were exported from Australia), it was South Australia that benefited most and, of course, suffered most when the crash finally came in late 1929. Rutherglen struggled on, its luscious tokays and muscats fortifying it against any further decline in its fortunes, until the 1960s, when the wine volcano began to erupt once more. But as the boom has progressed from red table wines to white, Rutherglen has not been well equipped to receive the benefits. Current fashion does not favour its best products, Tokay and Muscat, which have often been called Australia's most distinctive wines. This is a great pity. It is just as well that 'big' reds have always had their followers, as Rutherglen's reds are no laggards in this respect.

Today, Rutherglen has sixteen wineries, two of which (St Leonards and All Saints) have historic associations with Wahgunya, whose fruit is still vinified under their labels. Both vineyards are now owned by Brown Brothers of Milawa, who have amalgamated them administratively and are now running them under the name All Saints Estate.

Location: latitude 36°30'S, longitude 146°32'E, about 240 km north-east of Melbourne.
Elevation: The vineyards of the region are between 160 and 250 metres in altitude.
Topography and soils: The region is mainly flat, although there are slight undulations. Part of the Shepparton formation, its soils consist mainly of alluvial clay, silt, sand and gravel deposits spread over older marine sediments. They are accompanied in some places by lacustrine (lake) and aeolian (wind) deposits and are extremely deep, at places more than 50 metres. They have been mostly deposited by older river systems flowing west and north-west from the Victorian Alps. The two major soil types were classified in 1961 by Poutsma and Skene as Rutherglen Loam and (less prosaically) as Black Dog Fine Sandy Loam, the latter soil occurring in the southern part of the region. These soils are distinctive to the region and differ markedly from those in the Corowa area, across the River Murray, and soils to the south in the Glenrowan area of the Warby Ranges.
Climate: MJT 22.3°C, MAR 15.4, HDD 1775, AR 590 mm (Oct–Mar 258 mm), RH 50%, AI 375 mm, SH 9.3 (Dry & Smart), MJT 22.4°C, MAR na, HDD 1580 (adjusted for vine sites), AR 608 mm (Oct–Apr 311 mm), RH 26%, AI na, SH 9.6 (Gladstones), MJT 22.35°C (local), MAR 14.45°C (local), HDD 1817 (raw from Gladstones' data), AR 597.2 mm (local), RH 48% (local). Rutherglen undoubtedly has a very warm growing season with a substantial amount of its annual rainfall falling during that season. It has also been stressed that the region enjoys ripening temperatures comparable with other great fortified wine producing areas of the world,

e.g. Frontignan in Southern France and Setubal in Portugal. What is perhaps more important is that in Rutherglen's case, its low relative humidity leads to a partial shrivelling (without botrytis) of the berries during and after ripening. Such shrivelling results in an intense, very sweet style, but without the complexity of botrytis cinerea. A low natural humidity is also important in the control of downy mildew and less noble types of botrytis. Another factor differentiating its climate from areas nearer the coast is an absence of cooling afternoon breezes, cut off as it is from any maritime influences, though Wahgunyah, sitting on a bend in the Murray River, does sometimes experience a cooling river breeze in the evenings called the 'Wahgunyah Doctor'.

Irrigation is not essential for winegrowing in this region, but as in most other Australian sites, it is recommended certainly for the establishment of young vineyards and for times of moisture stress thereafter. Drip irrigation is found in many vineyards, water being supplied either from the Murray River or from private surface dams. The usual spray programs are adopted to counteract mildews. As for other problems, the Rutherglen region is frost-prone so vines tend to be trained high and clean cultivation techniques adopted. Colin Campbell allows about a 5 per cent crop loss every year for frosts and birds.

Harvest time: typical ripening dates are: chardonnay—in the east of region, second week of March, in the west of region, mid-March. Shiraz—in the east of region, end of March, in the west of region, end of March/early April. Cabernet sauvignon—in the east of region, mid-April, in the west of region, third week of April.

Principal varieties: White—chardonnay, muscadelle, riesling, semillon, trebbiano; Red—cabernet sauvignon, durif, greusche, muscat àpetits grains rouge, shiraz, touriga

Total area ha: na

Major wine styles: Historically, Rutherglen had two major wine styles: the first and most important being the marvellously rich fortified Muscats, Tokays (from the muscadelle variety) and port style; the second, the huge tannic dry reds, which were formidably big wines, and required equally heroic palates to consume them. Such wines often needed many years' cellaring to come into balance, if, indeed, they ever did. It is regrettable that during the past 25 years, popular taste has moved away from fortified wines, however good they may be and also, with some exceptions, from Australian reds that need long cellaring. But such is fashion. It is hoped that Rutherglen makers persist in their traditional styles, especially in making those luscious fortifieds!

The Muscats, made from the Rutherglen brown muscat (muscat a petits grains rouges) usually present a tawny brown hue and show that indescribable mix of muscat and rancio characters on nose and palate. The Tokays made from the muscadelle grape are usually an aged golden brown in shade with distinctive aromas of cold tea and, again, that marvellous integration of old wood, old spirit and old wine called 'rancio'. Such fascinating characters are replicated on palate. The port styles, whether tawny or vintage, can only be compared to those of McLaren Vale, but the vintage style is usually more earthy and less driven by blackberry fruit.

Though today those superb fortified styles are still produced, they need time, skill and the economic motive to continue in such production. Unless the pendulum of fashion swings away from table wines and in their favour, Rutherglen winemakers will not waste their time producing fortified wines they cannot sell. That is why there is a move afoot, supported by all the Rutherglen makers and also large companies such as Southcorp and Orlando-Wyndham, to standardise the quality and nomenclature of muscat into four classifications, which are from lowest to highest, Rutherglen, Classic, Grand and Rare. Such a scheme is of course aimed at popularising Muscat and sweeping away any mysteries and confusion in the minds of its consumers.

Apart from the fortifieds and the big reds, the region also produces honestly made white wines, Chardonnays and Semillons typical of warmer areas, which are good present drinking, but hardly ever memorable.

All Saints Estate   **R8.5**

All Saints Road, Wahgunyah, Vic 3687
Ph 02 6033 1922, Fax 02 6033 3515

Owner: Peter Brown
Chief winemaker:
Year of foundation: 1864
Tonnes crushed on average each year: 480
Location: Wahgunyah
Area: 57.52 ha
Soils: sandy loam over clay
Varieties planted: White—chardonnay, chenin blanc, marsanne, muscadelle, orange muscat, riesling, sauvignon blanc, semillon;
Red—cabernet franc, cabernet sauvignon, durif, malbec, merlot, meunier, muscat a petits grains rouges, pinot noir, ruby cabernet, shiraz
Leading wines: All Saints has two wine ranges: All Saints Estate-Heritáges Classic Release, Estate Selection, Show Reserve, Museum and St Leonards Kalara, Wahgunyah Shiraz and Carlyle. St Leonards has four ranges:
St Leonards (6 white and red table wines), Wine in Wood, Show Reserve and Museum Release (the last three all fortifieds).
Notes: All Saints Estate is an amalgamation of All Saints and St Leonards, though each label still appears. The wine ranges are given above. Both wineries having been retired from active winemaking (this takes place at the Kindergarten Winery at Brown Brothers Milawa) and each now has a studied tranquillity. All Saints is still very imposing with its red brick castellated winery and nearby

St Leonards is gracefully sheltered on the banks of a lagoon of the Murray River. Apart from their tranquil aspects, the Shiraz under each label remains excellent and towards the top of the region's standings, while the fortifieds are rich and luscious. All Saints cellar door sales: Mon–Sat 9am–5.30pm, Sun 10am–5.30pm. In addition The Terrace restaurant is open for a la carte lunch, morning and afternoon tea 10am–5pm. St Leonards cellar door sales: Thurs–Sun and Victorian public holidays 11am–3pm. Le Bistro is open Sat–Sun 11am–3pm.

Anderson's Winery   **NR**

Chiltern Road, Rutherglen, Vic 3685
(2 km from Rutherglen Post Office)
Ph 02 6032 8111

Owner: Anderson family
Chief winemaker: Howard Anderson
Year of foundation: 1993
Tonnes crushed on average each year: 25
Location: Rutherglen
Area: 3 ha
Soils: clay loam with 'buckshot' over clay base
Varieties planted: White—none; Red—shiraz
Leading wines: Anderson Winery Shiraz, Sparkling Shiraz, Methode Champenoise (a blend of pinot noir and chardonnay), Sparkling Chenin Blanc, Cabernet Sauvignon, Liqueur Muscat, Liqueur Tokay
Notes: Howard Anderson spent 14 years at Seppelt Great Western and still puts his

sparkling expertise to good use in Rutherglen by making three sparkling wines at his winery. Sparkling whites are not often made in this region so it is not surprising that some of the fruit used for this purpose comes from the King Valley. There are of course other sparkling reds in the region, usually made from shiraz and/or durif. Cellar door sales: 7 days 10am–5pm.

Buller's Calliope Winery   **R8.5**

Three Chain Road, Rutherglen, Vic 3685 (about 5 km west of the town)
Ph 02 6032 9660, Fax 02 6032 8055

Owners: Buller family
Chief winemaker: Andrew Buller
Year of foundation: 1921
Tonnes crushed on average each year: 80
Locations: Rutherglen and Indigo Valley within the Rutherglen region
Area: 22.81 ha at Rutherglen and 10 ha planted at Indigo Valley with 40 ha more available there
Soils: (Rutherglen) light red loam over clay. (Indigo Valley) granitic sand over red loamy subsoil
Varieties planted: (Rutherglen) White—chasselas, muscadelle, white frontignac; Red—cinsaut, grenache, mondeuse, muscat a petits grains rouge, shiraz. (Indigo Valley) White—chardonnay, marsanne, sauvignon blanc;
Red—cabernet franc, cabernet sauvignon, durif, merlot, pinot noir
Leading wines: Buller Museum Muscat, Museum Tokay, Calliope Shiraz, Mondeuse-Shiraz, Grenache-Cinsaut
Notes: Buller is an old and respected name in Rutherglen, not quite as old perhaps as the originals, Morris, Chambers and Campbell, but its non-irrigated Rutherglen vineyard makes great fortified wines in the same style. The Indigo Valley vineyard is drip irrigated and situated at 250 m in altitude in an attempt to

avoid the often extreme heat of the plains and to capture more fruit delicacy in its table wines. This is of course a departure from tradition and an effort to cater for the modern table wine market. May they both succeed! Cellar door sales: 7 days 10am–5pm except Christmas Day and Good Friday.

Campbell's Winery   **R8.5**

Murray Valley Highway, Rutherglen, Vic 3685
Ph 02 6032 9458, Fax 02 6032 9870

Owners: Campbell family
Chief winemaker: Colin Campbell
Year of foundation: 1870
Tonnes crushed on average each year: 850 (250 tonnes of which is purchased in the region)
Location: Rutherglen
Area: 60 ha
Soils: red clay loam
Varieties planted: White—chardonnay, muscadelle, riesling, semillon, sylvaner, trebbiano; Red—cabernet sauvignon, durif, muscat a petits grains rouge, ruby cabernet, shiraz
Leading wines: Campbell's Chardonnay, Cabernet, Riesling, Barkly Durif, Bobbie Burns Shiraz, Merchant Prince Muscat, Isabella Tokay, Allen's Port
Notes: The Campbell winery was founded by John Campbell, a Scottish goldminer who came to the region in 1858. Like all good Scots, he had a great respect for Bobbie Burns and named his winery after him. The reds are typical of the big ripe tannic styles of the region and the quality of the fortified wines is superlative. Cellar door sales: Mon–Sat 9am–5pm, Sun 10am–5pm.

Chambers Rosewood Winery   **R9**

Barkly Street, Rutherglen, Vic 3685
Ph 02 6032 8641, Fax 02 6032 8101

Owner: Bill Chambers
Chief winemaker: Bill Chambers
Year of foundation: 1858
Tonnes crushed on average each year: 150
Location: Rutherglen
Area: 55 ha
Soils: red brown earths
Varieties planted: White—muscadelle,
palomino, riesling; Red—cabernet sauvignon,
cinsaut, grenache, muscat a petits grains
rouge, shiraz, touriga
Leading wines: Chambers Rosewood Muscat,
Tokay, Cabernet Sauvignon, Shiraz
Notes: Chambers Rosewood is one of the
magic names of north-east Victorian fortified
wines, always vying with Morris as the
quintessence of Rutherglen Muscat style. If
anything, the Chambers style is lighter and a
touch more elegant, but both wines are
fantastically good and Bill Chambers,
winemaker and senior wine judge, is one of
the stalwarts of the industry. Cellar door sales:
Mon–Sat 9am–5pm, Sun 10am–5pm.

Cofield Wines **NR**

Distillery Road, Wahgunyah, Vic 3687
Ph/Fax 02 6033 3798

Owner: Max Cofield
Chief winemaker: Max Cofield
Year of foundation: 1990
Tonnes crushed on average each year: 70
(some shiraz bought in)
Location: Wahgunyah (2 vineyards)
Area: 3.2 ha
Soils: light free-draining sandy soil in one
vineyard, and heavier clay loam in the other
Varieties planted: White—chardonnay,
semillon; Red—cabernet sauvignon, merlot,
shiraz
Leading wines: Cofield Sparkling Shiraz,
Semillon
Notes: Max Cofield is specialising in Sparkling
Shiraz and finds that semillon suits the region.
Cellar door sales: Mon–Sat 9am–5pm, Sun

10am–5pm, closed Christmas Day, Boxing Day
and Good Friday.

Fairfield Vineyard **NR**

Murray Valley Highway, Brown's Plains,
via Rutherglen, Vic 3685
Ph 02 6032 9381

Owner: Mrs M. Morris-Slamen
Chief winemaker: contract
Year of foundation: 1859
Tonnes crushed on average each year: 50
Location: Brown's Plains
Area: 15 ha
Soils: reddish clay loam
Varieties planted: White—muscadelle, riesling,
trebbiano; Red—cabernet sauvignon, durif,
muscat a petits grains rouge, shiraz
Leading wines: Fairfield Vineyard White
Hermitage, Shiraz, Durif, Cabernet Sauvignon
Notes: This is the former home of George
Francis Morris, one of the pioneers of the
Rutherglen region, and a showplace of the
district. He was, like many, an unsuccessful
miner but, like very few, a most successful
general merchant and later vigneron. His great-
granddaughter Melba Morris-Slamen purchased
Fairfield in a ruined state in 1970 and has
painstakingly restored it. The vineyards too
have been re-established but not on their
former scale. Some of the nineteenth century
winemaking equipment is still in use at
Fairfield. The Durif has scored well in recent
wine shows and the Muscat also. Cellar door
sales: Mon–Sat 10am–5pm and some Sundays
noon–5pm.

Gehrig Wines **NR**

Cnr Murray Valley Highway and
Howlong Road, Barnawartha, Vic 3688
Ph 02 6026 7296, Fax 02 6026 7424

Owner: Gehrig family
Chief winemaker: Brian Gehrig
Year of foundation: 1858

Tonnes crushed on average each year: 120
Location: Barnawartha
Area: 14 ha
Soils: loam over clay base, water retentive
Varieties planted: White—chardonnay, chenin blanc, riesling, trebbiano; Red—cabernet sauvignon, durif, muscat, pinot noir, shiraz
Leading wines: Gehrig Estate Chardonnay, Chenin Blanc, Riesling, Cabernet Sauvignon, Shiraz, Vintage Port
Notes: This is one of the pioneer vineyards of the region with a historic winery now being modernised. Cellar door sales: Mon–Sat 9am–5pm, Sun 10am–5pm.

Jones Winery   NR

Chiltern Road, Rutherglen, Vic 3685
Ph 02 6032 8496, Fax 02 6032 8495

Owner/chief winemaker: Les Jones
Year of foundation: founded in 1860 and purchased by the Jones family in 1927
Tonnes crushed on average each year: not disclosed but estimated at 80
Location: Rutherglen
Area: 16 ha (dryland)
Soils: red clay
Varieties planted: White—chardonnay, Rutherglen pedro, trebbiano; Red—cabernet sauvignon, merlot, muscat a petits grains rouge, ruby cabernet, shiraz
Leading wines: Jones ports, muscats and sherries of varying styles
Notes: A maker of table wines and the fortified styles traditional to the region. Cellar door sales: Mon–Sat 9am–5pm, Sun and holidays 10am–5pm.

Morris Wines   R10

Mia Mia Road, Rutherglen, Vic 3685
Ph 02 6026 7303, Fax 02 6026 7445

Owner: Orlando Wyndham
Chief winemaker: David Morris
Year of foundation: 1859

Tonnes crushed on average each year: 500, plus about 200 tonnes of other fruit purchased locally
Location: Rutherglen
Area: 86 ha consisting of two vineyards of 43 ha each about a kilometre apart
Soils: red loam over red-yellow podsolic subsoil
Varieties planted: White—muscadelle, palomino, semillon; Red—cabernet sauvignon, cinsaut, durif, muscat a petits grain rouge, shiraz, touriga
Leading wines: There are three Morris ranges. The Morris Wine Selection consists of Morris Chardonnay, Semillon, Shiraz, Cabernet Sauvignon, Durif, Sparkling Shiraz-Durif. The Morris Canister range comprises Liqueur Muscat, Liqueur Tokay and Old Tawny Port. The Morris Black Label range has Liqueur Muscat and Old Tawny Port.
Notes: Fortifieds embody the true spirit of Rutherglen and the Morris fortifieds are 'the tops', rivalled only perhaps by Chambers within the region and by Bailey's of Glenrowan outside it. A Morris Liqueur Muscat is the taste experience of a lifetime. Cellar door sales: Mon–Sat 9am–5pm, Sun 10am–5pm.

Mount Prior Vineyard   NR

Cnr River Road and Popes Lane, Rutherglen, Vic 3685
Ph 02 6026 5591, Fax 02 6026 5590

Owner: Jim Sawyer
Chief winemaker: Anthony Lacy
Year of foundation: 1860
Tonnes crushed on average each year: 120, but will increase to 250, as new plantings come into bearing
Location: Rutherglen
Area: 47 ha
Soils: red loam over shale rock and red loam over clay
Varieties planted: White—chardonnay, chenin blanc, semillon; Red—cabernet sauvignon, durif, grenache, malbec, merlot, shiraz

Leading wines: Mount Prior Chardonnay, Shiraz, Cabernet-Merlot, Durif

Notes: Mount Prior has a gracious old Rutherglen house built in the booming 1880s and now run as a guest house with five rooms and an award-winning restaurant using top local produce, all set in two hectares of garden—an excellent place to taste its wines. It is open to the public on weekends, but cellar door sales are 7 days 10am–5pm.

Pfeiffer Wines R7

Distillery Road, Wahgunyah, Vic 3687
Ph 02 6033 2805, Fax 02 6033 3158

Owners: Chris and Robyn Pfeiffer
Chief winemaker: Chris Pfeiffer
Year of foundation: 1984
Tonnes crushed on average each year: 300
Location: Wahgunyah
Area: 22 ha
Soils: alluvial sandy soil over gravel base
Varieties planted: White—chardonnay, frontignac, muscadelle, riesling; Red—cabernet franc, cabernet sauvignon, gamay, merlot, muscat a petits grains rouge, pinot noir, shiraz, touriga and small areas of 26 other Portuguese varieties
Leading Wines: Pfeiffer Riesling, Chardonnay-Semillon, Chardonnay, Frontignac, Ensemble (a rosé style), Gamay, Pinot Noir, Shiraz, Cabernet Sauvignon, Auslese Tokay, Christophers Vintage Port, Old Distillery Port (a tawny), Old Distillery Muscat, Old Distillery Tokay, Fino Sherry. There is also the lesser priced Carlyle range made from fruit purchased in the district.
Notes: Chris Pfeiffer, as one would expect from an ex-Lindemans fortified winemaker, makes excellent fortifieds and there is a full range including that rarity, Fino Sherry. There is also a full range of table wines. Cellar door sales: Mon–Sat 9am–5pm, Sun 11am–4pm, closed Christmas and Boxing Days, Good Friday and Anzac Day morning.

St Leonards

Wahgunyah, Vic 3687 (see All Saints Estate)

Stanton and Killeen Vineyard R7.5

Jacks Road off Murray Valley Highway, Rutherglen, Vic 3685
Ph 02 6032 9457, Fax 02 6032 8018

Owner: Killeen family
Chief winemaker: Chris Killeen
Year of foundation: 1875
Tonnes crushed on average each year: 200
Location: Rutherglen
Area: 22 ha
Soils: red loams a metre deep over clay
Varieties planted: White—chardonnay, muscadelle; Red—cabernet sauvignon, durif, merlot, muscat a petits grains rouge, shiraz, tinta baroca, tinta cao, touriga nacional
Leading wines: Stanton & Killeen Shiraz, Cabernet-Shiraz, Durif, Vintage Port, Muscat, Tokay, Tawny Port
Notes: A very good maker of reds and fortifieds which are firmly in the mainstream of regional style. Cellar door sales: Mon–Sat 9am–5pm, Sun 10am–5pm.

G Sutherland Smith & Sons NR

Cnr Murray Valley Highway and Falkiners Road, Rutherglen, Vic 3685 (7 km east of the town)
Ph 02 6032 8177, Fax 02 6026 5923

Owner: George Sutherland Smith and Sons Pty Ltd
Chief winemaker: George Sutherland Smith
Year of foundation: 1993
Tonnes crushed on average each year: 20
Location: Rutherglen
Area: 5 ha consisting of three vineyards, at Glenrowan, Wooragee near Beechworth and Rutherglen
Soils: (Rutherglen vineyard) red loam over red-yellow podsol

Varieties planted: White—riesling, traminer;
Red—cabernet sauvignon, merlot, shiraz
Leading wines: Sutherland Smith Riesling,
Chardonnay, Josephine Riesling-Traminer,
Cabernet-Shiraz, Cabernet-Shiraz-Merlot,
Tawny Port
Notes: After losing All Saints in 1991, George
Sutherland Smith has set up once more in
Rutherglen, these days on a much smaller
scale. Cellar door sales: weekends, Victorian
school holidays and public holidays 11am–5pm.

Warrabilla Wines NR

Murray Valley Highway, Rutherglen,
Vic 3685 (18 km west of the town)
Ph/Fax 02 6035 7242

Owners: Andrew and Carol Sutherland Smith
Chief winemaker: Andrew Sutherland Smith
Year of foundation: 1991
Tonnes crushed on average each year: 40, all
of which are used for Warrabilla's own labels
Location: Brimin, in the west of the region
Area: 3.5 ha
Soils: sandy loam on a clay base with
'buckshot'
Varieties planted: White—none; Red—durif,
shiraz
Leading wines: Warrabilla Glenrowan Cabernet,
Brimin Cabernet Shiraz
Notes: Warrabilla makes rich and tannic reds,
very much in the spirit of its region. Cellar
door sales: 7 days 10am–5pm.

KING VALLEY AND ALPINE VALLEYS (PROPOSED REGION)

King Valley

The King Valley is a proposed region developed in the 1970s as a winegrowing area
chiefly by Italian farmers who wished for an alternative to an ever-shrinking tobacco
market and by graziers who wished to diversify from beef production. Its most famous
early wines were the Koombahla Rieslings and Cabernets made by Brown Brothers
in the 1970s and 1980s. That company later went on to develop the high altitude
Whitlands vineyard while continuing to purchase substantial amounts of fruit from
local growers.

Location: Wangaratta, see Ovens Valley. Whitfield, latitude 36°47'S, longitude
146°20'E, about 200 km from Melbourne
Elevation: Whitfield (valley floor 200 m) steeply ascending to Whitlands (800 m)
Topography and soils: The King River flows north-north-west to meet the Ovens near
Wangaratta. At its source, in the Alpine National Park, the country is mountainous,
but the vineyards commence some 40 km to the north around Cheshunt and
Whitfield. Around Whitfield there is extremely steep and undulating country which
remains hilly and undulating until the river reaches flood plains near Milawa. Around
Whitlands the soils are volcanic brown loams over clay. At lower altitudes to the
north the soils have formed on river deposits derived from Ordovician sedimentary
rock and from rock formed from acid lava flows during the Devonian period. When
the river leaves its valley and debouches on to the plain, there are deep red alluvial
loams (Milawa).
Climate: Wangaratta (see Ovens Valley below). Whitlands (altitude 800 m) Mean

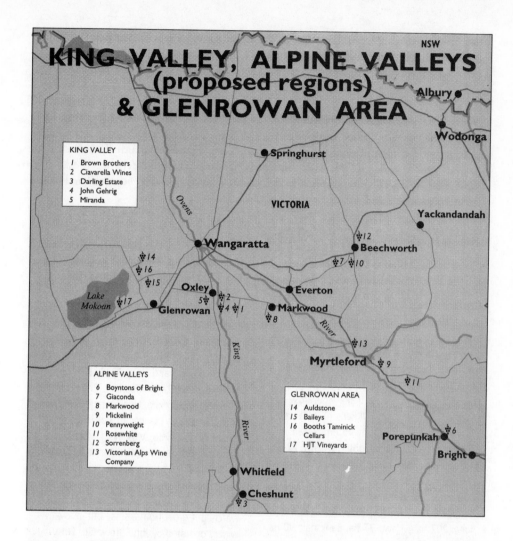

KING VALLEY, ALPINE VALLEYS (proposed regions) & GLENROWAN AREA

KING VALLEY

1 Brown Brothers
2 Ciavarella Wines
3 Darling Estate
4 John Gehrig
5 Miranda

NSW

Albury

Wodonga

Springhurst

VICTORIA

Yackandandah

Wangaratta

Beechworth

14
16
15

Oxley
5 2
4 1

Everton

Markwood
8

Lake
Mokoan 17

Glenrowan

River

13

Myrtleford 9

11

ALPINE VALLEYS

6 Boyntons of Bright
7 Giaconda
8 Markwood
9 Mickelini
10 Pennyweight
11 Rosewhite
12 Sorrenberg
13 Victorian Alps Wine
   Company

GLENROWAN AREA

14 Auldstone
15 Baileys
16 Booths Taminick
   Cellars
17 HJT Vineyards

Porepunkah 6

Bright

King River

River

Whitfield

Cheshunt
3

Temperature Warmest Month (MTWM) 19°C, HDD na, AR 1410 mm, RH na. Banksdale, central King Valley (altitude 450 m) MTWM 20.6°C, HDD na, AR 900 mm, RH na. Milawa (altitude 155 m) MTWM 22.8°C, HDD na, AR 660 mm, RH na. Other climatic information: Whitfield AR 1097 mm (Oct–April 463 mm). On its plains, therefore, the King River Valley seems a fairly warm area, but becomes increasingly cooler as the river is followed upstream to its source. Whitlands at 800 m in altitude has proved to be an excellent area for the production of sparkling base wine and for delicate table wines.

Phylloxera remains a grave risk here and vines must be planted on an appropriately resistant rootstock. Frosts too are a serious risk. See notes on Ovens Valley.

Harvest time: This will vary with altitude. Chardonnay: at 150 m late February, at 200 m early March, at 600 m 3rd week of March, at 800 m end of first week of April. Cabernet sauvignon: 150 m mid-March, at 200 m 3rd week of March, at

600 m 3rd week of April. At 800 m, cabernet sauvignon will not ripen fully and probably should not be planted at altitudes in excess of 600 m.

Principal varieties: White—chardonnay, sauvignon blanc; Red—cabernet sauvignon, shiraz

Area: na

Major wine styles: except for some Brown Brothers and Miranda wines, very little table wine appears under the King River Valley GI. Much more is purchased by outside wine companies and disappears into bigger blends of South East Australian origin, which is a pity for the proposed region produces excellent chardonnay, sauvignon blanc, cabernet sauvignon and shiraz—far too good to be consigned to the anonymity of a brand.

Brown Brothers   **R9.5**

Snow Road, Milawa, Vic 3678
Ph 03 5720 5500, Fax 03 5720 5511

Owners: Brown family
Chief winemaker: John G. Brown
Year of foundation: 1889
Tonnes crushed on average each year: not disclosed, but estimated at 4000 (including All Saints Estate and Mystic Park)
Locations: there are four major vineyards—Mystic Park (see Swan Hill Region), Milawa (lower King Valley, altitude 155 m, Mean Temperature Warmest Month (MTWM) 22.8°C, AR 660 mm), Banksdale (King River Valley, altitude 400–485 m, MTWM 20.6°C, AR 900 mm), and Whitlands (upper King Valley, altitude 800 m, MTWM 19°C, AR 1410 mm).
Area: 202 ha (Milawa 77 ha, Banksdale 90 ha, Whitlands 35 ha)
Soils: (Milawa) alluvial red sandy clay loam to a depth of 1.2 m, moderate pH; (Banksdale) Tertiary Eocene basalt, slightly acidic; (Whitlands) volcanic brown loam/clay loam to a depth of 2 m over Kaolin clay, low to moderate pH.
Varieties planted: (Milawa) White—chardonnay, chenin blanc, gewurztraminer, riesling, sauvignon blanc, white frontignac; Red—barbera, cabernet franc, cabernet sauvignon, dolcetto, fer, graciano, merlot, mondeuse, muscat a petits grains rouge, pinot noir, shiraz.

(Banksdale) White—chardonnay, pinot gris; Red—barbera, cabernet sauvignon, shiraz.
(Whitlands) White—chardonnay, gewurztraminer, pinot gris, riesling, sauvignon blanc; Red—cabernet franc, cabernet sauvignon, malbec, merlot, meunier, pinot noir
Leading wines: Brown Brothers Late Harvested Orange Muscat and Flora, Noble Riesling, Family Reserve Range (Riesling, Chardonnay, Cabernet Sauvignon), Non-Vintage Pinot Noir and Chardonnay (sparkling), Italian Varietal Range Pinot, Grigio, Moscato, Dolcetto, Nebbiolo, Barbera, Fortified Range Muscat, Port, Tokay
Notes: Brown Brothers is one of the great wineries of Victoria. For over 30 years I have watched it grow from a small but innovative winery operated by John Brown Snr with the assistance of his four sons to the modern regional giant it is today. Remarkably it is still strongly family-owned and there is a large variety of wines ranging from the most elegant sparkling styles to the sweet botrytised and fortifieds. It is all a question of the right varieties grown in the right places and Brown Brothers over many years has come to know North East Victoria very well. Cellar door sales: daily 9am–5pm. There is also an excellent restaurant (the Epicurean Centre), open daily from 11am–3pm.

Ciavarella Wines **R6.5**

Evans Lane, Oxley, Vic 3678
Ph/Fax 03 5727 3384

Owners: Cyril and Jan Ciavarella
Chief winemaker: Cyril Ciavarella
Year of foundation: 1978
Tonnes crushed on average each year: 15
Locations: Oxley and North Wangaratta
Area: 6 ha
Soils: sandy loams
Varieties planted: White—chardonnay, chenin blanc, semillon; Red—cabernet sauvignon, shiraz
Leading wines: Ciavarella Chardonnay (lightly wooded), Chenin Blanc, Shiraz, Cabernet Sauvignon, Dolcino (a sweet red), Late Harvest Chenin Blanc
Notes: A small winery and vineyard making a very pleasant lightly wooded Chardonnay. Cellar door sales: Mon–Sat 9am–6pm, Sun 10am–6pm.

Darling Estate **NR**

Nambucca Vineyard, Whitfield Road, Cheshunt, Vic 3678
Ph/Fax 03 5729 8396

Owner: H. G. and M. T. Darling
Chief Winemaker: H. G. Darling
Year of foundation: 1990
Tonnes crushed on average each year: 8
Locations: Koombahla Vineyard, Whitfield and Nambucca Vineyard, Cheshunt
Area: 21.5 ha consisting of two vineyards, Koombahla (20 ha) and Nambucca (1.5 ha)
Soils: (Koombahla) clay loam of volcanic origin; (Nambucca) similar soils
Varieties planted: (Nambucca) White—chenin blanc; Red—gamay, pinot noir. (Koombahla) White—chardonnay, riesling, sauvignon blanc, semillon; Red—cabernet franc, cabernet sauvignon, merlot, pinot noir, shiraz
Leading wines: Darling Estate Pinot Noir
Notes: Guy Darling is the pioneer of

winegrowing in the King Valley, which these days is one of the larger Victorian winegrowing regions. For years the fruit from Koombahla Vineyard was virtually all sold to Brown Brothers of Milawa and their Koombahla label became quite famous. These days the fruit sales are more widely spread, though such sales still constitute a major part of vineyard activity. Cellar door sales by appointment.

John Gehrig **NR**

Off the Snow Road, Oxley, Vic 3678
Ph 03 5727 3395, Fax 03 5727 3699

Owners: John and Elizabeth Gehrig
Chief winemaker: John Gehrig
Year of foundation: 1976
Tonnes crushed on average each year: 90
Location: Oxley
Area: 6 ha
Soils: alluvial sandy loam on a clay subsoil
Varieties planted: White—chardonnay, chenin blanc, riesling; Red—cabernet franc, cabernet sauvignon, durif, malbec, merlot, muscat a petits grains rouge, pinot noir, petit verdot
Leading wines: John Gehrig Pinot Noir, Merlot
Notes: A consistent bronze medallist at the Rutherglen Show. Cellar door sales: daily 9am–5pm.

Miranda **R8**

Cnr Snow Road and Whitfield Road, Oxley, Vic 3678
Ph/Fax 03 5727 3399

Owner: Miranda Wines Pty Ltd
Chief winemaker: Luis Simian
Year of foundation: (vineyards) 1997, (winery) 1998
Tonnes crushed on average each year: 1500 and increasing, all of which are used for Miranda's own labels
Location: Oxley
Area: 35 ha
Soils: sandy clay loam

Varieties planted: White—chardonnay; Red—cabernet sauvignon, merlot, petit verdot, shiraz
Leading wines: Miranda High Country Chardonnay, Riesling, Sauvignon Blanc, Cabernet Sauvignon, Merlot, Shiraz
Notes: Since 1995, the Miranda High Country range has exploded onto the premium wine scene, in that time winning two trophies and over 110 awards at various Australian and international wine shows. Cellar door sales: from mid-1999.

Alpine Valleys

Like most of the North East Victorian wine zone, the Ovens Valley was an area settled by graziers in the 1840s. Gold transformed it and Beechworth in the 1850s was one of the most famous Victorian fields. As a wine-producing area, its history is much more recent. There have been wine references to it since the 1960s and 1970s when Wynn's Ovens Valley 'Burgundy', made of local shiraz, gained quite a following. At the same time, Brown Brothers sold its Everton Hills (also in the Ovens Valley) range of reds. In the past decade, mainly due to the efforts of Rick Kinzbrunner, its Beechworth area has gained an excellent reputation for a fuller style of Pinot Noir and an elegant, rather reserved Chardonnay. As a winegrowing region it is naturally complementary to the adjoining King River Valley, and recently the newly formed Alpine Valleys Wine Co has erected a winery near Myrtleford. In contention at the time of writing is its name—'Ovens Valley' is not entirely acceptable. Some prefer 'Mount Buffalo Ranges'.

Location: Beechworth: latitude 36°21'S, longitude 146°41'E, about 250 km north-east of Melbourne; Wangaratta: latitude 36°21'S, longitude 146°19'E, about 200 km north-east of Melbourne
Elevation: Beechworth: 552 m; Wangaratta: 150 m; Bright 300–350 m
Topography and soils: In the Ovens River catchment area, four distinct river terraces and a recent flood plain have been identified. There are two more elevated terraces associated with Mount Buffalo. The soils on the present flood plain commence at 300 m elevation upstream of Eurobin in the Ovens and Buckland Valleys and upstream from Nug Nug in the Buffalo River Valley to a 180 m elevation downstream from Rocky Point Bridge. Such soils have no profile development and are the most fertile soils. They can be described as recent alluvial soils consisting mostly of sandy loams and fine sandy clay loams. Such soils produce high yields of grapes of lesser value to winemakers than fruit produced on higher terrace soils.

The soils on the lowest river terrace are greyish-brown gradational soils, still very young and highly fertile with little soil profile development. Soil types are similar to those on the flood plain. The elevation of these soils is 180–200 m.

On the second lowest terrace, soils are again greyish-brown to brown gradational. Soils here show more profile surface features ranging from fine sandy loam to fine sandy clay loam with a slight increase in texture at a quarter of a metre depth but not exceeding a clay loam. In soils on the lowest and second lowest river terrace, vigour control is necessary to produce fruit of very good quality. Sites where soil textures become lighter than fine sandy loam at a depth of three-quarters of a metre or more will aid vigour control, as some moisture stress can be imposed during January and February. The elevation of this terrace is about 220 m.

The second highest terrace has duplex soils on older sediments. Its soils vary greatly between upstream and downstream locations. Upstream from Rocky Point Bridge there are lighter soils of a yellowish-brown to reddish-brown colour, with soil textures not exceeding clay loams in the B horizon, whereas downstream from that bridge there are much heavier soil features with medium clay B horizons quite common. In elevation these soils vary from 240 m down to 180 m. Vigour control is less necessary because of the clay layers in the profile and the vines can be stressed. The fruit produced is usually of excellent quality.

The highest terrace has duplex reddish-brown to red-brown soils. These soils are at an elevation of 240–250 m and soil features change abruptly from fine sandy clay loams to reddish or red-brown medium clays with stable structure. As the soils are fairly fertile, some vigour control may still be necessary, but the fruit produced is of very high quality.

Forming a ring around Mount Buffalo, there are very old dark-red duplex soils. These soils are on ancient river terraces at an elevation of 300 m and in some slightly higher areas (320 m) are overlain with colluvial material. Though vigour control has to be practised, these too produce excellent fruit.

On the hills, soils vary from gradational to duplex and in colour from yellowish-brown to reddish-brown. They occur at an elevation of 300–340 m upstream of Rocky Point Bridge and at an elevation of 240–280 m downstream of this bridge. They have less depth in profile and gravel with medium clay is often found at depths of less than one metre. Here vine vigour is more easily managed because of lower fertility and moisture stress during January and February. Gently sloping hills with an easterly to north easterly aspect are favoured because there is often a deeper layer of surface soil. Around Beechworth, there are red duplex and gravelly clay loams.

Climate: Beechworth MJT 20.1° C, MAR na, HDD (raw) 1484, 1566 (cut off and adjusted for latitude daily temperature range and vine sites), AR 929 mm (Oct–Apr 437 mm), RH 41% 3pm, AI na, SH 9.3 (Gladstones). Wangaratta MJT 22.6°C, MAR na, HDD (raw) 1874, 1580 (adjusted for vine sites), AR 640 mm (Oct–Apr 325 mm), RH 26% (3pm), AR 640 mm (Oct–Apr 325mm), RH 26% 3pm, AI na, SH 9.5 (Gladstones). Bright (300 m altitude) MJT 20.4°C, MAR 13.6°C, HDD (raw) 1608, 1246 adjusted, AR 1218 mm (Oct–Apr 617 mm), RH na (Ovens Research Station).

Wangaratta is the Valley's 'bottom end', close to the junction of the King and Ovens Rivers. The table wines of Wangaratta are typified by the rather warm, full-bodied, tannic Shiraz styles of Milawa and nearby Oxley. Beechworth is due east of Wangaratta, but much more elevated with a much higher annual rainfall, making 'finer' table wines. Giaconda Pinot Noir and Chardonnay are styles in point. The southern end of the Valley (Bright and Porepunkah) is also very suitable for the production of excellent 'cool area' table wines, particularly Chardonnays.

In these alpine valleys, which basically run from the Victorian Alps (altitude about 2000 m) in the south-east to the north-west, vineyard site selection should be made with extreme care as there is a considerable risk of frost. Sites with free air drainage should be chosen to avoid streams of cold air which flow in springtime along the valleys to the flatter lands around Wangaratta. Throughout North Eastern Victoria, phylloxera is an ever-present risk and all vineyards should be established on phylloxera-resistant rootstocks.

Harvest time: (Bright) chardonnay late March–early April, shiraz late April–early May, late May.

Principal varieties: White—chardonnay; Red—cabernet sauvignon, merlot, shiraz

Area: na

Major wine styles: Chardonnay, Cabernet Sauvignon, Shiraz

Boyntons of Bright R7.5

Ovens Valley Highway, Bright, Vic 3747
Ph 03 5756 2356, Fax 03 5756 2610

Owners: Kel and Carolien Boynton
Chief winemaker: Kel Boynton
Year of foundation: 1987
Tonnes crushed on average each year: 225
Location: Bright
Area: 45 ha
Soils: red gravelly loams more than 3 m deep
Varieties planted: White—chardonnay, pinot gris, riesling, sauvignon blanc, semillon; Red—cabernet sauvignon, durif, merlot, meunier, shiraz
Leading wines: Boynton's of Bright Chardonnay, Pinot Gris, Riesling, Shiraz, Merlot
Notes: Ten kilometres west of Bright and high in the Ovens Valley beneath Mount Buffalo, Kel Boynton's vineyard is very cool and ripens April–May. It made a great initial impression at the Victorian Wine Show a few years ago. Since then, though the vineyards have expanded significantly and yields correspondingly increased, the wines have retained their quality. Cellar door sales: daily 10am–5pm.

Giaconda R10

McClay Road, Beechworth, Vic 3747
Ph/Fax 03 5727 0246

Owner/chief winemaker: Rick Kinzbrunner
Year of foundation: 1985
Tonnes crushed on average each year: 15
Location: Beechworth
Area: 2.5 ha
Soils: mixture of gravel and clay
Varieties planted: White—chardonnay; Red—cabernet sauvignon, pinot noir
Leading wines: Giaconda Chardonnay, Pinot Noir
Notes: A minute vineyard with huge standards of quality. Its Pinot style is different to the strawberry-plummy styles of Southern Victoria; it is slightly warmer, fuller and riper as befits a slightly warmer site. Its Chardonnay is a reserved, slightly closed style, made to cellar, one feels, very differently from the open, buttery, run-of-the-mill commercial style. These wines are fascinating expressions of their 'climat'. Cellar door sales by appointment only.

Markwood NR

Morris Lane, Markwood, Vic 3678
Ph/Fax 03 5727 0361

Owner/chief winemaker: Rick Morris
Year of foundation: 1971
Tonnes crushed on average each year: 15
Location: Markwood
Area: 4 ha
Soils: alluvial grey loam
Varieties planted: White—chardonnay, riesling; Red—cabernet sauvignon, shiraz

Leading wines: Markwood Cabernet Sauvignon
Notes: Cellar door sales, 7 days 9am–5pm.

Mickelini **NR**

Great Alpine Road, Myrtleford, Vic 3737
Ph/Fax 03 5751 1990

Owner: Vallunga Pty Ltd
Chief winemaker: contract
Year of foundation: 1982
Tonnes crushed on average each year: 900
Location: Myrtleford (winery), Buckland Valley,
Porepunkah (vineyards)
Area: 36 ha
Soils: red loam
Varieties planted: White—chardonnay;
Red—marzemino, merlot, pinot noir
Leading wines: Mickelini Chardonnay, Merlot,
Marzemino-Merlot
Notes: A new winery and cellar door outlet
was opened early in 1998 by the Mickelini
family which has its origins in the Trentino
province of north-east Italy. They previously
sold most of their fruit to Orlando-Wyndham.
For the lover of rare grape varieties, the
Marzemino-Merlot blend may be worth
a detour. Cellar door sales: weekends
10am–5pm, at other times telephone ahead.

Pennyweight **NR**

Pennyweight Lane, Beechworth, Vic 3747
Ph 03 5728 1747, Fax 03 5728 1704

Owners: Stephen and Elizabeth Morris
Chief winemaker: Stephen N Morris
Year of foundation: 1982
Tonnes crushed on average each year: 15
Location: Beechworth
Area: 3 ha
Soils: red duplex
Varieties planted: White—palomino, riesling,
semillon; Red—cabernet sauvignon, gamay,
pinot noir, shiraz
Leading wines: Pennyweight Pinot Noir, Shiraz,
Cabernet Blend, Riesling, Fortifieds

Notes: Stephen Morris is a member of the
famous Morris family, whose founder
G. F. Morris first arrived in the Rutherglen area
140 years ago. Pennyweight follows organic
principles and is non-irrigated. Cellar door
sales: Thurs–Tues 10am–5pm, Sun 11am–5pm,
closed Wednesdays, Good Friday and
Christmas Day.

Rosewhite **NR**

Happy Valley Road, Rosewhite, Vic 3737
Ph 03 5752 1077

Owner: Ron and Joan Mullett
Chief winemaker: Joan Mullett
Year of foundation: 1983
Tonnes crushed on average each year: 10
Location: Rosewhite
Area: 2.5 ha
Soils: shaley on a slope with good drainage
Varieties planted: White—chardonnay,
gewurztraminer; Red—cabernet sauvignon,
pinot noir, shiraz
Leading wines: Rosewhite Pinot Noir
Notes: Cellar door sales, weekends and public
holidays 10am–5pm and during January, also
mail order.

Sorrenberg **R6.5**

Alma Road, Beechworth, Vic 3747
Ph/Fax 03 5728 2278

Owners: Barry and Jan Morey
Chief winemaker: Barry Morey
Year of foundation: 1984
Tonnes crushed on average each year: 20
Location: Beechworth
Area: 2.5 ha
Soils: granitic
Varieties planted: White—chardonnay, riesling,
sauvignon blanc, semillon; Red—cabernet
franc, cabernet sauvignon, gamay, merlot
Leading wines: Sorrenberg Sauvignon Blanc
Semillon, Chardonnay, Gamay, Cabernet
Sauvignon, Cabernet Franc, Merlot

Notes: My last acquaintance with Sorrenberg was a pleasantly fruity Gamay. Cellar door sales: weekends 1pm–5pm, otherwise by appointment.

Victorian Alps Wine Co NR

Cnr Great Alpine and Snow Roads, Gapstead, Vic 3737
Ph 03 5729 8358

Owners: Victorian Alps Wine Co (a venture of Kingston Estate, Shayne Cunningham, four King Valley growers and one Buffalo Valley grower)
Chief winemaker: Shayne Cunningham
Year of foundation: 1997

Tonnes crushed on average each year: 1500
Location: (winery) Myrtleford
Area: 10 ha
Soils: a south-west facing slope with reddish-brown fine loam to sandy clay loam over shale and quartz
Varieties planted: White—none; Red—cabernet sauvignon, merlot
Leading wines: Black Ridge Cabernet-Merlot
Notes: This new corporate entity involves principals who bring together their own individual skills in an arrangement for the common good. The new winery will crush and vinify some of the considerable quantities of fruit now emanating from the Alpine Valleys. Cellar door sales: weekends 10am–7pm.

GLENROWAN AREA

Glenrowan is another area of North East Victoria which may one day become a region in its own right (see the map on p. 137). Certainly its fortified wine styles, as typified by Baileys, are distinctive.

Auldstone NR

Booths Road, Taminick, Vic 3675
Ph 03 5766 2237, Fax 03 5766 2131

Owners: Michael Reid and Nancy Reid
Chief winemaker: Michael Reid
Year of foundation: 1891 as Herceynia; 1987 as Auldstone
Tonnes crushed on average each year: 100, about half of which are used for Auldstone's own labels
Location: Taminick
Area: 20 ha
Soils: deep red granite sandy loams
Varieties planted: White—chardonnay, riesling, traminer; Red—cabernet sauvignon, merlot, muscat a petits grains rouge, shiraz
Leading wines: Auldstone Cabernet, Sparkling Shiraz, Shiraz, Muscat
Notes: The Reids are great enthusiasts for the Taminick area and demonstrated this by spending several years restoring the old Herceynia Winery and its surrounding vineyard. Cellar door sales: Thurs–Sat 9am–5pm, Sun 10am–5pm. Lunch is also available at weekends.

Baileys R10

Cnr Taminick Gap Road and Upper Taminick Road, Glenrowan, Vic 3675
Ph 03 5766 2392, Fax 03 5766 2596

Owner: Mildara Blass Ltd
Chief winemaker: Allen Hart
Year of foundation: 1870
Tonnes crushed on average each year: 650
Location: Taminick

Area: 72 ha (of which 17 are not presently bearing).

Soils: an overall dominance of deep, friable, well-structured, drained and aerated, red sub-plastic clayey soil while on the ridges there is a higher decomposed granite component.

Varieties planted: White—chardonnay, muscadelle; Red—cabernet sauvignon, muscat a petits grains rouge, shiraz, touriga

Leading wines: Baileys Founders Liqueur Muscat, Winemakers Selection Old Liqueur Muscat, 1920 Shiraz, 1904 Shiraz, Phantoms Lake Chardonnay, Cabernet-Shiraz

Notes: This vineyard and winery has a grand old reputation for its Muscat and its 'Hermitage'—a name no longer permissible but certainly unforgettable in the minds of older red wine drinkers. It was a red that needed many years to mature and was occasionally described as 'food, wine and a good cigar'. The years 1920 and 1904 refer to the age of the vineyards and not the respective vintages. The Muscat is also memorable, one of the great treasures of North East Victoria and matched only by a very few of the superb Muscats of Rutherglen. Cellar door sales: 7 days 9am–5pm.

Booths Taminick Cellars NR

Booths Road, Taminick, Vic 3675
Ph 03 5766 2282, Fax 03 5766 2151

Owners: Booth family
Chief winemaker: Peter Booth
Year of foundation: 1904
Tonnes crushed on average each year: 90
Location: Taminick
Area: 16 ha
Soils: granite soils
Varieties planted: White—chardonnay,

trebbiano; Red—cabernet sauvignon, merlot, muscat a petits grains rouge, shiraz

Leading wines: Booths Cabernet-Merlot, Shiraz

Notes: A producer of the traditional 'big' red style of the North East. Cellar door sales: Mon–Sat 9am–5pm, Sun 10am–5pm.

HJT Vineyards NR

Keenan Road, Glenrowan, Vic 3675
Ph 03 5766 2252, Fax 03 5766 3260

Owner: Tinson family
Chief winemaker: Wendy Tinson
Year of foundation: 1979
Tonnes crushed on average each year: 15
Location: Glenrowan
Area: 2 ha
Soils: free-draining red soil, very deep, above an ancient riverbed, containing red spherical aggregate

Varieties planted: White—chardonnay, chenin blanc, riesling; Red—cabernet sauvignon, merlot, pinot noir

Leading wines: HJT Vineyards Chardonnay, Cabernet Sauvignon

Notes: The vineyard is sited on a peninsula surrounded on three sides by Lake Mokoan, which provides both cooling lake air and an advantageous moisture. Ripening in this cool and moist microclimate is somewhat later than other vineyards in the district.

This is the vineyard of the late Harry Tinson— and his retirement occupation when he left Baileys. It has had some marvellous days including a narrow miss for its 1984 Chardonnay in the judging of the Farmer Brothers Trophy at the National Wine Show in 1986. These days it has a lower profile. Cellar door sales: Fri–Sat 10am–5pm. Sundays during school holidays.

❦ From gold to gold

As has been often stated in Australian wine history, the wine followed the mine and, though in Rutherglen's case this situation might just have been the reverse, miners were generally a thirsty lot and usually a purveyor of victuals found his gold much more easily than any digger. It is true that gold was found in the main street of Rutherglen but before, not after, the settlement of the town. Afterwards, the only ones to find it in the streets of Rutherglen were the merchants. The streets were never quite paved with gold and when miners did ultimately tire of mining in one place, the unlucky moved on to the next whispered Eldorado while the more successful settled where they were. Very few places had more than one goldrush though Rutherglen was an exception. After the gold craze of the late 1850s and early 1860s, the region settled down to an agricultural stability, during which successful vineyards were developed.

The wine styles which suited the region were obviously the heavy alcoholic reds and fortifieds that were also in favour in London in the last thirty years of the century. They travelled well—the existing level of alcohol and a little more added for the journey saw to that. So by the late 1880s an export trade was developing, aided by the opening of the railway to Melbourne. Though the local gentry favoured 'Champagne' such as that made by Mr Hans Irvine of Great Western, the less discerning local palates (much to the disgust of Mr Hubert de Castella of the Yarra Valley), later favoured richer, more alcoholic wines, just the kind that Rutherglen was making its speciality. It was about this time that Rutherglen's second goldrush began and also that the region's Muscats and Tokays began to make their mark. In a minute way they still do, for the best of the region's muscats may contain a fraction of the dark green muscaty essence of wine that first made its appearance a century ago. Such wines are unique and if there are degrees of uniqueness—which pedagogues say there most certainly are not—then the Tokays of the region are even more unique, for nowhere else in the world are there similar wines made from muscadelle, a minor Bordeaux white variety. The wines of the same name made in Hungary are superficially similar, but these are not made from muscadelle.

So how are Muscats and Tokays made? The method of making is quite similar, though of course the grape varieties are different. Tokay, as we have seen, is made from muscadelle, a bit-player in the making of Sauternes in the Bordeaux region of France. Muscat is made from muscat a petits grains rouges (the muscat with little red berries). The grapes are picked at their ripest, depending on season. This may be as low as 15° Baume or as high as 20° Baume. By that time they are shrivelled but should not be botrytised. Noble rot is no part of this style. They are fermented for 1–2 days on skins in the normal manner of red wine, but such a fermentation usually reduces the Baume by only 1–2 degrees. The juice, still very sweet, is then run off and the must is pressed. Both free-run and pressings are added together. The wines, very high in natural sugar, are then fortified with a neutral high strength grape spirit to about 18.5% alcohol. The purpose of this is to stabilise what would otherwise be a very unstable liquid and to preserve the sweetness. Having been placed in large old oak vats for about 12 months to clarify, they are then graded and placed in small old oak barrels where they age and evaporate for many years. It is during this period that they gain their complexity, intensity of flavour and lusciousness. They are then examined once more and, for the very best wines, refreshed with younger material before bottling.

Both Muscats and Tokays range in quality and price. The cheapest wines are usually of the youngest average age (about 4–5 years). The most expensive may be a blend of very old wines (average 60+ years) and much younger wines (3–4 years) and therefore average about 30 years. They do not improve in bottle and may, due to relatively high alcohol content, cause their cork to disintegrate if kept too long. They are usually served at room temperature, though younger wines served slightly chilled do have their admirers. After opening they retain their character for several weeks before losing freshness. Companion foods are usually dried fruits and nuts and, in the case of Muscats, rich desserts such as Christmas puddings. Nor should we forget creamy blue cheeses, such as Gippsland Blue, for which an old Muscat can make a perfect partner. As for Tokay, it goes well with such confections as creme caramel.

What are the typical characters of such wines? In colour, Muscats of young average age are pinky red to amber in hue. Older wines are more tawny and verge into olive green on the edges of the glass. In Tokay, its colour varies from gold-amber in young wines to deep brown in aged wines, also with tinges of green on the edges.

Aromatically, young Muscats smell of raisins or muscatels with occasional orange peel overtones, though this must not be confused with the typical botrytis nose. With age their nose becomes very complex with intense muscatel characters and also 'rancio' (a mixture of old wine, spirit, volatility due to years of evaporation, and old oak). Young Tokays, on the other hand, show confectionery aromas, caramel, toffee and the merest hint of muscat (after all, muscadelle is a card-carrying family member). With age these change to 'cold tea' and later to more complex butterscotch and rancio characters.

On palate, a young Muscat is distinctly grapey and fresh with intense flavours that suggest nothing else but muscat. Though a sweet wine, it should finish relatively dry and clean and should not cloy. Its senior colleague, like the mousse of a good old Champagne, hits the tongue with an explosion of flavour. Old raisins, fruit peel, rancio and old spirit all clamour for attention in a luscious liquid that lasts and lasts. In its youth, Tokay has sweet toffee characters. With age, it gains complexity and must, like Muscat, to retain its freshness. Unlike Muscat, it is never quite as complex and, though those butterscotch, cold tea and rancio characters are present, it does not quite have that Muscat intensity, lingering rather than exploding on the palate.

There is another point. Both Muscats and Tokays have excellent 'legs'. Swirl the glass around and watch those viscous streams of old wine trickle treacle-like into the bottom of the glass. And a word of warning—old fortified wines can be very hard on the teeth, pricking into every cavity and playing the very devil with the gums. But don't let this worry you; old Muscats and Tokays are a never-to-be-forgotten experience and these days they are the only gold that you will find on the streets of Rutherglen.

❦ NORTH WEST VICTORIA ZONE

This is an improbable wine zone which, without irrigation, can only be described as arid. It is due to the devotion of the 19th century Chaffey Brothers to irrigation engineering on the Murray River that it exists at all. This zone is centred upon the city of Mildura in the extreme north west of Victoria and further to the south east, Swan Hill. It encompasses the wine regions of Murray–Darling and Swan Hill, each of which cross the Murray into New South Wales. Apart from its irrigation country, this area is a desert, with some wheat grown in the southern parts. It is largely an area producing good to average quality white wine, especially Chardonnay and Semillon.

MURRAY–DARLING REGION

Perhaps that brilliant young nineteenth century lawyer/journalist/politician Alfred Deakin should be credited with the idea of first using irrigation in Australia on a large commercial scale. He had visited California in the 1880s and had viewed for himself the work of two irrigation engineers, George and William Chaffey. He invited them to visit Victoria. On their arrival in Mildura they immediately recognised the suitability of the red plains for irrigation. But the Chaffeys required land and water rights and the Victorian bureaucracy retarded the process of acquiring those rights so much that in frustration they turned to Renmark in neighbouring South Australia and began an irrigation scheme there. Their departure to South Australia proved to be just the spur that the Victorian government required. Within two months the red tape had been cut away and an offer was made to the Chaffeys. After its commencement in 1887, the Mildura scheme rapidly expanded and within a few months about 200 hectares had been cleared for occupation, about 27 kilometres of main irrigation channel established and temporary pumping stations erected. The population had also increased to 270. However, many problems confronted the settlers in getting their produce to the Melbourne market. Carriage of goods by road was slow and perishable produce often suffered in the process. River transport to areas where the produce could be transshipped by rail was often spasmodic due to low or non-existent river heights. It was not until the arrival of the railway in 1903 (when transport times to Melbourne could be reduced from over a week to one day) that the problems were permanently solved.

From the start, horticulture was highly important in the region. Though some wines (chiefly fortified) were made very early in the region's history (from 1891), the emphasis was on dried fruits. Later in the twentieth century, though dried fruits have remained important, this has switched to citrus and multi-purpose grapes. These days wine grapes have become even more important as imported citrus concentrate drives citrus growers away from that industry and there is greater demand for specialised wine grapes.

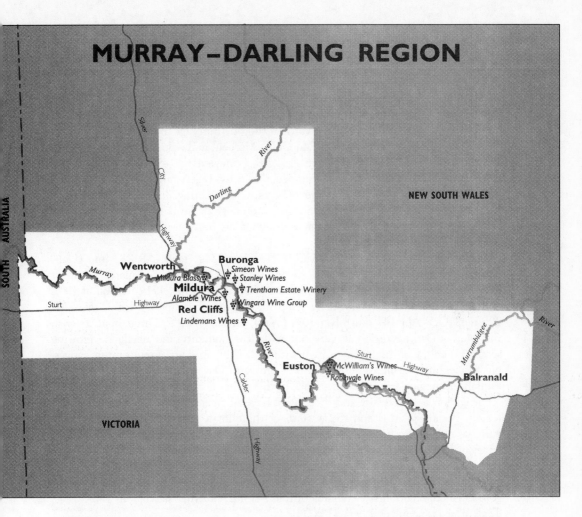

MURRAY–DARLING REGION

The first winery in the region, the Mildura Wine Co at Merbein, was established by W B Chaffey in 1888, its name being changed to Mildara in 1938. McWilliam's followed suit in 1952 at Robinvale, Hungerford Hill Wines began its winery (now owned by BRL Hardy) in 1963 and later Lindemans (now part of Southcorp Wines) erected Karadoc in 1974. Since then six other wineries have come into production in the region. Nine wineries within a region as large as this may not sound too many, but their production is enormous. It can be said that Murray-Darling is the industrial heartland of Australian wine production. In 1996, the region produced 188 650 tonnes of wine grapes, only 14 930 tonnes of which were red.

In wine terms, the region is known as a producer of good average quality Chardonnays, mostly marketed at keen prices, a reputation now supplanting that of producer of softpack white wine. The region is in the process of transformation from an area of multi-purpose grapes for common white wine to one of good to very good (but not outstanding quality) varietal white wine grapes.

Location: Mildura latitude 34°7'S, longitude 142°7'E, about 450 km north-west of Melbourne, is the commercial centre of this large region. It runs in a south easterly direction about 350 km from the South Australian border along the Murray to its junction with the Wakool River in New South Wales, encompassing lands on both the Victorian and New South Wales sides of the River Murray. Other viticultural areas forming part of it are Wentworth, Dareton, Buronga, Balranald and Euston (NSW) and Robinvale, Nangiloc, Red Cliffs, Merbein and Lake Cullulleraine (Vic).

Elevation: (general) 30–100 m above sea-level, (vineyards) 50–85 m.

Topography and soils: On first acquaintance, the region is generally flat and featureless, but subtle differences in height are important in affecting drainage. Occasionally breaking the flatness of the terrain are gentle dune-swale formations. Its soils are the typical pink-brown 'Mallee' type quite common in north-west Victoria. These sit over a limestone and clay subsoil.

Climate: Sunraysia MJT 23.6°C, MAR 13.7, HDD 2244 (raw), AR 283 mm (Oct–March 134 mm), RH 49% (9am), AI 637 mm, SH 9.7 (Dry & Smart). Contrast Gladstones Merbein MJT 23.3°C, MAR na, HDD 2191 (raw), 1719 (cut-off at 19°C and adjusted for latitude and daily temperature range but not for vine sites), AR 275 mm (Oct–Apr 147 mm), RH 30% (3pm), AI na, SH 9.8. Throughout its area, the Murray-Darling region is very hot with low humidity and negligible growing season rainfall. Continentality is high with wide shifts in diurnal temperature ranges, but not enough to make spring frosts a problem. Due to its dry climate and low rainfall, the region has lower incidence of disease than cooler wetter areas.

Irrigation is a necessity and there are a large number of such schemes within the region. Because of this and the warmth of the climate, fairly heavy crops of some varieties are able to be ripened. Such fruit is sought primarily by wineries for bottled wines of lesser price brackets and for current-drinking soft-pack wines.

Harvest time: chardonnay, mid-February, other varieties correspondingly later

Principal grape varieties: (over 3000 tonnes crushed in 1996) White—sultana, muscat gordo blanco, chardonnay, colombard; Red—shiraz, cabernet sauvignon

Total area: (winegrapes 1997) 21 000 ha

Major wine styles: Although Semillon of good quality has been reported from Lake Culluleraine, from the region itself, only Chardonnay can be said to be of interest. Its style is ripe and usually fairly forward and should be drunk within two years of vintage.

Alambie Wines **R6.5**

Campbell Ave, Irymple, Vic 3498
Ph 03 5024 6800, Fax 03 5024 6605

Owner: The Alambie Wine Co Ltd
Chief winemaker: Bob Shields
Year of foundation: 1977
Tonnes crushed on average each year: 4500
for Alambie's own brands
Location: (winery) Irymple. No vineyards are
owned. All grapes are purchased.
Soils: terra rossa over limestone and red loam
over yellow clay
Leading wines: Milburn Park Chardonnay,
Cabernet Sauvignon, Grenache, Salisbury
Chardonnay, Cabernet Sauvignon, Cabernet-
Merlot, Castle Ridge Colombard-Chardonnay,
Shiraz-Malbec-Mourvedre
Notes: This is a medium to large winery by any
other than local standards. Milburn Park is its
most prestigious brand with a gold medal and
trophy for its 1996 Chardonnay at the 1996
Melbourne Wine Show but with a consistent
minor award performance at other major wine
shows. Cellar door sales: Mon–Sat
10am–4.30pm.

Lindemans Wines **R7.5**

Eddy Road, Karadoc, Vic 3496
Ph 03 5024 0303, Fax 03 5024 0204

Owner: Southcorp Wines
Chief winemaker: Phillip John
Year of foundation: 1974
Tonnes crushed on average each year: storage
capacity 85 000 000 litres, crush not disclosed
but estimated to be at least 50 000 tonnes
Location: Karadoc (vineyard and winery), Lake
Culluleraine (vineyard)
Area: 108.1 ha (Karadoc), 200.8 ha (Lake
Culluleraine)
Soils: (Karadoc) red-brown earths over grey
loamy clay. (Lake Culluleraine) sand loam over
clay base with limestone marl
Varieties planted: (Karadoc) White—canada

muscat, chardonnay, riesling, sauvignon blanc,
semillon; Red—muscat a petits grains rouge,
rubired. (Lake Culluleraine) White—
chardonnay, semillon; Red—merlot
Leading wines: Lindemans Bin 65 Chardonnay,
other wines in the Lindemans Bin range,
Cawarra range (all usually South East
Australian wines)
Notes: Karadoc is a catchment for Southcorp
white wines from many sources. Even the use of
the word 'wine' is inappropriate, for not only do
wine and grapes come to Karadoc, but also
musts and juices. Its importance is as a
production and storage centre for chardonnay—
grapes, musts and wines. Other white varieties
such as Lake Culluleraine semillon are also
processed there. What is being phased out is the
very purpose of the winery's original
construction—wine cask production. These days
the emphasis is on Chardonnay, especially for
the production of that world leader—Bin 65.
Apart from this, little more can be said about
Karadoc, except that it is vast.

McWilliam's Wines **NR**

22 Moore Street, Robinvale, Vic 3549
Ph 03 5026 4004, Fax 03 5026 4479

Owner: McWilliam's Wines Pty Ltd
Chief winemaker: Matthew McWilliam
Year of foundation: 1963
Tonnes crushed on average each year: 10 000
Location: Robinvale
Area: no local vineyards owned, all fruit is
purchased from local growers
Leading wines: various McWilliam's fortified
wines
Notes: This is a production facility only with a
winemaking emphasis on fortified wine. Cellar
door sales: 7 days 10am–12 noon, 1pm–5pm.

Mildara Blass **R7**

Wentworth Road, Merbein, Vic 3505
Ph 03 5025 2303, Fax 03 5025 3300

Owner: Mildara Blass Ltd
Chief winemaker: Steve Guy
Year of foundation: 1888
Tonnes crushed on average each year: 10 000
Location: Irymple, Parkers Field (planted
1994–97)
Area: 244 ha consisting of 4 ha (Irymple),
240 ha (Parkers Field)
Soils: red sandy loams over a calcareous base
Varieties planted: (Irymple) White—chardonnay;
Red—none. (Parkers Field) White—chardonnay;
Red—cabernet sauvignon, merlot, petit verdot,
shiraz
Leading wines: Mildara Chardonnay, Church
Hill Chardonnay
Notes: This is the original winery of the Mildura
district founded by W G Chaffey in 1888. Its
chief source vineyard is Parkers Field which
produces in excess of 4000 tonnes of grapes,
mostly chardonnay. Cellar door sales: 7 days
10am–5pm except Christmas Day and Good
Friday.

Robinvale Wines NR

Lot 43b Sealake Road, Robinvale, Vic 3549
Ph 03 5026 3955, Fax 03 5026 1123

Owner: Caracatsonoudis family
Chief winemaker: William Caracatsonoudis
Year of foundation: 1976
Tonnes crushed on average each year: 350
Locations: Robinvale (winery and vineyard) and
Swan Hill (vineyard)
Area: 46.8 ha (Robinvale 36 ha), (Swan Hill
10.8 ha)
Soils: sandy loams over limestone organically
cultivated
Varieties planted: White—chardonnay, chenin
blanc, gordo blanco, sauvignon blanc, sultana;
Red—cabernet franc, cabernet sauvignon,
merlot, ruby cabernet, shiraz, touriga, zinfandel
Leading wines: Robinvale Wines Zinfandel-
Merlot, Chardonnay, Classic Dry White and a
range of non-alcoholic carbonated grape
beverages

Notes: Robinvale Wines is a member of the
Organic Vignerons Association of Australia and
specialises in bio-dynamically grown grapes. It
makes both alcoholic wines and non-alcoholic
beverages and has won many minor awards at
the Swan Hill Show. Cellar door sales:
Mon–Sat 9am–6pm, Sun 1pm–6pm.

Simeon Wines NR

Buronga Hill, NSW 2739
Ph 03 5022 2344, Fax 03 5024 1076

Owner: Simeon Wines Ltd (a publicly listed
company)
Chief winemaker: Brett McKinnon
Year of foundation: 1983 (Orlando), 1994
(Simeon Wines)
Tonnes crushed on average each year: 57 000
and increasing
Location: Buronga (winery)
Leading wines: no wines are sold direct to the
public, only to the trade in bulk
Notes: No vineyards are owned. All grapes are
purchased. This is predominantly a producer of
bulk wines, all of which are sold to the trade
including the winery's former owner, Orlando.

Stanley Wines NR

Silver City Highway, Buronga, NSW 2648
Ph 03 5023 4341, Fax 03 5023 4344

Owner: BRL Hardy Ltd
Chief winemaker: Neil Lindsay
Year of foundation: 1963 (Hungerford Hill),
1984 (Thomas Hardy & Sons)
Tonnes crushed on average each year: 47 000
and increasing
Location: Lake Culluleraine
Area: 180 ha
Soils: sandy loams over limestone
Varieties planted: White—semillon;
Red—cabernet sauvignon, merlot, shiraz
Leading wines: Stanley soft pack wines
Notes: Chiefly engaged in soft pack production
but crushes other quantities of grapes for

bottled wines in the BRL Hardy ranges. Cellar door sales: 10am–4pm weekdays, Sat 10.30am–4pm, Sun 12pm–4pm.

Trentham Estate Winery R7

Sturt Highway, Trentham Cliffs, NSW 2738
Ph 03 5024 8888, Fax 03 5024 8800

Owner: Murphy family
Chief winemaker: Anthony Murphy
Year of foundation: 1909 (first vineyard planted), 1988 (winery)
Tonnes crushed on average each year: 780
Location: Trentham Cliffs
Area: 30 ha
Soils: sandy loams and clay loams over limestone
Varieties planted: White—chardonnay, colombard, gewurztraminer, riesling, sauvignon blanc, taminga; Red—cabernet sauvignon, grenache, merlot, pinot noir, shiraz
Leading wines: Trentham Estate Chardonnay, Merlot, Shiraz
Notes: Certainly one of the leading wineries in this region, produces both reds and whites of consistently good quality. Cellar door sales: weekdays 8.30am–5pm, weekends 9.30am–5pm. Restaurant and barbecue Tues–Sun 11am–3pm.

Wingara Wine Group R7

Kulkyne Way, Red Cliffs, Vic 3496
Ph 03 5029 1666, Fax 03 5024 3316

Owner: Wingara Wine Group Pty Ltd
Chief winemaker: Mark Zeppel
Year of foundation: 1980
Tonnes crushed on average each year: 11 000 for Deakin Estate labels
Location: Red Cliffs
Area: 346 ha
Soils: typical sandy loams often over limestone
Varieties planted: White—chardonnay, colombard, doradillo, gewurztraminer, muscat gordo blanco, riesling, sauvignon blanc, semillon; Red—cabernet sauvignon, merlot, ruby cabernet, shiraz
Leading wines: Deakin Estate Chardonnay, Cabernet Sauvignon
Notes: A large winery by most standards with a high quality and two brands, Deakin Estate and Sunnycliff (export). Since 1987, Deakin Estate has won 10 gold medals and many more minor medals for its wines. There are no cellar door sales, but there is a lake for picnicking.

SWAN HILL REGION

Like much of the rest of Victoria, Swan Hill was first explored by that indefatigable Surveyor General of New South Wales, Major Thomas Mitchell, in 1836. Describing its soil as 'of the richest description . . . and capable of being converted into good wheat land and easily irrigated at any time by the river (Murray)', Mitchell named it Swan Hill after a 'point of ground between the two rivers (Murray and Little Murray)' where there was a 'shallow lagoon' with 'swans and waterfowl so abundant that . . . their noise disturbed us throughout the night'. As predicted by Mitchell, landowners in the Swan Hill area were irrigating their lands as early as the 1880s and the planting of muscats and sultanas for dried fruit production in the Nyah district commenced in 1900. However, early irrigation schemes were often insufficient and unreliable, resulting in the salinity of certain areas and the financial failure of

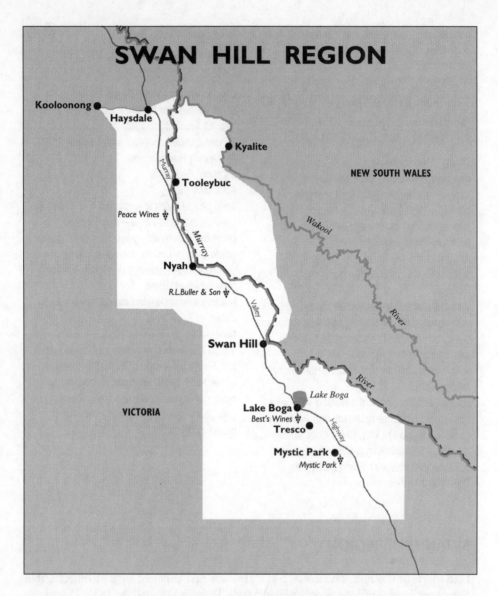

SWAN HILL REGION

Kooloonong

Haysdale

Kyalite

NEW SOUTH WALES

Murray

Tooleybuc

Peace Wines

Murray

Wakool

Nyah

R.L.Buller & Son

Valley

River

Swan Hill

River

VICTORIA

Lake Boga

Lake Boga

Best's Wines

Tresco

Highway

Mystic Park

Mystic Park

some irrigation trusts and private companies formed to subdivide agricultural land and supply water. The region's first winery, St Andrews, was built in 1930 at Tresco by the Thomson family. After the Second World War, many Sicilian immigrants planted wine grapes and stone fruits in the district. In 1951, when many wine areas in Australia were suffering acute economic stress, R L Buller & Son showed its faith in the future of wine and in the region by erecting Swan Hill's second winery at Beverford. There are now three wineries operating in the region and, in addition, Brown Brothers of Milawa with its Mystic Park Estate has established a substantial presence in the region.

Location: latitude 35°20'S, longitude 143°15'E, about 370–400 km north-west of Melbourne and 180 km south-east of Mildura, being partly in Victoria and partly in New South Wales, straddling the Murray River. Its northern boundary is the junction of the Murray and Wakool Rivers.

Elevation: 60–85 m above sea-level

Topography and soils: The region is generally flat. Calcareous earths are quite common throughout. These consist of red-brown loamy sand, sandy loam (Tachera) or loam surface soils above subsoils of sandy clayey loams, associated with the ancient miocene sea-bed and overlying lake, river and wind-borne deposits. These are over 80 m deep. Surface soils are neutral to alkaline; subsoils strongly alkaline. Surface soils are usually permeable, but permeability is restricted in all but the most sandy of subsoils. Rarer soils in the region are sandy earths, hard red duplex and brownish sands.

Climate: MJT 23.6°C, MAR 14.3°C, HDD (raw) 2138, AR 345 mm, RH 52%, AI 497 mm, SH 9.3 (Dry & Smart). Compare Gladstones' MJT 23.4°C, MAR na, HDD (raw) 2181, 1718 (cut off and adjusted for latitude and daily temperature range), AR 345 mm (Oct–Apr 178 mm), RH 29%, AI na, SH 9.7. Mystic Park Mean Temperature Warmest Month 23.5°C (Brown Bros). Though undeniably a hot region, Swan Hill is slightly cooler than Sunraysia and has a higher natural rainfall (345 mm p.a.). Its higher Mean Annual Range (MAR) temperature indicates a longer and slower ripening period. Irrigation is provided by three schemes within the region. Nyah is fed directly from the Murray River through pumps in the Nyah township. Tresco and Woorinen are supplied through the Torumbarry Scheme, which diverts water from the Murray near Echuca and channels it 160 km via a series of canals, creeks, weirs and lakes to its points of use. Other growers within the region obtain water either direct from the Murray River or from Kangaroo Lake. The region has no major climatic problems. Its chief concern is water quality and in particular the degree of salinity occurring during run-off after flooding of upstream rivers or heavy local rain.

Harvest time: late February–mid-March for most wine varieties

Principal grape varieties: White—chardonnay, colombard, riesling and chenin blanc, sultana, muscat gordo blanco; Red—shiraz, cabernet sauvignon, grenache and mataro

Total area: 484 ha and many more of multipurpose varieties such as sultana and muscat gordo blanco

Major wine styles: Shiraz, Chardonnay

Best's Wines Pty Ltd   R6.5

St Andrews, Lake Boga, Vic 3584
Ph 03 5037 2154

Owner: Best's Wines Pty Ltd
Chief winemaker: Viv Thomson
Year of foundation: 1930
Tonnes crushed on average each year: 390
Location: Lake Boga

Area: 29 ha
Soils: light sandy loam over limestone
Varieties planted: White—chardonnay, chenin blanc, colombard, muscadelle, muscat gordo blanco, riesling; Red—cabernet sauvignon, muscat a petits grains rouge, grenache, shiraz
Leading wines: Best's Victoria Chenin Blanc, Best's Victoria Cabernet Sauvignon

Notes: This was the first winery established in the Swan Hill region in 1930. Wines under the Victoria label are either 100% from Swan Hill or blends of Best's Swan Hill and Concongella vineyards (see Grampians).

R L Buller & Son Pty Ltd R6

Murray Valley Highway, Beverford, Vic 3590
Ph 03 5037 6305, Fax 03 5037 6803

Owner: R L Buller & Son Pty Ltd
Chief winemaker: Richard Buller
Year of foundation: 1951
Tonnes crushed on average each year: 1750
Location: Beverford
Area: 24 ha
Soils: sandy loam over limestone
Varieties planted: White—colombard, frontignac, muscat gordo blanco, pedro ximenes, semillon; Red—cabernet sauvignon, grenache, shiraz, touriga
Leading wines: Magee Dry Red, Buller's Beverford Cabernet Sauvignon
Notes: The second oldest winery in the region, specialising in reds. Wines made at Beverford are kept separate from the company's other wines made at Rutherglen. Cellar door sales: Mon–Sat 9am–5pm, Sun and public holidays 10am–4pm.

Mystic Park (vineyard only)

Gorton Drive, Mystic Park, Vic 3581

Owner: Brown Brothers
Year of foundation: 1968
Tonnes produced on average each year: 1000

Location: Mystic Park
Area: 61 ha
Soils: tachera sandy loam to a depth of one metre
Varieties planted: White—chenin blanc, colombard, flora, orange muscat, semillon; Red—cabernet sauvignon, grenache, shiraz, tarrango
Leading wines: Brown Brothers Orange Muscat, Tarrango
Notes: This large vineyard helps to satisfy the fruit needs of Brown Brothers. No local cellar door sales.

Peace Wines R6.5

Murray Valley Highway, Piangal, Vic 3597
Ph 03 5030 5291, Fax 03 5030 5605

Owner: Garacama Pty Ltd
Winemaker: Andrew Peace
Year of foundation: 1980
Tonnes crushed on average each year: 2500
Location of vineyard: Piangal
Area: 58 ha
Soils: sandy loam and river loam over limestone
Varieties planted: White—chardonnay, crouchen, riesling, semillon; Red—cabernet sauvignon, grenache, malbec, mataro, pinot noir, ruby cabernet, shiraz
Leading wines: Ashwood Grove Lady Hamilton Chardonnay, Shiraz, Grenache, Murphy's Block Red
Notes: This winery has a rising chardonnay reputation, based on the high quality of its Lady Hamilton Chardonnay 1995 and the good 1996. Cellar door sales by appointment.

PART II

TASMANIA

❦ Wine in Tasmania

Wine was produced in Tasmania as long ago as 1826, but the vine suffered obvious disadvantages in the island colony. Its extremely cool climate, the lack of skilled labour and viticultural knowledge, and a very small market were factors that greatly discouraged the development of a viable industry. By 1850, viticulture in Tasmania was extinct, and the only subsequent flicker of interest occurred later in the 19th century when an Italian entrepreneur planned to plant grapes on Maria Island, a venture that was ultimately abandoned.

The industry's rebirth occurred during the 1950s and 1960s as a result of persistence by two migrants, the French engineer, Jean Miguet, who planted vines near Launceston and Claudio Alcorso, an Italian, who started plantings further south on the Derwent River just west of Hobart. In 1967, vines appeared once more in the Tamar Valley, when Graham Wiltshire established a vineyard near Legana. By 1974 Dr Andrew Pirie was pioneering the Pipers Brook area.

Since then, bearing in mind its climatic limitations and the consequent restrictions on grape varieties that will ripen fully in that climate, Tasmanian viticulture has expanded quite rapidly. Pinot Noir, Chardonnay and, to a lesser extent, Riesling are some of the varieties that have been particularly successful, but as a rule only locations with a favourably warm and long season (parts of the Tamar Valley and the East Coast) will ripen Cabernet Sauvignon. The result is that Tasmanian Cabernet rarely, if ever, rivals the mainstream styles of Australian Cabernet.

By 30 June 1996, Tasmania could boast of 67 licensed wine producers, 77 individual vineyards and 17 commercial wineries, encompassing an area of 413 ha. The 1995 vintage produced over 2000 tonnes of winegrapes, and in 1996 a slightly lower quantity of 1874 tonnes was produced. As can readily be appreciated from the number of vineyards and the area of plantings, Tasmanian vineyards are not large, having an average area of less than 6 ha. Only 11 vineyards have an area greater than 10 ha and many are struggling to be self-supporting. But, on the whole, it is an enthusiastic and expanding industry with its sights firmly fixed upon quality.

Both as an 'appellation' under the Tasmanian government scheme and as a Geographical Indication, Tasmania is a single wine zone without, as yet, any wine regions or sub-regions. However, I have for convenience and differentiation of areas, divided Tasmania into three wine 'regions', as does, in fact, the Vineyard Association of Tasmania. In the national context, Tasmania will probably never be other than a niche player, its importance lying in the quality of its Chardonnays, Pinots and sparkling wines.

Location: The North East latitude 41°07'S, longitude 147°05'E (Pipers River); latitude 42°05'S, longitude 148°05'E (Swansea–Bicheno). The Tamar Valley and the North West, latitude 41°25'S, longitude 147°10'E (Launceston). The South latitude 42°65'S, longitude 147°30'E (Derwent Valley); latitude 42°60'S, longitude 147°40'E (Coal River); latitude 43°02'S, longitude 147°E (Huon Valley).

Elevation: Pipers Brook, 120 m; Swansea–Bicheno, 25 m; The Tamar Valley, 80 m; Derwent Valley, 60 m; Coal River Valley, 65 m; Huon Valley, 50 m

Topography and soils: Tasmania is, of course, an extension of the Australian mainland, separated only recently in geological time by Bass Strait. Its topography is very similar to south-eastern New South Wales and southern Victoria with quite mountainous terrain in the western and central parts of the island and warmer coastal aspects on its eastern side. Its southerly situation also means that it is constantly exposed to the predominantly southerly and westerly winds of the Roaring Forties. Tasmania also shares many of the soil types of the mainland. Generally, in the north there are deep sandy earths of a reddish colour, while in the south, soils are thinner and sandstone-based.

Climate: *North and east.* Launceston MJT 17.7°C, MAR na, HDD (raw) 1155 and 1281 (cut off and as adjusted for latitude, daily temperature range and vine sites), AR 725 mm (Oct–Apr 348 mm), RH 46% (3pm Jan), AI na, SH 7.6 (Gladstones), Cf MJT 17.2°C, MAR 10.3°C, HDD (raw) 1020, AR 788 mm (Oct–Mar 311 mm), RH 65% (9am Jan), AI 224 mm, SH 7.3 (Dry & Smart). St Helens MJT 16.7°C, MAR na, HDD (raw) 1017 and 1264 (cut off and as adjusted for latitude, daily temperature range and vine sites), AR 782 mm (Oct–Apr 431 mm), RH 59% (3pm Jan), AI na, SH 7.6. *South.* Risdon MJT 16.8°C, MAR na, HDD (raw) 1039 and 1182 (cut off and as adjusted for latitude, daily temperature range and vine sites), AR 596 mm (Oct–Apr 356 mm), RH 51% (3pm Jan), AI na, SH 6.8. Hobart MJT 16.7°C, MAR na, HDD (raw) 1019 and 1158 (cut off and adjusted for latitude, daily temperature range and vine sites), AR 622 mm (Oct–Apr 359 mm), RH 52% (3pm Jan), AI na, SH 6.7. I have mentioned that generally Tasmania is an extremely cool zone. It is interesting to note, however, that most of Tasmania's modern viticultural development took place during the 1980s and that in *Viticulture and Environment* Dr Gladstones quite reasonably postulates Tasmania is becoming warmer.

The question should therefore be asked, is Tasmania's viticulture being reborn during a false dawn? Will the trend continue or be reversed? Whatever the answers may be, Tasmania's future vine sites will continue to need the most careful planning and the present ones all the protection that they can obtain from late spring frosts and high winds.

Harvest time: *North and east.* Pinot noir and chardonnay early to mid-April, cabernet sauvignon late May, riesling slightly earlier. *South.* Pinot noir and chardonnay early April, riesling early May

Principal varieties: White—chardonnay, riesling, sauvignon blanc; Red—pinot noir, cabernet sauvignon

Other varieties: White—gewurztraminer, muller thurgau, pinot gris, semillon. Red—cabernet franc, gamay, merlot meunier, petit verdot, shiraz

Total area as at 1996: 413 ha (322 ha bearing, 91 ha non-bearing)

Major wine styles: Pinot Noir, Chardonnay, Riesling, Sparkling White (Champagne style)

WINERIES WITHOUT VINEYARDS SPECIALISING IN MAKING WINE FROM TASMANIA-WIDE SOURCES

Fishburn and O'Keefe **R7**

16 Pioneer Avenue, New Norfolk,
Tas 7140
Ph 03 6286 1238, Fax 03 6261 4029

Owner: Fishburn and O'Keefe Wines Pty Ltd
Chief winemaker: Greg O'Keefe
Year of foundation: 1991
Tonnes crushed on average each year: 50
Location: no vineyards owned or leased
Area: na
Varieties planted: none, all grapes are
purchased from outside growers
Leading wines: Fishburn and O'Keefe Riesling,
Pinot Noir Brut, Trout (a non-vintage sparkling
white), Trout White (a blended still white),
Chardonnay, Pinot Noir, Cabernet Sauvignon
Notes: Greg O'Keefe makes wine from all over
Tasmania, both as a contract winemaker and
on his company's own behalf. He is especially
keen on Riesling and his Sparkling White styles
are champenised on the premises. His
enthusiasm shows in the wines. No cellar door
sales.

Wellington Wines **R9**

Cnr Richmond and Denholms Roads,
Cambridge, Tas 7170
Ph 03 6248 5844, 03 6243 7320,
Fax 03 6243 0226

Owners: Andrew and Jennifer Hood
Chief winemaker: Andrew Hood
Year of foundation: 1990
Tonnes crushed on average each year: 200
(about 50 for Wellington's own label, the rest
as contract winemaker for about 30 vineyards
throughout Tasmania)
Location: no vineyards owned or leased
Area: na
Varieties planted: na
Leading wines: Wellington Riesling,
Chardonnay, Pinot Noir, Iced Riesling
Notes: Andrew Hood is primarily a contract
winemaker for many small vineyards
throughout Tasmania. In his own right, he
concentrates on fine-fruit styles of Riesling,
Chardonnay and Pinot Noir, which are of
excellent quality. He also makes a freeze-dried
sweeter style of Riesling. Cellar door sales by
appointment.

NORTHERN TASMANIA (TAMAR VALLEY AND PIPERS RIVER)

Brook Eden Vineyard **NR**

Adams Road, Lebrina, Tas 7254
Ph 03 6395 6244

Owners: John and Sheila Bezemer
Chief winemaker: John Bezemer
Year of foundation: 1988 (vineyard), 1993
(winery)
Tonnes crushed on average each year: 8

Location: Lebrina
Area: 2 ha
Soils: Red kraznozems
Varieties planted: White—chardonnay, riesling;
Red—cabernet sauvignon, pinot noir
Leading wines: Brook Eden Vineyard
Chardonnay, Pinot Noir
Notes: A small vineyard and winery that is part

of a larger pastoral property. Cellar door sales: 10am–5pm daily.

Cliffhouse NR

RSD 457 Kayena, Tas 7270
Ph 03 6394 7454, Fax 03 6394 7419

Owners: Geoff and Tracey Hewitt
Chief winemaker: Alain Rousseau (contract)
Year of foundation: 1983
Tonnes crushed on average each year: 40
Location: Kayena, Tamar Valley
Area: 4 ha
Soils: ironstone gravel over clay
Varieties planted: White—chardonnay, riesling; Red—cabernet sauvignon, pinot noir
Leading wines: Cliffhouse Riesling, Pinot Noir
Notes: Geoff Hewitt is dedicated to producing classic, cool area table wines, which, unfortunately, I have not tasted. Cellar door sales by appointment.

Clover Hill R9

Clover Hill Road, Lebrina, Tas 7254
Ph 03 6395 6114, Fax 03 6395 6257

Owner: John Goelet (owner of Taltarni)
Chief winemakers: Shane Clohessy (Taltarni) and Chris Markel (Clos du Val-California)
Year of foundation: 1986
Tonnes produced on average each year: 100
Location: Lebrina, about 10 minutes drive south-west of Pipers Brook and about 20 minutes north-east of Launceston
Area: 20 ha
Soils: volcanic soil of dark red colour tending to be acid
Varieties planted: White—chardonnay; Red—meunier, pinot noir
Leading wine: Clover Hill (a sparkling wine made by the champagne method)
Notes: Only one wine is produced, although Clover Hill fruit does find its way into other non-Tasmanian Taltarni sparkling wines. The grapes are crushed at Clover Hill and undergo

their primary fermentation there. The resultant blended wines are then transported to Taltarni for champenisation and a minimum 30 months maturation on lees. Clover Hill is the archetypal Tasmanian sparkling white, extremely elegant and often tending to acidity when young. With some bottle age it becomes quite creamy and makes a marvellous aperitif style. Cellar door sales: daily 10am–5pm.

Dalrymple Vineyard NR

1337 Pipers Brook Road, Pipers Brook, Tas 7254
Ph/Fax 03 6382 7222

Owners: Bertel and Anne Sundstrup and Jill Mitchell
Chief winemaker: contract under the guidance of Bert Sundstrup
Year of foundation: 1987
Tonnes crushed on average each year: 45, but will increase as new plantings come into bearing
Location: Pipers Brook
Area: 10 ha
Soils: Situated upon rich red basaltic soil on the edge of an extinct volcano crater with a clay subsoil over a high underground water table, the vineyard enjoys a favourable north-east aspect and so maximum sunshine hours are obtained
Varieties planted: White—chardonnay, sauvignon blanc; Red—pinot noir
Leading wines: Dalrymple Vineyard Chardonnay, Sauvignon Blanc, Chardonnay
Notes: Having won trophies from time to time for all three of its wines, Dalrymple hopes to continue its winning ways in its new winery, completed in 1997. Cellar door sales: daily 10am–5pm except Christmas Day.

Delamere **R7**

4238 Flinders Highway, Pipers Brook,
Tas 7254
Ph 03 6382 7190, Fax 03 6382 7250

Owners: Richard and Dallas Richardson
Chief winemaker: Richard Richardson
Year of foundation: 1983
Tonnes crushed on average each year: 20
Location: Pipers Brook
Area: 3 ha
Soils: kraznozem, a deep well-structured, well-drained soil, having good moisture retention and a pH that is neutral to slightly acid
Varieties planted: White—chardonnay; Red—pinot noir
Leading wines: Delamere Pinot Noir, Chardonnay
Notes: Like all the wisest red producers of Pipers Brook, Richard Richardson specialises in pinot noir, producing a fine-boned, fruit driven red. He also makes tiny amounts of chardonnay. Cellar door sales: daily 10am–5pm.

Glenbothy Vineyard **NR**

RSD 175 Glenwood Road, Relbia,
Tas 7258
Ph/Fax 03 6343 0773

Owners: Mike and Philippa Sharman
Chief winemaker: Andrew Hood (contract)
Year of foundation: 1987
Tonnes produced on average each year: 8, but will increase as recent plantings come into production
Location: Relbia (just south of Launceston)
Area: 3.2 ha
Soils: shallow sandy loam overlying neutral to alkaline clay, which reduces the vigour of the vines, but with a good aspect. Plantings are closely spaced with vertical shoot positioning. New plantings will employ the Smart-Dyson pruning system.
Varieties planted: White—chardonnay, riesling, sauvignon blanc, schonburger; Red—cabernet sauvignon, pinot noir
Leading wines: Glenbothy Vineyard Chardonnay, Pinot Noir, Riesling
Notes: Cellar door sales by appointment only.

Grey Sands **NR**

Glengarry, Tas 7275

Owners: Robert and Rita Richter
Chief winemaker: none yet
Year of foundation: 1989
Tonnes produced on average each year: 3.5 (in 1997), but will increase as the vineyard comes into full bearing
Location: Glengarry, in the Supply River Valley (a tributary of the Tamar)
Area: 2 ha
Soils: Robert Richter, a graduate of Roseworthy, has endeavoured to match variety to soil-type. Thus the pinot gris is planted on silty grey loam over hardpan and clay, the merlot on heavy brown clay over mudstone and the pinot noir on a lighter brown clay soil interspersed with pebbly rocks.
Varieties planted: White—pinot gris; Red—merlot, pinot noir
Leading wines: none yet
Notes: The Richters have taken things slowly and carefully so far, but their intelligent approach in matching variety and soil should prove beneficial. Hopefully, wine production should commence in 1998. No cellar door sales.

Heemskerk Wine Group

See the following Tasmanian entries—Heemskerk, Kayena, Loira and Rochecombe

Notes: All wines of the group are usually blended and there are no single, 'estate-grown' wines. Accordingly a rating is only given to Heemskerk.

Heemskerk R8

Pipers Brook Road, Pipers Brook,
Tas 7254
Ph 03 6382 7133, Fax 03 6382 7242

Owner: Pipers Brook Vineyard Ltd
Chief winemaker of the Group: Dr Andrew Pirie
Year of foundation: 1976
Tonnes crushed on average each year: the vineyard is being redeveloped, but it is estimated that the 1998 vintage will be about 220 tonnes
Location: Pipers Brook
Area: 42 ha
Soils: red kraznozems
Varieties planted: White—chardonnay, pinot gris, riesling; Red—meunier, pinot noir
Leading wines: Jansz (sparkling—until April 1998), Heemskerk Chardonnay, Pinot Noir
Notes: Purchased in early 1998, Heemskerk (one of the pioneers of grapegrowing in the area along with Pipers Brook), is now part of Pipers Brook Vineyard Ltd, which is rapidly expanding its winemaking activities. The rather austere Jansz sparkling white made from the classic Champagne varieties, chardonnay, pinot noir and meunier, is Heemskerk's flagship. (The Jansz brand was sold to Yalumba in April 1998. Presumably Yalumba will continue to obtain fruit from existing sources in Tasmania.) Cellar door sales: 7 days 10am–5pm.

Holm Oak Vineyards R7

Rowella, Tas 7270
Ph 03 6394 7577, Fax 03 6394 7350

Owners: Nicholas and Cynthia Butler
Chief winemaker: Nicholas Butler
Year of foundation: 1983
Tonnes crushed on average each year: 42
Location: Rowella (Tamar Valley)
Area: 6.2 ha
Soils: alluvial soils over gravelly, ironstone clays
Varieties planted: White—riesling;

Red—cabernet franc, cabernet sauvignon, merlot, pinot noir
Leading wines: Holm Oak Pinot Noir, Cabernet Sauvignon (a blend of the 'Bordeaux' varieties), Pinot Noir-Chardonnay (a still pink wine), Riesling
Notes: Now one of the Tamar Valley's older vineyards, Holm Oak is located in a very favourable position for ripening cabernet sauvignon. Its fuller-style Cabernet is of very good quality and helps keep the 'Bordeaux' flag flying in this very cool state. Cellar door sales: daily 10am–5pm.

Ironpot Bay NR

Rowella Vineyard
West Bay Road, Rowella, Tas 7250
Ph 03 6394 7320, Fax 03 6394 7346

Owner: Rod Cuthbert
Chief winemaker: Andrew Hood (contract)
Year of foundation: 1988
Tonnes crushed on average each year: 35
Location: Deviot (Tamar Valley)
Area: 4.1 ha
Soils: loam over clay
Varieties planted: White—chardonnay, gewurztraminer, pinot gris, sauvignon blanc, semillon; no red
Leading wines: Ironpot Bay Chardonnay, Semillon-Sauvignon Blanc, Pinot Grigio
Notes: Ironpot Bay specialises in unwooded whites and has won many awards for such wines. Cellar door sales by appointment.

Kayena Vineyard (vineyard only)

Kayena, Tas 7270

Owner: JAC Group (Mr Joseph Chromy)
Year of foundation: 1994
Tonnes produced on average each year: The vineyard is not yet mature and is also subject to redevelopment. The estimated 1998 vintage is 48 tonnes.
Location: Kayena (Tamar Valley)

Area: 21 ha
Soils: grey, sandy clayey loam to sandy loam
Varieties planted: White—chardonnay, pinot gris, riesling, sauvignon blanc; Red—cabernet sauvignon, merlot, pinot noir
Leading wines: no wines are made under this label
Notes: No cellar door sales.

Lake Barrington Estate NR

Kentish Park, West Kentish, Tas 7306
Ph 03 6491 1249, Fax 03 6334 2892

Owner: Maree Taylor
Chief winemakers: Andrew Hood (still wines), Steve Lubiana (sparkling) (contract)
Year of foundation: 1986
Tonnes crushed on average each year: 8
Location: West Kentish
Area: 4 ha (2 ha of which are non-bearing)
Soils: red clay
Varieties planted: White—chardonnay, riesling; Red—cabernet sauvignon, pinot noir
Leading wines: Lake Barrington Chardonnay, Pinot Noir, Alexandra (sparkling) and in exceptional years, Riesling and Cabernet Sauvignon
Notes: Alexandra has won a trophy as Tasmania's Best Sparkling Wine for its 1993 and 1994 vintages at the Tasmanian Wine Show. In addition there have been bronze medals for the Chardonnay and Pinot Noir at the same show. The vineyard adjoins Lake Barrington and has a superb view. Cellar door sales: weekends and public holidays 10am–5pm.

Lalla Gully NR

Brooks Road, Lalla, Tas 7267
Ph 03 6331 2325, Fax 03 6331 7948

Owners: Rod Ascui and Kim Seagram
Chief winemakers: Kim Seagram and Andrew Hood (contract)
Year of foundation: 1988

Tonnes crushed on average each year: 25
Location: Lalla (southern end of Pipers River area)
Area: 3 ha
Soils: a thin layer of dark loam over mudstone, well-drained and not very vigorous
Varieties planted: White—chardonnay, sauvignon blanc; Red—pinot noir
Leading wines: Lalla Gully Pinot Noir, Sauvignon Blanc
Notes: An excellent site for sauvignon blanc, as vintages 1995 and 1996 have shown. Cellar door sales at Ripples (restaurant), Launceston, 7 days. Vineyard visits by appointment only.

Loira (vineyard only)

Sidmouth, Tas 7270

Owner: Pipers Brook Vineyard Ltd
Chief winemaker: Andrew Pirie
Year of foundation: 1986
Tonnes produced on average each year: estimated at 57 tonnes for 1998 vintage
Location: Sidmouth (Tamar Valley)
Area: 9 ha
Soils: grey sandy loam over sandy clay
Varieties planted: White—chardonnay, pinot gris, riesling, sauvignon blanc; Red—cabernet sauvignon, pinot noir
Leading wines: none are produced under this label
Notes: This was formerly the Buchanan vineyard, owned by Don Buchanan, who is now chief winemaker at Arrowfield in the Hunter Valley. There are no cellar door sales.

Marion's Vineyard R8

Foreshore Drive, Deviot, Tas 7275
Ph/Fax 03 6394 7434

Owners: Mark and Marion Semmens
Chief winemaker: Marion Semmens
Year of foundation: 1980
Tonnes crushed on average each year: 40
Location: Deviot (Tamar Valley)

Area: 11 ha
Soils: doleritic and ironstone gravel. As Mark Semmens says, 'a lot of rock!'.
Varieties planted: White—chardonnay, gewurztraminer, muller-thurgau, pinot gris; Red—cabernet sauvignon, cascade (labrusca cross), pinot noir, zinfandel
Leading wines: Marion's Vineyard Cabernet Sauvignon
Notes: Tipperary is a long way, but so too is Tasmania if you come from California, as Mark and Marian Semmens did. Arriving initially as tourists, they were entranced by the Tamar and decided to return permanently to a 30-acre rocky, bush block above the river. Nearly two decades later, they can point to an 11-hectare vineyard and winery as their own piece of Tasmania, 'a very protected macropocket', which ripens cabernet sauvignon, as Mark points out, 'even in bad years'. The Cabernet Sauvignon is good and so is the Pinot Noir, but the only 'cascade' I've tasted is the more usual amber liquid, which Mark and Marion do not make. Cellar door sales: daily 10am–5pm. There is also a restaurant.

Notley Gorge NR

Loop Road, Glengarry, Tas 7275
Ph 03 6396 1166, Fax 03 6396 1200

Owner: Dr M Beamish
Chief winemaker: Andrew Hood (contract)
Year of foundation: 1982
Tonnes crushed on average each year: 50, of which about 35 are used for Notley Gorge's own labels
Location: Glengarry, about 6 km west of Exeter
Area: 8 ha
Soils: duplex soils over a clay base
Varieties planted: White—chardonnay, sauvignon blanc; Red—cabernet sauvignon, merlot, pinot noir
Leading wines: Notley Gorge Pinot Noir
Notes: The present Notley Gorge estate is an amalgamation of the former Notley Gorge and Glengarry vineyards. It sprang to prominence with a top gold for Pinot Noir at the Royal Melbourne Wine Show, an award that can but underscore Tasmania's reputation as a producer of fine Pinot Noir and Andrew Hood as one of its leading makers. Cellar door sales: by appointment.

Peacock NR

Rowella Road, Rowella, Tas 7250
(vineyard only)

Owner: Fred Peacock
Chief winemaker: Steve Lubiana (contract)
Year of foundation: 1991
Tonnes crushed on average each year: 15, but will increase as the vineyard comes to maturity
Location: Rowella (Tamar Valley)
Area: 4 ha
Soils: grey silt clay loam, mudstone derived and drip irrigated
Varieties planted: White—chardonnay; Red—cabernet sauvignon, pinot noir
Leading wines: see Bream Creek entry
Notes: This vineyard is not yet individually named and has only just come into bearing. Presently all fruit is vinified as Bream Creek. When yields increase, this vineyard and its wines may assume their own personalities and labels. No cellar door sales.

Pipers Brook R9.5

3959 Bridport Highway, Pipers Brook via Lebrina, Tas 7254
Ph 03 6382 7197, Fax 03 6382 7226

Owner: Pipers Brook Vineyard Ltd
Chief winemaker: Dr Andrew Pirie
Year of foundation: 1974
Tonnes crushed on average each year: 500
Location: There are seven vineyards, three at Pipers Brook, two at Pipers River, two at Rosevears in the Tamar Valley, and now also Heemskerk.

Area: 82 ha planted and 65 ha in bearing in 1997
Soils: kraznozems (deep friable tertiary basaltic soils)
Varieties planted: White—chardonnay, gewurztraminer, pinot gris, riesling, sauvignon blanc, semillon; Red—cabernet franc, cabernet sauvignon, merlot, pinot noir
Leading wines: Pipers Brook Vineyard Pellion (premium Pinot Noir), Summit Chardonnay, Opimian (a Cabernet-Merlot blend), Riesling, Pinot Gris
Notes: Pipers Brook Vineyard began its life in 1974, after its founder, Dr Andrew Pirie, had completed a massive study of cool-area sites in south eastern Australia. In 1989, the company's capital base was expanded and it became an unlisted public company. Though Pipers Brook Vineyard cannot claim to be the founder of modern Tasmanian viticulture, it was certainly the first Tasmanian wine company to operate nationally. Its standards of quality are very high, with its Pinot Noir and Chardonnay being particularly noteworthy. Ninth Island (its second label) is also very well known in mainland Australia. In early 1998, it purchased the Heemskerk, Loira and Rochecombe vineyards and wineries from Mr Joseph Chromy's JAC Group. Cellar door sales at Pipers Brook Winery: Mon–Fri 10am–5pm year long, weekends 11am–5pm (Nov 1 to April 30 only). The restaurant is open for lunch December 1 to Easter. Cellar Door Sales at Strathlynn, Rosevears Drive, Rosevears Ph 03 6330 2388; open daily 10am–5pm except Christmas Day. Restaurant open for lunch 12 noon–3pm each day except Christmas Day.

Powercourt Vineyard NR

Upper McEwans Road, Legana, Tas 7277
Ph 03 6330 1225, Fax 03 6330 2161

Owner/chief winemaker: Ralph Power
Year of foundation: 1972

Tonnes crushed on average each year: 12
Location: Legana (Tamar Valley)
Area: 2.5 ha
Soils: a sloping vineyard of doleritic soil on a yellow clay subsoil with a north-east aspect
Varieties planted: White—none; Red—cabernet sauvignon, pinot noir
Leading wines: Elmslie Cabernet Sauvignon, Pinot Noir
Notes: Ralph Power uses Elmslie (once the name of the property) as a label for his wines. Cellar door sales: by mail order or by appointment.

Providence Vineyards NR

236 Lalla Road, Lalla, Tas 7267
Ph 03 6395 1290, Fax 03 6395 2088

Owner: Stuart Bryce
Chief winemaker: Andrew Hood (contract)
Year of foundation: 1956
Location: Lalla
Area: 3 ha
Soils: A heavy clay doleritic loam. The older vines are trellised on vertical screens, one metre apart with rows 1.5 metres apart; the younger vines are trained to Carbonneau Open Lyre, 1 metre apart with 3.5 metres between rows. The vineyard is drip irrigated.
Varieties planted: White—chardonnay, riesling, semillon; Red—pinot noir
Leading wines: Providence Chardonnay (lightly wooded), Pinot Noir
Notes: During the late 1980s and early 1990s, when the French became unusually litigious in efforts to protect the fair name of their wines, any non-French wine using a word that even remotely suggested a region of France was pounced upon and held up as an example of 'passing-off'. One such word was 'La Provence', the name of Tasmania's first modern-day vineyard, founded in 1956 by a French migrant, Jean Miguet. Miguet, a pioneer in an Anglo-Celtic society more accustomed to sheep than wine, established a

one hectare vineyard and produced wine for several years. He sold his vineyard in 1975 and returned to France, dying there soon afterwards. In 1980, Stuart Bryce purchased the property and continued to trade under the name La Provence. In 1994 he became the target of litigation by the French, but fortunately persisted in his defence against what proved to be an unsuccessful action. However, in 1996, as a precaution against any future legal action, for Stuart Bryce is a vigneron and not a professional litigant, he changed his vineyard's name to Providence Vineyards. Stuart's wines regularly win bronze medals at local shows. Cellar door sales: 7 days 10am–5pm. The cellar door also caters for other small growers who have limited cellar door operations or none at all. Currently these are: Lalla Gully, Springvale, Winstead, Lake Barrington, Ironpot Bay and Rotherhythe.

Rochecombe R7

40 Baxters Road, Pipers River, Tas 7252
Ph 03 6382 7122, Fax 03 6382 7231

Owner: Pipers Brook Vineyard Ltd
Chief winemaker: Dr Andrew Pirie
Year of foundation: 1983
Tonnes crushed on average each year: the vineyard is subject to redevelopment, but produced about 160 tonnes in the 1998 vintage.
Location: Pipers River
Area: 25 ha
Soils: red kraznozems
Varieties planted: White—chardonnay, pinot gris, riesling, sauvignon blanc; Red—cabernet franc, cabernet sauvignon, merlot, pinot noir
Leading wines: Rochecombe Pinot Noir, Riesling, Rochecombe RV (a sparkling wine)
Notes: Originally owned by a Swiss family who sold in 1994 to the JAC Group, which in turn sold to Pipers Brook in 1998, Rochecombe seems to have overcome the great difficulties with frost that it experienced in its earlier

years. As well as the wines mentioned, from time to time an excellent Sauvignon Blanc is made. Cellar door sales: 7 days 10am–5pm,. There is also a restaurant.

Rotherhythe Vineyard R8

Henderson's Lane, Gravelly Beach,
Tas 7276
Ph 03 6294 4869

Owner: John Ferguson Vincent
Chief winemaker: Greg O'Keefe (contract)
Year of foundation: 1986
Tonnes crushed on average each year: 30, about half of which is used for Rotherhythe's labels
Location: West Tamar
Area: 4 ha
Soils: reddish loams and gravelly loams
Varieties planted: White—chardonnay; Red—cabernet sauvignon, merlot, pinot noir
Leading wines: Rotherhythe Chardonnay, Pinot Noir, Cabernet Sauvignon
Notes: Rotherhythe has changed hands recently, but the winemaking, which saw tremendous success in recent Tasmanian Wine Shows, remains constant. The Cabernet Sauvignon is particularly good. No cellar door sales.

Sterling Heights Vineyard NR

Faulkners Road, Winkleigh, Tas 7275
Ph/Fax 03 6396 3214

Owners: Geoff and Jenny Wells
Chief winemaker: Alain Rousseau (contract)
Year of foundation: 1988
Tonnes produced on average each year: 10, of which half is used for the Sterling Heights label
Location: Winkleigh, in the sub-district locally referred to as Glengarry
Area: 1.5 ha
Soils: grey sandy loam over varying subsoils with an east-north-east aspect
Varieties planted: White—chardonnay, riesling;

Red—cabernet franc, meunier, pinot noir
Leading wines: Sterling Heights Pinot Noir
Notes: For Geoff Wells, Sterling Heights Pinot
Noir has been a consistent performer at wine
shows, winning a gold medal for the 1993
vintage and several bronze awards for the
1994 vintage. Cellar door sales by appointment
only.

St Matthias **NR**

Rosevears Drive, West Tamar, Tas 7277
Ph 03 6330 1700, Fax 03 6330 1975

Owner: a syndicate of Hobart businessmen
with Tim Goddard as Chief Executive
Chief winemaker: Alain Rousseau
Year of foundation: 1982
Tonnes produced on average each year: 82

Location: West Tamar (Tamar Valley)
Area: 9 ha
Soils: The vineyard has reddish-brown clayey
loams intermixed with ironstone and is
well-sited above the Tamar with a warm
north-east aspect.
Varieties planted: White—chardonnay,
gewurztraminer, riesling; Red—cabernet
sauvignon, merlot, pinot noir
Leading wines: Moorilla Chardonnay, Cabernet
Sauvignon, St Matthias Chardonnay
Notes: St Matthias is the home of Moorilla's
trophy-winning Chardonnay, always a 'must'
for Chardonnay enthusiasts. Its excellent
Cabernet Sauvignon is also well-known in
Tasmania. Cellar door sales: daily
10am–5pm.

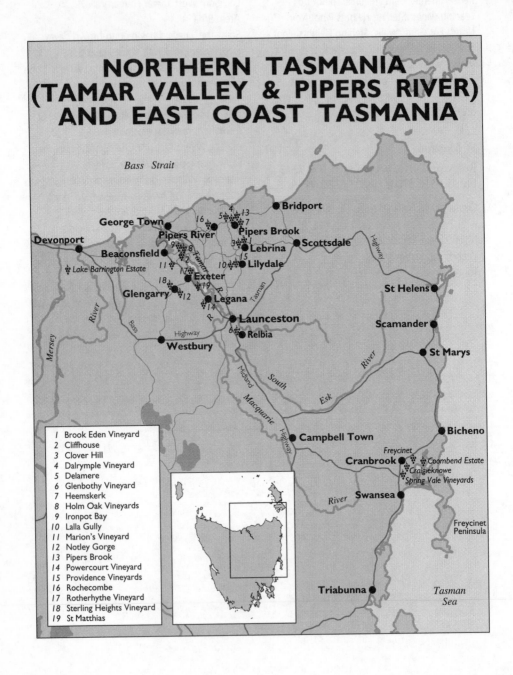

NORTHERN TASMANIA
(TAMAR VALLEY & PIPERS RIVER)
AND EAST COAST TASMANIA

Bass Strait

Bridport

George Town

Pipers River
Pipers Brook

Devonport

Beaconsfield
Lebrina
Scottsdale

Lake Barrington Estate
Lilydale

Exeter

Glengarry
Legana

St Helens

Launceston
Scamander

Relbia
Westbury
St Marys

Bicheno

Campbell Town
Freycinet
Cranbrook
Coombend Estate
Craigieknowe
Spring Vale Vineyards

Swansea

Freycinet
Peninsula

Triabunna
Tasman
Sea

1	Brook Eden Vineyard
2	Cliffhouse
3	Clover Hill
4	Dalrymple Vineyard
5	Delamere
6	Glenbothy Vineyard
7	Heemskerk
8	Holm Oak Vineyards
9	Ironpot Bay
10	Lalla Gully
11	Marion's Vineyard
12	Notley Gorge
13	Pipers Brook
14	Powercourt Vineyard
15	Providence Vineyards
16	Rochecombe
17	Rotherhythe Vineyard
18	Sterling Heights Vineyard
19	St Matthias

EAST COAST TASMANIA

Apsley Gorge Vineyard **NR**

Rosedale Road, Bicheno, Tas 7215
Ph 03 6375 1221, Fax 03 6375 1589

Owners: Brian Franklin and Greg and Maureen Walch
Chief winemaker: Andrew Hood (contract)
Year of foundation: 1988
Tonnes crushed on average each year: 18, but will increase as recently planted vines come into bearing
Location: Bicheno
Area: 6 ha
Soils: heavy clay over broken sandstone
Varieties planted: White—chardonnay; Red—cabernet franc, cabernet sauvignon, merlot, pinot noir
Leading wines: Apsley Gorge Chardonnay, Pinot Noir
Notes: A small vineyard with very positive show results, proving once again how suitable this area of east coast Tasmania is for pinot noir and chardonnay. As the vines have aged there has been a steady rise to excellence. The 1993 vintage received bronzes, 94 silvers, 95 golds and one trophy at the 1995 Royal Hobart Show. The 1996 Chardonnay also won gold at the Tasmanian Wine Show. It is quite evident that the climate is the secret here. The vineyard has been established in a north-east facing valley almost at the entrance to the Apsley Gorge National Park. Vintage is extremely late, picking sometimes not being completed until early June. Cellar door sales are from The Gulch, a tourist facility at Bicheno. Vineyard visits are by appointment.

Coombend Estate **NR**

Swansea, Tas 7190
Ph 03 6257 8256, Fax 03 6257 8484

Owners: AJ and JL Fenn-Smith
Chief winemaker: Andrew Hood (contract)

Year of foundation: 1986
Tonnes produced on average each year: 12
Location: Swansea
Area: 3.25 ha
Soils: This vineyard is adjacent to Freycinet, but its soils are slightly different—brownish on a clay base with a good northerly aspect and excellent drainage
Varieties planted: White—riesling, sauvignon blanc; Red—cabernet sauvignon
Leading wines: Coombend Cabernet Sauvignon
Notes: Coombend Estate vineyard is part of a much larger pastoral property. It has gained a good reputation for its Cabernet Sauvignon, being located in one of the few Tasmanian areas that do in fact suit that late-ripening variety. Farm cottage accommodation is available on the property and cellar door sales are daily from 9am–6pm and by mail order.

Craigie Knowe **R7**

80 Glen Gala Road, Cranbrook, Tas 7190
Ph 03 6259 8252, Fax 03 6223 5009

Owner/chief winemaker: John Austwick
Year of foundation: 1979
Tonnes crushed on average each year: 5, but will increase as new plantings come into bearing
Location: Cranbrook, between Swansea and Bicheno
Area: 5.1 ha (most not yet bearing)
Soils: friable red loams over dolerite (Kraznozems), as John Austwick says 'great for vegetables and grapes'
Varieties planted: White—riesling; Red—cabernet franc, cabernet sauvignon, merlot, petit verdot, pinot noir
Leading wines: Craigie Knowe Cabernet (a blend of the 'Bordeaux' varieties mentioned above)
Notes: The east coast (together with the more

sun-endowed areas of the Tamar Valley) is one of the rare spots in Tasmania that seems capable of ripening cabernet sauvignon and perhaps even later varieties like petit verdot. John Austwick is a self-confessed 'Bordeaux' man and accordingly very patient in a Tasmanian climate that often makes life very difficult for 'Bordeaux' cultivars. His Cabernet, like that of near neighbour, Geoff Bull of Freycinet, is long and full-flavoured. Cellar door sales: weekends or by appointment.

Freycinet R10

Tasman Highway, Bicheno, Tas 7215
Ph 03 6257 8574, 03 6257 8384,
Fax 03 6257 8454

Owners: Geoff and Susan Bull
Chief winemakers: Claudio Radenti
Year of foundation: 1980
Tonnes crushed on average each year: 50, but production will increase to 100 by 2000 as newly planted vineyards come into production
Location: Bicheno (18 km south)
Area: 9 ha
Soils: rocky podsolic loam over a well-drained clay subsoil
Varieties planted: White—chardonnay, muller thurgau, riesling; Red—cabernet sauvignon, merlot, pinot noir
Leading wines: Freycinet Pinot Noir, Chardonnay, Cabernet Sauvignon
Notes: Freycinet is one of the great success stories of Tasmanian viticulture, proving in that zone that climate and exposure are critical in the ripening of quality grapes. Freycinet is situated in a natural amphitheatre, which faces north, being open to the mildest of Tasmanian east coast weather. It is sheltered from cold southerly and westerly winds, and is also in a rain shadow, which means that supplementary irrigation is often necessary during the growing

season. Its Pinot Noir is powerful and concentrated, and its Cabernet Sauvignon is arguably the 'biggest' in Tasmania, with little of the leafy, capsicum-like 'green' attributes of leaner Cabernets. Its Chardonnay also is excellent. The pity of it is that production is so limited, but hopefully this is about to change. Soon there will also be a premium sparkling wine. Cellar door sales: August–May, weekdays 9am–5pm, weekends 10am–5pm. June–July, open weekdays only 9am–4.30pm.

Spring Vale Vineyards NR

Cranbrook, Tas 7190
Ph 03 6257 8208, Fax 03 6257 8598

Owners: Rodney and Lyn Lyne
Chief winemaker: Andrew Hood (contract)
Year of foundation: 1986
Tonnes crushed on average each year: 15, but increasing to 35 by 1999
Location: Cranbrook
Area: 4 ha (only 3 ha bearing in 1998)
Soils: a rich, red-brown loam over porous clay with a tendency to promote excessive vigour in the vines. Its fertility is controlled by trellising and strict attention to bud numbers.
Varieties planted: White—chardonnay, gewurztraminer, pinot gris; Red—pinot noir
Leading wines: Spring Vale Pinot Noir, Chardonnay
Notes: Spring Vale, part of a much larger pastoral property owned by the Lyne family since 1875, is another of those fortunate vineyards that share the marvellous viticultural climate of Tasmania's east coast. Like its neighbours Apsley Gorge, Freycinet and Coombend, Spring Vale has built an excellent reputation for rich and full-flavoured Pinot Noir. Cellar door sales: weekends, school and public holidays 10am–5pm or by prior appointment.

SOUTHERN TASMANIA

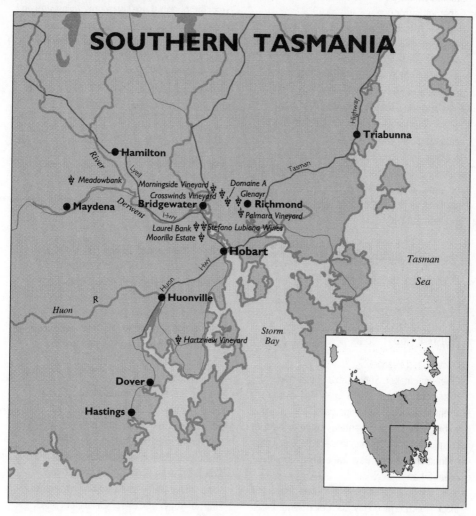

Domaine A

 R8

Tea Tree Road, Campania, Tas 7026
Ph 03 6260 4174, Fax 03 6260 4390

Owners: Ruth and H Peter Althaus
Chief winemaker: H Peter Althaus
Year of foundation: 1973
Tonnes crushed on average each year: 80
Location: Campania (Coal Valley)
Area: 10 ha
Soils: still often called Stoney Vineyard (the

name is used as a label for its more current
drinking wines), the soils are, as the former
vineyard name suggests, quite stony with a
thin layer of black clay over strongly weathered
dolerite and sandstone. They are also quite
well-drained

Varieties planted: White—sauvignon blanc;
Red—cabernet franc, cabernet sauvignon,
merlot, petit verdot, pinot noir

Leading wines: Domaine A Pinot Noir, Cabernet Sauvignon

Notes: H Peter Althaus uses two labels, Domaine A for wines of quality that should be cellared, and Stoney Vineyard for wines of good quality that are current drinking or to be drunk within two years. Together with the east coast and the Tamar Valley, the Coal River Valley is another Tasmanian site that in good years can ripen cabernet sauvignon satisfactorily. Indeed Domaine A makes award winning Cabernet Sauvignons, sometimes with the addition of a little cabernet franc, merlot and petit verdot. Cellar door sales by appointment only.

Bream Creek Vineyard NR

Marion Bay Road, Bream Creek, Tas 7175
Postal address (sales) GPO box 2020
Hobart Tas 7001
Ph/Fax 03 6231 4646

Owner: Fred Peacock
Chief winemaker: Steve Lubiana (contract)
Year of foundation: 1973
Tonnes crushed on average each year: 35, but will increase as new plantings come to maturity
Location: Bream Creek (close to the east coast overlooking Marion Bay due east of Hobart)
Area: 6 ha
Soils: brown basaltic clay loam over basalt and black self-mulching clay loam of dolerite base, drip-irrigated
Varieties planted: White—chardonnay, riesling, traminer; Red—cabernet sauvignon, pinot noir
Leading wines: Bream Creek Riesling, Pinot Noir
Notes: Except for fairly recent plantings of chardonnay, pinot noir and traminer, the first crops of which were picked in 1995, Bream Creek is a mature vineyard and by Tasmanian standards quite old. For many years it supplied fruit to Moorilla Estate, but this arrangement ceased in 1990. Due chiefly to adverse winds,

it has had its share of difficulties over the years, although these seem now to have been overcome. Since 1992, it has retained all fruit for the Bream Creek label. Chardonnay and Pinot Noir, both consistent bronze medallists are the highlight wines. No cellar door sales. Visits by appointment only. For sales write to the above post office box number.

Crosswinds Vineyard NR

Tea Tree, Tas 7017
Ph/Fax 03 6265 1091

Owner: Andrew and Rose-Marie Vasiljuk and Dr Fergus Mitchell
Chief winemaker: Andrew Vasiljuk
Year of foundation: 1990
Tonnes crushed on average each year: 20
Locations: Tea Tree and Brookfield (20 km south of Hobart)
Area: 3 ha (1 ha Tea Tree, 2 ha Brookfield)
Soils: *Tea Tree* shallow clay loam over dolerite; *Brookfield* deep red loam on a river flat
Varieties planted: White—chardonnay; Red—pinot noir
Leading wines: Crosswinds Pinot Noir
Notes: Another Tasmanian vineyard yet again pointing out that pinot noir is eminently suitable to most Tasmanian areas. Both the 1995 and 1996 vintages of Crosswinds Pinot Noir have been successful at recent wine shows. The 1996 won a trophy for the best Pinot of show at Cowra. Cellar door sales: 7 days 10am–5pm.

Elsewhere Vineyard NR

40 Dillons Hill Road, Glaziers Bay, Tas 7109
Ph/Fax 03 6295 1509

Owners: Eric and Jette Phillips
Chief winemakers: Andrew Hood (still wines) and Steve Lubiana (sparkling wines)
Year of foundation: 1984
Tonnes crushed on average each year: 40

Location: Glaziers Bay (the estuary of the Huon River), about 65 km south of Hobart
Area: 9 ha
Soils: light sandy loam, a clay subsoil over limestone and granite
Varieties planted: White—chardonnay, riesling; Red—pinot noir
Leading wines: Elsewhere Vineyard Pinot Noir (a still red), Methode Champenoise
Notes: Located in a very cool area, the amusingly named Elsewhere Vineyard is yet another Tasmanian estate with a great reputation for its Pinot Noir, surely the only red varietal that is totally suited to Tasmania. No cellar door sales.

Geebin Vineyard (formerly Milnathort) NR

3729 Channel Highway, Birches Bay, Tas 7162
Ph 03 6267 4750, Fax 03 6267 4601

Owners: Ken and Barbara Jones
Chief winemaker: Andrew Hood (contract)
Year of foundation: 1983
Tonnes crushed on average each year: 0.3
Location: D'Entrecasteaux Channel, 3 km south of Woodbridge
Area: 0.25 ha
Soils: clayey loam
Varieties planted: White—riesling; Red—cabernet sauvignon
Leading wines: Geebin Riesling
Notes: Ken Jones claims that Geebin is the smallest commercial vineyard in Australia. I have not tasted its hard-to-find wines and they will always remain so unless you live virtually next door, but it is remarkable to see cabernet sauvignon so far south. Bed and breakfast accommodation is available, but no cellar door sales.

Glenayr NR

Back Tea Tree Road, Richmond, Tas 7025
Ph 03 6260 2388, Fax 03 6260 2691

Owners: Janet and Bill Casimaty
Chief winemaker: Chris Harrington
Year of foundation: 1975
Tonnes crushed on average each year: 4
Location: Richmond (Coal Valley)
Area: 1 ha
Soils: duplex soils ranging from a heavy black cracking clay to sandy loam
Varieties planted: White—riesling; Red—cabernet franc, cabernet sauvignon, merlot, pinot noir, shiraz
Leading wines: Glenayr Pinot Noir, Chardonnay, Riesling, Cabernet-Shiraz-Merlot
Notes: Adjacent to the much larger Tolpuddle vineyard, Glenayr wines are made at Domaine A by Chris Harrington, vineyard manager of both. Glenayr Chardonnay is made from purchased Tolpuddle grapes. Cellar door sales: Mon–Fri 8am–5pm.

Hartzview Vineyard NR

70 Dillons Road, Gardners Bay, Tas 7112
Ph 03 6295 1623, Fax 03 6295 1723

Owners: Robert and Anthea Patterson
Chief winemaker: Andrew Hood (contract), Robert Patterson
Year of foundation: 1988
Tonnes crushed each year on average: not disclosed, but estimated at 15 tonnes
Location: Gardners Bay, Huon Valley
Area: 3 ha
Soils: yellow podsols gradational verging on duplex
Varieties planted: White—none; Red—pinot noir
Leading wines: Hartzview Pinot Noir
Notes: Hartzview is a wine centre selling not only its own wine, but also the wines of other local winemakers. The range of wines is

extensive. Spacious accommodation is available for up to six people in a colonial-style homestead. Cellar door sales: 9am–5pm each day except Christmas Day.

Jollymont Vineyard NR
Pullens Road, Woodbridge, Tas 7162
Ph 03 6267 4594

Owners: Peter Kreet and Heather Creet
Chief winemaker: Andrew Hood (contract)
Year of foundation: 1989
Tonnes crushed on average each year: the vineyard is in its development stages and less than 2 tonnes have been produced each year so far
Location: Woodbridge
Area: 1.4 ha
Soils: dolerite and mudstone
Varieties planted: White—chardonnay, chasselas; Red—pinot noir
Leading wines: wine production commenced in 1998 with Pinot Noir
Notes: Jollymont is on a northern slope with an annual rainfall of about 900 mm. It employs a split trellis system with vine spacing at 0.8 m and rows 3 m apart. It is not irrigated. There are no cellar door sales as yet.

Kinvarra Estate NR
1211 Glenora Road, Plenty, Tas 7140
Ph 03 6286 1333

Owners: Sue and David Bevan
Chief winemaker: Andrew Hood (contract)
Year of foundation: 1990
Tonnes crushed on average each year: 6
Location: Plenty
Area: 1 ha
Soils: dolerite-based loams
Varieties planted: White—riesling; Red—pinot noir
Leading wines: Kinvarra Estate Riesling, Pinot Noir
Notes: Only very small amounts of wine are

produced under the Kinvarra label, the majority of the fruit being sold. No cellar door sales.

Laurel Bank NR
130 Black Snake Lane, Granton, Tas 7030
Ph 03 6263 5977, Fax 03 6263 3117

Owner: Kerry Carland
Chief winemaker: Andrew Hood (contract)
Year of foundation: 1985
Tonnes crushed on average each year: 4
Location: Granton
Area: 2 ha (one hectare established and one yet to bear)
Soils: Quite complex soils ranging from deep black cracking clays with limestone particles which are alkaline through shallower loamy soils (of more normal pH) to shallow dry sandy loam with sub-surface sandstone 'floating' rock (slightly acidic in pH)
Varieties planted: White—sauvignon blanc; Red—cabernet franc, cabernet sauvignon, merlot, pinot noir
Leading wines: Laurel Brook Cabernet-Merlot
Notes: Kerry Carland has proceeded cautiously with Laurel Bank trying, where possible, to match varieties to soil types. His Mariafeld pinot noir clone flourishes in the black clay. Cellar door sales by appointment.

Meadowbank R8
Glenora, Tas 7140
Ph 03 6286 1234, Fax 03 6286 1133

Owners: Gerald Ellis and Jim Cartledge
Chief winemaker: Greg O'Keefe (contract)
Year of foundation: 1974
Tonnes crushed on average each year: 90
Location: Glenora
Area: 11.7 ha (with an additional 8.4 ha vineyard being developed for sparkling wine production)
Soils: sandy loam over clay
Varieties planted: White—chardonnay, riesling,

sauvignon blanc; Red—cabernet sauvignon, meunier, pinot noir
Leading wines: Meadowbank Pinot Noir, Chardonnay
Notes: One of the older established Tasmanian vineyards, Meadowbank seems now to be getting a second wind with the development of a new vineyard to be used exclusively for sparkling wine production. Its Pinot Noir is usually very good, especially the premium Henry James Pinot (named after Henry James Ellis and not the novelist). Its Chardonnay is also first-class. Cellar door sales: 7 days 11am–5pm.

Milford Vineyard NR

Tasman Highway, Cambridge, Tas 7025 (opposite the Tasmanian Golf Club)
Ph 03 6248 3029, Fax 03 6224 2331

Owners: Charles Lewis, Jonathon Dakin, Clive Ockenden and Peter Last
Chief winemaker: Andrew Hood (contract)
Year of foundation: 1984
Tonnes crushed on average each year: 2.5
Location: Richmond (Coal Valley)
Area: 1 ha
Soils: deep calcareous sandy soil over a clay base
Varieties planted: Red—pinot noir; no white
Leading wine: Milford Pinot Noir
Notes: Milford is a well-sheltered site, located in the lower reaches of the Coal River Valley and, in common with Tasmania's better sites, seemingly very suitable for pinot noir. No cellar door sales.

Moorilla Estate R9

655 Main Road, Berriedale, Tas 7011
Ph 03 6249 2949, Fax 03 6249 4093

Owners: a syndicate of Hobart businessmen with Tim Goddard as Chief Executive
Chief winemaker: Alain Rousseau
Year of foundation: 1958

Tonnes crushed on average each year: 30 (of estate-grown fruit)
Location: Berriedale, Derwent Valley
Area: 3.5 ha
Soils: clayey loam, with an excellent aspect
Varieties planted: White—gewurztraminer, riesling; Red—pinot noir
Leading wines: Moorilla Pinot Noir, Riesling
Notes: Arguably the founding vineyard of modern Tasmanian wine, Moorilla has recently undergone two unexpected changes. Long in the ownership of the Alcorso family, it was sold late in 1995. It also, sadly, had to deal with the tragic death of its former winemaker, Jason Winter, in the Port Arthur shootings in 1996. However, having withstood these blows, it continues to produce two of the most respected wines in Tasmania, the Pinot Noir and Riesling, which have a fine national reputation. About 200 tonnes are crushed at Moorilla winery (35 from its estate plantings, about 85 from its St Matthias vineyard and the balance is purchased). Moorilla's restaurant is open for lunch every day except Mondays. Cellar door sales: 7 days 10am–5pm.

Morningside Vineyard NR

Middle Tea Tree Road, Tea Tree, Tas 7017
Ph 03 6268 1748

Owners: Peter and Brenda Bosworth
Chief winemaker: Peter Bosworth
Year of foundation: 1980
Tonnes crushed on average each year: 5
Location: Tea Tree, Coal River Valley
Area: 1.5 ha
Soils: dolerite on limestone-based subsoil
Varieties planted: White—chardonnay, riesling; Red—cabernet franc, cabernet sauvignon, petit verdot, pinot noir
Leading wines: Morningside Pinot Noir, Riesling
Notes: So named because of its aspect, the morning sun falling upon the vineyard, Morningside is fairly closely planted (1.8 m

between rows and 1.25 m between vines). Sales by mail order. Cellar door sales by appointment only.

Palmara Vineyard NR

1314 Richmond Road, Richmond, Tas 7025
Ph 03 6260 2462

Owner: AR Bird Pty Ltd
Chief winemaker: Allan Bird
Year of foundation: 1984
Tonnes crushed on average each year: 3.5, but up to 7 tonnes is anticipated when all varieties are mature and fully bearing
Location: Richmond (Coal Valley)
Area: 1 ha
Soils: variable soils of great age with some volcanic ash content overlying an ancient sandstone and dolerite seabed and pHs varying from 5.2 to over 8; quite fertile in the main with vine vigour controlled by a naturally low rainfall (less than 500 mm per annum)
Varieties planted: White—chardonnay, ehrenfelse, semillon, siegerrebe; Red—cabernet sauvignon, pinot noir
Leading wines: Palmara Pinot Noir
Notes: A typical, small Tasmanian vineyard now progressing from an experimental stage. As might be expected, pinot noir is proving most reliable and has enjoyed show success. Cellar door sales: summer, open weekends and holidays 12 noon–6pm; spring and autumn, weekends and holidays 12noon–4pm; closed during winter (June, July, August). Appointments may be made.

Stefano Lubiana Wines NR

Rowbottoms Road, Granton, Tas 7030
Ph 03 6263 7457, Fax 03 6263 7430

Owners: Steve and Monique Lubiana
Chief winemaker: Steve Lubiana
Year of foundation: 1990
Tonnes crushed on average each year: 150
Location: Granton
Area: 8 ha
Soils: poor, grey, gravelly soils
Varieties planted: White—chardonnay, pinot gris, sauvignon blanc; Red—merlot, pinot noir
Leading wines: Stefano Lubiana Pinot Noir, Sparkling
Notes: Stefano Lubiana Wines sells most of its fruit, retaining about 30 tonnes for its own wine production, both sparkling and still, Pinot Noir. Cellar door sales: Thurs–Mon 9am–5pm.

Tolpuddle Vineyard (vineyard only)

C/- Strathayr Instant Lawns, Back Tea Tree Road, Richmond, Tas 7025

Owners: Bill Casimaty, Dr Tony Jordan and Garry Crittenden
Year of foundation: 1988
Tonnes produced on average each year: 100
Location: Richmond (Coal Valley)
Area: 14 ha
Soils: duplex soils ranging from a black cracking clay to sandy loam
Varieties planted: White—chardonnay; Red—pinot noir
Leading wines: no Tolpuddle wines are produced
Notes: Tolpuddle is the largest vineyard in Southern Tasmania. Its production is largely specialised for sparkling wine only and sold to leading makers such as Domaine Chandon. Other grapes are sold to the adjoining Glenayr Vineyard.

PART III

SOUTH AUSTRALIA

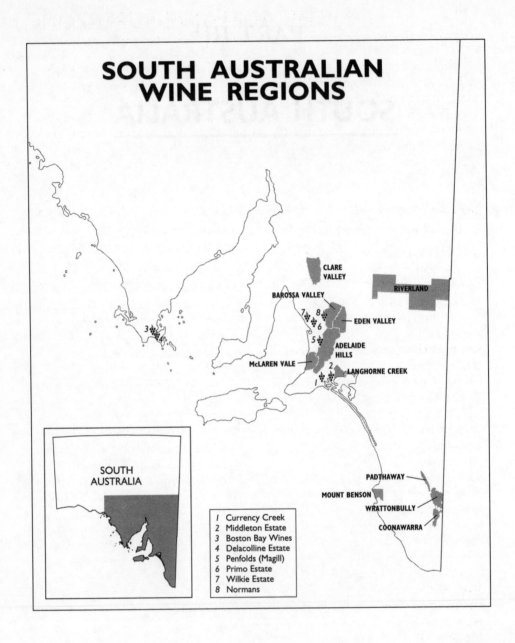

SOUTH AUSTRALIAN WINE REGIONS

CLARE VALLEY

RIVERLAND

BAROSSA VALLEY

7 8
6   EDEN VALLEY
5
ADELAIDE HILLS

McLAREN VALE

2   LANGHORNE CREEK

1

3

SOUTH AUSTRALIA

PADTHAWAY

MOUNT BENSON

WRATTONBULLY

COONAWARRA

1 Currency Creek
2 Middleton Estate
3 Boston Bay Wines
4 Delacolline Estate
5 Penfolds (Magill)
6 Primo Estate
7 Wilkie Estate
8 Normans

❦ THE ADELAIDE SUPERZONE

'Adelaide' is an umbrella zone including 'Barossa', 'Fleurieu' and 'Mount Lofty Ranges' and allows winemakers within those zones to use the name 'Adelaide' instead of their zonal description. In some senses, this seems anomalous, but it does accommodate wine-producing areas such as Adelaide Plains and the very few remaining suburban vineyards of Adelaide, such as Magill, which were once such a force in the growth of South Australian winemaking. It also includes the very new vineyard areas of Kangaroo Island. All wineries in the superzone are marked on the state map.

Normans (vineyard only) ❦

Evanston Vineyard, Gawler, SA 5118

Owner: Normans Wines Limited
Chief winemaker: Roger Harbord
Year of foundation: 1952
Tonnes produced on average each year: 550
Location: Evanston, near Gawler
Area: 45 ha
Soils: heavy brown loam over gravel (floodplain of Gawler River)
Varieties planted: White—chardonnay, chenin blanc, riesling, sauvignon blanc; Red—cabernet sauvignon, pinot noir, shiraz
Leading wines: Normans Old Vine Shiraz, Unwooded Chardonnay, White label range, Bin C106 Cabernet, Bin C207 Chardonnay
Notes: The Normans wineries are at Clarendon (in the McLaren Vale region) and at Lone Gum (Riverland), but this vineyard provides most of Normans' own fruit (and about one-third of its total requirements). Its leading wine is Old Vine Shiraz (a blend usually of Padthaway, Langhorne Creek and Evanston fruit). Unwooded Chardonnay also has had an impressive show career, winning trophies and medals at various wine shows. No cellar door sales here.

Penfolds ❦ R10

78 Penfold Road, Magill, SA 5072
Ph 08 8301 5400, Fax 08 8301 5562

Owner: Southcorp Wines
Chief winemaker: John Duval
Year of foundation: 1844
Tonnes crushed on average each year: not disclosed but estimated at about 35
Location: Magill
Area: 6.5 ha
Soils: red loam over slate with limestone reefs running through the vineyard
Varieties planted: White—none; Red—shiraz
Leading wines: Penfolds Magill Estate Shiraz
Notes: Magill Estate is where Penfolds began. Dr Christopher Penfolds original Grange cottage, recently restored, stands as a South Australian viticultural landmark and the dry-grown shiraz vineyard, whose vine-age averages 50 years, is the last of Adelaide's truly suburban vineyards. Its vines sometimes contribute to Grange Hermitage, but its more usual product is the excellent Magill Estate Shiraz, made in the historic adjoining cellars. Cellar door sales: 7 days 10am–4.30pm. There is also a restaurant.

Patritti (see McLaren Vale)

Primo Estate R10

Old Port Wakefield Road, Virginia,
SA 5120
Ph 08 8380 9442, Fax 08 8380 9696

Owners: Joe and Dina Grilli
Chief winemakers: Joe Grilli and Grant Harrison
Year of foundation: 1979
Tonnes crushed on average each year: 350
Location: Virginia
Area: 16 ha
Soils: free draining alluvial red loam
Varieties planted: White—chardonnay,
colombard, riesling, semillon; Red—barbera,
cabernet sauvignon, grenache, nebbiolo, shiraz
Leading wines: Primo Estate Colombard,
Adelaide Shiraz, Joseph Sparkling Red
Notes: Primo Estate is a winery of finesse and
style existing in the baking heat of the
Adelaide Plains. What Joe Grilli achieves with
colombard (a white variety recommended for
holding its acidity in the warmest of areas but
not much else) is nothing short of miraculous.
In its best years, it is as crisp as the best
sauvignon blanc with many of its herbaceous
characters in common and equally good with
seafood. His reds also, both sparkling and still,
are excellent. Cellar door sales: 15 June to
31 August only and within that period open
Mon–Sat 10am–4.30pm. Otherwise sales by
mail order.

Wilkie Estate NR

Lot 1 Heaslip Road, Penfield, SA 5121
Ph 08 8284 7655, Fax 08 8284 7618

Owners: BH and MJ Wilkie and TJ Spurr
Chief winemaker: Barossa Valley Estates
(Natasha Mooney) (contract)
Year of foundation: 1974 re-established 1988
Tonnes crushed on average each year: 60
Location: Virginia
Area: 7.2 ha
Soils: red-brown earths with sandy loam about
50 cm deep
Varieties planted: White—verdelho; Red—
cabernet sauvignon, merlot, ruby cabernet
Leading wines: Wilkie Estate Cabernet Merlot
Notes: Wilkie Estate is a certified organic
vigneron. The wines are shown and win
medals regularly at Adelaide, Melbourne and
Rutherglen. They are distributed from Adelaide
and there are no cellar door sales.

❦ BAROSSA ZONE

With the exception of Adelaide and Reynella, this zone is the birthplace of South Australian wine. It remains even today as one of its major production areas in terms of wineries, if not in grape production. It folds neatly into two wine regions—Barossa Valley and Eden Valley.

BAROSSA VALLEY REGION

Originally called 'Barrossa' by Colonel William Light in 1837 after a Spanish battle in which he had fought during the Peninsular War, the Valley soon lost its first 'r' due to the early colonists both misspelling and mispronouncing it. This situation was regularised by bureaucracy in 1846 when the hundred of 'Barossa' was proclaimed. Prior to this, during early exploratory work, the expatriate German geologist Johann Menge had favourably reported that the area north-east of Adelaide known as the Barrossa Ranges was first-class farming country, enthusiastically describing it as 'the real cream of South Australia'. In 1839, he persuaded his former employer George Fife Angas, founder of the South Australian Company, to allow his secretary Charles Flaxman to accompany him on a further tour of the area. Flaxman confirmed Menge's report and soon after, acting as Angas' agent, purchased 28 000 acres at one pound per acre.

The South Australian Company, wishing to establish a free colony of smallholders and artisans, insisted that every settler paid in full for his land, which was not to exceed 32 ha in extent. Convict labour and free land grants were certainly not welcome in South Australia. George Fife Angas, however, favoured a superstratum of landed gentry (men of property and capital who could afford to take up large tracts of lands). The latter class could purchase much larger tracts of land on two conditions, the first being that they were prepared to subdivide and sell land back to smaller settlers when they had the capital to purchase it, and the second that they retained at least 1600 ha of their original purchase (obviously as a source of employment for more of the farm labourers and artisans, the more successful of whom were already settling the Valley floor. Few blocks as large as this existed on the Valley floor. There were many more in the hills to the east. So the net result of the two policies was that the smallholders purchased smaller, more fertile blocks chiefly in the Valley and engaged in intensive crop farming, dairying, horticulture and day labour while the gentry bought broadacres mainly in the Hills for grazing, though a few of the latter class, such as Joseph Gilbert and Henry Evans, later diversified into wine production. The national origin of the settlers was also different. The smallholders and artisans were largely German or Silesian Lutherans who had left Prussia in protest against a new Lutheran service ordained by Kaiser Friedrich Wilhelm III. The graziers were almost entirely Anglo-Celtic and re-created the orderly estates with which they were familiar in Britain. There was therefore a broad social and economic division between the inhabitants of the Valley and those

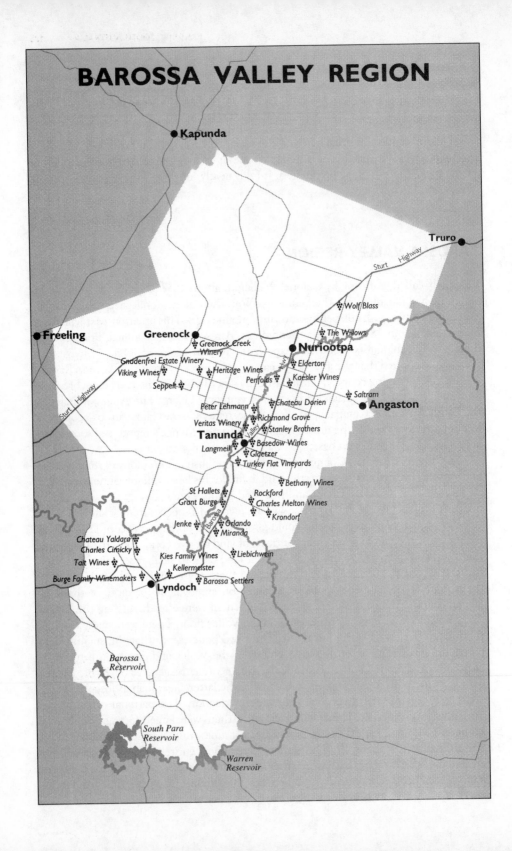

BAROSSA VALLEY REGION

Kapunda

Truro

Sturt Highway

Freeling

Greenock

☙ Wolf Blass

☙ The Willows

Greenock Creek
Winery

Nuriootpa

Gnadenfrei Estate Winery

☙ Elderton

Viking Wines

☙ Heritage Wines

☙ Kaesler Wines

Penfolds

Seppelt

☙ Saltram

☙ Chateau Dorien

Angaston

Peter Lehmann

Richmond Grove

Veritas Winery

Stanley Brothers

Barossa Valley

Tanunda

Basedow Wines

Langmeil

☙ Glaetzer

☙ Turkey Flat Vineyards

☙ Bethany Wines

St Hallets

Rockford

Grant Burge

☙ Charles Melton Wines

☙ Krondorf

Jenke

Orlando

Barossa

Miranda

Chateau Yaldara

Charles Cimicky

Tait Wines

Kies Family Wines

☙ Liebichwein

Kellermeister

Burge Family Winemakers

Lyndoch

Barossa Settlers

*Barossa
Reservoir*

*South Para
Reservoir*

*Warren
Reservoir*

of the Hills (the Barossa Ranges). The factor that would tend to unite them—though this must not be overstated, for few settlers were prepared in the 1840s to risk a whole livelihood upon it—was a common cognisance of wine.

By the 1840s the first vineyards were appearing both in the Valley and to a lesser extent in the Hills. In 1843, a Silesian family, the Aldenhovens, settled in Bethany and are believed to have planted grapes. By 1847, local wines were being exhibited at the Tanunda and Angaston shows. In the same year, Johann Gramp planted near Jacob's Creek and Joseph Gilbert also began his vineyard at Pewsey Vale in the Hills. Samuel Smith followed with the first vines at Yalumba two years later. Both the gentry and the German smallholders were accustomed to wine with their meals. So winegrowing, for which the country and climate were quite favourable, became popular as one of the general disciplines of local farming life, although by no means the most important one. Indeed, winemaking was to become too popular twenty years afterwards, as the later history of South Australia was to prove.

Winegrowing received a tremendous fillip in 1858 with the enactment of the Wark Act by the South Australian legislature which, mistakenly as it turned out, wished to encourage wine production. The Act permitted expansion of distillery licensing (most wines of this period relied on the addition of some spirit at least for their stability). The result was an explosion of vineyards (vineyard area increased from 300 ha in 1858 to 2650 ha in 1866) and subsequently a general lowering of winemaking standards. As the *Adelaide Observer* pointed out, 'there were prospects that failure would teach them [the vintners] to produce an article which would be prized in the markets of the world'. But markets outside South Australia were extremely hard to find and the local market was flooded.

Left to itself the overproduction stimulated by this legislation may soon have petered out were it not for the irrational optimism generated by the Gladstonian budget of 1860, whereby Australian colonial wines were encouraged to enter Britain because of more favourable duties.

Nonetheless it was during this period (1850 to 1870) that many of the patriarchal families that dominated Australian winemaking for the ensuing century became established—families of German origin such as Seppelt, Gramp and Henschke, and those of Anglo-Saxon heritage such as Smith and Salter. There were of course many others, whose descendants are still resident in the Valley and its vicinity. The Wark legislation was repealed in 1877 and this in turn caused an exodus of the lesser-skilled from the South Australian industry and induced others to concentrate on grape-growing.

By this time export markets were beginning to flourish for Barossa wine. The chief wine styles were a heavy dry red, which would withstand the rigours of a 19 000 km voyage and the often neglectful behaviour of the London dockers at the other end, and fortified sweet reds and whites, the 'ports' and 'sherries' which were to become beloved by the British working classes. By 1900, South Australia was producing about ten million litres of wine annually and the Barossa nearly half of this total.

Despite many anti-German outbursts, prohibition campaigns from temperance groups and British Empire jingoism, the First World War proved only the mildest hiccup in Barossa wine production. The twenties provided yet another boost to the Barossa economy, thanks to peace, the 1924 export bounty of the Federal government and Winston Churchill's beneficent 'Empire preference' budget of 1925 in favour of Empire fortifieds over Spanish and Portuguese. Yet overproduction and speculation saw a severe decline in the British market from 1928. The whole structure came crashing down during the Great Depression and wine exports (fortified, of course) only recovered immediately prior to the Second World War. Though this war severely curtailed exports, the domestic market became quite buoyant. There was a beer shortage and the soldiers, both Australian and American, substituted fortified wine for their traditional tipple.

This time, the war's end and another victorious peace brought little improvement to a rather flat export market. Indeed, the British seemed to favour lighter European table wines and the traditional fortifieds of Portugal and Spain. At home things began to change, ever so slightly, at first. Lighter style white wines such as Ringold (more refreshing than the heavily alcoholic fortifieds) began to be accepted though in a minor way. There was even talk in the industry of red table wines becoming popular. In 1950, Penfolds dispatched Max Schubert on a study tour to Bordeaux and the lasting result—following much intervening work on the part of its creator—was Grange Hermitage.

During this decade and the 1960s, the Barossa remained the production centre of the Australian wine industry, but there were to be changing emphases especially in white wine handling. Arguably, the greatest of these was a German invention, the pressure fermentation tank, first imported into Australia by Orlando Wines in 1952. Other technical tours de force included inert gas cover of fermenting must, refrigeration, the increasing use of stainless steel and cold stabilisation. One wine result of these technical triumphs was the production of a sparkling white wine of virtually mass appeal—Barossa Pearl. Thousands of young Australians were introduced to wine by this party fizz and millions of bottles were produced. There were also vast social changes taking place in Australia. The post-war immigration scheme was in full swing, encouraging settlement not only by Anglo-Celts but also by Italians, Germans and other central Europeans, most of whom had at least some familiarity with wine. And then, in the mid-1960s, came the long awaited red wine boom. By 1970, table wine consumption surpassed fortified for the first time.

During the 1970s and 1980s, the Barossa maintained its wine production ascendancy, though now in the Valley and amongst its growers there was a sense of neglect by the large companies. During the 1980s many such companies looked beyond the Valley to outside sources, such as the Riverland and the booming Coonawarra and Padthaway regions, for grapes which were lighter and more delicate for the table wine styles that they were producing. The domestic market was now very buoyant and, by the early 1980s, per capita wine consumption exceeded 20 litres annually. In the Barossa a sense of regional identity was stirring, inspired by winemakers such as Peter Lehmann, whose primary winemaking ethics were not only quality but also loyalty to his Barossa growers. By 1990, there were many smaller producers reliant almost entirely on local grapes for wine production and a re-awakening among the larger companies of the awareness of the value of local fruit for robust reds, wood-matured whites and fruity, flavoursome

Rieslings. Both large and small wine companies are now proud of proclaiming the Barossa origin of a wine. The future of the Barossa Valley wine region and its growers seems assured.

Location: latitude 34°35'S, longitude 139°00'E, about 80 km north-east of Adelaide
Elevation: varying from south to north from about 300 m at Williamstown to 200 m at Lyndoch, 250 m at Tanunda and 270 m at Nuriootpa; and from east to west 400 m at Mengler's Hill, 250 m at Dorrien, 300 m at Patterson Hill and 380 m at Belvidere. Traditionally, the eastern boundary of the Barossa Valley, separating it from the Eden Valley, has followed the 400-metre contour line, which approximates the ridge of the Barossa Range and differentiates the predominant soils of the Barossa (see below) from the rocky, podsolic soils of the Eden Valley.
Topography and soils: Geologically, the Barossa Valley is an inter-montane basin, having an extensive area of Tertiary deposited sediments. On its eastern side, overlooking the Valley, there is a belt of metamorphosed Cambrian limestone (Angaston marble), adjacent to the northern section of the Kanmantoo trough, where there is also a strong development of high grade metamorphic rock, including gneisses and gneissic granites which form the Barossa Ranges.

In the Valley, there are two dominant soil types: (i) grey and brown clays, red-brown earths, brown earths or black earths over red-brown clay subsoils; and (ii) calcareous solodised solonetz (yellow sands) over red clay subsoils. In the west and north-west of the region (the country around Gomersal), the grey and brown clay soils are less suitable for viticulture due to their cracking characters. The red-brown earths of the hills around Marananga and Greenock and the northern hills in the vicinity of Truro and Stockwell are ideally suited. However, the yellow sands, wherever situated, have a lower water retention capacity and, unless irrigation is available, are not regarded as suitable.
Climate: Nuriootpa MJT 21.2°C, MAR16.8, HDD raw 1703, AR 504 mm (Oct–Apr 200 mm), RH 49% 9am, 31% 3pm (Nuriootpa Viticultural Research Centre). Williamstown MJT 19.3°C, MAR 11.6, HDD raw 1336, AR 756 mm (Oct–Apr 266 mm), RH 56% 9am, 33% 3pm (Mount Crawford Forest); compare with Barossa: MJT 21.4°C, MAR 12.6°C, HDD raw 1715, AR 503 mm (Oct–Mar 161 mm), RH 47% (9am), AI 464 mm, SH 8.8 (Dry & Smart); compare with Nuriootpa: MJT 20.8°C, MAR na, HDD raw 1575, 1443 (as cut-off and adjusted for latitude and daily temperature range), AR 506 mm (Oct–Apr 204 mm), RH 36% (3pm Jan), AI na, SH 8.6 (G).

Undoubtedly Nuriootpa is a warm area, but the Barossa Valley as a whole varies widely in climate. Its north-western areas (adjacent to the northern Adelaide Plains) are as a rule even warmer than Nuriootpa, but the more southerly Williamstown district, being higher, is cooler and wetter.

The Valley is located within the catchment of the North Para River and to a lesser extent that of the Light River, which constitutes part of its northern boundary. Its groundwater is recharged by water from the North Para River and by the higher rainfall and infiltration from the Eden Valley. Because of limited resources, irrigation is tightly controlled in the Barossa Valley. New bores and surface dams are prohibited in order to maintain the sustainability of underground aquifers. All present bores are metered and limited in usage to 100 megalitres per hectare per annum, while present dams are restricted in volume to the ability of the owner to collect natural run-off and to harvest water from transitory stream flows. In the Barossa Valley aquifer, water quality is described as 'good quality at depth, saline at the surface'.

Viticultural problems in the form of heat stress can arise as a result of hot northerly winds during the ripening season, though occasional westerly sea breezes can be an ameliorating factor. Disease risk from downy and powdery mildew and botrytis is low. Starlings, however, are a major problem. Like other older viticultural areas, growers in those areas of the Barossa Valley where there is no risk of soil erosion practise clean cultivation rather than sod culture for moisture retention, but this is gradually changing. As for pruning and harvesting, these are carried out mechanically for all but the youngest and oldest vines. As excessive vine vigour does not present much of a problem, there is little canopy or bunch thinning, though there is some slashing carried out in summer. As a result, canopy and trellis management is carried out on traditional lines to satisfy as much as possible the demands of mechanical harvesting, though some growers are experimenting with more modern Scott-Henry techniques. Many bush-pruned vines still remain and premium wines produced from 'old vines', especially shiraz, have become a speciality of the Valley.

Harvest time: generally in the 7-week period from late February to mid to late April. Typical ripening dates: chardonnay early to mid-March; riesling mid-March; shiraz late March; cabernet sauvignon early to mid-April.

Principal varieties: (1996 vintage, over 1000 tonnes produced) White—semillon, riesling, chardonnay, chenin blanc, muscadelle, muscat blanc; Red—shiraz, grenache, cabernet sauvignon, pinot noir.

Total area: 6413 ha (1996) (may be slightly overstated as the boundary between Barossa Valley and Eden Valley cuts through the hundred of Moorooroo and all of the Moorooroo vine area has been included in the Barossa Valley area).

Major wine styles: (from grapes of Barossa origin) White—Semillon (a fuller style often matured in new American oak), Riesling, Chardonnay (usually oaked), Semillon-Chardonnay (a blend); Red—Shiraz (full-bodied and ripe, often matured in American oak) with Old Vines Shiraz a speciality of many vineyards, Cabernet Sauvignon (full-bodied and rich), Grenache (a full, fruity style usually intended for reasonably early drinking), Shiraz-Grenache-Mataro (a blend) and Cabernet-Merlot (a blend); also, traditionally, fortified reds (of port style), which are at the present time in market disfavour.

Barossa Settlers NR

Trial Hill Road, Lyndoch, SA 5351
Ph 08 8524 4017, Fax 08 8524 4519

Owners: Howard and Joan Haese
Chief winemaker: Howard Haese

Year of foundation: 1983
Tonnes produced on average each year: not disclosed but estimated at 250 (most grapes are sold); estimated crush for Barossa Settlers labels, 10 tonnes

Location: Lyndoch
Area: 32 ha
Soils: loam with red clay subsoil
Varieties planted: White—chardonnay, riesling, semillon; Red—cabernet sauvignon, grenache, shiraz
Leading wines: Barossa Settlers Shiraz, Riesling
Notes: A very small family operated winery specialising in the traditional red of the Barossa Shiraz. Its vineyard contains shiraz vines planted in 1887, which play a major part in its Barossa Settlers Shiraz. Cellar door sales: Mon–Sat 10am–4pm, Sun 11am–4pm.

Barossa Valley Estate R 7

Heaslip Road, Angle Vale, SA 5117
Ph 08 8284 7000, Fax 08 8284 7219

Owner: Valley Growers' Co-operative Ltd, owned by 65 Barossa Valley grapegrowers
Chief winemaker: Natasha Mooney
Year of foundation: 1985
Tonnes crushed on average each year: 3000, of which 1200 are utilised for the Barossa Valley Estates labels
Location: no vineyard area is owned by the Co-operative, only by its many members; grape origin is from many parts of the Barossa Valley and is confined to the Valley
Area: none, see above
Varieties planted: White—chardonnay, frontignac, muscadelle, riesling, sauvignon blanc, semillon, traminer, trebbiano; Red—cabernet sauvignon, grenache, merlot, pinot noir, shiraz
Leading wines: E&E Black Pepper Shiraz, Sparkling Shiraz, Ebenezer Cabernet Merlot, Chardonnay, Shiraz
Notes: This is one of the last (and arguably the biggest) of the co-operatively owned wineries in Australia, and has enjoyed great success with its ultra-rich Black Pepper Shiraz. Cellar door sales: 7 days 9am–5pm.

Basedow Wines R6.5

161–165 Murray Street, Tanunda, SA 5352
Ph 08 8563 0333, Fax 08 8563 3597

Owners: Terry and Jill Hill
Chief winemakers: Craig Stansborough, Grant Burge (consultant)
Year of foundation: 1896
Tonnes crushed on average each year: 4000
Location: Tanunda
Area: no vineyards owned, all fruit purchased from growers
Varieties planted: none
Leading wines: Basedow Semillon, Shiraz, Riesling, Cabernet, Bush Vine Grenache, Sauvignon Blanc
Notes: This winery was founded in 1896 and remained in Basedow family hands until 1971. John Basedow, the last family owner-winemaker, won a Jimmy Watson trophy in 1970. In the ensuing 27 years, there have been four proprietors, the latest being the Hill family. It owns no vineyards but has a broad range of wines of good quality overall and keenly priced. Perhaps Basedow's most famous table wine of recent years has been its 'Oscar's White Burgundy', now varietally labelled, a lemon and vanilla-scented Semillon matured in American oak with a full-flavoured palate, very typical of the up-front Barossa Semillon style. Cellar door sales: weekdays 10am–5pm, weekends and public holidays 11am–5pm.

Bethany Wines R8

Bethany Road, Tanunda, SA 5352
Ph 08 8563 2086, Fax 08 8563 0046

Owners: Schrapel families
Chief winemakers: Robert and Geoff Schrapel
Year of foundation: 1977
Tonnes crushed on average each year: 350
Location: Bethany (south-east of Tanunda)
Area: 40 ha made up of four vineyards—

Homestead, Bethanian, Manse (Barossa) and
Trial Hill (Eden Valley)
Soils: (Homestead) alluvial soil over red-brown
clay and limestone; (Bethanian) rich top soil
(a metre deep) over clay, some Biscay soil;
(Manse) flood plain top soil well drained over a
clay base; (Trial Hill) rich top soil from ½ m to
1 m deep over rocky clay subsoil
Varieties planted: White—chardonnay,
frontignac, muscadelle, riesling, semillon;
Red—cabernet franc, cabernet sauvignon,
grenache, merlot, shiraz
Leading wines: Bethany Riesling, Shiraz,
Chardonnay, Cabernet Merlot, Semillon
Notes: Bethany is the heartland of the Barossa
Valley and the Schrapel family, whose
ancestors arrived in 1844, are very much part
of its history. After many years as growers, the
family constructed its winery in 1977. As might
be expected, the Wood-Aged Semillon is very
good, as is the Shiraz. Cellar door sales:
Mon–Sat 10am–5pm, Sun 1pm–5pm.

Burge Family Winemakers   R8.5

Barossa Valley Way, Lyndoch, SA 5351
Ph 08 8524 4644, Fax 08 8524 4444

Owners: Richard, Bronwyn and Noel Burge
Chief winemaker: Rick Burge
Year of foundation: 1928
Tonnes crushed on average each year: 60 rising
to 100 by the year 2000
Location: Lyndoch
Area: 10 ha
Soils: clay loam over limestone to sandy loam
over red clay
Varieties planted: White—muscat blanc,
riesling, semillon; Red—cabernet sauvignon,
grenache, merlot, mourvedre, shiraz
Leading wines: Burge Family Winemakers
Draycott Shiraz, Olive Hill Semillon, Grenache-
based reds
Notes: Rick Burge is a self-confessed admirer of
Rhone-style reds, most of which are grenache-
based, and believes that his region is ideally

suited to reproduce the warmth and generosity
of that style. However, he does not ignore
shiraz and Draycott is one of the best of the
Barossa. Cellar door sales: 7 days 10am–5pm.

Cellarmaster   R7

Dorrien Estate, cnr Siegersdorf Road and
Barossa Valley Way, Tanunda, SA 5352
Ph 08 8561 2200, Fax 08 8561 2299

Owner: Cellarmaster Wines Pty Ltd (a division
of Mildara Blass Ltd)
Chief winemaker: Wayne Dutschke
Year of foundation: 1983
Tonnes crushed on average each year: 400
(all used for own labels)
Locations: there are two vineyards, Dorrien
Estate, Barossa (5.6 ha) and Eden Valley
(32 ha)
Area: 37.6 ha
Soils: sandy loam over light to medium reddish
clay
Varieties planted: White—chardonnay;
Red—cabernet sauvignon, shiraz
Leading wines: Cellarmaster Dorrien Bin 7
Cabernet-Shiraz, New Eden Shiraz
Notes: Cellarmaster Wines was originally set up
to service the requirements of the American
Express Wine Club, whose members either
lacked the confidence to make their own wine
selections at retail liquor shops, were too busy
or simply preferred to use their phone and
have selections made for them. It proved to be
a successful marketing undertaking and grew
markedly during the late 1980s and early
1990s. Even after a dispute terminated the
agreement between Cellarmaster and
American Express it retained other direct sales
contracts and remained a success. It was
purchased by Mildara Blass in 1997. Its wines
have been of fair to good commercial quality
overall. No cellar door sales.

Charles Cimicky R7

Gomersal Road, Lyndoch, SA 5351
Ph 08 8524 4025, Fax 08 8524 4772

Owner: Charles Cimicky
Chief winemaker: Charles Cimicky
Year of foundation: 1972
Tonnes crushed on average each year: 450
Location: Lyndoch
Area: 26 ha
Soils: red loam over limestone
Varieties planted: White—none; Red—cabernet sauvignon, merlot, shiraz
Leading wines: Charles Cimicky Shiraz, Merlot
Notes: Charles Cimicky features a Signature Shiraz, which is typical of the generous style of the region. Cellar door sales: Tues–Sun 10.30am–4.30pm.

Charles Melton Wines R9

Krondorf Road, Tanunda, SA 5352
Ph 08 8563 3606, Fax 08 8563 3422

Owners: Virginia and Charlie Melton
Chief winemaker: Charlie Melton
Year of foundation: 1984
Tonnes crushed on average each year: 125
Locations: Tanunda and Lyndoch
Area: 16.5 ha (two vineyards, Tanunda 4.5 ha and Lyndoch 12 ha)
Soils: (Tanunda) heavy clays; (Lyndoch) sandy loams to heavy clays
Varieties planted: White—none; Red—cabernet franc, cabernet sauvignon, grenache, shiraz
Leading wines: Charles Melton Nine Popes, Shiraz, Rose of Virginia, Sparkling Red
Notes: The Barossa Valley owes its 1980s revival to staunch individuals, such as Charlie Melton, Rocky O'Callaghan and Peter Lehmann, who were prepared to rely on the natural richness of Barossa red style when many other wineries had downgraded the Barossa as an area of quality grapegrowing. The fact that they have now been joined by many others only reinforces the Valley's renaissance as a region of excellence. The Charles Melton style is robust, traditional and very good. Cellar door sales: 7 days 11am–5pm.

Chateau Yaldara R6.5

Gomersal Road, Lyndoch, SA 5351
Ph 08 8524 4200, Fax 08 8524 4112

Owners: Thumm family
Chief winemaker: Hermann Thumm, Robert Thumm (winemaker)
Year of foundation: 1947
Tonnes crushed on average each year: 6000
Location: Lyndoch
Area: 53 ha (with a further 50 ha in course of planting)
Soils: red fertile light loam through to loamy clay over alluvials
Varieties planted: White—chardonnay, crouchen, riesling, sauvignon blanc, semillon; Red—cabernet sauvignon, grenache, merlot, pinot noir, shiraz
Leading wines: The premium range used to be Lakewood, though the top spot in the Yaldara order of merit now seems to have been taken by The Farms range and this appears to be justified by recent wine show results. Nevertheless the Lakewood range remains consistently good
Notes: Built on the ruins of an old Barossa flour mill by its founder Hermann Thumm, Chateau Yaldara has always been a showplace in the Barossa Valley and today it boasts its own motel and restaurant, in addition to its Garden Bistro and extensive gardens. Cellar door sales: 7 days 9am–5pm.

Elderton R8

Murray Street, Nuriootpa, SA 5355
Ph 08 8562 1058, Fax 08 8562 2844
Toll free sales line 1800 888 500

Owner: Elderton Vineyards Pty Ltd
Chief winemaker: James Irvine (contract)

Year of foundation: 1985
Tonnes crushed on average each year: not disclosed, but estimated at 400
Location: Nuriootpa
Area: 32 ha
Soils: deep river silt over limestone varying to red-brown earth away from the river
Varieties planted: White—chardonnay, riesling; Red—cabernet sauvignon, merlot, shiraz
Leading wines: Elderton Command Shiraz, Estate Riesling, Cabernet-Shiraz-Merlot, Merlot (100%)
Notes: The outstanding wine here is Command Shiraz, a big yet smooth Barossan style, matured in American oak and made from vines about 60 years old. Elderton has won many trophies with this wine and also a Jimmy Watson 1993 with a Cabernet Sauvignon. Cellar door sales: Mon–Fri 8.30am–5pm, weekends and public holidays 11am–4pm

Glaetzer 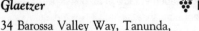 R8

34 Barossa Valley Way, Tanunda, SA 5352
Ph 08 8563 0288, Fax 08 8563 0218

Owner: Glaetzer Wines Pty Limited
Chief winemaker: Colin Glaetzer
Year of foundation: 1996
Tonnes crushed on average each year: 50
Location: Tanunda
Area: no vineyards are owned or leased
Varieties planted: none
Leading wines: Glaetzer Semillon, Shiraz, Malbec-Cabernet Sauvignon, 'Bishop' Shiraz, Grenache-Mourvedre and a range of sparkling wines, Pinot Noir and Shiraz
Notes: This new winery was established by Colin Glaetzer, former winemaker of Barossa Valley Estates, in 1996. As you would expect of wines from a skilled Barossa hand, his wines are full and flavoursome and all Barossa, the fruit being sourced from the Ebenezer area. Cellar door sales: Mon–Fri 10.30am–4.30pm, Sundays and public holidays 11.30am–4.30pm.

Gnadenfrei Estate Winery NR

Seppeltsfield Road, Marananga via Tanunda, SA 5352
Ph 08 8562 2522, Fax 08 8562 3470

Owners: Malcolm and Joylene Seppelt
Chief winemaker: Malcolm Seppelt with assistance from Rolf Binder
Year of foundation: 1979
Tonnes crushed on average each year: 26
Location: Marananga
Area: 3.2 ha
Soils: heavy clay loam overlying dark red friable clay and gravelly loam and sandy loam
Varieties planted: White—none; Red—grenache, malbec, meunier, pinot noir, shiraz
Leading wines: Gnadenfrei Estate Shiraz, Shiraz-Grenache
Notes: This small family cellar specialises in the reds grown on its own vineyard. In addition there are whites and other reds made from grapes purchased locally and from the Eden Valley. There is a restaurant open for lunch from 12.30pm to 3pm every day except Monday unless it is a public holiday. Cellar door sales: 10am–5.30pm except Monday, unless it is a public holiday.

Grant Burge R8.5

Barossa Valley Way, Jacobs Creek, SA 5352
Ph 08 8563 3700, Fax 08 8563 2807

Owners: Grant and Helen Burge
Chief winemaker: Grant Burge
Year of foundation: 1988
Tonnes crushed on average each year: 5000 (about 1000 used for Grant Burge labels)
Locations: Bethany, Jacobs Creek, Krondorf, Lyndoch (5 vineyards), Williamstown
Area: 300 ha
Soils: (Bethany) duplex, Biscay over heavy clays; (Jacobs Creek) duplex, sandy loam over heavy clays; (Krondorf) duplex, loamy clays over heavy red clays; (Lyndoch) duplex, alluvial soil over

red-brown clays; (Williamstown) duplex, sand and sandy loam over heavy clays

Varieties planted: White—chardonnay, chenin blanc, muscadelle, riesling, traminer, sauvignon blanc, semillon, viognier, white frontignac; Red—cabernet franc, cabernet sauvignon, grenache, malbec, merlot, mourvedre, petit verdot, shiraz

Leading wines: Grant Burge Meshach Shiraz, Barossa Ranges Chardonnay, Merlot

Notes: Meshach is an excellent Shiraz, made in the typically rich Barossan way. Very ripe fruit and American oak in abundance give a big, mouth-filling style, which obviously pleased the judges at the 1997 Adelaide Wine Show where it was awarded the Montgomery Trophy. Cellar door sales: 7 days 10am–5pm, except Good Friday and Christmas Day.

Greenock Creek Vineyard and Cellars **NR**

Radford Road, Seppeltsfield, SA 5360
Ph 08 8562 8103, Fax 08 8562 8259

Owners: Michael and Annabelle Waugh
Chief winemaker: Michael Waugh
Year of foundation: 1989
Tonnes crushed on average each year: 45 tonnes but will increase to 120 tonnes as new vines come into bearing
Locations: Seppeltsfield and Marananga (three vineyards, two in Seppeltsfield, one in Marananga)
Area: 18 ha
Soils: deep red earth to sandy loam to bluestone shale
Varieties planted: White—chardonnay; Red—cabernet sauvignon, grenache, shiraz
Leading wines: Greenock Creek Vineyard Unwooded Chardonnay, Chardonnay (oaked), Cornerstone Grenache, Cabernet Sauvignon, Seven Acre Shiraz, Creek Block Shiraz
Notes: Once quite small, this family winery is now growing quickly. Its vineyards are not irrigated. Its wines, made solely from Greenock

Creek fruit, are crushed and made off-site and then returned to the cellars for maturing. Its Shiraz, made in the generously flavoured Barossa manner, is most popular. A faithfully restored cottage, Miriam's, is available for bed and breakfast. Cellar door sales: Wed–Mon 11am–5pm.

Heritage Wines **R7**

Seppeltsfield Road, Marananga, SA 5355
Ph 08 8562 2880, Fax 08 8562 2692

Owners: Stephen and Christine Hoff
Chief winemaker: Stephen Hoff
Year of foundation: 1984
Tonnes crushed on average each year: 85
Location: Marananga
Area: 4 ha
Soils: red-brown earth over clay
Varieties planted: White—none; Red—cabernet sauvignon, malbec, shiraz
Leading wines: Heritage Semillon, Chardonnay, Shiraz, Cabernet-Malbec, Cabernet Sauvignon
Notes: With the assistance of the grapes of his growers, Stephen Hoff crushes some 85 tonnes and produces a full range of Barossa styles. His reds are his own fruit and usually of excellent quality and value. Cellar door sales: 7 days 11am–5pm.

Jenke   **R9**

Jenke Road, Rowland Flat, SA 5352
Ph 08 8524 4154, Fax 08 8524 5044

Owner/chief winemaker: Kym Jenke
Year of foundation: vineyard 1926, winery 1989
Tonnes crushed on average each year: 100
Location: Rowland Flat
Area: 45 ha
Soils: alluvial river silt, very deep
Varieties planted: White—chardonnay, riesling, semillon; Red—cabernet franc, cabernet sauvignon, grenache, merlot, shiraz
Leading wine: Jenke Semillon

Notes: Kym Jenke is descended from an old Barossa grapegrowing family who arrived in 1854. His vineyard, dating only from 1926, is therefore a comparative youngster but its quality is outstanding, especially its semillon. Jenke Semillon is an excellent white, ripe in the best Barossa tradition but never fat or over-blown. Cellar door sales: 7 days 10am–4.30pm.

Kaesler Wines R7

Barossa Valley Way, Nuriootpa, SA 5355
Ph 08 8562 2711, Fax 08 8562 2788

Owners: T.C. and T.K. Hueppauff
Chief winemaker: Toby Hueppauff
Year of foundation: 1990
Tonnes crushed on average each year: 50
Location: Nuriootpa
Area: 11.5 ha
Soils: red-brown loam over clay
Varieties planted: White—palomino, semillon; Red—cabernet sauvignon, mataro, shiraz
Leading wines: Kaesler Semillon, Shiraz
Notes: This vineyard has venerable shiraz vines 105 years old. Even the 'young' vines average 60 years. The wines are the Barossa specialities, Shiraz and Semillon. There is a restaurant and cottage accommodation is available. Cellar door sales: 7 days 10am–5pm.

Kellermeister R7

Barossa Valley Way, Lyndoch, SA 5351
(about 1.5 km east of the town)
Ph 08 8524 4303, Fax 08 8524 4880

Owners: Ralph and Val Jones
Chief winemaker: Trevor Jones
Year of foundation: 1975
Tonnes crushed on average each year: 100
Location: Lyndoch
Area: 4.4 ha
Soils: red loam clay and limestone over black loam over soft schist rock
Varieties planted: White—none; Red—cabernet sauvignon, shiraz

Leading wines: Kellermeister Chardonnay, Shiraz, Riesling, Cabernet Sauvignon, Colombard, Cabernet Sauvignon-Merlot
Notes: Kellermeister offers a typical range of Barossa table wines with Shiraz, matured in American oak, amongst its best. Cellar door sales: 9am–5pm each day, except Christmas Day and Good Friday.

Kies Family Wines NR

Barossa Valley Way, Lyndoch, SA 5351
Ph/Fax 08 8524 4110

Owners: Kies family
Chief winemaker: James Irvine (contract)
Year of foundation: 1880 (vineyard), 1969 (winery)
Tonnes crushed on average each year: 100 tonnes for Kies Family labels, balance of fruit is sold
Location: Lyndoch and Hoffnungsthal
Area: 80 ha
Soils: dark brown soil (Hoffnungsthal), heavy to sandy loams (Lyndoch)
Varieties planted: White—chardonnay, chenin blanc, muscadelle, muscat of alexandria, sauvignon blanc, semillon, traminer, white frontignac; Red—cabernet franc, cabernet sauvignon, grenache, merlot, shiraz
Leading wine: Kies Family Wines 1908 Old Vineyard Shiraz
Notes: The Kies Family are chiefly grapegrowers, their ancestors first planting their vineyards in 1880. Today these vineyards are a treasured legacy. One of their grape purchasers is Penfolds and Kies shiraz has made a contribution to Grange Shiraz. Cellar door sales: Mon–Fri 10am–4.30pm, weekends and public holidays 10am–5pm. There are also barbecue facilities and a gazebo.

Krondorf R7

Krondorf Road, Tanunda, SA 5352
Ph 08 8563 2145, Fax 08 8562 3055

Owner: Mildara Blass
Chief winemaker: Nick Walker
Year of foundation: 1978
Tonnes crushed on average each year: 5000
(includes the crush from Krondorf's own
vineyards)
Location: Tanunda
Area: 104 ha
Soils: red-brown earth sandy loams over
medium clays. Biscay soils, shallow mud over
medium clays
Varieties planted: White—chardonnay, white
frontignac, semillon; Red—cabernet sauvignon,
grenache, shiraz
Leading wines: Krondorf Chardonnay,
Coonawarra Shiraz
Notes: Most wines are multiregional blends of
good quality and keenly priced. Cellar door
sales: 7 days 10am–5pm.

Langmeil NR

Langmeil Road, Tanunda, SA 5352
Ph 08 8563 2595, Fax 08 8563 3622

Owner: Langmeil Winery
Chief winemaker: Paul Lindner
Year of foundation: 1932
Tonnes produced on average each year: 65
Location: Tanunda
Area: 5 ha
Soils: red loamy clay with limestone and
ironstone
Varieties planted: White—none; Red—shiraz
Leading wine: Langmeil Shiraz
Notes: Estate production of 65 tonnes is part
of a much larger crush of 500 tonnes, the
balance being fruit purchased from local
growers. Cellar door sales: 7 days 11am–5pm,
except Christmas Day and Good Friday.

Peter Lehmann R9.5

Samuel Road, Tanunda, SA 5352
Ph 08 8563 2500, Fax 08 8563 3402

Owner: Peter Lehmann Wines Ltd
Chief winemaker: Andrew Wigan
Year of foundation: 1978 (as Masterson,
renamed Masterson Barossa Vignerons in
1979, then named Peter Lehmann Wines Ltd in
1982)
Tonnes crushed on average each year: 12 500
(own use 7300, contract crush 5200)
Location: (winery) Tanunda; (vineyards)
Stonewell (17.5 ha), The Crossing (18 ha)
(Barossa); Clare (20 ha)
Area: 55.5 ha (see above)
Soils: (Stonewell) variable Biscay soil over shale
and red-brown loam over limestone; (The
Crossing) red duplex over clay; (Clare) Trillions
Hill, grey brown shallow soil over shale
Varieties planted: (Stonewell) White—
chardonnay; Red—cabernet sauvignon,
grenache, malbec, merlot, shiraz; (The
Crossing) White—chardonnay, frontignac,
semillon; Red—cabernet franc, cabernet
sauvignon, shiraz; (Clare) White—none; Red—
cabernet sauvignon, malbec, merlot, shiraz
Leading wines: Peter Lehmann Stonewell
Shiraz, Mentor, Clancy's
Notes: Peter Lehmann, publicly corporatised or
not, is a Barossa Valley patriot, a single-minded
independent in a multinational world. Though
most of his fruit is purchased from growers
(over 200 from all over the Valley), the only
'outside' fruit that comes into the winery is
from the adjacent Eden Valley region and the
company's own vineyard at Clare, which will
provide some of the red source for its other
premium brand, Clancy's. Corporate existence
has often been difficult since the company's
inception in 1978, but the philosophy has not
wavered. His leading wines are red, Stonewell
Shiraz and the very smart Cabernet blend,
Mentor, though the Lehmann Eden Valley
Rieslings age very gracefully. Cellar door sales:
weekdays 9.30am–5pm, weekends and public
holidays 10.30am–4.30pm.

Liebichwein NR

Steingarten Road, Rowland Flat,
SA 5352
Ph/Fax 08 8524 4543

Owners: Liebich family
Chief winemaker: Ron Liebich
Year of foundation: 1985 (vineyard), 1992 (winery sales)
Tonnes crushed on average each year: 18
Location: Rowland Flat
Area: 25 ha
Soils: The vineyard is divided by a creek. Its northern side is Biscay, south of creek is red-brown earth
Varieties planted: White—chardonnay, muscat gordo, riesling, semillon, traminer; Red—cabernet sauvignon, grenache, merlot, mourvedre, pinot noir
Leading wines: Liebichwein Cabernet Sauvignon, Riesling-Traminer, Bush Vine Grenache, Shiraz
Notes: Liebichwein is a small family winery whose wines are consistent bronze medallists at local wine shows. As the extent of the vineyard suggests, many more grapes are grown (in total 150 tonnes per year) than are used for the Liebichwein label. Cellar door sales: weekends 11am–5pm, other times by appointment.

Miranda (previously Rovalley) R8

Barossa Valley Way, Rowland Flat,
SA 5352
Ph 08 8524 4537, Fax 08 8524 4066

Owner: Miranda Wines
Chief winemaker: David Norman
Year of foundation: 1919
Tonnes crushed on average each year: 1500
Location: Rowland Flat
Area: 50 ha
Soils: Four vineyards, all at Rowland Flat, varying from deep loam through light to heavy clay to Biscay soil

Varieties planted: White—chardonnay, riesling; Red—cabernet franc, cabernet sauvignon, shiraz
Leading wines: Miranda Show Reserve Series, Grey Series
Notes: It must be the Italian influence. Just as the De Bortoli family added new dimensions of excellence to Yarra Valley winemaking, so the Mirandas have put their own quality imprint on the Barossa. Show success has been widespread for both whites and reds. Cellar door sales: weekdays 9.30am–4.30pm, weekends and public holidays 10.30am–4.30pm.

Orlando R9

Barossa Valley Way, Rowland Flat,
SA 5352
Ph 08 8521 3111, Fax 08 8521 3100

Owner: Orlando Wyndham
Chief winemaker: Philip Laffer
Year of foundation: 1847
Tonnes crushed on average each year: not disclosed but in excess of 10 000
Location: Rowland Flat (winery)
Area: as well as purchasing local fruit, Orlando has several vineyards in the Barossa Valley. These are Jacobs Creek (26 ha), Bungalow (21 ha), Kluges Estate (34 ha) and Lyndoch Estate (7 ha), 88 ha in all. (See also Eden Valley)
Soils: (Jacobs Creek) red-brown earth with sandy loam; (Bangalow and Kluges) same as Jacobs Creek; (Lyndoch Estate) dark cracking clays with self-mulching surface soil.
Varieties planted: (Jacobs Creek) White—riesling; Red—pinot noir, shiraz; (Bungalow) White—none; Red—cabernet sauvignon; (Kluges Estate) White—chardonnay, riesling; Red—cabernet franc, shiraz
Leading wines: Gramps Chardonnay, Gramps Cabernet Merlot, the Jacobs Creek range
Notes: Having celebrated its sesquicentenary in 1997, Orlando is the oldest wine company

resident in the Barossa Valley and one of Australia's largest. It is now world-famous for its excellent value Jacobs Creek brand, very little of which originates from its picturesque vineyard of the same name. Cellar door sales: weekdays 10am–5pm, weekends and public holidays 10am–4pm.

Penfolds   **R10**

Tanunda Road, Nuriootpa, SA 5355
Ph 08 8560 9389, Fax 08 8560 2494

Owner: Southcorp Wines
Chief winemaker: John Duval
Year of foundation: 1844
Tonnes crushed on average each year: (from the company's own Barossa vineyards) not disclosed but estimated at 1500 tonnes
Locations: (in the Barossa Valley) Kalimna, Koonunga Hill, Stonewell Road
Area: 200.7 ha in total—137.2 ha (Kalimna), 30.3 ha (Koonunga Hill), 33.2 ha (Stonewell Road)
Soils: (Kalimna) varying from deep sandy soil on sloping areas to sandy loam and heavy red-brown clays on the flats; (Koonunga Hill) red-brown earth over deep red clays; (Stonewell Road) mainly deep red clays with some shallow silt-based top soils
Varieties planted: White—(Stonewell Road) chardonnay, riesling, semillon; Red—(Kalimna) cabernet sauvignon, mourvedre, petit verdot, sangiovese, shiraz; (Koonunga Hill) cabernet sauvignon, shiraz; (Stonewell Road) cabernet sauvignon, grenache, shiraz
Leading wines: Penfolds Grange, Kalimna Bin 28, Cabernet Shiraz Bin 389 and many other famous Penfolds reds; Barossa-sourced wines: Penfolds Barossa Valley Semillon-Chardonnay, Barossa Valley Old Vine Grenache-Shiraz-Mourvedre
Notes: The Penfolds Nuriootpa winery (or perhaps it should be called 'establishment') is the engine room of Australia's largest wine company. It crushes over 30 000 tonnes of grapes annually for other companies within the group as well as for itself. Penfolds leading reds are usually blends from more than one region, including the world-renowned Grange which relies on the low-yielding Kalimna vineyard for its 'backbone', as does Kalimna Bin 28. Recently more of Penfolds wines are waving the Barossa banner of origin. Penfolds whites are of increasing interest, the best of which are now sourced from the Adelaide Hills. Cellar door sales: Mon–Sat and public holidays 10am–5pm, Sun 1pm–5pm.

Richmond Grove   **R8**

Para Road, Tanunda, SA 5352
Ph 08 8563 2204, Fax 08 8563 2804

Owner: Orlando Wyndham
Chief winemaker: John Vickery
Year of foundation: 1897
Tonnes crushed on average each year: 80
Location: Tanunda
Area: 7 ha, also sources fruit from its own Coonawarra vineyard (see entry) and purchases elsewhere (notably from Watervale in the Clare region)
Soils: red duplex, red-brown earth on a clay base
Varieties planted: White—none; Red—cabernet sauvignon
Leading wines: Richmond Grove Barossa Shiraz, Coonawarra Cabernet Sauvignon, Watervale Riesling
Notes: Richmond Grove is a rather peripatetic label. It has moved without difficulty from the Hunter to the Barossa Valley where its latest home is the century-old Orange Grove (Chateau Leonay) winery in Tanunda. It is also the workplace of eminent winemaker John Vickery, who is responsible for among others its excellent Watervale Rieslings. It is now the South Australian 'red' winery for the Orlando-Wyndham group with the Rowland Flat facility as the 'white'. Its Cabernet Sauvignon sourced from Coonawarra is also quite good. Cellar

door sales: weekdays 9am–4.30pm, weekends and public holidays 11am–4.30pm.

Rockford R9

Krondorf Road, Tanunda, SA 5352
Ph 08 8563 2729, Fax 08 8563 3787

Owner: Tanunda Vintners Pty Ltd
Chief winemaker: Robert O'Callaghan
Year of foundation: 1984
Tonnes crushed on average each year: 350
Location: Tanunda
Area: none, all grapes purchased from private growers
Varieties crushed: White—riesling, semillon; Red—grenache, shiraz
Leading wines: Rockford Black Shiraz, Basket Press Shiraz
Notes: Barossa tradition is very much the theme at Rockford. An 1850s stone settler's cottage and winemaking equipment almost as old add to the antique atmosphere, but it all works wonderfully and the reds are full-bodied, typically Barossan and not to be missed. Cellar door sales: each day except Sunday 11am–5pm.

St Hallett R10

St Halletts Road, Tanunda, SA 5352
Ph 08 8563 2319, Fax 08 8563 2901

Owners: Lindner McLean Vineyards and Cellars Pty Ltd, Bob McLean, managing director
Chief winemaker: Stuart Blackwell
Year of foundation: 1944
Tonnes crushed on average each year: 2800
Location: St Hallett Valley, Tanunda
Area: 4 ha
Soils: alluvial silty loam, red duplex over clay
Varieties planted: White—chardonnay, sauvignon blanc, semillon; Red—cabernet sauvignon, grenache, merlot, mourvedre, shiraz, touriga
Leading wines: St Hallett Old Block Shiraz,

Faith Shiraz, Blackwell Shiraz, Semillon-Sauvignon Blanc, Cabernet Merlot, Chardonnay, Poachers Blend, Gamekeepers Reserve
Notes: 'Big Bob' McLean is one of the irrepressible characters of the Australian wine industry. In less than a decade he has taken St Hallett from relative mediocrity to the top of the tree. There have been two compelling reasons for this meteoric rise. The first, as always, is hard work; the second is a realisation of the combined worth of old shiraz vines and Barossa tradition. Old Block Shiraz is a rich style typical of generous Barossa fruit and sourced from several vineyards over 50 years old, that is deceptively drinkable after only a few years yet matures well over a decade. This type of red has certainly struck a responsive chord in red wine consumers with the result that Old Block has many flattering imitations in warmer Australian wine regions. Cellar door sales: 7 days 10am–5pm.

Saltram R7.5

Angaston Road, Angaston, SA 5353
Ph 08 8564 3355, Fax 08 8564 3384

Owner: Mildara Blass
Chief winemaker: Nigel Dolan
Year of foundation: 1859
Tonnes crushed on average each year: 7000 and growing
Location: Angaston
Area: 50 ha
Soils: sands over medium clay and deep silty loam and red-brown earth over limestone and red clay
Varieties planted: White—chardonnay; Red—cabernet sauvignon, pinot noir, shiraz
Leading wines: Saltram No 1 Shiraz, Mamre Brook, Metala, Mr Pickwick Port
Notes: Saltram is an old and respected Barossa name which, during a generation, has passed through several hands—Seagram, Rothbury Estate and now Mildara Blass—with a

corresponding effect on quality, that is, until recently. Now with an excellent winemaker, Nigel Dolan, wine quality is again in the ascendant. Cellar door sales: 7 days 9am–5pm.

Seppelt R9.5

Seppeltsfield Road, Seppeltsfield via Tanunda, SA 5352
Ph 08 8568 6200, Fax 08 8562 8333

Owner: Southcorp Wines
Chief winemaker: James Godfrey
Year of foundation: 1851
Tonnes crushed on average each year: not disclosed but estimated at 800
Locations: Seppeltsfield, Dorrien, Chateau Tanunda
Area: 105.5 ha in total (Seppeltsfield 95.3 ha, Dorrien 6.25 ha, Chateau Tanunda 3.6 ha)
Soils: (Seppeltsfield) light red-brown loam over limestone; (Dorrien and Chateau Tanunda) heavy red-brown clays
Varieties planted: (Seppeltsfield) White— palomino; Red—cabernet sauvignon, grenache, shiraz, touriga. (Dorrien) White—none; Red—cabernet sauvignon. (Chateau Tanunda) White—chardonnay, riesling; Red—none
Leading wines: Seppelts Dorrien Cabernet Sauvignon, Show Sherries, Show Tawny DP 90
Notes: Seppelt is another of the old established Barossa wine companies now part of the Southcorp empire. Seppeltsfield is famous for its nineteenth century cellars, full of old fortifieds, which are a joy to the palate and especially to their maker, James Godfrey, a self-confessed Sherry fanatic. His Dorrien Cabernet Sauvignon, a rich, long-living cabernet style, is also especially good.
Cellar door sales: weekdays including public holidays 10am–5pm, Sat 10am–4.30pm, Sun 11am–4pm.

Stanley Brothers NR

Barossa Valley Way, Tanunda, SA 5352
Ph 08 8563 3375, Fax 08 8563 3758

Owners: LG & LJ Stanley
Chief winemaker: Lindsay Stanley
Year of foundation: 1994
Tonnes crushed on average each year: 200 of which 100 are used for Stanley Brothers labels
Location: Tanunda
Area: 50 ha
Soils: sand over permeable yellow-clay, water retentive
Varieties planted: White—chardonnay; Red—cabernet sauvignon, shiraz
Leading wines: Stanley Brothers Thoroughbred Cabernet, John Hancock Shiraz, Chardonnay Pristine
Notes: Lindsay Stanley was the winemaker of the former Anglesey Estate in the Adelaide Plains. Cellar door sales: 7 days 9am–5pm.

Tait Wines ⚹ NR

Yaldara Drive, Lyndoch, SA 5351
Ph 08 8524 5000

Owners: Tait family
Chief winemaker: David Tait
Year of foundation: 1994
Tonnes crushed on average each year: 60
Location: Lyndoch
Area: 5 ha
Soils: red-brown clay over a loamy slaty base
Varieties planted: White—chardonnay, frontignac; Red—cabernet sauvignon, grenache, pinot noir, shiraz
Leading wines: Tait Chardonnay, Cabernet, Shiraz, Grenache
Notes: The Tait family have been connected with the Barossa Valley for more than 100 years, albeit as coopers, not winemakers. The small family-owned winery has been in operation since 1994. Cellar door sales: 7 days 10am–5pm.

The Willows Vineyard R8

Light Pass Road, Light Pass, SA 5355
Ph 08 8562 1080, Fax 08 8562 3447

Owners: Scholz family
Chief winemakers: Peter and Michael Scholz
Year of foundation: 1989
Tonnes crushed on average each year for own label: 85 and increasing
Location: Light Pass
Area: 32 ha
Soils: alluvial loams, red-brown earth over clay, sand over clay
Varieties planted: White—chardonnay, riesling, semillon; Red—cabernet sauvignon, grenache, malbec, pinot noir, shiraz
Leading wines: The Willows Semillon, Shiraz
Notes: The vineyard is extensive and grape sales still constitute the major part of the Scholz family's viticultural activities. Indeed the family have been grapegrowers for over 60 years. However, as a 'value-adding' concept, the family introduced 'The Willows' label in the late 1980s and it has been very successful. The wines are now made by Peter and Michael Scholz at the Peter Lehmann winery. Both the Semillon and Shiraz are typically smooth, easy-drinking Barossa styles. Cellar door sales: 10.30am–4.30pm most days.

Turkey Flat Vineyard R8

Bethany Road, Tanunda, SA 5352
Ph 08 8563 2851, Fax 08 8563 3610

Owners: Peter and Christie Schulz
Chief winemaker: Peter Schulz
Year of foundation: 1990
Tonnes crushed on average each year: 150
Location: Tanunda
Area: 17 ha
Soils: red-brown sandy loam over limestone
Varieties planted: White—semillon;
Red—cabernet sauvignon, grenache, mourvedre, shiraz
Leading wines: Turkey Flat Cabernet

Sauvignon, Semillon, Grenache, Shiraz, Rose
Notes: Named after the bush turkeys that roamed the Barossa in the nineteenth century, Turkey Flat opened its cellar door facilities in 1993 but Turkey Flat Vineyard is much more ancient. The vineyard originated about 1847 and still has some shiraz vines over 150 years old. It came into the Schulz family about 1870 and has been owned by them ever since. The red wine styles are typically rich and smooth. Cellar door sales: 7 days 11am–5pm.

Veritas Winery NR

94 Langmeil Road, Tanunda, SA 5352
Ph 08 8563 2330, Fax 08 8563 3158

Owners/chief winemakers: Rolf and Christa Binder
Year of foundation: 1955
Tonnes crushed on average each year: 235 but increasing as new plantings come into bearing
Location: Tanunda
Area: 38 ha in total (Chri-Ro Estate 20 ha, Western Ridge 8 ha, new plantings 10 ha)
Soils: shallow sandy loams over limestone
Varieties planted: White—chardonnay, chenin blanc, riesling, sauvignon blanc, semillon; Red—cabernet franc, cabernet sauvignon, grenache, malbec, merlot, mourvedre, shiraz
Leading wines: Veritas Chardonnay, Cabernet Sauvignon-Merlot, Mourvedre Grenache, Hanisch Vineyard Shiraz
Notes: This medium sized winery is now in its second generation of family ownership. The reds have won trophies at the Barossa Show. Cellar door sales: weekdays 9am–5pm, weekends 11am–5pm.

Viking Wines NR

Seppeltsfield Road, Marananga, SA 5352
Ph 08 8562 3842, Fax 08 8562 4266

Owners: Thord and Charmaine Soderstrom
Chief winemaker: Rolf Binder (contract)
Year of foundation: 1993

Tonnes crushed on average each year: 20
Location: Marananga
Area: 8 ha
Soil: red clay
Varieties planted: White—chardonnay, riesling;
Red—cabernet sauvignon, shiraz
Leading wines: Viking Wines Chardonnay,
Riesling, Cabernet Sauvignon, Shiraz
Notes: Thord and Charmaine Soderstrom are
Swedes with a background in submarines. So it
was entirely logical that, when they decided to
come ashore for the last time in 1993, they
should buy an old bush-vine vineyard in the
Barossa Valley as a weekender. The vineyard
has been rehabilitated and Viking's wines are
starting to be noticed in the Barossa, as well as
in Sweden where they are exported, and they
are no doubt in the mainstream of Valley style.
Cellar door sales: 7 days 11am–5pm.

Wolf Blass **R8.5**

Bilyara Vineyard, Sturt Highway,
Nuriootpa, SA 5355
Ph 08 8562 1955, Fax 08 8562 2156

Owner: Mildara Blass

Chief winemakers: White (Chris Hatcher),
Red (John Glaetzer)
Tonnes crushed on average each year: 30 000
(about 6000 of which originate from the
Barossa and Eden Valleys)
Locations: Nuriootpa, Eden Valley
Area: 356 ha in total, 8 ha (Nuriootpa), 177 ha
(Eden Valley), 98 ha (Eden Valley), 73 ha
(Sevenhill)
Soils: (Nuriootpa) red-brown earth over
limestone clay; (Eden Valley) loamy sands and
sandy loam over red-brown clays and
decomposed parent material
Varieties planted: White—(Eden Valley) riesling;
Red—(Nuriootpa and Eden Valley) cabernet
sauvignon, shiraz
Leading wines: Wolf Blass range of reds and
whites, including Black Label Cabernet
Sauvignon
Notes: the Bilyara winery is the home of the
famous Wolf Blass multi-area reds, which John
Glaetzer has masterminded for many years.
The winery receives fruit from many other sites
including Clare. Cellar door sales: 7 days,
9.15am–4.30pm weekdays, 10am–4.30pm
weekends and public holidays.

EDEN VALLEY REGION

The Eden Valley, which can be broadly described as the upland country above 400
metres in altitude adjacent to the Barossa's eastern boundary, shares its historical
roots with the Barossa. In the 1840s, as the Barossa Ranges, it became the broadacre
grazing country settled by the new colony's Anglo-Celtic gentry, two of whom—
Joseph Gilbert at Pewsey Vale (1847) and Henry Evans at Evandale (1852)—
subsequently established vineyards on their properties. At the perimeter of the new
region (Angaston), Samuel Smith planted vines in 1849. The nomenclature 'Eden
Valley' came into use in the 1860s as a township subdivision, settled by William
Lillecrap. The region also became known utlimately as Eden Valley, but not until
the 1950s.

In 1862, Johann Christian Henschke settled near present-day Keyneton, then
called North Rhine. As part of his general farming activities, he too planted a small
vineyard. At this time also, there were both large and small wineries and distilleries
in the general area, especially Pewsey Vale which was gaining quite a reputation for

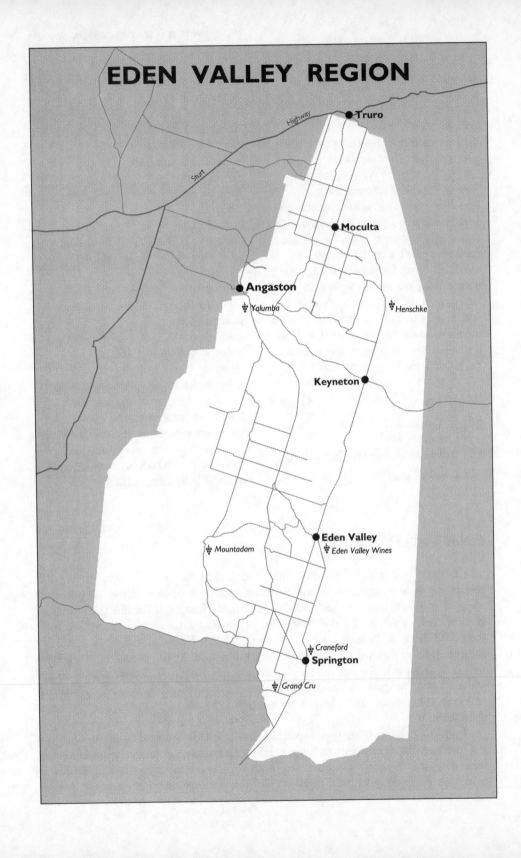

EDEN VALLEY REGION

Truro

Moculta

Angaston
🍇 *Yalumba*

🍇 *Henschke*

Keyneton

Eden Valley
🍇 *Eden Valley Wines*

🍇 *Mountadam*

🍇 *Craneford*
Springton

🍇 *Grand Cru*

its 'Hocks' and 'Rieslings', as well as 'its Shiraz and Carbonet [sic]' reds (Ebenezer Ward). The region expanded substantially during the nineteenth century but never threatened its lowland neighbour in production, nor in popular taste which was then beginning to favour fortified reds rather than table wines. By the 1920s the southern parts of Eden Valley had reverted to grazing; sheer economics had overwhelmed the production of delicate table wine. The Henschke family, however, maintained its link with wine throughout, though it too produced fortified wine in the economically adverse middle years of the twentieth century. The renascence of Eden Valley as a table wine producing area occurred in the 1950s when Cyril Henschke, one of the most skilled and enlightened winemakers of his age, began to market the region's delicate table wines in the eastern states. Soon after this, Eden Valley Rieslings, delicately crafted by the young John Vickery, were also available. Today, the region's forte is still riesling, though in its warmer northern parts, around Keyneton and Moculta, shiraz is extremely successful. Most cool area grape varieties are cultivated and its name is synonymous with style and delicacy.

Location: latitude 34°35'S, longitude 139°E, about 75 km north east of Adelaide.
Elevation: 380–550 m
Topography and soils: Part of the northern Kanmantoo Trough, the region is hilly and exhibits a strong development of high-grade metamorphic rock amongst which are gneisses and gneissic granites. Its soils are chiefly grey-brown duplex or yellow podsolic skeletal, sharing common characteristics with many other south-eastern and south-western Australian vineyard soils, though in places the soils of the region tend towards infertile leached sands.
Climate: MJT 19.3°C, MAR na, HDD raw 1365, 1251 (cut off and adjusted for latitude and daily temperature range but not for vine sites) (Gladstones), AR (Henschke, Moculta) 534 mm (about 225 mm of which falls Oct–Apr), but further south and at greater altitude higher (Jim Irvine at Eden Valley reporting 680 mm pa), RH 39% (3pm Jan), AI na, SH 8.3. Eden Valley is a cool and dry region, having, in common with other higher altitude areas, great temperature variability, a relatively high number of sunshine hours and low summer rainfall and humidity.

The Valley is a natural drainage basin for two river systems, the North Para, flowing into the Barossa Valley, and the nostalgically named Rhine which flows eastwards into the Murray. Irrigation is a must in the Valley and reliance is placed chiefly on surface dams filled by rainfall rather than on bores, as groundwater flow is often limited, quite poor in quality and often saline. New surface water storage dams in areas which debouch into the Para system have now been limited by legislation to less than 5 million litres in capacity.

In contrast to the more conservative, warm area practices of the Barossa Valley, the winegrowers of Eden Valley have followed the advice of modern viticulturalists and adopted modern, cool area viticultural techniques such as canopy management, vine planting widths and row orientation. Sod culture, which has the benefits of minimising erosion, water run-off and soil compaction, has also largely replaced clean cultivation. Both under-vine and inter-row mulching are also being utilised to retain moisture and build up nitrogenous material in the soil. In the Eden Valley, as in other cool areas, modern methods of vertical trellising such as Scott Henry and Smart Dyson, which minimise vine vigour and maximise sunlight penetration, are gaining in popularity while leaf plucking also assists in sunlight exposure. In its warmer northern areas, such as Moculta, however, the more traditional techniques of Barossan viticulture still exist. Pruning and harvesting are carried out chiefly by machine except on the steepest vineyard blocks.

Viticultural problems encountered in the Valley include botrytis and powdery mildew, which are counteracted by modern spray programs during the growing season. The region's grapes are also the unwelcome target of hungry birds, especially starlings, rosellas and crows, while young vines can be particularly delectable to rabbits and hares which raid from the protection of surrounding bushland. Other afflictions are the Light Brown Apple Moth and eutypa (die-back), a disease caused by a fungus that is often fatal to older vines and results from careless pruning. Spring frosts can also pose problems.

Harvest time: generally for all relevant varieties about 3–4 weeks later than on the floor of the Barossa Valley. Typical are shiraz second week in April, riesling end of April, cabernet sauvignon end of April.

Principal varieties: (1996 vintage over 1000 tonnes produced) White—riesling; Red—shiraz.

Total area: (1996) 452 ha (may err slightly on the low side due to vine area of the hundred of Moorooroo being included entirely in the Barossa Valley wine region).

Major wine styles: Except in the region's north and along its western and south-western edges, the Eden Valley must be classified generally as a white wine production area. In the north (the Moculta–Keyneton district), greater warmth and old vines produce marvellous fuller-bodied Shiraz reds (Hill of Grace, Mount Edelstone excel). Cabernet sauvignon grows very successfully on the western rim of the Valley (the Woodbury vineyard of Tollana and Mountadam are cases in point) with a fullness of berry flavour, atypical of the region as a whole which generally produces Cabernets of lighter berry and leaf flavours (Pewsey Vale). Pinot noir is the region's third most widely grown red variety.

With a reputation over a century old, the region produces what is generally regarded as Australia's classic riesling style, high flavoured yet elegant wines of floral-lime characters which age over a decade into 'honey and toast' styles, treasured by lovers of older rieslings. Chardonnay is also grown quite widely but, as most Chardonnays these days rely on winemaking technique for complexity, it is difficult to gauge its regional as opposed to its technical characteristics. This variety and pinot noir are also utilised for sparkling wine production.

Craneford R7

Main Street, Springton, SA 5235
Ph 08 8568 2220, Fax 08 8568 2538

Owners: Alan and Jacqui Williams
Chief winemaker: contract

Year of foundation: 1978
Tonnes crushed on average each year: 30
Location: Eden Valley
Area: 7 ha
Soils: sandy soils over rock

Varieties planted: White—riesling; Red—shiraz
Leading wines: Craneford Riesling, Shiraz,
Chardonnay, Cabernet Sauvignon
Notes: The recent change of ownership has
been beneficial to Craneford. Its 1997 Riesling
won a well-deserved gold medal and the
trophy for the best small producer wine at the
1997 Barossa Wine Show. Cellar door sales:
Wed–Mon 11am–5pm.

Eden Valley Wines **NR**

Main Street, Eden Valley, SA 5235
Ph 08 8564 1111, Fax 08 8564 1110

Owner: Eden Valley Wines Pty Ltd
Chief winemaker: Vicky Barteer
Year of foundation: 1994
Tonnes crushed on average each year: 100 but
increasing
Location: Eden Valley
Area: 132 ha
Soils: sand over sandstone
Varieties planted: White—chardonnay,
frontignac, riesling, semillon; Red—cabernet
sauvignon, mataro, merlot, malbec, pinot noir,
shiraz
Leading wines: Eden Valley Riesling
Notes: A large extension to its vineyard near
Eden Ridge was commenced in late 1997 with
the emphasis very much on riesling, which is,
after all, the leading white grape of the region.
As a result, Eden Valley Wines will specialise in
bottle-aged Riesling, its other varietals making
their appearance at cellar door only. It is
envisaged that, by 2001, the winery will be
crushing 1500 tonnes. Cellar door sales: 7 days
10am–5pm. There is also a large restaurant
and function room and cottage
accommodation is available.

Grand Cru **R7**

Dewell's Road, Springton, SA 5235
Ph 08 8568 2378, Fax 08 8568 2799

Owner: Karl Seppelt
Chief winemaker: Petaluma Winery (contract)
Year of foundation: 1981
Tonnes crushed on average each year: 100
Location: Springton
Area: 9 ha
Soils: schist–yellow grey loam duplex podsolic
skeletal rocks
Varieties planted: White—chardonnay;
Red—cabernet sauvignon, merlot, pinot noir
Leading wines: Grand Cru Chardonnay,
Cabernet Sauvignon, Chardonnay Brut, Brut
Sauvage, Sparkling Shiraz
Notes: Australian wine owes a great debt to
Karl Seppelt, who has spent all his working life
in the wine industry. It was he who helped
'discover' the Drumborg and Padthaway wine
regions in the early 1960s. Grand Cru, drip
irrigated with salt-free water and on the
southern boundary of the Eden Valley region,
is only a kilometre away from the Adelaide
Hills region. Karl believes it shares more
climatic common ground with the latter than
the former and was intended, he says, as a
retirement hobby. His vineyard has since
become much more and, with 60 tonnes of his
own fruit used for his own wines, is now quite
a large boutique. The Chardonnay is a lightly
wooded style. The Cabernet in warm years can
be quite powerful and concentrated, but
usually softens into an accessible drinking style
after 4–5 years' cellaring. The sparkling wines
are also consistent medal winners. There are
also fortified reds (vintage and tawny 'ports')
and a fino 'sherry'. Cellar door sales: 7 days
10am–5pm

Grant Burge (vineyard only) **NR**

(see Barossa Valley entry)
Summer's Hill, Eden Valley, SA 5235

Location: Eden Valley
Tonnes produced on average each year: 250
Area: 32 ha

Soils: podsolic soils, sandy topsoil over yellow-brown clay, acidic
Varieties planted: White—chardonnay, riesling; Red—pinot noir
Leading wine: Grant Burge Barossa Ranges Chardonnay

Heggies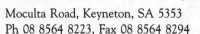

(see Yalumba)

Henschke R10

Moculta Road, Keyneton, SA 5353
Ph 08 8564 8223, Fax 08 8564 8294

Owner: C A Henschke & Co
Chief winemaker: Stephen Henschke
Year of foundation: 1868
Tonnes crushed on average each year: 600
Location: Keyneton
Area: 100 ha
Soils: (Eden Valley) sandy loam over schisty clay; (Hill of Grace) deep alluvial silty loam; (Mount Edelstone) podsolic skeletal rock over red clay; (Tilly) shallow loamy clay over heavier clay; (Homegarden) shallow sandy loam over heavy clay
Varieties planted: White—chardonnay, gewurztraminer, riesling, sauvignon blanc, semillon; Red—cabernet sauvignon, malbec, merlot, shiraz
Leading wines: Henschke Hill of Grace, Cyril Henschke Cabernet Sauvignon, Mount Edelstone (all red); Tilly's Vineyard, Louis Eden Valley Semillon, Julius Eden Valley Riesling, Eden Valley Chardonnay, Sauvignon Blanc-Semillon, Joseph Hill Gewurztraminer
Notes: A pioneer maker in the Eden Valley, Henschke is one of the older family-owned wine companies in Australia and a famous name indeed for its shiraz reds, the magnificent Hill of Grace and marvellous Mount Edelstone, whose greatness was initiated by the late Cyril Henschke. Since his own accession as winemaker, Stephen

Henschke has commemorated his father with the Cyril Henschke Cabernet Sauvignon, a powerful but very stylish red. Today Stephen is one of Australia's leading winemakers and his wife, Pru, is an eminent viticulturist. Cellar door sales: weekdays 9am–4.30pm, Sat 9am–12 noon, public holidays 10am–3pm, closed Sundays, Good Friday and Christmas Day.

Hill-Smith Estate

(see Yalumba)

Irvine NR

Springhill Vineyard, Basil Roeslers Road, Eden Valley, SA 5235
Ph/Fax 08 8564 1046

Owners: James and Marjorie Irvine
Chief winemaker: James Irvine
Year of foundation: 1980
Tonnes crushed on average each year: 100
Location: Eden Valley
Area: 9.6 ha but closer spacing has enabled 2175 vines per hectare to be planted (the region's usual planting is 1500 vines per hectare) and therefore the vineyard area is effectively 13.5 ha
Soils: grey-brown podsolic soil over skeletal schisty rock
Varieties planted: White—chardonnay, meslier, pinot gris; Red—merlot, zinfandel
Leading wines: Irvine Grand Merlot
Notes: James Irvine is a vastly experienced winemaker and one of Australia's leading wine consultants. Sited on a hillside with ancient grey-brown podsolic soil (quite thin in parts) over gravelly subsoil, Springhill is drip irrigated and relatively close-planted with vine spacing at 1 m and row spacing at 2.2 m. Its trellising is a mixture of traditional two wire vertical and the Smart-Dyson system. Jim's most recent triumph has been a first prize at the 1st World Merlot Competition in Switzerland among such prestigious Merlot names as Petrus and others.

Apart from his Merlot success, he grows about 5% of the world's supply of meslier, a highly acid white variety from the Aube. It seems to be in disfavour elsewhere in Champagne (where there is usually plenty of acidity) but is very useful in warmer sparkling winemaking areas. No cellar door sales.

Leo Buring (vineyard only)   R9

Tanunda Road, Nuriootpa, SA 5355

Owner: Southcorp Wines
Chief winemaker: Geoff Henricks
Year of establishment: 1931
Tonnes produced on average each year: not disclosed but estimated at 550
Location: High Eden Vineyard, Eden Valley
Area: 57 ha
Soils: variations of three podsolics: sand over sandy loam; sandy loam over clay; sandy loam over mottled; clay overlying impermeable sandstone
Varieties planted: White—chardonnay, riesling, sauvignon blanc; Red—pinot noir
Leading wines: Leo Buring Leonay, Show Reserve Rieslings
Notes: Now made by Geoff Henricks, the delicacy of the riesling tradition commenced by John Vickery goes on. There have been a few finetunings, however. The old, confusing bin numbering system has been dropped and there are three rieslings, Eden Valley, Clare and top-of-the-tree, Leonay, which can come from either region but not from both. Cellar door sales: see Penfolds Nuriootpa.

Mountadam   R8.5

High Eden Ridge, Eden Valley, SA 5235
Ph 08 8564 1101, Fax 08 8564 1064
(Adelaide office
Ph 08 8361 3300, Fax 08 8361 3400)

Owner: David & Adam Wynn Pty Ltd
Chief winemaker: Adam Wynn
Year of foundation: 1972 (first vintage 1984)

Tonnes crushed on average each year: 700
Location: High Eden Ridge in the south of Eden Valley
Area: 50 ha
Soils: sand over schist and quartz
Varieties planted: White—chardonnay (over 50% of the vineyard area), pinot gris (experimental), viognier (experimental); Red—cabernet sauvignon, merlot, pinot noir, shiraz
Leading wines: Mountadam Chardonnay (still), Pinot Noir-Chardonnay (sparkling), Pinot Noir (still red), Merlot, The Red (a blend of cabernet sauvignon and merlot). After the Mountadam range comes the David Wynn range. Its leading wine is Patriarch Shiraz. There is a third range of organically grown wines, Eden Ridge.
Notes: The Wynn Family has been associated with Australian wine and winemaking for over 80 years. Adam Wynn carries on its involvement into a third generation. His late father, David, has long been recognised as the rescuer and resuscitator of present-day Coonawarra. Against his own father Samuel's recommendation, he purchased the run-down Riddoch winery and vineyards in 1951, building Wynns 'Coonawarra Estate' into a very popular brand and in the process making Coonawarra a nationally known region. S Wynn & Co subsequently became a publicly listed company which is now part of Southcorp Wines. Mountadam, now completing its first quarter-century of existence, might be described as the realisation of the late David Wynns retirement dream. His son, Adam, now in control of the estate and winemaker since its first vintage, has been immensely successful with his Chardonnay, which, among its Eden Valley brethren, is certainly *primus inter pares*. All the Mountadam wines are sourced entirely from the estate. Cellar door sales: 11am–4pm each day.

Orlando (vineyard only)   R9

Karra Yerta Road, Eden Valley, SA 5235

Owner: Orlando Wyndham Pty Ltd
Chief winemaker: (white) Philip Laffer
Year of foundation: 1968
Tonnes produced on average each year: 250
Locations: Eden Valley (2)
Area: 62.6 ha, Karra Yerta Road (61 ha) and
Steingarten (1.6 ha)
Soils: (Karra Yerta) sandy loam over weathered
sandy clay; (Steingarten) decomposed schisty
rock
Varieties planted: White—riesling, traminer;
Red—none.
Leading wines: St Helga Riesling, Steingarten
Riesling, Jacob's Creek Riesling (part)
Notes: Orlando is blessed by two outstanding
Rieslings from this Region. St Helga is from the
Karra Yerta Road vineyard which is one of the
most reliable Eden Valley sites, always
producing high quality Riesling. Steingarten
Riesling is sourced from its eponymous Eden
Valley vineyard but regrettably is available only
in minute quantities. Cellar door sales: see
Orlando Barossa entry.

Pewsey Vale

(see Yalumba)

Tollana   R9

Tanunda Road, Nuriootpa, SA 5355
Ph 08 8560 9389, Fax 08 8560 2494

Owner: Southcorp Wines
Chief winemaker: Neville Falkenberg
Tonnes crushed on average each year: 1200
Location: (vineyards) Eden Valley
Area: 120 ha, Roesler's (14.4 ha) and
Woodbury (105.6 ha)
Soils: similar to Leo Buring soils
Varieties planted: (Roesler's) White—riesling,
sauvignon blanc, semillon; Red—meunier,
shiraz. (Woodbury) White—chardonnay,

gewurztraminer, riesling; Red—cabernet
sauvignon, pinot noir, shiraz
Leading wines: Tollana range of Eden Valley
wines
Notes: Tollana is one of the lesser-known
treasures of Southcorp. Its Cabernet Sauvignon
TR222 and its Botrytis Riesling are never less
than very good. Cellar door sales: as for
Penfolds Barossa.

Wolf Blass (vineyards only)

(see Barossa Valley entry)

Yalumba   R9

(see also Coonawarra, Koppamurra and
Riverland SA)
Eden Valley Road, Angaston, SA 5353
Ph 08 8561 3200, Fax 08 8561 3393

Owners: Hill Smith family
Chief winemaker: Simon Adams
Year of foundation: 1849
Tonnes crushed on average each year: 8000
Locations: Angaston (the winery sits in the
Eden Valley wine region on the boundary of
the Barossa Valley region), Eden Valley,
Coonawarra, Koppamurra, Oxford Landing
(Qualco) est 1958

i) Angaston vineyards

(Shorts and Old Triangle)

Tonnes crushed on average each year: 40
Location: Angaston
Area: 7.16 ha
Soils: red-brown earth over clay limestone base
Varieties planted: White—riesling, semillon;
Red—cabernet sauvignon, shiraz
Leading wines: previously incorporated in the
Yalumba Family Reserve range, now part of
the new release Yalumba range

ii) Heggies (vineyard only)   **R9**

off Flaxman's Valley Road, Eden Valley, SA 5253

Chief winemaker: Simon Adams
Year of foundation: 1971
Tonnes crushed on average each year: 200
Location: Eden Valley
Area: 48.5 ha
Soils: grey loam over gravel clay base with rocky outcrops
Varieties planted: White—chardonnay, riesling; Red—merlot
Leading wines: Heggies Vineyard wines

iii) Hill-Smith Estate
(vineyard only)   **R9**

Off Flaxman's Valley Road, Eden Valley, SA 5253

Chief winemaker: Tony Davis
Year of foundation: 1971
Tonnes crushed on average each year: 100
Location: Eden Valley
Area: 23.25 ha
Soils: grey loam over gravel
Varieties planted: White—chardonnay, sauvignon blanc; Red—none
Leading wines: Hill-Smith Estate wines

iv) Pewsey Vale (vineyard only)   **R8**

Brownes Road, Eden Valley, SA 5235

Chief winemaker: Louisa Rose
Year of foundation: 1963 (the original Pewsey Vale ceased production about 1927)
Tonnes crushed on average each year: 350
Location: Eden Valley
Area: 58.6 ha
Soils: grey loam over gravel and clay
Varieties planted: White—riesling;

Red—cabernet sauvignon
Leading wines: the Pewsey Vale Vineyard wines
Notes: Yalumba is the oldest family owned wine company in Australia. Its founder, Samuel Smith, was a Dorsetshire brewer who settled near Angaston in 1848 and ultimately prospered. His was a typical pioneer's story: very little initial capital but, after working as an orchardist for George Fife Angas, saved enough to buy a smallholding (12 ha) and plant a small vineyard. A trek to the goldfields followed, and modest success after great effort. More land was purchased and some capital improvements made. By the late 1880s, Yalumba had gained quite a reputation for its 'port', which reflected the contemporary change in public taste to stronger reds and fortified wines. So Yalumba continued into the twentieth century, producing strong reds and fortifieds to satisfy its local and overseas markets, though some table wines were made for the then small band of enthusiasts. By 1960 Yalumba, in common with the other established wine companies of that time, was preparing for a table wine revival. As Joseph Gilbert had over a century earlier, it saw its opportunity in Pewsey Vale in the Barossa Ranges, establishing its vineyard there in 1963. Later, in 1971, Yalumba planted its two other 'Hills' vineyards and has subsequently established vineyards at Coonawarra and Koppamurra (see entries). Today it remains one of the larger family-owner Australian wine companies, crushing about 20 000 tonnes of grapes annually. All wines of the company are produced and sold at its Angaston winery.
Cellar door sales: weekdays 8.30am–5pm, Saturdays and public holidays 10am–5pm, Sundays 12 noon–5pm.

❦ Cabernet Sauvignon & Co

Cabernet sauvignon is a grape variety that has received universal recognition. In Bordeaux where it originated, it is blended to a greater or lesser extent with its cohabitant, merlot, but there is often a leavening of its other colleagues, cabernet franc, malbec and petit verdot. It has been present in Australia since 1832, but the migration of its companions, with the exception of malbec, has been much more recent. Merlot and cabernet franc have been present in Australia barely twenty years and petit verdot is even newer. So it is scarcely remarkable that we have not yet seen the best of them in blends. But we are beginning to see them.

At the same time as the acclimatisation of these 'new' varieties, we have witnessed the creation in one case and the rebirth and consolidation in other cases of 'cooler' wine-growing areas. Coonawarra has expanded vastly in the past 30 years. We have seen the growth of Margaret River as one of Australia's premium areas. Mount Barker is also widely respected and the Yarra Valley has been reborn. In all four areas, cabernet sauvignon is a major variety and there is a certain rivalry among the areas for cabernet supremacy. As the prize for such supremacy is increased public recognition and acceptance of that area (and greater sales), it is necessary to examine the cabernet styles of each of the regions to see how they differ. As each has also from time to time made claims to be Australia's 'Medoc', we should examine the significant climate factors of each for any justification of that claim.

The table shows comparisons between the altitudes, the relevant mean daily temperatures, effective degree days, annual mean rainfall, relative humidity and total sunshine hours.

	Medoc	Coonawarra	Margaret River	Yarra Valley (Healesville)	Mt Barker (WA)
Altitude (m)	47	59	90	130	253
Daily mean temp (°C)	Apr 11.7	Oct 12.6	13.5	13.0	13.1
	May 15.4	Nov 14.8	15.8	15.2	15.6
	Jun 18.3	Dec 17.0	18.0	17.0	17.6
	Jul 20.5	Jan 19.3	20.0	17.9	19.0
	Aug 20.5	Feb 19.6	20.3	18.2	19.0
	Sept 18.3	Mar 17.4	18.8	16.8	17.7
	Oct 13.3	Apr 14.5	16.5	13.3	15.7
Effective degree days adjusted for vine sites	1453	1333	1557	1352	1488

	Medoc	Coonawarra	Margaret River	Yarra Valley (Healesville)	Mt Barker (WA)
Average annual rainfall (mm)					
Apr–Oct	427	Oct–Apr 257	274	597	285
Nov–Mar	406	May–Sept 371	918	411	471
Total	833	628	1192	1008	756
Relative humidity (July)	59% (3pm)	48% (Jan)	56%	57%* (9am Jan)	54%
Sunshine hours	1472	1593	1626	1490	1518

Note: All data according to Gladstones, *Viticulture and Environment*, except for Yarra Valley relative humidity*.

Such comparisons prove little, however, and only tend to emphasise differences rather than similarities. In degree day terms, both Coonawarra and the Yarra Valley are much cooler than the Medoc, while Margaret River is substantially warmer. Mount Barker is closest in degree days, but greater in total sunlight hours. In that respect, the Medoc and the Yarra Valley are least blessed but close, while Coonawarra and Margaret River enjoy a superiority. Both the Medoc and Margaret River have similarities in relative humidity. Margaret River would otherwise be a paradise for botrytis were it not for its dry summer, a condition which does not always come to the rescue of the Yarra Valley. It should also be noted that the Medoc warms much more quickly than any comparable Australian site, for example, 66 degree days in April which virtually triples in May to 181. Coonawarra heat degree days in October (86) are not quite doubled by November and in cooling rates too the Medoc falls more rapidly than Coonawarra (Medoc Sept—253, Oct—133; Coonawarra March—224, Apr—142), though the differences in corresponding latitudes (Coonawarra is more than 5 degrees closer to the equator than the Medoc) would certainly have an influence.

In broad terms there are similarities between the Medoc and Coonawarra. In location, both are reasonably close to the sea, though the Medoc is a peninsula subject to greater air moisture and therefore subject to less frost risk. Altitudes are similar and terrains of both are flat. Coonawarra is on the whole much drier and more liable to frost after budburst; the Medoc warms more quickly; the soils are quite different in nature though similar in drainage (well-drained terra rossa above limestone in the case of Coonawarra's best country and, on the whole, well-drained silty pebbly alluvial soils on a clayey subsoil in the case of Medoc). So perhaps we may simply conclude our climate study with 'Vive la difference!'. If Australia cannot pretend to any 'Medoc' homoclimes, we do at least have magnificent but distinct cabernet styles of our own from the four Australian regions mentioned.

In Margaret River, David Hohnen makes Cape Mentelle Cabernet Sauvignon from the original 1970 five-hectare planting and believes that the best Margaret River cabernet sauvignon must be picked ripe but equally should retain its acid balance. Irrigation has helped produce a balanced, stress-free wine, which means good structure, but soft tannins. He leaves his wine in contact with skins for 3–4 weeks. By the end of the first week, his Cabernet has extracted all the tannin it will take and the next 2–3 weeks are really a maceration period, softening and integrating the tannins. Then the wine is inoculated (so that it undergoes immediate malolactic fermentation), blended into approximately its final form and then transferred into small oak, half of which is new and all of which is French. Eighteen months is spent in barrel, during which the wine is racked several times and egg-white fined when necessary. It is finally assembled and coarsely filtered immediately prior to bottling and then bottle-aged for two more years. It is released between 3 and 4 years of age, designed to be drunk after 10 years and to live for 20. The factor that separates Margaret River from the rest, according to David, is a mulberry, blackberry leafiness that pervades its flavour, together with a full but never harsh tannic finish.

In Coonawarra, Ralph Fowler, formerly of Leconfield, seeks complexity in Cabernet Sauvignon. Simple pleasant fruitiness should be no part of Coonawarra cabernet sauvignon. He makes four or five pickings based on flavour criteria. He seeks and usually finds a mulberry character in the early flavour profile of Coonawarra cabernet. Aromas at this stage are predominantly 'rose-petal' and the baume (although Ralph does not regard this as a criterion) is between 11.5 and 12 degrees. This picking usually accounts for about 20% of the crop. At the next level of flavour ripeness (usually between 12.5 and 13 degrees), he notices berry-cassis flavours with similar aromas and picks about 40% of the fruit. Finally at super-maturity (13 degrees plus), he finds liquorice and leather characters and picks the balance at this point. As for merlot, he uses this variety as an 'alcohol' additive, ripening it as much as possible. It usually forms between 6% and 15% of the final wine. His other chosen variety, petit verdot, with its quite distinct 'green' flavours, ripens very late anyway and forms 4% to 7%. As for skin contact, Ralph leaves the wine macerating on skins for 4–5 weeks. The oak used is predominantly American (about 55%) and the rest French. The early picked cabernet is put into older oak, which does not dominate its more delicate flavours; the riper material is put into new. Over a period of about 3 months after vintage, the various parcels of wine, including merlot and petit verdot, are put together. The wine then spends at least 15 more months in barrel and is ready to bottle at 20 months of age. A zero sulfur regime is maintained during barrel maturation, but the wine before bottling receives about 20 parts per million. Ralph expects such a wine to come to maturity between 4 and 7 years of age depending on vintage and to live about 15 years. To him, Coonawarra's input into cabernet sauvignon is its 'terroir' and in that terroir there is an intensity of berry and earth flavour which, in Bordeaux terms, I liken to Pauillac.

In the Great Southern, John Wade at Howard Park also picks on flavour. He seeks out the riper traits—dark berry-cassis—seeing a natural progression of ripeness from capsicum (underripe), green-apple (almost), berry (just ripe), dark berry-cassis (properly ripe). These flavours often, but not always, have corresponding baume levels, but John never picks on baume. He looks for a total fermentation and skin-contact period of between 18 and 31 days in good years and less of course in lighter years. After inoculation for malolactic fermentation, his cabernet sauvignon goes into new French oak (Troncais or Allier or similar coarse-grained oak) for 6 months before its first racking. At this time also, the final wine is virtually assembled. This includes all the portions of cabernet sauvignon chosen, which constitute about 70% of the wine, about 25% merlot or shiraz (shiraz has been used in place of merlot in three of the eleven years that John has made his Cabernet) and about 5% cabernet franc. John is presently assessing petit verdot as a component of future Cabernet Merlots. The wine then receives another 12 months in barrel before its second racking. After this, there is a further maturation period in oak of about 6 months before it is coarsely filtered and prepared for bottling. After bottling there is a rest period of about 2 months before release. John expects his Howard Park Cabernet Merlots to drink softly and supplely for the first six months. They then usually 'tighten up' for about two years, coming to maturity between five and seven years of age. He expects their ultimate life span to be between 15 and 20 years. So what factor sets Mount Barker cabernet apart from the others? Well, perhaps none. John prefers to talk in terms of similarity, especially with Coonawarra, his other old stamping-ground. They share an earthy-berry flavour that is the hallmark of good cabernet. The difference, John feels, is that Howard Park Cabernet Merlot has more generosity on palate.

At Coldstream Hills in the Yarra Valley, James Halliday produces an estate-grown Cabernet Sauvignon, blended, when the vintage demands it, with about 10% merlot, but often 100% cabernet sauvignon. He does not pick on flavour alone. He looks very carefully at both vine and grape condition. To James, a favourable aspect, such as that of Coldstream's Amphitheatre vineyard, is critical when growing cabernet sauvignon in the Yarra. In nine out of ten years, he has noted that the vine leaves in the north-facing Amphitheatre are still 'active' at the time of picking; baumes are between 12.5 and 13.5 degrees and flavours are 'sweet berry', balanced by sufficient acidity. When he makes his cabernet sauvignon, about 60% is open-fermented and then run off into French oak to finish primary fermentation. The balance is left in closed vats to macerate on skins for 7–14 days. And the differentiating factors of Yarra Cabernet? According to Halliday, there is both finesse and fineness in Yarra Cabernet, finesse in its berry, leaf and mint flavours, fineness in the quality of its tannins. To use a Bordeaux comparison, in Cabernet the Yarra is Australia's Margaux commune.

✤ LIMESTONE COAST ZONE

The Limestone Coast is aptly named, for it mostly encompasses ancient sea beds of the Southern Ocean. Its wine regions are Mount Benson, Coonawarra, Wrattonbully and Padthaway.

ROBE

Robe is part of the Limestone Coast wine zone and not presently entitled to any more specific designation. Southcorp Wines has a vineyard here of 150.4 ha, consisting of the following grape varieties: (white) chardonnay, sauvignon blanc and semillon; (red) cabernet sauvignon and merlot. First vintage was in 1997 and the vineyard is not yet in full bearing, but when this is achieved it will yield an estimated 1500 tonnes. Its end use has not yet been decided. There are no local wineries. Climatic information would be similar to nearby Mount Benson (see entry).

BORDERTOWN

Bordertown is also part of the Limestone Coast zone. Though there are no local wineries, it is growing rapidly and had 340 hectares of vines in 1997. The area is irrigated. There are two major vineyards in the general area. As this area is likely to become a region, some basic climatic detail is given: MJT 22°C, MAR 12.3°C, HDD na, AR 557 mm, AI 358 mm, RH 48%.

Cuppa Cup Vineyard (vineyard only)   **NR**

Bordertown, SA 5268

Owner: Global Vineyards
Manager: Southcorp Wines
Chief winemaker: various winemakers within Southcorp Wines
Year of foundation: 1988
Tonnes crushed on average each year: not disclosed but estimated at 2800
Location: Bordertown
Area: 175 ha
Soils: terra rossa over limestone

Varieties planted: White—chardonnay; Red—cabernet sauvignon, merlot, petit verdot
Leading wines: the fruit has contributed to various wines made within the Southcorp group, for example, Lindemans Bin 65 Chardonnay, Penfolds Bins 707 and 407 Cabernet Sauvignon and Bin 389 Cabernet Shiraz
Notes: This is a valued contributor to some of Southcorp's leading wines. There are no local cellar door sales.

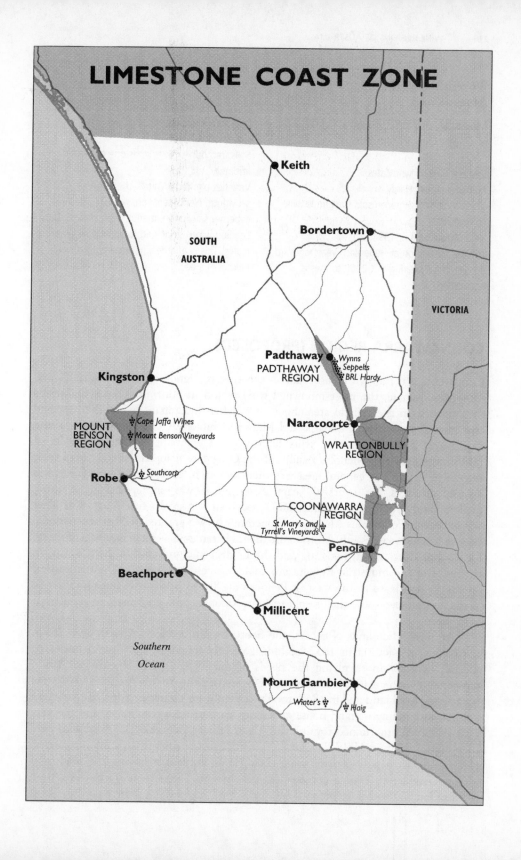

LIMESTONE COAST ZONE

Keith

Bordertown

SOUTH
AUSTRALIA

VICTORIA

Kingston

Padthaway
PADTHAWAY
REGION

Wynns
Seppelts
BRL Hardy

Naracoorte

MOUNT
BENSON
REGION

Cape Jaffa Wines
Mount Benson Vineyards

WRATTONBULLY
REGION

Robe

Southcorp

COONAWARRA
REGION

St Mary's and
Tyrrell's Vineyards

Penola

Beachport

Millicent

Southern
Ocean

Mount Gambier

Winter's   Haig

Wirrega Vineyard
(vineyard only)   **NR**

Mundulla, SA 5270, about 10 km south
of Cuppa Cup Vineyard

Owners: various syndicates
Manager: Geoff Hardy
Chief winemaker: grapes sold to various wine
companies
Year of foundation: 1994
Tonnes crushed on average each year: vineyard
not yet in full bearing but 2300 tonnes is
anticipated

Location: Mundulla
Area: 163.4 ha
Soils: red duplex over limestone marl, drip
irrigated
Varieties planted: White—chardonnay,
sauvignon blanc, semillon, verdelho; Red—
cabernet sauvignon, merlot, petit verdot, shiraz
Leading wines: fruit sold to various winemakers
Notes: This is a large vineyard in a relatively
unknown area. There are no local cellar door
sales.

COONAWARRA REGION (PROPOSED)

Coonawarra is certainly the most famous cabernet sauvignon region in Australia and,
some would argue, the most renowned wine region in Australia per se. Europeans
first touched on the general area about 1800, when Lieutenant James Grant named
two inland peaks Mount Schank and Mount Gambier. A closer inspection of the
region was made about two years later when Lieutenant Matthew Flinders of
HMS *Investigator* and Nicholas Baudin of the *Geographe* mapped the coast from their
respective ships. The general area was then forgotten, except by sealing boats and
escaped convicts, for over 40 years. After all it was unprepossessing country,
predominantly swampy in summer and flooded in winter. Its first squatter at what
was to become Penola was Alexander Cameron, who was granted the first occupational
licence in south-east South Australia in 1844. He ran considerable numbers of sheep,
for wool production was booming and the English midland and northern towns, in
the midst of the Industrial Revolution, could scarcely get enough. The first settlers
on the Yallum lease to the west of Penola were the Austins, who later sold to the
Wells. In October 1861, they resold to John Riddoch, who continued to populate it
with sheep.

Like many thousands of others, the Scottish-born Riddoch arrived, aged 25, in
the colony of Victoria in 1852, seeking gold. He found it, after initial fossicking
success, basically in supplying the needs of miners on the goldfields and was a
prosperous merchant in Geelong when he purchased the Yallum run for $60 000. He
became the local laird and in 1865 stood successfully for parliament. In 1880, he spent
$28 000 in building a grand house at Yallum Park which exists today, and the very
next year even entertained royalty, the young Princes George and Albert, who were
then midshipmen on HMS *Bacchante*. Yet Riddoch was more than a minor grandee.
He was in fact a politician of some skill. He succeeded in having the road from
Mount Gambier to Penola constructed and later in 1885 secured a rail link from
Mount Gambier to Naracoorte.

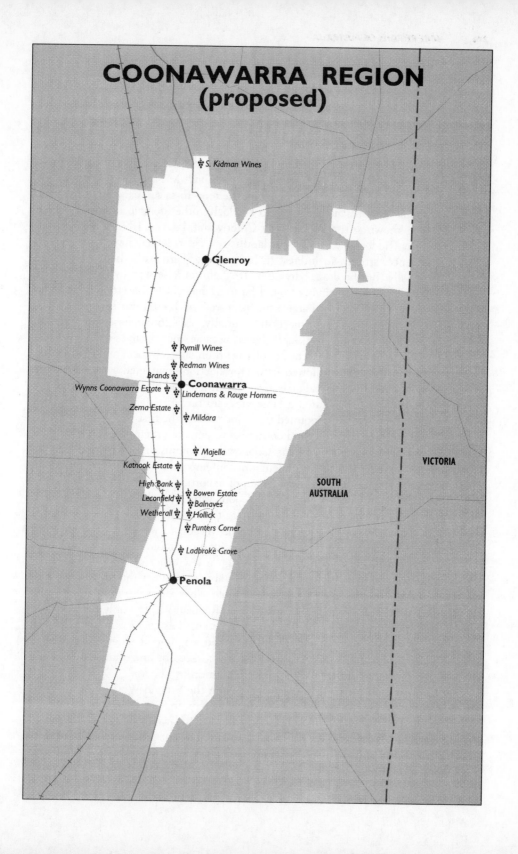

Though sheep provided his chief source of income, his interests were not devoted solely to them. By this time, they extended to arboriculture (he acclimatised the radiata pine in the region) and horticulture. In his horticultural endeavours, he was assisted by William Wilson, a Scot, who had also succeeded (rather more modestly than Riddoch) on the goldfields. Wilson had spent some years in vineyards in France and Spain and had later established an excellent Penola garden that, according to a contemporary observer (obviously anticipating the *Guide Michelin*) was 'worth a long journey to see'. The garden was developed on the terra rossa soil existing in the area. There was similar country further north in Riddoch's other domain, Katnook, which was to become known as the Penola Fruit Colony and, later in 1897, Coonawarra.

Exactly why Riddoch subdivided his land is not clear. It may have been, due to Wilson's influence, strictly an interest in horticulture. Perhaps he had overreached himself financially. But he did subdivide in 1890 after a false start in 1889. First, he divided 459 ha into blocks varying from 4 ha to 32 ha on the limestone ridge about 10 kilometres north of Penola. Later a further parcel of 324 ha was subdivided. His subdivision was not spectacularly successful. Initially, only 26 purchasers were found. For the Penola fruit colonists, as the purchasers became known, times rapidly became harder. The Australia-wide bank crashes of 1893 soon affected them and their prices. Droughts later in the 1890s followed by overproduction completed a dismal picture of poor economic returns, but Riddoch in the meantime had fulfilled his undertakings to his purchasers. He had planted a large vineyard on his neighbouring lands, had erected a substantial winery, appointed two winemakers (the first was William Salter, soon followed by Ewen McBain) and continued to purchase their grapes. Viticultural assistance was always available to his Coonawarra 'colonists'. But beyond that he could not go, for he too was dependent on contemporary market forces. Riddoch died in 1901, having realised his own dream of exporting his wine to England.

Without Riddoch's driving force, the Coonawarra viticultural dream began to fade rapidly and his winery was used merely for the making of base wine for brandy distillation. Only a young Bill Redman, who had begun to work for Riddoch a few months before his death, was able later to continue to produce wine by purchasing a 16 ha vineyard block from the estate, though a few other growers struggled on. Their grapes went to the still but Redman was able to prevent the total collapse of table wine making by the sale to Adelaide of table wines for export and later by sales to Woodley Wines of Adelaide. For many years Redman was the only name known outside the district and even then to very few people. His cause was not helped in the 1930s by a state government which instituted a vine-pull scheme designed to convert Coonawarra into a dairying area, but was assisted by one of his reds winning overseas recognition at an Inter-Dominion Exhibition in London.

Yet Coonawarra's turn was to come again, after the Second World War. In 1951, the Wynn family purchased the old Riddoch winery and its vineyards and David Wynn publicised the region so successfully that 'Coonawarra' became a buzzword among the few 'claret' drinkers of the time. A minute but growing public curiosity about Coonawarra and red wine generally awakened in turn the interest of Wynns rival producers. Mildara in particular began to purchase land on the terra rossa ridge. Penfolds too purchased vineyard blocks. Later Wynns itself began to increase its holdings substantially and by the mid-1960s Lindemans had also entered Coonawarra, this time by purchasing Rouge Homme, as the Redman family winery and winemaking business had come to be known.

Since then the Coonawarra land boom has continued, not only in the terra rossa country but also in the adjoining intermediate and poorly drained black rendzina soils. What has eventuated, with a logic that is sometimes rare in the wine industry, is that grape varieties for which Coonawarra is traditionally respected—cabernet sauvignon and shiraz—have for the most part been planted on the well-drained terra rossa soils and transitional soils. The white varieties such as chardonnay, sauvignon blanc and semillon and red varieties used for sparkling wine base such as pinot noir have been chiefly planted on the black rendzina.

It was once alleged that soils had little relevance in Australian winemaking. What was important was superior winemaking technique. In Coonawarra's case, that is quite wrong. Coonawarra's winemakers are as technically skilled as any others in Australia but, in red winemaking, their typical terra rossa soils give them a decided edge.

Coonawarra's road to regional status has not been without controversy. Not that it was ever doubted that it should be a region. What was in contention were its boundaries. The first formal declaration of these was at the annual general meeting of the Viticultural Council of the South East of South Australia on 25 October 1984, where it was decided that the Hundreds of Penola and Comaum should be regarded as the boundaries of Coonawarra. At the ensuing annual general meeting (21 October 1985), this decision was reaffirmed. In addition, in the rules of the Coonawarra Vignerons' Association, which was incorporated on 12 November 1985, membership was made available 'to holders of producers' licences, as defined in the Liquor Licensing Act, in the Coonawarra viticultural area, within the Hundreds of Penola and Comaum . . .'. On 18 May 1988, the Viticultural Council repeated its definition in a letter to Karl Seppelt, who was at that time engaged in defining the viticultural regions of South Australia on behalf of the Australian Wine and Brandy Corporation. The Viticultural Council again confirmed the definition of Coonawarra at its meeting on 17 July 1991. It is perhaps unfortunate that nowhere in these resolutions is there any mention of soil type, merely the hundred boundaries of Comaum and Penola and in the 1980s the area had been growing rapidly. However, thought was obviously being given to this problem. The Coonawarra Grapegrowers' Association Inc (CGA) was formed on 11 August 1993. Its qualification for membership rather mysteriously confers eligibility upon growers of wine grapes within the area known as Coonawarra, which is defined as 'that area within the Hundreds of Penola and Comaum and more particularly that wine grape growing area known as Coonawarra . . . which area shall be determined by members at a special general meeting from time to time'. Though, as a definition, it suffers logically in that it is defined in terms of itself (how can Coonawarra be defined by 'members', who may or may not be within its boundaries?) it does allow the CGA to vary its area from time to time. The new boundaries as shown on the map (p. 217), were approved by members on 1 December 1995.

Today, within its delimited boundaries, Coonawarra has approximately 3300 ha of vineyard, producing about 35 000 tonnes of grapes. There are 13 wineries and

20 sales outlets, a far cry from my first visit to the region in 1967 when there were four wineries and one sales outlet.

Location: latitude 37°18'S, longitude 140°50'E, about 360 km south-east of Adelaide
Altitude: 59 m
Topography and soils: The general area of which Coonawarra is part is a series of former coastal dunes, rising slightly to the north-east and descending to the south-west, ultimately to the present sea-level, at Beachport, about 90 km away. The region itself is set on a limestone ridge only centimetres above flat country which, prior to various drainage schemes during the early twentieth century, was prone to flooding during winter rainfall, as there were no rivers or creeks in the region to carry the water away naturally. This low plain with its consequent, vigorous growth of grass provided good summer pasture for sheep and cattle. The limestone ridge slightly above was selected for settlement and for the building of roads, because of its superior drainage.

The limestone ridge of Coonawarra is distinct, apparently created about 650 000 years ago in a different geological age to other such ridges in the general area. This distinction lies in the differences in its age, its slightly higher clay content and organic matter. It extends from just to the south of Penola northwards about 16 kilometres. It is nowhere more than 2 kilometres wide and is often much narrower. Its surface is a layer of rich red loam, commonly called terra rossa (classified by KH Northcote as consisting of two soils (Uf 5.31 and Um 6.41)) varying in depth from 5 centimetres to about 60. It is superimposed on pieces of limestone intermixed with clay down to about two to three metres. In turn, this sits above a pure water table, beneath which there is a bed of sandstone. Generally to the west there is a heavier black loam, called black rendzina, which sits above similar substrata. However, both red and black topsoil areas on the eastern boundary are somewhat intermingled. The crucial difference between the soils is their drainage capacity.

The black rendzina soils (often called groundwater or, as classified by KH Northcote, Ug 5.14) are much inferior in this aspect. It has been said that such soils can hold six times as much water as an equivalent depth of sand. Though vines may be grown on the black rendzina (indeed it has been noted that such soils promote excessive growth and sometimes overcropping), its poorer drainage means that the soils warm later than the red soils and therefore that vines grown on it may have a later budburst, a later flowering and even perhaps an imperfect ripening. This would be critical in later-ripening red varieties such as cabernet sauvignon and petit verdot. So the comparatively early ripening white and red varieties such as chardonnay, pinot noir and meunier (all eminently suitable for sparkling wine base) may be grown satisfactorily. Indeed, satis-factory white wine may be made from other early ripening white varieties not customarily used for sparkling wine base (all, it should be noted, with reasonable and not excessive crop levels). Quality red production should not, however, be expected from such soils. There are also brown rendzina soils found in the Coonawarra region. These are similar to terra rossa in all respects except colour and are called in the region 'transitional' soils. They have been planted to grapes quite successfully.

Within the delimited area, to the east of the limestone ridge and as far as the

Victorian border, there are duplex red sandy soils over a clay base (Northcote Dr 2.23). Again, they are intermixed with small banks of terra rossa and the brown 'transitional' soils. Drainage is satisfactory and vineyard development as part of the Coonawarra region is permitted here.

Climate: MJT 19.3°C, HDD raw 1363, 1333 (cut off and as adj for lat, daily temp range and for vine sites) MAR na, AR 628 mm (Oct–Apr 257 mm), RH 40% (Jan 3pm), AI na, SH 7.5 (G). MJT 19.6°C, MAR 9.8°C, HDD raw 1432, AR 646 mm (Oct–Mar 218 mm), RH na, AI 52 mm, SH 7.8 (D&S). (Local) 18.85°C (av between 3 stations (north, central and south)), MAR 9.75°C (again based on same av), RH 49% (av Jan). Coonawarra is a cool but sunny area with a low January relative humidity. The climate has been described as Mediterranean and is uniform throughout the region. About 35–40% of its annual rainfall falls in the growing season (Oct–Mar) and can occasionally affect vintage, especially in the south of the region. Irrigation is from bores and is controlled and licensed by statute according to type of crop. Such bores are replenished by groundwater flow and by a shallow water table only 2 metres beneath the surface. A confined aquifer (the Dilwyn Formation) exists about 150 metres beneath the surface, but is not presently used for irrigation. Local lore regards Anzac Day (25 April) as a watershed in ripening, as the weather sometimes changes dramatically after that date. It is said, particularly of cabernet sauvignon, that 'if it is not ripe by Anzac Day, forget it!'. Viticultural problems include spring frosts which can be severe, and powdery and downy mildew, both usually controlled by fungicide sprays. On the bigger properties, pruning and harvesting is usually by machine. For cabernet sauvignon on the classical soils, ripening times are reasonably uniform throughout the centre of the region, though slightly earlier in the north and correspondingly later in the south. Picking for cabernet sauvignon typically commences in the second to third week of April.

Harvest time: generally from late March to early May

Principal grape varieties: White—chardonnay, riesling, sauvignon blanc, semillon; Red—cabernet franc, cabernet sauvignon, merlot, pinot noir, petit verdot, shiraz

Total area: 3000 ha and growing

Principal wine styles: Cabernet Sauvignon (which may include up to 15% of merlot, cabernet franc and petit verdot in total), Cabernet Merlot (which may include less than 85% cabernet sauvignon, but must include merlot as a predominant secondary variety), Cabernet Verdot (similarly with verdot as predominant secondary variety), Shiraz, Chardonnay.

Balnaves **R7.5**

Riddoch Highway, Coonawarra, SA 5263 (4 km north of Penola on right-hand side between Haselgrove and Bowen Estate)
Ph 08 8737 2946, Fax 08 8737 2045

Owners: Doug, Annette, Kirsty and Peter Balnaves

Chief winemaker: Peter Bissell
Year of foundation: 1976 (vineyard), first vintage 1990
Tonnes crushed on average each year: 400; (own label 80)
Location: Coonawarra
Area: 40 ha

Soils: red clay loam over limestone and friable red loam over clay and also sandy soil over clay
Varieties planted: White—chardonnay; Red—cabernet franc, cabernet sauvignon, merlot, shiraz
Leading wines: Balnaves of Coonawarra Cabernet Sauvignon
Notes: Doug Balnaves is a Coonawarra winegrower of great experience, formerly the viticulturalist for the Coonawarra vineyard of Hungerford Hill, which is now a Southcorp brand. Since 1996, there has been a new winery on site, though Doug still sells 80% of his grapes to other wineries. Cellar door sales: weekdays 9am–5pm, weekends and public holidays 10am–5pm.

Bowen Estate R8.5

Main Road (now the Riddoch Highway), Coonawarra, SA 5263
Ph 08 8737 2229, Fax 08 8737 2173

Owners: Doug and Joy Bowen
Chief winemaker: Doug Bowen
Year of foundation: 1972. First vintage 1975
Tonnes crushed on average each year: 140
Location: Coonawarra
Area: 32 ha
Soils: red clay based loam over limestone
Varieties planted: White—chardonnay; Red—cabernet franc, cabernet sauvignon, merlot, petit verdot, shiraz
Leading wines: Bowen Estate Shiraz, Bowen Estate Cabernet Sauvignon
Notes: After Eric Brand and Owen Redman, Doug Bowen was one of the first 'boutique' producers of Coonawarra. Restricting cropping levels to about 6 tonnes per hectare for his reds, he makes concentrated yet supple reds and has built a very fine reputation for his Shiraz and Cabernet Sauvignon over the years. Cellar door sales: 7 days 10am–5pm except at Christmas and Good Friday.

Brands R8.5

Riddoch Highway, Coonawarra, SA 5263
Ph 08 8736 3260, Fax 08 8736 3208

Owner: McWilliam's Wines Pty Ltd
Winemakers: Jim Brand and Bruce Gregory
Year of foundation: 1965
Tonnes crushed on average each year: 700 (1997) and growing, reaching about 3000 tonnes about the year 2000
Location: Coonawarra
Area: 240 ha in bearing and awaiting bearing
Soils: red clay loam over limestone
Varieties planted: White—chardonnay, riesling; Red—cabernet franc, cabernet sauvignon, merlot, petit verdot, pinot noir, shiraz
Leading wines: Brand's Family Reserve Chardonnay, Brand's Family Reserve Cabernet Sauvignon
Notes: By taking over Rouge Homme Wines in 1965, Lindemans inadvertently started a new era for Eric Brand. He had previously been a Coonawarra orchardist with a few acres of shiraz grapes, which he had sold to his father-in-law, Bill Redman. As a new winemaker with little winemaking knowledge, Eric converted the back of his garage into a winery, borrowed some equipment from Hardy's and also some experience from Owen Redman and made a stunning 1966 Shiraz. Fortune had smiled and Brand's Laira Shiraz 1966 is one of my lasting wine memories. Cellar door sales: weekdays 8am–4.30pm, weekends and public holidays 10am–4pm.

BRL Hardy (vineyards only) NR

Riddoch Highway, Coonawarra, SA 5263
Ph 08 8736 5144, Fax 08 8736 5110

Owner: BRL Hardy Ltd
Chief winemaker: Peter Dawson
Year of foundation: 1971
Tonnes crushed on average each year: not disclosed but estimated (1997) at 300 tonnes, which will increase dramatically once all

planted vineyard comes into bearing
Location: Coonawarra (three vineyards)
Area: Weatherall Vineyard 24.7 ha of which
7.7 ha are interplanted; 24 ha (planted 1995),
and further 80 ha was planted during 1996–7;
27 ha leased 1996
Soils: (Weatherall Vineyard) terra rossa and
black rendzina; 80 ha vineyard terra rossa and
brown soils over clay; 27 ha vineyard, terra
rossa
Varieties planted: White—none; Red—cabernet
sauvignon, merlot, shiraz
Leading wines: Thomas Hardy Cabernet
Sauvignon (at present not wholly Coonawarra
cabernet, as sufficient fruit is not yet available)
Notes: Among the bigger Australian wine
companies, BRL Hardy has always found it
difficult to source sufficient fruit from
Coonawarra for its red winemaking needs.
Recent vineyard plantings should solve that
problem around the year 2000. No cellar door
sales.

Haselgrove

Formerly owners of 40 hectares of vineyard
which were sold recently, Haselgroves are now
concentrating their attentions on the McLaren
Vale and Koppamurra regions, where they
have substantial vineyards. They are winding
down Coonawarra, where less than one
hectare of vineyard remains.

Highbank   R8
Riddoch Highway, Coonawarra, SA 5263
Ph 08 8737 2020, Fax 08 8736 3122

Owners: Dennis and Bonnie Vice
Chief winemaker: Trevor Mast (contract)
Year of foundation: 1986
Tonnes crushed on average each year: 25
Location: Coonawarra
Area: 4.8 ha
Soils: terra rossa without variation

Varieties planted: White—none; Red—cabernet
franc, cabernet sauvignon, merlot
Leading wines: Highbank, Cabernet Blend,
Merlot
Notes: Dennis Vice is a lecturer in viticulture at
the South East Institute of Technical and
Further Education and practises hands-on
viticulture at Highbank. His chief wine is a
smooth Cabernet blend, but when there is
sufficient merlot, a 100% Merlot is also made.
An excellent Highbank Cabernet Sauvignon
1996 was tasted in November 1997. Some
accommodation is available at Honeysuckle
Rise, set among the Highbank vines. Cellar
door sales: long weekends and public holidays
10am–5pm, other times by appointment.

Hollick   R8
Racecourse Road, Penola, SA 5277
Ph 08 8737 2318, Fax 08 8737 2952

Owners: IB & WC Hollick
Chief winemaker: Ian Hollick
Year of foundation: 1983
Tonnes crushed on average each year: 500
Location: Penola
Area: 54 ha
Soils: terra rossa
Varieties planted: White—chardonnay, riesling;
Red—cabernet sauvignon, malbec, merlot,
pinot noir, shiraz
Leading wines: Ravenswood Cabernet
Sauvignon, Hollick, Cabernet Sauvignon Merlot,
Reserve Chardonnay, Unoaked Chardonnay,
Shiraz Cabernet Sauvignon
Notes: By Coonawarra standards, Hollick is an
estate of modest size but of excellent
reputation. Winning the 1985 Jimmy Watson
trophy in only its third year of operation did
not hurt at all. Ian Hollick makes some of
Coonawarra's best reds. In particular, the
Ravenswood Cabernet Sauvignon, which makes
its appearance only in Coonawarra's best years,
is outstanding.

Katnook Estate **R9**

Riddoch Highway, Coonawarra, SA 5263
(about halfway between Penola and
Coonawarra)
Ph 08 8737 2394, Fax 08 8737 2397

Owner: Wingara Wine Group Pty Ltd
Chief winemaker: Wayne Stehbens
Year of foundation: 1979
Tonnes crushed on average each year: 1500
Location: Coonawarra
Area: 237.5 ha
Soils: essentially terra rossa but also chocolatey
terra rossa soils
Varieties planted: White—chardonnay, riesling,
sauvignon blanc; Red—cabernet sauvignon,
merlot, pinot noir, shiraz
Leading wines: Katnook Cabernet Sauvignon,
Merlot, Chardonnay, Sauvignon Blanc
Notes: Katnook is named after one of John
Riddoch's properties, part of which is the
original Coonawarra subdivision. Indeed,
Katnook's second label (usually very good
value) is Riddoch Estate. Katnook produces an
excellent Cabernet Sauvignon, a complex
Chardonnay and one of the better Sauvignon
Blancs from this region. A new and quite
recent addition to the range is the excellent
Coonawarra Merlot. Cellar door sales: Mon–Fri
9am–4.30pm, Sat 10am–4.30pm, Sun
12noon–4.30pm, closed Christmas Day, Boxing
Day and Good Friday.

S Kidman Wines **NR**

John Riddoch Highway, Coonawarra, SA
5263 (about 12 km north of Coonawarra
township)
Ph 08 8736 5071, Fax 08 8736 5070

Owners: Sid and Suzie Kidman
Chief winemaker: Sid Kidman
Year of foundation: 1984
Tonnes crushed on average each year: 100 of
which 74 are used for the Kidman label
Location: Coonawarra

Area: 15 ha
Soils: terra rossa and sandy loam over red clay
Varieties planted: White—riesling, sauvignon
blanc; Red—cabernet sauvignon, shiraz
Leading wines: Kidman Cabernet Sauvignon,
Shiraz, Riesling, Sauvignon Blanc
Notes: Formerly called 'The Ridge Wines', this
is quite a small estate by Coonawarra
standards. Cellar door sales: 9am–5pm daily.

Ladbroke Grove **NR**

Riddoch Highway, Penola, SA 5277
Ph 08 8737 2082, Fax 08 8737 3236

Owner: Ladbroke Grove Wines Pty Ltd
Chief winemaker: Ken Ward (contract)
Year of foundation: 1982
Tonnes crushed on average each year: 10
Location: Coonawarra
Area: 1 ha
Soils: terra rossa
Varieties planted: White—riesling; Red—shiraz
Leading wines: Ladbroke Grove, Premium
Shiraz, Shiraz, Riesling
Notes: A very small boutique with cellar door
sales: 7 days 10am–4.30pm.

Leconfield **R9.5**

Riddoch Highway, Coonawarra, SA 5263
Ph 08 8737 2326, Fax 08 8737 2285

Owner: Richard Hamilton Wines Pty Ltd
Chief winemaker: Philippa Treadwell
Year of foundation: 1974
Tonnes crushed on average each year: 450
Location: Coonawarra
Area: 40 ha
Soils: terra rossa plus a little black rendzina
Varieties planted: White—chardonnay, riesling;
Red—cabernet franc, cabernet sauvignon,
merlot, petit verdot, shiraz
Leading wines: Leconfield, Cabernet, Shiraz,
Chardonnay, Riesling
Notes: Since the days of former proprietor Syd
Hamilton, Leconfield's wine of renown has

been Cabernet, a benchmark of the region, which is now a blend of cabernet sauvignon, merlot, petit verdot and sometimes cabernet franc, which accounts for 78% of its Coonawarra production. In recent times, there has also been a great demand for its excellent Shiraz. Cellar door sales: 7 days 10am–5pm, except Christmas Day and Good Friday.

Lindemans **R10**

Riddoch Highway, Coonawarra, SA 5263
Ph 08 8736 3205, Fax 08 8736 3250

Owner: Southcorp Wines
Chief winemaker: Greg Clayfield
Year of foundation: 1971
Tonnes crushed on average each year: not disclosed but estimated at 1350
Location: Coonawarra
Area: 132.6 ha
Soils: classic central strip terra rossa
Varieties planted: White—chardonnay, riesling, sauvignon blanc; Red—cabernet franc, cabernet sauvignon, malbec, merlot, shiraz
Leading wines: Limestone Ridge Shiraz Cabernet, St George Cabernet Sauvignon, Pyrus
Notes: Lindemans have been located in Coonawarra since 1965, when the former Lindemans public company purchased Rouge Homme Wines. It did not really begin to market its own Coonawarra brands till the mid-1970s when Limestone Ridge 1971 was released and the reds that have become famous, the Lindemans trio—St George, Limestone Ridge and Pyrus. Of the three, I have a sneaking preference for Limestone Ridge, which for me epitomises classic Coonawarra character, though St George Cabernet Sauvignon and Pyrus (a multi-blend of cabernet sauvignon, cabernet franc, merlot and malbec) have had their moments of triumph. A Jimmy Watson trophy was won in 1981 for the 1980 St George and the same trophy for 1985 Pyrus in 1986. All three are

individual vineyard wines. Lindemans Coonawarra whites can also be very good, but the reds have always been the raison d'etre for the company's presence in Coonawarra. May they long continue! Cellar door sales: 7 days 10am–4pm.

Majella **R8.5**

Lynn Road, Coonawarra, SA 5263
Ph 08 8736 3055, Fax 08 8736 3057

Owners: Brian, Anthony, Ros and Teresa Lynn
Chief winemaker: Bruce Gregory (contract)
Year of foundation: 1968
Tonnes crushed on average each year: 300 (60 of which are used for the Majella label)
Location: Coonawarra
Area: 43 ha
Soils: terra rossa running off to sandy loam at the rear of the property
Varieties planted: White—none; Red—cabernet sauvignon, merlot, shiraz
Leading wines: Majella, Shiraz, Cabernet
Notes: Majella is now one of the older and more mature red vineyards of the Coonawarra region and supplied excellent fruit to Wynns for many years, some of which found its way into the early John Riddoch Cabernets. It continues to sell most of its fruit, but since 1991 has made excellent Shiraz and Cabernet reds under its own label. Cellar door sales: 7 days 10am–4.30pm.

Mildara **R8.5**

Riddoch Highway, Coonawarra, SA 5263
Ph 08 8736 3380, Fax 08 8736 3307

Owner: Mildara Wines Ltd
Winemaker: David O'Leary
Year of foundation: 1955
Tonnes crushed on average each year: 3038
Location: Coonawarra
Area: (landholding) 312 ha
Soils: terra rossa with some black rendzina soils to the west

Varieties planted: White—chardonnay, sauvignon blanc; Red—cabernet sauvignon, malbec, merlot, pinot noir, shiraz

Leading wines: Mildara Alexanders, Robertson's Well Cabernet Sauvignon, Jamieson's Run Red and Jamieson's Run Chardonnay

Notes: Historically Mildara is one of Coonawarra's most important names. As the first large Australian wine producer to purchase land in the region after Wynns, it helped in a small way (in the early 1960s) to promote the red boom that awakened Australia to table wine in the late 1960s. It is equally important to understand how Mildara (in the 1930s and 1940s a leading producer of fortified wines) became involved in table wine per se. The late Ron Haselgrove, chairman of Mildara in the 1950s, believed that red table wine was at that time set to return to market favour. Consequently, Mildara became a keen purchaser of Coonawarra red from Bill Redman in the early 1950s to blend with other material purchased from McLaren Vale and the Hunter Valley. Redman ultimately advised Mildara that his own production was limited and that Mildara should really acquire its own vineyard land on the red bank and make its own red. Its first of many such land purchases was in 1955. In 1963, it erected its winery (the third in the region, after Rouge Homme and Wynns) and its first famous red (a Cabernet Sauvignon) of that vintage was appropriately nicknamed 'Peppermint Patty' because of its intense peppermint character on nose and palate. It is fair to say that no other Mildara Coonawarra red has been as famous since, but the quality of Alexanders (a blend of cabernet sauvignon, merlot and malbec) and Robertson's Well Cabernet Sauvignon remains high. Cellar door sales: weekdays 9am–4.30pm, Saturdays, Sundays and public holidays 10am–4pm.

Orlando (vineyards only) R9

Riddoch Highway, Coonawarra, SA 5263

Owners: Orlando and Richmond Grove
Chief winemaker: Phil Laffer
Year of foundation: 1977
Tonnes crushed on average each year: 600
Location: Coonawarra (three separate vineyards)
Area: 130 ha
Soils: terra rossa, plus dark chocolate soil over limestone
Varieties planted: White—chardonnay, riesling; Red—cabernet franc, cabernet sauvignon, merlot, pinot noir, shiraz
Leading wines: St Hugo Coonawarra Cabernet Sauvignon, Richmond Grove Coonawarra Cabernet, Russet Ridge, Jacaranda Ridge Cabernet Sauvignon
Notes: Orlando is another large winemaker, which came late to Coonawarra. Its St Hugo Cabernets are of high quality and always reliable, while its super-flagship from Coonawarra, Jacaranda Ridge, makes rather more spasmodic but sensational appearances. Richmond Grove Coonawarra Cabernet is also a recent arrival and usually excellent value. There are no cellar door sales.

Parker Coonawarra Estate R9

Riddoch Highway, Coonawarra, SA 5263
Ph 02 9357 3376, Fax 02 9358 2527

Owners: Parker Coonawarra Vineyard Partnership and Pepper Tree Wines Pty Ltd
Chief winemaker: Chris Cameron
Year of foundation: 1985
Tonnes crushed on average each year: 45 (the balance of fruit, about 150 tonnes, is sold or made under other labels)
Location: Coonawarra
Area: 20 ha
Soils: terra rossa varying in colour from deep red to brown
Varieties planted: White—none; Red—cabernet

franc, cabernet sauvignon, merlot, petit verdot
Leading wines: Parker Coonawarra Estate Terra Rossa First Growth, Parker Coonawarra Estate Terra Rossa Cabernet Sauvignon
Notes: From the varieties planted, it is easy to see that the Parker wines are variations on a theme of Coonawarra Cabernet Sauvignon and are major products indeed. Very rich and powerful in fruit with equally impressive oak, they are certainly made to cellar for an extended period (say 8–10 years). There are no cellar door sales.

Penfolds (vineyard only) R10

Riddoch Highway, Coonawarra, SA 5263

Owner: Southcorp Wines
Chief winemaker: John Duval
Year of foundation: 1957
Tonnes crushed on average each year: not disclosed but estimated at 1300
Location: Coonawarra
Area: 130.5 ha
Soils: terra rossa
Varieties planted: White—chardonnay, riesling; Red—cabernet sauvignon, shiraz
Leading wines: Penfolds Coonawarra Shiraz Bin 128 and superb special releases from time to time, such as Bin 620 Cabernet Shiraz 1966 and other more recent wines
Notes: With ownership of its Coonawarra vineyard dating from the Coonawarra revival of the late 1950s, Penfolds is one of the veterans of the region. Bin 128 Coonawarra Shiraz has been a consistent though not outstanding performer over the years, but the special releases made from time to time more than warrant my rating. No local cellar door sales.

Penley Estate (vineyard only) R9.5

McLeans Road, Coonawarra, SA 5263
Ph 08 8231 2400, Fax 08 8231 0589

Owner: Penley Estate
Chief winemaker: Kym Tolley

Year of foundation: 1988
Tonnes crushed on average each year: 750
Location: Coonawarra
Area: 81 ha
Soils: terra rossa and brown sandy loam and overlying limestone
Varieties planted: White—chardonnay; Red—cabernet franc, cabernet sauvignon, merlot, pinot noir, shiraz
Leading wines: Penley Coonawarra Cabernet Sauvignon, Coonawarra Pinot Noir Sparkling, Chardonnay, Hyland Shiraz
Notes: Kym Tolley is a winemaker not only by vocation but also by ancestry, being descended from the Penfold and Tolley families. When Coonawarra is added to this winemaking heritage, the results are reds of sumptuous style and whites of elegance. The Penley Estate Coonawarra Cabernet Sauvignon can be simply magnificent. Cellar door sales: none at Coonawarra, tasting by appointment in Adelaide.

Petaluma R10

Riddoch Highway, Coonawarra, SA 5263
Ph 08 8339 4122, Fax 08 8339 5253

Owner: Petaluma Ltd
Chief winemaker: Brian Croser; (winemaker) Constantinos Moshos

i) Evans Vineyard

Year of foundation: 1969
Tonnes crushed on average each year: 62
Location: Coonawarra
Area: 7.35 ha
Soils: terra rossa, clay loam well structured over former or highly calcareous material
Varieties planted: White—none; Red—cabernet sauvignon, merlot
Leading wines: Petaluma Coonawarra (Red), Petaluma Coonawarra Merlot
Notes: A blend of cabernet sauvignon and merlot, the Petaluma Coonawarra is a superb

premium red. It is made in the best traditions of its region without the massive structure of some of its counterparts but with the added style and elegance that one expects from any Petaluma wine. Bordeaux comparisons are odious but Petaluma Coonawarra plays the Lafite of the region. No local cellar door sales.

ii) *Sharefarmers Vineyard*

Penola Hundred Line Road, Coonawarra, SA 5263

Year of foundation: 1983
Tonnes crushed on average each year: 210
Location: Coonawarra (see notes)
Area: 40 ha
Soils: terra rossa similar to Evans Vineyard
Varieties planted: White—chardonnay, sauvignon blanc, semillon; Red—cabernet franc, cabernet sauvignon, malbec, merlot, pinot noir
Leading wines: Sharefarmers White, Sharefarmers Red
Notes: At the time of writing, this is a vineyard of much controversy. The vineyard is within the hundred of Struan, outside what is now the regional boundary of Coonawarra and outside the Penola hundred on the opposite side of the road, although it was planted before the 'official' definition of the Coonawarra boundary was made by the Viticultural Council of SE South Australia in October 1984. Its wines are of excellent quality and go under the Sharefarmers label and sometimes into the Petaluma brands. No local cellar door sales.

Punters Corner **R7.5**

Riddoch Highway and Racecourse Road, Coonawarra, SA 5263
Ph/Fax 08 8737 2007

Owner: Timbercorp Securities Pty Ltd
Chief winemaker: Balnaves' (contract)
Year of foundation: 1975 (as James Haselgrove), 1993 as Punters Corner

Tonnes crushed on average each year: 200 of which 60 is utilised for the Punters Corner label
Location: Coonawarra
Area: 43.75 ha in two blocks, one on Victoria and Albert Lane and the other surrounding the cellar door sales area
Soils: terra rossa and shallow sand over clay (V & A Lane)
Varieties planted: White—chardonnay; Red—cabernet sauvignon, malbec, merlot, shiraz
Leading wines: Cabernet Sauvignon, Shiraz, Chardonnay
Notes: Located at the southern end of the famous terra rossa bank, its address is the clue to the unusual name of this vineyard—the Penola Racecourse is a few hundred metres away. From my experience of the Cabernet Sauvignon, the wines are considerably better than a good each-way bet. Cellar door sales: 10am–5pm each day, except June, July and August when hours are 10am–4pm weekdays and 10am–5pm weekends and holidays.

Redman Wines **R7**

Riddoch Highway, Coonawarra, SA 5263
Ph 08 8736 3331, Fax 08 8736 3013

Owners: Redman family
Chief winemakers: Bruce and Malcolm Redman
Year of foundation: 1966
Tonnes crushed on average each year: 250
Location: Coonawarra
Area: 33.5 ha
Soils: terra rossa virtually 100%
Varieties planted: White—none; Red—cabernet sauvignon, merlot, shiraz
Leading wines: Redman Shiraz, Redman Cabernet Sauvignon, Redman Cabernet Sauvignon Merlot
Notes: Redman Wines came into being soon after the sale of Rouge Homme Wines to Lindemans in 1965, when Owen Redman purchased Arthur Hoffman's 70-year-old shiraz

block, which in 1966 yielded some superb wine, as it did again in 1969. Plantings of cabernet sauvignon made in the late 1960s came to fruition in 1970. The first vintages off the new cabernet block were excellent. I well remember the 1971, bottled in magnum. During the later 1970s and 1980s, wine standards declined but more recently there have been distinct signs of improvement. Cellar door sales: Mon–Fri 9am–5pm, weekends 10am–4pm.

Rosemount (vineyard only) R9

Kirri Billi Vineyard, Riddoch Highway, Coonawarra, SA 5263

Owner: Rosemount Estate Pty Ltd
Chief winemaker: Philip Shaw
Year of foundation: 1982
Tonnes crushed on average each year: not disclosed but estimated at 280
Location: Coonawarra
Area: 108 ha (80 ha planted in 1997 and not yet bearing)
Soils: (Kirri Billi) classic terra rossa; (Abbey) patches of terra rossa, clay loams, outcrops of sandy loam to sand
Varieties planted: White—none; Red—cabernet sauvignon, merlot
Leading wines: Reserve Cabernet
Notes: In a little under 30 years, Rosemount has become a national wine company with, I imagine, all the aspirations accompanying such a status. Naturally one of those should be a quality Coonawarra red, appearing annually. One of my Rosemount disappointments has been that great Coonawarra reds have not appeared often enough from Rosemount's older Coonawarra vineyard. With new vineyard plantings in Coonawarra of 80 ha complementing the existing 28 ha and ultimately producing over 1000 tonnes, this should ensure that this comes about more regularly.

Rouge Homme R8

Riddoch Highway, Coonawarra, SA 5263
Ph 08 8736 3205, Fax 08 8736 3250

Owner: Southcorp Wines
Chief winemaker: Paul Gordon
Year of foundation: 1908 as John Redman & Sons (Bill Redman) and 1954 as Rouge Homme Wines Pty Ltd
Tonnes crushed on average each year: not disclosed but estimated at 600
Location: Coonawarra
Area: 60 ha
Soils: terra rossa
Varieties planted: White—chardonnay; Red—cabernet franc, cabernet sauvignon, merlot, petit verdot, pinot noir, shiraz
Leading wines: Cabernet Sauvignon, Pinot Noir, Shiraz Cabernet, Richardson's Red Block (a blend of the 'Bordeaux' red varieties and in this sense a 'younger brother' of Lindemans Pyrus with talents of its own, winning the Jimmy Watson trophy in 1994)
Notes: Rouge Homme Wines was purchased by Lindemans in 1965 and has since become a 'brand', though a very good one, sourcing its fruit from the Coonawarra region. The Richardson's Block wines are not individual vineyard wines but may contain material from the Rouge Homme Richardson's Block, together with other Coonawarra material. The petit verdot mentioned among the varieties planted is not yet an active participant in any of the reds.

Rymill Wines R8

The Riddoch Run Vineyard, Coonawarra, SA 5263
Ph 08 8736 5001, Fax 08 8736 5040

Owners: Rymill family
Chief winemaker: John Innes
Year of foundation: 1972
Tonnes crushed on average each year: 1500
Location: Coonawarra

Area: 161 ha in two vineyards (Winery) 101 ha, (Three Milehome) 60 ha
Soils: (Winery) terra rossa of variable depth; (Three Milehome) part terra rossa and sandy loam over limestone
Varieties planted: White—chardonnay, sauvignon blanc, traminer; Red—cabernet franc, cabernet sauvignon, merlot, meunier, pinot noir, shiraz
Leading wines: Rymill Cabernet Sauvignon, Merlot Cabernet Franc and Cabernet Sauvignon, Shiraz
Notes: Peter Rymill is of Riddoch descent, formerly using 'Riddoch Run' as his label. As there are at least two other labels which celebrate the memory of his ancestor, to avoid confusion Peter Rymill has phased out 'Riddoch Run' on the Australian market. It is still used, however, on wines intended for export. The Rymill winery is located in an outstanding, modern building with facilities for visitors to view every part of the process. The Rymill Cabernet Sauvignon is worthy of the highest respect. Cellar door sales: 7 days 10am—5pm except Good Friday and Christmas Day.

Southcorp Wines

Remaining vineyards owned by Southcorp in the Coonawarra region include the Terra Rossa Vineyard, located north of Coonawarra, which was established in 1968. It is 45.3 ha in extent, producing about 450 tonnes (not disclosed, but my estimate) of chardonnay, cabernet sauvignon and shiraz. Its production is used variously by Penfolds. There are other vineyards at various places within the region owned by Southcorp Wines. They encompass 198.2 ha, producing on my estimate about 2000 tonnes of chardonnay, riesling, cabernet sauvignon, merlot, petit verdot, pinot noir and shiraz. The production is utilised in Penfolds reds, Seaview sparkling wines and Tollana Botrytis Riesling. Soils are chiefly terra rossa but vary in places to podsolic sands over clay. There are no cellar door outlets in Coonawarra for these vineyards.

Wetherall R7

Riddoch Highway, Coonawarra, SA 5263
Ph 08 8737 2104, Fax 08 8737 2105

Owners: MT and MC Wetherall and BA and MJ Wetherall
Chief winemaker: Michael T Wetherall
Year of foundation: 1965
Tonnes crushed on average each year: 500
Location: Coonawarra
Area: 70 ha
Soils: Terra rossa and red sandy loam over sandstone
Varieties planted: White—chardonnay; Red—cabernet sauvignon, shiraz
Leading wines: Wetherall Cabernet Sauvignon, Shiraz, Chardonnay
Notes: Ninety per cent of the Wetherall grape production is sold to other winemakers, only about 50 tonnes being used for the Wetherall label. Cellar door sales: 7 days, usual business hours.

Wynns Coonawarra Estate R10

Memorial Drive, Coonawarra, SA 5263
Ph 08 8736 3266, Fax 08 8736 3202

Owner: Southcorp Wines
Chief Winemaker: Sue Hodder
Year of foundation: 1891, as Wynns Coonawarra Estate 1951
Tonnes crushed on average each year: not disclosed but estimated at 7200
Location: Coonawarra
Area: 719.5 ha
Soils: terra rossa varying to black rendzina on western edges
Varieties planted: White—chardonnay, riesling; Red—cabernet sauvignon, merlot, shiraz
Leading wines: Wynns John Riddoch Cabernet Sauvignon, Michael Hermitage, Coonawarra Estate Black Label Cabernet Sauvignon,

Coonawarra Estate Hermitage, Cabernet Shiraz, Merlot, Riesling, Chardonnay
Notes: Wynns is without doubt the largest winegrower and producer in the Coonawarra region. Yet the lack of quality that is sometimes associated with large production is nowhere to be seen in the Wynns range of magnificent regional wines. In every sense, Wynns (now in the proprietorship of Southcorp Wines) has realised what might be called John Riddoch's dream. It occupies the winery that he erected though it is now many times bigger. Since the Wynn family purchased 'Wynns Coonawarra Estate' in 1951, and due largely to David Wynns promotional efforts in the 1950s and 60s, Coonawarra has become without doubt Australia's premium red production area. The superb John Riddoch Cabernet Sauvignon is arguably Australia's most opulent Cabernet Sauvignon.

Yalumba (vineyard only)   R9

Riddoch Highway, Penola, SA 5263

Owners: Hill-Smith family
Chief winemaker: Simon Adams
Year of foundation: 1993
Tonnes crushed on average each year: 300
Location: Penola
Area: 31.35 ha in two vineyards (Menzies) 17.71 ha and (Hawthorns) 13.64 ha
Soils: terra rossa
Varieties planted: (Menzies) White—none; Red—cabernet sauvignon. (Hawthorns) White—none; Red—cabernet sauvignon, merlot, shiraz
Leading wines: Yalumba 'The Menzies' Coonawarra Cabernet Sauvignon
Notes: The 'Menzies' Cabernet is named after Sir Robert Menzies, a former Australian prime minister, who at a dinner once publicly endorsed the quality of a Yalumba Cabernet. No local cellar door sales.

Zema Estate   R8

Riddoch Highway, Coonawarra, SA 5263 (just south of Coonawarra township)
Ph 08 8373 3010, Fax 08 8736 3219

Owners: Zema family
Chief winemakers: Matt and Nick Zema
Year of foundation: 1982
Tonnes crushed on average each year: 150 but will increase as younger vines come into bearing
Location: Coonawarra
Area 43.85 ha
Soils: terra rossa
Varieties planted: White—sauvignon blanc; Red—cabernet franc, cabernet sauvignon, malbec, merlot, nebbiolo, shiraz
Leading wines: Zema, Family Selection Cabernet Sauvignon, Cabernet Sauvignon, Shiraz, Cluny (a blend of the 'Bordeaux' varieties, cabernet sauvignon, cabernet franc, merlot and malbec)
Notes: The Zema Estate is a twentieth century version of many a story of the nineteenth—the immigrant made good. Demetrio Zema arrived in Australia in 1959 to marry his fiancee, Francesca. He intended to stay only two years and return to Italy with his new wife. In the meantime, he employed himself as a painter in Penola, becoming quite successful. He was so successful, in fact, that he decided to follow in the footsteps of his father and grandfather and plant a vineyard, not in his native land but right here in Coonawarra. The older vineyards have no supplementary irrigation. The younger vines are irrigated to assist in their establishment. The Zema Cabernet Sauvignon is in the midstream of good Coonawarra reds, the Family Reserve sometimes outstanding.
Cellar door sales: 7 days 9am–5pm, except Christmas Day and Good Friday.

PADTHAWAY REGION

The region was first settled by squatters in the 1840s and pastoral leases were issued by the South Australian government in 1851. In that year also, Scottish immigrant Robert Lawson named his grazing run (47 square miles) 'Padthaway', a name derived from the local Aboriginal word *Potaruwt*, meaning 'good water'. Except for sleeper-cutting, grazing continued to be the primary occupation of the district from then until the mid-1930s. This was despite the fact that, in 1926, a Royal Commission report concluded that the area was too valuable to be allowed to remain purely in pastoral occupation. Yet official reports do occasionally emerge from pigeonholes and, from 1936, the area began to be further subdivided and some cereal-growing commenced. The end of the Second World War brought yet more subdivision in the form of soldier-settlement, the establishment of the township of Padthaway in 1952 and, from the mid-1950s, the utilisation of irrigation from the underground aquifers for pasture seed production and stock-fattening.

By the 1960s most wine companies were well aware that their red wine sales were improving. Those established in areas such as Coonawarra knew that they had suitable sites and climate to satisfy this boom. For others not in Coonawarra or other suitable red wine producing areas, and cash-strapped as most family wine companies tended to be, the quandary was whether to buy quite expensive land in such areas or seek new (but basically similar) lands elsewhere at a cheaper price. Seppelt was just such a company. After a close study of the area, inspired by a CSIRO report almost 20 years before, Seppelt purchased land at Keppoch (then a name commonly used for the area) and planted its first experimental vineyard in 1963. Its commercial plantings began the following year. The modern era of Padthaway had begun. Seppelt was followed by Hardy's and Lindemans in 1968.

Early wines began to come from the region in the late 1960s and early in the following decade. Though the country was roughly similar to Coonawarra in soils, its early wines were most definitely not. They were tremendously disappointing—thin red wines coming from over-irrigated callow vines, which proved very difficult to sell. It was with a sense of relief that the companies then established in Padthaway turned with the majority of Australian winedrinkers to white wines later in the 1970s. Following major plantings of riesling, its whites were more successful and Chardonnay too was becoming increasingly desirable in the marketplace. Padthaway's reputation was finally established as a white wine producing area, indeed, later in the mid-1980s as a premium Chardonnay region. In the past decade, however, it has shot forward as a producer of premium Shiraz.

Today, all the major wine companies have substantial vineyards in the region as well as several smaller growers. There are also two wineries, Eliza Padthaway Estate (a small winery specialising in sparkling wines) and BRL Hardy's Stonehaven (a very modern winery with a 10 000-tonne capacity), completed in 1998.

The major disadvantage that Padthaway has suffered over the years is a lack of identity, as large companies tend to use their wines from this region in major blends. Except for very poor reds in its early days and Lindemans excellent Padthaway Chardonnays in more recent years, Padthaway identity has usually remained a closely kept corporate secret.

Location: latitude 36°37'S, longitude 140°28'E, about 290 km south-east of Adelaide
Elevation: 35–90 m
Topography and soils: Similar to Wrattonbully and Coonawarra to its south, Padthaway was once part of the ancient sea-beds adjoining south-eastern South Australia, after an inundation of the sea 40 million years ago. About 15 million years later, the sea began to recede, leaving the Gambier limestone deposits commonly found in the region. After a further inundation, climatic changes and an uplift of the land surface some 2 million years ago caused the sea to retreat finally, leaving a series of ridges which are the remains of ancient coastal sand dunes parallel to the present coastline. One of these ridges, running from the northern to the southern end of the region, is known as the West Naracoorte Ridge and forms its eastern boundary.

The interdunal plain to its west comprises about 80% of the region. It is quite flat and at an altitude of about 37 metres above sea-level. Its soils are variable. Most common is red duplex (Dr 2.23 Northcote), which is alkaline in nature. The soils of the West Naracoorte Ridge, which rises on average to about 87 metres elevation, are on their slopes red-brown sandy loams (Uc 6 and Um 6 Northcote) of less than half a metre in depth limestone.

Climate: MJT 20.3°C, MAR 11.25°C, HDD raw 1603, AR 524 mm (Oct–Apr 199 mm), RH 56% (9am Jan) (Bureau of Meteorology), MJT 20.4°C, MAR 11.4°C, HDD raw 1606, AR 526 mm (Oct–Mar 178 mm), RH 65% (9am Jan), AI 475 mm, SH 8.2 (Dry & Smart). MJT 20.2°C, MAR na, HDD raw 1560, 1479 (cut off and as adjusted for vine sites), AR 509 mm (Oct–Apr 208 mm), RH 35% (3pm Jan), AI na, SH 8.1 (Gladstones). MJT 20.1°C, MAR 10.5°C, HDD na, AR 528 mm (Oct–Apr na), RH 60% (Lindemans local meteorological station).

Variable MJTs between 20.1°C and 20.4°C certainly point to a difference in recording sites, but the raw HDD (1603–1606) makes Padthaway one of the warmer regions of the Limestone Coast zone. Even so, it is scarcely hot and so lends itself well to the production of medium to full-bodied dry white and dry red styles. Frosts are a local hazard as they are virtually throughout the Limestone Coast zone and are generally countered by overhead spray irrigation. Despite this, serious frost damage occurs on a 'one year in ten' basis, with damage occurring more frequently in isolated vineyard depressions. The region is also one of the driest in the zone, irrigation being necessary and practised throughout. In the past, this was carried out by overhead sprinklers, travelling irrigators and flood, but in recent years the region has committed itself to convert all irrigation systems to drip by the year 2000, except overhead sprinklers used for frost control. The source of irrigation is from bore holes tapping into underground aquifers. Irrigation licences are now required and it has also been suggested that a local winter-flowing creek be diverted to recharge the aquifer throughout the year.

Doubtless the recent vast improvement in Padthaway reds is due to the advent of drip irrigation and the practice of controlled stress applied to the vineyards from budburst to the completion of flowering, which is now reducing yields to about 10 tonnes to the hectare where premium quality is required. With such regimes in place, the future of Padthaway as a quality red area seems assured.

Harvest time: chardonnay early to mid-March, shiraz late March to early April

Principal varieties: (areas over 100 ha) White—chardonnay, riesling; Red—shiraz, cabernet sauvignon, pinot noir
Total area: (1996) 2665 ha
Major wine styles: Chardonnay is definitely the most important wine style of the region. Such wines are usually of the fig-peach spectrum of aromas and flavours, are medium to full-bodied, have excellent length of palate and mature well over 3–5 years. Lindemans has established the region's excellent reputation for this variety.

The Pinot Noirs are light fresh-drinking reds of distinctive pinot character with light strawberry aromas and flavours. They are not to be kept long. Lindemans is the principal exponent of this style.

Shiraz from Orlando Wyndham in particular (Lawson's), are full-bodied reds exhibiting great depth of ripe berry-pepper character both on nose and palate. Also part (50%) of the Eileen Hardy Shiraz 1995, winner of the Jimmy Watson trophy in 1996. Wines such as these are recommended for cellaring for 8–10 years.

Cabernet Sauvignon is rarely seen unblended. It is released either blended with merlot or with cabernet sauvignon from other areas. By itself it has decent berry characters but is rather plain and simple, even disappointing when compared with the wealth of rich berry-blackcurrant character shown by the cabernets of Coonawarra to the south.

Merlot is still to be finally evaluated in the region but is very promising, producing fruity plummy reds of medium to full body when not overcropped.

BRL Hardy   NR

Stonehaven, Keith-Naracoorte Road,
Padthaway, SA 5271
Ph 08 8765 6060, Fax 08 8765 6008

Owner: BRL Hardy
Chief winemaker: Tom Newton
Year of foundation: vineyards 1968, winery 1998
Tonnes crushed on average each year: 5000
Location: Padthaway
Area: 411.4 ha, 80 ha of which are not yet bearing
Soils: red duplex over limestone, but varies to sand over limestone on ridges
Varieties planted: White—chardonnay, riesling, sauvignon blanc, semillon, verdelho, viognier; Red—cabernet franc, cabernet sauvignon, merlot, pinot noir, shiraz
Leading wines: all of BRL Hardy's Padthaway wine is blended into their premium and mid-range bottled wine. Padthaway Shiraz from this vineyard recently composed half of the Eileen

Hardy Shiraz which won the Jimmy Watson trophy in 1996
Notes: Padthaway is a valued contributor to the various BRL Hardy blends. No cellar door sales.

Browns of Padthaway
(vineyard only)   R7

Keith-Naracoorte Road, Padthaway,
SA 5271
Ph 08 8765 6063, Fax 08 8765 5083

Owner: Brown family
Chief winemaker: Rymill Winery and Heathfield Winery (contracts)
Year of foundation: 1970
Tonnes crushed on average each year: 2000, about 500 of which are used for Browns of Padthaway's own labels
Location: Padthaway
Area: 286 ha, of which 136 ha are new plantings not yet in bearing

Soils: red sandy loam over clay over limestone
Varieties planted: White—chardonnay, riesling,
sauvignon blanc, verdelho; Red—cabernet
sauvignon, malbec, shiraz
Leading wines: Browns of Padthaway Family
Reserve Cabernet Sauvignon, Riesling,
Chardonnay, Shiraz
Notes: This is a large independent grower,
which has about a quarter of its crop made
into its own label wines. Wine quality is good.
Cellar door sales at Eliza Padthaway Estate.

Eliza Padthaway Estate R8

Padthaway Estate, Padthaway, SA 5271
Ph 08 8765 5039, Fax 08 8765 5097

Owners: Dale Baker and Ian Gray
Chief winemaker: Nigel Catt (contract)
Year of foundation: 1980
Tonnes crushed on average each year: 650,
about 200 of which are used for its own labels
Location: Padthaway
Area: 40 ha
Soils: red duplex above limestone
Varieties planted: White—chardonnay;
Red—pinot noir
Leading wines: Eliza Pinot Chardonnay Cuvee,
Pinot Noir Brut, Sparkling Burgundy,
Chardonnay (both wooded and unwooded)
Notes: The charming homestead dating from
1845 offers excellent accommodation and fine
food in the manner of one of the better
French Relais. It is what the French might also
term a *monocru*, a small (but only in
comparison with its neighbours) estate making
its own sparkling wine. Its winery, located in
an old woolshed, has one of the few
traditional square Champagne presses in
Australia. Cellar door sales: 7 days
10am–4.30pm.

Mildara Blass (vineyard only) NR

Padthaway SA 5271

Owner: Mildara Blass
Chief winemaker: Ivan Hogg

Year of foundation: 1989 (by both Tolley and
Andrew Garrett both subsequently purchased
by Mildara Blass)
Tonnes crushed on average each year: not
disclosed but estimated at 1700
Location: Padthaway
Area: total 122 ha in two vineyards (Tolley 44
ha and Garrett 78 ha)
Soils: (Garrett) red loam over limestone; (Tolley)
sand over red clay over limestone
Varieties planted: (Tolley) White—chardonnay,
riesling; Red—cabernet sauvignon, shiraz.
(Garrett) White—chardonnay, riesling,
sauvignon blanc; Red—cabernet franc, pinot
noir
Leading wines: There are no separately
released Mildara Blass Padthaway wines. The
wines are component parts of many of its
premium and semi-premium wine ranges
Notes: No local cellar door sales.

Orlando Wyndham (vineyard only) R10

Padthaway, SA 5271

Owner: Simeon Wines Ltd leased and managed
by Orlando Wyndham
Chief winemaker: Phil Laffer
Year of foundation: 1968
Tonnes crushed on average each year: 2300
Location: Padthaway
Area: 167 ha
Soils: varied, sandy loam over limestone
(Lawsons); red duplex over limestone
Varieties planted: White—chardonnay,
sauvignon blanc; Red—cabernet franc,
cabernet sauvignon, malbec, merlot, shiraz
Leading wines: Lawsons Shiraz, St Hilary
Chardonnay. In addition Orlando Wyndham
Padthaway fruit forms part of many premium
and semi-premium blends made by the
company, including Gramp's Cabernet Merlot,
Wyndham Estate Bin 444 Cabernet Sauvignon,
Bin 555 Shiraz, Jacob's Creek Shiraz Cabernet
and Cabernet Sauvignon

Notes: Rated for its magnificently concentrated Lawsons Shiraz and the often very successful St Hilary Chardonnay. Orlando's Padthaway fruit is an essential ingredient in many of their successful wines. No local cellar door sales.

Southcorp (vineyard only) R10

Padthaway, SA 5271

Owner: Southcorp Wines
Chief winemakers: various within the Southcorp Wines Group
Years of foundation: 1963 (Seppelt vineyard), 1968 (Lindeman vineyard), 1968 (now Penfolds vineyard but formerly Wynns and before Wynns, Glenloth)
Tonnes crushed on average each year: not disclosed but estimated at 18 000
Location: Padthaway
Area: total 1188 ha. There are three large vineyard areas, which for convenience and for the sake of history I shall call Seppelt 283.6 ha, Lindemans 596.1 ha and Penfolds (formerly Wynns) 307.8 ha
Soils: various; red duplex and red-brown sandy loams

Varieties planted: (Seppelts) White—chardonnay, muscat a petits grains, riesling, semillon; Red—cabernet sauvignon, merlot, pinot noir, shiraz. (Lindemans) White—chardonnay, muscat a petits grains, riesling, sauvignon blanc, semillon; Red—cabernet sauvignon, merlot, pinot noir, shiraz. (Penfolds) White—chardonnay, riesling, sauvignon blanc, semillon; Red—cabernet sauvignon, shiraz
Leading wines: (Seppelts), part of Terrain range, part of Moyston range; (Lindemans) Padthaway Chardonnay, Sauvignon Blanc, Cabernet-Merlot, part of the Bin range; (Penfolds) part of Bin range, part of Koonunga Hill Range, part of Rawson's Retreat range and part of Bin 202 (export)
Notes: The output of Southcorp's production in Padthaway is chiefly divided between three of the group's major entities, Lindemans, Seppelts and Penfolds. Details of Padthaway's enormous quality contribution to the various Southcorp ranges are listed above. The rating is based on the superb consistency of Lindemans Padthaway Chardonnay. There are no local cellar door sales.

WRATTONBULLY (PROPOSED REGION)

Like most of south-eastern South Australia, the early history of the Wrattonbully region was pastoral. The area of what is now the town of Naracoorte was first settled in 1842 by George Ormerod and called the Naracoorte Run. Adjoining this area is Struan, settled at the same time by the Robertson brothers who prospered from grazing and timber-milling, converting local red-gum forests into many thousands of sleepers which were sold to the South Australian Railways. Like John Riddoch at nearby Yallum Park, the Robertsons became the lairds of the district, building a fine mansion and entertaining royalty. Again like Riddoch they subdivided and used part of their land, not for fruit growing and viticulture but for grazing, and smaller grazing properties came into being.

Situated immediately to the north of Coonawarra with its urban centre Naracoorte adjacent to but not forming part of it, Wrattonbully had a history of pastoral and forestry activity until the early 1990s, when the vast growth of its neighbour and the generally like nature of its terrain caused obvious viticultural interest. There had, however, been viticultural development as early as 1968 when the Wrattonbully Vineyard in the southern part of the proposed region was established. Further plantings took place in the early 1970s, but the upsurge did not really begin until 1993. From then until 1997, 950 hectares of vineyard have been established. About 90% of the vines planted have been red. There is currently only one winery within the proposed region, most wine being made outside it. This region, previously to be called Koppamurra, faced legal difficulties concerning the use of its name. 'Koppamurra' is registered as a trademark and cannot be used as a regional description without the consent of the owner of the trademark.

Wrattonbully is an area of modern viticultural techniques yet with an air of caution. Vineyard trellising has been arranged to accommodate vertical shoot positioning: 1.1 metre, single or double wire or Scott Henry. Planting density varies from row widths of 2.2 m to 2.75 m averaging 2000–2700 vines per hectare and Yalumba has taken the precaution of planting 80% of its vines on phylloxera resistant rootstocks.

Location: latitude 36°57'S, longitude 140°46'E, about 310 km south-east of Adelaide
Elevation: 55 to 130 m with most vineyards located between 75 and 100 m above sea-level
Topography and soils: the Naracoorte area is generally recognised to be the most inland of a series of ranges representing the ancient coastal dunes and sea-bed from which the Limestone Coast wine zone derives its name. It is a district of flat lands with undulating rises, having very similar soils to those of Coonawarra to its immediate south. Red sandy clay to clay loams over limestone (terra rossa) are interspersed with red-brown earths and podsols.
Climate: (from Bureau of Meteorology records over a 12-year period) MJT 19.75°C, MAR 10.7°C, HDD raw 1481, AR 565 mm (Oct–Apr 227 mm), RH 49% (Jan 9am), AI na, SH na. Its climate varies only slightly from the premium growth region of Coonawarra to the south, though the important Padthaway region to its north is warmer. Its average summer ripening temperature is one degree warmer than Coonawarra and one degree cooler than Padthaway. Its vineyards are slightly higher in elevation than those of Coonawarra with better air drainage and a consequent lower frost risk, though there is significant frost risk in April–May and mid-August to October. Its climate and lower relative humidity mean a slightly drier vine environment with less risk of botrytis, downy mildew, phomopsis, black spot and other fungal diseases. The chief risk is powdery mildew, which is likely to occur every year.

Irrigation is essential and efficient drip irrigation is employed throughout the region. Though water quality from bores is very good, such usage is restricted by government regulation and irrigation licences are necessary. Such licences have been issued to the maximum permissible amount set by the South Australian government and no additional licences to take water will be granted. Any new winegrower must purchase an existing licence.
Harvest time: Wrattonbully is situated midway between Coonawarra and Padthaway, and harvest dates are similarly placed: chardonnay, sauvignon blanc fourth week of

March; merlot, shiraz second week of April; cabernet sauvignon third week of April. *Principal varieties planted*: White—chardonnay, sauvignon blanc, semillon and a little riesling; Red—cabernet sauvignon, shiraz, merlot, smaller areas of cabernet franc, pinot noir and meunier

Area: 950 ha approx (1997)

Major wine styles: It is too early to prophesy what the region's major styles will be. However, unless there have been major miscalculations, they will undoubtedly be red (as 90% of the vineyard area planted has been to red cultivars) and most probably cabernet sauvignon-dominant.

Australian Premium Wines (vineyard only)   NR

Koppamurra, SA

Owner: Australian Premium Wines
Chief winemaker: Nick Haselgrove
Year of foundation: 1995
Tonnes crushed on average each year: not yet in full bearing but estimated to reach 350
Location: Koppamurra
Area: 40 ha
Soils: vineyard is located mostly on terra rossa dune
Varieties planted: White—none; Red—cabernet sauvignon, merlot shiraz
Leading wines: see notes
Notes: As no wines from this vineyard have yet been released, it is too early to assess their quality. There are no local cellar door sales.

BRL Hardy Ltd (vineyard only) NR

Elderslie Road, Naracoorte, SA 5271

Owner: BRL Hardy Ltd
Chief winemaker: Peter Dawson
Years of foundation: 1994–95
Tonnes crushed on average each year: not yet fully bearing but estimated to produce 1650
Location: Koppamurra
Area: 155 ha consisting of two vineyards (Elderslie Road 82 ha and Burgess 73 ha)
Soils: terra rossa clay over limestone (70%), red and brown sandy loams over clay (30%)
Varieties planted: (Elderslie Road) White—

chardonnay; Red—cabernet sauvignon, pinot noir, shiraz. (Burgess) White—chardonnay; Red—cabernet sauvignon, meunier, pinot noir, shiraz
Leading wines: the vineyards provide component parts of the Sir James sparkling range but no wines of sole Koppamurra origin have yet been released
Notes: The vineyard already plays some part in the making of the Sir James range but it is envisaged that it will also form part of the Eileen Hardy and Thomas Hardy wines in the future. No local cellar door sales.

Heathfield Ridge Winery   NR

Cnr Caves Road and Riddoch Highway, South Naracoorte, SA 5271 (10 km south of the town within the Koppamurra wine region)
Ph 08 8762 4133, Fax 08 8762 0141

Owners: Tidswell family
Chief winemaker: Pat Tocaciu
Year of foundation: 1998
Tonnes crushed on average each year: no Wrattonbully vineyard yet bearing; there is a vineyard of 150 ha that is 30 km south-west of Naracoorte on the Bool Lagoon Road, outside Wrattonbully but within the Limestone Coast zone, which forwards its fruit to the Heathfield Ridge Winery for making
Location: (winery) Koppamurra
Area: Koppamurra vineyard not yet fully planted

Soils: terra rossa over limestone
Varieties planted: White—chardonnay, sauvignon blanc; Red—cabernet sauvignon, merlot, shiraz
Leading wines: no wines yet released
Notes: Heathfield Ridge winery was erected early in 1998 to act as a contract crushing centre, but is otherwise fully equipped for winemaking. In due course it will vinify the grapes from its own vineyards. Cellar door sales may eventuate in the future.

Koppamurra Wines NR

Joanna, 7 km east of Struan, SA 5271
Ph 08 8271 4127, Fax 08 8271 0726

Owner: Koppamurra Wines Pty Ltd
Chief winemaker: John Greenshields
Year of foundation: 1991
Tonnes crushed on average each year: 60
Location: Joanna
Area: 8.4 ha
Soils: terra rossa over limestone
Varieties planted: White—chardonnay, riesling; Red—cabernet franc, cabernet sauvignon, merlot, meunier, shiraz
Leading wines: Koppamurra Wines Cabernet-Merlot, Two Cabernets, Chardonnay
Notes: The wine is not made at the vineyard but at Norton Summit near Adelaide. Cellar door sales by appointment only.

Mildara Blass (vineyard only) NR

Langkoop Road, Koppamurra, SA 5271

Owner: Mildara Blass Ltd
Chief winemakers: David O'Leary, Toni Stockhausen, Fiona Purnell

Year of foundation: 1994
Tonnes crushed on average each year: 1400
Location: Koppamurra
Area: 400 ha consisting of three local vineyards (not yet fully bearing)
Soils: terra rossa (the old dunes), red-brown loams and duplex soils (lighter sandy soil over clay), these latter soils being interdunal
Varieties planted: White—none; Red—cabernet sauvignon, merlot, petit verdot, shiraz
Leading wines: Flanagan's Ridge range
Notes: These vineyards are another huge investment of Mildara Blass scheduled to produce over 4000 tonnes of premium red varieties within the next 3–4 years. The Flanagan's Ridge range is currently their path to market. No local cellar door sales.

Yalumba (vineyard only) NR

Cnr Davies Edwards Road and Old Caves Road, Koppamurra, SA 5271

Owners: Hill-Smith family
Chief winemaker: Simon Adams
Year of foundation: 1995
Tonnes crushed on average each year: not yet in full bearing but estimated at 950 (for the presently planted 85 ha)
Location: Koppamurra
Area: 85 ha with a further 80 ha to be planted between 1998 and 2000
Soils: terra rossa over limestone
Varieties planted: White—chardonnay, sauvignon blanc, semillon; Red—cabernet sauvignon, merlot, shiraz
Leading wines: none yet released
Notes: No local cellar door sales.

MOUNT BENSON REGION

Mount Benson, a name unfamiliar to most wine lovers, is destined to become much more famous. It has the same French connection as the more illustrious Margaret River and arguably even more potential. A compact region situated on the south-east coast of South Australia between Kingston and Robe, it was first explored in April 1802 in a piece of Anglo-French cooperation unusual for its time (the early days of the Napoleonic Wars) by the French navigator, Nicolas Baudin, in *Geographe* and Lieutenant Matthew Flinders in HMS *Investigator*. They had met, not surprisingly, in Encounter Bay when both were mapping the southern coast of Australia. Had they been closer to Europe, they might have tried to blast each other out of the water, but were infinitely more civilised, recalling their presence in the region by naming prominent landmarks along the coast. Thus Lacepede and Guichen Bays and Cape Jaffa were named by Baudin and Baudin Rocks by Flinders, who already had his own name immortalised by the island in Bass Strait.

By 1840, the area had become part of the stock route from Portland to Adelaide. Mount Benson itself was named after a stockman, Harry Benson, and in 1845 the region was settled. The first local industry was grazing and later in the nineteenth century black wattle bark was harvested for the extraction of tannin. Late twentieth-century industries include cray-fishing and afforestation, but that other source of tannin, the grapevine, was not to appear until 1978 when Colin Kidd, viticultural manager of Lindemans, planted a trial vineyard of 80 vines (four rows of 20 vines each of cabernet sauvignon, riesling, traminer and chardonnay) at Cape Jaffa Almond Orchard. All grew well. The first commercial vine planting occurred in 1989 when the first vines of the Mount Benson Vineyard were established.

Currently, the Mount Benson region encompasses 112.6 ha of vineyards and has one winery and cellar door sales outlet (Cape Jaffa) in operation. A further expansion of vineyard area (66 ha) took place in 1997. Though it is not yet a region on the tip of every wine lover's tongue and is still quite small, its prospects and those of the other satellite regions around Coonawarra are extremely exciting.

Location: latitude 37°5'S, longitude 139°45'E, about 300 km south-east of Adelaide
Altitude: 10–40 m
Topography and soils: The region is generally undulating with limestone outcrops. Its soils are of 'terra rossa' type similar to the Coonawarra region, which are friable dark brown to dark red subplastic clays above a medium to heavier clay brown-red subsoil and a typical limestone crust. Drainage is generally good.
Climate: (Noolook Forest over 22 years) MJT 18.2°C, MAR na, HDD raw 1226, AR 657 mm (Oct–Apr 222 mm), RH na, AI na, SH na. Mount Benson is a very cool area with obvious maritime influences, southerly sea breezes predominating during summer and autumn. Annual rainfall is 657 mm, falling mainly between April and November. Water of excellent quality for drip irrigation is supplied by two sources, one virtually on top of the other. The first and more shallow is the Gambier Limestone aquifer, in some places as close to the surface as 2 m and in others as deep as 35 m. This aquifer is recharged annually, chiefly by local rainfall occurring between May

and November. The second and deeper is the Dilwyn Formation, semi-artesian in nature and believed to be recharged by water from the Gambier Limestone formation and by sources as far away as Western Victoria. Frosts occurring after periods of drought can be a problem in spring, as can strong sea breezes at budburst and flowering. Normal precautions such as wind breaks are taken to obviate wind damage. Compared with Coonawarra, 100 km to the south-east, Mount Benson's growing season starts earlier and finishes later. For example, chardonnay budburst is a week earlier (first week of September), flowering a week later (second week of November), veraison two and a half weeks later (around 7 February) and harvest about 10 days later (around 1 April).

Harvest time: late March to the end of April

Principal grape varieties: White—chardonnay, sauvignon blanc, semillon, verdelho; Red—cabernet franc, cabernet sauvignon, merlot, petit verdot, shiraz

Total area: (1997) 178.6 ha and growing rapidly

Major wine styles: Cabernet Sauvignon.

Cape Jaffa Wines R7

Limestone Coast Road, Mount Benson, SA 5276
Ph 08 8768 5053, Fax 08 8768 5040

Owners: Hooper and Fowler families
Chief winemaker: Derek Hooper
Year of foundation: 1993
Tonnes crushed on average each year: 50 and rising, as more vines are planted and come into bearing
Location: Mount Benson
Area: 19 ha
Soils: terra rossa
Varieties planted: White—chardonnay, sauvignon blanc, semillon; Red—cabernet franc, cabernet sauvignon, merlot, petit verdot, shiraz
Leading wines: Cabernet Sauvignon, Shiraz, Chardonnay
Notes: My most recent experience of Cape Jaffa Wines was its extremely enjoyable Cabernet Sauvignon 1995, vibrant and fruity yet with the balance and weight of tannin to ensure its improvement over 3–4 more years and this off very young vines. Further wines from this vineyard are eagerly awaited. No cellar door sales.

Cellarmaster Wines (vineyard only) NR

Balmoral Vineyard, Mount Benson via Kingston SE, SA 5275
Ph 08 8768 6264

Owner: Cellarmaster Wines Pty Ltd (Mildara Blass)
Chief winemaker: Peter Thompson
Year of foundation: 1993
Tonnes crushed on average each year: 60 (1997) and increasing to 500 as vines mature and vineyard is fully planted
Location: Mount Benson
Area: 170 ha
Soils: terra rossa
Varieties planted: White—chardonnay, sauvignon blanc, verdelho; Red—cabernet franc, cabernet sauvignon, merlot, shiraz, petit verdot
Leading wines: Cabernet Sauvignon, Cabernets (a blend of cabernet sauvignon, merlot, cabernet franc and petit verdot), Shiraz, Merlot, Chardonnay, Verdelho and Sauvignon Blanc
Notes: Balmoral has all the ingredients of a classic Limestone Coast vineyard, good water, good terra rossa soil and a maritime climate

which can turn scorching days into cool nights, though it does create the necessity for wind breaks during the more wind-sensitive times of the grape-growing season. Strangely for a region so close to the sea, spring frosts may be a problem when the earth is cold and the nights are clear. A cellar door sales outlet is planned by 1999 in the old Balmoral Post Office, which was erected in 1878.

Mount Benson Vineyards NR

Wright's Bay Road, Mount Benson, via
Kingston SE, SA 5275
Ph/Fax 08 8768 6251

Owners: WR and CM Wehl
Chief winemaker: Bruce Gregory (Brand's, contract)
Year of foundation: 1989
Tonnes crushed on average each year: 10 and rising, as more vines come into bearing
Location: Mount Benson
Area: 8 ha
Soils: terra rossa
Varieties planted: White—none; Red—cabernet sauvignon, merlot
Leading wines: Cabernet Sauvignon
Notes: Mount Benson Vineyard pioneered this new region. Its cellar door is 3 km from the sea and midway between Kingston and Robe. Its reds are obviously of merit and it has wasted no time in exhibiting them, gaining a silver medal from the Royal Hobart Wine Show in 1995 and a bronze medal in the Jimmy Watson class at the Royal Melbourne Show. No cellar door sales.

Prosperine (vineyard only) NR

PO Box 85, Kingston SE, SA 5275
Robe Road, Mount Benson via Kingston
SE, SA 5275
Ph/Fax 08 8766 0070

Owners: Oliver Trading, Robin Ling, James Ling, Neil Jones

Chief winemaker: to be selected, when sufficient fruit is harvested
Year of foundation: 1993
Tonnes crushed on average each year: first vintage (1997) 8 tonnes and rising to 100 tonnes by 1999, as vines come to maturity
Location: Mount Benson
Area: 20 ha
Soils: terra rossa
Varieties planted: White—sauvignon blanc; Red—cabernet sauvignon, shiraz
Leading wines: no wines yet made under the Prosperine label
Notes: It is early days at Prosperine as it is for the region as a whole. Cellar door sales are not yet planned, but will probably happen by the year 2000. There are some problems because of salt-bearing sea breezes, but these are manageable by planting on east-facing slopes and by plantations of trees acting as wind breaks. Another problem is occasional frost damage, unusual in a region only 5 km from the sea. The local aquifer, however, is delivering irrigation water, which at 270 ppm salt is far better than some metropolitan water supplies. No winery is presently planned.

Terossa Vineyards (vineyard only) NR

Limestone Coast Road, Mount Benson
via Kingston SE, SA 5275
Ph 08 8768 5028

Owner: Brian and Alison Addison
Chief winemaker: all grapes are presently sold to winemakers
Year of foundation: 1992
Tonnes crushed on average each year: (1996) 61 and increasing to 200 as vines come to maturity
Location: Mount Benson
Area: 19 ha
Soils: terra rossa
Varieties planted: White—chardonnay; Red—cabernet sauvignon, shiraz

Leading wines: no current plants for a Terossa label

Notes: As its name suggests, Terossa is a

flourishing vineyard on terra rossa soil, 7 km from the Southern Ocean. No cellar door sales.

OTHER LIMESTONE COAST VINEYARDS AND WINERIES

Haig **NR**

Square Mile Road, Mount Gambier, SA 5290

Ph 08 8725 5414, Fax 08 8725 0252

Owners: AR and HM Haig

Chief winemaker: Nick Haselgrove (contract)

Year of foundation: 1982

Tonnes crushed on average each year: 20, of which about 8 are used for the vineyard label

Location: near the famous Blue Lake, Mount Gambier

Area: 4 ha

Soils: rich, black, volcanic soils over limestone

Varieties planted: White—chardonnay; Red—cabernet sauvignon, gamay, pinot noir

Leading wines: Haig Chardonnay, Pinot Noir

Notes: Pinot noir, gamay and chardonnay seem very suitable for this location. Cellar door sales: 7 days 11am–5pm.

St Mary's **NR**

Victoria and Albert Lane, west of Coonawarra, SA 5263

Ph 08 8736 6070, Fax 08 8736 6045

Owner: Barry Mulligan

Chief winemaker: Barry Mulligan

Year of foundation: 1986

Tonnes crushed on average each year: not disclosed

Location: out of the defined Coonawarra region to the west

Area: 9.6 ha

Soils: terra rossa soils very similar to the ridge within the defined Coonawarra region

Varieties planted: White—chardonnay, riesling; Red—cabernet franc, cabernet sauvignon, merlot, petit verdot, shiraz

Leading wines: St Mary's House Block (a Cabernet Sauvignon), Shiraz, Chardonnay, Riesling

Notes: The St Mary's vineyard, located west of the defined Coonawarra region but on one of the very similar ridges of terra rossa soils that roll westward towards the coast, is jointly owned by the Mulligan family and Tyrrells Vineyards though the brand St Mary's is owned solely by the Mulligan family. Cellar door sales: 7 days 10am–4pm, closed Christmas Day and Good Friday.

Tyrrells Vineyards (vineyard only) **NR**

St Mary's, Victoria and Albert Lane, west of Coonawarra, SA 5263

Owner: Tyrrells Vineyards Pty Ltd

Chief winemaker: Andrew Spinaze

Year of foundation: 1995

Tonnes crushed on average each year: 160

Location: west of Coonawarra

Area 14.4 ha

Soils: see St Mary's entry above

Varieties planted: see St Mary's entry above

Leading wines: no wines yet released

Notes: This is another instance of Tyrrells expansion to national winemaking status. At the time of writing no wines had been released but a 1996 red is certain to be released soon. No cellar door sales.

Winter's R6.5

Clarke Road, O B Flat, via Mount
Gambier, SA 5290
Ph/Fax 08 8726 8255

Owners: Martin and Merrilee Winter
Chief winemaker: Brand's (contract)
Year of foundation: 1988
Tonnes crushed on average each year: 20, of
which 15 are used for the vineyard's own label
Location: O B Flat, 6 km south of Mount
Gambier

Area: 8 ha
Soils: well-drained, volcanic sandy loams
Varieties planted: White—chardonnay; Red—
cabernet franc, cabernet sauvignon, pinot noir
Leading wines: Winter's Cabernet Sauvignon
Notes: Winter's is certainly one of South
Australia's most southerly vineyards, but this
does not seem to prevent cabernet sauvignon
from thriving in this location. A dusty, leafy
1994 tasted in 1996 was a good style. Cellar
door sales: weekends 10am–4pm, other times
by appointment, closed Christmas Day.

❦ Shiraz

The origin of shiraz is to say the least obscure. There is a city in Iran of the same name and a city in Sicily called Syracuse. Did shiraz originate in Persia and proceed via Sicily to Roman Gaul? Who knows and who can ever ascertain its origin except by DNA testing of modern shiraz against current Persian grapevines (if any are left under the Muslim mullahs). When the myths and legends come away, what we are left with is a Northern Rhone grape variety of very respectable reputation, which is solidly ensconsed in many parts of Australia.

Not that its establishment has always been secure. One of the great swings in the popularity pendulum in the past twenty years has been that of shiraz. From the degradation of grubbing-out or grafting in the late 1970s to the exaltation of increasing vineyard area in the late 1990s, such has been its lot. Who now remembers the shiraz muffins of the 1970s? In the late 1970s there was little public excitement in red wines and that was concentrated entirely on cabernet sauvignon. Now there is much more, as Australians recognise just how good our red wines are and how well suited most of our wine regions are to shiraz. Cabernet sauvignon, except for its wines from premium regions, has begun to take a back seat. Merlot has not yet really made an impact (though it promises much in certain regions) and pinot noir remains, if not an outright disappointment, then an expensive enigma to most consumers.

Where are our best shiraz regions? It all depends on the climates and also the consumers' expectations of the variety. Perhaps the most common hope is for a deeply coloured, aromatically arousing, opulently flavoured wine, richly endowed with berry and pepper fruit, vanillan oak and firm but not hard tannin, a macho red, soft enough to drink comparatively young (2–3 years old), youthfully generous, but not aggressive, on the palate, a wine that will also age gracefully for perhaps another 5–7 years, revealing in due course its complex varietal nuances on nose and palate. For such wines, the shiraz enthusiast should seek out warm to hot climates in areas such as McLaren Vale (incomparable for shiraz in good years), Clare (big shiraz styles with longevity), the Barossa Valley and perhaps the Hunter Valley (although the Hunter style is often more savoury and rarely as rich as the South Australian areas mentioned). In more moderate climates, there are the Bendigo, Heathcote and Great Western regions of central and western Victoria, which make firm shiraz reds of balanced fruit and tannin again long-living and mellow in their more senior years, which some see as having peculiar eucalypt aromas, as well as the more customary black pepper. So too, there are 'cooler' areas such as Sunbury, whose outstanding Shiraz representative is the historic Craiglee, Geelong, where Bannockburn often produces outstandingly 'cool' Shiraz. Also the Yarra Valley, not usually a name dangling from everyone's lips when shiraz is mentioned, is extremely complex in that what are usually seen as 'berry' aromas turn into 'plum' and its 'pepper' transmogrifies from 'black' to 'white'. De Bortoli and Seville Ente are the outstanding names here. But let us not leave Western Australia out of calculations. That state also has an excellent shiraz subregion, Mount Barker, which shows the typical black pepper, berry and spice characters of Central Victoria, though without that idiosyncratic eucalyptus overlay that is sometimes noticed.

What are the problems of shiraz today? Very few unless you regard 'too much of a good thing' as a problem. Shiraz seems to flourish virtually everywhere in vinous Australia. Only in our coolest areas does it fail to ripen satisfactorily, producing rather thin 'green' wines. And perhaps in extremely hot areas it occasionally 'bakes' into overripeness, though this is rare. The most common fault is in winemaking—a tendency to use far too much American oak, so that all the nose and palate perceive are lashings of 'coconut', which totally dominate fruit and destroy any claim to finesse that the wine may have. However, our better shiraz makers today seem to be shunning the extremes of American oak and seeking a more subtle path for what might well be called our native wine.

❧ FLEURIEU ZONE

Fleurieu is a considerable area of South Australia, encompassing, as one would expect, the Fleurieu Peninsula. It extends from Glenelg (metropolitan Adelaide) in the north, south along the peninsular coast as far east as the Murray River mouth and pushes back into the hills above McLaren Vale as far as Clarendon. It includes the wine regions of Langhorne Creek and McLaren Vale.

LANGHORNE CREEK REGION

The name commemorates Alfred Langhorne, an early overlander, who drove cattle from Sydney in 1841. Having been attacked by Aborigines near the Rufus River, he saw the cattle safely down to what is now the Langhorne Creek area to country he held as a squatter. The spot where he crossed the Bremer River was thereafter known as Langhorne's Crossing and later, after the bridge was built, Langhorne's Bridge or Langhorne's Creek.

In 1850, the South Australian government surveyed and subdivided the area and one of the original purchasers of a selection in that year was Frank Potts, who had arrived in Adelaide aboard the *Buffalo* in 1836. The country selected was part of the flood plain of the Bremer River, which has its sources in the eastern slopes of the Adelaide Hills and flows into Lake Alexandrina, outlet also of the Murray-Darling system. As a flood plain, it not only had the Bremer overflowing its banks nearly every winter but had been the recipient of rich alluvial soil, possibly for many centuries. The first settlers realised this, noting the rich natural grasslands which were ideal for grazing and the soil beneath, excellent for the growth of cereal crops.

Vines were first planted possibly with the encouragement of that ardent South Australian propagator of the vine, Thomas Hardy, who was rising to prominence in the 1860s. Though the exact year is unknown, Frank Potts was one of the first to plant vines (mainly shiraz and verdelho) about that time. Another early grower was Edward Hector of Montura. There is also contemporary diary evidence that Thomas Hardy began to buy wine from Potts in the mid to late 1860s and wine production is confirmed by an 1869 report in a local newspaper that 'a large quantity of wine is being made in the neighbourhood this season. Messrs Hector and Potts, the two largest and most successful growers in the district, are just about to finish their gathering'. In 1883 William Formby bought the land which he later (in 1892) planted with shiraz and cabernet sauvignon and called Metala, some of the original vines of which survive today.

Though the winter flood of the Bremer provided natural irrigation and soaked the deep alluvial soils of the plain, Frank Potts created an innovation and, in so doing, one of Australia's first irrigation schemes. This was the building of an ox-drawn pumping system which harnessed the spring and summer flow of the Bremer

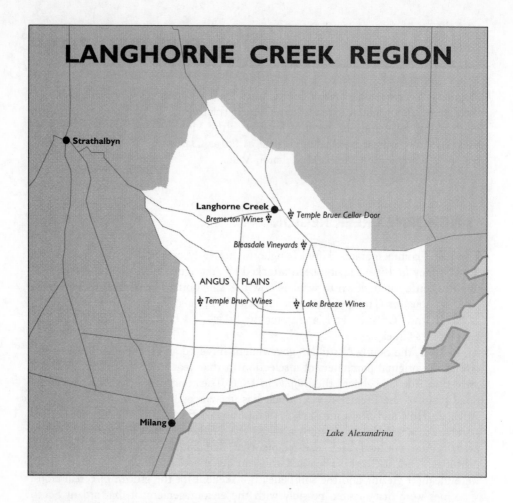

by diverting a flow equivalent to 50 cubic metres an hour into a main channel conveying it to the vineyard. In the twentieth century, the development of irrigation in the region continued with the building of levees. They held back the water diverted from the river by way of channels cut into the river banks or the overflow from the river if the winter flood was high enough. In the period from the 1930s to the 1970s, four weirs were built across the river to enable its full flow to be diverted onto the flood plain so that winter and spring irrigation could take place in the vineyards. The region's irrigation capacity was also increased in the late 1950s when wells were bored, though the salinity levels of this supply increased over the next 20 years. In 1980 restrictions were placed on water use and, for a few years after, these restrictions—and encouragement from the South Australian government to recharge the basin with low salinity flood water from its supplying rivers (the Bremer and the Angas)—enabled viticulturalists to use good quality water. But at this time also to ensure the establishment of new young vine varieties and the continuity of economic crop levels, permanent trickle irrigation was introduced. Once more the sub-artesian system began to suffer, water salinity began to increase and the amount available for irrigation began to reduce. This severe problem began to be solved when access to Murray-Darling water from Lake Alexandrina was made available to irrigators in exchange for their entitlements to water from the Angas-Bremer system. At first little water was taken and then only by irrigators close to Lake Alexandrina, but since the early 1990s pipelines of great length (the longest over 35 km) have been built to allow irrigation of land close to Langhorne Creek. Thus, for the time being, the pressure has been taken off the flagging sub-artesian basin of the Angas-Bremer system.

Meanwhile, the Potts family—whose winery and vineyard 'Bleasdale' was named after Dr John Bleasdale, a leading Victorian cleric, who spread the temperance gospel by encouraging the growth of vineyards and the moderate consumption of table wine—was expanding its wine and fortifying spirit production. Though this trade was chiefly in bulk, the Potts family reserved very small quantities of its best wines for its own label. The 1920s and its export demands for fortified reds met the Potts' bulk sale requirements exactly. The 1930s and the Great Depression brought an end to this flourishing trade and later they were compelled to distil over a million litres of wine. Yet they persisted in winemaking and by the 1960s, though the pendulum was swinging back to table wine, the region had been reduced to this one winery only. However, the excellent Metala reds of Saltram also kept this then obscure area on the map and Lindemans produced a soft Shiraz-Ouillade blend from the area.

Its time came in the late 1960s when a young German winemaker, Wolf Blass, decided to 'go solo', making his own red blends in masterly style. Langhorne Creek red was usually one of Wolf's essential building blocks and Wolf's three successive Jimmy Watson trophies brought it to the fore. Since the Blass success, many other wine companies have utilised the region's fruit for blending purposes, though few, save local wineries, seem disposed to market a 100% Langhorne Creek wine.

With the availability and certainty of irrigation water from the Murray-Darling system, Australia's larger wine companies swarmed into the region during the 1990s. Mildara-Blass, Orlando, Rosemount and BRL Hardy have all made significant plantings there. In addition, many smaller local growers have increased plantings and irrigators who once specialised in other crops have made the transition to vines. Today there are four wineries within the region.

Location: latitude 35°13'S, longitude 139°05'E, about 60 km south-east of Adelaide, bounded by the Mount Lofty Ranges to the west and north and Lake Alexandrina to the south
Altitude: from virtually sea-level to 50 m, averaging about 20 m
Topography and soils: Resting on and resulting from the alluvial outwash from the Mount Lofty Ranges, Langhorne Creek is generally flat with very fertile soils. It has a general elevation from about 1 metre (on the shores of Lake Alexandrina, its southern boundary) grading upwards to and bounded by a 50-metre contour line in the north of the region. There are also slight undulations due to sandy loam rises caused by wind action. The light sandy soils of the original outwash are traversed and drained by two rivers, the Bremer and the Angas, which in turn have made their

own contributions to the soil complexities of the region, by depositing silts and clays on the plain during flooding. This in turn has given rise to pockets of silts, loams, clay loams and clay overlying the original sands and clays.

Climate: (Note: Gladstones and Smart and Dry appear to have used Strathalbyn weather station about 12 km away for their MJTs. The 'local' readings are those of Bill Potts of Early Day Vineyards from his own weather station in the midst of his vineyard. Such data, however, have only been gathered for about 10 years.) MJT 19.2°C, MAR 9°C, HDD raw 1458, AR 388 mm (Oct–Mar 145 mm), RH 60%, AI 383 mm, SH 8.3 (local), MJT 19.9°C, MAR 10.3°C, HDD raw 1521, AR 410 mm (Oct–Apr 135 mm), RH 60% (9am Jan), AI 443 mm, SH 8.3 (Dry & Smart), MJT 19.9°C, MAR na, HDD raw 1655, 1606 as cut off and adjusted for latitude daily temperature range and for vine sites), AR 495 mm (Oct–Apr 204 mm), RH 43% (3pm Jan). AI na, SH 8.2 (Gladstones). Langhorne Creek has a deceptively mild climate with little variation across its region—deceptive because one would imagine such a region of low rainfall, where vineyard areas are flat and virtually at sea-level, to have little air movement and to be extremely warm. It is certainly not so. It is much cooler than, say, McLaren Vale. There are two reasons for this. The large expanse of water, Lake Alexandrina, is immediately to the south and a prevailing south-west sea breeze blowing across the lake moderates temperatures in Langhorne Creek in summer, a breeze that is apparently much less frequent in Strathalbyn. In winter the lake's influence is also to be felt, again moderating the cold nights that would otherwise make the area more frost-prone. The lake also accounts for the high relative humidity of the region.

The annual rainfall of 388 mm (of which only about 145 mm falls during the growing season (Oct–March)) is low and irrigation is necessary during this season (see above for a brief history of the region's irrigation). There are three sources of irrigation: (A) the area watered by the unique annual flooding of the Bremer and Angas systems; (B) water pumped by pipelines from Lake Alexandrina; and (C) water drawn from the Angas-Bremer sub-artesian basin.

Source A flooding is carried out through a series of floodgates and leveee banks which divert water from the rivers and onto surrounding vineyard land, where it remains from 1–2 days until the vineyard soil is saturated. One soaking usually suffices for the ensuing growing season. Water quality, however, varies considerably depending on the salinity of the water in the volume of flow and the time of year in which it occurs. Large flows usually occurring in winter and early spring carry less salinity (about 100 ppm). Smaller earlier flows have much higher salinity (as much as 1800 ppm). Source B has caused many pipelines to be established, including a major pipeline that is utilised by over 40 different landholders. It is available year-round, reliable and its salinity during the last three years has varied from 260 to 340 ppm. This water source alone has caused a major expansion of the Langhorne Creek area, about 80% of the currently planted area being presently irrigated from this source. Source C (the sub-artesian basin of the Angas-Bremer system) is now much diminished as a source of irrigation, though some vineyards do use a mix of this source and lake water for this purpose. Its salinity also can be much higher (250 to 2500 ppms).

Viticultural problems that may occur include excess vine vigour, frost (a slight risk) and mildews, both powdery and downy, but the usual spray program should hold these in check.

Harvest time: Typical phenological dates for Langhorne Creek are cabernet sauvignon, late March to mid to late April, shiraz, similarly

Principal grape varieties: (1996) cabernet sauvignon (947.42 ha), shiraz (609.16 ha), chardonnay (241.27 ha), merlot (130 ha)

Total area: (1996) 1961.8 ha rising to 2500 ha by 1998

Principal wine styles: A difficult question as Langhorne Creek wines are mostly blended with the wines of other regions, the wines of Bleasdale being a notable exception. However, the region's Cabernet Sauvignon and Shiraz reds are distinguished by an accessibility of nose and a suppleness of palate, having good fruit-tannin integration. They not only make excellent blending material but also very good early drinking. Good examples are Bleasdale, Saltram Metala Shiraz Cabernet and Blass Grey Label Cabernet Sauvignon and Shiraz. Malbec also as made by Potts can be a supple, harmonious style. The region's two major varieties can be described as follows: Cabernet Sauvignon possessing classical mint, blackcurrant and chocolate characters; Shiraz typically plummy, earthy and chocolatey.

Bleasdale Vineyards R8

Wellington Road, Langhorne Creek, SA 5255 (about 1.5 km east of the town)
Ph 08 8537 3001, Fax 08 8537 3224

Owner: Bleasdale Vineyards Pty Limited
Chief winemaker: Michael Potts
Year of foundation: 1850
Tonnes crushed on average each year: 1000 made up of 700 produced from Bleasdale's own vineyards and the rest purchased from other growers
Location: Langhorne Creek
Area: 50 ha
Soils: rich alluvial flood soils
Varieties planted: White—chardonnay, riesling, verdelho; Red—cabernet franc, cabernet sauvignon, grenache, malbec, oeuillade, petit verdot, pinot noir, red frontignac, shiraz, tinta madeira
Leading wines: Bleasdale Frank Potts Cabernet, Merlot, Malbec, Cabernet Franc, Mulberry Tree Cabernet Sauvignon, Bremerview Shiraz, Sandhill Verdelho
Notes: The first and oldest winery in the region and for a long time the only one, Bleasdale has a wide selection of table wines with the

emphasis on supple reds, of which Bleasdale Malbec is often a very good spicy example.
Cellar door sales: Mon–Sat 9am–5pm, Sun 11am–5pm.

Bremerton Wines NR

Strathalbyn Road, Langhorne Creek, SA 5255
Ph 08 8537 3093, Fax 08 8537 3109

Owners: Craig and Mignonne Willson
Chief winemaker: Rebecca Willson
Year of foundation: 1988
Tonnes crushed on average each year: 120 but increasing
Location: Langhorne Creek
Area: 114 ha
Soils: part black-grey river loam and part sand over clay
Varieties planted: White—chardonnay, sauvignon blanc, semillon, verdelho;
Red—cabernet sauvignon, malbec, merlot, petit verdot, shiraz
Leading wines: Bremerton Wines Old Adam Shiraz, Cabernet Sauvignon, Cabernet, Shiraz, Merlot

Notes: Bremerton's cellar door area is a stone 1860s horse stable and barn, faithfully restored. Bremerton is also a consistent medal winner at wine shows, its Cabernet Sauvignon 1996 striking gold at McLaren Vale and silvers at Hobart and Stanthorpe, its Old Adam Shiraz was a top selection for *Winestate* magazine for 1996, while its Cabernet Shiraz Merlot is a regular award winner. Cellar door sales: 7 days from 10am; lunch available on weekends at Mignonne's Mood Food but booking is essential.

BRL Hardy (vineyard only)   NR
Langhorne Creek, SA 5255

Owner: BRL Hardy Limited
Chief winemaker: Peter Dawson
Year of foundation: 1995
Tonnes crushed on average each year: vineyard not yet fully bearing, but when vines come to maturity, crush should well exceed 1000 tonnes
Location: Langhorne Creek
Area: 94 ha
Soils: alluvial, red loamy clays, silty sands
Varieties planted: White—none; Red—cabernet franc, cabernet sauvignon, merlot, shiraz
Leading wines: see notes
Notes: Like the rest of the 'big battalions', BRL Hardy gathered its first substantial crop from its recent plantings in 1998 and, until the vineyards reach maturity, the wines made will in all probability be blended into the general run of BRL Hardy reds. No local cellar door sales.

Lake Breeze Wines   R7.5
Step Road, Langhorne Creek, SA 5255
(3 km south of the town)
Ph 08 8537 3017, Fax 08 8537 3267

Owners: Follett family
Chief winemaker: Greg Follett

Year of foundation: vineyard 1930s, winemaking 1987
Tonnes crushed on average each year: 750, with 95 being utilised for the Lake Breeze labels and this will be increased to 150 tonnes and more in succeeding vintages
Location: Langhorne Creek
Area: 65 ha
Soils: alluvial, black-brown soils
Varieties planted: White—chardonnay, white frontignac; Red—cabernet sauvignon, grenache, merlot, shiraz
Leading wines: Lake Breeze Cabernet Sauvignon; Bernoota Shiraz-Cabernet Sauvignon
Notes: The Follett family began farming in Langhorne Creek in the 1880s, originally growing currants for drying and then replacing them with port and sherry grape varieties in the 1930s, which in turn were replaced by the present table wine varieties 20–30 years ago. Since 1994, Lake Breeze wines have received five trophies and 27 gold medals. The Lake Breeze Cabernet Sauvignon is especially good. Cellar door sales: 10am–5pm each day.

Mildara Blass (vineyard only)   NR
Lake Plains Road, Langhorne Creek, SA 5255

Owner: Mildara Blass Limited
Chief winemaker: Chris Hatcher
Year of foundation: 1994
Tonnes crushed on average each year: estimated to be 5500 tonnes by 2004
Location: Langhorne Creek
Area: 170 ha plus long-term lease of the Metala vineyard totalling 250 ha
Soils: rich alluvial loams and sandy clay
Varieties planted: White—none; Red—cabernet sauvignon, merlot, shiraz plus trial plantings of other reds
Leading wines: Saltram Metala Reds and Blass Grey Label Cabernet
Notes: Within a decade the Mildara Blass

production from Langhorne Creek will be enormous, but as Viticultural Director, Vic Patrick says, 'Mildara's presence in this region is small by comparison to others'. No local cellar door sales.

Orlando Wyndham (vineyard only)   NR

Clements Road, Langhorne Creek, SA 5255

Owner: Orlando Wyndham
Chief winemaker: Phil Laffer
Year of foundation: 1995
Tonnes crushed on average each year: 1998 first vintage, a small commercial crop was picked, but this will increase substantially in coming years
Location: Langhorne Creek
Area: 306 ha
Soils: loamy sands to sandy loams of varying depth over sandy clay loam
Varieties planted: White—chardonnay; Red—cabernet franc, merlot, shiraz
Leading wines: Orlando Jacobs Creek range
Notes: For Orlando, its Langhorne Creek vineyard represents a very large investment. As well as the vineyard, it has involved the construction of a long water pipeline, but it should return several thousand tonnes of fruit on maturity of the vines. No local cellar door sales.

Rosemount (vineyard only)   NR

Alexandrina, Milang Road, Angas Plains, SA 5255

Owner: Rosemount Estate
Chief winemaker: Philip Shaw
Year of foundation: 1993
Tonnes crushed on average each year: presently about 1500 but the vineyard is only recently in bearing and the crop will at least double
Location: Angas Plains

Area: 320 ha
Soils: deep alluvial sandy loams, red sandy loams over limestone
Varieties planted: White—chardonnay; Red—cabernet sauvignon, merlot, petit verdot, shiraz
Leading wines: At present, blended into Diamond label varietals, but when the vines mature, there may be a 100% Langhorne Creek red
Notes: Intended to supplement Rosemount's mid-range of red wines, this is another very young vineyard not quite in full bearing. No local cellar door sales.

Temple Bruer Wines   NR

Milang Road, Strathalbyn, SA 5255
Ph 08 8537 0203, Fax 08 8537 0131

Owners: Barbara and David Bruer
Chief winemaker: David Bruer
Year of foundation: 1981
Tonnes crushed on average each year: 230 but increasing as new vines come into bearing
Location: Langhorne Creek
Area: 24 ha consisting of two vineyards, the old 8 ha and the new 16 ha
Soils: alluvium on top of Mallee sand over limestone marl
Varieties planted: White—chenin blanc, riesling, verdelho, viognier; Red—cabernet franc, cabernet sauvignon, grenache, malbec, merlot, petit verdot, shiraz
Leading wines: Temple Bruer Cabernet Merlot, Shiraz-Malbec, Grenache
Notes: Temple Bruer old vineyard is a certified organic vineyard, as will be the new vineyard which is just coming into bearing and employs the Smart-Dyson trellising system to counteract greenhouse effect. Generally Temple Bruer is managed according to techniques which will assist sustainability. There is also a commercial grapevine nursery, which supplies vineyards throughout Australia. Cellar door sales: Tues–Sun 10am–4.30pm.

McLAREN VALE REGION

One of the first areas to be settled south of Adelaide (1839), the McLaren Vale region was, prosaically enough, initially named after its first surveyor, John McLaren. It was a name that had some difficulty catching on, the hamlets originally named Gloucester and Bellevue having greater local currency. However, by the 1920s, the name McLaren Vale became commonly accepted.

As was customary in early Australian rural settlements, the pioneers were generally prepared to experiment with any crop that might be of value either domestically or to the local economy. Such was the case with viticulture, where the usual practice was to plant a few vines to see what happened. So it was with the first English settlers who worked their mixed farms south of Adelaide, but none were prepared to risk an entire livelihood on the vine. John Reynell was typical of such settlers. He is reputed to have planted vines on his Reynella farm as early as 1838.

Medicine has often walked arm in arm with the vine. So it was in South Australia, at Magill, east of Adelaide, with Dr Penfold in 1844. Similarly south of Adelaide, where Dr Alexander Kelly planted a vineyard on his Trinity farm near Morphett Vale perhaps even earlier than Dr Penfold. By 1845, there was little doubt that most temperate and explored parts of South Australia appeared eminently suitable for viticulture. By 1850 what is now McLaren Vale witnessed the planting of its first 'commercial' vineyard—12 hectares at Hope Farm (now Seaview) established by George Manning. Five years later, Manning made his first wine, but he still relied on wheat as his principal crop. By 1860 South Australia was about to experience its first wine boom. Dr Kelly saw great export opportunities and, utilising most of his own capital and enlisting the financial support of some of the magnates of Adelaide, such as Sir Thomas Elder, Sir Samuel Davenport and Sir Edward Sterling, he organised the purchase of Crown land near McLaren Vale late in 1862. Tintara, which began to be planted the following year, was to be the region's first truly commercial vineyard and London was to be its market. A decade later, amid recriminations, the company had ground slowly to a halt. In 1873 it closed its doors for the last time. It was 'picked up' quite cheaply in 1876 by an immigrant boy made good, Thomas Hardy, aged 46, then reaching the peak of his commercial activity.

Hardy, a Devonshire lad, had reached Adelaide in 1850 at the age of 20. After time in the goldfields, where he made money, not from gold but from droving cattle to feed the miners, he bought 'Bankside' on the Torrens near Adelaide in 1853. By the late 1850s he was a small but thriving horticulturalist and winemaker and was even exporting small quantities of wine to London. Hardy trod carefully through the depressed 1860s. Tintara was most likely his introduction to McLaren Vale and fortuitously his purchase of Tintara coincided with a general upturn in the South Australian economy as a whole, which had been depressed due to drought, the discovery of gold in Victoria and New South Wales (which caused a drift of South Australian population to those two eastern colonies) and the non-discovery of gold in South Australia (which would have more than reversed the trend). The presence of a successful wine company—for Thomas Hardy & Sons was very successful by

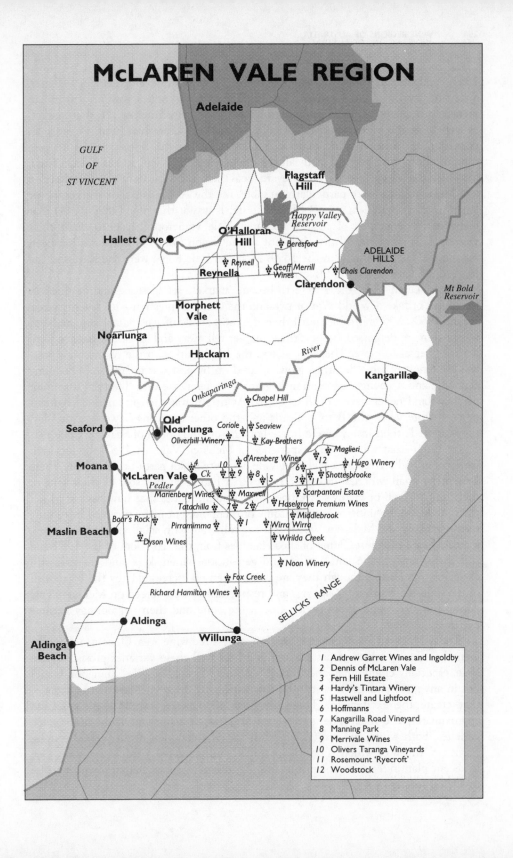

McLAREN VALE REGION

Adelaide

GULF
OF
ST VINCENT

Flagstaff
Hill

Happy Valley
Reservoir

Hallett Cove ●

O'Halloran
Hill

🍇 Beresford

ADELAIDE
HILLS

🍇 Reynell

🍇 Geoff Merrill
Wines

🍇 Chais Clarendon

Reynella

Clarendon ●

Mt Bold
Reservoir

Morphett
Vale

Noarlunga

River

Hackam

Kangarilla ●

Onkaparinga

🍇 Chapel Hill

Seaford ●

Old
Noarlunga

Coriole 🍇 🍇 Seaview

Oliverhill Winery 🍇 🍇 Kay Brothers

🍇 Maglieri

Moana ●

4   10   🍇 d'Arenberg Wines   🍇 12   🍇 Hugo Winery

McLaren Vale ● Ck   🍇 9   🍇 8   5   6 🍇   🍇 Shottesbrooke

Pedler

🍇 Marienberg Wines   🍇 Maxwell   3 🍇 🍇 11   🍇 Scarpantoni Estate

Tatachilla 🍇   7 🍇 🍇 2   🍇 Haselgrove Premium Wines

Boar's Rock 🍇   Pirramimma 🍇   🍇 1   🍇 Wirra Wirra   🍇 Middlebrook

Maslin Beach ●

🍇 Dyson Wines   🍇 Wirilda Creek

🍇 Noon Winery

🍇 Fox Creek

Richard Hamilton Wines 🍇

SELLICKS RANGE

● Aldinga

Willunga ●

Aldinga
Beach ●

1	Andrew Garret Wines and Ingoldby
2	Dennis of McLaren Vale
3	Fern Hill Estate
4	Hardy's Tintara Winery
5	Hastwell and Lightfoot
6	Hoffmanns
7	Kangarilla Road Vineyard
8	Manning Park
9	Merrivale Wines
10	Olivers Taranga Vineyards
11	Rosemount 'Ryecroft'
12	Woodstock

1880—undoubtedly influenced the progress of viticultural development in McLaren Vale and by the 1890s, a new viticultural boom was under way, as Australian vignerons began to exploit new opportunities in the British market. In that market, as well as in the various Australian colonial markets, there had been a change in popular taste to heavier and more alcoholic wines. For the British, it was a swing towards cheap fortifieds and medically recommended 'tonic burgundies' (heavy reds), for which the warmer Australian vineyard areas such as the Barossa Valley, Rutherglen and McLaren Vale were particularly suitable. For the Australian wine market, never large, it was probably an aping of British taste. It was at this time (1890–1914) that many of the ancestors of today's McLaren Vale vignerons began to plant their vineyards. Thomas Hardy's involvement in the region from 1876 onwards has been mentioned, but prominent in the 1890s McLaren Vale boom were the Kays and the Johnstones. Later came the Osborns.

For McLaren Vale, these were to become markets set in stone and destined to last—give or take a World War or two and the Great Depression—for seventy years. By the 1960s, McLaren Vale, until then the most stable of Australian wine markets, was once more depressed as the British market fell away and as a consequence local wineries began to close. This time it was the local market to the rescue, as a post-war awareness of wine began to grow, spurred on by post-war migration, a booming economy and a younger generation beginning to be aware of a 'lifestyle' that their parents could never have hoped to enjoy. At first it was a cognisance of charmat-process white wine, the Barossa Pearls and the other sparkling 'jewels' of the day, then 'dry red', then in my case a home-bottling of a hogshead of Seaview Cabernet-Shiraz 1964—that was my first experience of McLaren Vale. By 1967, the local red wine boom had arrived and McLaren Vale was very much part of it. Suddenly, there were many small wineries, unknown names that had previously sold all their wine or their fruit to Emu or Hardy's or Gilbey's of London, names that now needed to sell their product or go under. Go under some of them did, but many survived by turning to winemaking and McLaren Vale began to proliferate with small, interesting names, scarcely heard of before. Some of those families from the red boom of the 1960s are still there, now in the hands of second generation winemakers, and they are still extremely interesting, though they are being eaten up increasingly by the bigger fish of the industry. Further replantings and restructurings were forced on McLaren Vale during the 1970s and 1980s, when first white wine and then chardonnay became extremely popular.

Today McLaren Vale remains predominantly a red wine area. Of course there are many hectares of white grapes planted and how well these varieties prosper in the Vale, especially chardonnay and, though not quite as consistently, sauvignon blanc! But in any good vintage, it is still the reds, especially shiraz and cabernet sauvignon, that create the excitement. There are over 40 wineries in McLaren Vale and approximately 270 independent growers, who grow all major and many minor grape varieties, both white and red. Average annual production is about 30 000 tonnes, about two-thirds of which is crushed, vinified and marketed as McLaren Vale. Due to recent plantings yet to come into bearing, the average annual crop will increase to 43 000 tonnes by 1999.

Location: latitude 35°03', 35°17'S, longitude 138°30' to 138°40', about 40 km south of Adelaide

Altitude: generally from 50 m to 350 m: in the north 100 m around Reynella to 200 m in the Blewitt Springs area with isolated vineyards in the Mount Lofty Ranges to 350 m; in the south, closer to the sea, there are lower vineyards, which commence at 50 m altitude

Topography and soils: Viewed from the town, McLaren Vale has a flat to undulating landscape, rising gently to the north and the east, but rather more steeply to the north-east. Most of its vineyards are planted within a radius of 12 km from the sea in the general area of McLaren Vale–McLaren Flat–Willunga on a wide variety of soils. There are fertile red-brown earths, common podsolic soils of low fertility, terra rossa, rendzinas, solodic and cracking soils. Geologically, the region is divided into two systems: the hard rocks of the Mount Lofty Ranges consisting of shales, siltstone, quartzite, dolomite and tillite and overlying Cambrian carbonate metasediments such as limestone, dolomite and siltstone; and the unconsolidated sediments of the St Vincent Basin, typified by the Willunga and Noarlunga Embayments. Sand deposits are common around the North and South Maslin areas. Tertiary remnants, though extensively eroded over millions of years, still cap the hills and there the old land surface has been ferruginised to form the red-brown ironstone so admired by the original Thomas Hardy, who thought he could taste it in the reds.

Climate: MJT 21°C, MAR 10.8, HDD raw 1913, AR 656 mm (Oct–Mar 182 mm), RH 49% (9am mid Jan), AI 418 mm, SH 8.6 (Dry & Smart). McLaren Vale is a warm to hot region with dry summers, but it is important to stress that it is bounded on its west by the St Vincent Gulf, which exerts a beneficial cooling effect with its on-shore breezes. Its winters are moderate in temperature and wet (474 mm of rain falling between April and September). Relative humidity is low at 49% and supplementary irrigation is necessary. This is usually carried out by drippers, which have as their water source either surface dams or bores from underground aquifers, the chief of which is the Willunga Basin Aquifer, a source of good water quality, which drains into the Gulf via a small number of streams. About 2% of vineyards are irrigated through mains water. It is to be noted that there is a proposal to limit irrigation to 170 mm per year. Regional temperature variability is less than 1.5°C. Air drainage is generally quite good and frost is virtually unknown. Because of the warm, dry climate in spring and summer, mildews are also rarely a problem, though most vineyards are sprayed periodically. There are isolated sandy areas where nematodes exist, but these can be combated by planting on rootstocks. Light brown apple moth is also present from time to time.

Harvest time: chardonnay early–mid-March, sauvignon blanc mid-March, shiraz late March, cabernet sauvignon late March and grenache late April; harvest times can vary by up to two weeks in the various areas within the region

Principal grape varieties: White—chardonnay, riesling, semillon, sauvignon blanc; Red—shiraz, cabernet sauvignon, grenache, merlot

Total area: (1996) 3616 ha

Principal wine styles: The shiraz of McLaren Vale is rich, ripe, generous and soft, yet paradoxically 'long' with acids and tannins firm enough usually to ensure a cellaring life of 5–10 years. Often the wines seem precocious and can be drunk at 1–2 years of age, but they keep excellently. Predominant flavours are blackberry, black pepper and dark chocolate. Traditionally, shiraz was often blended with varieties such as grenache and mourvedre and made into 'Burgundy' or, by itself or blended with grenache, fortified and made into a long-living 'port' style.

The chardonnays have ripe peachy fruit characters both in aroma and flavour that adapt to oak very harmoniously, making the McLaren Vale style one of the best warm area examples of the variety. But McLaren Vale Chardonnay should not usually be kept beyond 3 years.

Again, the cabernet sauvignons are a very ripe style of red with dark berry, blackcurrant aromatics and flavours and 'dark chocolate'. It is sometimes blended with its 'Bordeaux' brothers, cabernet franc, merlot and petit verdot. Some tasters also find a savoury black olive character on nose and palate. Ageing potential similar to shiraz.

The mystery with sauvignon blanc is why in an area so warm as McLaren Vale, it conforms so well to its grassy, high acid varietal specifications (which after all are based on sauvignon's performance in relatively cool areas) as to make it notable in three years out of five. Why should McLaren Vale sauvignon show its typical herbaceous-tropical characters in such a warm area? The answer is based on two factors. Firstly McLaren Vale predominantly grows the old shy-bearing clone of sauvignon blanc. The small amount of fruit produced therefore is never overcropped and conforms excellently in most years to sauvignon's typical parameters. Secondly, the foliage produced by such vines is generally luxuriant, giving shaded, methoxypyrazine characters to the small crops of sauvignon blanc, which do not become overripe, though they reach quite high baumes. The best of McLaren Vale Sauvignon Blanc should be drunk young—up to eighteen months of age.

Andrew Garrett Wines   R7

Kangarilla Road, McLaren Vale, SA 5171
Ph 08 8323 8853, Fax 08 8323 8550

Owner: Mildara Blass
Chief winemaker: Phillip Reschke
Year of foundation: 1983
Tonnes crushed on average each year: 1600
(includes production from contract growers and
other regions)
Locations: Tamar Vineyard (McLaren Flat)
32 ha; Padthaway 78 ha (part of Mildara Blass)
Area: 32 ha
Soils: (McLaren Flat) loamy clay, bleached
sands; (Padthaway) terra rossa, grey bleached
sands
Varieties planted: White—chardonnay;
Red—cabernet sauvignon, shiraz

Leading wines: Andrew Garrett Sparkling
Burgundy, Bold Style Shiraz
Notes: Andrew Garrett Wines is another
Mildara Blass facility, which sources a majority
of its fruit from outside the McLaren Vale
region, though Bold Style Shiraz often does
contain enough McLaren Vale fruit to make it
representative of its region. Cellar door sales:
7 days 10am–5pm.

Beresford   R7

49 Fraser Avenue, Happy Valley, SA 5159
Ph 08 8322 3611, Fax 08 8322 3610

Owner: Crestview Pty Ltd
Chief winemaker: Rob Dundon

Year of foundation: 1985
Tonnes crushed on average each year: 1900
Locations: McLaren Vale and Langhorne Creek
Area: 110 ha (Langhorne Creek)
Soils: sandy loam with alluvial deposit, deep
sand over clay loam and heavy alluvial soils
Varieties planted: White—chardonnay,
sauvignon blanc, semillon; Red—cabernet
sauvignon, merlot, petit verdot, pinot noir,
sangiovese, shiraz
Leading wines: Beresford Semillon Sauvignon
Blanc, Cabernet Merlot, Chardonnay, Shiraz. In
addition there are four other ranges: Beresford
Katherine Hills, Beresford Highwood, Beresford
Saints (Estelle, Yvette and Helene) and
Beresford Beacon Hill
Notes: Beresford is managed by Rob Dundon, a
winemaker of many years' experience with
Hardy's. It occupies the old Horndale winery,
built in 1896, one of the McLaren Vale boom
years of the 1890s. Part buried in the side of a
hill, it used the favoured mode of wine
movement in those days before electric
pumps—gravity. Horndale was also a distillery
for some years in the 1930s. Wine standards
are satisfactory and recently have been raised a
notch, as witnessed by the silver medal won in
the 1997 Adelaide Show by St Yvette
Chardonnay. Cellar door sales: 7 days
11am–5pm.

Boar's Rock **NR**

Lot 50, Tatachilla Road, McLaren Vale,
SA 5171
Ph 08 8323 9955, Fax 08 8323 9966

Owners: group of McLaren Vale businesspeople
Chief winemaker: Mike Farmilo
Year of foundation: 1997
Tonnes crushed on average each year: 3500
anticipated for 1998 vintage
Location: Tatachilla Road, McLaren Vale
Area: no vineyards are owned
Varieties planted: no vineyards are owned

Leading wines: no wines are produced for
commercial sale to the public
Notes: A crushing and winemaking facility
directed by former Seaview chief winemaker,
Mike Farmilo, that will be undoubtedly very
busy. There are no cellar door sales.

Chais Clarendon (see also Normans, Adelaide Plains, Riverland) **R8.5**

Grants Gully Road, Clarendon, SA 5157
Ph 08 8383 6138, Fax 08 8383 6089

Owner: Normans Wines Limited
Chief winemaker: Roger Harbord
Year of foundation: (Normans) 1853
Tonnes crushed on average each year: 30
Location: Clarendon
Area: 4 ha
Soils: clay loam interspersed with 'buckshot'
Varieties planted: White—chardonnay;
Red—cabernet sauvignon
Leading wines: Chais Clarendon Chardonnay,
Cabernet Sauvignon
Notes: Normans is one of Australia's medium-
sized wineries. In addition to 30 tonnes of its
own Adelaide Hills fruit used chiefly for Chais
Clarendon wines, the company utilises fruit
from its newly acquired McLaren Vale vineyard,
its older 45 ha vineyard at Evanston on the
Adelaide Plains and from growers in McLaren
Vale, Langhorne Creek, Coonawarra,
Padthaway and the Adelaide Hills. The
Clarendon winery crushes about 1500 tonnes
in total. Cellar door sales: Mon–Sat
10am–5pm, Sun 11am–5pm.

Chapel Hill **R10**

Chapel Hill Road, McLaren Vale,
SA 5171
Ph 08 8323 8429, Fax 08 8323 9245

Owner: Gerard Industries Pty Limited
Chief winemaker: Pam Dunsford
Year of foundation: 1979

Tonnes crushed on average each year: 500
Location: McLaren Vale
Area: 84 ha consisting of four vineyards;
Chapel Hill (14 ha), Kangarilla (30 ha), Bakers
Gully (32 ha) and Merrivale (8 ha)
Soils: (Chapel Hill and Merrivale) red-brown
earths over shale with ironstone; (Kangarilla)
duplex sand over mottled clays with ironstone;
(Bakers Gully) red-brown earth over clay with
ironstone
Varieties planted: White—chardonnay, riesling,
verdelho; Red—cabernet sauvignon, malbec,
merlot, shiraz
Leading wines: Chapel Hill Reserve
Chardonnay, McLaren Vale Shiraz, Reserve
Cabernet-Shiraz, The Vicar (a Cabernet-Shiraz
blend), Unwooded Chardonnay, Verdelho,
Eden Valley Riesling
Notes: The fruit intake of Chapel Hill is
primarily sourced from McLaren Vale, but it is
supplemented by fruit from other premium
regions such as Coonawarra, Padthaway and
Eden Valley. Its wines are made by one of
Australia's leading winemakers, Pam Dunsford.
Chapel Hill has become, thanks to her efforts,
one of the premium wineries of McLaren Vale,
whose wines always merit respect and more
importantly impart a great deal of pleasure.
Recently, Chapel Hill embarked upon a
considerable expansion, more than tripling its
size in one vintage. Doubtless Pam Dunsford
has taken it all in her stride. Cellar door sales:
7 days 11am–5pm.

Coriole R8

Chaffeys Road, McLaren Vale, SA 5171
Ph 08 8323 8305, Fax 08 8323 9136

Owners: Lloyd family
Chief winemaker: Stephen Hall
Year of foundation: 1968
Tonnes crushed on average each year: 360 but
increasing to 440 from 1998 vintage
Location: McLaren Vale
Area: 20 ha increasing to 25 ha in 1998

Soils: red-brown earth over capped limestone;
deep red clay (Lloyd Reserve vineyard)
Varieties planted: White—chenin blanc,
semillon; Red—cabernet sauvignon, merlot,
sangiovese, shiraz
Leading wines: Coriole Lloyd Reserve Shiraz,
Mary Kathleen (a Merlot Cabernet), Redstone
(shiraz cabernet grenache blend)
Notes: Coriole is located in the 'Seaview' area
of McLaren Vale, distinctive for its red-brown
earths above a limestone substructure. Such
soils produce excellent reds and Coriole is
renowned for its Shiraz both Reserve and
standard. Cellar door sales: Mon–Fri 9am–5pm,
weekends and public holidays 11am–5pm.

d'Arenberg Wines R8

Osborn Road, McLaren Vale, SA 5171
Ph 08 8323 8206, Fax 08 8323 8423

Owner: FE Osborn & Sons Pty Ltd
Chief winemaker: Chester Osborn
Year of foundation: 1912
Tonnes crushed on average each year: 450 but
increasing to 1000-plus by the year 2000 as
new plantings come into bearing
Location: McLaren Vale
Area: 119.2 ha, consisting of two vineyards;
Osborn Vineyard (67.2 ha) and Pedler's Divide
Vineyard (52 ha)
Soils: varying soils dominated by duplex
red-brown loamy sand and grey-brown loamy
sands
Varieties planted: (Osborn Vineyard) White—
chardonnay, marsanne, riesling, sauvignon
blanc, viognier; Red—cabernet sauvignon,
chambourcin, grenache, mourvedre, shiraz.
(Pedler's Divide Vineyard) White—chardonnay,
marsanne, roussanne, sauvignon blanc,
viognier; Red—cabernet sauvignon, grenache,
mourvedre, petit verdot, shiraz
Leading wines: d'Arenberg markets a wide
range of table wines and fortifieds, of which
the pick are Old Vine Shiraz and d'Arry's
Original Shiraz-Grenache

Notes: d'Arenberg is a McLaren Vale veteran and in a sense a reticule of the Vale tradition with its big smooth red styles, a fortified Shiraz ('port') and also a Fine Old Tawny, but all the essential white trappings of modernity are there also—a Chardonnay, a Sauvignon Blanc and a 'sticky', made as most superior botrytised sweet whites should be from riesling. Its renaissance as a McLaren Vale table wine specialist began in the late 1960s with one spectacularly performing red, the 1967 Burgundy, a blend of grenache and shiraz which set fire to the contemporary show scene by winning many trophies throughout Australia. In addition to the great selection of reds, there is d'Arry's Verandah, a restaurant with a modern regionally-based cuisine and a menu changing daily which is open year round, except for August, for lunch Wednesdays to Sundays inclusive and for dinner Friday and Saturday nights. Cellar door sales: weekdays 9am–5pm, Saturdays and public holidays 10am–5pm, Sundays noon–4pm.

Dennis of McLaren Vale R7

Kangarilla Road, McLaren Vale, SA 5171
Ph 08 8323 8665, Fax 08 8323 9121

Owners: PS & SIH Dennis
Chief winemaker: Peter Dennis
Year of foundation: 1970
Tonnes crushed on average each year: 125 (about 100 of which are used for Dennis labels)
Location: McLaren Vale
Area: 13.5 ha
Soils: varying sandy loams
Varieties planted: White—chardonnay, sauvignon blanc, white muscat; Red—cabernet sauvignon, grenache, merlot, shiraz
Leading wines: Dennis Shiraz, Chardonnay
Notes: The Dennis family is another of those grapegrowing families that took to winemaking during the red wine boom of the mid to late 1960s. The winery also has an

excellent reputation for Chardonnay, rich and ripe in the usual McLaren Vale manner. Cellar door sales: Mon–Sat 10am–5pm, Sun and public holidays 11am–5pm.

Dowie Doole R7

182 Main Road, McLaren Vale, SA 5171
Ph 08 8323 8100, Fax 08 8323 0100

Owners: Tintookie Vineyards Pty Ltd and N & J Doole
Chief winemaker: Brian Light (contract)
Year of foundation: 1996
Tonnes crushed on average each year: 400 (about 10% of which is used for the Dowie Doole labels)
Locations: McLaren Vale and Blewitt Springs
Area: McLaren Vale 26 ha, Blewitt Springs 16 ha
Soils: (Blewitt Springs) sand over clay; (McLaren Vale) sandy loam
Varieties planted: White—chenin blanc, sauvignon, semillon; Red—cabernet sauvignon, merlot, pinot noir, shiraz
Leading wines: Dowie Doole Semillon-Sauvignon Blanc, Shiraz
Notes: It is often said that McLaren Vale is a region of small winemakers. Dowie Doole must be its latest although, with a crush of 400 tonnes, it is not so small at all. Its wines are in the mainstream of McLaren Vale quality and I have noticed an attractively full-flavoured Semillon-Sauvignon Blanc. No cellar door sales.

Dyson Wines NR

Sheriff Road, Maslin Beach, SA 5171
Ph 08 8386 1092, Fax 08 8327 0066

Owner/chief winemaker: Allan Dyson
Year of foundation: 1977
Tonnes crushed on average each year: 40
Location: Maslin Beach, about 8 km west of McLaren Vale
Area: 6 ha
Soils: brown loam over red clay

Varieties planted: White—chardonnay, sauvignon blanc, semillon, viognier; Red—cabernet sauvignon
Leading wines: Dyson Cabernet Sauvignon, Chardonnay, Sauvignon Blanc-Semillon
Notes: Situated only 2.5 km from St Vincent Gulf, Dyson Wines is a true wine estate, wine being made only from estate-grown fruit and bottled at the winery. Cellar door sales: 7 days 10am–5pm.

Fern Hill Estate NR
Ingoldby Road, McLaren Flat, SA 5171
Ph 08 8383 0167, Fax 08 8383 0107

Owner: Saidwick Pty Ltd
Chief winemaker: Grant Burge (contract)
Year of foundation: 1975
Tonnes crushed on average each year: not disclosed but estimated at 10; a further quantity (about 50 tonnes) of fruit is bought in
Location: McLaren Flat
Area: 33 ha
Soils: heavy loam graduating to sand over clay
Varieties planted: White—none; Red—cabernet sauvignon
Leading wines: Fern Hill Estate Cabernet Sauvignon, Chardonnay, Semillon, Shiraz
Notes: Formerly owned by Wayne Thomas, Fern Hill Estate is now part of the Hill International wine group, with Basedow and Marienberg. The Fern Hill Cabernet style was a typically rich, chocolatey red, but I have not tasted it under its new ownership. Cellar door sales: 7 days 10am–5pm.

Fox Creek R8
Malpas Road, Willunga, SA 5171
Ph 08 8556 2403, Fax 08 8556 2104

Owners: J and H Watts, P and H McDonald, J and L Roberts, M and A McKinnon and P Watts
Chief winemakers: Sarah and Sparky Marquis
Year of foundation: 1994
Tonnes crushed on average each year: 725, of which 135 are used for the Fox Creek label
Location: Willunga (four separate vineyards)
Area: 120 ha
Soils: black clays (terra nera) very sticky when wet, powdery when dry
Varieties planted: White—chardonnay, chenin blanc, sauvignon blanc, semillon, verdelho; Red—cabernet franc, cabernet sauvignon, grenache, merlot, shiraz
Leading wines: Fox Creek Reserve Shiraz, Reserve Cabernet Sauvignon, Vixen (a sparkling red), Verdelho, Chardonnay
Notes: This is an exciting new McLaren Vale winery, which burst onto the scene in 1995. Its Shiraz reds, as one would expect from their McLaren Vale origin, have done extremely well, in particular winning the local Bushing Festival with the 1994, the award for best one-year-old red for 1995 and its 1996 Reserve won two trophies and four golds. Its vineyard is quite modern, using Scott Henry and vertical shoot positional trellising. For water stress management, neutron probe water measurement and computer plotted water deficit drip irrigation is employed. Cellar door sales: 11am–5pm daily.

Geoff Merrill Wines R8
Mount Hurtle Winery, 291 Pimpala Road, Woodcroft, SA 5161
Ph 08 8381 6877, Fax 08 8322 2244

Owner: Geoff Merrill
Chief winemakers: Geoff Merrill and Goe di Fabio
Year of foundation: 1980 (Mount Hurtle Winery, originally built in 1897, was re-opened in 1986)
Tonnes crushed on average each year: 1400 (including many tonnes of fruit purchased from local sources)
Location: Reynella
Area: 12 ha
Soils: sandy loam to red-brown earth topsoil over red clays

Varieties planted: White—chardonnay, sauvignon blanc; Red—cabernet sauvignon, merlot

Leading wines: Geoff Merrill Reserve Chardonnay, Reserve Cabernet Sauvignon, Reserve Semillon, Premium Sauvignon Blanc, Chardonnay, Grenache (a rose), Cabernet Merlot, Shiraz

Notes: The ebullient Geoff Merrill is one of the established characters of the Australian wine industry. Paradoxically, his wine styles (in particular his Reserve Chardonnay and Reserve Cabernet Sauvignon) tend to elegance rather than exuberance. The Mount Hurtle label, which was more characteristically McLaren Vale in style than the Reserve, has now been discontinued and the Geoff Merrill Premium range substituted. So McLaren Vale style continues. Cellar door sales: Mon–Fri 9am–5pm, Sun 10am–5pm, closed Sat.

Hardy's Tintara Winery (winery only)

Main Road, McLaren Vale, SA 5171
Ph 08 8323 8676, Fax 08 8323 0151

Owner: BRL Hardy Ltd
Chief winemaker: Peter Dawson; red winemaker Stephen Pannell
Year of foundation: 1876
Tonnes crushed on average each year: 6500
Location: McLaren Vale
Area: see Reynell entry
Varieties planted: see Reynell entry
Leading wines: Eileen Hardy Shiraz, Thomas Hardy Cabernet Sauvignon, Tintara Shiraz
Notes: This is not Dr Alexander Kelly's original Tintara winery but an old flour mill so renamed by Thomas Hardy in 1876. Today it is BRL Hardy's winemaking facility for virtually all the red grapes processed by the group from McLaren Vale, Coonawarra, Padthaway, Yarra Valley and many other areas. The leading wines mentioned are usually made from at

least 50% of McLaren Vale fruit. Cellar door sales: 7 days 10am–4.30pm.

Haselgrove Premium Wines R7

Cnr Foggo and Kangarilla Roads, McLaren Vale, SA 5171
Ph 08 8323 8706, Fax 08 8323 8049

Owner: Australian Premium Wines Ltd
Chief winemaker: Nick Haselgrove
Year of foundation: 1981
Tonnes crushed on average year: 1200 (700 used for the Haselgrove labels)
Location: McLaren Vale
Area: 17 ha
Soils: sand over clay
Varieties planted: White—chardonnay, chenin blanc, sauvignon blanc, viognier; Red— cabernet sauvignon, grenache, merlot, shiraz
Leading wines: There are three ranges: H Reserve Chardonnay, Botrytis Semillon, Sparkling Garnet (shiraz), Pinot Noir Chardonnay; Haselgrove Picture Label Chardonnay, Chenin Blanc, Sauvignon Blanc, Grenache-Shiraz, Cabernet-Merlot-Shiraz; Sovereign Chardonnay, Grenache, Cabernet Sauvignon
Notes: This is another winery run by a scion of an old-established winemaking family. Wine quality is usually very good, H Reserve Chardonnay and Reserve Shiraz being the pick. Cellar door sales: Mon–Fri 9am–5pm, weekends and public holidays 10am–5pm.

Hastwell and Lightfoot 🍇 NR

Foggos Road, McLaren Vale, SA 5171
Ph 08 8323 8692, Fax 08 8323 8098

Owners: M & W Hastwell and M & J Lightfoot
Chief winemaker: Nick Haselgrove (contract)
Year of foundation: 1988
Tonnes crushed on average each year: 165 rising to 200 by the year 2000 (6 tonnes presently used for the Hastwell & Lightfoot labels)

Location: McLaren Vale
Area: 17 ha
Soils: sand over clay
Varieties planted: White—chardonnay, semillon, viognier; Red—cabernet franc, cabernet sauvignon, shiraz
Leading wines: Hastwell & Lightfoot Chardonnay, Cabernets Sauvignon and Franc blend
Notes: Though an established grapegrower, this is a fairly new McLaren Vale winemaker whose object in winemaking is to grow fruit of good flavour and to take that flavour through to the wine. The prescription sounds excellent. Cellar door sales by appointment.

Hoffmanns **NR**

Ingoldby Road, McLaren Flat, SA 5171
Ph/Fax 08 8383 0232

Owners: Peter and Anthea Hoffmann
Chief winemaker: Nick Holmes (contract)
Year of foundation: 1978 (vineyard), 1995 (as label)
Tonnes crushed on average each year: 30 (10 for Hoffmans label)
Location: McLaren Flat
Area: 4 ha
Soils: varying from sandy loams to heavy grey clay
Varieties planted: White—none; Red—cabernet sauvignon, shiraz
Leading wines: Hoffmanns Cabernet Sauvignon
Notes: A small family-owned winery. Cellar door sales: daily 11am–5pm.

Hugh Hamilton Fine Wines (vineyards only) **R7**

McMurtrie Road, McLaren Vale, SA 5171
Ph 08 8323 8689, Fax 08 8323 9488

Owner/chief winemaker: Hugh Hamilton (wine made elsewhere)
Year of foundation: 1991
Tonnes crushed on average each year: crush has been variable due to re-establishment of the vineyards from 1995–97, but should be 60 tonnes in 1998, rising to 180 by 2001
Location: McLaren Vale
Area: 14 ha
Soils: a dark shrinkable clay Biscay
Varieties planted: White—chardonnay; Red—cabernet sauvignon, merlot, shiraz
Leading wines: Hugh Hamilton Unwooded Chardonnay, Shiraz, Merlot, Cabernet Sauvignon
Notes: Hugh Hamilton is a member of the winemaking Hamilton family of Adelaide. His ancestor was Richard Hamilton, who planted a vineyard near Glenelg in 1838 and has always been considered one of the earliest, if not the first, winemaker in South Australia. Hugh's wines are very much in the midstream of McLaren Vale and I have usually found the Unwooded Chardonnay and Shiraz to be of excellent quality. There are no cellar door sales. Sales by mail order are available by writing to PO Box 615, McLaren Vale, SA 5171.

Hugo Winery **R7**

Elliott Road, McLaren Flat, SA 5171
Ph 08 8383 0098, Fax 08 8383 0446

Owners: John and Liz Hugo
Chief winemaker: John Hugo
Year of foundation: 1982
Tonnes crushed on average each year: 170
Location: McLaren Flat
Area: 20.4 ha
Soils: red loam over clay
Varieties planted: White—chardonnay, sauvignon blanc; Red—cabernet franc, cabernet sauvignon, grenache, shiraz
Leading wines: Hugo Shiraz
Notes: This is another winery which produces good McLaren Vale Shiraz, rich, chocolatey and vanillan with all the size that one expects from the region. Cellar door sales: 10.30am–5pm Sun–Fri, Sat noon–5pm.

Ingoldby R8

Kangarilla Road, McLaren Vale, SA 5171
Ph 08 8323 8853, Fax 08 8323 8550

Owner: Mildara Blass
Chief winemaker: Phil Reschke
Year of foundation: 1972
Tonnes crushed on average each year: 300
(42 tonnes of which comes from the Ingoldby
vineyard, the balance from local growers)
Location: McLaren Vale
Area: 7 ha
Soils: friable alluvial loam
Varieties planted: White—none; Red—cabernet
sauvignon, grenache, shiraz
Leading wines: Ingoldby Shiraz, Chardonnay,
Cabernet Sauvignon
Notes: Another recent acquisition by the well-
funded Mildara Blass organisation, Ingoldby has
a respected name, making an excellent
Chardonnay from local contract-grown fruit. Its
Shiraz too is very much in the spirit of the
Vale. Cellar door sales: weekdays 9am–5pm,
weekends and public holidays 11am–5pm.

Kangarilla Road Vineyard and Winery NR

Kangarilla Road, McLaren Flat, SA 5171
Ph 08 8383 0533, Fax 08 8383 0044

Owners: Kevin and Helen O'Brien
Chief winemaker: Kevin O'Brien
Year of foundation: 1975
Tonnes crushed on average each year: 100
Location: McLaren Flat
Area: 7 ha
Soils: predominantly red loam with creek bed
stones
Varieties planted: White—chardonnay;
Red—carbernet franc, shiraz, zinfandel
Leading wines: Kangarilla Road Chardonnay,
Shiraz, Cabernet Sauvignon, Zinfandel
Notes: Formerly the Cambrai winery, Kangarilla
Road's claim to fame is that it is one of the
few producers of Zinfandel in the region. Cellar

door sales: weekdays 10am–5pm, weekends
and public holidays 11am–5pm.

Kay Brothers R7.5

'Amery', Kays Road, McLaren Vale,
SA 5171
Ph 08 8323 8211–01, Fax 08 8323 9199

Owners: Kay family
Chief winemaker: Colin Kay
Year of foundation: 1890
Tonnes crushed on average each year: 100
Location: McLaren Vale
Area: 14 ha
Soils: sandy, lateritic, gravelly, very variable
Varieties planted: White—sauvignon blanc;
Red—cabernet sauvignon, merlot, mourvedre,
pinot noir, shiraz
Leading wines: Kay Brothers Amery Block 6
Shiraz, Cabernet Sauvignon, Block 4 Shiraz,
Very Old Tawny Port
Notes: The winery was completed in 1895 and
a vineyard commenced a few years before and
they are now very much part of McLaren
Vale's and Australia's wine history. Its cellars
are built on the side of a hill according to a
model designed by John Kelly (son of
Alexander) employing the gravity flow principle,
very useful when the only pumps commonly
available were manual. (Steam pumps were
used by some wineries, but they were quite
expensive.) Crushers are on the top level,
fermenters on the second level and, below,
casks and storage tanks. Kay Brothers were for
many years involved in the export to the UK of
heavy reds and fortifieds, which were the forte
of McLaren Vale at that time. In 1926 over
200 000 litres of 'London Blend' (a heavy
fortified red) were exported. Today the Block 6
Shiraz, made from 1892 plantings, is a classic
McLaren red. Cellar door sales: weekdays
9am–5pm, weekends and public holidays
noon–5pm.

Maglieri R8.5

Douglas Gully Road, McLaren Flat,
SA 5171
Ph 08 8383 0177, Fax 08 8383 0136

Owner: Mildara Blass
Chief winemaker: John Loxton
Year of foundation: 1972
Tonnes crushed on average each year: 3500,
about 2000 of which are crushed for Maglieri's
own labels
Locations: McLaren Flat and McLaren Vale
Area: 150 ha
Soils: (McLaren Flat) deep sand; (McLaren Vale)
Biscay
Varieties planted: White—chardonnay, riesling,
semillon; Red—cabernet sauvignon, grenache,
merlot, shiraz
Leading wines: Maglieri Shiraz, Cabernet
Sauvignon, Merlot, Chardonnay, Semillon,
Lambrusco
Notes: Maglieri is a leading producer of
Australian Lambrusco style, but such
production tends to conceal a deeper quality—
that of the McLaren Vale region. The top of
the range Steve Maglieri Shiraz is of excellent
quality and ages well, as testified by the 1990
which won best red wine of the show at
Melbourne in 1996. The younger Maglieri
Shiraz are equally capable of top wine show
performances. Cellar door sales: Mon–Sat
9.30am–4pm, Sun and public holidays
11am–4pm, closed Christmas Day, Good
Friday, Easter Sunday.

Manning Park NR

Cnr Oliver's and Chalk Hill Roads,
McLaren Vale, SA 5171
Ph 08 8323 8209, Fax 08 8323 9474

Owners: W Randall, W Ward and A Fletcher
Chief winemaker: Warren Randall
Year of foundation: 1993
Tonnes crushed on average each year: 40, of

which about 10 are used for the Manning Park
labels
Location: McLaren Vale
Area: 10 ha
Soils: rich alluvial red earth
Varieties planted: White—chardonnay, riesling;
Red—cabernet sauvignon, grenache, shiraz,
merlot
Leading wines: Manning Park Savage
Grenache, Wild Shiraz
Notes: With such distinctively feral titles, one
might initially approach such wines with great
caution, but experienced former Seppelt and
Andrew Garrett winemaker, Warren Randall,
obviously feels that good McLaren Vale wine
should not be tame. Cellar door sales: 7 days
10am–5pm.

Marienberg Wines R6

2 Chalk Hill Road, McLaren Vale,
SA 5171 (Cellar door)
Ph 08 8323 9666, Fax 08 8323 9600

Owner: The Hill Wine Group
Chief winemaker: Grant Burge (contract)
Year of foundation: 1966
Tonnes crushed on average each year: 400
Location: McLaren Vale
Area: 32 ha
Soils: heavy loam graduating to sand over clay
Varieties planted: White—chardonnay;
Red—cabernet sauvignon, grenache, shiraz
Leading wines: There are two wine ranges,
Marienberg Reserve and Cottage. The Reserve
Range embodies Chardonnay, Shiraz and
Cabernet Sauvignon. 'Cottage' has a Riesling, a
blended white and a blended red.
Notes: Though the Marienberg whites and reds
are full of flavour, they seem to my palate
rather broad and somewhat old-fashioned with
a tendency to too much oak. Despite this, they
are consistent winners of silver and bronze
awards at wine shows. Cellar door sales:
7 days 10am–6pm except Christmas Day and
Good Friday.

Maxwell R8

Cnr Olivers Road and Chalk Hill Road,
McLaren Vale, SA 5171
Ph 08 8323 8200, Fax 08 8323 8900

Owner: Maxwells Wines
Chief winemaker: Mark Maxwell
Year of foundation: 1979
Tonnes crushed on average each year: 250
(100 of which is used for the Maxwell label)
Location: McLaren Vale
Area: 8.5 ha
Soils: brown loam over limestone, well drained
Varieties planted: White—sauvignon blanc,
semillon; Red—cabernet sauvignon, merlot,
shiraz
Leading wines: Maxwell Ellen Street Shiraz
Notes: Reinforcing the rise of its reputation,
Maxwell erected a new winery in 1997. Its
Ellen Street Shiraz is one of the better reds of
McLaren Vale, rich, berry-flavoured and
chocolatey, and it also produces an excellent
unwooded Semillon. Mead is another string to
the Maxwell bow. Cellar door sales: 7 days
10am–5pm, closed Christmas Day and Good
Friday.

Merrivale Wines NR

Olivers Road, McLaren Vale, SA 5171
Ph 08 8323 9186, Fax 08 8323 9746

Owner: Gerard Industries
Chief winemaker: Pam Dunsford (consultant)
Year of foundation: 1973
Tonnes crushed on average each year: 120, of
which 40 are used for Merrivale's own labels
Location: McLaren Vale
Area: 40 ha at two vineyards, Bakers Gully
32 ha, Merrivale 8 ha
Soils: red-brown earth over shale with
ironstone
Varieties planted: White—chardonnay, riesling;
Red—cabernet sauvignon, shiraz
Leading wines: Tapestry Cabernet Sauvignon

Bin 338, Shiraz Bin 388, Chardonnay Bin 288,
Riesling Bin 228
Notes: Formerly owned by Brian and Kay Light,
Merrivale was purchased by Gerard Industries
in 1997 and there has been a change of
winemaker. Knowing the standards of
Merrivale's consultant winemaker, the wines
are certain to be of very high quality. Cellar
door sales: 7 days 11am–5pm.

Middlebrook R7.5

10 Sand Road, McLaren Vale, SA 5171
Ph 08 8383 0004, Fax 08 8383 0470

Owner: Walter Clappis Nominees Pty Ltd
Chief winemaker: Walter Clappis
Year of foundation: 1900 (by the Hardy family)
Tonnes crushed on average each year: 475, of
which 300 are used for Middlebrook labels
Location: McLaren Vale (2 km east of the
town)
Area: 39 ha
Soils: Biscay and loam over clay
Varieties planted: White—chardonnay,
sauvignon blanc, semillon; Red—cabernet
franc, cabernet sauvignon, merlot, shiraz
Leading wines: Middlebrook Cabernet
Sauvignon, Shiraz
Notes: Middlebrook was purchased in 1993 by
Walter and Kerry Clappis and used as a
storage facility until their Ingoldby winery was
sold to Mildara Blass in 1995. Since then,
Walter Clappis has completely refurbished
Middlebrook and it is once again a working
winery. Walter is an experienced McLaren Vale
maker and Middlebrook's current wines are
within the mainstream of McLaren Vale style.
Cellar door sales: 7 days 10am–5pm. There is
also a restaurant.

Noon Winery NR

Rifle Range Road, McLaren Vale,
SA 5171
Ph/Fax 08 8323 8290

Owner/chief winemaker: Drew Noon
Year of foundation: 1976
Tonnes crushed on average each year: 48
Location: McLaren Vale
Area: 2 ha
Soils: brown loam over red clay, duplex
Varieties planted: White—none;
Red—grenache
Leading wines: Noon Grenache-Shiraz,
Cabernet Sauvignon
Notes: This is a small family-run winery which
once produced big reds in the traditional Vale
style. Drew Noon recently took over the family
property and continues to concentrate entirely
on reds. Cellar door sales: each day
10am–5pm.

Norman's Wines (vineyard only) NR

Kangarilla Road, Bakers Gully, McLaren
Vale, SA 5171

Owner: Norman's Wines Ltd
Chief winemaker: Roger Harbord
Year of foundation: c1920
Tonnes crushed on average each year: 200
Location: Baker's Gully
Area: 40 ha presently planted (with a further
80 ha to be planted by the year 2000)
Soils: sandy soils over ironstone
Varieties planted: White—chardonnay; Red—
cabernet sauvignon, grenache (old bush vines),
merlot, nebbiolo, shiraz
Leading wines: Norman's Bush Vine Grenache,
with other varieties contributing to other
Norman's wines
Notes: This vineyard was purchased by
Norman's in 1998 and is remarkable for its
25 hectares of 70-year-old bush vine grenache,
which is extremely low-bearing (less than
5 tonnes to the hectare). Its wines are made at
the nearby Clarendon winery. No cellar door
sales here.

Oliverhill Winery NR

Seaview Road, McLaren Vale, SA 5171
Ph/Fax 08 8323 8922

Owners: Stuart and Linda Miller
Chief winemaker: Stuart Miller
Year of foundation: 1973
Tonnes crushed on average each year: 50
(some fruit is bought in)
Location: McLaren Vale
Area: 6 ha
Soils: chiefly clay loam over limestone
Varieties planted: White—none; Red—cabernet
sauvignon, grenache, shiraz
Leading wines: Oliverhill Cabernet, Sparkling
Red, Shiraz, Grenache
Notes: A small family-owned winery with cellar
door sales weekdays 10am–4pm, weekends
and public holidays 10am–5pm.

Olivers Taranga Vineyards NR

Cnr Olivers and Warners Roads,
McLaren Vale, SA 5171
Ph/Fax 08 8323 8498

Owner: Oliver Nominees Pty Limited
Chief winemaker: contract
Year of foundation: c1840 (not quite known,
but the Olivers were early grape growers in the
region); winemaking began in 1994
Tonnes crushed on average each year: 450
(about 8 tonnes are used for Olivers Taranga
labels)
Location: McLaren Vale
Area: 60 ha
Soils: sandy loam over clay over limestone
Varieties planted: White—chardonnay, chenin
blanc, crouchen, sauvignon blanc; Red—
cabernet sauvignon, grenache, merlot, pinot
noir, shiraz
Leading wines: Olivers Taranga Vineyards
Shiraz
Notes: By heritage, the Olivers are a family of
grape growers, having farmed in the McLaren
Vale region virtually since its first settlement.

Winemaking is relatively low profile. No cellar door sales.

Patritti NR

13–23 Clacton Road, Dover Gardens, SA 5048
Ph 08 8296 8261, Fax 08 8296 5088

Owner: G Patritti & Co Pty Ltd
Chief winemaker: Geoff Patritti and consultants
Year of foundation: 1926
Tonnes crushed on average each year: 900
Location: McLaren Vale
Area: 80 ha on two vineyards (Aldinga 40 ha, Blewitt Springs 40 ha)
Soils: (Aldinga) light loam over limestone; (Blewitt Springs) deep sand
Varieties planted: White—none; Red—cabernet sauvignon, grenache, shiraz
Leading wines: Patritti Blewitt Springs Estate Shiraz-Cabernet, Grenache
Notes: One of the last of Adelaide's suburban wineries, but really of McLaren Vale identity with two large vineyards within the region. Cellar door sales: Mon–Sat 9am–6pm.

Pertaringa Wines R8.5

Hunt and Rifle Range Roads, McLaren Vale, SA 5171
Ph 08 8323 8125, Fax 08 8323 7766

Owners: Ian Leask and Geoff Hardy
Chief winemaker: Geoff Hardy (with the assistance of Ben Riggs from Wirra Wirra under contract)
Year of foundation: 1980
Tonnes crushed on average each year: 600
Location: McLaren Vale
Area: 27 ha
Soils: sandy loam over red clays, dense loam over heavy clay
Varieties planted: White—chardonnay, riesling, sauvignon blanc, semillon; Red—cabernet franc, cabernet sauvignon, shiraz

Leading wines: Pertaringa Cabernet Sauvignon, Semillon, Shiraz, Sauvignon Blanc
Notes: Pertaringa is owned by leading viticulturalists Ian Leask and Geoff Hardy, who sell most of their fruit. Only about 30 tonnes of grapes are crushed for the Pertaringa and Geoff Hardy labels, but they are some of the best that McLaren Vale produces. As a consequence, because of low volume, Pertaringa wines are rarely entered in wine shows, but the 1996 Pertaringa Shiraz did win a gold medal at the McLaren Vale show in 1997. No cellar door sales.

Pirramimma R9

Johnston Road, McLaren Vale, SA 5171
Ph 08 8323 8205, Fax 08 8323 9224

Owner: AC Johnston Pty Ltd
Chief winemaker: Geoffrey Johnston
Year of foundation: 1892
Tonnes crushed on average each year: 2500, of which 750 are used for own label
Location: McLaren Vale
Area: 177 ha
Soils: very variable, heavy black clay loams, red-brown loams, grey loam to light sand over friable clay subsoil
Varieties planted: White—chardonnay, riesling, sauvignon blanc, semillon; Red—cabernet franc, cabernet sauvignon, grenache, merlot, petit verdot, shiraz
Leading wines: Pirramimma Chardonnay, Hillsview Cabernet Merlot, Petit Verdot, Shiraz
Notes: Pirramimma is part of the soul of McLaren Vale, in the Johnstone family's hands since 1892. For the first seventy years of its existence, it made and sold big reds and fortifieds for the London trade, but in the 1960s and 1970s made a successful switch into local markets, at first as a grape grower, then as a maker of excellent reds. Though it is still predominantly a grape grower and a contract crusher for other wineries, its reds are some of the best (and the best value) in the

region, particularly Hillsview Cabernet-Merlot. It was also a pioneer in the introduction of chardonnay to McLaren Vale in 1977 and of petit verdot in 1983 which, unlike its counterpart in Bordeaux, has little trouble ripening in McLaren Vale. Today, it is one of the few winemakers to produce a 100% Petit Verdot in Australia. Cellar door sales: weekdays 8.30am–5pm, Sat 11am–5pm. Sun and public holidays 11.30am–4pm.

Reynell R9

Reynella Road, Reynella, SA 5161
Ph 08 8392 2222, Fax 08 8392 2202

Owner: BRL Hardy Ltd
Chief winemaker: Peter Dawson; red winemaker Stephen Pannell; white winemaker Tom Newton; sparkling winemaker Ed Carr
Year of foundation: 1853
Tonnes crushed on average each year: not disclosed but estimated at 250, many more tonnes are purchased from growers in McLaren Vale
Locations: two vineyards, Reynella and Yeenunga
Area: 42.8 ha (Reynella 10.8 ha and Yeenunga, which is close to Seaview, 32 ha)
Soils: (Reynella) grey sandy loam over red-brown clay; (Yeenunga) grey loamy sand over shaly red-brown clay
Varieties planted: White—chardonnay, palomino; Red—cabernet sauvignon, grenache, malbec, merlot, shiraz
Leading wines: Reynell Merlot, Cabernet Sauvignon, Shiraz
Notes: Present-day BRL Hardy headquarters, the former Chateau Reynella, is the site of the first vineyard planted in what is now the McLaren Vale region in 1838 and also the oldest wine cellar in the region (the Old Cave Cellar constructed in 1845). It is also where Thomas Hardy, then a young immigrant aged 20, became a farm labourer for a few months in 1850. His employer was John Reynell, the

local squire. The wheel was ultimately to turn full circle for, in 1982, Thomas Hardy and Sons Pty Ltd purchased Chateau Reynella. Recently BRL Hardy has initiated the Reynell premium range of reds, the successor to the former Chateau Reynella Basket Pressed range, which were always of excellent quality and mostly of Reynella vineyard origin. Cellar door sales: 7 days 10am–4.30pm.

Richard Hamilton Wines R8.5

Main Road, Willunga, SA 5172
Ph 08 8336 2288, Fax 08 8336 2868

Owners: Dr Richard and Mrs Jette Hamilton
Chief winemaker: Philippa Treadwell
Year of foundation: 1972
Tonnes crushed on average each year: 600 (all of which are used for the Richard Hamilton labels)
Location: Willunga
Area: 55 ha (consisting of three vineyards, Hut Block, Winery Block and Farm Block)
Soils: red clay loams over limestone
Varieties planted: White—chardonnay, chenin blanc, riesling, sauvignon blanc, semillon; Red—cabernet sauvignon, grenache, merlot, shiraz
Leading wines: Richard Hamilton Chardonnay, Hut Block Cabernet, Old Vines Shiraz
Notes: Reversing the more usual south-north journey, the Richard Hamilton crop travels south to its Leconfield winery in Coonawarra for making, but the wines are kept quite distinct. Quality of all wines, as one would expect from Ralph Fowler, is excellent. Cellar door sales: 7 days 10am–5pm, except Good Friday and Christmas Day.

Rosemount 'Ryecroft' R9

14 Ingoldby Road, McLaren Flat, SA 5171
Ph 08 8383 0001, Fax 08 8383 0456

Owner: Rosemount Estates
Chief winemaker: Philip Shaw

Year of foundation: 1888
Tonnes crushed on average each year: (from the company's own vineyards) not disclosed but estimated at 1500
Area: 163 ha
Soils: varying from Biscay to sand over red clay
Varieties planted: White—chardonnay, chenin blanc, riesling, sauvignon blanc, semillon, traminer; Red—cabernet sauvignon, grenache, malbec, merlot, pinot noir, shiraz
Leading wines: Rosemount Traditional (a red blend of cabernet sauvignon, merlot and petit verdot), Grenache Shiraz Mourvedre, Balmoral Shiraz
Notes: Rosemount purchased Ryecroft in 1991 and since then has been re-appraising Ryecroft in the marketplace. As a result what was the Ryecroft range has all but disappeared, being now restricted to Flame Tree red and white, two 'fighting' blends in the lower price range of the market. The name 'Rosemount' is now seen on two of its McLaren Vale reds—Traditional (a cabernet sauvignon blend) and Grenache-Shiraz-Mourvedre (paradoxically rather more traditional in the McLaren Vale region than any cabernet blend). There is also the very fine 'Balmoral', a premium McLaren Vale Shiraz by any standards. Cellar door sales: weekdays 10am–5pm, weekends and public holidays 11am–5pm.

Scarpantoni Estate R8

Scarpantoni Drive, McLaren Flat, SA 5171
Ph 08 8383 0186, Fax 08 8383 0490

Owners: Domenico, Paula, Michael and Filippo Scarpantoni
Chief winemakers: Michael and Filippo Scarpantoni
Year of foundation: 1979
Tonnes crushed on average each year: 225
Location: McLaren Flat
Area: 32 ha

Soils: deep sand and shallower sand over ironstone
Varieties planted: White—chardonnay, riesling, sauvignon blanc; Red—cabernet sauvignon, gamay, merlot, shiraz
Leading wines: Scarpantoni Estate Shiraz, Sauvignon Blanc, Cabernet Sauvignon, School Block (a Cabernet-Shiraz-Merlot blend), Chardonnay, Unwooded Chardonnay, Black Tempest (a sparkling red), Fleurieu (a sparkling white), Gamay
Notes: A producer well in the mainstream of McLaren Vale style, producing very good Shiraz as witness its trophy for best varietal Shiraz at the 1997 McLaren Vale wine show and good Chardonnay, both wooded and unwooded. Cellar door sales: weekdays 9am–5pm, weekends and public holidays 11am–5pm.

Seaview R9

Chaffey's Road, McLaren Vale, SA 5171
Ph 08 8323 8250, Fax 08 8323 9308

Owner: Southcorp Wines
Chief winemaker: Steve Chapman
Year of foundation: 1850 (as Hope Farm)
Tonnes crushed on average each year: (from the company's own vineyards) not disclosed but estimated at 1400
Location: in six vineyards (McLaren Vale, Seaview, CPL, Bethany, Blencowe, Chapel Hill, Park Hill)
Area: 146.7 ha
Soils: (CPL) duplex red-brown earth; (Bethany) dark self-mulching clay loam with a tendency to surface cracking, quite fertile; (Blencowe, Chapel Hill, Park Hill, Seaview) ranging from duplex red-brown earth on Blencowe and Chapel Hill to more sandy red-brown earth on Seaview
Varieties planted: White—chardonnay, riesling, sauvignon blanc, semillon; Red—cabernet sauvignon, grenache, shiraz
Leading wines: Edwards and Chaffey

Chardonnay, Cabernet Sauvignon, Shiraz, the Seaview range of sparkling wines

Notes: From a small McLaren Vale winery in the mid-1960s, Seaview has achieved national and international recognition, especially for sparkling wines. Very little, if any, of the base wine for the Seaview sparkling range originates in McLaren Vale, but the quality has risen beyond all comparison to price and those wines at the top of the sparkling range are generally considered to be among Australia's best. The Edwards and Chaffey range of premium table wines, which does originate within the region, is also top class. Cellar door sales: weekdays 9am–4.30pm, Sun 11am–4pm, Sat and public holidays 10am–5pm.

Shottesbrooke **R8.5**

Bagshaws Road, McLaren Flat, SA 5171
Ph 08 8383 0002, Fax 08 8383 0222

Owners: CJ and NG Holmes
Chief winemaker: Nick Holmes
Year of foundation: 1981
Tonnes crushed on average each year: 250
Location: McLaren Flat
Area: 20 ha
Soils: varying from deep sandy loam to deep sand over clay
Varieties planted: White—chardonnay, sauvignon blanc; Red—cabernet sauvignon, merlot, shiraz
Leading wines: Shottesbrooke Eliza Shiraz, Sauvignon Blanc, Cabernet Merlot Malbec
Notes: Former Ryecroft winemaker Nick Holmes now concentrates entirely on his own winery, Shottesbrooke, which sprang to fame in the mid-1980s. The reds are excellent and the whites very good. Cellar door sales: weekdays 10am–4.30pm, weekends and public holidays 11am–5pm.

Simon Hackett Wines **R6.5**

283 Wakefield Street, Adelaide, SA 5000
Ph 08 8232 4305, Fax 08 8223 3714

Owner: Simon Hackett Wines Pty Limited
Chief winemaker: Simon Hackett
Year of foundation: 1981
Tonnes crushed on average each year: 180 (includes 70 tonnes crushed from the Barossa Valley)
Location: (vineyards) McLaren Vale and Willunga
Area: 5.5 ha
Soils: loam over gravel over limestone
Varieties planted: White—none; Red—cabernet sauvignon, shiraz
Leading wines: Simon Hackett Anthony's Reserve Shiraz, Foggo Road Cabernet Sauvignon
Notes: Simon Hackett leases his vineyard in McLaren Vale and also winemaking facilities. In addition a quantity of fruit is purchased from growers. Nonetheless, his McLaren Vale reds are typical of their area. No cellar door sales yet.

Tatachilla **R7**

151 Main Street, McLaren Vale, SA 5171
Ph 08 8323 8656, Fax 08 8323 9096

Owner: Tatachilla Winery Pty Ltd
Chief winemaker: Michael Fragos
Tonnes crushed on average each year: 4660 (for Tatachilla labels 1460)
Location: (winery) McLaren Vale, (vineyard) Clarendon
Area: 14.4 ha
Soils: shallow clay loam over ironstone
Varieties planted: White—chardonnay; Red—cabernet sauvignon, merlot, pinot noir
Leading wines: Tatachilla Keystone Grenache-Shiraz
Notes: Tatachilla is another name of considerable importance in the Vale's history. It was founded in the year of Federation and was

one of the keystones of export sales to the United Kingdom. Indeed its 'Keystone Burgundy' was the centre of a London legal battle in 1908 in which the French endeavoured unsuccessfully to stop the Australian use of the generic name 'Burgundy'. Later Tatachilla was purchased by Penfolds and became its McLaren Vale winery for many years until 1961 when it was closed. Then began a rollercoaster of ownership until 1993 when it was purchased and refurbished by the present owners. Present-day 'Keystone' is considerably lighter, I imagine, than its pre-First World War ancestor, but the blend of grenache and shiraz is probably much the same. Tatachilla has one vineyard at Clarendon and many growers throughout McLaren Vale. Cellar door sales: Mon–Sat 10am–5pm, Sun and public holidays 11am–5pm.

Tyrrells (vineyard only) **NR**
Main Road, Willunga, SA 5172

Owner: Tyrrells Vineyards Pty Limited
Chief winemaker: Andrew Spinaze
Year of foundation: 1994
Tonnes crushed on average each year: 600
Location: Willunga
Area: 38.9 ha
Soils: clay loam
Varieties planted: White—chardonnay, sauvignon blanc; Red—cabernet sauvignon, grenache, merlot, pinot noir, shiraz
Leading wines: Rufus Stone Shiraz
Notes: This Willunga vineyard is part of Tyrrells 1990s change of identity from Hunter Valley winemaker to Australian winemaker. Not that the Tyrrell family will ever allow the Hunter Valley to become subsidiary to any other Australian region. The Rufus Stone Shiraz is very interesting, commemorating the place in New Forest where in 1100 the dastardly King William Rufus, while out hunting, became fair game himself, receiving an arrow between the eyes (or was it between the shoulders, no-one

quite knows) reputedly from the bow of an ancient Tyrrell. No local cellar door sales.

Wirilda Creek **NR**
McMurtrie Road, McLaren Vale, SA 5171
Ph 08 8323 9688, Fax 08 8323 9260

Owners: Kerry Flanagan and Karen Shertock
Chief winemaker: Kerry Flanagan
Year of foundation: 1993
Tonnes crushed on average each year: 32
Location: McLaren Vale
Area: 3 ha
Soils: gravelly sand with some clay over limestone
Varieties planted: White—none; Red—cabernet sauvignon, malbec, merlot, shiraz
Leading wines: Wirilda Creek Shiraz Rare, Cabernet-Merlot, Cabernet-Shiraz-Malbec
Notes: This small winery has a good red reputation. Its 1994 Shiraz finished in the top 10 in the Great Australian Shiraz Challenge and the Cabernet Merlot 1993 won the trophy for the best red blend at the McLaren Vale show. A vineyard has also been planted recently on Kangaroo Island. Cellar door sales: 7 days 10.30am–5.30pm.

Wirra Wirra **R9**
McMurtrie Road, McLaren Vale, SA 5171
Ph 08 8323 8414, Fax 08 8323 8596

Owner: RG & RT Trott Pty Limited
Chief winemaker: Ben Riggs
Year of foundation: orginally 1893 then re-established in 1969
Tonnes crushed on average each year: 900
Location: McLaren Vale
Area: 61 ha consisting of Bethany (McLaren Vale) 22 ha, Scrubby Rise (McLaren Vale) 14 ha, and Moray Park (McLaren Flat) 25 ha
Soils: (Bethany) sand over clay; (Scrubby Rise) black Biscay clay; (Moray Park) deep red clay loams
Varieties planted: White—chardonnay, riesling,

sauvignon blanc, semillon; Red—cabernet sauvignon, grenache, merlot, pinot noir, shiraz

Leading wines: Wirra Wirra RSW Shiraz, Church Block, Chardonnay, Semillon-Sauvignon Blanc, The Cousins (a sparkling blend of pinot noir and chardonnay)

Notes: At once a blend of the ancient and modern of McLaren Vale, Wirra Wirra was founded in 1893 by RS Wigley, after whom RSW Shiraz is named, and flourished until 1924 when he died. Winemaking ceased in 1936 and the land was later sold off piecemeal by his family. The winery block (2.8 ha and the derelict winery) was purchased in 1969 by cousins Greg and Roger Trott from the son of Wigley's foreman. Today Wirra Wirra enjoys a very high reputation for quality in both whites and reds. Cellar door sales: Mon–Sat 10am–5pm, Sun and public holidays 11am–5pm.

Woodstock R7.5

Douglas Gully Road, McLaren Vale, SA 5171

Ph 08 8383 0156, Fax 08 8383 0437

Owners: Collett family

Chief winemaker: Scott Collett

Year of foundation: 1974

Tonnes crushed on average each year: 250

Location: Douglas Gully

Area: 21 ha

Soils: White sandy soils of varying depth over clay

Varieties planted: White—chardonnay, riesling, semillon; Red—cabernet sauvignon, grenache, shiraz

Leading wines: Woodstock Cabernet Sauvignon, 'The Stocks' Shiraz, Botrytis Sweet White

Notes: Woodstock produces typical McLaren Vale wines, the Chardonnay full-flavoured and generous, the reds full bodied and reliable, and the 'sticky' luscious and sweet. There are rarely half-measures here. Cellar door sales: weekdays 9am–5pm, weekends and public holidays noon–5pm. The Coterie, a restaurant and function centre, is open on Sundays for lunch.

CURRENCY CREEK AREA

Situated in the Lower Fleurieu peninsula, this area was for many years viewed as a poor cousin of McLaren Vale, and it was always on the 'other side of the tracks', that is, the wrong side of the Sellick's Hill range, closer to Strathalbyn than McLaren Vale. However, when 'critical mass' is achieved and this should be within the next five years, as there are many new vineyards being currently planted there, it will probably attain regional status. There are two wineries presently in existence—Currency Creek and Middleton Estate.

Currency Creek R6.5

Winery Road, Currency Creek, SA 5214, about 10 km from Goolwa

Ph 08 8555 4069, Fax 08 8555 4100

Owners: Wally and Phillip Tonkin

Chief winemaker: Phil Tonkin

Year of foundation: 1969

Tonnes produced on average each year: 300, of which about 95 are used for Currency Creek labels
Location: Currency Creek
Area: 45 ha
Soils: deep sand about 4–5 metres deep over clay
Varieties planted: White—chardonnay, riesling, sauvignon blanc, semillon; Red—cabernet sauvignon, gamay, pinot noir, shiraz
Leading wines: Currency Creek Sauvignon Blanc, Shiraz, Chardonnay, Cabernet Sauvignon, Methode Traditionale, Sparkling Shiraz
Notes: This winery has had several names since its foundation by Wally Tonkin nearly 30 years ago. Currency Creek (the name of its general area) seems now to have stuck. Its best wines are usually its whites, particularly its Chardonnay. Cellar door sales: 7 days 10am–5pm. There is a restaurant open every day for lunch and dinner, as well as six accommodation units.

Middleton Estate NR

Flagstaff Hill Road, Middleton, SA 5213
Ph 08 8555 4136, Fax 08 8555 4108

Owners: Nigel and Debra Catt
Chief winemaker: Nigel Catt
Year of foundation: 1979
Tonnes crushed on average each year: 120, of which 50 are used for the Middleton Estate labels
Location: Middleton
Area: 25 ha
Soils: sandy loams to heavier loams over clay with some ironstone
Varieties planted: White—riesling, semillon; Red—cabernet sauvignon, merlot, shiraz
Leading wines: Middleton Estate Shiraz, Riesling
Notes: Middleton Estate is located in a north–south oriented valley just 7 km from the Southern Ocean with vines running east–west and cool maritime breezes to add a necessary touch of humidity. Nigel Catt describes his site as 'perfect'. Cellar door sales: Fri–Sun 10am–5pm. There is also a restaurant. In fact there are two, the second being on the beach at Port Elliot about 10 km away.

❧ THE PENINSULAS ZONE

This zone includes the Yorke and Eyre Peninsulas of South Australia. A wine region that may in the future be delimited is that area surrounding Port Lincoln, which long ago was touted as the capital of South Australia but to no avail. There are small vineyards there at present.

Climate: MJT 20°C, MAR na, HDD raw 1722 (1583 cut off and adjusted for latitude, daily temperature range and vine sites), AR 486 mm (Oct–Apr 161 mm), RH 53%, AI na, SH 7.5 (Gladstones)

Boston Bay Wines NR
Lincoln Highway, Port Lincoln, SA 5606
Ph/Fax 08 8684 3600

Owners: Graham and Mary Ford and family
Chief winemaker: David O'Leary (contract)
Year of foundation: 1984
Tonnes crushed on average each year: 35
Location: Port Lincoln, Southern Eyre Peninsula
Area: 5.6 ha
Soils: brown sandy loam over clay over limestone
Varieties planted: White—chardonnay, riesling; Red—cabernet sauvignon, merlot, shiraz
Leading wines: Boston Bay Riesling, Cabernet Sauvignon, Merlot
Notes: Boston Bay is a maritime vineyard. Graham Ford says he can throw a stone into the sea from it. He says Riesling is well suited to the area as is his straight Merlot.
Cellar door sales: 11.30am–4.30pm weekends, public holidays and school holidays. Special functions are catered for and there is a picnic area.

Delacolline Estate NR
Whillas Road, Port Lincoln, SA 5606
Ph 08 8682 6579, Fax 08 8683 4195

Owner: Ian Fletcher
Chief winemaker: Andrew Mitchell (contract)
Year of foundation: 1984
Tonnes crushed on average each year: 30
Location: Port Lincoln
Area: 5 ha
Soils: gravelly red soils over clay and some sandy limestone country
Varieties planted: White—chardonnay, riesling, sauvignon blanc, semillon; Red—cabernet sauvignon, merlot, shiraz
Leading wine: Delacolline Estate Semillon-Sauvignon Blanc
Notes: Delacolline Estate, Port Lincoln's other winery, is 5 km from the sea and at an elevation of 160 m. Cellar door sales: weekends and public holidays 1.30pm–4pm.

❧ LOWER MURRAY ZONE

This is a large arid stretch of land, extending from the Victorian border west to the foothills of the Mount Lofty Ranges. Its lifeblood is the water of the River Murray. It has one wine region, Riverland.

RIVERLAND REGION

The region was first discovered by Charles Sturt in 1830 when he sailed down the Murrumbidgee, into the Murray River (which he named) and on to Lake Alexandrina and its confluence with the sea in Encounter Bay. As a horticultural and viticultural area, it began with the establishment of an irrigation area at Renmark by the Chaffey Brothers in 1887 (see Murray-Darling region). Similar small irrigation settlements were started along the river during the 1890s and in the years following until the First World War. Viticulture had also commenced at this time and, in 1910, Angove's established a distillery at Renmark and a winery at Lyrup three years later. They were followed by Chateau Tanunda (the Adelaide Wine Company) which, in 1914, erected a distillery. This was sold in 1916 on the liquidation of the Adelaide Wine Co to what was to become the Renmark Growers Co-operative. Thomas Hardy & Sons built two wineries in 1915–16 (one at Waikerie, the other at Murray View) and there were the beginnings of the Berri Co-operative in 1918. The years after the Second World War brought soldier settlement blocks, much more planting and increased production as South Australia enjoyed a boom in strong red and fortified wines. As in the early days of the Murray-Darling region, there was an emphasis on distillation and the doradillo variety was widely planted. By 1927 the quantity of Riverland fruit produced outstripped that of the Barossa Valley for the first time.

Though the Great Depression brought considerable hardship, the region was fortunate in that there was a continuing demand for brandy and fortified wines. In the 1950s, vineyard development in the region continued. Orlando planted at Ramco in 1952. By 1958 when it became clear that the pendulum of public taste was swinging back to lighter table wines, the Berri Co-operative constructed a winery intended entirely for that purpose. Other large vineyards were established at that time, such as Seppelt near Qualco and Yalumba at Oxford Landing. By the 1970s and 1980s, wine casks (soft pack) had made an indelible mark on the wine industry and many millions of litres of Riverland wine were employed to fill them. These days, with the emphasis on bottled table wines, the region produces many varietal table wines of good quality and of particularly good value, as well as its traditional brandies and fortifieds, though in much smaller quantity than previously.

Location: latitude 34°27'S, longitude 140°36'E about 200 km north-east of Adelaide
Elevation: 10–20 m (River valley terraces), 35–50 m (Mallee country above)

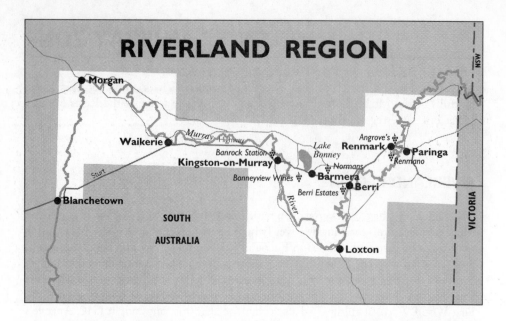

Topography and soils: The region consists of gently undulating Mallee Highlands and dissected river valley terraces of various heights. The terrace soils are grey and brown clays frequently lying above layers of coarse sand where sandbars and sandhills previously existed. Such soils are present in Renmark, Cobdogla and Lyrup.

The Mallee Highlands are constituted by a series of discontinuous east-west parallel sand dunes. Soils here are chiefly deep red sands or loamy sands with moderate calcium carbonate content about 0.5 to 1 metre deep. On the flatter areas and in the depressions of the Mallee, the soils are of heavier texture to sandy clay loams, and heavier often overlying layers of calcium carbonate at a depth of half a metre. Such soils often contain shallow water tables which require the construction of tile drains to remove effluent, which is pumped into evaporation basins. The Highland soils occur in Berri, Waikerie and Loxton. The soils are normally deficient in nitrogen and zinc; the former can be corrected by the growth of cover crops, the latter by the use of foliar sprays.

Climate: Riverland MJT 23°C, MAR 13.2°C, HDD raw 2084, AR 274 mm (Oct–Mar) 130 mm, RH 51% 9am, AI 510 mm, SH 9.6 (Dry & Smart). Berri MJT 23°C, MAR na, HDD raw 2144, 1745 (cut off and adjusted for latitude and daily temperature range), AR 269 mm (Oct–Apr 139 mm), RH 24% 3pm (Gladstones), AI na, SH 9.4. Though the Riverland is undoubtedly a hot area, it is the coolest of all Australian fully-irrigated regions during ripening. All vineyards are irrigated, about 80% by sprinkler or drip and the balance by flood, though flood is slowly disappearing, as all new vineyards must be under micro or drip irrigation. Viticultural problems which may be encountered include downy and powdery mildew, though increasing use of trickle irrigation may counter the onset of downy mildew to some extent. In addition normal spray regimes are employed. Other pests in certain areas include nematodes, which may reduce yields, and light brown apple moth.

Harvest time: chardonnay third week of February, shiraz first week of March, cabernet sauvignon mid-March.

Major varieties: 1996 (over 500 ha planted) White—chardonnay, muscat gordo blanco, sultana; Red—cabernet sauvignon, grenache, shiraz

Total area: (1996) c13 400 ha (including table grapes, drying and all-purpose varieties)

Principal wine styles: Chardonnay, a reputation established and maintained by Renmano. This is a wine which has changed in style considerably in the past decade from a hugely oaked ripe almost fat style to something much more lean and almost fine, very good considering the warmth of the area. Angove also produces a reliable range of varietal wines as well as a very fine aged Brandy, St Agnes Seven Star XO. Otherwise current drinking bottled and soft pack table wines.

Angove **R7.5**

Bookmark Avenue, Renmark, SA 5341
Ph 08 8595 1311, Fax 08 8595 1583

Owners: Angove family
Chief winemaker: Garry Wall
Year of foundation: 1886
Tonnes crushed on average each year: 15 000 and increasing
Location: Nanya Vineyard is at Murtho Road, Paringa
Area: 480 ha
Soils: red mallee sands bolstered by the addition of grape marc and fertiliser over heavy clay
Varieties planted: White—chardonnay, chenin blanc, colombard, doradillo, palomino, riesling, sauvignon blanc, sylvaner, traminer, trebbiano, white grenache; Red—barbera, cabernet sauvignon, carignan, grenache, melbec, pinot noir, ruby cabernet, shiraz
Leading wines: Angove Classic Reserve Varietals, Butterfly Ridge range, St Agnes 7 Star XO Brandy
Notes: Angove is a producer of good quality table wines at reasonable prices. St Agnes 7 Star XO Brandy is arguably Australia's best.
Cellar door sales: Mon–Fri 9am–5pm.

Austvin **NR**

Bookpurnong Road, Loxton SA 5333
Ph 08 8584 7236, Fax 08 8584 6876

Owner: Simeon Wines Ltd
Chief winemaker: Kevin Pfeiffer
Year of foundation: 1993
Tonnes crushed on average each year: 44 000 and increasing
Location: Loxton vineyards (Morgan, Qualco, Waikerie)
Area: 1403 ha (Morgan 371.7 ha, Qualco 591.3 ha, Waikerie, 440 ha)
Soils: (Morgan) heavy loams over clay; (Qualco) red sands over calcrete; (Waikerie) river cliff soil, marly
Varieties planted: (Morgan) White—chardonnay, doradillo, gewurztraminer, muscat gordo blanco; Red—shiraz. (Qualco) White—chardonnay, muscadelle, reisling; Red—cabernet sauvignon, grenache, muscat a petit grains rouge, shiraz. (Waikerie) White—chardonnay, semillon; Red—cabernet sauvignon, merlot, petit verdot, shiraz
Leading wines: Simeon Wines is a producer of bulk wine for other wine companies and for export
Notes: Cellar door sales, Mon–Sat 9am–5pm.

Banrock Station R6.5

Kingston on Murray, SA 5331
Ph 08 8583 0235, Fax 08 8583 0265

Owner: BRL Hardy Ltd
Chief winemaker: Peter Dawson
Year of foundation: small plantings in 1955,
vastly extended in 1995–96
Tonnes produced on average each year:
estimated at 3500
Location: Kingston on Murray
Area: 230.7 ha
Soils: sandy loam varying in depth over
limestone
Varieties planted: White—chardonnay, riesling,
sauvignon blanc, semillon; Red—cabernet
sauvignon, shiraz
Leading wines: Banrock Station Shiraz,
Unwooded Chardonnay, Shiraz-Cabernet,
Semillon-Chardonnay
Notes: This vineyard produces large quantities
of fruit made at Renmano into competent reds
and whites and some soft-pack. Cellar door
sales: 7 days 10am–4.30pm.

Berri Estates R5

Sturt Highway, Berri, SA 5343
Ph 08 8582 0300, Fax 08 8583 2224

Owner: BRL Hardy Ltd
Chief winemaker: Paul Kassebaum
Year of foundation: 1918
Tonnes crushed on average each year: 70 000
Location: Berri (winery), no vineyards owned
Leading wines: Berri estate soft-pack wines
Notes: Though it was once the leader of table
wine production in the region and has a Jimmy
Watson trophy to its credit, it was a long time
ago. These days Berri Estates is a producer of
bulk wine and soft-pack material. Cellar door
sales: Mon–Sat 9am–5pm.

Bonneyview Wines NR

Sturt Highway, Barmera, SA 5345
Ph 08 8588 2279, Fax 08 8588 1577

Owner: Robert Minns
Chief winemaker: Noel Sibley
Year of foundation: 1975
Tonnes crushed on average each year: 60, all
of which are used for Bonneyview's own labels
Location: Barmera
Area: 3.5 ha
Soils: 'Murray' sand
Varieties planted: White—chardonnay,
sauvignon blanc, white frontignac; Red—black
frontignac, cabernet sauvignon, malbec,
merlot, petit verdot, red frontignac, ruby
cabernet, shiraz, touriga
Leading wines: Bonneyview Cabernet Blend,
Cabernet-Petit Verdot, Shiraz-Petit Verdot,
Chardonnay, Fortifieds
Notes: For the region, Bonneyview is a tiny
winery, but it acquits itself well, winning
awards at the Riverland Wine Show for its reds
and fortifieds. Cellar door sales: 7 days
9am–5.30pm. There is also a restaurant.

Kingston Estate R7.5

Sturt Highway, Kingston on Murray,
SA 5331
Ph 08 8583 0244, Fax 08 8583 0304

Owners: Moularadellis family
Chief winemaker: Rod Chapman
Year of foundation: 1979
Tonnes crushed on average each year: 10 000,
all of which are used for Kingston Estate labels
and at the present time mostly supplied by 180
growers, whose fruit is strictly selected. Five of
these growers are 'Reserve' growers, who work
on an incentive producing fruit for the
Kingston Estate Reserve range
Location: Kingston on Murray
Area: 120 ha (most not yet bearing)
Soils: shallow loam to sandy loam over
limestone

Varieties planted: White—chardonnay; Red—cabernet sauvignon, merlot, petit verdot, shiraz
Leading wines: Kingston Estate Reserve Chardonnay, Chardonnay, Semillon-Sauvignon Blanc, Reserve Cabernet-Merlot, Merlot, Shiraz, Sarantos Chardonnay
Notes: For this region, Kingston Estate is a medium to large winery with a small to medium sized vineyard, most of which is not yet bearing. Its wines are widely exported and are of excellent quality for their price. No cellar door sales.

Mildara Blass (vineyard only)   NR
Qualco, SA

Owner: Mildara Blass Ltd
Chief winemaker: Chris Hatcher
Year of foundation: 1960
Tonnes crushed on average each year: 950
Location: Qualco
Area: 84 ha
Soils: deep red sand over limestone
Varieties planted: White—chardonnay, riesling; Red—cabernet sauvignon, shiraz
Leading wines: a contributor to Mildara Blass' commercial table wines
Notes: The former DA Tolley vineyard was acquired when Mildara Blass bought DA Tolley a few years ago. These days the fruit forms part of lower priced bottled wines in the Mildara Blass ranges. No local cellar door sales.

Normans   R6.5
Lone Gum Winery, Nixon Road, Monash, SA 5342
Ph 08 8583 5255, Fax 08 8583 5444

Owner: Normans Wines Limited
Chief winemaker: Roger Harbord
Year of foundation: 1994
Tonnes crushed on average each year: 20 000 all purchased from growers
Location: Monash (winery)
Area: no vineyards owned

Leading wines: Lone Gum Chardonnay, Shiraz, Chandlers Hill Shiraz
Notes: The Lone Gum Winery is the engine room for Normans middle and lower range labels. Cellar door sales: Mon–Fri 9am–4.30pm.

Orlando   NR
Qualco Road, Sunlands, SA 5322

Owner: Orlando Wyndham Pty Ltd
Chief winemaker: Phil Laffer
Year of foundation: 1952
Tonnes produced on average each year: 2500
Location: Ramco
Area: 140 ha
Soils: discontinuous east-west parallel sand dunes of loamy sands with lower areas of shallower heavy-textured soils of sandy clay loam overlying calcium carbonate (calcrete)
Varieties planted: White—chardonnay, muscat gordo blanco, sauvignon blanc, semillon, white frontignac; Red—ruby cabernet, shiraz
Leading wines: part of Jacobs Creek Dry Red, part of Jacobs Creek Shiraz, part of Jacobs Creek Cabernet
Notes: This is a source vineyard for part of the massive production of the Jacobs Creek range. No local cellar door sales.

Renmano   R7
Sturt Highway, Renmark, SA 5341
Ph 08 8586 6771, Fax 08 8586 5939

Owner: BRL Hardy Ltd
Chief winemaker: Frank Newman
Year of foundation: 1914 (Adelaide Wine Co), 1916 (Renmark Growers Co-op)
Tonnes crushed on average each year: 20 000 all purchased from local growers
Location: Renmark
Leading wines: Renmano Chairmans Selection Chardonnay, Renmano 2-litre casks
Notes: Renmano has no vineyards of its own but can be said to have established Chardonnay as one of the benchmarks of this

region. It originated as a forward opulent style, but recently has become considerably more lean and hungry. I must say I prefer the present style.

Southcorp *(vineyards only)* **NR**
Waikerie, SA 5330

Owner: Southcorp Wines
Chief winemaker: John Duval
Years of foundation: winery 1915, vineyards Markaranka 1969
Tonnes crushed on average each year: not disclosed but estimated at 4500
Location: Waikerie (winery), Markaranka (vineyard)
Area: 167.1 ha
Soils: red sands over calcrete
Varieties planted: White—chardonnay, muscat gordo blanco; Red—cabernet sauvignon, grenache
Leading wines: lower priced bottled and soft-pack throughout the group
Notes: For Southcorp, Riverland is an area of massive production which finds its way into soft-pack wines and lower priced bottles, both still and sparkling of many Southcorp brands. No local cellar door sales.

Yalumba *(vineyard only)* **R7**
Waikerie Cadell Road, Oxford Landing, SA 5321
Ph 08 8541 9155, Fax 08 8541 9288

Owner: S Smith & Son Pty Ltd
Chief winemaker: Simon Adams
Year of foundation: 1958
Tonnes produced on average each year: 5000
Location: Oxford Landing
Area: 280 ha
Soils: deep red sand over limestone
Varieties planted: White—chardonnay, chenin blanc, colombard, riesling, sauvignon blanc, semillon, viognier; Red—cabernet sauvignon, merlot, ruby cabernet, shiraz
Leading wines: Oxford Landing Chardonnay, Sauvignon Blanc, Semillon-Sauvignon Blanc, Cabernet-Shiraz
Notes: Oxford Landing is theoretically the bottom rung of the Yalumba ladder. Yet it is always of good quality and well-priced. Its Chardonnay is one of the benchmark products of the region. No local cellar door sales.

❧ Chardonnay, Brian Croser and the Adelaide Hills

It is probably correct to say that the commercial exploitation of chardonnay began throughout Australia about 1980, when sufficient chardonnay vines had been planted to satisfy (in a very small way) a growing demand which, later that same decade, became almost insatiable. Before that time it was really a phenomenon of the Hunter Valley where it had been 'discovered' in the late 1960s by Murray Tyrrell. It was successfully fermented in barrel (a traditional Burgundian technique) in 1973, a year that should perhaps be commemorated as the date of introduction of modern Chardonnay technique to Australia.

Since 1980, with the assistance of Burgundian experience (where, after all, chardonnay probably originated), and with the objective of achieving greater complexity in Australian Chardonnay, our winemakers have shown their characteristic cleanliness and skill and have left few chardonnay stones unturned. For barrel fermentation and maturation, there have been flirtations with many types of French Oak, Nevers, Limousin, Allier and Vosges, not to mention American and German, as well as more exotic kinds such as Yugoslav, Hungarian, Portuguese and even (in the late 1990s) Russian. Then there came into vogue various degrees of wood-charring, light-, medium- and heavy-toast. Then it was realised that it was not perhaps the type of oak or the charring that was ultimately important, but the quality and the seasoning of the wood and perhaps even the skill of the French coopers. So we sought out the coopers who made the barrels for the Burgundians. During this time of oak experimentation, many other technical developments occurred in chardonnay making: skin contact, malolactic fermentation, low sulfurs, no sulfurs, oxidative handling, non-oxidative handling, maturation on still and stirred lees, whole bunch pressing, early bottling, late bottling and, in the last few years, unwooded chardonnay with or without malolactic fermentation.

As all these technical advances continued, chardonnay came to be planted in every wine-growing region in Australia and virtually everywhere it has been planted it has succeeded, for chardonnay is, in Brian Croser's words, 'a very forgiving variety'. If Murray Tyrrell may be termed the modern 'discoverer' of Australian chardonnay, Brian Croser must at least be its patron saint. He is certainly the modern pioneer of the viticultural possibilities of the Piccadilly Valley in particular and the Adelaide Hills region in general. Croser, who has made over 20 chardonnay vintages, long ago realised that great chardonnay was made in the vineyard, not necessarily the winery.

In 1996, Croser revealed what he considered to be the essential factors of site selection for great Australian chardonnay. The soil, aspect and climatic requirements of the site were, he contended, as follows:

• the slope must be free-draining of both air (to prevent frost) and moisture (to avoid 'wet feet') in the vines

- the soil should be of a bright red or white colour, which is light reflective in nature
- the soil should be old (in the geological sense) and of moderate fertility so that the vine spends its time ripening a moderate crop rather than trying to ripen an excessive crop or to produce excessive foliage. New volcanic soils are to be avoided
- the slope should be as steep as is manageable, facing to the north-east (in Australia, the aspect most favourable in harnessing and maximising the early morning sunlight hours to ripen chardonnay, while protecting it from the extremes of cold southerly and extremely hot or cold westerly or hot northerly winds
- the climate should be Mediterranean (i.e. a wet, cold winter and a dry summer of moderate humidity)
- the region should be cool enough to delay ripening into mid to late autumn, conditions favouring retention of grape acidity and the development of the fine but intense aromatics that typify great chardonnay
- such sites are likely to occur in a cool region of 900 to 1250 degree days (few sites in Australia are as cool as 900—perhaps a HDD of 1000 is more realistic).

Croser was convinced that such sites are found only in 'cool' regions, where chardonnay budburst, flowering, veraison (the colouring and ripening of the grapes) are as late as possible in their cycle and harvest is close to autumn leaf fall, but within that area, the 'distinguished site' will be the warmest (a 'hot spot').

In addition, there are ten other viticultural and meteorological criteria which that 'hot spot' must have in order to become distinguished.

1 steep hillside rows which maximise sunlight intensity, such rows being oriented north-south for even ripening on both sides of the vine
2 a close spacing of the vineyard to spread the vineyard's natural spacing of shoots
3 a vertical canopy for full interception of sunlight
4 leaf stripping from just above the fruiting zone when the vine has stopped growing (usually about a month before veraison) to allow sunlight penetration and ventilation to the fruit
5 protection from wind to limit the amount of water sucked through the vine (to replenish dehydration)
6 cool flowering conditions to achieve natural crop control at a level of 6–9 tonnes per hectare (to achieve small bunches consisting of large and small berries, which is extremely important, for small berries ripen more easily and give a higher skin to juice flavour. In this way, what the French call 'millerandage' and the Australians 'hen and chicken' can be beneficial.)
7 vines of ten years' age or more to achieve full root exploitation of the soil and provide old wood carbohydrate storage
8 a summer dry enough to stop the vine growing and to induce some stress (but not too much)
9 a long, cool air, sunny, dry autumn during which the grapes mature completely before the onset of rain
10 the uniqueness, conferred by a discrete, obviously different location.

Such were Croser's conclusions after a visit to Burgundy, based on a comparison he made between his own Piccadilly Valley vineyards and the hill of Aloxe-Corton in the Cote de Beaune. So we may ask what sort of Chardonnays such an Australian vineyard site is likely to produce. Fine-textured wines of intense aromatics and great finesse that most certainly need years in bottle to develop ultimate complexity. Where in Australia are such vineyard sites to be found? Some already exist in the Adelaide Hills, the Yarra Valley and northern Tasmania. Others are still to be located, maybe at altitude, the Snowy Mountains and Central Tablelands of New South Wales or perhaps much closer to sea-level in southern Victoria or the far south-east of South Australia or the south-west of Western Australia.

In his chardonnay making, Brian Croser is very fortunate in that he has a number of quality 'sites' from which to select his raw material. Such a number of quality sites within one region increases vastly the number of options that a maker of chardonnay has at vintage time.

It is common knowledge that the modern chardonnay maker never makes only one wine. Depending upon the resources of chardonnay fruit (whether from different vineyards within the same sub-region, region, wine zone, state or perhaps all of Australia), there is a multitude of options. As regards parts of the final wine, the maker may direct that the fruit be picked at varying stages of ripeness; it may be crushed or be subject to whole bunch ferment; it may be left in contact with skins; the juice may be clarified; it may be left on 'solids'. It may be fermented anaerobically or subject to a degree of oxidation. At what temperature has the must been fermented? What degree of sulfuring has it had? After fermentation in tank or in new or older oak, it may be stored in stainless steel or matured in that same barrel or barrels. And the maturation oak itself, as pointed out above, may be new or older and have many different national provenances or even diverse origins within the same country (as witness the different types of French oak with their variations of flavour). And what of the imprint of the cooper? What degree of 'toasting' has the oak undergone? Has the wine undergone malolactic fermentation? And indeed what length of maturation and what treatment within that period of maturation has the wine experienced? Have its 'lees' been still or stirred? Has it been 'cleaned up' and taken totally off 'lees'? Has its sulfur been adjusted or is it virtually sulfur-free? As you will readily appreciate, depending on resources, the winemaker may finish with forty or fifty different chardonnays, all in varying quantities—lots of detail in which to complete the big picture or a miniature if desired. But in either case the dominant feature of that picture will be complexity, in the greatest possible degree that the winemaker can achieve in the regional or sub-regional wine, through tasting, monitoring and differentiating quality at several stages during the winemaking and maturation process. Fairly soon, the 'top' components for the final wine or wines will emerge and will then be subject to the final dab of the brush, a slight oak adjustment perhaps here and there, some parts to spend a little more time in oak and some to come out and remain in stainless steel for a while. The final blending will take place some time thereafter. And there are still other decisions to be made. Will it be filtered prior to bottling? How long should it remain in bottle prior to release? Such attention to minutiae has made Australian winemakers sought-after the world over.

And what of the rest of the wine? There may be a second Chardonnay label available for some further part of it, but what is rejected will be sold or blended with another variety or varieties to form a lower-priced and lesser-quality wine. Such is present-day Chardonnay.

☙ MOUNT LOFTY RANGES ZONE

The broad uplands of South Australian viticulture. An important zone containing old and new wine regions—the Clare Valley and the Adelaide Hills.

ADELAIDE HILLS REGION

By 1830, what is today the Adelaide coast and its hinterland of steep hills had become quite well-known to explorers and sealers and the first inland explorations had begun to take place. In 1830 Charles Sturt navigated the Murray River to its mouth in Lake Alexandrina and Captain Barker climbed Mount Lofty the following year. After settlement of the coastal plain in 1836, early colonists, both Anglo-Celt and German, wasted little time in heading for the hills behind what was to become the city of Adelaide. By 1844, the Hills' first wines began to appear, made in all probability by Walter Duffield who, in 1848, became South Australia's first wine exporter by shipping a case of his wine, now famous as the 'Echunga hock', to Queen Victoria. By 1871, the Hills region was reportedly producing over 700 000 litres of wine from a vineyard area of 536 ha. From then on, the region went into a slow but persistent decline, though not due, as in some other Australian areas, to phylloxera. This time the causes were most probably the lack of consistent quality, the rise of the prohibition movement, non-existence of export markets and over-supply of local ones, and a gradual change in public taste in favour of fortified wines and big reds. By 1910, however, viticulture had become a minor economic activity and by 1930 had ceased altogether. In the half-century following, the region became highly regarded for its fruit and vegetables, for which there was a much more constant demand from nearby Adelaide than there had ever been for wine.

The viticultural renaissance of the Adelaide Hills was due to one man, who was conscious of the history of the region and ever confident in its suitability for the making of sparkling and delicate table wines. Brian Croser built its first winery, Petaluma, and planted its surrounding vineyards at Piccadilly in the late 1970s. From then on a second rush to the Hills swiftly gained momentum. Today there are over 80 winegrowers and 20 wineries in the region and the numbers are rapidly increasing.

Location: latitude 34°56'S, longitude 138°45'E, about 14 km directly east of Adelaide, a long narrow swathe of land on a north–south axis, located in the southern Mount Lofty Ranges, about 75 km long and 20 km wide
Elevation: averaging about 400 m with peaks at 730 m and gullies at 350 m
Topography: the main feature is the southern Mount Lofty Ranges which run north–south through the central west of the wine region. West-facing are a series of steep scarps or tiers, ultimately descending to the Adelaide plain, but ascending to summits

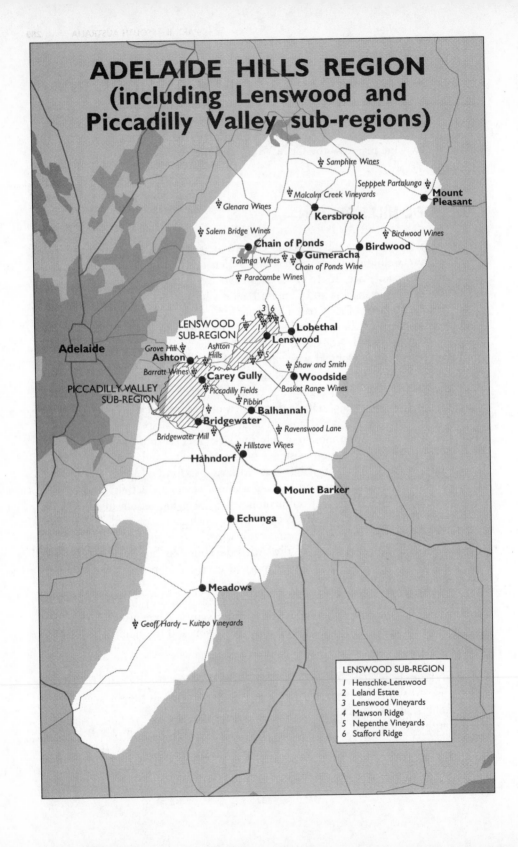

ADELAIDE HILLS REGION
(including Lenswood and Piccadilly Valley sub-regions)

�‴ Samphire Wines

Seppelt Partalunga �‴

�‴ Malcolm Creek Vineyards

Mount Pleasant

�‴ Glenara Wines

Kersbrook

�‴ Salem Bridge Wines

�‴ Birdwood Wines

Chain of Ponds

Gumeracha

Birdwood

Talunga Wines �‴

Chain of Ponds Wine

�‴ Paracombe Wines

3 6
4 2
1
LENSWOOD SUB-REGION

Lobethal

Lenswood

Adelaide

Grove Hill �‴

Ashton Hills

Ashton

5

�‴ Shaw and Smith

Barratt Wines �‴

Carey Gully

Woodside

PICCADILLY VALLEY SUB-REGION

�‴ Piccadilly Fields

Basket Range Wines

�‴ Pibbin

Balhannah

Bridgewater

�‴ Ravenswood Lane

Bridgewater Mill �‴

�‴ Hillstave Wines

Hahndorf

Mount Barker

Echunga

Meadows

�‴ Geoff Hardy – Kuitpo Vineyards

LENSWOOD SUB-REGION

1 Henschke-Lenswood
2 Leland Estate
3 Lenswood Vineyards
4 Mawson Ridge
5 Nepenthe Vineyards
6 Stafford Ridge

at the centre and then east of the peaks, more gentle slopes on the descent to the east. The whole area is undulating with local peaks and fertile gullies.

Soils differ greatly throughout the region with variations occurring both north–south and east–west. In the north of the wine region, the underlying rock is Aldgate Sandstone, upon which there have developed yellow, gritty clays and dark grey sandy loams. In the creeks and gullies, there are alluvial deposits and deep schistic clays with dark red-brown loams. In the centre are bedrocks of Torrens Sandstone on which there are skeletal grey and yellow podsols with alluvial deposits in the gullies and on the creek flats, while to the south and east there are meadow podsols. Most country is free-draining.

Climate: Belair (western foothills) MJT 20.4°C, MAR na, HDD raw 1727, 1625 (cut off and adjusted for latitude and daily temperature range), AR 755 mm (Oct–Apr 282 mm), RH 51% (3pm Jan), AI na, SH 8.2. Stirling (high Hills) MJT 17.7°C, MAR na, HDD raw 1183, 1213 (as adjusted for latitude, daily temperature range and vine sites), RH 52% (3pm Jan), AI na, SH 8.3. Mount Barker (eastern foothills) MJT 18.8°C, MAR na, HDD raw 1433, 1337 (cut off and adjusted for latitude, daily temperature range and vine sites), RH 39% (3pm Jan), AI na, SH 8.1. The Adelaide Hills region has basically a Mediterranean climate with variations in some microclimates, due to altitude. There are three basic areas with the coolest and wettest vineyard sites in the high Hills north and north-east of Stirling (1121 mm annual rainfall) about as far north as Uraidla and as far north-east as Lenswood. The warmest and driest areas are in the western foothills (Belair, 755 mm annual rainfall) and in the northern part of the region (north of Gumeracha), though the eastern foothills (Mount Barker) are also warm and dry (781 mm annual rainfall). The whole region has a maritime influence due to weather changes from the west and south-west. It is cold and sometimes bleak in winter with some higher areas receiving occasional dustings of snow. Often cold even in January, it can be generally described as a cool area. Rainfall is between 750 mm and 1200 mm depending on location, the western (highest) edge of the high Hills being normally the wettest. Most falls are in winter and spring; about 15% falls in summer, but is unreliable. Supplementary irrigation is essential, especially when establishing vineyards. Drip or micro-spray irrigation is by bore water from extremely local aquifers or water from private surface dams, though the latter are now being restricted due to the fact that the region is a watershed for the Adelaide metropolitan area. Salinity is generally not a problem but some bores do return unacceptably saline water.

Spring frosts after budburst are a difficulty on the bottoms of valleys and on river flats with some growers retarding pruning in an attempt to avoid frost damage. Birds too present problems because of the relatively small size of vineyards and their proximity to orchards and forests.

The growing season sees budburst (depending on variety) from mid-September to mid-October, flowering mid to late November and veraison mid to late February.

Harvest time: late March to early May, though occasionally earlier, with auslese pickings extending into late May

Principal grape varieties: White—chardonnay, riesling, sauvignon blanc, semillon; Red—cabernet sauvignon, merlot, pinot noir, shiraz (increasingly respected, especially in the southern and northern areas of the Adelaide Hills, see entry on Geoff Hardy, Kuitpo Vineyards)

Total area: 420 ha

Principal wine style: The Adelaide Hills region is arguably the leading quality region in Australia for chardonnay. Usually, its wines are beautifully structured, aromatic, long-palated and crisp-finishing with very good cellaring capacity.

Ashton Hills R8

Tregarthen Road, Ashton, SA 5137
Ph/Fax 08 8390 1243

Owner: Peter Van Rood
Chief winemaker: Stephen George (most of the wine), some made by contract at Petaluma
Year of foundation: 1981
Tonnes crushed on average each year: 21
Location: Ashton
Area: 3 ha
Soils: shallow sandy clay loam over well-draining ancient sandstone
Varieties planted: White—chardonnay, riesling, sauvignon blanc; Red—cabernet franc, cabernet sauvignon, merlot, pinot noir
Leading wines: Ashton Hills, Pinot Noir, Riesling, Chardonnay
Notes: Stephen George is a winemaker of two distinct district personalities. The first is the supple elegance of wines such as Ashton Hills Riesling, the second the monumental strength of the Clare reds of Wendouree, where he is a consultant winemaker. He also has his own Galah label, not as flippant as its name may suggest, under which he makes and markets interesting parcels of red and white wine from the Adelaide Hills and Clare areas. Cellar door sales: Fri–Sun 10am–5pm.

Barratt Wines NR

Uley Vineyard, Cornish Road off Collins Road, Summertown, SA 5141
Ph/Fax: 08 8390 1788

Owners: Lindsay and Carolyn Barratt
Chief winemaker: Jeffrey Grosset (contract)

Year of foundation: 1993
Tonnes crushed on average each year: 5.26 in 1996 but will increase as vines come to maturity and plantings are extended
Location: Summertown
Area: Uley 5.15 ha, Bonython 3.43 ha
Soils: (Uley) ranging from sandy loam at top to light clay over sandstone at bottom; (Bonython) sandy loam
Varieties planted: White—chardonnay, sauvignon blanc; Red—pinot noir
Leading wines: Chardonnay, Pinot Noir
Notes: The Uley Vineyard is still very young, but in a region of excellence it has very good show results with its Pinot Noir and Chardonnay. No cellar door sales.

Basket Range Wines (vineyard only) NR

Blockers Road, Basket Range, SA 5138
Ph 08 8390 1515

Owner-chief winemaker: Philip Broderick
Year of foundation: 1980
Tonnes crushed on average each year: 5
Location: Basket Range
Area: 2 ha
Soils: sandy loam over sandstone, acidic
Varieties planted: White—none; Red—cabernet franc, cabernet sauvignon, malbec, merlot (petit verdot is to be planted in the near future)
Leading wine: Basket Range Cabernet Blend
Notes: Basket Range is a very small vineyard concentrating its resources on a Bordeaux-style red. No cellar door sales.

Birdwood Wines NR

Mannum Road, Birdwood, SA 5234
Ph 08 8263 0986

Owners: Oli and Susan Cucchiarelli
Chief winemaker: Oli Cucchiarelli, but not on site
Year of foundation: 1980 (first wine 1988)
Tonnes crushed on average each year: 20 but increasing as young vines come into bearing
Location: Birdwood
Area: 10 ha
Soils: sandy loams over yellow clay
Varieties planted: White—chardonnay, riesling, sauvignon blanc; Red—cabernet franc, cabernet sauvignon, merlot
Leading wines: Chardonnay, Cabernet Sauvignon
Notes: An oenology graduate of Charles Sturt University (Wagga), Oli Cucchiarelli is proud of his Chardonnay. No cellar door sales.

Chain of Ponds Wines R9

Adelaide Road, Gumeracha, SA 5233
Ph 08 8389 1415, Fax 08 8336 2462

Owners: Caj and Genni Amadio
Chief winemaker: Caj Amadio
Year of foundation: 1993
Tonnes crushed on average each year: 60 and increasing, although a large proportion of the fruit grown is sold to another wine company
Location: Gumeracha
Area: 63 ha
Soils: red-brown loam topsoil over light-medium permeable clay and shale
Varieties planted: White—chardonnay, sauvignon blanc, semillon; Red—cabernet franc, cabernet sauvignon, grenache, merlot, pinot noir, sangiovese, shiraz
Leading wines: Chain of Ponds Chardonnay, Semillon, Sauvignon Blanc-Semillon, Riesling, Cabernet Sauvignon, Novello Rosso
Notes: This is a very exciting vineyard in a very exciting region. Chain of Ponds 1995

Chardonnay hit Sydney like a bombshell in 1996. Cellar door sales: weekends and holidays 10.30am–4.30pm.

Glenara Wines R8

126 Range Road North, Upper Hermitage, SA 5131
Ph/Fax 08 8380 5056

Owners: LE and JL Verrall
Chief winemaker: Trevor Jones
Year of foundation: 1971
Tonnes crushed on average each year: 70
Location: Upper Hermitage and Montacute
Area: 12 ha
Soils: dark brown loam over red clay over siltstone
Varieties planted: (Upper Hermitage)
White—chardonnay, riesling, sauvignon blanc; Red—cabernet franc, cabernet sauvignon, merlot, pinot noir, shiraz. (Montacute)
White—chardonnay, semillon; Red—pinot noir
Leading wines: Glenara Bottle Fermented Pinot Noir, Riesling, Unwooded Chardonnay, Sauvignon Blanc-Semillon, Shiraz, Cabernet-Merlot, Merlot, Riesling Auslese
Notes: Glenara has been in the Verrall family for over 70 years, though a vineyard only since 1971. Recently it has been approved as an organic vineyard by the Organic Vignerons Association of Australia and all vintages since 1993 have been certified as organically grown. Cellar door sales: 7 days 11am–5pm.

Geoff Hardy—Kuitpo Vineyards R9

Tynan Road, Kuitpo, SA
Ph 08 8388 3700, Fax 08 8388 3564

Owner: Geoff Hardy
Chief winemaker: Geoff Hardy, Ben Riggs (consultant)
Year of foundation: 1987
Tonnes crushed on average each year: 25
Location: Kuitpo
Area: 40 ha (most fruit is sold to other makers at the present time)

Soils: old podsolic duplex, gravelly, quartzite
Varieties planted: White—chardonnay, sauvignon blanc, semillon; Red—cabernet franc, cabernet sauvignon, merlot, pinot noir, shiraz
Leading wines: Geoff Hardy Cabernet, Shiraz (made only in good years)
Notes: Geoff Hardy's 1993 Kuitpo Shiraz was the winner of the inaugural Qantas Great Australian Shiraz Challenge, a remarkable achievement for a cool-area Shiraz. It is necessary, however, to restrict shiraz to a low crop in Kuitpo to ripen it fully. Kuitpo, located in the southern area of the region, is expanding rapidly as McLaren Vale winemakers move up into the Hills. At the time of writing, three properties adjoining that of Geoff Hardy have each been planted with 25 hectares of vines. No cellar door sales.

Grove Hill NR

120 Old Norton Summit Road, Norton Summit, SA 5136
Ph/Fax 08 8390 1437

Owner: Marguerite Giles
Chief winemaker: Roman Bratasiuk
Year of foundation: 1978
Tonnes crushed on average each year: (est) 5
Location: Norton Summit
Area: 2 ha close planted
Soils: clay loam, acidic
Varieties planted: White—chardonnay, riesling; Red—pinot noir
Leading wines: Grove Hill Marguerite Pinot Chardonnay (sparkling), Chardonnay, Riesling
Notes: Grove Hill is a close-planted vineyard, located on a property owned for over 150 years by the Giles family. At about 400 metres in altitude, it has its own very cool microclimate. Its riesling is not irrigated and other varieties are irrigated only when absolutely necessary. No cellar door sales.

Henschke-Lenswood R10

Cnr Coldstore and Croft Roads, Lenswood, SA 5240
Ph 08 8564 8223, Fax 08 8564 8294

Owners: Stephen and Prue Henschke
Chief winemaker: Stephen Henschke
Year of foundation: 1981
Tonnes crushed on average each year: 60
Location: Lenswood
Area: 16 ha
Soils: schisty sandy loam with shale fragments
Varieties planted: White—chardonnay, riesling; Red—cabernet franc, cabernet sauvignon, merlot, pinot noir
Leading wines: Abbott's Prayer (a merlot-cabernet blend), Giles Pinot Noir, Croft Chardonnay, Green's Hill Riesling
Notes: If ever any doubt is expressed about the suitability of the Lenswood region for superlative reds, simply utter 'Abbott's Prayer' and any such doubts are instantly allayed. The Giles Pinot Noir is always complex and interesting, while the Croft Chardonnay and the Green's Hill Riesling are never less than excellent. No cellar door sales at Lenswood. Wines are available for sale at Henschke, Keyneton.

Hillstowe Wines R8.5

104 Main Road, Hahndorf, SA 5245
Ph 08 8388 1400, Fax 08 8388 1411

Owner: Hillstowe Wines Pty Limited
Chief winemaker: Chris Laurie
Year of foundation: 1984
Tonnes crushed on average each year: 25
Location: Carey Gully
Area: 14.6 ha (most of the fruit produced is sold)
Soils: ancient weathered podsols
Varieties planted: White—chardonnay, sauvignon blanc; Red—merlot, pinot noir
Leading wines: Udy's Mill Chardonnay, Pinot Noir

Notes: Since 1991 when it launched its own label, Hillstowe has rapidly built a reputation of excellence for its elegantly styled Udy's Mill Chardonnay. Its Udy's Mill Pinot Noir is never far behind. It now has its own production facility at Mount Torrens, which also produces McLaren Vale wines from its Buxton vineyard. Cellar door sales: 7 days 10am–5pm.

Leland Estate **R8**

Neudorf Road, Lenswood, SA 5240
Ph 08 8389 6928

Owner/chief winemaker: Robb Cootes
Year of foundation: 1986
Tonnes crushed on average each year: 16
Location: Lenswood
Area: 3 ha
Soils: red-brown earth, duplex, podsolic
Varieties planted: White—sauvignon blanc;
Red—pinot noir
Leading wines: Adele Sparkling, Neudorf Sauvignon Blanc, Neudorf Pinot Noir
Notes: Robb Cootes, former senior winemaker of Yalumba, is another winemaker-proprietor who has decided to be his own man. His Sauvignon Blanc is a white of great quality. No cellar door sales.

Lenswood Vineyards **R10**

Crofts Road, Lenswood, SA 5240
Ph 08 8389 8111, Fax 08 8389 8553

Owners: Tim and Annie Knappstein
Chief winemaker: Tim Knappstein (the wines are not made on site, but under Tim Knappstein's supervision and control at Knappstein Wines in Clare, except for Pinot Noir, which is made at Nepenthe Vineyards, Lenswood)
Year of foundation: 1981
Tonnes crushed on average each year: 130 increasing to 200 by the year 2000
Location: Lenswood
Area: 26.67 ha

Soils: old soils; duplex, grey-brown and red-brown loam over crumbly clay subsoils with sandstone over quartz gravel, generally of low fertility
Varieties planted: White—chardonnay, sauvignon blanc, semillon; Red—cabernet sauvignon, malbec, merlot, pinot noir
Leading wines: Lenswood Vineyards Pinot Noir, Chardonnay, Sauvignon Blanc
Notes: This is another exciting Adelaide Hills vineyard in one of the coolest areas of the region, so cool that Tim Knappstein feels that the Bordeaux varieties—semillon, cabernet sauvignon, merlot and malbec—find the Lenswood climate a little too chilly for comfort and accordingly do not fully ripen. Pinot noir, chardonnay and sauvignon blanc, however, seem to regard it as ideal. No cellar door sales.

Malcolm Creek Vineyard **R8**

Bonython Road, Kersbrook, SA 5231
Ph/Fax 08 8389 3235

Owners: RL and EM Tolley
Chief winemaker: RL Tolley at Barossa Vintners
Year of foundation: 1982
Tonnes crushed on average each year: 9
Location: Kersbrook
Area: 2 ha
Soils: schistic loam over clay
Varieties planted: White—chardonnay;
Red—cabernet sauvignon
Leading wines: Malcolm Creek Cabernet Sauvignon, Chardonnay
Notes: What do winemakers do when they retire from winemaking? Make wine! What else? After many years of winemaking at Tolley's Pedare, Reg Tolley has gone back to winemaking, but on a smaller scale. The wines are supple and always have some bottle age. Cellar door sales: weekends and public holidays 11am–5pm.

Mawson Ridge (vineyard only) NR

Mawson Road, Lenswood, SA 5240
24–28 Main St, Hahndorf (sales)
Ph 08 8362 7826, Fax 08 8462 7588

Owners: Raymond and Madeleine Marin
Chief winemaker: Peter Leske (contract)
Year of foundation: 1994
Tonnes crushed on average each year: 1998
was the first vintage
Location: Lenswood
Area: 3 ha
Soils: heavy loam over shale, highly acidic
Varieties planted: White—chardonnay, pinot
gris, sauvignon blanc; Red—cabernet franc,
merlot, pinot noir
Leading wines: first vintage 1998
Notes: It is early days for Dr Ray Marin, but the
area is very good and the varieties spot-on.
I look forward to seeing them. Cellar door
sales from August 1999 at Hahndorf.

Nepenthe Vineyards R9

Vickers Road, Lenswood, SA 5240
Ph/Fax 08 8389 8218

Owners: Twedell family
Winemaker: Peter Leske
Year of foundation: 1994
Tonnes crushed on average each year: 120 and
increasing as recently planted areas of the
vineyard come into bearing
Location: Lenswood
Area: 24 ha
Soils: duplex red podsols over clay of varying
depth
Varieties planted: White—chardonnay, pinot
gris, riesling, sauvignon blanc, semillon;
Red—cabernet sauvignon, merlot, pinot noir,
zinfandel
Leading wines: Nepenthe Chardonnay, Pinot
Noir, Sauvignon Blanc (barrel fermented)
Notes: Nepenthe is only the second winery
with full crushing facilities to be built in the
Adelaide Hills (the first was Petaluma in 1979).

Two of its 1997 vintage whites (Sauvignon
Blanc and Unwooded Chardonnay) were
tasting well in late 1997. Cellar door sales from
late 1998.

Paracombe Wines R8

Paracombe Road, Paracombe, SA 5132
Ph 08 8380 5058

Owners: Paul and Kathy Drogemuller
Chief winemaker: reds (Paul Drogemuller);
sparkling, whites (Petaluma contract)
Year of foundation: 1983
Tonnes crushed on average each year: 20
Location: Paracombe
Area: 12 ha
Soils: varying from brown sandy loam and
ironstone over clay and quartz rock to brown
loam over 'buckshot' over yellow pipe clay
Varieties planted: Whites—chardonnay,
sauvignon blanc; Red—cabernet franc,
cabernet sauvignon, merlot, pinot noir, shiraz
Leading wines: Sauvignon Blanc, Cabernet
Franc, Shiraz-Cabernet, Chardonnay, Pinot-
Chardonnay (sparkling)
Notes: Paul Drogemuller is currently the only
winemaker in Paracombe, an old and respected
name in South Australia. He has built a solid
reputation for his wines and though there are
no cellar door sales, there is a mailing list and
an annual wine release day (usually the last
Sunday in October) on which mailing list
members can taste and purchase wines.

Petaluma R10

Spring Gully Road, Piccadilly, SA 5151
.(winery)
Mount Barker Road, Bridgewater,
SA 5155 (sales)
Ph 08 8339 4122, Fax 08 8339 5253
(winery and sales)

Owner: Petaluma Limited
Chief winemaker: Brian Croser
Years of foundation: 1976 (label), 1978 (first

Piccadilly Valley vineyard), 1979 (winery)
Tonnes crushed on average each year: 250, of
Adelaide Hills fruit
Location: Piccadilly Valley
Area: 60 ha
Soils: the Petaluma vineyards overlie various
geological strata. Most lie on Woolshed Flat
shale rather than the sandstone and siltstone
rocks of the Castambul. Fortunately, the rest
save one lie above Basket Range sandstone or
alluvium. Uniquely the Tiers vineyard rests upon
Calc-silicates. Top soil over general sandy loam
to sandy clay loam over brown to orange clay
Varieties planted: White—chardonnay;
Red—pinot noir
Leading wines: (from Adelaide Hills fruit)
Petaluma Chardonnay, Tiers Chardonnay,
'Croser' (a vintage sparkling wine, made by the
classical method, usually of 50/50 pinot noir
and chardonnay, though these proportions are
sometimes varied)
Notes: Petaluma is the fount of modern
winemaking both in the Adelaide Hills and
Australia as a whole. Since its erection in 1979,
the Piccadilly winery has seen a steady stream
of postgraduate winemaking talent flow out to
the Australian wine industry and indeed the
world. The inspiration for this has been Brian
Croser, who has devoted his professional
career to ensuring that Petaluma has only one
standard—the highest. Croser was drawn to
the Hills in his search for a region to make the
finest of Australian sparkling wine. No one can
deny that in the making of 'Croser', he has
succeeded brilliantly. In the course of so doing,
he has made excellent table wines from other
regions under the Petaluma label, a riesling
from Clare and excellent reds from
Coonawarra. It is, however, Petaluma
Chardonnay that always excites Australian
palates. It is a standard by which other
Australian chardonnays are judged and it has
originated solely from the Adelaide Hills region
since 1990. Although Brian Croser has often
said that he reserves the right to include

material from other regions if such material is
in his mind better, I somehow doubt that this
will ever happen. Cellar door sales at
Bridgewater Mill, Mon–Fri 9.30am–5pm,
weekends 10am–5pm.

Pibbin R8

Greenhill Road, Balhannah, SA 5242
Ph 08 8388 4794, Fax 08 8388 0015

Owners: Roger and Lindy Salkeld
Chief winemaker: Roger Salkeld
Year of foundation: 1985
Tonnes crushed on average each year: 20
Location: Verdun and Balhannah
Area: 2.4 ha (Verdun), 1 ha (Balhannah)
Soils: gravelly quartz and ironstone over clay
Varieties planted: White—viognier; Red—pinot
noir
Leading wines: Pibbin Pinot Noir (a still red),
Sparkling Pinot Noir (white), Pinot Noir (whole
bunch pressed made as a still white)
Notes: The Verdun vineyard occupies a
northerly slope on ironstone loam, close
planted 2.1 × 1.5 m, with vertical shoots and
minimally sprayed. It is a warmer site within a
cool area and Roger Salkeld is optimistic about
its suitability for viognier. Cellar door sales:
weekends 11am–5.30pm.

Piccadilly Fields R8

185 Piccadilly Road, Piccadilly, SA 5151
Ph 08 8370 8800, Fax 08 8232 5395

Owners: Vigara family
Chief winemaker: Temple Bruer (contract)
Year of foundation: 1985
Tonnes crushed on average each year: 50 for
winemaking under the Piccadilly Fields label,
but more as fruit sold to other winemakers
Location: Piccadilly, Uraidla, Balhannah,
Lenswood
Area: 125.5 ha, (13 ha Piccadilly, 18 ha
Uraidla, 30 ha Balhannah, 1.5 ha Lenswood,
40 ha Woodside, 23 ha Lobethal)

Soils: (Piccadilly) gravelly clays vary to clay loam on hill; (Balhannah) deep clay loam; (Woodside) clay and sandy loam over bluestone; (Lobethal) sandy loam over deep clay; (Uraidla) gravelly clays; (Lenswood) high clay loam
Varieties planted: (Piccadilly) White—chardonnay; Red—cabernet sauvignon, gamay, merlot, meunier, pinot noir. (Uraidla) White—chardonnay; Red—meunier, pinot noir. (Balhannah) White—sauvignon blanc; Red—merlot, pinot noir. (Lenswood) White—sauvignon blanc; red—none
Leading wines: Piccadilly Fields Chardonnay, Merlot-Cabernet Sauvignon (a red blend)
Notes: Though Piccadilly Fields with nearly 60 ha of vineyards is one of the larger vineyard plantings in the region, most of its production is sold to other winemakers and some wine is exported to Europe. The result is that its wines are not widely available in Australia. Piccadilly Fields Chardonnay is the pick of them. No cellar door sales.

The Range Vineyard (vineyard only)   NR
The Range Road, Willunga, SA 5172

Owner: Rosemount Estate Pty Ltd
Chief winemaker: Philip Shaw
Year of foundation: 1994
Tonnes crushed on average each year: not yet fully bearing but expected to produce about 300 tonnes
Location: Willunga
Area: 30 ha
Soils: red-brown loam over grey clay, podsolic
Varieties planted: White—chardonnay, sauvignon blanc; Red—none
Leading wines: a contributor to Diamond Sauvignon Blanc.

Ravenswood Lane   R9
Ravenswood Lane, Hahndorf, SA 5245
Ph 08 8388 1250, Fax 08 8388 7233

Owners: John and Helen Edwards
Winemaker: BRL Hardy (contract)
Year of foundation: 1993
Tonnes crushed on average each year: 100 and rising
Location: Hahndorf
Area: 24 ha
Soils: sandy loam over porous red clay and granitic sand over rock
Varieties planted: White—chardonnay, sauvignon blanc; Red—cabernet sauvignon, merlot, shiraz
Leading wines: Ravenswood Lane Sauvignon Blanc, Chardonnay (at the time of writing, no reds had been released)
Notes: Ravenswood Lane at 425 m in altitude is about 50 m lower than vineyards in the Piccadilly Valley. Accordingly, though Chardonnay here is crisp and fine-boned and Sauvignon Blanc exhibits classical gooseberry flavours, it is also an excellent red area, being slightly warmer and brighter than Piccadilly. John Edwards is particularly excited about his Shiraz. All wines will be available at cellar door and, in time, at fine restaurants throughout Australia. No cellar door sales. Orders by phone or fax.

Salem Bridge Wines   NR
Salem Bridge Road, Lower Hermitage, SA 5131
Ph/Fax 08 8380 5240

Owner: Barry Miller
Chief winemaker: contract
Year of foundation: 1989
Tonnes crushed on average each year: projected 100 but plantings are not yet fully bearing; about 10 tonnes is presently used for Salem Bridge labels
Location: Lower Hermitage
Area: 13 ha
Soils: loam over clay, schisty rock and ironstone
Varieties planted: White—none; Red—cabernet franc, cabernet sauvignon, merlot, shiraz

Leading wines: Salem Bridge Cabernet Franc, Cabernet Sauvignon
Notes: Another new name in the rapidly growing Adelaide Hills region. No cellar door sales.

Samphire Wines and Pottery   NR

Watts Gully Road, Kersbrook, SA 5233
Ph 08 8389 3183

Owner: TW and VR Miller Pty Ltd
Chief winemaker: Tom Miller
Year of foundation: 1979
Tonnes crushed on average each year: 4
Location: Watts Gully
Area: 0.34 ha
Soils: micaceous schist, quartz
Varieties planted: White—riesling; Red—none
Leading wine: Samphire Riesling
Notes: Adjacent to the picturesque Heysen trail, tiny Samphire is located near the northern boundary of the Adelaide Hills region, not far from Eden Valley. Hence Tom Miller's understandable affection for riesling. Cellar door sales by appointment.

Seppelt Partalunga (vineyard only)   R9.5

North East Road, Mount Pleasant, SA 5235

Owner: Southcorp Wines
Chief winemaker: Ian McKenzie
Year of foundation: 1982
Tonnes crushed on average each year: not disclosed but estimated at 750
Location: Mount Pleasant
Area: 82 ha
Soils: sand over sandy loam, podsolics not dissimilar to Leo Buring Eden Valley soils
Varieties planted: White—chardonnay, pinot blanc, riesling, sauvignon blanc; Red—cabernet sauvignon, merlot, meunier, pinot noir, shiraz
Leading wine: Partalunga Chardonnay
Notes: Planted in 1982 by Seppelt, then family-owned, Partalunga has built an excellent

reputation for its small range of wines, in particular its Chardonnays which have been very impressive in recent years. Cellar door sales: see Seppeltsfield Barossa Valley entry.

Shaw and Smith   R9.5

Woodside Vineyard, Woodside, SA 5244
Ph 08 8370 9911, Fax 08 8370 9339

Owners: a unit trust owned principally by Shaw and Smith and the Hill-Smith family
Chief winemaker: Martin Shaw
Year of foundation: 1989
Tonnes crushed on average each year: 250
Location: Woodside together with contract growers at Lenswood and Kuitpo
Area: (Woodside) 26.5 ha
Soils: duplex red-brown sandy loam over clay with some gravel and quartz
Varieties planted: White—chardonnay, sauvignon blanc; Red—merlot
Leading wines: Shaw and Smith Unoaked Chardonnay, Reserve Chardonnay (oaked), Sauvignon Blanc
Notes: With the consummate winemaking skill of 'flying winemaker', Martin Shaw, and the unerring palate of Michael Hill-Smith MW, how can Shaw and Smith go wrong? Of the styles to be drunk young, the Unoaked Chardonnay is refreshing and full of fruit, the Sauvignon Blanc is zingy and alive in the mouth (though in 1996 and 1997 without quite the intensity of previous years) while the Reserve Chardonnay, made with restraint and elegance, needs only patience and some 4–5 years in the bottle to reveal its almost 'Burgundian' complexity. No cellar door sales.

Stafford Ridge   R10

Stafford Road, Lenswood, SA 5240
Ph 08 8272 2105, Fax 08 8271 0177

Owners: Geoff and Judy Weaver
Chief winemaker: Geoff Weaver
Year of foundation: 1982

Tonnes crushed on average each year: 75
Location: Lenswood
Area: 10.7 ha
Soils: podsolic sandy loam over permeable
yellow clay, old and relatively infertile
Varieties planted: White—chardonnay, riesling,
sauvignon blanc; Red—cabernet sauvignon,
merlot, pinot noir
Leading wines: Stafford Ridge Chardonnay,
Sauvignon Blanc
Notes: Formerly chief winemaker at Hardy's,
since 1992 Geoff Weaver has concentrated his
considerable energies and skills at Stafford
Ridge. The results, especially the complex,
almost Burgundian Chardonnay and the fresh,
gooseberry-toned Sauvignon Blanc, have been
outstanding. No cellar door sales.

Talunga Wines   **NR**

Adelaide Mannum Road, Gumeracha,
SA 5233
Ph 08 8389 1222, Fax 08 8389 1233

Owners: di Cesare and Scaffidi families
Chief winemaker: Vince Scaffidi and contract
Year of foundation: 1988
Tonnes crushed on average each year: 1000, of
which 25 are used for Talunga label purposes
Location: Gumeracha
Area: 62 ha
Soils: loam to dark red shaley soil on the slopes
Varieties planted: White—chardonnay, riesling,
sauvignon blanc, semillon, verdelho; Red—
cabernet franc, cabernet sauvignon, gamay,
grenache, merlot, nebbiolo, pinot noir,
sangiovese, shiraz
Leading wines: Talunga Shiraz, Cabernet
Sauvignon, Chardonnay
Notes: This is a large vineyard with a
considerable production, most of which is sold
to other winemakers. Two bronze medals have
been won at recent wine shows. Cellar door
sales: Wed–Sun and public holidays
11am–5pm. There is also a restaurant.

Lenswood Sub-region

The Adelaide Hills were settled soon after the foundation of South Australia in 1836 and from as early as 1844 in Echunga there was a history of winemaking. Such was not the case with Lenswood (formerly called Jerry's Flat), where from 1861 early agricultural activities were horticulture, market gardening and grazing and, later, dairying. Orcharding, however, remained the major activity and by 1982 the area produced 95% of South Australia's apples. Yet even before 1982 interest in orcharding was diversifying to cherries, flowers and, of course, vines.

Inspired by Brian Croser's planting of a vineyard in the Piccadilly Valley in the late 1970s, the interest in producing wine spread rapidly to other areas in the Hills and especially Lenswood where Tim Knappstein planted a commercial vineyard in 1981. He was soon followed by Stephen Henschke and Geoff Weaver in the following year. The first Lenswood grapes were produced in 1985 and since then Lenswood wines have been conspicuous winners in local and national wine shows with Chardonnay, Pinot and Sauvignon Blanc leading the varietal charge. In 1997, Nepenthe, the sub-region's first winery, began operation. An important factor in the development of Lenswood was the involvement of experienced winemakers and wine show judges, such as Tim Knappstein, Geoff Weaver and Stephen Henschke, in the achievement of high professional standards of winemaking, a participation which has added a final gloss to the polish of the sub-region. Lenswood is a sub-region of significant quality.

Location: latitude 34°57'S, longitude 138°48'E, about 25 km east of Adelaide, its boundaries are contours, set at a base elevation of 400 m, extending to an upper altitude of 560 m

Elevation: 400–560 m. Such boundaries exist because there is no country in the sub-region above 560 m and grape-growing conditions in the valleys below 400 m are distinctly different.

Topography and soils: part of the South Mount Lofty Ranges, running north-east to south-west, the Lenswood sub-region consists of a range of hills, its boundaries being wholly situated within the catchment of the Onkaparinga River. The Lenswood vineyards are generally planted east-facing close to the tops of the hills to benefit from more mild and even-temperature conditions and to avoid the potential frost problems of the valleys. Suitable slopes are limited in availability and much of the region is very steep and afforested by old eucalypt woodland.

The soils are podsolic with a leached sandy loam topsoil between 1 and 1.5 metres deep over a subsoil of generally yellow clay. They are characterised by (a) low fertility, important in restraining the vigour of the vine, a restraint in turn critical in the production of quality fruit, and (b) good water-holding capacity in the clays with restricted release, giving the vines a slow but steady supply of water ensuring constant but moderate activity.

Climate: MJT 19.3°C, HDD 1350, MAR na, AR 920 mm, RH na, AI na, SH na. Lenswood is a cool and wet sub-region, cooler and wetter in fact than all the rest of the Adelaide Hills region except the Piccadilly Valley. It has a low diurnal range of temperatures and such cool but even temperatures yet sufficient warmth in most years allow all but the latest-ripening grape varieties to ripen. Importantly its rainfall during March and April is low again enabling ripening and the prevention of rots and mildews.

Irrigation is required but only sparingly, as water stress during the growing season is low and such irrigation is obtained from private dams and from bores. However, official approval is now required to drill bores or construct dams and is also required for the clearing of native vegetation.

Harvest time: sauvignon blanc and pinot noir third week of March to second week of April; chardonnay first to third week of April; cabernet sauvignon third week of April to first week of May

Principal grape varieties: White—chardonnay, sauvignon blanc; Red—pinot noir

Total area: (1997) 145 ha

Major wine styles: Chardonnay, Sauvignon Blanc, Pinot Noir

Wineries and vineyards within the sub-region: The following winery and vineyards using their own labels were situated within the Lenswood sub-region at the time of writing: Henschke-Lenswood, Leland Estate, Lenswood Vineyards, Mawson Ridge, Nepenthe Vineyards and Winery and Stafford Ridge. See above for individual notes.

Piccadilly Valley Sub-region

Dominated by the summit of Mount Lofty, so called by Matthew Flinders when commanding HMS *Investigator* in 1802, the Piccadilly Valley was first settled in 1837.

Early on it was called The Tiers, a name now commemorated by a premium single-vineyard chardonnay made by Petaluma.

Quite presciently, Robert Cock, one of the first explorers and settlers in the district, remarked in 1838 that its hillsides 'seemed well-adapted for vineyards'. However, its first industry was timber-getting, the local stringybark being considered ideal for basic fencing and bush dwellings. Such logging operations were the beginning of the township of Crafers, named after one David Crafer, who opened the Norfolk Arms Hotel there in 1839. Timber-getting continued, though small farms soon sprang up. To encourage access to the area, the construction of the Great Eastern (Mount Barker) Road was begun in 1841 and Cox's Creek Village (near the present town of Bridgewater) was founded soon after. This road, however, was not considered satisfactory, being replaced by a new Mount Barker Road in 1851, which passed through the present-day towns of Stirling, Aldgate and Bridgewater and was the precursor of the modern South-Eastern Freeway. Subdivision of Stirling followed during the 1850s, though sales were slow due to the poor quality of the land. To the north, however, around present-day Piccadilly and Summertown, the country was of greater fertility and towards the end of the 19th century began to be used for horticulture and market gardening. These activities continued well into the 20th century.

Save for the 19th century vineyard of Brooklyn at Summertown, there is little or no evidence of widespread viticultural activity before the 1980s. In the 19th century, popular belief held that viticulture was suitable only for warmer sites and the Piccadilly Valley, mostly settled by Anglo-Celts without a native wine tradition, was most likely considered too cold for that purpose and in any case Adelaide was a close and prosperous market for the fruit and vegetables that grew so well in the area.

In the modern era, grape growing began in the 1970s. By 1978 Brian Croser was planting Petaluma to chardonnay and pinot noir for the making of still and sparkling table wines. The sub-region began to boom in the 1980s, with Stephen George planting at Ashton Hills in 1981, Piccadilly Fields being commenced in 1984, and the Woodshill Vineyard being established in 1987–88. Chardonnay and pinot noir have remained the dominant plantings. This sub-region is bounded by the sub-region of Lenswood to the east and north-east.

Location: latitude 34°58'S, longitude 138°47'E, the Piccadilly Valley is located about 18 km south-east of Adelaide
Elevation: elevation varies from about 400 m to 710 m (the summit of Mount Lofty)
Topography and soils: the base rocks of the sub-region are very old, being of the palaeoproterozoic era and mostly consisting of quartz-mica-feldspar schists and gneisses, overlain by Basket Range sandstone, Woolshed flat shale, the Castambul Formation siltstone and Stonyfell quartzite.

Its topographies and soils are variable, being recently described as having three dominant landforms BC, BA and AC. The BC presence is categorised as 'low hills formed on sandstones with surface ironstone. The main soils are sandy loam over brown clay on rock and loam over orange clay on rock'. BA and AC occur with equivalent frequency. BA is described as 'low hills and slopes formed on medium to coarse grained sandstones with chief soils of sandy loam over brown clay, shallow loamy sand on rock'. AC is depicted as 'low hills and hills of the high rainfall inner ranges, the soils of which are loam over brown clay on rock'.

Of more infrequent occurrence are landforms CA, DB, SC and BB. CA is 'rolling to steep low hills and slopes formed on coarse grained sandstones with main soil of stony sand over clayey sand grading to yellow sandy clay on rock'. DB is 'low hills to hills in the high rainfall inner ranges with main soil being loam over orange to brown friable clay forming on shale'. Stringybark forest is a typical vegetation. SC has drainage depressions and lower slopes on coarse-grained alluvium with main soil of gravelly loamy sand over yellow, red and grey clay. BB comprises rocky hillslopes formed on coarse-grained sandstones with main soil of shallow stony coarse sands on rock.

Climate: climate information is complicated by the fact that the weather recording station at Stirling was closed in 1985 and moved to Mount Lofty. So two sets of data are given, one current for 22 years until 1985, the more recent only since 1991 at Mount Lofty. Stirling (until 1985) MJT 18.65°C, HDD 1260 (cut off at 19°C where necessary but not adjusted for latitude, altitude, daily temperature or vine sites), MAR na, AR 1118.2 mm (Oct to Apr 425.9 mm), RH 64% (9am) and 50% (3pm), AI na, SH 1771 (Gladstones). Mount Lofty from 1991 MJT 16°C, HDD 898.4 (cut-offs were unnecessary here but no other adjustments were made), MAR na, AR 1225.6 mm (Oct–Apr 470 mm), RH 76% (9am) and 62% (3pm), AI na, SH na. Other rainfall information: Ashton (65 years to 1998) AR 1054.5 mm (Oct–Apr 388 mm). Uraidla (108 years to 1998) AR 1087.1 mm (Oct–Apr 379.9 mm).

Though the sub-region is quite close to St Vincents Gulf (about 15 kilometres in a direct line), it is considered to have a climate that is continental rather than maritime, because of the intervening Mount Lofty Range. It is obviously a very cool viticultural area and its boundary approximates the 1000 mm average rainfall line, which means that Piccadilly Valley fruit can virtually be grown without supplementary irrigation. However, supplementary irrigation, sourced from wells of high quality water, is necessary when establishing vineyards and is an obvious insurance factor even in the Piccadilly Valley for the occasional drought years.

Generally, the sub-region has few disease problems, provided the usual spray regimes are adhered to. Netting for protection from birds seems to be unnecessary, nor are other bird-scaring devices employed.

Harvest time: chardonnay, mid to late April, generally varying because of aspect, topography, soil type and 'cultural control', i.e. vine management. This last factor is an amalgam of pruning regime, the amount of irrigation, crop loads and canopy manipulation and is very variable.

Principal grape varieties: White—chardonnay (75.6 ha), riesling (0.8 ha); Red—pinot noir (47.6 ha), meunier (12.4 ha), gamay (1.6 ha), merlot (1.2 ha), cabernet sauvignon (0.8 ha). Chardonnay seems to be the premium variety of the sub-region and totally suited to it.

Total area 1998: 140 ha

Major wine styles: Chardonnay, Sparkling

Wineries and vineyards within the sub-region: Barratt Wines, Petaluma, Piccadilly Fields.

❧ Riesling

Can it be said that the decline of Australian riesling has been stemmed? Not that it ever declined in quality terms. But even wine of excellent quality cannot be made forever, if its sales disappear. Though the sales curve may still be declining, the future of Australian riesling seems secure enough, at least in its three classic areas, the Eden Valley, the Clare Valley and the Great Southern. If they are indeed 'classic' areas for riesling, what makes them so?

Riesling has often been described as the archetypal 'continental' grape variety. Is this description justified? The table compares the three Australian areas mentioned with Geisenheim in the Rheingau, another 'classic' riesling area.

	Geisenheim		Clare Valley		Eden Valley*	Mount Barker (WA)
Altitude	100 m		398 m		450 m	253 m
Effective degree	Apr	23	Oct	143	72	120
days	May	171	Nov	225	140	175
	June	265	Dec	279	211	244
	July	279	Jan	279	258	279
	Aug	279	Feb	252	235	252
	Sep	182	Mar	279	225	277
	Oct	26	Apr	156	110	210
	Total	1225		1613	1251	1557
Average rainfall (mm)						
April–Oct	333		Oct–April 245		243	285
Nov–Dec	185		May–Sept 387		415	471
Total	518			632	658	756
Relative humidity (3pm)	56%**		37%**		44%**	54%**
Sunshine hours	1333		1870		1764	1518
Continentality***	11.8		8.5		7.2	5.7

* Eden Valley degree days not adjusted for vine sites.

** All relative humidity averaged over the growing season.

*** In this instance, not the difference between the mean January temperature and the mean July temperature, but the difference between daily mean temperature averaged from October to April and daily mean temperatures averaged for the other five months of the year in Australia. In the northern hemisphere, the relevant months are of course reversed.

Note: All statistics are after Gladstones, *Viticulture and Environment*.

As is commonly said, there are lies, damned lies and statistics. Certainly from the continentality aspect, Geisenheim is much more 'continental'. It warms very quickly from April to May, much more speedily than October to November in any Australian site mentioned. It is also the coolest site in degree day terms with fewest sunshine hours. As well, it has the highest relative humidity and the highest growing season rainfall. Among the Australians, Clare is by far the warmest in degree day terms with the greatest number of sunshine hours. (But see the Clare regional entry—the Clare HDD may be distorted or at least not representative of the Clare regional areas where riesling is grown.) Clare is also the driest, both in annual rainfall and in relative humidity with the highest Australian 'continentality'. Eden Valley is the highest site of the four and, of the Australians, the coolest and second driest. As for Mount Barker, it has a relative humidity of 54% (approaching that of Geisenheim), the least 'continentality' and is relatively warm, yet with the second lowest number of sunshine hours. So there is no statistical consistency overall (perhaps one should not expect it), but there are similarities in degree days between Geisenheim and Eden Valley, for both areas can produce rieslings which have been described as 'steely' and which mature slowly. Indeed the only factors in common between Clare and Eden Valley are similar altitudes, a high continentality (in Australian terms) and low humidities. Are these factors the climatic reasons for classic Australian riesling?

John Vickery, now of Richmond Grove in the Barossa Valley and a renowned maker of Australian riesling, thinks not. His experience of the riesling of both areas extends over 40 years and to him, humidity-stressed vines give concentrated but not better flavours. In his opinion, there are indeed differences between Clare and Eden Valley rieslings, but they are primarily brought about by soil divergencies, not climate. He prefers to use fruit that is not moisture-stressed. In Clare, he sees citrus characters in riesling, brought about by Clare's alluvial red-brown soils, which sit over a marly limestone subsoil. In Eden Valley, the sandy, schisty, less fertile soils give riesling a more aromatic floral and spice character. He fully understands the misapprehensions of some writers who allege that Eden Valley rieslings are sometimes 'improved' by a non-disclosed and substantial addition of traminer, but knows that such allegations are quite wrong.

So the differences in Australian rieslings cannot be attributed to climatic factors alone. The differences in the wines are as usual the product of a multitude of other things, with soils, climate and winemaking technique all playing interactive roles.

CLARE VALLEY REGION

The early history of the Clare region is a little obscure. Perhaps it was Mr Hill—who named the Hutt River but about whom not much else is known—who first visited the area, but it is certain that, in May 1839, Edward Eyre, a young man of 24, rode north from Adelaide. Like Blaxland, Wentworth and Lawson in New South Wales a quarter of a century before, he was in search of new pastoral land. He surmounted the Flinders Ranges, reaching as far as the dry Lake Torrens, having passed through what was to become a few years later the village of Clare. In 1840 another Englishman, John Horrocks, like Eyre a pastoralist/explorer, also arrived. He settled Hope Farm in what is now the Clare Valley, named the village of Penwortham after his birthplace in Lancashire and is credited, through the labours of one of his servants, no doubt, with planting the first few vines there. Mount Horrocks commemorates him. In 1841, the Hawker brothers also established their Bungaree station just north of Clare and there too a few vines were planted. The foundation of the town of Clare (or Clareville as it was initially called) must be laid at the feet of an Irishman, Edmund Burton Gleeson, born where else but in County Clare. He had arrived in the district in 1840 and six years later he planned a village near a property of his, Inchiquin. He too was vinously inclined, having subscribed five pounds to Captain Sturt's Vine Association, a sum which gained him over 500 vines which he planted at Inchiquin. But regions and their villages and vineyards, in order to grow, need an economic imperative and this was provided by the discovery of copper at Burra in 1845. The copper was transported to the sea, not via Adelaide but across country by a road to Port Wakefield in the north of the Gulf of St Vincent, which traversed the countryside south of the settlement at Clare through present-day Mintaro, Watervale, Leasingham and Auburn, all of which, including the small village of Clare, enjoyed a copper-inspired prosperity. This copper boom, while not creating the wave of excitement that was to swamp Australia by the discoveries of gold in the eastern colonies a few years later, certainly provided a solid economic base for the permanence of the area. On the basis of this modest mining prosperity, the Clare district and its more southerly regions grew and when later the copper 'boom' was renewed by discoveries in the late 1850s at Moonta and Wallaroo, the prosperity remained. Though Clare suffered in the economic downturn of South Australia in the 1860s, it would rise again in the 1870s to enjoy the wheat boom of that period by becoming the rural centre for the mid-north wheatfields. There were, however, other influences that would also affect Clare.

Arriving in 1848, seeking respite from religious persecution, the Society of Jesus introduced a religious element into the Clare equation and initially settled near Neagle's Rock, south-west of the town. In 1851, intending to create a Catholic educational and cultural centre in emulation of Rome, the Jesuit Order founded a college south of Clare which they named Sevenhill in imitation of the Seven Hills of the Eternal City. Later the college became a school which educated as many as 450 boys, closing in 1887 due to competition from Adelaide. It was also a seminary for the training of priests. For sacremental purposes, the brothers planted vines in

CLARE VALLEY REGION

🍇 Emerald Estate

Jim Barry Wines 🍇

🍇 Knappstein Wines

● **Clare**
🍇 Leasingham

🍇 Wendouree Cellars
🍇 Tim Adams Wines

Sevenhill Cellars 🍇   🍇 Pikes

● **Sevenhill**   🍇 The Wilson Vineyard

Eldredge 🍇   🍇 Stringy Brae
                    Wines   🍇 Pauletts

Skillogalee 🍇   🍇 Waninga
Jeanneret Wines 🍇 🍇 Pearson Vineyards   Reilly's Wines 🍇
    Mitchell 🍇 ● **Penwortham**   ● **Mintaro**
Penwortham Cellars 🍇   🍇 Mintaro Wines

Olssens of Watervale 🍇
Crabtree of Watervale 🍇   🍇 Quelltaler Estate
                    ● **Watervale**

                    🍇 Clos Clare

Leasingham ● 🍇 Tim Gramp Wines

                    🍇 Taylors

                ● **Auburn**
                🍇 Grosset
                🍇 Mount Horrocks

Barrier   Highway

1852 and dug the first wine cellar in the region. In 1862, building began on the Collegiate Church, which was consecrated in 1875. Unlike school-teaching, however, winemaking was to continue to the present day.

About the same time as the foundation of Sevenhill, a wandering Cornishman, Francis Treloar, who had been modestly successful in a sojourn on the Victorian goldfields, decided to settle near present-day Watervale. He called his property Springvale and he too planted vines in 1853. By the 1890s, after passing through several hands, that property with a considerably enlarged vineyard was renamed Quelltaler by its owners Messrs Buring and Sobels.

The 1890s also saw a general wine boom throughout South Australia, with Clare playing a considerable part. One large and one small winery in particular were to endure to the present decade. The smaller was Birks Wendouree, Australia's first boutique winery. It was dedicated to quality then and remains so. Though it has undergone a change of ownership, it is otherwise unchanged to this day. The Stanley Wine Co was formed to fulfil a need that had been discerned earlier that decade— a winery to crush the many tonnes of grapes which were not subject to contract by the small number of wineries then present in the region. For this purpose the principals, including the outspoken John Christison (owner of the local brewery) had purchased and equipped an old jam factory. It suited well enough, but they continually lamented the vast amounts of money that it was consuming and its lack of return on capital. By 1912 it was under the control of one man, JH Knappstein. It was his family that took the Stanley Wine Co through the thick of the early and mid-twenties boom and the thin of the Great Depression until the next wine boom of the 1960s and ultimate sale by the Knappstein family to the Heinz Co in 1971. Another merger at this time also saw Quelltaler become part of the Melbourne wine distributor Nathan and Wyeth and later Remy Martin.

At this time also, Taylor's, a huge new vineyard and winery complex in Auburn at the southern end of the Clare Valley, was established. For its pains, the Taylor family, a very few years later, felt the anguish of the swing in Australian wine taste from red to white in the mid-1970s. The sale of Stanley paradoxically saw the rise of the Enterprise Wine Co, a venture of Tim Knappstein, in the same old brewery building that had once housed the original venture of John Christison. The wheel had turned full circle.

The 1990s see Mildara Blass in control of Quelltaler, Petaluma in possession of the Tim Knappstein Wines (formerly Enterprise), BRL Hardy owning Stanley (now renamed Leasingham), Taylor's remaining Taylor-made and the hand of God still upon Sevenhill. There are also many large companies with broadacres of vines, but wineries outside the Clare region. In addition there are many smaller winemaker/proprietors (all highly qualified former employees of large wine companies) with their own vineyards of varying sizes and many grower/proprietors with their own labels, who use their winemaking services. Today, there are over 25 wineries and vineyards with their own labels.

Location: latitude 33°50'S to 34°3'S, longitude 138°42'E to 138°44'E, about 140 km north of Adelaide. The Clare Valley region commences at Auburn in the south

(100 km north of Adelaide) and runs further north 40–45 km more, the vineyards ending just north of the town of Clare.

Elevation: 300–550 m

Topography and soils: Part of the northern Mount Lofty Ranges, the Clare Valley region is a central valley (through which the Main North Road passes) running basically south-north. As this valley runs north, it rises to a watershed around Sevenhill, and thereafter the main valley falls with a shallow gradient to the north. The principal townships of the Valley, Leasingham, Watervale, Penwortham, Sevenhill and Clare, all lie along this axis. To the west the regional boundary largely follows the 300 m contour, while between this boundary and parallel with the central valley is the important Skillogalee Valley. Altitudes in this area reach 450–550 m. To the east is an undulating ridge reaching altitudes of 450 m and further east still a more consistent ridge attains 500 m. This ridge incorporates Quarry Hill, Lodge Hill and Stony Point. In the middle of the region, to the east of the main valley, rises the highest point of the region, Mount Horrocks (608 m), which forms the head of the Hill River catchment, while the Camel's Hump Range comprises its right. Auburn, the first town of the Valley as one approaches from the south, lies on the Wakefield River at an altitude of 330 m. Here the country is much flatter, but the hills to the west mark the continuation of the Skillogalee Valley. The soils are quite variable. Red and yellow podsolic (Dr & Dy) soils often prevail on the hillsides, while on the valley floors there are red-brown earths with good water-holding capacity. In addition there are areas of deep friable black soil said to be specially suited to merlot. Subsoils also vary from clay through limestone to slatey shaley rock.

Climate: MJT 21.9°C, MAR 13.6°C, HDD raw 1774, AR 634 mm (Oct–Mar 182 mm), RH 47% (9am Jan) AI 426 mm, SH 8.8 (D&S), MJT 21.3, MAR na, HDD raw 1779, 1613 (cut off and adjusted for latitude daily temperature range and vine sites), AR 632 mm (Oct–Apr 245 mm), RH 32% (3pm Jan), AI na, SH 8.8 (Gladstones). The Clare climate is a paradox. The Dry & Smart HDD portrays Clare as a very warm viticultural area. Though Gladstones' HDD is more favourable to the production of the robust red table wines and fine rieslings, which after all are the Clare Valley's forte, he still suggests that his statistics relate to vineyards with a comparable altitude and latitude to that of the weather station. He also suggests that its location might have distorted the true vineyard situation to some extent (it was formerly sited at the post office in an enclosed courtyard on concrete paving in the centre of the town, close to such causes of urban warming as buildings and roads about 398 m in altitude). Thus he seems to imply that most of the region is cooler.

There may be other factors at work. One may be higher altitude, for example, such vineyards as Petaluma's Hanlins Hill Vineyard and others at Penwortham and Polish Hill River are nearly 100 m higher. A second factor is a different, more southerly latitude, for example, Watervale which has a similar altitude to Clare but is 15 km further south. A third may be the incidence of a cooling south-westerly sea breeze. A fourth could be different topographies, some vineyards being located on ridges with free air drainage in all directions, thus offsetting any tendencies to excessive heat. So perhaps the individual differences among the vineyards are the important factors, not any attempt to apply a uniform HDD to an entire region.

Traditionally (that is, pre-1975) viticulture in the Clare Valley was a dryland activity, confined to those areas where rainfall was highest and the vineyard soils sufficiently moisture-retentive (that is, valley bottoms or contour planted hillsides). However, the late 1970s and the 1980s saw the widespread introduction of drippers and the consequent increase in the areas considered suitable for viticulture. The ensuing demand for water witnessed such depletion of both underground and surface water resources that it caused great concern. In 1995 a 12-month moratorium was imposed on new water resource use, followed in July 1996 by a proclamation that limited any greater use of water to 500 kL per annum from proclaimed surface and/ or groundwater sources other than for domestic or stock purposes unless a licence was held. Water supplies also had to be metered. Thus vineyards within the proclaimed area must be managed within a limited water budget and therefore crop levels controlled. This of course has a beneficial effect on resultant fruit quality. It is for this reason that the Proclaimed Water Area boundary corresponds to that of the Clare Valley region.

Harvest time: Like other aspects of Clare regional viticulture, these are quite variable. Riesling in warmer areas of the region can ripen as early as the first week of March, but in cooler areas can be as late as mid-April. Shiraz has broadly the same ripening parameters—from second week of March in warmer areas to third week of April in those that are cooler. Cabernet sauvignon ripens from the fourth week of March in warmer locations to the end of April in colder spots.

Principal varieties: (1996) shiraz 664.15 ha, riesling 523.15 ha, cabernet sauvignon 517.42 ha, chardonnay 361.68 ha, semillon 164.81 ha

Total area: (1996) 2552.62 ha

Principal wine styles: It is an ancient cliché to speak of iron fists within velvet gloves, but regrettably such a cliché does fit Clare Shiraz. A young Clare Shiraz should be redolent of berries and black pepper, a nose which given time changes to ripe berries, but not to leather. Its youthful palate should have a good weight of open berry flavour and a firm but not harsh or extractive structure of tannin and acid. With bottle age the palate should soften and harmonise, retaining a soft and silky berry fruitiness. Again such wines can be aged up to 15 years.

In its best years, a young Riesling from Clare shows marginally tropical aromas which soon change to lime citrus with a light floral overlay and then, after a year or so in bottle, to a very slight 'toast' character. The palate should be fresh, again lime citrusy in flavour but tending after a little time to broader floral-lime flavours. Finishing acidity may be crisp, but should at all times be integrated and not harsh, neither should the wine be too soft and round in the mouth. With bottle age the wine becomes toasty, both on nose and palate, though never giving the impression of tiredness or oxidation. The best Clare Rieslings can live for 8–12 years.

Clare Cabernet Sauvignon is usually bigger and firmer in most respects than Clare Shiraz, having a deep purple colour, a nose of berries, mint and spice and a similar youthful palate with size, concentration and firmness to match. With age (12–15 years), such reds soften into a velvety harmony of berries and mint, though always giving the impression of ripeness and warmth, albeit with a certain firmness on finish.

Semillon usually wood-matured, a sophistication that increases harmony and adds distinction. The nose of young wooded Clare Semillon should show ripe lemon and vanilla aromas, its palate will be of similar flavours though revealing a soft fullness that makes such wines excellent drinking after 1–2 years. I have not tasted such wines of any age and am reluctant to recommend any ageing period beyond 2–3 years, as I doubt whether they have the structure of, say, Hunter Semillon in its best years.

Perhaps Chardonnay, a variety often described as 'most forgiving', is at its least lenient in Clare. Not that it always makes bad wine—the excellent Clare Chardonnays of Hardy's and Penfolds prove the contrary—but perhaps it is somehow aware that, standing as it does in the shadow of a great Riesling tradition, it is often undistinguished.

Brian Barry (vineyard only) R7

Farrell Flat Road, Clare, SA 5453
Ph 08 8363 6211, Fax 08 8362 0498

Owner: Brian Barry
Chief winemaker: Brian Barry
Year of foundation: 1976
Tonnes crushed on average each year: 170, of which 95 are used for the Brian Barry labels
Location: East Clare
Area: 33 ha
Soils: rich red loam over limestone, deep friable black soils
Varieties planted: White—chardonnay, riesling; Red—cabernet sauvignon, merlot, shiraz
Leading wines: Brian Barry Jud's Hill Riesling, Chardonnay, Cabernet Sauvignon, Merlot
Notes: Brian Barry is one of Australia's most experienced winemakers and wine judges and now makes his own wines using the facilities of Petaluma. Jud's Hill, 500 m in altitude and planted on red and black loam over limestone, is a typical dry grown Clare vineyard about 1.5 km east of the town. Unusually in this age of mechanisation, all grapes are hand-picked. His Rieslings are among my favourites and with the Cabernet Sauvignon are consistent medal winners. Five wines entered at the 1997 Clare Valley Wine Show won five awards. No cellar door sales.

Clos Clare NR

Government Road, Watervale, SA 5452
about 1 km south of town
Ph/Fax 08 8843 0161

Owner: Noel Kelly
Chief winemaker: Jeffrey Grosset (riesling, contract); Barossa Valley Estates (shiraz, contract)
Year of foundation: 1993
Tonnes crushed on average each year: 12, about half of which are used for the Clos Clare label
Location: Watervale (part of the old Leo Buring Florita vineyard)
Area: 2.125 ha
Soils: terra over limestone
Varieties planted: White—riesling, sauvignon blanc; Red—none
Leading wines: Clos Clare Riesling, Shiraz
Notes: Clos Clare is a small vineyard whose wines, being made by Jeffrey Grosset, are assured of a certain pedigree. The Clos Clare Shiraz is made from purchased grapes. Cellar door sales: weekends and public holidays 10am–5pm.

Crabtree of Watervale R6.5

North Terrace, Watervale, SA 5452
Ph 08 8843 0069, Fax 08 8843 0144

Owner: Robert and Elizabeth Crabtree
Chief winemakers: Robert Crabtree and Stuart Bourne

Year of foundation: 1981
Tonnes crushed on average each year: 95,
about 85 of which are used for the Crabtree
of Watervale own labels
Location: Watervale (winery)
Area: 13.5 ha
Soils: There are three types of soil on the
Crabtree vineyard, loam on a limestone and
shale base (riesling), a lighter sandy loam
(shiraz) and heavier black soils (cabernet
sauvignon)
Varieties planted: White—pedro ximenes,
riesling, semillon; Red—cabernet sauvignon,
grenache, shiraz
Leading wines: Crabtree of Watervale Riesling,
Shiraz-Cabernet Sauvignon
Notes: Robert Crabtree is an experienced Clare
vigneron and his Riesling is well in the
mainstream of Clare style. Cellar door sales:
7 days 11am–5pm, occasionally closed
Tuesdays or Wednesdays.

Eldredge NR

Spring Gully Road, Clare, SA 5453
Ph/Fax 08 8842 3086

Owners: Leigh and Karen Eldredge
Chief winemaker: Leigh Eldredge
Year of foundation: 1992
Tonnes crushed on average each year: 50
(presently purchased from growers)
Location: Clare
Area: 2 ha but plantings will increase
Soils: sandy loams over gravel and schist
Varieties planted: White—none as yet;
Red—sangiovese, shiraz
Leading wines: Eldredge Vineyards Watervale
Riesling, Cabernet Sauvignon, Semillon-
Sauvignon Blanc, Blue Chip Shiraz, New Age
Grenache, Clare Valley Gold Late Harvest
Riesling
Notes: Only established since 1992, Leigh
Eldredge has had a marvellous run in wine
shows in the past few years. A gold at the
Adelaide Wine Show and Hyatt Wine of the

Year for 1997 Riesling, and a gold at Clare. His
Cabernet 95 was also the winner of a gold
and the trophy at Adelaide for best varietal
Cabernet. Cellar door sales: 7 days 11am–5pm.
Restaurant also open for lunch, Friday,
Saturday, Sunday and public holidays.

Emerald Estate NR

Main North Road, Stanley Flat, Clare,
SA 5453
Ph 08 8842 3296, Fax 08 8842 2220

Owners: DC and GC Carroll
Chief winemaker: Tim Adams (contract)
Year of foundation: 1990
Tonnes crushed on average each year: 143 and
increasing (of which 32 tonnes are currently
used for Emerald Estate labels)
Location: Stanley Flat
Area: 18 ha
Soils: terra rossa over limestone and dark river
loam
Varieties planted: White—chardonnay, riesling,
semillon; Red—cabernet sauvignon, pinot noir,
shiraz
Leading wines: Emerald Estate Shiraz,
Chardonnay, Cabernet Sauvignon, Riesling
Notes: A Clare name new to me and most of
its fruit is sold, but Tim Adams is an excellent
winemaker. Cellar door sales: Thurs–Mon
10am–5pm.

Grosset R10

1 Manoora Road, Auburn, SA 5451
Ph 08 8849 2175, Fax 08 8849 2292

Owner/chief winemaker: Jeffrey Grosset
Year of foundation: 1981
Tonnes crushed on average each year: 200,
about 140 of which are used for the Grosset
labels
Location: (winery) Auburn, (vineyards)
Watervale, Polish Hill River Valley
Area: 9 ha
Soils: (Polish Hill) clay over gravel with

underlying shale and slates; (Watervale) red
loam over limestone
Varieties planted: White—riesling; Red—
cabernet franc, cabernet sauvignon, merlot
Leading wines: Grosset Polish Hill Riesling,
Watervale Riesling, Gaia (a red blended from
the red varieties mentioned above), Piccadilly
Chardonnay
Notes: Jeffrey Grosset is a winemaker of
excellence, commended internationally for his
Rieslings and also for Gaia, a superbly
structured Clare red that combines the wealth
of blackcurrent richness of Clare cabernet
sauvignon with elegant structure of cabernet
franc and the soft, plummy generosity of
merlot. It has been compared to a young
Bordeaux, but such comparisons are odious.
It is something quite different—a perfectly
ripened Clare cabernet blend showing strength,
complexity and elegant style, which can stand
quite independently of foreign comparison.
It is a red that is uniquely Clare. He also makes
another acclaimed white—Piccadilly
Chardonnay. Cellar door sales: from the first
weekend in September, Wed–Sun 10am–5pm
while stocks last.

Jeanneret Wines NR

Jeanneret Road, Sevenhill, SA 5453
Ph 08 8843 4308, Fax 08 8843 4351

Owners: Patricia and Denis Jeanneret
Chief winemaker: Ben Jeanneret
Year of foundation: 1994
Tonnes crushed on average each year: 45
Location: Sevenhill
Area: 4 ha
Soils: varying from red clay over limestone to a
rich dark sandy loam
Varieties planted: White—riesling, semillon;
Red—cabernet sauvignon, muscat, shiraz
Leading wines: Jeanneret Riesling, Semillon,
Cabernet Sauvignon, Shiraz
Notes: This is a small family-operated winery in
an attractive lakeside setting. All practice is

organic and all fruit is dry grown. Cellar door
sales: each day 9am–5pm except Christmas
Day and Good Friday.

Jim Barry Wines R8

Main North Road, Clare, SA 5453
Ph 08 8842 2261, Fax 08 8842 3752

Owners: Jim Barry family
Chief winemaker: Mark Barry
Year of foundation: 1959
Tonnes crushed on average each year: 1000
Location: Clare
Area: 160 ha
Soils: chiefly red-brown loam over clay and
limestone; some cracking clay (Biscay)
Varieties planted: White—chardonnay, riesling,
sauvignon blanc, semillon; Red—cabernet
sauvignon, malbec, merlot, shiraz
Leading wines: The Armagh (Shiraz), McCrae
Wood Shiraz, McCrae Wood Cabernet-Malbec,
Port
Notes: Peter Barry notices a great demand for
reds these days both at home and overseas
and with styles such as The Armagh and
McCrae Wood Shiraz, it is no wonder.
Cellar door sales: 7 days 9am–4pm.

Knappstein Wines R9

2 Pioneer Ave, Clare, SA 5453
Ph 08 8842 2600, Fax 08 8842 3831

Owner: Petaluma Limited
Chief winemaker: Andrew Hardy
Year of foundation: 1976
Tonnes crushed on average each year: 650
Location: Clare
Area: 95 ha
Soils: red-brown loam over limestone (terra
rossa)
Varieties planted: White—chardonnay,
gewurztraminer, riesling, sauvignon blanc,
semillon; Red—cabernet franc, cabernet
sauvignon, malbec, merlot, shiraz
Leading wines: Knappstein Hand Picked

Riesling, Enterprise Cabernet Sauvignon, Enterprise Shiraz

Notes: Founded by eminent winemaker and show judge Tim Knappstein, who now makes excellent wines in the Adelaide Hills, the winery was sold to Wolf Blass Wines some years ago and later sold to Petaluma, the present owner. Its wines, now made by Andrew Hardy, former disciple of Brian Croser, are excellent. On the Clare scale, the whites are crisp and refreshing rather than full-bodied and the reds also tend to elegance rather than weight. Cellar door sales: weekdays 9m–5pm, Sat 11am–5pm, Sun 11am–4pm, all public holidays except Christmas Day and Good Friday.

Leasingham **R10**

7 Dominic Street, Clare, SA 5453
Ph 08 8842 2555, Fax 08 8842 3293

Owner: BRL Hardy Limited
Chief winemaker: Richard Rowe
Year of foundation: 1893
Tonnes crushed on average each year: 4000 (about 2000 tonnes of which are used for Leasingham labels)
Location: Clare (winery), with Rogers vineyard 7 km north-east, Provis vineyard 4 km east and Dunn's 4 km south-east of the town; Leasingham (Schobers vineyard 3 km south of the village)
Area: 350 ha
Soils: (Rogers and Provis) variable soils, predominantly red loam over limestone and slate with some areas of shallow grey soils over slate; (Dunn's) predominantly deep terra rossa with small areas of shallow grey soils over grey slate; (Schobers) 30 cm of red loam over limestone with shaley slate sections on an exposed wind-swept hill in a rain shadow
Varieties planted: White—chardonnay, chenin blanc, riesling, sauvignon blanc, semillon; Red—cabernet franc, cabernet sauvignon, grenache, malbec, merlot, pinot noir, shiraz
Leading wines: Leasingham Classic Clare

Shiraz, Riesling, Cabernet Sauvignon; Bin range, Bin 7 Riesling, Bin 37 Chardonnay, Bin 42 Semillon-Sauvignon Blanc, Bin 56 Cabernet-Malbec

Notes: Leasingham winery is the old Stanley winery which was established in the heady South Australian wine boom days of 1893 and was for years owned by the Knappstein family and later by Heinz. After its purchase by BRL Hardy, it dropped the Stanley name some years ago and has since been successfully transformed into a 'boutique' (though it still crushes about 4000 tonnes of grapes a year). It crushes only local fruit and maximises the quality reputation of the Clare region for delicate Rieslings, and massive, almost earth-moving Shiraz and Cabernet reds which, despite their 'size', retain an amazing fruit softness on palate. Quality over the whole range is excellent. Cellar door sales: Mon–Fri 8.30am–5pm, weekends and public holidays 10am–4pm.

Mintaro Wines **R7.5**

Leasingham Road, Mintaro, SA 5415
Ph 08 8843 9046, Fax 08 8843 9050

Owner/chief winemaker: Peter Houldsworth
Year of foundation: 1985
Tonnes crushed on average each year: 40
Location: Mintaro, about 13 km south-east of Clare
Area: 10 ha
Soils: terra rossa over limestone
Varieties planted: White—riesling; Red—cabernet franc, cabernet sauvignon, shiraz
Leading wines: Mintaro Wines Riesling
Note: This is a small but consistently good performer at regional and state wine shows, whose best product is usually Clare's speciality—Riesling. Cellar door sales: 7 days 9am–5pm.

Mitchell R9

Hughes Park Road, Sevenhill, SA 5453
Ph 08 8843 4258, Fax 08 8843 4340

Owners: Andrew and Jane Mitchell
Chief winemaker: Andrew Mitchell
Year of foundation: 1975
Tonnes crushed on average each year: 500
Locations: Sevenhill and Watervale
Area: 55 ha
Soils: (Sevenhill) sandy loam over gravelly
subsoil; (Watervale) red loam over deep
crumbly limestone
Varieties planted: White—riesling, semillon;
Red—cabernet sauvignon, grenache, shiraz
Leading wines: Mitchell Sevenhill Vineyard
Cabernet, Watervale Riesling, Peppertree
Vineyard Shiraz, Growers Grenache, Growers
Semillon
Notes: Mitchell is one of the leading smaller
wineries of the Clare region (indeed with a
crush of 500 tonnes, not so small these days).
The Cabernet and Shiraz reds, when young,
are rich and robust and age harmoniously.
They are typical of the top wines of the region.
The Riesling is aromatic and charming, easy to
drink when youthful, but with the usual
regional ability to age very gracefully. Cellar
door sales: 7 days 10am–4pm (as the maker
adds, 'when stocks are available').

Mount Horrocks R8

Auburn Railway Station, Auburn,
SA 5451
Ph/Fax 08 8849 2243, 08 8849 2202

Owner/chief winemaker: Stephanie Toole
Year of foundation: 1982
Tonnes crushed on average each year: 80
Location: (vineyard) Watervale
Area: 7 ha
Soils: red loam over limestone
Varieties planted: White—chardonnay, riesling,
semillon; Red—shiraz
Leading wines: Mount Horrocks Riesling,
Cordon Cut Riesling, Shiraz
Notes: Stephanie Toole has owned the Mount
Horrocks label for some years and using her
partner Jeffrey Grosset's nearby winery she
makes excellent Rieslings, both dry and sweet.
In addition she has now made her first Shiraz,
a 1996, which, in a search for subtlety and
style, has been matured in French oak rather
than American. In other times, the railway
station was the most important building in
town. These days, the trains rarely run on
time—or at all. So Stephanie Toole conceived
the marvellous idea of making the local station
popular again. Her Auburn refreshment rooms
are open for tasting on weekends and public
holidays, 11am–5pm. But do not try to arrive
by train.

Old Station Vineyard (vineyard only) NR

Watervale, SA 5452
Ph/Fax 02 9144 1925

Owners: Bill and Noel Ireland
Chief winemaker: David O'Leary (contract)
Year of foundation: vineyard planted 1926, Old
Station label from 1995
Tonnes crushed on average each year: 59
Location: Watervale
Area: 6 ha
Soils: red loam over limestone
Varieties planted: White—pedro, riesling;
Red—grenache, shiraz
Leading wines: Old Station Riesling, Shiraz,
Grenache Shiraz
Notes: This is a 'retirement' diversion for
former Sydney retailer Bill Ireland, who
obviously enjoys his life in wine. The pedro
ximenes will be grafted to shiraz in the next
2–3 years. No cellar door sales.

Olssens of Watervale NR

Unnamed road, an extension of North
Terrace, Watervale, SA 5452 (about
3 km north-west of the village)
Ph/Fax 08 8843 0065

Owners: Kevin and Helen Olssen
Chief winemaker: Andrew Mitchell (contract)
with assistance from Kevin Olssen
Year of foundation: vineyard 1979, label 1994
Tonnes crushed on average each year: 45 (of
which about 10 are used for the Olssen label);
this is likely to increase as new plantings come
into full bearing
Location: Watervale
Area: 5 ha
Soils: variable but chiefly red clay loams over
slatey, shaley rock
Varieties planted: White—chardonnay, riesling,
semillon; Red—caberent franc, cabernet
sauvignon, merlot
Leading wines: Olssens of Watervale Riesling,
Cabernet Sauvignon-Cabernet Franc-Merlot,
Semillon
Notes: Yet another of the footsoldiers of
Australian viticulture, this is a small family
owned vineyard whose proprietors are keenly
interested in their region and its quality. Such
vineyards are so essential to the growth and
development of Australian wine and help to
maintain the enthusiasm and momentum of
the Australian wine industry. The Olssens have
not shown their wines until recently when their
Riesling won a creditable bronze at the Clare
Valley Wine Show. Cellar door sales: (subject to
change) Mondays, Fridays, weekends and
public holidays 11am–5pm, other times by
appointment.

Pauletts R8

Polish Hill River Road, via Sevenhill,
SA 5453
Ph 08 8843 4328, Fax 08 8843 4202

Owners: Neil and Alison Paulett
Chief winemaker: Neil Paulett
Year of foundation: 1983
Tonnes crushed on average each year: 200
Location: Polish Hill River Valley
Area: 10 ha
Soils: variable red-brown clayey loam, grey
sandy loam and Biscay over slatey sandstone;
subsoil acidic
Varieties planted: White—chardonnay, riesling,
sauvignon blanc; Red—cabernet sauvignon,
merlot, shiraz
Leading wines: Paulett Riesling, Shiraz
Notes: Neil Paulett is an experienced and skilful
winemaker. He began his winemaking self-
employment in 1983, a year of turmoil for
Clare with bushfires and floods all manifesting
before and during vintage. However, Pauletts is
now firmly established and making excellent
award-winning Riesling and Shiraz which after
all is the mainstream of Clare winemaking.
Cellar door sales: 7 days 10am–5pm, except
Christmas Day and Good Friday.

Pearson Vineyards NR

Main North Road, Penwortham,
SA 5453 (western side of main road
in the village)
Ph 08 8843 4234, Fax 08 8843 4141

Owners: Jim and Trish Pearson
Chief winemaker: Jim Pearson
Year of foundation: 1993
Tonnes crushed on average each year: 15
Location: Penwortham
Area: 2 ha
Soils: clayey-loam soils
Varieties planted: White—riesling, semillon;
Red—cabernet franc, cabernet sauvignon,
malbec
Leading wines: Pearsons Riesling, Cabernet
Franc
Notes: This is a tiny vineyard of dry-grown,
hand-pruned and harvested vines and a winery
planned for the 1998 vintage. Cellar door

sales: weekdays noon–5pm, weekends and public holidays 11am–5pm.

Penfolds Clare Estate (vineyard only) R9

Quarry Road, Clare, SA 5453

Owner: Southcorp Wines
Chief winemaker: John Duval
Year of foundation: 1980
Tonnes crushed on average each year: not disclosed but estimated at 1800
Location: Clare
Area: 179.4 ha
Soils: shallow red-brown earth over broken clay and slate subsoils, red-brown earth clay loam over clay Biscay on creek flats
Varieties planted: White—chardonnay, riesling, semillon; Red—cabernet franc, cabernet sauvignon, malbec, merlot, petit verdot
Leading wines: Penfolds Clare Estate Chardonnay, Penfolds Organic Red, Organic White
Notes: The Clare Estate produces a consistently good blend of the classic 'Bordeaux' red varieties, which tends to elegance rather than weight. However, it is well worth cellaring for the medium term. The Chardonnay is also good, but sometimes a rather simple style without the ultimate complexity of Penfolds Chardonnays from the Adelaide Hills. No local cellar door sales.

Penwortham Cellars NR

Government Road, Penwortham, SA 5453
Ph 08 8843 4345, Fax 08 8843 4100

Owners: Richard and Anne Hughes
Chief winemaker: Richard Hughes
Year of foundation: 1985
Tonnes crushed on average each year: 13
Location: Penwortham
Area: 8 ha (5 ha of which are not yet bearing)
Soils: an undulating vineyard with heavy loam soils over limestone

Varieties planted: White—riesling; Red—cabernet sauvignon, shiraz
Leading wines: Penwortham Riesling, Unwooded Cabernet Sauvignon, Unwooded Shiraz
Notes: Penwortham Cellars is another small maker whose Rieslings have won medals at capital city and regional shows. Unusually there is also an Unwooded Cabernet Sauvignon and an Unwooded Shiraz. Cellar door sales: Sat 10am–5pm, Sun and public holidays 10am–4pm.

Petaluma (vineyard only) R10

Hanlin's Hill, Clare, SA 5453

Owner: Petaluma Limited
Chief winemaker: Brian Croser
Year of foundation: (vineyard) 1968
Tonnes crushed on average each year: 200
Location: Hanlin's Hill and Yertabulti about 3 km east of Clare
Area: 29.7 ha
Soils: red-brown loam over slate
Varieties planted: White—chardonnay, riesling, sauvignon blanc; Red—malbec, shiraz
Leading wine: Petaluma Riesling
Notes: The quintessential estate white has come from the same source since the vineyard's acquisition by Petaluma with never a sign of being blended with riesling from elsewhere. Typical of and often the elegant best of its region. When young it is usually a pale green colour with an attractive lime-citrus nose and a crisp refreshing palate, but such a description is mere generalisation. The wine must be tasted. It ages well also. The other varieties are usually blended into the Bridgewater Mill range. No local cellar door sales.

Pikes R8

Polish Hill River Road, Sevenhill, SA 5453
Ph 08 8843 4370, Fax 08 8843 4353

Owners: Pike family
Chief winemaker: Neil Pike
Year of foundation: 1984
Tonnes crushed on average each year: 375
Location: Polish Hill River Valley
Area: 34 ha
Soils: red-brown earth over clay with slate and broken bluestone subsoil, well drained
Varieties planted: White—chardonnay, riesling, sauvignon blanc, semillon; Red—cabernet franc, cabernet sauvignon, merlot, pinot noir, sangiovese, shiraz
Leading wines: Pikes Riesling, Shiraz, Chardonnay, Cabernet-Merlot, Sauvignon Blanc
Notes: Neil Pike produces very good whites (Riesling in particular) and reds (excellent Shiraz), which are typical of the region.
Cellar door sales: 7 days 10am–4pm.

Quelltaler Estate   **R9**

Quelltaler Road, Watervale, SA 5452
Ph 08 8843 0003, Fax 08 8843 0096

Owner: Mildara Blass
Chief Winemaker: Alan Hart
Year of foundation: 1853
Tonnes crushed on average each year: 3600
Locations: Watervale and Polish Hill River
Area: 320 ha
Soils: red loam over limestone and red loam over slate
Varieties planted: White—chardonnay, riesling, semillon; Red—cabernet franc, cabernet sauvignon, merlot, petit verdot, shiraz
Leading wines: Annies Lane Riesling, Cabernet-Merlot, Chardonnay, Shiraz, Semillon
Notes: The Quelltaler Estate is a treasure indeed with the old bluestone winery (commenced in 1863) solidly ensconsed on its hill overlooking Watervale. The original vineyard on the site was planted in 1853 by John Treloar, who called it 'Springvale'. It was later sold to Sir Walter Hughes, a mining magnate, who left it by will to his nephew, JM Richman. He in turn sold to the partnership

of Hermann Buring and Carl Sobels in 1890 and they germanicised the name to Quelltaler. For much of the twentieth century it was owned by Buring and Sobels, which had by that time become a company. Its famous products included Quelltaler Hock and Granfiesta Sherry but, by 1960, it had become effectively merged with its national distributor, Nathan and Wyeth. That company itself was taken over by the cognac producer, Remy Martin, which in 1990 sold the estate to Mildara Blass. For a time in the 1980s and 1990s, the wines held a low profile and the Quelltaler name was all but forgotten. Today Riesling is still an important part of its production (for Watervale is wholeheartedly riesling country). The brand name Annies Lane is named after Annie Wayman, whose horse and cart became bogged one day almost a century ago when on her way to feed some pruners. Cellar door sales: weekdays 8.30am–5pm, weekends and public holidays 11am–4pm.

Reilly's Wines   **NR**

Cnr Hill and Burra Streets, Mintaro, SA 5415
Ph 08 8843 9013, Fax 08 8337 4111

Owner: Reilly's Wines (a partnership)
Chief winemaker: Justin Ardill
Year of foundation: 1994
Tonnes crushed on average each year: 24
Location: Mintaro
Area: 5 ha
Soils: rich red loam over limestone or shale
Varieties planted: White—riesling; Red—cabernet sauvignon, grenache, shiraz
Leading wines: Reilly's Wines Old Bush Vine Grenache, Riesling (dry and late-picked), Dry Land Shiraz, Port
Notes: This is a small dry land vineyard and winery concentrating on older vines, in particular bush vines, so prized now in older areas of South Australia (contrast the vine pull

scheme of 1986 when many hectares of such vines of then unfashionable varieties were uprooted). The resultant reds are usually big and generous in flavour. Reilly's Wines also markets its own olive oil gathered from the wild olive trees so prevalent in those warmer climates of the state. Cellar door sales: weekends and public holidays 10am–5pm.

Sevenhill Cellars R9.5

College Road, Sevenhill, SA 5453
(7 km south of Clare)
Ph 08 8843 4222, Fax 08 8843 4382

Owner: Society of Jesus
Chief winemaker: Brother John May SJ
winemaker John Monten
Year of foundation: 1851
Tonnes crushed on average each year: 400
Location: Sevenhill
Area: 59 ha
Soils: variable, Biscay, red loam over limestone, light sandy shaley soils and red loam over clay
Varieties planted: White—chardonnay, chenin blanc, frontignac (red, white, black and brown), muscadelle, pedro ximines, riesling, semillon, verdelho; Red—cabernet franc, cabernet sauvignon, grenache, malbec, merlot, ruby cabernet, shiraz, touriga
Leading wines: Sevenhill Cellars Cabernet Sauvignon, Shiraz, St Ignatius (a blend of the 'Bordeaux' varieties mentioned above), St Aloysius (a rare blend of chardonnay, chenin blanc and verdelho), and sacramental wine
Notes: Sevenhill Cellars is the oldest wine establishment in the Clare region and its wines epitomise the spirit of the region. When wineries and distilleries belonging to religious orders are mentioned we imagine cowled monks hurrying along ivied cloisters with secret formulas. Certainly there are buildings which evoke that atmosphere but, thanks to Brother John May, Sevenhill today is a technically advanced, very modern winery. Its reds in particular are of an excellent standard. Cellar

door sales: weekdays 8.30am–4.30pm, Saturdays and public holidays 9am–4pm, closed Sundays, Christmas Day, New Year's Day and Good Friday.

Skillogalee R7.5

off Hughes Park Road, Sevenhill via Clare, SA 5453
Ph 08 8843 4311, Fax 08 8843 4343

Owners: Dave and Diana Palmer
Chief winemaker: Dave Palmer
Year of foundation: 1969
Tonnes crushed on average each year: 95
Location: Skillogalee Valley, west of the Main North Road, about 8 km south of Clare
Area: 25 ha
Soils: red podsols
Varieties planted: White—chardonnay, riesling, traminer, white frontignac; Red—cabernet franc, cabernet sauvignon, malbec, shiraz
Leading wines: Skillogalee Riesling, Shiraz, The Cabernets
Notes: Bounded on the west by the Spring Gully National Park, Skillogalee enjoys a charming setting in its secluded valley at the western end of the Sevenhill area, having a slightly cooler location and a slightly higher rainfall than the valleys to the east. It is a consistent award winner at wine shows, its specialities being those of the region as a whole—flavoursome, full-bodied reds and good Riesling. It has a restaurant open for lunch, morning and afternoon tea. Cellar door sales: 7 days 10am–5pm.

Stephen John Wines NR

Watervale, SA 5452 (about 1 km west of the Watervale Hotel)
Ph/Fax 08 8843 0105

Owners: Rita and Stephen John
Chief winemaker: Stephen John
Year of foundation: 1994
Tonnes crushed on average each year: 100,

about half of which is used for the Stephen John labels

Locations: Watervale and Clare

Area: 5.5 ha (Watervale), 16 ha (Clare)

Soils: terra rossa on limestone and slate, Biscay over limestone

Varieties planted: White—chardonnay, pedro ximines, riesling; Red—cabernet sauvignon, shiraz

Leading wines: Stephen John Watervale Riesling, Watervale Chardonnay, Clare Valley Shiraz, Clare Valley Cabernet Sauvignon, Sparkling Red NV, Watervale Pedro Ximines (a lightly oaked dry white)

Notes: Stephen John is a member of the well-known Barossa family of coopers and winemakers. In his own right he is an eminent wine judge and a well-known winemaker, formerly employed as chief winemaker at Quelltaler by Mildara Blass. Having taken the road to independence, he has chosen the prestigious Watervale area to pursue his profession. His extremely cool Watervale vineyard, east-facing and 500 m in altitude, has seen snow three times in the last seven years and, like most of Watervale, favours riesling. No cellar door sales as yet.

Stringy Brae Wines NR

Sawmill Road, Sevenhill, SA 5453
Ph/Fax 08 8843 4313

Owners: Donald and Sally Wilson

Chief winemaker: Andrew Mitchell (contract)

Year of foundation: 1991

Tonnes crushed on average each year: 20 but increasing to 110 tonnes by 2000

Location: Sevenhill

Area: 9 ha

Soils: loam limestone and clay

Varieties planted: White—riesling; Red—cabernet sauvignon, shiraz

Leading wines: Stringy Brae Riesling, Shiraz, Cabernet Sauvignon

Notes: Stringy Brae is a low-key family-operated winery with plans for expansion. It has just started to show its wines and wisely relies on the staple grape varieties of the Clare region. At the 1997 Clare Show, it received a gold for Shiraz and a bronze for Riesling. Cellar door sales: weekends and public holdiays 10am–5pm, at other times refer to road signs.

Taylors R7

Taylors Road, Auburn, SA 5451
Ph 08 8849 2008, Fax 08 8849 2240

Owner: Taylors Wines Pty Limited

Chief winemaker: Neil Jericho (acting)

Year of foundation: 1969

Tonnes crushed on average each year: 2500

Location: Auburn

Area: 480 ha but growing (another 240 ha will be planted in the near future)

Soils: red-brown loam over limestone

Varieties planted: White—chardonnay, crouchen, riesling; Red—cabernet sauvignon, pinot noir, shiraz

Leading wines: Taylors Cabernet Sauvignon, Shiraz

Notes: Taylors was founded at the height of the red wine boom in the late 1960s. The subsequent progression of Australian tastes to white wine caused a certain disturbance to Taylors' red wine plans, but the company subsequently overcame this. In style, Taylors' Riesling conforms very pleasantly to Clare quality and the reds are usually offered with a little bottle maturity and this makes for easier drinking (which is no bad thing). However, they tend to be on the lighter side when compared to the mainstream of Clare regional reds. Cellar door sales: weekdays 9am–5pm, Saturdays and public holidays 10am–5pm, Sundays 10am–4pm, closed Christmas Day and Good Friday.

Tim Adams Wines R9

Warenda Road, Clare, SA 5453
(about 3 km south of the town)
Ph 08 8842 2429, Fax 08 8842 3550

Owners: Tim Adams, Pam Goldsack, Grant and
Jackie Crawley
Chief winemaker: Tim Adams
Year of foundation: 1987
Tonnes crushed on average each year: 250
Location: Clare
Area: 8.4 ha two vineyards, Winery (0.4 ha)
and She Oaks (8 ha), 15 km south of Clare
Soils: varying from friable red loam over
limestone to dark podsolic over dark clay
Varieties planted: White—riesling, semillon;
Red—cabernet franc, cabernet sauvignon,
grenache, malbec, shiraz
Leading wines: Tim Adams Aberfeldy Shiraz,
Semillon, The Fergus (a blend of grenache and
other red varieties), Riesling
Notes: Since his departure from Hardy's
Leasingham winery over 10 years ago, Tim
Adams has built a formidable reputation for
Shiraz. His grenache-dominant blend The
Fergus is also excellent, as is the Semillon,
which is complex and very worthy of the
much-maligned epithet 'classic'. This just leaves
his Riesling, which is always very good. As well
as making his own wines, Tim does
considerable amounts of contract winemaking.
Cellar door sales: weekdays 10.30am–5pm,
weekends and public holidays 11am–5pm.

Tim Gramp Wines NR

Mintaro Road, Leasingham, SA 5452
(2 km south of Watervale)
Ph 08 8843 0199

Owner: Tim Gramp
Chief winemaker: Tim Gramp
Year of foundation: 1990
Tonnes crushed on average each year: 50
Location: Leasingham
Area: 2 ha

Soils: brown to red loam over limestone, sandy
loam over limestone
Varieties planted: White—none; Red—cabernet
sauvignon
Leading wines: Tim Gramp Riesling, Shiraz,
Cabernet Sauvignon
Notes: Tim Gramp has five generations of
winemaking ancestry so it was only natural
that one day he would wish to make his own
wine. He began in 1991 with a tremendous
Tim Gramp Shiraz, not from Clare but from
McLaren Vale, a place for which he still has
more than a passing regard. In early 1996, Tim
purchased the Mount Horrocks site at
Leasingham with 2 ha of adjacent cabernet
sauvignon vineyard. With this fruit in addition
to other growers' fruit, Tim is beginning to
establish his Clare identity, though McLaren
Vale fruit will feature on the menu for some
time yet. Cellar door sales: weekends and
public holidays 10.30am–4.30pm.

Waninga NR

Hughes Park Road, Sevenhill via Clare,
SA 5453
Ph/Fax 08 8843 4395

Owners: Graham and Ethel Mill, Bob Ling, Ken
Foggo, Hilary Taylor
Chief winemakers: Tim Adams, Jeffrey Grosset
(contract)
Year of foundation: (vineyard) 1979, (cellar
door sales) 1989
Tonnes crushed on average each year: 250 of
which 25 are used for the Waninga labels
Location: Sevenhill, west of the Main North
Road, in the Skilly Hills midway between
Sevenhill and Penwortham
Area: 38 ha
Soils: red-brown loam over rock and clay with
sandy loams elsewhere
Varieties planted: White—chardonnay, chenin
blanc, riesling, semillon; Red—cabernet
sauvignon, shiraz

Leading wines: Waninga riesling, Shiraz, Chardonnay

Notes: Waninga is a large vineyard supplying fruit to, among others, Tim Adams and Jeffrey Grosset who are its contract winemakers. Its wines are consistent medal winners at the Clare Regional Wine Show. Cellar door sales: weekends, public and school holidays 10am–5pm.

Wendouree Cellars R10

Wendouree Road, Clare, SA 5453 (about 3 km south-east of town, adjacent to the isolated Stony Point Range)
Ph 08 8842 2896

Owners: Liberman family
Chief winemaker: Tony Brady
Year of foundation: 1893
Tonnes crushed on average each year: 50
Location: Clare
Area: 10.5 ha
Soils: friable red loam over clay, and shallow soils over limestone
Varieties planted: White—muscat of Alexandria; Red—cabernet franc, cabernet sauvignon, malbec, mourvedre, shiraz
Leading wines: Wendouree Shiraz, Shiraz-Mataro (Mourvedre), Shiraz-Malbec, Cabernet Sauvignon
Notes: In a sense, Wendouree Cellars is Australia's oldest boutique vineyard. Its wines I imagine are much the same as they were a century ago—quintessentially Clare and of course red, big wines intended for people with cellars and patience, much the same as people were a century ago. In the meantime, the Birks family has come and gone from Wendouree and Tony and Lita Brady carry the Wendouree

torch and the Birks' tradition, in much the same way as the Olympic torch is carried, reverently and with great care. The reds are still made beautifully and intended for medium- to long-term cellaring, about 10 years minimum. Cellar door sales by arrangement.

The Wilson Vineyard R8

Polish Hill River, Sevenhill, SA 5453
Ph 08 8843 4310

Owners: Wilson family
Chief winemaker: John Wilson
Year of foundation: 1974
Tonnes crushed on average each year: 95
Location: Polish Hill River
Area: 13 ha
Soils: acidic red-brown clayey loam over decomposing slate
Varieties planted: White—chardonnay, gewurztraminer, riesling, semillon; Red—cabernet sauvignon, malbec, merlot, nebbiolo, petit verdot, shiraz, zinfandel
Leading wines: The Wilson Vineyard Gallery Series Riesling, Gallery Series Cabernet Sauvignon, Hippocrene, Chardonnay, Zinfandel
Notes: John Wilson is an articulate man who writes a delightful newsletter and is yet another of the legion of Australian medical men bewitched by the vine, an enchantment which has now lasted for over twenty years. His vineyard has a whole pharmacopoeia of grape varieties, but the best of them are—as usual for Clare—riesling, shiraz and cabernet sauvignon. He may not agree with me about the grape varieties, but the Gallery Series Riesling and Cabernet Sauvignon are consistently good. Cellar door sales: weekends between May and October 10am–4pm.

PART IV

WESTERN AUSTRALIA

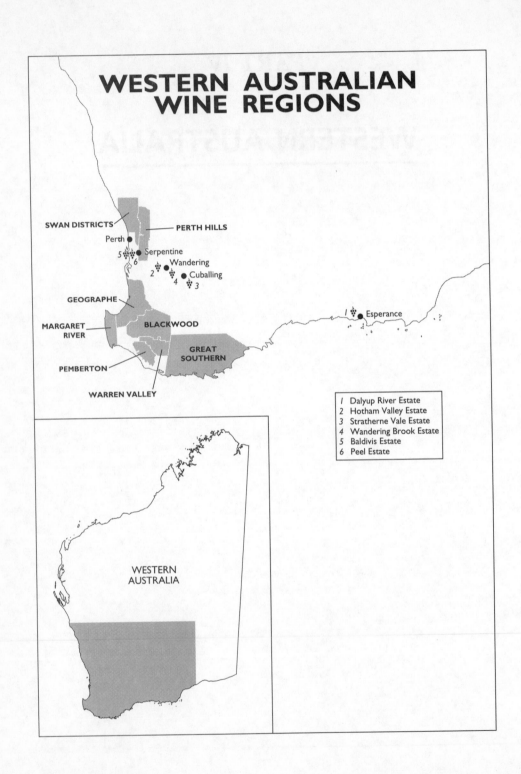

WESTERN AUSTRALIAN WINE REGIONS

SWAN DISTRICTS

Perth

PERTH HILLS

5

Serpentine

6

Wandering

2

Cuballing

4

3

GEOGRAPHE

Esperance

MARGARET
RIVER

BLACKWOOD

PEMBERTON

GREAT
SOUTHERN

WARREN VALLEY

1	Dalyup River Estate
2	Hotham Valley Estate
3	Stratherne Vale Estate
4	Wandering Brook Estate
5	Baldivis Estate
6	Peel Estate

WESTERN
AUSTRALIA

❧ EASTERN PLAINS, INLAND AND NORTH OF WESTERN AUSTRALIA

This is a vast area (in fact, all of Western Australia except the temperate south-west) which so far has no wine significance.

❧ WEST AUSTRALIAN SOUTH EAST COASTAL ZONE

This is a long, lonely east-west stretch of the Western Australian coastline beginning near Bremer Bay about 120 km east of Albany, travelling through Esperance (the natural centre of the zone) and ending some 250 km further east (about halfway to the western border of South Australia). At the time of writing, Esperance had applied for but not yet granted wine regional status. There are relatively few vineyards in this zone, but there is no reason why, given sufficient irrigation, there should not be many more.

Dalyup River Estate   **NR**

Esperance, WA

Ph/Fax 08 9076 5027

Owner/chief winemaker: Tom Murray
Year of foundation: 1987
Tonnes crushed on average each year: 10, of which 8 are used for Dalyup River labels
Location: Esperance
Area: 2.8 ha
Soils: silty loam A horizon about 0.8 m deep over clay loam subsoil

Varieties planted: White—chardonnay, riesling, sauvignon blanc; Red—cabernet sauvignon, shiraz
Leading wines: Dalyup River Estate Shiraz, Sauvignon Blanc (wooded)
Notes: Some 600 km south-east of Perth, Dalyup River Estate is one of the most remote vineyards in Australia. Yet it flourishes, winning a gold award for its 1995 Shiraz at the 1997 Mount Barker Wine Show. Cellar door sales: weekends and public holidays 10am–4pm.

❦ SOUTH WEST AUSTRALIA ZONE

This is the heartland of Western Australian viticulture. Its cooler areas such as Margaret River produce excellent reds of marvellous fruitiness and high quality whites; those that are warmer make fuller-bodied reds of good character. Currently, this zone comprises four registered wine regions, Great Southern, Margaret River, Geographe and Blackwood Valley with perhaps three more in the offings as a result of the fracture of the proposed former region—Pemberton. These three presently unregistered regions are Pemberton, Warren Valley and Manjimup.

The Great Southern region has three registered sub-regions—Mount Barker, Albany and Porongurups. In addition two more subregions are proposed—Denmark and Frankland.

GEOGRAPHE REGION

The Geographe region was often previously called the South West Coastal Plain, but is now enlarged to encompass the foothills of the Darling Range and the country to its south-east around Donnybrook-Kirup. It is named after Geographe Bay, most of which it fronts, the bay itself deriving its name from one of the two vessels under the command of Nicholas Baudin who explored much of the coast of south-western and southern Australia in the early years of the nineteenth century. The other ship was the *Naturaliste* which gave its name to a cape at the western end of Geographe Bay.

There was little tradition of grape-growing in the region until the inter-war period of the 1920s and 1930s, when small vineyards and wineries were established around the town of Harvey by Italian migrants. With the onset of the Second World War, many of these vignerons were interned and their vineyards fell into neglect, being grazed by dairy cows and never re-established after the war.

The modern viticultural era of the Geographe region began in 1973 when Dr Barry Killerby planted a vineyard at Stratham, 15 km south of Bunbury. He was followed a year later by Dr Peter Pratten, who commenced planting at Capel Vale on the Capel River just west of the town of Capel and in 1976 by Gil Thomas. Soon after a vineyard was established on the South West Highway between Donnybrook and Kirup.

So the region remained until 1995 when Rob Bowen of Capel Vale and Matt Aldridge then of Killerby began to encourage local grape-growing interest by the formation of the Geographe Vignerons Association. As a result, there are now many more young vineyards in the region with one vineyard over 40 ha in extent. There are two major wineries in the region, Capel Vale and Killerby, as well as another recently established winery, Donnybrook Valley, and several growers who wish to market some or all of their own grapes as wine under their own label.

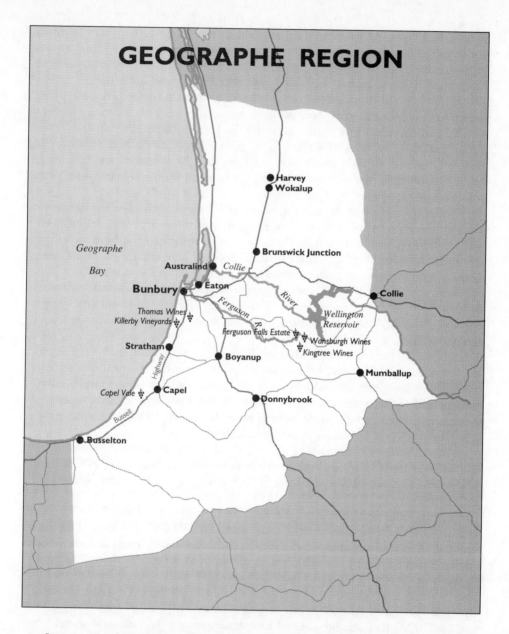

GEOGRAPHE REGION

Location: Bunbury (centre of region) latitude 33°18'S, longitude 115°38'E. Busselton (south-west of region) latitude 33°38'S, longitude 115°22'E. Collie (east of region) latitude 33°21'S, longitude 116°08'E. Wokalup (north of region) latitude 33°08'S, longitude 115°53'E. Bunbury is about 150 km south of Perth.

Elevation: from sea-level to 200 m

Topography and soils: The country rises gradually from the west (the coast) to the east (the Darling Range) about 200–250 m, but rather less so to the south-east and south. Along the coastal strip and at virtually sea-level is the 'tuart country', characterised by growths of *Eucalyptus gomphocephala* (the tuart gum). This consists of deep yellow sands over limestone. These are well-drained, iron-stained, siliceous sands usually over 2 metres deep. They are suitable for viticulture, but are of low natural fertility and need building up in respect to organic matter. They also often require nutrition as nutrients leach easily.

The major river systems of the region are the Harvey, Collie, Preston and Capel. Along the banks of these rivers are found brown loamy earths and brown sandy earths. These are alluvial, usually over 2 metres deep, well-drained and inherently fertile. Topsoils comprise rich brown loamy sands, sandy loam and loam passing into red or brown clay loamy or clayey subsoil.

As the altitude increases and the slopes and valleys of the Darling Range are reached, there are friable red-brown loamy earths together with brown loamy earths and brown deep loam duplex soils. These are 1–2 metres deep and have formed on the gneiss and granite of the Yilgarn Block. Topsoils here usually consist of sandy loams or loams above clays, which are usually porous and well structured.

Further upwards still on hills and ridges are located loamy gravels and moderately deep sandy gravels. These are lateritic and consist of loamy sands and sandy loams containing 20–80% rounded ironstone gravel above red or yellow-brown clayey subsoils about 50 cm thick.

In the south (adjacent to the Margaret River region) and south-east of the region, the increase in altitude is not so pronounced. Busselton is flat and its soils are poorly drained. Further south, around Chapman's Hill, the soils are often gravelly 'marri' country and suitable for viticulture, while in the south-east in the vicinity of Donnybrook and Kirup, there are gravelly sandy loams very suitable for wine grapes. However, frosts in this locality present a considerable problem.

Climate: Bunbury (centre) MJT 21.2°C, MAR na, HDD raw 1875, 1685 (cut off and adjusted for latitude, daily temperature range and for vine sites), AR 881 mm (Oct–Apr 185 mm), RH 54%, AI na, SH 8.8 (Gladstones). Busselton (south) MJT 20.9°C, MAR na, HDD raw 1779, 1589 (cut off and adjusted for latitude, daily temperature range and vine sites), AR 838 mm (Oct–Apr 179 mm), RH 51% (3pm Jan), AI na, SH 8.4. Donnybrook (south-east) MJT 21.7°C, MAR na, HDD raw 1878, 1657 (cut off and adjusted for latitude, daily temperature range and vine sites), AR 1019 mm (Oct–Apr 221 mm), RH 31% (3pm Jan), AI na, SH 8.6 (Gladstones). Collie (east) MJT 21.6°C, MAR na, HDD raw 1779, 1611 (cut off and adjusted for latitude, daily temperature range and vine sites), AR 988 mm (Oct–Apr 221 mm), RH 34% (3pm Jan), AI na, SH 8.7. Wokalup (north) MJT 22.6°C, MAR na, HDD raw 2057, 1707 (cut off and adjusted for latitude, daily temperature range and vine sites), AR 1010 mm (Oct–Apr 224 mm), RH 41% (3pm Jan), AI na, SH 8.9 (Gladstones).

The climate of the region may be termed Mediterranean, that is, generally warm and dry between October and April with less than a quarter of its annual rainfall occurring during this period. The MJTs become warmer, as a general rule, to the north, east and south-east as one moves inland from Bunbury. Only Busselton is marginally cooler in January.

Around Bunbury, the climate during the growing season is warm, though maritime influences keep temperatures equable. Favourable relative humidities due to sea breezes emanating from the Indian Ocean are also maintained. Frosts are rare.

The area to the south of Busselton, which adjoins the Margaret River region, is Chapman's Hill. Here, the rain shadows of the more southerly Whicher range and the westerly ridge running north–south from Cape Naturaliste to Cape Leeuwin have resulted in a warm, dry and sunny climate not unlike that of the coastal area nearer Bunbury.

South-east of Bunbury around Donnybrook, the locality has good surface water catchments and its climate appears to favour full-bodied red and light fortifieds. Its relative humidity is low, increasing the risk of water stress during ripening but reducing risks of mildew. There is also a frost risk in spring and site selection for vineyards must be carried out very carefully to ensure that there is maximum air drainage.

Inland from Bunbury are the towns of Burekup and Dardanup. Suitable vine sites here for medium- to full-bodied whites and reds appear to be Henty Brook (south-east of Burekup) and the Ferguson Valley and Crooked Brook (south-east of Dardanup). Winter–spring rainfall is generous and reliable and there are good surface water catchments. The locality is also mostly free of frosts. Already in the Ferguson Valley there is an explosion of vineyards, including the largest in the region (presently 40 ha, but planned to extend to 100). As one proceeds north, the region becomes hotter. Wokalup is typical and seems more suited to fortifieds than the more southerly parts, though the cooling and humidifying influences of the prevailing sea breeze still has a beneficial effect.

There are relatively few other viticultural problems, though powdery mildew does occur. It is treated in the usual way by sulfur spray. Insect pests include wingless grasshoppers and garden weevils. Open range guineafowl have proved most effective in reducing their numbers.

Principal varieties: White—chardonnay, verdelho; Red—shiraz, merlot, cabernet sauvignon

Harvest time: chardonnay mid-February to third week of March, shiraz third week of March, cabernet sauvignon week of March, merlot third week of March to first week of April

Total area: (Oct 1997) 150 ha

Principal wine styles: What has come from the region so far is largely represented by its largest makers, Capel Vale and Killerby. Capel Vale makes excellent Chardonnays and also very good full-bodied Shiraz reds, though many of these have emanated from Mount Barker. Killerby likewise has made a name for its local reds in recent years. Cabernet Sauvignon, however, produces only adequate wines which lack the tannic fullness and varieties of Cabernet from, say, Margaret River. Merlot is a variety relatively new to the district, which is showing excellent promise. There is no reason to suppose that Merlot should not become a major wine style of the region.

Blinman Estate NR

Gardincourt Drive, Ferguson Valley,
WA 6236
Ph 08 9728 0068

Owners: Dewar family
Chief winemaker: no wine yet produced
Year of foundation: 1997
Tonnes crushed on average each year: vines
not yet bearing but production should be 800–
1000 tonnes when all vines are fully bearing
Location: Ferguson Valley near Dardanup
Area: 40 ha expanding to 100 ha by 2002
Soils: strong gravelly red loams over a porous
clay base
Varieties planted: White—chardonnay, chenin
blanc, sauvignon blanc, semillon; Red—
cabernet sauvignon, grenache, merlot, shiraz
Leading wines: no wines yet made
Notes: The Ferguson Valley is yet another
Australian instance of great vineyard
expansion. Jeff Dewar has also planned a
substantial winery for the site. No cellar door
sales yet.

Capel Vale R9

Stirling Estate, Mallokup Road, Capel,
WA 6271
Ph 08 9727 1986, Fax 08 9727 1904

Owners: Dr Peter and Mrs Elizabeth Pratten
Chief winemakers: Rob Bowen and Krister
Jonsson
Year of foundation: 1975
Tonnes crushed on average each year: 850,
being the crush from Whispering Hill in Mount
Barker, Sheldrake in Pemberton-Warren,
Stirling Estate and fruit purchased from
growers
Location: Capel
Area: 25 ha
Soils: deep loam over limestone
Varieties planted: White—chardonnay;
Red—merlot, shiraz

Leading wines: Capel Vale Frederick
Chardonnay
Notes: Peter Pratten's Capel Vale Vineyard is
one of the veterans of the region and now
produces one of Australia's best
Chardonnays—Frederick, wholly sourced from
the Stirling Estate vineyard (Capel). There are
four ranges of wines. The first is the flagship
range of mostly single estate reds and whites:
Frederick Chardonnay, Kinnaird Shiraz (Mount
Barker), Howcroft Merlot Cabernet (merlot
from Capel and cabernet from Margaret River),
Whispering Hill Riesling (Mount Barker) and
Sevenday Road Sauvignon Blanc (Pemberton).
The second range is the Grey label consisting
of Riesling, Sauvignon Blanc-Semillon,
Chardonnay, Merlot, Shiraz and Cabernet
Sauvignon. Lower down the scale is the Flying
Duck range which has Unwooded Chardonnay,
Sauvignon Blanc-Chardonnay, CV Shiraz and
CV Cabernet-Merlot. The fourth range is
Layman's Hut composed of Classic White,
Chenin, Fronti and Classic Red. Cellar door
sales: 10am–4pm daily.

Donnybrook Valley Wines NR

Lot 384 South Western Highway,
Newlands, WA 6239
Ph/Fax 08 9731 6349

Owners: Lawrance and Wise families
Chief winemaker: Siobhan Lynch
Year of foundation: 1988
Tonnes crushed on average each year: 80
Location: Donnybrook
Area: 12 ha
Soils: gravelly loams over clay
Varieties planted: White—chardonnay,
colombard, sauvignon blanc, verdelho; Red—
cabernet franc, cabernet sauvignon, merlot
Leading wines: Wise Vineyards Merlot,
Chardonnay
Notes: All wines are sold under the Wise
Vineyards labels. There are no cellar door sales

(see Wise Vineyards in the Margaret River region).

Ferguson Falls Estate NR

Pile Road, Ferguson Valley via Dardanup, WA 6236
Ph/Fax 08 9728 1083

Owners: Peter and Margaret Giumelli
Chief winemaker: James Pennington (contract)
Year of foundation: 1983
Tonnes crushed on average each year: 6
Location: Ferguson Valley via Dardanup
Area: 3 ha (of which 1 ha is not yet producing)
Soils: lateritic gravels and sandy gravel slopes, well drained and quite steep
Varieties planted: White—chardonnay; Red—cabernet sauvignon, merlot
Leading wines: Ferguson Falls Cabernet Sauvignon, Chardonnay
Notes: Cellar door sales by appointment.

Killerby Vineyards R8

Lakes Road, Capel, WA 6230
Ph 08 9795 7222, Fax 08 9795 7835, (Perth office) 08 9481 1133

Owner: Killerby Vineyards Pty Ltd
Chief winemaker: Paul Boulden
Year of foundation: 1973
Tonnes crushed on average each year: 150
Location: Stratham
Area: 20 ha
Soils: 'tuart', free-draining sandy loam over limestone
Varieties planted: White—chardonnay, semillon; Red—cabernet franc, cabernet sauvignon, merlot sauvignon, shiraz
Leading wines: Killerby Vineyards Shiraz, Cabernet Sauvignon, Chardonnay
Notes: This is the pioneer of the Geographe region, or the South West Coastal Plain as the area was once called, and a maker of good Chardonnay, Shiraz and Cabernet Sauvignon. Cellar door sales: 10am–5pm daily.

Kingtree Wines NR

Kingtree Road, Wellington Mills, WA 6236
Ph 08 9728 3050, Fax 08 9728 3113

Owners: David and Cheryl Rourke
Chief winemaker: Krister Jonsson, Capel Vale (contract)
Year of foundation: 1991
Tonnes crushed on average each year: 30 but will increase to 45 (about 10 tonnes presently used for Kingtree's own labels)
Location: Ferguson Valley
Area: 4 ha
Soils: rich, gravel loams, amply watered by a surface catchment dam, filled by a rainfall of 1000 mm per annum
Varieties planted: White—riesling, sauvignon blanc; Red—cabernet sauvignon, merlot
Leading wines: Kingtree Sauvignon Blanc, Riesling, Cabernet Sauvignon-Merlot
Notes: Located on the edge of the Darling Scarp in the newly booming Ferguson Valley, Kingtree, though hardly 7 years old, is already a veteran of the district. With its wines made by Krister Jonsson and a guest lodge that accommodates four couples, it is already a favourite tourist destination. Cellar door sales: daily noon–5.30 pm.

Thomas Wines NR

Crowd Road, Gelorup, WA 6233
Ph/Fax 08 9795 7925, 08 9795 7085 (home), 08 9721 7228 (business)

Owners: Gill and Janet Thomas
Chief winemaker: Gill Thomas
Year of foundation: 1976
Tonnes crushed on average each year: 10 (some grapes also bought in)
Location: Gelorup
Area: 2.2 ha
Soils: 'tuart' country
Varieties planted: White—none; Red—pinot noir

Leading wines: Briar Holme Cabernet Sauvignon, Pinot Noir

Notes: Gill Thomas is not only a winemaker but a very busy pharmacist and blue water sailor. A seven-days-a-week pharmacy and sailing take time, as does winemaking, so his Briar Holme label has not been seen as frequently as it used to be. It will certainly continue but will probably be confined to Pinot Noir in the future. Cellar door sales by appointment.

Wansburgh Wines **NR**

Pile Road, Ferguson, WA 6236
Ph 08 9728 3104, Fax 08 9728 3091

Owners: Brian and Jan Wansburgh
Chief winemaker: Willespie Wines (contract)
Year of foundation: 1986
Tonnes crushed on average each year: 15, the balance of fruit is sold
Location: Ferguson Valley
Area: 6 ha (2 ha not yet bearing)
Soils: sandy gravelly lateritic ('marri') loam on a steep, well-drained slope
Varieties planted: White—chardonnay, riesling, sauvignon blanc, semillon; Red—cabernet sauvignon, shiraz
Leading wines: Wansburgh Sauvignon Blanc, Cabernet-Shiraz
Notes: Brian Wansburgh retired recently. Now he is very much back to work 7 days a week. Cellar door sales: weekends 11am–5pm.

MARGARET RIVER REGION

Early exploration of the coasts of the region was carried out by Dutch navigators in the early seventeenth century and more extensive mapping in the early nineteenth century by the British and French (Matthew Flinders in the *Investigator*, Nicolas Baudin in *Geographe* and Freycinet in *Naturaliste*). Hence the names Geographe Bay and Cape Naturaliste. Though there are reports of Margaret River wine being bartered for tea, coffee and bolts of gingham in the 1850s, early history is sketchy. More substantiated is the planting by an Italian farmer, Jimmy Meleri, of 4 hectares of doradillo in 1914. However, Margaret River really sprang to life as a vineyard region as a result of two research reports. Californian viticulturalist Professor Harold Olmo and the Western Australian scientist Dr John Gladstones are the researchers to whom credit is due. Olmo was commissioned by the Western Australian government in 1955 to evaluate the state's wine industry and to advise on its future. As with most reports, the government response was most notable for its absence but finally, in 1962, it resolved to act by planting an experimental vineyard at Forest Hill near Mount Barker in the Great Southern region. Sufficient interest had, however, been aroused in the Margaret River region by Olmo's report to cause Dr John Gladstones of the University of Western Australia to carry out further research in that region in 1965. His enthusiastic report stimulated Perth cardiologist Dr Tom Cullity to plant his Vasse Felix vineyard near Willyabrup in 1967. His first vintage was in 1971 and his vigorous pursuit of the Margaret River vine inspired others. Dr Bill Pannell began to plant Mosswood in 1970, followed by Dr Kevin Cullen and his wife Di in 1971. In 1978, the region, led by Dr Kevin Cullen, was among the first in Australia to adopt regional certification of wines as a means of improving local wine quality.

MARGARET RIVER REGION

1. Abbey Vale Vineyards
2. Amberley Estate
3. Arlewood Estate
4. Ashbrook Estate
5. Brookland Valley
6. Cape Clairault
7. Chapman's Creek
8. Cullen Wines
9. Driftwood
10. Evans & Tate
11. Fermoy Estate
12. Gralyn Cellars
13. Happs
14. Hay Shed Hill
15. Hunt's Foxhaven Estate
16. Lenton Brae
17. Moss Brothers
18. Moss Wood Winery
19. Palmer Wines
20. Pierro
21. Ribbon Vale Estate
22. Rivendell Vineyard
23. Sandalford Wines
24. Treeton Estate
25. Vasse Felix
26. Vasse River Wines
27. Wild
28. Willespie
29. Wise Vineyards
30. Woodlands Wines
31. Woody Nook
32. Wright's Winery
33. Yungarra Estate

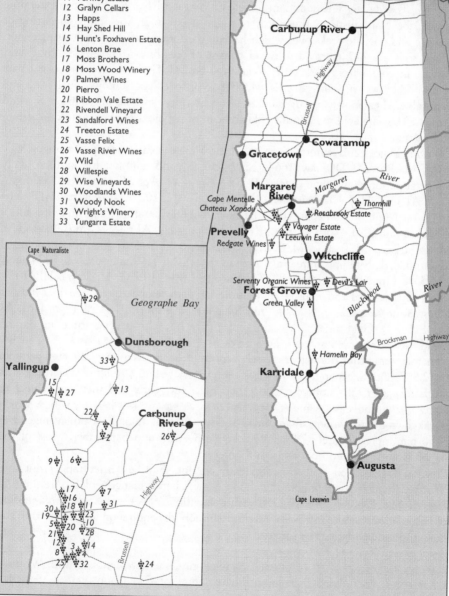

Today, the region has over 100 vineyards and 40 wineries and there are 55 winemaking and winegrowing members of the Margaret River Wine Industry Association. The region is rightly regarded, with Coonawarra and the Yarra Valley, as one of the three premium cabernet sauvignon areas in Australia.

Location: the region south of Perth and west of longitude 115°18'E, approx 33°42'S, about 250 km south-south-west of Perth

Elevation: 90 m

Topography and soils: The dominant feature of Margaret River is a low ridge extending from Cape Naturaliste in the north to Cape Leeuwin in the south consisting of granitic and gneissic rocks over which laterite has formed. It is an undulating region whose soils are 1–2 metres thick and consist of grey-brown gravelly, sandy loams, varying in colour from dark grey to dark red-brown. These surface soils cover pale yellow or brown sub-surface soils which pass into clayey subsoils. Such soils are permeable when moist, but difficult to wet when dry, and are also subject to wind erosion. They are acid to neutral in pH and can be deficient in phosphorus, potassium and calcium.

Climate: (Major centres north to south in the Margaret River region) Yallingup MJT 20°C, MAR na, HDD raw 1664, 1629 (cut off and adjusted for latitude, daily temperature range and vine sites), AR 1083 mm (Oct–Apr 232 mm), RH 55% (3pm Jan), AI na, SH 7.9 (Gladstones). Willyabrup MJT 20.2°C, MAR na, HDD raw 1649, 1601 (cut off and adjusted for latitude, daily temperature range and vine sites), AR 1138 mm (Oct–Apr 253 mm), RH 54% (3pm Jan), AI na, SH 7.8 (Gladstones). Margaret River MJT 20°C, MAR 7.2°C, HDD raw 1597, 1557 (cut off and adjusted for latitude, daily temperature range and vine sites), AR 1192 mm (Oct–Apr 274 mm), RH 53% (3pm Jan), AI na, SH 7.7. Karridale MJT 19.1°C, MAR na, HDD raw 1529, 1507 (cut off and adjusted for latitude and daily temperature range only without adjusted for vine sites), AR 1200 mm (Oct–Apr 294 mm), RH 55% (3pm Jan), AI na, SH 7.2 (Gladstones). A warm but rarely hot climate, maritime in nature, paradoxically regarded as 'cool' because of its long slow ripening season. The reality is that winter in Margaret River is rarely very cold, as witness its mean July temperature of 12.8°C (Dry & Smart). But it is quite often very wet, as a result of which its vines are hardly ever fully dormant, burst their buds very early and then are subject to many spring and early summer dangers, such as strong, salt-bearing winds, which wreak havoc with young chardonnay shoots. Annual rainfall is on average over 1150 mm, approximately 70% falling between April and September. Most of the region is drip irrigated from dams and bores.

Principal varieties: Red—cabernet sauvignon, merlot, shiraz, cabernet franc, pinot noir; White—chardonnay, semillon, sauvignon blanc, chenin blanc, verdelho, riesling

Harvest time: February to mid April with a variation of 3–4 weeks in the maturation of cabernet sauvignon and 2–3 weeks for semillon, depending on location within the region, the north being the earliest

Total area: 800 ha (1997)

Principal wine styles: Red—Cabernet Sauvignon, Cabernet-Merlot, Shiraz; White—Chardonnay, Semillon, Sauvignon Blanc, Semillon-Sauvignon Blanc, Verdelho.

Cabernet Sauvignon has been particularly successful within the region, either as a single wine or blended with Merlot and Cabernet Franc. Shiraz reds are still not common, but are growing in popularity among makers. Pinot Noir has in my opinion been generally a disappointment. Of the whites, Sauvignon Blanc and Semillon when blended or when bottled separately show typically herbaceous and/or tropical characters and are very racy and refreshing. Chardonnay too is very good.

Abbey Vale Vineyard **R8**

Lot 392 Wildwood Road, Yallingup, WA 6282
Ph 08 9755 2277, Fax 08 9755 2286

Owners: Pamela and William McKay
Chief winemaker: Dorham Mann (contract)
Year of foundation: 1986
Tonnes crushed on average each year: 200
Location: Yallingup
Area: 25 ha
Soils: gravelly loam over clay
Varieties planted: White—chardonnay, chenin blanc, sauvignon blanc, semillon, verdelho; Red—cabernet sauvignon, merlot, shiraz
Leading wines: Abbey Vale Verdelho, Chardonnay, Cabernet
Notes: Bill McKay has literally careered around the world—as an engineer working in Uganda for the British Foreign Office, the owner of a private electronics business, which was later taken over by another company, a stint in Canada, then five years' study to qualify as a clinical psychologist. He then moved to Western Australia and finally to Margaret River, where his son, Kevin, had become interested in viticulture. As grapegrowers, the McKays first sold their fruit to Houghtons, reserving a little for their own label, then the study bug hit Bill again and he enrolled in a summer course in brewing at UC Davis, later to establish the Moonshine brewery at Abbey Vale. After all this, Abbey Vale may be an anti-climax, but the whites are accessible and full of flavour. Cellar door sales: each day 10.30am–5pm.

Amberley Estate **R8**

Thornton Road, Yallingup, WA 6282
Ph 08 9755 2288, Fax 08 9755 2171

Owner: Amberley Estate Pty Ltd
Chief winemaker: Eddie Price
Year of foundation: 1986
Tonnes crushed on average each year: 450 including purchased fruit
Location: Yallingup
Area: 31.5 ha
Soils: gravelly loams, 'marri' country
Varieties planted: White—chardonnay, chenin blanc, sauvignon blanc, semillon; Red—cabernet franc, cabernet sauvignon, merlot, shiraz
Leading wines: Amberley Estate Semillon-Sauvignon Blanc, Cabernet Sauvignon
Notes: Founded by Albert Haak, a South African who settled in Margaret River in 1985 and has since retired from the company, Amberley is one of the larger estates of this region with an average crush of 450 tonnes and a current folio of nine wines, ranging from a slightly sweet Chenin style to an excellent Chardonnay in the whites, while the reds include a velvety Cabernet Merlot. Cellar door sales: each day 10am–4.30pm.

Arlewood Estate **R7**

Harman's Road South, Willyabrup, WA 6284
Ph/Fax 08 9755 6267
Mobile 0417 931 089

Owner: John Wojturski
Chief winemaker: Juerg Muggli (Chateau Xanadu contract)

Year of foundation: 1988
Tonnes crushed on average each year: 20
Location: Willyabrup
Area: 4 ha, with 2 ha not yet bearing
Soils: pea gravel loam over clay
Varieties planted: White—sauvignon blanc, semillon; Red—cabernet franc, cabernet sauvignon, merlot, shiraz
Leading wines: Arlewood Estate Semillon, Cabernet Sauvignon
Notes: An impressive 1995 Semillon, made in the usual elegant Margaret River manner, has been the only Arlewood wine that I have seen to date. Cellar door sales by appointment.

Ashbrook Estate R9

Harman's Road South, Willyabrup, WA 6284
PO Box 320, Cowaramup, WA 6284
Ph 08 9755 6262, Fax 08 9755 6290

Owners: Devitt family
Chief winemakers: Tony and Brian Devitt
Year of foundation: 1975
Tonnes crushed on average each year: 120
Location: Willyabrup
Area: 12 ha
Soils: gravelly red loam
Varieties planted: White—chardonnay, riesling, sauvignon blanc, semillon, verdelho; Red—cabernet franc, cabernet sauvignon, merlot
Leading wines: Ashbrook Chardonnay (wooded), Semillon, Sauvignon Blanc, Verdelho, Cabernet Sauvignon
Notes: Fresh Semillon and Verdelho with its typically zingy Margaret River fruit are the highlights of the whites, while Ashbrook's only red, a Cabernet Sauvignon, matured in French oak, usually shows excellent complexity and palate length. Cellar door sales: each day 11am–5pm.

Brookland Valley R8.5

Caves Road, Willyabrup, WA 6284
Ph 08 9755 6250, Fax 08 9755 6214

Owners: M and D Jones and BRL Hardy Ltd
Chief winemaker: BRL Hardy Ltd
Year of foundation: 1984
Tonnes crushed on average each year: 190
Location: Willyabrup
Area: 20 ha
Soils: chiefly shallow loam over gravel ('marri'), deep sand, deep alluvial loams
Varieties planted: White—chardonnay, sauvignon blanc; Red—cabernet franc, cabernet sauvignon, merlot
Leading wines: Brookland Valley Chardonnay, Sauvignon Blanc, Cabernet Sauvignon-Merlot
Notes: Brookland Valley has been fortunate to have chosen the highly experienced Gary Baldwin as its winemaking consultant, and now has a national profile for excellent Chardonnays and Sauvignons, not to mention its very smooth Cabernet Sauvignon Merlot blend. A 100% Merlot was produced in 1997. Recently BRL Hardy purchased a 50% interest. Cellar door sales: each day 11am–4.30pm except Monday. There is also a restaurant, Flutes Cafe.

Cape Clairault R8.5

Henry Road, Willyabrup, WA 6280
Ph 08 9755 6225, Fax 08 9755 6229

Owners: Ian and Ani Lewis
Chief winemakers: Ian Lewis and Peter Stark
Year of foundation: 1976
Tonnes crushed on average each year: 90
Location: Willyabrup
Area: 11 ha
Soils: yellow-brown gravelly sandy loams
Varieties planted: White—chardonnay, riesling, sauvignon blanc, semillon; Red—cabernet franc, cabernet sauvignon, merlot
Leading wines: The Clairault (a premium red

blend), Sauvignon Blanc-Semillon, Sauvignon Blanc

Notes: If there are any valid comparisons to be made between wine regions of different countries, one must be between the different parts (or sub-regions) of the Margaret River region and those of Bordeaux, especially with regard to cabernet sauvignon and its blends. Around Bordeaux are the supple reds of Graves, most with a goodly proportion of merlot to make them attractive to drink at a comparatively youthful age (often 7–10 years). I like to comprare these wines to those of the Willyabrup 'sub-region' of Margaret River. Here merlot again shows how attractive it can be in partnership with cabernet sauvignon and cabernet franc. The results are soft and supple reds, accessible at a fairly early age (3–5 years). For those Bordeaux lovers who like firmer-structured cabernet sauvignon wines, go north of Bordeaux to Pauillac and especially to St Estephe. In Margaret River, go to the southern areas of the region, indeed Margaret River itself, and taste, say, Cape Mentelle Cabernet Sauvignon, made as David Hohnen directs to last 15–20 years. What has all this to do with Cape Clairault? Only that Ian Lewis makes a delightful Cabernet-Merlot blend called The Clairault, supple and chewy in the best Graves (or Willyabrup) manner. Cellar door sales: each day 10am–5pm.

Cape Mentelle R10

Off Wallcliffe Road, Margaret River, WA 6285
Ph 08 9757 3266, Fax 08 9757 3233

Owner: Cape Mentelle Vineyards Ltd
Chief winemaker: John Durham
Year of foundation: 1970
Tonnes crushed on average each year: 700
Location: Margaret River
Area: 76 ha
Soils: old granite-derived lateritic gravels, 'marri' country with wind blown sand pockets

Varieties planted: White—chardonnay, chenin blanc, sauvignon blanc, semillon; Red—cabernet sauvignon, merlot, shiraz, zinfandel

Leading wines: Cape Mentelle Cabernet Sauvignon, Shiraz, Semillon Sauvignon, Trinders Vineyard Cabernet Merlot

Notes: Now one of the veteran estates of the Margaret River region and, like its Cabernet Sauvignons which are made to last 15–20 years and twice winners of the Jimmy Watson trophy, ageing magnificently. Highly regarded also for its Shiraz and a stylishly tangy Semillon Sauvignon. Though the majority of its equity capital is owned by Veuve Clicquot Ponsardin of Reims, it is still very much under the day-to-day direction of its founder, David Hohnen. That direction remains unswerving in its continued search for even greater quality. Cellar door sales: each day 10am–4.30pm.

Chapman's Creek R9

Yelverton Road, Willyabrup, WA 6280
Ph 08 9755 7545, Fax 08 9755 7571

Owner: Tony Lord
Chief winemaker: Devil's Lair (contract)
Year of foundation: 1992
Tonnes crushed on average each year: 80
Location: Willyabrup
Area: 10 ha
Soils: sandy loam over gravel and some gravel structure

Varieties planted: White—chardonnay, chenin blanc, sauvignon blanc, semillon;
Red—cabernet sauvignon, merlot, shiraz

Leading wines: Chapman's Creek Unoaked Chardonnay, Chardonnay, Cabernet Sauvignon, Cabernet Merlot, Shiraz, Merlot

Notes: After many years and masses of words in *Decanter* about other people's wines, Tony Lord has returned home to Western Australia to do it all for himself. He is thrilled, as are many of his former readers, now turned consumers. Chapman's Creek Chardonnay

1995 was tasting extremely well in November 1997. Cellar door sales by appointment.

Chateau Xanadu **R8.5**

Terry Road, Margaret River, WA 6285
Ph 08 9757 2581, Fax 08 9757 3389

Owners: Lagan family
Chief winemaker: Jurg Muggli
Year of foundation: 1977
Tonnes crushed on average each year: 250
Locations: Margaret River, Rosa Brook
Area: 20 ha (Margaret River), 8 ha (Rosa Brook)
Soils: lateritic gravel 'marri' country
Varieties planted: White—chardonnay, chenin blanc, sauvignon blanc, semillon;
Red—cabernet franc, cabernet sauvignon, merlot, shiraz
Leading wines: Chateau Xanadu Secession (a blend of sauvignon blanc and semillon), Semillon (usually wood-matured), Cabernet Sauvignon
Notes: After many years of conventional vine cultivation using pesticides and chemical fertilisers, Chateau Xanadu is now treading the Integrated Production (IP) path. This organic approach aims to improve wine quality and consistency by returning the vineyard to more natural environmental practices. Thus manure-based fertilisers supplemented by natural mineral additions are now applied. Pesticide use has ceased and where possible predator-friendly spray programs such as pyrethrin have been substituted. In addition, ducks and other poultry are used for natural insect and snail control. Herbicides have been eliminated, straw mulching substituted and irrigation has been kept to a minimum. As for the wines, there is no change from Xanadu's good to very good quality. Cellar door sales: every day 10am–5pm.

Cullen Wines **R10**

Caves Road, Cowaramup, WA 6284
Ph 08 9755 5277, Fax 08 9755 5550

Owners: Cullen family
Chief winemaker: Vanya Cullen
Year of foundation: 1971
Tonnes crushed on average each year: 200
Location: Cowaramup
Area: 28 ha
Soils: lateritic gravel
Varieties planted: White—chardonnay, riesling, sauvignon blanc, semillon; Red—cabernet franc, cabernet sauvignon, merlot, pinot noir
Leading wines: Cullen Cabernet Sauvignon-Merlot, Chardonnay, Pinot Noir, Sauvignon Blanc-Semillon
Notes: In an age of drip irrigation, Cullen's holds to traditional dry-land viticulture. As Di Cullen points out, the region receives over 1150 mm of rain each year, so drip irrigation is probably unnecessary. The Cullen philosophy is one of absolute wine quality, a philosophy totally vindicated by wines such as Cullen Cabernet Sauvignon and Cullen Chardonnay. Cellar door sales: each day 10am–4pm.

Devil's Lair **R9**

Rocky Road, Witchcliffe, WA 6285
Ph 08 9757 7573, Fax 08 9757 7533

Owner: Southcorp Wines
Chief winemaker: John Duval
Year of foundation: 1981
Tonnes crushed on average each year: 250
Location: Witchcliffe
Area: 33.5 ha
Soils: gravelly lateritic loam over permeable clay
Varieties planted: White—chardonnay, sauvignon blanc, semillon; Red—cabernet franc, cabernet sauvignon, merlot, petit verdot, pinot noir
Leading wines: Devil's Lair Cabernet Sauvignon, Pinot Noir, Chardonnay, Fifth Leg (a blended white)

Notes: Renowned for its stylish Cabernet Sauvignon, when owned by Philip and Alison Sexton, Devil's Lair was regarded as a rising star. As Southcorp's first venture in the west, it will probably achieve superstar status. Cellar door sales by appointment.

Driftwood R8

Lot 13, Caves Road, Yallingup, WA 6282
Ph 08 9755 6323, Fax 08 9755 6343

Owner: Saruman Holdings Pty Ltd
Chief winemakers: Maria Melsom, Steve Pester
Year of foundation: 1989
Tonnes crushed on average each year: 200
Location: Yallingup
Area: 19 ha
Soils: variable, rich loams to gravelly loams to gritty sandy soils over ironstone and clay
Varieties planted: White—chardonnay, chenin blanc, sauvignon blanc, semillon; Red—cabernet sauvignon, pinot noir, shiraz
Leading wines: Driftwood Chardonnay, Semillon, Cabernet Sauvignon
Notes: Driftwood is another of those moderately large Margaret River estates which is showing lots of promise. Its vines are still comparatively young but, located as it is in Yallingup, in the 'white wine' area of Margaret River, it is certain to come to prominence. Its whites have already received due recognition overseas. Cellar door sales: each day 11am–4.30pm.

Evans & Tate R9.5

Cnr Metricup and Caves Roads, Willyabrup, WA 6280
Ph 08 9755 6244, Fax 08 9755 6283

Owner: Evans & Tate Ltd
Chief winemaker: Brian Fletcher
Year of foundation: 1971
Tonnes crushed on average each year: 1500
Locations: Willyabrup (Redbrook); its other

major vineyard in the region is Lionel's Vineyard at Jindong
Area: 64 ha (20 ha Redbrook, 44 ha Lionel's Vineyard)
Soils: Redbrook: lateritic gravel; Lionel: 'abba' fertile, red-orange light sandy loams with a low clay content over ironstone
Varieties planted: (Redbrook) White—chardonnay, sauvignon blanc, semillon, verdelho; Red—cabernet sauvignon, merlot, shiraz. (Lionel's Vineyard) White—chardonnay, sauvignon blanc, semillon; Red—none planted at this stage
Leading wines: Evans & Tate Margaret River Chardonnay, Margaret River Semillon, Margaret River Shiraz, Margaret River Merlot, Margaret River Cabernet Sauvignon
Notes: Evans & Tate is renowned for its marvellous Margaret River Semillon, an elegant nectar of lemony fragrance and supple, ever so slightly herbaceous, palate. Both Brian Fletcher, the current winemaker, and Krister Jonsson before him have brought this variety to ultimate fulfilment in Margaret River. In this region only the semillons of Moss Wood and Cullen are in the same elegant style. Cellar door sales: each day 10.30am–4.30pm.

Fermoy Estate R7

Metricup Road, Willyabrup, WA 6280
Ph 08 9755 6285, Fax 08 9755 6251

Owner: Fermoy Margaret River Unit Trust
Chief winemaker: Michael Kelly
Year of foundation: 1985
Tonnes crushed on average each year: 110
Location: Willyabrup
Soils: lateritic gravelly loam
Varieties planted: White—chardonnay, chenin blanc, sauvignon blanc, semillon;
Red—cabernet franc, cabernet sauvignon, malbec, merlot, pinot noir
Leading wines: Fermoy Cabernet Sauvignon, Semillon
Notes: In some years, I have occasionally noted

a firm almost hard character on the palate of Fermoy Cabernets which indicates a lack of harmony, but recent tastings show an improvement. Cellar door sales: 7 days 11am–4.30pm.

Flinders Bay Vineyard (vineyard only)

 NR

Karridale, WA 6288

Owners: Ireland and Gillespie families
Chief winemaker: Clive Otto (contract)
Year of foundation: 1995
Tonnes crushed on average each year: vines not yet bearing but 600 tonnes anticipated by 2002, first vintage 1998
Location: Karridale
Area: 48 ha
Soils: lateritic gravel 'marri' soils
Varieties planted: White—chardonnay (Mendoza Clone and Clone 1), sauvignon blanc, semillon; Red—cabernet sauvignon, malbec, merlot, shiraz
Leading wines: none yet, but probably will be a Cabernet Sauvignon dominant blend, a Chardonnay and a Sauvignon Blanc-Semillon
Notes: A partnership between former Sydney retailers Bill and Noel Ireland and experienced Witchcliffe viticulturalist Alistair Gillespie and his wife Colleen, Flinders Bay is a substantial vineyard set in the ultracool deep south of the Margaret River region. No cellar door sales on site, but wines will be available for tasting at Vasse Felix.

Gralyn Cellars

 NR

Caves Road, Willyabrup, WA 6284
Ph/Fax 08 9755 6245

Owners/chief winemakers: Graham and Merilyn Hutton
Year of foundation: 1975
Tonnes crushed on average each year: not disclosed but about 30 tonnes
Location: Willyabrup

Area: 4.5 ha
Soils: 'pea' gravel over clay
Varieties planted: White—riesling, semillon; Red—cabernet sauvignon, shiraz
Leading wines: Gralyn Cellars Cabernet Sauvignon, Cabernet-Shiraz, Fortifieds
Notes: Port style was originally the forte of Gralyn, but more recently the Huttons have had great success with their red table wines, winning a Sheraton Gold Award for 1995 Shiraz and a gold at the 1996 Perth Wine Show for Cabernet Shiraz. Cellar door sales: 7 days 10.30am–4.30pm.

Green Valley

 NR

Sebbes Road, Forest Grove, WA 6286
Ph 08 9757 7510, Fax 08 9384 3131

Owners: Ed and Eleonore Green
Chief winemakers: Vasse Felix and Chateau Xanadu (contract)
Year of foundation: 1979
Tonnes crushed on average each year: 50
Location: Forest Grove
Area: 9 ha
Soils: lateritic gravel ('marri'), sandy and also 'karri' loam
Varieties planted: White—chardonnay, chenin blanc, colombard, muller-thurgau, riesling; Red—cabernet sauvignon, merlot, shiraz
Leading wines: Green Valley Chardonnay, Cabernet Sauvignon
Notes: Green Valley is in the appropriately named Forest Grove area, a very cool, southerly district of Margaret River. The adjoining Boranup Forest and its birds have forced the Greens to net their entire vineyard, which will at least ensure that the Greens, not the birds, get the pick of the crop. Cellar door sales: Saturdays and public holidays 10am–6pm, Sundays 10am–4pm.

Hamelin Bay NR

Five Ashes Vineyard, RMB 116
McDonald Road, Karridale, WA 6288
Ph/Fax 08 9758 6779

Owners: Richard and Roslyn Drake-Brockman
Chief winemaker: Eddie Price, Amberley Estate
(contract)
Year of foundation: 1992
Tonnes crushed on average each year: 60 and
rising as more vines are planted and come into
bearing
Location: Karridale
Area: 25 ha
Soils: gravelly sandy loam
Varieties planted: White—chardonnay,
sauvignon blanc, semillon; Red—cabernet
sauvignon, merlot, shiraz
Leading wines: Hamelin Bay Chardonnay,
Sauvignon Blanc
Notes: Hamelin Bay's first vintage was 1996.
Karridale is a very cool, maritime area in the
far south of the Margaret River region. Cellar
door sales by appointment.

Happs R7.5

Commonage Road, Dunsborough,
WA 6281
Ph 08 9755 3300, Fax 08 9755 3846

Owner: Happs Pty Ltd
Chief winemakers: Erl Happ and Frank Kittler
Year of foundation: 1978
Tonnes crushed on average each year: 190
Locations: Dunsborough and Karridale
Area: 23.9 ha
Soils: (Dunsborough) 'Mungite' sand 'Jarrah'
soil sandy gravelly overlying kaolinitic clay.
(Karridale) sandy gravels, felspathic-quartzey
with a pink tint
Varieties planted: White—chardonnay, chenin
blanc, furmint, marsanne, muscadelle,
sauvignon blanc, semillon, verdelho, viognier;
Red—bastardo, brown muscat, cabernet franc,
cabernet sauvignon, gamay, graciano, malbec,

merlot, pinot noir, shiraz, souzao, tempranillo;
in addition, there are seven other varieties in
trial rows
Leading wines: Happ's Cabernet-Merlot,
Merlot, Shiraz, Chardonnay, Verdelho,
Semillon-Verdelho, Fuschia (Rose), Fortis
(vintage port style)
Notes: As may be seen from the list of varieties
planted, Erl Happ has an intense interest in
varieties and their distinctive flavours and the
wines made reflect this interest. A vineyard
much larger than the home vineyard at
Dunsborough is presently being developed at
Karridale, 60 km south and much cooler. Cellar
door sales: 7 days 10am–5pm.

Hay Shed Hill R7

Harman's Mill Road, Willyabrup,
WA 6280
Ph 08 9755 6234, Fax 08 9755 6305

Owners: Barry and Liz Morrison
Chief winemaker: Peter Stanlake
Year of foundation: 1988
Tonnes crushed on average each year: 100
Location: Willyabrup
Area: 18 ha
Soils: chiefly lateritic gravel with some loam
over clay and sand pockets
Varieties planted: White—chardonnay,
sauvignon blanc, semillon; Red—cabernet
franc, cabernet sauvignon, merlot, muscat,
petit verdot, pinot noir
Leading wines: Hayshed Hill Cabernet
Sauvignon, Semillon, Sauvignon Blanc,
Pitchfork Pink, Chardonnay, Pinot Noir
Notes: This was formerly Sussex Vale, now
completely refurbished as Hay Shed Hill with
the added advantage of a supple, easy drinking
Cabernet Sauvignon off 20-year-old vines, a
delightful red very much in the style of its
Willyabrup origin. Cellar door sales: Sat–Mon,
Wed and public holidays 10am–5pm.

Hunt's Foxhaven Estate NR

Canal Rocks Road, Yallingup, WA 6282
Ph 08 9755 2232, 08 9755 2249

Owners: David and Libby Hunt
Chief winemaker: David Hunt
Year of foundation: 1978
Tonnes crushed on average each year:
9, increasing to 20
Location: Yallingup
Area: 3.2 ha and increasing
Soils: sandy clay loams alkaline
Varieties planted: White—riesling, sauvignon
blanc, semillon; Red—cabernet franc, cabernet
sauvignon, merlot
Leading wines: Hunt's Foxhaven Yallingup
Classic White, Cabernet Sauvignon
Notes: This is a small family-operated winery
with a cellar door outlet and an emphasis on
white wines. Cellar door sales: weekends and
public holidays 11am–5pm.

Leeuwin Estate R10

Stevens Road, Margaret River, WA 6285
Ph 08 9757 6253, Fax 08 9757 6364

Owner: Rural Developments Pty Ltd
Chief winemaker: Robert Cartwright
Year of foundation: 1975
Tonnes crushed on average each year: 500
Location: Margaret River
Area: 100 ha in bearing, 40 ha not yet bearing
Soils: old granite derived lateritic gravel—
'marri-jarrah' for red, 'marri-karri' for white
Varieties planted: White—chardonnay, riesling,
sauvignon blanc; Red—cabernet sauvignon,
pinot noir and very small quantities of malbec,
merlot and petit verdot
Leading wines: Art Series Chardonnay,
Cabernet Sauvignon, Riesling
Notes: The showplace of Margaret River,
Leeuwin Estate has an obsession—quality. Its
Art Series Chardonnay in particular is a
benchmark for the Australian style. An
excellently structured white that matures well,
even when released, as it usually is, at four
years of age. It is aromatically rich but elegant,
with a palate that matures into a fig-peach
ripeness without fatness. Cellar door sales:
10.30am–4.30pm each day. There is also a
restaurant.

Lenton Brae NR

Caves Road, Willyabrup, WA 6284
Ph 08 9755 6255, Fax 08 9755 6268

Owners: Bruce and Jeanette Tomlinson
Chief winemaker: Edward Tomlinson (Gary
Baldwin, consultant)
Year of foundation: 1982
Tonnes crushed on average each year: 90
Location: Willyabrup
Area: 12 ha
Soils: gravelly loam, 'marri' country
Varieties planted: White—chardonnay,
sauvignon blanc, semillon; Red—cabernet
franc, cabernet sauvignon, merlot, petit verdot
Leading wines: Lenton Brae Chardonnay,
Cabernet Merlot, Sauvignon Blanc, Semillon,
Sauvignon Blanc, Cabernet Sauvignon
Notes: Bruce Tomlinson makes both serious
and light-hearted wines, not that the latter are
any sort of joke. He simply believes that
present-day society requires lighter enjoyable
wines to accompany its preference for
Mediterranean style foods. More traditional
cellaring styles are not ignored, however, as
witness Lenton Brae's Chardonnay and
Cabernet Sauvignon.

Marybrook Vineyards NR

Vasse Yallingup Road, Marybrook,
WA 6280
Ph 08 9755 1143, Fax 08 9755 1112

Owners: Aubrey and Jan House
Chief winemaker: Mike Davies (contract)
Year of foundation: 1988
Tonnes crushed on average each year: 10
Location: Marybrook

Area: 4 ha
Soils: black and red alluvial loam 1–2 metres deep over gravelly clay
Varieties planted: White—chardonnay, verdelho; Red—bastardo, cabernet franc, cabernet sauvignon, grenache
Leading wines: Marybrook Verdelho, Cabernet
Notes: No cellar door sales at this small winery.

Moss Brothers **NR**

Lot 1 Sussex Location 341
Caves Road, Willyabrup, WA 6280
Ph 08 9755 6270, Fax 08 9755 6298

Owners: Fay, Jeff, Peter and David Moss
Chief winemakers: David and Jane Moss
Year of foundation: 1984
Tonnes crushed on average each year: 80
Location: Willyabrup
Area: 6.6 ha
Soils: 'mean' gravelly soils
Varieties planted: White—chardonnay, sauvignon blanc, semillon; Red—cabernet franc, grenache, merlot, pinot noir
Leading wines: Moss Brothers Semillon, Sauvignon Blanc, Cabernet-Merlot, Pinot Noir
Notes: This name is not without controversy because of nearby Moss Wood and not without its amusing side because of the world-famous clothes hire firm in London. However, as Jeff Moss says, a family should be entitled to use its own name and so it does. In a region where pinot noir is not regarded as a success, Moss Bros is an exception and makes a good Pinot Noir. Cellar door sales: each day 9am–5.30pm.

Moss Wood Winery **R10**

Metricup Road, Willyabrup, WA 6280
Ph 08 9755 6266, Fax 08 9755 6303

Owner: Moss Wood Pty Ltd
Chief winemaker: Keith Mugford
Year of foundation: 1969
Tonnes crushed on average each year: 80

Location: Willyabrup
Area: 8.5 ha (1.75 ha to come into bearing)
Soils: gravelly loam about 1–2 metres deep over clay
Varieties planted: White—chardonnay, semillon; Red—cabernet franc, cabernet sauvignon, merlot, petit verdot, pinot noir
Leading wines: Moss Wood Cabernet Sauvignon, Semillon, Chardonnay, Pinot Noir
Notes: Moss Wood is another very famous Margaret River winery, for many years owned by Dr Bill Pannell, like Keith Mugford a talented winemaker-proprietor. The most famous wines here are the Semillon in the whites—elegant and stylish like most Margaret River Semillons—and the Cabernet Sauvignon. Though Margaret River is rather warm for the variety, Keith Mugford also makes a light and very flavoursome Pinot Noir. Cellar door sales by appointment.

Palmer Wines **NR**

Caves Road, Willyabrup, WA 6280
Ph 08 9797 1881, Fax 08 9797 0534

Owners: Helen and Steve Palmer
Chief winemaker: Amberley Estate (contract)
Year of foundation: 1977
Tonnes crushed on average each year: 65
Location: Willyabrup
Area: 10.2 ha
Soils: old gravelly soils over clay
Varieties planted: White—chardonnay, sauvignon blanc, semillon; Red—cabernet franc, cabernet sauvignon, merlot
Leading wines: Palmer Chardonnay, Semillon, Cabernet Sauvignon
Notes: The story of Palmers is almost biblical: a struggle against nature in the form of a cyclone, which wiped out the first planting of cabernet sauvignon, and then the veritable plague of grasshoppers, which devoured the regrowing shoots. Thus ended the Palmers' first viticultural lesson in 1977. Steve's other love, horse-racing, led him into the

thoroughbred industry for a time and then it was back into the wine industry in the mid-1980s, as Margaret River began to boom. Steve's neighbour, Mike Peterkin, supervised the planting of the new vineyard and the first vintage came on stream in 1989. Early Palmer Chardonnays, made by Mike Peterkin, were tremendously successful, the 1991 winning a trophy at the Mount Barker Show. Since 1994, the winemaking has been supervised by Eddie Price at Amberley and success continues. Cellar door sales by appointment.

Pierro R10

Caves Road, Willyabrup, WA 6280
Ph 08 9755 6220, Fax 08 9755 6308

Owner/chief winemaker: Dr Mike Peterkin
Year of foundation: 1980
Tonnes crushed on average each year: 130
Location: Willyabrup
Area: 7 ha
Soils: lateritic gravelly loam over friable clay subsoils
Varieties planted: White—chardonnay, sauvignon blanc, semillon; Red—cabernet franc, cabernet sauvignon, merlot, petit verdot, pinot noir
Leading wines: Pierro Chardonnay, Cabernets, Semillon-Sauvignon Blanc
Notes: Mike Peterkin is a winemaking medical practitioner, renowned for Pierro Chardonnay, one of the best examples of the variety anywhere in Australia, a lively semillon-sauvignon blanc blend and a supple and stylish cabernet, made from the classic Bordeaux brotherhood, cabernet sauvignon, cabernet franc, merlot and petit verdot. Cellar door sales: each day 10am–5pm.

Redgate Wines R6

Boodjidup Road, Margaret River, WA 6285
Ph 08 9757 6488, Fax 08 9757 6308

Owner: WW Ullinger
Chief winemaker: Andrew Forsell and Paul Ullinger
Year of foundation: 1977
Tonnes crushed on average each year: 150
Location: Margaret River
Area: 16 ha
Soils: light lateritic gravel varying to sand in the valley
Varieties planted: White—chardonnay, chenin blanc, sauvignon blanc, semillon;
Red—cabernet franc, cabernet sauvignon, merlot, pinot noir, shiraz
Leading wines: Redgate Chardonnay, Sauvignon Blanc, Cabernet Sauvignon, Shiraz
Notes: Cabernet is the accepted wisdom at Margaret River but Redgate Shiraz, winner of gold medals at Hobart and Stanthorpe, is certainly making its mark. This old established winery (old, that is, by Margaret River standards) is also well known for its herbaceous Sauvignon Blanc. Cellar door sales: each day 10am–5pm.

Ribbon Vale Estate R7

Lot 5 Caves Road, Willyabrup, WA 6280
Ph 08 9755 6272, Fax 08 9755 6337

Owner: John James
Chief winemaker: Michael Davies (contract)
Year of foundation: 1977
Tonnes crushed on average each year: 60
Location: Willyabrup
Area: 6.8 ha
Soils: lateritic gravel overlying kaolinised granite gneiss
Varieties planted: White—sauvignon blanc, semillon; Red—cabernet franc, cabernet sauvignon, merlot
Leading wines: Ribbon Vale Sauvignon Blanc, Merlot
Notes: Ribbon Vale is so named not only because it has delightful views over the Willyabrup valley but primarily because of its shape, 185 m wide and 1.3 km long. Fresh

Sauvignon Blanc, lemony herbaceous Semillon and plummy Merlot are the hallmarks of this estate. Cellar door sales: weekends and public holidays 10am–5pm.

Rivendell Vineyard NR

Wildwood Road, Yallingup, WA 6282
Ph 08 9755 2235, Fax 08 9755 2295
Mobile 0417 977 192

Owners: Mark and Wendy Standish
Chief winemakers: Mike and Jan Davies (contract)
Year of foundation: 1987
Tonnes crushed on average each year: 35 and increasing
Location: Yallingup
Area: 12.5 ha
Soils: lateritic gravel 'marri' country
Varieties planted: White—sauvignon blanc, semillon, verdelho; Red—cabernet franc, cabernet sauvignon, merlot, shiraz
Leading wines: Rivendell Cabernets, Semillon-Sauvignon Blanc, Verdelho
Notes: Rivendell is another family-run vineyard in the Margaret River 'white wine belt' at Yallingup. Verdelho seems to be its speciality at the moment. Cellar door sales: each day 10am–5pm.

Rosabrook Estate R7

Rosabrook Road, Margaret River, WA 6285
Ph 08 9757 2286, Fax 08 9757 3634

Owner: John Shepherd
Chief winemaker: Simon Keall
Year of foundation: 1993
Tonnes crushed on average each year: 60
Location: Margaret River
Area: 15 ha
Soils: deep sandy loam varying to deep sandy gravel loam over clay
Varieties planted: White—chardonnay, riesling, sauvignon blanc, semillon; Red—cabernet franc, cabernet sauvignon, malbec, merlot, shiraz
Leading wines: Rosabrook Semillon-Sauvignon Blanc, Cabernet-Merlot, Shiraz
Notes: A very promising newcomer to Margaret River, Rosabrook is already building a strong reputation for its reds. Cellar door sales: summer only, Thurs–Sun 11am–4pm.

Sandalford Wines R7.5

Metricup Road, Willyabrup, WA 6284
Ph 08 9755 6233, Fax 08 9755 6294

Owner: Sandalford Wines Pty Ltd
Chief winemaker: Bill Crappsley
Year of foundation: 1973 (Margaret River vineyard)
Tonnes crushed on average each year: 600
Location: Willyabrup
Area: 107.95 ha
Soils: lateritic gravel 'marri' country
Varieties planted: White—chardonnay, chenin blanc, riesling, sauvignon blanc, semillon, verdelho; Red—cabernet sauvignon, shiraz
Leading wines: Most Sandalford reds and whites are blends of Margaret River and Mount Barker fruit. One present exception to this is Sandalford Margaret River Verdelho.
Notes: Sandalford is one of the West's senior wine producers, dating its establishment year as 1840. Its Margaret River vineyard has experienced a number of problems over the years, the most serious of which has been the small, almost meagre, production of its vines. This is now being addressed and quantity is improving. Quality has never been in doubt and certainly at some time in the future, if Bill Crappsley has his way, there will be a premium Margaret River red. Cellar door sales: each day 11am–4pm.

Sandstone R6

Caves and Johnson Roads, Willyabrup, WA 6280
Ph 08 9755 6271, Fax 08 9755 6292

Owners: Jan and Mike Davies and partners
Chief winemakers: Jan and Mike Davies
Year of foundation: 1988
Tonnes crushed on average each year: 10
Location: Willyabrup (not yet in full production)
Area: 6 ha
Soils: lateritic gravel, 'jarrah-marri' country
Varieties planted: White—semillon; no reds planted
Leading wines: Sandstone Semillon, Cabernet Sauvignon
Notes: Mike and Jan Davies conduct a flourishing business as contract winemakers and bottlers for numerous local winegrowers. The Sandstone Semillon is always among the better whites of the region. No cellar door sales.

Serventy Organic Wines NR

Valley Home Vineyard, Rocky Road, Witchcliffe, WA 6286
Ph/Fax 08 9757 7534

Owners: Peter and Lyn Serventy
Chief winemaker: Peter Serventy
Year of foundation: 1984
Tonnes crushed on average each year: 15
Location: Witchcliffe
Area: 7 ha
Soils: 'Karri' loam over gravel
Varieties planted: White—chardonnay, sauvignon blanc; Red—pinot noir, shiraz
Leading wines: Serventy Chardonnay, Pinot Noir, Shiraz
Notes: Serventy is currently the only certified organic vineyard in the Margaret River region. Cellar door sales: Fri–Sun and holidays 10am–4pm.

Thornhill NR

The Berry Farm, Bessell Road, Margaret River, WA 6285
Ph/Fax 08 9757 5054

Owners: Andrea and Eoin Lindsay
Chief winemaker: Eoin Lindsay

Year of foundation: 1983
Tonnes crushed on average each year: 8
Location: Margaret River
Area: 4 ha
Soils: varying from clay alluvial to sandy loam without gravel
Varieties planted: White—sauvignon blanc, semillon; Red—cabernet sauvignon
Leading wine: Thornhill Cabernet Sauvignon
Notes: Thornhill is a berry farm; all sorts of berries and kiwi fruit are used in the making of fruit wines and naturally fermented fruit vinegars. Though the vineyard is an offshoot of the farm, it is taken very seriously and Eoin Lindsay is very proud of his Cabernet Sauvignon. It is produced in the Chapman Valley, a very cool microclimate of Margaret River. Cellar door sales: 7 days 10am–4.30pm.

Treeton Estate NR

North Treeton Road, Cowaramup, WA 6284
Ph 08 9755 5481, Fax 08 9755 5051

Owner/chief winemaker: David McGowan
Year of foundation: 1987
Tonnes crushed on average each year: 33 and increasing as further vines are planted
Location: Cowaramup
Area: 8.5 ha, will increase to 15 ha
Soils: pebbly lateritic loam
Varieties planted: White—chardonnay, chenin blanc, sauvignon blanc; Red—cabernet sauvignon, shiraz
Leading wine: Shiraz
Notes: This typical family-operated Margaret River winery is beginning to expand and, with a 50-tonne or more crush, will certainly occupy all David McGowan's time. Watch out for the Shiraz, hitherto understandably unfashionable in Margaret River because of the quality of its cabernet, but now well worth attention. Cellar door sales: 7 days 10am–6pm.

Vasse Felix R8.5

Cnr Caves and Harmans Roads,
Willyabrup, WA 6280
Ph 08 9755 5242, Fax 08 9755 5425

Owner: Heytesbury Pty Ltd
Chief winemaker: Clive Otto
Year of foundation: 1967
Tonnes crushed on average each year: 500
Location: South Cowaramup
Area: 15 ha
Soils: lateritic gravelly loam over a clay base
Varieties planted: White—riesling, semillon,
verdelho; Red—cabernet sauvignon, malbec,
shiraz
Leading wines: Vasse Felix Cabernet Sauvignon,
Shiraz
Notes: This is the first vineyard of modern
Margaret River. Founded in 1967 by Dr Tom
Cullity, it became an icon and was famous at
that time for its Cabernet Sauvignon. More
recently, ownership has passed to Heytesbury,
the Holmes à Court family company, and the
range of wines has been extended. Its Shiraz is
now among the best in the west. Cellar door
sales: 7 days 10am–4.30pm.

Vasse River Wines NR

Bussell Highway, Carbunup, WA 6280
Ph/Fax 08 9755 1111

Owners: Credaro family
Chief winemaker: Robert Credaro with
consultancy advice
Year of foundation: 1988
Tonnes crushed on average each year: 35 but
increasing from 1998
Location: Carbunup
Area: 25 ha, mostly young non-bearing vines
Soils: red gravelly loam over clay
Varieties planted: White—chardonnay,
semillon, verdelho; Red—cabernet sauvignon,
merlot, shiraz
Leading wines: Vasse River Cabernet Merlot,
Chardonnay

Notes: Robert Credaro is the third generation
of the family, which has been farming this
property since 1922. Some fruit is sold each
vintage, but Robert is anticipating a crush in
excess of 150 tonnes in the near future, a
challenge which he is honing his winemaking
skills to meet. Cellar door sales: 7 days
10am–5pm.

Virage Wines NR

13B Georgette Road, Gracetown,
WA 6284
Ph/Fax 08 9755 5318

Owners: Bernard and Pascale Abbott
Chief winemaker: Bernard Abbott
Year of foundation: 1991
Tonnes crushed on average each year: 20
Location: Margaret River
Leading wines: Virage Cabernet Merlot,
Semillon-Chardonnay
Notes: Though Virage is quite small (only about
1000 cases are produced), there are no cellar
door sales and all marketing is done directly to
retailers in Perth and Sydney. No vineyard is
owned.

Voyager Estate R8

Steven's Road, Margaret River, WA 6285
Ph 08 9757 6358

Owner: Michael Wright
Chief winemaker: Stuart Pym
Year of foundation: 1978
Tonnes crushed on average each year: 300
Location: Margaret River
Area: 40 ha and expanding
Soils: gravelly loam over permeable clay
Varieties planted: White—chardonnay, chenin
blanc, sauvignon blanc, semillon;
Red—cabernet franc, cabernet sauvignon,
merlot, shiraz
Leading wines: Voyager Estate Chardonnay,
Cabernet Sauvignon, Merlot
Notes: Michael Wright purchased the former

Freycinet Estate in 1991 and has since expanded it into one of the showplaces of the region. Yet it is not all show, but serious stuff—the whites, especially the Chardonnay, are excellent and the red Cabernet Sauvignon Merlot is positively outstanding. The sweeter style Chenin Blanc, however, leaves me a little cold. Cellar door sales: daily 11am–5pm.

Wild NR

Caves Road, Yallingup, WA 6282
Ph 08 9755 2066, Fax 08 9754 1389

Owner: Glen Brook Pty Ltd
Chief winemaker: Mark Lane
Year of foundation: 1985
Tonnes crushed on average each year: 35
Location: Yallingup
Area: 6.5 ha
Soils: gravelly loam over clay
Varieties planted: White—chardonnay, chenin blanc, sauvignon blanc, semillon,
Red—cabernet franc, cabernet sauvignon, gamay, merlot, pinot noir
Leading wines: Wild Semillon (lightly oaked), Classic (a white blend), Honeydew (a sweet table white), Simply Red (merlot and pinot noir), Cabernet Sauvignon, Franc, Merlot
Notes: Cellar door sales: 7 days 9.30am till late. There is also a restaurant.

Willespie R7.5

Harman's Mill Road, Willyabrup,
WA 6280
Ph 08 9755 6248, Fax 08 9755 6210

Owners: Kevin and Marian Squance
Chief winemaker: Peter Lemmes
Year of foundation: 1976
Tonnes crushed on average each year: 100
Location: Willyabrup
Area: 20 ha
Soils: chiefly gravelly loam over clay, loam over clay
Varieties planted: White—sauvignon blanc,

semillon, verdelho; Red—cabernet sauvignon
Leading wines: Willespie Cabernet Sauvignon, Verdelho, Semillon, Semillon-Sauvignon Blanc
Notes: Full-bodied Cabernet reds, a complex dry Verdelho, a grassy Semillon and a fresh white blend of semillon and sauvignon blanc are the highlights of the excellent Willespie range. Cellar door sales: 7 days 10.30am–5pm.

Wise Vineyards NR

Eagle Bay Road, Meelup, WA 6281
Ph 08 9756 8098, Fax 08 9755 3979

Owner: Ron Wise
Chief winemaker: Siobhan Lynch
Year of foundation: 1986
Tonnes crushed on average each year: 150
Location: Cape Naturaliste Peninsula, 5 km north of Dunsborough
Area: 20 ha
Soils: gravelly loams over clay, richer loam over clay, sand over clay
Varieties planted: White—chardonnay, chenin blanc, sauvignon blanc, semillon;
Red—cabernet sauvignon, merlot, pinot noir, sangiovese, shiraz
Leading wines: Wise Vineyards Chardonnay, Semillon, Cabernet Sauvignon
Notes: This winery and its restaurant with a spectacular view over Geographe Bay presently produces soft accessible reds (Merlot and Pinot Noir). Fruit is also brought in from Donnybrook in the Geographe region, and from Pemberton. Cellar door sales: 7 days 10.30am–4.30pm.

Woodlands Wines R6.5

Caves Road, Willyabrup, WA 6280
Ph 08 9755 6226 (winery),
08 9274 6155, Fax 08 9321 6385

Owners: David and Heather Watson
Chief winemaker: David Watson
Year of foundation: 1973
Tonnes crushed on average each year: 10 (the rest of the fruit is sold)

Location: Willyabrup
Area: 4.8 ha
Soils: red-brown gravelly loam over clay
Varieties planted: White—chardonnay;
Red—cabernet franc, cabernet sauvignon,
malbec, merlot, pinot noir
Leading wine: Woodlands Cabernet Sauvignon
Notes: Another veteran of the region,
Woodlands is at the heart of Willyabrup's best
cabernet country and its Cabernets are
sometimes astounding in their quality. But
production is small and during the 1980s was
irregular. Cellar door sales: weekends by
appointment.

Woody Nook NR

Metricup Road, Metricup, WA 6284
Ph/Fax 08 9755 7547

Owners: Jeff and Wyn Gallagher
Chief winemaker: Neil Gallagher
Year of foundation: 1982
Tonnes crushed on average each year: 30
Location: Metricup
Area: 8 ha
Soils: lateritic gravelly loam over clay
Varieties planted: White—chardonnay, chenin
blanc, sauvignon blanc, semillon, verdelho;
Red—cabernet franc, cabernet sauvignon,
merlot, shiraz
Leading wines: Woody Nook Classic Dry White,
Cabernet Sauvignon
Notes: This small maker's great care in the
upbringing of its wines is rewarded by show
success. Cellar door sales: 7 days
10am–4.30pm.

Wright's Winery R6

Harman's Road South, Cowaramup,
WA 6284
Ph 08 9755 5314, Fax 08 9755 5459

Owners: HC and MBB Wright
Chief winemaker: Henry Wright
Year of foundation: 1973

Tonnes crushed on average each year: 65
Location: Cowaramup
Area: 11.5 ha
Soils: an undulating vineyard with variable soils
rising from red loam over clay to gravelly
lateritic loam over clay
Varieties planted: White—chardonnay, riesling,
semillon; Red—cabernet sauvignon, shiraz
Leading wines: Wright's Shiraz, Cabernet
Sauvignon, Premium Estate (a semillon-
chardonnay blend), White Port (from riesling),
Vintage Port (from shiraz)
Notes: As a young man, Henry Wright worked
as a British colonial officer in Kenya and
Zimbabwe. So winemaking is really only the
second chapter of a very interesting life. Yet he
is already a veteran of Margaret River, being
one of the first six to plant in the region.
Wright plans no expansion to the winery or
vineyard, being content to remain of modest
but certainly not minute size. He has also been
and remains an enthusiastic proponent of
shiraz for the Margaret River region. Cellar
door sales: 7 days 10am–4.30pm.

Yungarra Estate NR

2 Yungarra Drive, Dunsborough,
WA 6281
Ph 08 9755 2153, Fax 08 9755 2310

Owners: Gerry and Wendy Atherden
Chief winemaker: Erl Happ (contract)
Year of foundation: 1988
Tonnes crushed on average each year: 80 and
rising, as the vineyard matures
Location: Dunsborough
Area: 8 ha
Soils: gravelly loam over clay, lateritic
Varieties planted: White—chenin blanc,
sauvignon blanc, semillon, verdelho;
Red—cabernet franc, cabernet sauvignon,
merlot, pinot noir
Leading wines: Cabernet Merlot, Semillon
Notes: Despite its first vintage being as recent
as 1992, Yungarra is already making a name

for its elegant Cabernet Merlot—subtle, fruity and not too weighty—as witness its successes in Perth's Sheraton Awards and the Top 100 of the Sydney International Wine Competition. Cellar door sales: 7 days 10am–4pm.

GREAT SOUTHERN REGION

Albany, the largest city in the Great Southern region, is also the oldest settlement in Western Australia, being founded on Christmas Day 1826. The suitability of the region for vines was assessed much later, thanks largely to the pioneering report of Professor Olmo in 1955, made for the Western Australian government, further work by John Gladstones in 1963 (see the introduction to Margaret River) and the ongoing enthusiasm shown by Bill Jamieson, the Western Australian state viticulturalist at that time. Its vineyard beginnings are generally acknowledged to have commenced in 1965 with the planting of the first cuttings at Forest Hill on land leased to the Western Australian Department of Agriculture by local farmers, Tony and Betty Pearse. The initial plantings of a little over a hectare each of riesling and cabernet sauvignon were unsuccessful due to excessive spring rainfall. Notwithstanding that setback, the vines were replanted the following year and succeeded. Its first wines in 1972 were pretty much a family affair, the riesling being made by Dorham Mann at Sandalford, and the cabernet at Houghton's in 1972 by his father Jack, the doyen of the Western Australian wine industry, then making his 51st and last vintage before retirement. About the same time (1967), John Roche, an Adelaide businessman, was planting one hectare each of cabernet and riesling on his Frankland River property, Westfield. Local grazier Tony Smith also caught the mood by planting his Bouverie vineyard near Denbarker with a hectare of cabernet sauvignon and one of shiraz in 1968. The Roche plantings today form a very small part of the Houghton Wine Co Frankland River Vineyard and those of Smith form a fraction of the Plantagenet vineyard.

In 1975, Plantagenet made its first wines at Mount Barker and the region was firmly established, there being seven vineyards in operation between Mount Barker and Frankland River. Soon after, vineyards in the Porongurups area were being developed, as well as others around Denmark. Today there are 26 vineyards and eight wineries in the region, which is highly regarded for its Riesling and Shiraz wines, though Pinot Noir is also very successful.

Location: Albany latitude 35°02'S, longitude 117°42'E, about 400 km south-east of Perth; Mount Barker latitude 34°36'S, longitude 117°38'E, about 350 km south-east of Perth
Elevation: from sea-level to about 400 m in fairly uniform gradients. The Porongurups apart, the region is gently undulating.
Topography and soils: Topographically, from Albany and the southern coast, the region climbs gently northward to the plateau of the Yilgarn Rock in the west and in the east traverses another slightly rising plain of tertiary sediments to the Porongurups and Stirling Ranges in the north. Its soils seem nicely divided by the north–south

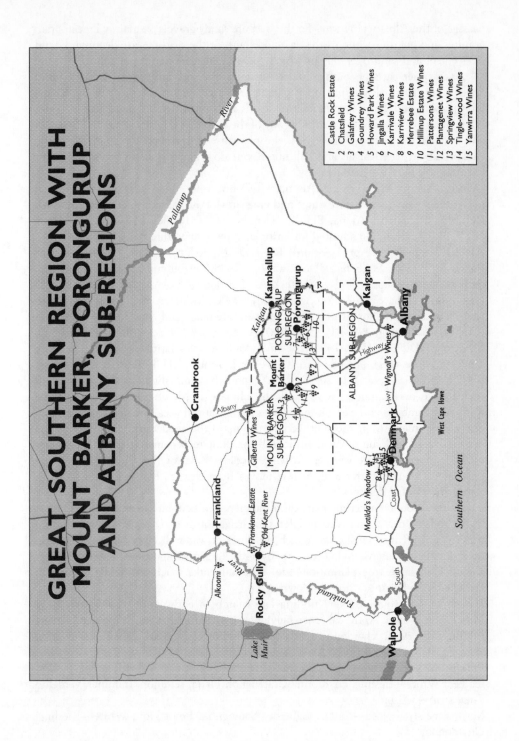

GREAT SOUTHERN REGION WITH MOUNT BARKER, PORONGURUP AND ALBANY SUB-REGIONS

1   Castle Rock Estate
2   Chatsfield
3   Galafrey Wines
4   Goundrey Wines
5   Howard Park Wines
6   Jingalla Wines
7   Karrivale Wines
8   Karriview Wines
9   Merrebee Estate
10 Millinup Estate Wines
11 Pattersons Wines
12 Plantagenet Wines
13 Springview Wines
14 Tingle-wood Wines
15 Yanwirra Wines

Pallanup

River

Kalgan

Kamballup

Kalgan

Kalgan

Porongurup

PORONGURUP
SUB-REGION

Albany

ALBANY SUB-REGION

Highway

Albany

Cranbrook

Mount
Barker

MOUNT BARKER
SUB-REGION

Gilberts Wines

Denmark

Wignall's Wines

Hwy

West Cape Howe

Frankland

Frankland Estate

Old Kent River

Matilda's Meadow

Coast

Alkoomi

River

Rocky Gully

Southern Ocean

Lake
Muir

Frankland

South

Walpole

passage of the Albany Highway. To the west are sandy gravels on mainly Precambrian granites and gneisses while to the east and south of the Stirlings are deep sand, sand over gravel and sand over clay on chiefly tertiary siltstones and spongolites.

As in other parts of south-western Australia, the soils are generally divided into 'marri' and 'karri' depending on the prevalent tree, 'marri' being gravelly, sandy, lateritic soils and 'karri' heavier, clayey loams with much less, if any, gravel.

Drainage of the western part is by way of the Frankland, Kent, Denmark, Sleeman and Hay Rivers. Between the rivers, the plateau country is poorly drained. To the east of Albany, the Kalgan and Pallinup Rivers do drain this district to some extent but drainage here is generally poor.

Climate: Albany MJT 19°C, MAR na, HDD raw 1495, 1533 (cut-off and adjusted for latitude, daily temperature range and vine sites), AR 800 mm (Oct–Apr 303 mm), RH 54% (3pm Jan), AI na, SH 7.9. Denmark MJT 18.7°C, MAR na, HDD raw 1471, 1461 (cut-off and adjusted for latitude, daily temperature range and vine sites), AR 1012 mm (Oct–Apr 354 mm), RH 65% (3pm Jan), AI na, SH 6.6. Mount Barker MJT 19°C, MAR na, HDD raw 1440, 1488 (cut-off and adjusted for latitude, daily temperature range and vine sites), AR 756 mm (Oct–Apr 285 mm), RH 49% (Jan 3pm), AI na, SH 7.1. Porongurups MJT 19°C, MAR na, HDD raw 1441, 1446 (cut-off and adjusted for latitude, daily temperature range and vine sites), AR 748 mm (Oct–Apr 310 mm), 49% RH (3pm Jan), AI na, SH 7.1. Rocky Gully MJT 19.8°C, MAR na, HDD raw 1530, 1494 (cut-off and adjusted for latitude, daily temperature range and vine sites), AR 687 mm (Oct–Apr 215 mm), RH 43% (3pm Jan), AI na, SH 7.6 (all Gladstones). In such a large region there are slight local differences in temperature and rainfall, but overall the climate is Mediterranean, experiencing warm, dry summers and wet winters. As a generalisation, it can be said that the more one moves inland from the south coast, the more the moderating influence of the sea is reduced and the more 'continental' the climate becomes (that is, in summer inland temperatures are warmer, in winter, colder). As for the rainfall, the coastal areas are of course wetter and, as one moves from west to east and from south to north, the rainfall declines.

As the Mount Barker area sits on an ancient sea-bed and areas of salt still exist in the soil, salinity presents its problems for irrigation from rivers and bores. Surface water is run off into local dams which, in times of water shortage, are used for drip irrigation. Local hazards include damage by birds, kangaroos and emus, where vineyards are close to large tree plantations and national parks (such as the Porongurups). Frosts after budburst are not unknown.

Harvest time: (Mount Barker) riesling late March to early April, chardonnay early March, shiraz early April, cabernet sauvignon early to mid-April. (Frankland River) riesling early April, chardonnay early March, shiraz early April, cabernet sauvignon early April.

Principal varieties: Red—shiraz, cabernet sauvignon, pinot noir, cabernet franc, merlot, malbec; White—riesling, chardonnay, sauvignon blanc, semillon, traminer, verdelho

Total area: 4500 ha

Major wine styles: Red—Shiraz, Cabernet Sauvignon, Pinot Noir; White—Riesling, Chardonnay

Alkoomi R9

Wingeballup Road, Frankland, WA 6396
Ph 08 9855 2229, Fax 08 9855 2284

Owners: Merv and Judy Lange and family
Chief winemaker: Michael Staniford
Year of foundation: 1971
Tonnes crushed on average each year: 500
Location: Frankland River
Area: 40 ha
Soils: free draining gravel over clay, 'marri'
country
Varieties planted: White—chardonnay, riesling,
sauvignon blanc, semillon, verdelho;
Red—cabernet sauvignon, merlot, malbec,
cabernet franc, shiraz
Leading wines: Alkoomi Sauvignon Blanc,
Riesling, Chardonnay, Cabernet Sauvignon,
Shiraz
Notes: Alkoomi is one of the veterans of the
once remote Frankland River area. Its excellent
Sauvignon Blanc is usually a pungent reminder
of the variety at its tart and refreshing best. Its
Riesling is delightfully delicate and varietally
correct. Its reds, particularly its Cabernet
Sauvignon, are deep-flavoured and age well up
to 10 years and sometimes longer.

Castle Rock Estate R7.5

Porongurup Road, Porongurup, WA 6324
Ph 08 9853 1035, Fax 08 9853 1010

Owners: Angelo and Wendy Diletti
Chief winemaker: Michael Staniford (contract)
Year of foundation: 1983
Tonnes crushed on average each year: 60
Location: Porongurup
Area: 9 ha
Soils: an undulating vineyard with red loam
over clay on its higher slopes and gravelly loam
over tight clay on its lower parts
Varieties planted: White—chardonnay, riesling,
sauvignon blanc; Red—cabernet franc,
cabernet sauvignon, merlot, pinot noir
Leading wines: Castle Rock Riesling, Cabernet

Sauvignon, Chardonnay, Pinot Noir, Estate
White
Notes: As its name implies, Castle Rock has
commanding views of the surrounding
countryside as far as the Stirling Ranges. In its
comparatively short existence, it has built up an
excellent reputation for aromatic Rieslings and
Cabernets of full berry flavour. Cellar door
sales: Wed–Sun and public holidays
10am–5pm.

Chatsfield R8

O'Neill Road, Mount Barker, WA 6324
Ph/Fax 08 9851 1704

Owners: Dr Ken and Mrs Joyce Lynch
Chief winemaker: Plantagenet Wines (Gavin
Berry, contract)
Year of foundation: 1976 as Waterman's,
renamed Chatsfield in 1985
Tonnes crushed on average each year: 33
Location: Mount Barker
Area: 17.2 ha consisting of two vineyards (old
8 ha and new 9.2 ha)
Soils: gravelly loam over clay
Varieties planted: White—chardonnay,
gewurztraminer, riesling, sauvignon blanc;
Red—cabernet franc, shiraz
Leading wines: Chatsfield Riesling, Shiraz
Notes: With some vines now over 20 years old,
Chatsfield is one of the quiet quality
performers of the Great Southern region. It
produces rich Shiraz wines, often medal
winners, and delicate Rieslings and Traminers.
Cellar door sales: Wed–Sun and public holidays
10am–5pm.

Forest Hill (vineyard only) R8.5

Muir Highway, Mount Barker, WA 6324

Owners: R McGrath, A Marton, T Lyons
Chief winemaker: Clive Otto (Vasse Felix)
Year of foundation: 1965
Tonnes crushed on average each year: 200
Location: Mount Barker

Area: 25 ha
Soils: gravelly loams over clay, 'marri' country
Varieties planted: White—chardonnay, riesling, sauvignon blanc; Red—cabernet sauvignon
Leading wines: Forest Hill Cabernet Sauvignon, Riesling
Notes: This is the original vineyard of Mount Barker, first planted in 1965 and re-established the following year after failure due to excessive spring rainfall. First wines from the vineyard were made in 1972 and immediately Mount Barker began to gain a national reputation for its Rieslings. The region suffered somewhat of a culture-shock when this icon was sold in 1989 to Heytesbury, the Holmes à Court family company, but, though the label changed, quality certainly did not suffer. The vineyard was sold once more in 1993 to its present owners, who continue to supply its fruit to Vasse Felix on a long-term contractual basis. No local cellar door sales.

Frankland Estate R8

Frankland Road, Frankland, WA 6396
Ph 08 9855 1555, Fax 08 9855 1583

Owners: Barrie Smith and Judi Cullam
Chief winemakers: Barrie Smith and Judi Cullam
Year of foundation: 1988
Tonnes crushed on average each year: 190
Location: Frankland
Area: 18.8 ha
Soils: well-drained gravelly soils over loam over clay about a metre deep
Varieties planted: White—chardonnay, riesling, sauvignon blanc; Red—cabernet franc, cabernet sauvignon, malbec, merlot, petit verdot, shiraz
Leading wines: Frankland Estate Riesling, Chardonnay, Olmo's Reward (a red blend, cabernets franc and sauvignon based), Isolation Ridge (shiraz)
Notes: Quite new in the region, Frankland Estate is already highly regarded for its

aromatic Riesling and harmonious Cabernet blend, named after Professor Olmo. Cellar door sales by appointment.

Galafrey Wines R6.5

Quangellup Road, Mount Barker, WA 6324
Ph 08 9851 2022, Fax 08 9851 2324

Owners: Ian and Linda Tyrer
Chief winemaker: Ian Tyrer
Year of foundation: 1975
Tonnes crushed on average each year: 75
Location: Mount Barker
Area: 11 ha
Soils: gravelly loam over clay
Varieties planted: White—chardonnay, muller-thurgau, riesling; Red—cabernet sauvignon, cabernet franc, merlot, pinot noir, shiraz
Leading wines: Chardonnay, Riesling, Cabernet Sauvignon, Pinot Noir, Shiraz
Notes: Now among the veterans of Mount Barker, Ian and Linda Tyrer recently moved Galafrey from its old wool store surrounds to new winery premises. Typically good Mount Barker Riesling. Cellar door sales: Mon–Sat 10am–5pm.

Gilberts Wines R7

Albany Highway, Kendenup, WA 6323
Ph 08 9851 4028

Owners: Jim and Beverley Gilbert
Chief winemaker: Gavin Berry (contract)
Year of foundation: 1985
Tonnes crushed on average each year: 30
Location: Albany Highway, 18 km north of Mount Barker
Area: 6 ha
Soils: gravelly loam over clay, 'marri' country
Varieties planted: White—chardonnay, riesling; Red—shiraz
Leading wines: Gilbert Riesling, Chardonnay, Shiraz
Notes: Jim and Beverley Gilbert run a mixed

farm north of Mount Barker and their vineyard is very much a hands-on operation. Their leading wines, in particular Shiraz and Riesling, share the strengths of the region. Cellar door sales: 7 days 10am–5pm.

Goundrey Wines R8

Muir Highway, Mount Barker, WA 6324
Ph 08 9851 1777, Fax 08 9851 1997

Owners: Jack Bendat and family
Chief winemaker: Keith Bown
Year of foundation: 1975
Tonnes crushed on average each year: 1800
Location: Langton, Mount Barker
Area: 220 ha and growing
Soils: gravelly loam over clay with some granitic and sandy areas
Varieties planted: White—chardonnay, riesling, sauvignon blanc, semillon; Red—cabernet sauvignon, merlot, pinot noir and shiraz
Leading wines: Goundrey Unwooded Chardonnay, Classic White, Cabernet Merlot
Notes: As may be seen from the scheduled increases in plantings, Goundrey, one of the older names in the region, is a winery in a hurry. By the new millennium, Jack Bendat plans to make Goundrey the west's number 2 producer in volume and no doubt number 1 in quality. Cellar door sales: Mon–Sat 10am–4.30pm, Sun 11am–4.30pm.

Harewood Estate R8

Scotsdale Road, Denmark, WA 6333
Ph 08 9840 9078, Fax 08 9840 9053

Owners: Keith and Margie Graham
Chief winemaker: John Wade (contract)
Year of foundation: 1988
Tonnes crushed on average each year: 50
Location: Denmark
Area: 7.75 ha
Soils: deep loam about 1.2 metres graduating to a 'karri-marri' gravelly mixture over friable clay

Varieties planted: White—chardonnay; Red—pinot noir
Leading wines: Harewood Estate Chardonnay, Pinot Noir
Notes: Harewood is a new name, sensibly assessing and establishing the qualities of its vineyard before launching into full-scale wine production. In 1996, only six tonnes of its fruit were utilised in its own wine production but, as the vines are maturing and wine is of consistently good quality, the amount of wine made will undoubtedly increase. No cellar door sales.

Houghton Wine Co Frankland River (vineyard only) R9

Netley Road, Frankland, WA 6396
Ph 08 9274 5100, Fax 08 9274 5372

Owner: Houghton Wines (lessee)
Chief winemaker: Larry Cherubino
Year of foundation: 1970
Tonnes crushed on average each year: 750
Location: Frankland
Area: 89.4 ha
Soils: gravelly sands over clay, 'marri' country
Varieties planted: White—chardonnay, riesling, semillon, verdelho; Red—cabernet sauvignon, malbec, merlot, pinot noir, shiraz
Leading wines: Houghton Riesling, Crofters Cabernet-Merlot, Reserve Shiraz, Wildflower Ridge Shiraz, 'Jack Mann' (a super premium red released in 1997 for the first time)
Notes: Houghton's Frankland River Vineyard is one of the larger and older vineyards in the region. Founded in 1970 and still owned by the Roche family, it was most certainly a gesture of confidence in the future for, by 1975, with the Great Southern region then relatively unknown, 58 ha of dryland vineyard had been established. When the vineyard was expanded in 1978 to approximately its present size, drip irrigation was also installed. This meant (in former wine maker Paul Lapsley's words) 'having to find enough fresh water to

do the job'. This was achieved by harvesting 600 ha of pasture land of the leach water by means of 9 km of drains. No local cellar door sales.

Howard Park Wines (winery only)   R10

Lot 377 Scotsdale Road, Denmark, WA 6333
Ph 08 9848 2345, Fax 08 9848 2064

Owners: J and A Burch and J and W Wade
Chief winemaker: John Wade
Year of foundation: 1986
Tonnes crushed on average each year: 500
Location: no vineyards owned, all fruit presently purchased
Leading wines: Howard Park Riesling, Chardonnay, Cabernet Merlot; other label, Madfish Bay
Notes: Howard Park is the 'professional rooms' of the Great Southern's foremost winemaker and consultant, John Wade, who has a widespread practice making other people's regional wines. He does this exceptionally well, as he does his own label Howard Park, whose Cabernet-Merlot and Riesling wines are often brilliant.

Jingalla Wines   R7.5

Bolganup Dam Road, Porongurup, WA 6324
Ph/Fax 08 9853 1023

Owners: Geoff and Nita Clark and Barry and Shelley Coad
Chief winemaker: Goundrey (contract)
Year of foundation: 1979
Tonnes crushed on average each year: 38
Location: Porongurup
Area: 8 ha
Soils: pea gravel, 'marri' country, and some red 'karri' loams deep granitic and ironstone 'jarrah' country
Varieties planted: White—riesling, semillon,

verdelho; Red—cabernet sauvignon, shiraz
Leading wines: Jingalla Verdelho, Semillon, Riesling, Shiraz, Cabernet Sauvignon
Notes: Located on the northern slopes of the spectacular Porongurup Range at 450 m altitude, Jingalla is ideally suited to produce excellent Rieslings, which it does consistently. Cellar door sales: 7 days 10.30am–5pm.

Karrilea Estate (vineyard only)   NR

RMB 905 Duck Road, Mount Barker, WA 6324
Ph 08 9851 1838

Owners: John and Jan Pickles
Chief winemaker: in times of wine production, Plantagenet Wines
Year of foundation: 1982
Tonnes crushed on average each year: 10, presently all grapes are sold
Location: Mount Barker
Area: 2 ha
Soils: gravelly loam over clay
Varieties planted: White—riesling, sauvignon blanc, traminer; Red—cabernet franc, cabernet sauvignon, merlot, pinot noir
Leading wines: no wine production at the present time, but it is anticipated that wine production may recommence soon
Notes: Karrilea is an organic vineyard, cultivated biodynamically. No cellar door sales.

Karrivale Wines   R8

Woodlands Road, Porongurup, WA 6324
Ph 08 9853 1009, Fax 08 9853 1129

Owners: Campbell and Annette McGready
Chief winemaker: Plantagenet (contract)
Year of foundation: 1979
Tonnes crushed on average each year: 20
Location: Porongurup
Area: 6.5 ha
Soils: 'karri' loam with some gravel over clay
Varieties planted: White—chardonnay, riesling; Red—cabernet sauvignon, shiraz

Leading wines: Karrivale Riesling, Chardonnay
Notes: As it is proud to claim, Karrivale is the
'vineyard with a view'. It is backed by the bald
domes of the Porongurups with a marvellous
northerly prospect of the Stirling Ranges, which
are sometimes capped by the only snow to fall
in Western Australia. Its rieslings are excellent,
too. Cellar door sales: Wed–Sun 10am–5pm.

Karriview Wines NR

Roberts Road, Denmark, WA 6333
Ph/Fax 08 9840 9381

Owners: Bruce and Mary Day
Chief winemaker: John Wade (contract)
Year of foundation: 1986
Tonnes crushed on average each year: 12
Location: Denmark
Area: 2 ha
Soils: 'karri' loam but with some gravel 'marri'
country over clay
Varieties planted: White—chardonnay;
Red—pinot noir
Leading wines: Karriview Chardonnay, Pinot
Noir
Notes: With ultra-close spacing of vines,
Karriview's crop is very low in quantity but
high in quality, highlighting the promise of
Denmark as a high-quality cool area for the
cultivation of chardonnay and pinot noir. At
800 cases in all, its wines will always be scarce
but well worth seeking out. Cellar door sales:
summer holidays 7 days 10am–5pm, Feb–April
Fri–Mon 10am–5pm.

Landsdale

Denmark Road, Mount Barker, WA 6324
(vineyard only under contract to
Sandalford Wines Pty Ltd)

Owner: Trentvale Pty Ltd
Chief winemaker: Bill Crappsley (Sandalford
Wines)
Year of foundation: 1989
Tonnes crushed on average each year: 600

Location: Mount Barker
Area: 52.3 ha
Soils: gravelly loam over clay, 'marri' country
Varieties planted: White—chardonnay, riesling;
Red—cabernet franc, cabernet sauvignon,
merlot, shiraz
Leading wines: Sandalford Wines is one of
Western Australia's bigger producers and
sources its fruit from this region and three
others—Margaret River, Pemberton and its
Caversham estate in the Swan Valley. Its wines
from this vineyard are presently blended with
wines from its other vineyards. No cellar door
sales.

Marribrook Wines NR

Rocky Gully Road, Frankland, WA 6396
Ph/Fax 08 9457 7885

Owners: Denis and Faye Brooks
Chief winemaker: Plantagenet Wines (contract)
Year of foundation: 1990
Tonnes crushed on average each year: 27
crushed in 1996 and rising
Location: Frankland
Area: 5.5 ha
Soils: gravelly sandy loam over clay, duplex
'marri' soils
Varieties planted: White—chardonnay,
marsanne, sauvignon blanc, semillon;
Red—cabernet franc, cabernet sauvignon,
malbec, merlot
Leading wines: Marribrook Unwooded
Chardonnay, Marsanne, Cabernet Sauvignon
Notes: The Brookses purchased the vineyard
from former Alkoomi winemaker Kim Hart
recently. No cellar door sales.

Matilda's Meadow NR

Hamilton Road, Denmark, WA 6333
Ph 08 9848 1951, Fax 08 9848 1957

Owners: Don Turnbull and Pamela Meldrum-
Turnbull
Chief winemaker: John Wade (contract)

Year of foundation: 1990
Tonnes crushed on average each year: 22 and
rising
Location: Denmark
Area: 6.8 ha
Soils: 'karri' loam
Varieties planted: White—chardonnay,
sauvignon blanc, semillon; Red—cabernet
franc, cabernet sauvignon, pinot noir, shiraz
Leading wines: Matilda's Meadow Chardonnay,
Pinot Noir, Cabernet Sauvignon
Notes: This vineyard shows excellent promise
for the future. Cellar door sales: Wed–Mon
10am–4pm. There is also a restaurant.

Merrebee Estate NR

St Werburgh's Road, Mount Barker,
WA 6324
Ph 08 9851 2424, Fax 08 9851 2425

Owner: Merilyn Basell
Chief winemaker: John Wade (contract)
Year of foundation: 1985
Tonnes crushed on average each year: 28 and
rising
Location: Mount Barker
Area: 3.75 ha and expanding
Soils: sandy gravelly loams over clay, 'marri'
country
Varieties planted: White—chardonnay, riesling;
Red—shiraz
Leading wines: Merrebee Estate Chardonnay,
Unwooded Chardonnay
Notes: Merilyn Basell is another of the
enthusiastic vignerons of Mount Barker. Cellar
door sales: weekends and public holidays
10am–4pm excluding Good Friday and
Christmas Day.

Millinup Estate Wines R8

Porongurup Road, Porongurup, WA 6324
Ph/Fax 08 9853 1105

Owner: Peter Thorn
Chief winemaker: Gavin Berry (contract)

Year of foundation: 1990
Tonnes crushed on average each year: 3
Location: Porongurup
Area: 1 ha
Soils: 'karri' loam with some 'marri' and some
'yate' country
Varieties planted: White—riesling;
Red—cabernet sauvignon
Leading wines: Riesling, Late Harvest Riesling,
Cabernet Sauvignon
Notes: Millinup is a very small estate, situated
in the marvellous Porongurups. My favourite is
Millinup Riesling, like all Porongurup Rieslings,
fresh and crisp when young, tending to
classical 'toastiness' when 3–4 years old. Cellar
door sales: weekends 10am–5pm.

Old Kent River R7

Turpin Road, Rocky Gully, WA 6397
Ph/Fax 08 9855 1589

Owners: Mark and Debra Noack
Chief winemaker: Michael Staniford (contract)
Year of foundation: 1985
Tonnes crushed on average each year: 25
(the balance of fruit produced is sold to
winemakers both locally and interstate)
Location: Rocky Gully
Area: 11 ha
Soils: ancient silty gravelly loam
Varieties planted: White—chardonnay,
sauvignon blanc; Red—pinot noir, shiraz
Leading wine: Old Kent River Pinot Noir
Notes: The Noacks are proud of their Pinot
Noir, both on the vine and in the bottle. As a
red, it performs well in shows. On the vine, it
has been purchased by such well-respected
winemakers as Domaine Chandon and
Houghton, among others. Importantly, as a
diversification from a depressed wool market, it
has been a winner. Cellar door sales by
appointment.

Omrah Vineyard
(vineyard only)
 NR

McSorley Road, Mount Barker,
WA 6324

Owner: Houghton Wines (part of BRL Hardy
group)
Chief winemaker: Larry Cherubino
Year of foundation: 1987
Tonnes crushed on average each year: 650
Location: Mount Barker
Area: 73 ha
Soils: gravelly loams over clay, 'marri' country
Varieties planted: White—chardonnay,
sauvignon blanc; Red—cabernet sauvignon,
shiraz
Leading wines: Houghton wines are often
blends of fruit from the company's vineyards
throughout Western Australia. Other Houghton
vineyards are located at Moondah Brook, Swan
Valley, Pemberton and Frankland River. No
local cellar door sales.

Pattersons Wines
 R8

St Werburgh's Road, Mount Barker,
WA 6324
Ph/Fax 08 9851 2063

Owners: AF and SM Patterson
Chief winemaker: Plantagenet Wines (contract)
Year of foundation: 1982
Tonnes crushed on average each year: 20
Location: Mount Barker
Area: 4 ha
Soils: sandy loam over ironstone and clay
Varieties planted: White—chardonnay;
Red—pinot noir, shiraz
Leading wines: Pattersons Wines Chardonnay,
Pinot Noir, Shiraz
Notes: Pattersons consistently produce
generously flavoured Chardonnays, which
mature well over 2–3 years. Cellar door sales:
Sun–Wed 10am–5pm.

Plantagenet Wines
 R9

Lot 45–46 Albany Road, Mount Barker,
WA 6324
Ph 08 9851 2150, Fax 08 9851 1839

Owner: Plantagenet Wines Pty Limited
Chief winemaker: Gavin Berry
Year of foundation: 1974
Tonnes crushed on average each year: 450
Locations: Bouverie, Harvey Road, Denbarker;
Wyjup, Spring Road, Denbarker; and Crystal
Brook, Spence Road, Narrikup
Area: 49 ha in all (Bouverie 7 ha, Wyjup 16 ha,
Crystal Brook, 26 ha)
Soils: (Bouverie) clay loam varying to gravelly
loam on hilltop; (Wyjup) chiefly gravelly loam;
(Crystal Brook) varying from lighter gravelly
loam to heavier conglomerate gravel
Varieties planted: White—chardonnay,
sauvignon blanc, riesling; Red—cabernet
sauvignon, cabernet franc, merlot, pinot noir,
shiraz
Leading wines: Riesling, Chardonnay, Cabernet
Sauvignon, Shiraz
Notes: Plantagenet is one of the pioneers of
the Great Southern and one of the larger
producers of the region. It is renowned for its
Shiraz and Cabernet Sauvignon. Its winemaker
Gavin Berry is also very busy contract
winemaking for other vineyards in the region.
Cellar door sales: Mon–Fri 9am–5pm,
weekends 10am–4pm.

Springviews Wines
 NR

Woodlands Road, Narrikup, WA 6326
Ph 08 9853 2088, Fax 08 9853 2098

Owners: Andy and Alice Colquhuon
Chief winemaker: John Wade (contract)
Year of foundation: 1987
Tonnes crushed on average each year: 6 (the
rest of the crop is sold to other winemakers)
Location: Narrikup
Area: 5 ha
Soils: old gravelly loams over yellow clay, acidic

Varieties planted: White—chardonnay, riesling;
Red—cabernet sauvignon
Leading wines: Springviews Chardonnay,
Riesling, Cabernet Sauvignon
Notes: Cellar door sales by appointment.

Tingle-wood Wines   **NR**

Glenrowan Road, Denmark, WA 6333
Ph/Fax 08 9840 9218

Owners: Robert and Judy Wood
Chief winemaker: John Wade (contract)
Year of foundation: 1976
Tonnes crushed on average each year: 18
Location: Denmark
Area: 4 ha
Soils: 'Karri' loam with rock
Varieties planted: White—riesling;
Red—cabernet sauvignon, shiraz
Leading wines: Tingle-wood Yellow Tingle
Riesling, Red Tingle Cabernet-Shiraz
Notes: I have heard great things about Tingle-
wood Riesling and, made by John Wade, it
should be excellent. Cellar door sales: 7 days
9am–5pm.

Whispering Hill (vineyard only)   **NR**

O'Neil Road, Mount Barker, WA 6324

Owners: Peter and Elizabeth Pratten of Capel
Vale
Chief winemakers: Rob Bowen and Krister
Jonnson
Year of foundation: 1985
Tonnes crushed on average each year: 200
Location: Mount Barker
Area: 26 ha
Soils: old 'marri' loams resulting from degraded
Porongurup granite
Varieties planted: White—riesling, sauvignon
blanc, semillon; Red—cabernet franc, cabernet
sauvignon, shiraz
Leading wines: This is one of Capel Vale's
several vineyards in Western Australia that
contribute to Capel Vale's ranges of wines.
Others are the Capel Stirling vineyard in the
Geographe wine region and the Sheldrake
vineyard near the Lefroy River in the
Pemberton–Warren wine region. When the
year permits, as it often does in the Great
Southern, an impeccable Riesling is produced
from Whispering Hill fruit. A Kinnaird Shiraz
also of 100% Mount Barker origin has recently
been released.
Notes: No local cellar door sales.

Wignall's Wines   **R8.5**

Lot 5384 Chester Pass Road, Albany,
WA 6330
Ph/Fax 08 9841 2848

Owners: Bill, Patricia and Robert Wignall
Chief winemaker: Robert Wignall
Year of foundation: 1982
Tonnes crushed on average each year: 80
Location: Albany
Area: 12 ha
Soils: chiefly gravel and sand over friable clay
base, 1 metre deep
Varieties planted: White—chardonnay,
sauvignon blanc; Red—pinot noir, cabernet
sauvignon
Leading wines: Wignall's Pinot Noir and
Chardonnay
Notes: Bill Wignall could be said to have
established Great Southern's reputation for
Pinot Noir. In good years, they are soft fleshy
wines of opulent flavour and always worth
drinking. Cellar door sales: 7 days noon–4pm.

Yanwirra Wines   **NR**

Redman Road, Denmark, WA 6333
Ph 08 9848 1802, Fax 08 9386 3578

Owners: Ian and Elizabeth McGlew
Chief winemaker: John Wade (contract)
Year of foundation: 1989
Tonnes crushed on average each year: 18
Location: Denmark

Area: 4 ha

Soils: 'karri' loams with some gravelly and sandy patches

Varieties planted: White—chardonnay, riesling, sauvignon blanc, semillon; Red—cabernet franc, cabernet sauvignon, merlot

Leading wines: Yanwirra Cabernet Merlot, Sauvignon Blanc, Riesling

Notes: Ian McGlew is another of the medical profession who has turned to the vine. Quite apart from the weekend commuting from Perth to Denmark, the establishment of Yanwirra has not been without its difficulties. Hail, strong winds, crows, all have left their imprint in various vintages. But he remains confident in the future of the Denmark area and in the elegant medium-bodied reds that he is producing. No cellar door sales.

Mount Barker Sub-region

This was the first sub-region in Australia to secure recognition.

Topography, soils and climate: The sub-region is located on the Plantagenet plateau with the Mount Barker hill at its centre. It varies in altitude from 180 to 250 m above sea-level. It is gently undulating and is distinguished from the other winegrowing areas of the Great Southern region—Frankland River, Denmark, Porongurups and Albany—by its comparatively poor 'marri' soils, that is, lateritic gravelly sandy loams or sandy loams directly derived from granite rock. Good drainage and soil warmth are their major contribution to the well-being of the vine. Vineyards are planted chiefly on the tops and sides of the hills, avoiding the valley bottoms because of increased salinity. For the same reason, irrigation dams have not been built in such valleys. These dams have tended to be constructed so they can be fed from road catchments.

The climate of the sub-region is classified as Mediterranean with the majority (471 mm) of its annual rainfall (756 mm) falling between May and September. HDD for vineyard sites is 1488. Sunshine hours are 1518 and 3pm relative humidity is 54%. During the growing season, the most likely month for frosts to occur is October and this risk increases as one travels from south to north. There is also an increase in sunshine hours and a decrease in rainfall and relative humidity in the same direction.

Harvest time: Here is a further point of distinction of Mount Barker from its co-occupants of the Great Southern region. Typical dates for early and late maturity of the Mount Barker crop are second week of March for chardonnay and pinot noir, last week of April for cabernet sauvignon. Areas to the south such as Albany and Denmark have budburst and harvest two weeks earlier, while the Porongurups harvest two weeks later.

Total area: over 2000 ha

Principal wine styles: Those two great 'continental' grape varieties, shiraz and riesling, have most definitely distinguished themselves at Mount Barker, though how their 'Mount Barker' qualities are distinct *per se* from the qualities of the rieslings and shiraz from Frankland River or the Porongurups is difficult to say and would certainly require very precise tasting from a panel of experts. But this observation apart, the Rieslings of Mount Barker usually have an intensely appealing 'lime-citrus' character on nose and palate and an ability to age which rivals those of the Eden and Clare Valleys. Shiraz too has its distinctions, being related more to the spicy Rhone Valley style than to the heavier berry and black-pepper warm area wines of McLaren Vale and the Barossa Valley. Mount Barker, through its Omrah Vineyard, can also lay claim to the introduction of the unwooded chardonnay style to the Australian consumer.

At present, the Mount Barker sub-region produces about 4000 tonnes of grapes each vintage, has 350 hectares under vine and three wineries. In addition large quantities of fruit are sent to Perth and other winemaking centres for processing. Wine producers utilising Mount Barker fruit and present in the sub-region are Goundrey, Plantagenet, Galafrey, Chatsfield, Houghton, Sandalford, Forest Hill, Gilberts, Patterson, Karrilea, Merrebee, Capel Vale and Blue Wren Estates (see individual entries).

Albany Sub-region

Though most of the credit for the early exploration of the southern Australian coast is due to Matthew Flinders and the French navigators Baudin and Freycinet, the inhabitants of Albany have certainly not forgotten the contribution of Captain George Vancouver who, in 1791, discovered and named such local features as King George Sound, Princess Royal Harbour and Oyster Harbour. Vancouver, who had sailed with Cook on his second and third voyages to the Pacific, was also responsible for the discovery and naming of Vancouver, British Colombia.

On Christmas Day, 1826, Major Edmund Lockyer, who had been despatched from Sydney, arrived at King George Sound in the brig *Amity* to claim the western part of the Australian continent for Great Britain. On his small square rigger, he brought with him 29 soldiers, 23 convicts, a surgeon, ship's captain and crew as well as six months' provisions. On the 21 January 1827, he duly raised the Union Jack and called his settlement Fredericks Town, a name later changed to Albany. After the founding of the Swan River Colony in 1829, civilian government eventually came to Albany in 1831, when the first magistrate, Alexander Collie, was appointed.

Besides the usual occupation of land for grazing, Albany was associated with whaling from its earliest days. Whaling ceased in 1978, but the whaling station remains as the world's largest whaling museum. Though it was common knowledge in the area that grapes grew well in Albany, the sub-region's first commercial vineyard, Redmond, did not appear until 1974. Its grapes were sold to Plantagenet. In 1982, Bill Wignall planted his King River vineyard. Its first vintage in 1985 was a tremendous success, the Pinot Noir receiving a gold medal at an interstate capital city wine show and the Chardonnay winning the SGIO trophy as WA's Best Table Wine. Such success, however, did not enthuse the local public and it was not until the mid-1990s that, in line with the growth of general Australian interest in vineyards, more vineyards began to be planted in the sub-region.

As at the end of 1998, there were 60 ha of vines planted in the sub-region with over 220 ha planned for the near future. The potential crop of the sub-region about the year 2005 is therefore over 3000 tonnes. There is one operating winery and cellar door outlet (Wignall's) within the sub-region and one cellar door outlet (Alkoomi, whose vineyards are not within the sub-region) in the town of Albany.

Topography and soils: The sub-region has been described as an area of 'sands and laterite on elongate crests' (CSIRO Groundwater Research 1979–1982) with intervening valleys lying on sedimentary rock that is not suitable for viticulture due to this fact and to poor drainage. Its geographical formations are chiefly Precambrian granites and gneisses and its basic soils are sandy gravels overlying a layer of laterite rock of varying thickness, which it is necessary to deep-rip for viticultural purposes. Below the laterite is a clay or clay loam, which has good rooting characteristics. The soils, however, have been modified by history. As the prevailing summer wind is easterly, the western slopes of the area have less sand in their soil profiles, while the eastern slopes have correspondingly more. Sites suitable for viticulture within the sub-region need to be carefully selected as drainage is restricted and this means that the areas suitable for viticulture are confined mostly to the slopes. Irrigation is available only from private water harvesting, which is usually by means of rainfall run off into dams. The elevation of the sub-region varies from 14–40 m.

Climate: For details, see the notes on the Great Southern region. Generally, however, the climate of the sub-region is quite uniform, though rainfall in the west, adjacent to the coast, is slightly higher than the east, and temperature is marginally lower closer to the coast than further inland due to sea breezes. Generally the climate can be described as Mediterranean with moist but cool rather than cold winters, and warm dry summers. Diurnal variation of temperature is generally slight once more due to maritime winds (the Albany Doctor, as such breezes are called locally). A further factor in this slight diurnal variation is the release from rocks after sunset of heat stored during sunlight hours. The particular virtue of the sub-region is that the middle of the day in summer is optimal for photosynthesis, a balance of reasonable humidity and reasonable heat ensuring that the leaf stomata of the vines do not close, but remain active with consequent efficient and satisfactory ripening.

Harvest time: Harvest usually commences early in March with pinot noir, followed 7–10 days later by chardonnay and then sauvignon blanc. Cabernet sauvignon usually ripens mid-April.

Total area: (end of 1998) 60ha

Principal wine styles: Because of the justifiable devotion of Bill Wignall to pinot noir, Wignall's King River Pinot Noir has created the red wine reputation of the sub-region. Chardonnay, however, is not far behind and regularly wins trophies and gold medals. Other promising varieties are sauvignon blanc and cabernet sauvignon. Little shiraz is yet grown in the sub-region.

Porongurup Sub-region

This is a further sub-region of the Great Southern Region. Its name is a corruption of the Aboriginal word Purringorep and means place of the spirits. It was formally settled about 1859, but in practice had been used by squatters for sheep grazing since about 1830, a practice that has continued to the present day. However, in the intervening 160 years, more and more farmers moved into the area with the consequence that pastoral activities expanded to include cattle, both for beef and dairying, as well as a variety of horticultural pursuits including orcharding, vegetable growing and very recently viticulture.

Interest in viticulture grew slowly but positively after the publication of the favourable viticultural reports of Harold Olmo and John Gladstones in the 1950s and 60s, the first vineyard in the sub-region, Bolganup, being planted to 2 ha of cabernet sauvignon in 1974. Others soon followed with the initial planting of the present Millinup Wines vineyard, being made to 1 ha of riesling in 1978. The following year Jingalla Wines was established with a vineyard of 3 ha, as was Karrivale with 1 ha of riesling vines. In the 1980s, vineyard expansion continued albeit in a restrained and careful way. 1983 saw the beginning of the Castle Rock Estate, and 1985 the commencement of Springviews. Since then, in common with the general Australian trend of the early 1990s, there has been a proliferation of smaller vineyards. There are no wineries presently within the sub-region, all wine for those vineyards with cellar door outlets being made outside the area. At the end of 1998, there were 57.2 ha of vineyards within the sub-region with one winery planned for 1999 vintage.

Topography and soils: The area has been described by John Gladstones as 'a small, isolated, range of intrusive granite'. The dominant feature of the sub-region is the Porongurup Range, a series of large, bare, granite knobs crowding one upon the other over a length of 12 km and a width of 3 km. The height of the range is about 600 m. The highest point is the Devils Slide at 670 m. These granite domes constitute the National Park. Most of the vineyards are planted on the northern slopes below the knobs at about 300 m in altitude on 'karri' loams as the soils derived from the weathered granite are commonly known. These are quite deep and lie above a clay subsoil. This sub-region differs from that of Mount Barker in that the Mount Barker soils are lateritic gravelly loams known as 'marri', and from the Albany sub-region where the soils are commonly sandy loams. The area has excellent air drainage.

Climate: Climatic data for this sub-region has been mentioned in the general notes concerning the regional climate of the Great Southern, but it is worth noting that, according to Gladstones, the sub-region develops a thermal zone '[i.e. a layer of warm night air] that sits above the inversion or fog boundary that caps the dense cold air that settles on the valley bottoms' because of 'its isolated and projecting hills'. Therefore it has less temperature variability and extremes during the ripening period. Rainwater from the granite slopes is usually run off into dams and most vineyards are drip-irrigated.

Harvest time: Harvesting usually begins about the middle of March and extends until the end of April, with individual varieties ripening one to two weeks later than their counterparts in the Mount Barker sub-region.

Total area: 57.2 ha

Principal wine styles: The main varieties grown in the sub-region are riesling, chardonnay, verdelho, cabernet sauvignon, shiraz, pinot noir, merlot, cabernet franc and semillon. The major wine style from a national point of view is probably riesling, a reputation gained from the early styles of Castle Rock, though cabernet also can be excellent.

At present, the sub-region produces about 600 tonnes of grapes, though this will grow. Growers with cellar door sales facilities within the sub-region are Castle Rock Estate, Jingalla Wines, Karrivale Wines, Millinup Estate Wines and Springviews Wines.

PEMBERTON REGION (PROPOSED)

Timber and apples were perhaps the first claims to fame of the Pemberton and Manjimup areas. Like the other cooler areas of South Western Australia wine zone, Pemberton owes a great debt of gratitude to Dr John Gladstones for his pioneering viticultural studies of this region, as well as those of Margaret River and the Great Southern. Until Gladstones' work in the 1960s, little was known of Pemberton's potential for viticulture, but Gladstones, noting the similarity between the mean temperatures and sunlight hours of Manjimup and Bordeaux, made the confident prediction that 'the wines produced from the appropriate grape varieties should be very much in the mainstream of Bordeaux styles'.

Thus the Western Australian Department of Agriculture—very much I suppose in a spirit of experimentation—established a pilot vineyard midway between Pemberton and Manjimup in 1977. It succeeded and so did the first commercial vineyard (Lefroy Brook) planted five years later near Pemberton. From 1985 to 1987, many more commercial plantings occurred, seven of them being in excess of 20 ha, and in 1988 the Pemberton Vignerons' Association was formed. By 1990, the first wines from Pemberton were being produced and in the ensuing vintage, the first wines from the nearby Manjimup area came on to the market. It was originally planned that there should be one region, but there was some dispute as to its proper name. Some favoured 'Pemberton', some favoured 'Warren Valley' and at a meeting of the Pemberton Vignerons' Association in October 1994, the name 'Pemberton' was found to be preferred by a majority of the vignerons, but this did not prove to be a lasting solution. More recently it has been decided that there should be two adjoining regions. However, debate continues and the matter has not been finally resolved.

The Pemberton and Warren Valley regions now boast over 600 ha of vines shared among over 50 vineyards. In addition there are six wineries within the regions and some regional wine is made outside them. In vintage 1996, the regions produced 3000 tonnes of grapes, their principal varieties being chardonnay, cabernet sauvignon, pinot noir and merlot.

Location: The town of Pemberton stands latitude 34°27'S, longitude 116°01'E, about 280 km virtually due south of Perth. It is linked to other south-western wine regions by the South West Highway (from Albany and Walpole) and by the Vasse Highway (from Margaret River and Busselton). Northcliffe is also a part of the region.
Elevation: Pemberton, about 171 m above sea-level with vineyards 60–200 m. Northcliffe about 100 m above sea-level, with its vineyards 100–120 m.
Topography and soils: Pemberton is an undulating region rising from an altitude of about 100 m in the south to about 200 m in its north. Local soils are 'karri' loams,

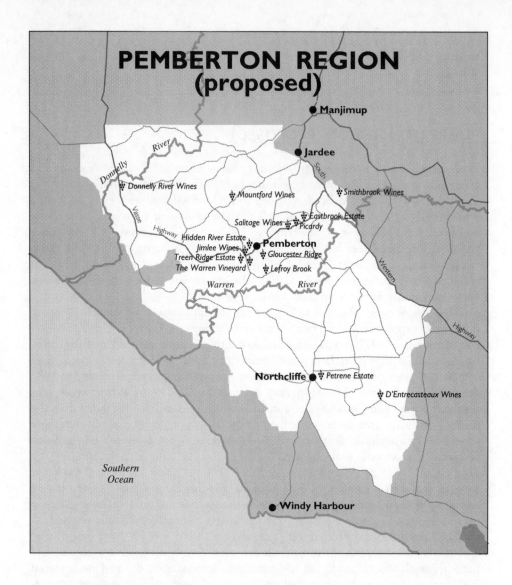

that is, those which have carried karri trees. The 'karri' loams are formed from gneissic rock, though outcrops of 'marri' soil occur on some of the higher slopes throughout the area. On the 'karri' loams also, viticulturalists need to be on guard against excess vine vigour.

Gravel content, much sought-after in this region for its drainage and soil-warming capabilities, is sometimes as high as 60% in the 'marri' soil and much lower or nil in the 'karri' loam. Subsoil is usually medium clay. Appropriate viticultural soils are characterised by good drainage with low to moderate water-holding capacity. Irrigation is generally, though by no means universally, practised.

Suitable red varieties for the Pemberton district which, though lower than Manjimup, is cooler include pinot noir and meunier, but not varieties ripening later than merlot. Cabernet sauvignon in this location seems to require a very warm exposure in order to ripen completely.

Climate: Pemberton MJT 19.2°C, MAR na, HDD raw 1403, 1421 (cut-off and adjusted for latitude, daily temperature range and vine sites), AR 1255 mm (Oct–Apr 361 mm), RH 48%, AI na, SH 6.7 (Gladstones). The Southern Ocean is the major influence on the region's climate, though its influences are tempered somewhat by the altitude of suitable viticultural sites. The regional climate can be described as Mediterranean, warm but rarely hot summers and cool, wet winters. Annual rainfall varies throughout the region from about 1255 mm (Pemberton) to about 1400 mm (Northcliffe). Generally, the more proximate the Southern Ocean, the more precipitation can be expected. The bulk (72%) of the annual rainfall occurs within the five months from May to September.

Water supply for irrigation is usually from large catchment dams, for which official permission is required, though some properties are permitted to irrigate direct from adjoining rivers such as the Donnelly River and Lefroy Brook. In addition, water supply for irrigation purposes may be permitted from bores. Rivers in the region with the exception of the Warren are largely unaffected by salinity. Birds (particularly silvereyes) are a problem in any location where native flowering gums bloom later than early-ripening grape varieties. Alternative food supplies and netting are the only solution. Nematodes may also occur in certain places, but are not considered a major problem.

Principal varieties: White—chardonnay, sauvignon blanc, verdelho; Red—cabernet sauvignon, pinot noir, merlot, cabernet franc (in descending order of area planted). Some chardonnay and pinot noir is used as sparkling wine base outside the region.

Harvest time: chardonnay, early–mid-March; pinot noir, late February; merlot, mid–late March; cabernet sauvignon, mid–late April

Total area: est 800 ha

Principal wine styles: It is rather early to speculate on the wine future of the Pemberton region, but Pinot Noir and Chardonnay will certainly play a prominent part, if only because of the personalities present in the region. It may be that the pinot noir variety in Pemberton has its own particular *goût de terroir*, a distinctive smokiness on nose and palate. Of other varieties verdelho seems to impress as a fresh young white style and sauvignon blanc is another variety of promise. As to cabernet sauvignon, perhaps the verdict is still awaited.

Big Brook and Channybearup Wines (vineyard only) NR

Channybearup Road, Pemberton,
WA 6260
Ph 08 9776 1556

Owner: Charlie Chodorowski
Chief winemaker: none yet appointed

Year of foundation: 1990
Tonnes crushed on average each year: 8
Location: West Pemberton
Area: 5 ha (planting yet to be completed)
Soils: 'karri' and blackbutt loams on a gravelly subsoil

Varieties planted: White—chardonnay, traminer, semillon, verdelho; Red—cabernet franc, cabernet sauvignon, merlot, pinot noir, meunier
Leading wines: none yet
Notes: Big Brook Vineyard, at 190 m altitude, is one of the highest in the Pemberton region and certainly in need of the wind breaks that Charlie Chodorowski has established. It is planted on an old cricket pitch in the middle of a trotting track. No wines are available and no cellar door facilities exist at the present time, but this will change in years to come.

CT Blakers (vineyard only) NR
Sevenday Road, Manjimup, WA 6258

Owner: CT Blakers Pty Ltd
Year of foundation: 1995
Tonnes crushed on average each year: 13 in 1997, but approximately 100 tonnes are anticipated as the vines mature and the vineyard is fully planted
Location: Fontys Pool
Area: 10.3 ha
Soils: gravelly loam
Varieties planted: White—chardonnay, sauvignon blanc, semillon; Red—cabernet sauvignon, shiraz
Leading wines: no present plans to make wine or to have wine made
Notes: This is a vineyard only. All grapes are sold. There are no cellar door facilities.

Bracken Ridge Estate (vineyard only) NR
Roche Road, Pemberton, WA 6260
Ph 08 9776 0016, Fax 08 9776 0017

Owner: Bracken Ridge Holdings Pty Ltd
Year of foundation: 1996
Tonnes crushed on average each year: vineyard not yet in bearing
Location: Pemberton

Area: 63.06 ha (planted 1996), 28 ha (planted 1997)
Soils: 'karri' and 'marri' loams
Varieties planted: White—chardonnay, sauvignon blanc, semillon, verdelho; Red—cabernet sauvignon, merlot, pinot noir, shiraz
Leading wines: no present plans to produce wine under a Bracken Ridge label
Notes: Bracken Ridge is presently one of the larger vineyards of the Pemberton region, but has no intention at the present time of erecting a winery or having any cellar door facilities.

Brocksopp Vineyard (vineyard only) NR
Glauder Road, Pemberton, WA 6260

Owner: John Brocksopp
Year of foundation: 1994
Tonnes crushed on average each year: 3, but will probably increase as 1997 was the first vintage
Location: Pemberton
Area: 2 ha or 5000 vines
Soils: gravelly loams
Varieties planted: Red—shiraz, mataro; experimental patches of whites
Leading wines: Shiraz
Notes: This vineyard is intended as a retirement diversion for the energetic John Brocksopp, who is the longstanding viticulturalist of Leeuwin Estate at Margaret River. John says that one day he will notice and enjoy the much reduced levels of stress. He has no plans to make his own wine or to increase the size of the vineyard. It will definitely be a one-man operation. Accordingly, there are no cellar door sales and little prospect of them. As for Shiraz, it is his favourite red.

Capel Vale *(vineyard only)*   **NR**

Sheldrake Vineyard, Appadene Road,
Nelson, WA 6260

Owners: Peter and Elizabeth Pratten
Chief winemaker: Rob Bowen
Year of foundation: 1995
Tonnes crushed on average each year: 200, but
this will probably double as vines mature and
the vineyard comes into full bearing
Location: Nelson
Area: 40 ha
Soils: deep 'karri' loams, fertile
Varieties planted: White—chardonnay,
sauvignon blanc, semillon, verdelho, viognier;
Red—merlot, pinot noir, shiraz
Leading wines: first vintage 1997
Notes: This is one of the middling to large
vineyards of the region. There is no winery on
site and it is not intended that there will be
any cellar door sales. The wines are made at
Capel Vale winery, but as Rob Bowen says, any
wines good enough will make the Capel Vale
Reserve label and be seen in their own right.
Otherwise they will be blended.

D'Entrecasteaux Wines   **NR**

Adjacent to Boorara Conservation Park,
Northcliffe, WA 6262
Ph 08 9776 7232

Owners: Rudd family
Chief winemaker: Eastbrook Estate (contract)
Year of foundation: 1988
Tonnes crushed on average each year: 20
Location: Northcliffe
Area: 4 ha
Soils: gravelly sandy loam 1–2 metres deep
over clay
Varieties planted: White—chardonnay,
sauvignon blanc; Red—cabernet sauvignon,
pinot noir
Leading wine: D'Entrecasteaux Chardonnay
Notes: D'Entrecasteaux is a small family
operation virtually in the midst of a virgin karri

forest. Close by are the Lane Pool Falls, 10 km
away is the D'Entrecasteaux National Park and
20 km distant the south-west coast. Cellar
door sales: public holidays.

Donnelly River Wines   **R6.5**

Donnelly River Bridge, Vasse Highway,
Pemberton, WA 6260
Ph 08 9776 2052, Fax 08 9776 2053

Owners: Matt and Anne Harsley
Chief winemaker: Blair Meiklejohn
Year of foundation: 1986
Tonnes crushed on average each year: 45,
increasing to 250
Location: Peerabeelup
Area: 11.5 ha
Soils: rich alluvial loam
Varieties planted: White—chardonnay,
sauvignon blanc, semillon, traminer; Red—
cabernet sauvignon, merlot, pinot noir, shiraz
Leading wines: Donnelly River Chardonnay,
Cabernet Sauvignon, Pinot Noir
Notes: Donnelly River is another farming
diversification story, where a property
purchased with retirement in mind by former
owner George Oldfield not only became a
vineyard but also the site of the region's
first winery. Cellar door sales: 7 days
9.30am–4.30pm.

Eastbrook Estate   **R7**

Lot 3, Vasse Highway, Eastbrook,
WA 6260
Ph/Fax 08 9776 1251

Owners: Kym and Jane Skipworth
Chief winemaker: Kym Skipworth
Year of foundation: 1990
Tonnes crushed on average each year: 20 and
rising as more vines are planted and come into
bearing
Location: Eastbrook
Area: 6 ha
Soils: gravelly loam over clay 'karri'

Varieties planted: White—chardonnay, sauvignon blanc; Red—pinot noir, shiraz
Leading wines: Chardonnay, Pinot Noir
Notes: Since 1990, Eastbrook has been a consuming passion for Kym and Jane Skipworth. They were formerly 'weekend warriors', committing themselves to the wearisome grind of a 700 km round trip from Perth, though with great 'enthusiasm and gusto'. They settled permanently at Eastbrook in 1994, having made their first vintage 'under primitive conditions' in 1993. Now the winery restaurant complex has been completed, Kym, very much a hands-on winemaker, can commit himself totally to his dry-grown 'Burgundian' grape types. Cellar door sales: Fri–Sun and public holidays 11am–3pm.

Fontys Pool Farm (vineyard only) NR

Sevenday Road, Manjimup, WA 6258
Ph 08 9777 1842, Fax 08 9777 1391

Owner: Fontys Pool Farm Pty Ltd
Year of foundation: 1989
Tonnes crushed on average each year: 580, but this will increase substantially as the planting of the vineyard is completed and the newly planted vines come into bearing
Location: Fontys Pool
Area: 38 ha but will grow to 100 ha by year 2000
Soils: 'karri' and 'jarrah' loams
Varieties planted: White—chardonnay, sauvignon blanc, semillon; Red—cabernet franc, cabernet sauvignon, merlot, pinot noir, shiraz
Leading wines: no wines produced
Notes: Fontys Pool Farm will certainly be one of the larger vineyards in the region, but there are no plans for any winemaking and consequently no cellar door facilities.

Gloucester Ridge R6.5

Burma Road, Pemberton, WA 6260
Ph 08 9776 1035, Fax 08 9776 1390

Owners: Don and Sue Hancock
Chief winemaker: John Wade (contract)
Year of foundation: 1985
Tonnes crushed on average each year: 50
Location: Pemberton
Area: 15 ha
Soils: deep gravelly loam
Varieties planted: Whites—chardonnay, sauvignon blanc; Red—cabernet franc, cabernet sauvignon, pinot noir
Leading wines: Gloucester Ridge Chardonnay, Cabernets, Cabernet Sauvignon, Sauvignon Blanc
Notes: Two of the pioneers of the Pemberton region, Don and Sue Hancock, are now solidly established and successful vignerons close to Pemberton town. Their 1994 Cabernet Sauvignon won a silver medal at the National Wine Show in Canberra while the 1995 Cabernet was judged by *Winestate* magazine as the equal best blend in Western Australia in its March 1997 edition. Gloucester Ridge has cellar door sales (7 days 10am–5pm) and cafe facilities.

Hidden River Estate NR

Millineaux Road, Pemberton, WA 6260
Ph/Fax 08 9776 1437

Owners: Phil and Sandy Goldring
Chief winemaker: Ian Tyrer of Galafrey (contract)
Year of foundation: 1994
Tonnes crushed on average each year: 7 (first vintage 1997), but a crop of 20–25 tonnes is anticipated when the vines are fully bearing
Location: Pemberton
Area: 2.2 ha
Soils: medium 'karri' loam over clay
Varieties planted: White—chardonnay (Gin Gin clone); Red—none

Leading wines: Hidden River Estate
Chardonnay, Unwooded Chardonnay, Cabernet
Sauvignon (from purchased fruit)
Notes: Phil Goldring's first vintage was 1997.
Cellar door sales by appointment.

Houghton Wines
(vineyard only)   NR

Stirling Road, Pemberton, WA 6260
Ph 08 9776 1526, Fax 08 9776 1519

Owners: BRL Hardy and others
Chief winemaker: Houghton Wines
Year of foundation: 1989
Tonnes crushed on average each year: 400 but
increasing to 700 by 1999 as the vineyard
comes into full production
Location: Pemberton
Area: 63.4 ha
Soils: 'karri' loam
Varieties planted: White—chardonnay,
verdelho; Red—cabernet sauvignon, merlot
Leading wines: Houghton Wines have as yet
marketed no wines wholly from this region.
No doubt, however, it will eventually happen.
Notes: This is a vineyard only and there are no
cellar door sales.

Jardee Wines   NR

PO Box 450, Manjimup, WA 6258
Ph/Fax 08 9777 1552

Owners: Steve Miolin and Paul McArdle
Chief winemaker: Barry Smith
Year of foundation: 1993
Tonnes crushed on average each year: 8
Location: Pemberton (vineyards from which
fruit is purchased)
Area: no vineyards are owned
Varieties crushed: White—chardonnay;
Red—pinot noir
Leading wines: Jardee Pinot Noir, Chardonnay
Notes: Jardee is a negociant operation, similar
to many French negociant businesses. There
are no cellar door sales.

Jennavale Vineyard (leased
to Donnelly River Wines)   NR

Vasse Highway, Peerabeelup, nr
Pemberton, WA 6260

Owner: Jupps Holdings
Chief winemaker: Blair Meiklejohn (contract)
Year of foundation: 1992
Tonnes crushed on average each year: 35 but
will increase as vines come to maturity
Location: Peerabeelup
Area: 4 ha
Soils: sandy alluvial loam
Varieties planted: Whites—chardonnay,
sauvignon blanc, semillon; Red—cabernet
sauvignon, pinot noir, shiraz
Notes: At the time of writing, this very young
vineyard was only in its second vintage.

Lefroy Brook   NR

Glauder Road, Pemberton, WA 6260
Ph 08 9386 8385

Owners: Holt family
Chief winemaker: Peter Fimmel (contract)
Year of foundation: 1982
Tonnes crushed on average each year: 6
Location: Pemberton
Area: 1.2 ha
Soils: 'karri' loam
Varieties planted: White—chardonnay;
Red—pinot noir
Leading wines: Lefroy Brook Chardonnay, Pinot
Noir
Notes: Patrick Holt is the pioneer of the
Pemberton region. His vineyard is 15 years old
and the beneficiary of a wealth of experience
of the habits of silver-eyes and kangaroos. As a
result, the vineyard is now permanently netted
and kangaroo-proof. Patrick is also a Burgundy
enthusiast. It shows in the varieties planted,
the close spacing of the vineyard, the lack of
irrigation and certainly in the wine style. There
are no cellar door sales.

Merum Vineyard NR

Hillbrook Road, Northcliffe, WA 6262
Ph 08 9777 1543

Owners: Melsom family
Chief winemakers: Michael and Maria Melsom
Year of foundation: 1996
Tonnes crushed on average each year:
approximately 100 is anticipated when planting
is completed and the vineyard is in full bearing
Location: Northcliffe, directly east of
Pemberton town, south of Manjimup and
north of Northcliffe on the Wheatley Coast
Road
Area: 6 ha, planned to increase to 10 ha
within 2 years
Soils: gravelly loam over clay
Varieties planted: White—chardonnay,
semillon; Red—merlot, shiraz
Leading wines: two wines only are planned,
Shiraz and Semillon-Chardonnay
Notes: First release is planned for year 2000,
though there will be no cellar door sales. The
Melsoms are aiming for high quality, low
quantity, super-premium wine. Sales will be by
mail order with wine directly distributed from
the winery. Contract winemaking facilities will
be used.

Mountford Wines R6.5

Bamess Road, Pemberton, WA 6260
Ph 08 9776 1345, Fax 08 9776 1439

Owner: Andrew Mountford
Chief winemaker: Andrew Mountford
Year of foundation: 1987
Tonnes crushed on average each year: 55
Locality: Pemberton
Area: 6 ha
Soils: 'karri' loams, well-drained
Varieties planted: White—chardonnay,
sauvignon blanc; Red—cabernet franc,
cabernet sauvignon, malbec, merlot, pinot noir

Leading wines: Sauvignon Blanc, Chardonnay,
Pinot Noir
Notes: Andrew Mountford is very much a
hands-on winemaker. The winery, cafe and
gallery were constructed from hand-made
mud-bricks with local timber hewn by his own
hands. All this and his own wine and cider,
too. Andrew shows his wines at Western
Australian wine shows and has been deservedly
successful, his major prize being an SGIO wine
award, made in 1992 for the best Pemberton
white. Cellar door sales: 7 days 10am–5pm.

Omodei Vineyard (vineyard only) NR

Vasse Highway, Eastbrook, WA 6260
Ph 08 9776 1214, Fax 08 9776 1121

Owners: Omodei family
Year of foundation: 1994
Tonnes crushed on average each year: 1997
saw the first vintage; when the vineyard is fully
in bearing about 90 tonnes are anticipated
Location: Eastbrook
Area: 9 ha
Soils: gravelly 'karri' loam over clay
Varieties planted: White—chardonnay,
sauvignon blanc, verdelho; Red—merlot, pinot
noir, shiraz
Leading wines: no wine made
Notes: There are no plans for a winery or to
have wine made at this stage. No cellar door
sales.

Petrene Estate NR

Muirillup Road, Northcliffe, WA 6262
Ph/Fax 08 9776 7145

Owners: Peter Hooker and Irene Wilson
Chief winemaker: Peter Fimmel (contract)
Year of foundation: 1994
Tonnes crushed on average each year: 1 (1997)
but expected to rise to 40 tonnes as plantings
are completed and the vineyard matures

Location: Northcliffe
Area: 2 ha presently and 2 ha later
Soils: deep gravelly loam ('karri') over clay loam or light clay
Varieties planted: White—chardonnay, sauvignon blanc; Red—pinot noir
Leading wine: Petrene Chardonnay
Notes: Petrene is a very new, quite small vineyard in a cool maritime climate. Cellar door sales every day except Tues 10.30am–4pm. Closed June, July and August.

Phoenicia Vineyard (vineyard only)   NR

Eastbrook Road, Pemberton, WA 6260

Owner: Graham Raad
Year of foundation: 1989
Tonnes crushed on average each year: 340
Location: Pemberton
Area: 34 ha
Soils: gravelly loam, well-drained
Varieties planted: White—chardonnay, sauvignon blanc, semillon; Red—cabernet franc, merlot, pinot noir, shiraz
Leading wines: no wines made
Notes: Phoenicia Vineyard is purely a grapegrower. There are no wines made and consequently no cellar door sales.

Picardy   9

Cnr South Western Highway and
Eastbrook Road, Pemberton, WA 6260
Ph/Fax 08 9776 0036

Owners: Pannell family
Chief winemakers: Dan Pannell, Bill Pannell
Year of foundation: 1992
Tonnes crushed on average each year: 5 (1996) but estimated to increase to 80 when the planting of the vineyard is completed and the vines are in full bearing
Location: Pemberton
Area: 8 ha
Soils: lateritic gravel on a ridge, well-drained
Varieties planted: White—chardonnay

(specifically clones 76, 95, 96 and 277); Red—cabernet franc, cabernet sauvignon (clone selected from Moss Wood), merlot, pinot noir (clones 114, 115, 277, O5V12 and a clone of pinot tordu, imported to Western Australia over 60 years ago), shiraz (a second generation selection from a Swan Valley clone made by John Kosovich)
Leading wines: Chardonnay, Pinot Noir, Merlot-Cabernet blend, Shiraz
Notes: As well as being a busy Perth medical practitioner, Bill Pannell has had a long and distinguished wine career. Almost thirty years ago he founded Moss Wood in Margaret River, which rapidly became one of the leading wineries in that region. He then sold that vineyard in 1985 to Keith Mugford and continued his wine interests as a member of a syndicate of Australian investors in the Domaine de la Pousse d'Or in the Volnay area of the Cote de Beaune. As a result of this, the syndicate developed the Smithbrook vineyard (see entry) near Pemberton. He then sold his interest in that syndicate and acquired a large area of land of which Picardy is now part, situated on an excellent lateritic gravel ridge. Early wines have been very promising. Its first vintage was in 1996 and its winery was completed only in 1997. With Bill Pannell's unfailing commitment to wine quality, I anticipate great things. No cellar door sales.

Salitage Wines   R8.5

Vasse Highway, Pemberton, WA 6260
Ph (winery cellar door) 08 9776 1195,
Fax 08 9776 1504

Owners: John and Jenny Horgan
Chief winemaker: Patrick Coutts
Year of foundation: 1989 (winery erected in 1994)
Tonnes crushed on average each year: 225
Location: near Eastbrook Road, Pemberton
Area: 20 ha
Soils: gravelly ironstone

Varieties planted: White—chardonnay, sauvignon blanc; Red—cabernet franc, cabernet sauvignon, merlot, petit verdot, pinot noir

Leading wines: Chardonnay, Pinot Noir

Notes: Salitage shares what is rapidly becoming known as the 'Pemberton Ridge', a long, low hill of lateritic gravel ('marri' country) about 12 km north-east of Pemberton. It is a hilltop site with excellent air drainage to avert frost-risk and good ripening aspect. It is also drip irrigated to prevent moisture stress. Salitage is already the quality pace-setter for the region in chardonnay and pinot noir. When its vines are mature, superb wines are expected. Cellar door sales: 7 days 10am–4pm.

Smithbrook Wines R8

Smith Brook Road, Pemberton, WA 6260
Ph 08 9772 3557, Fax 08 9772 3579

Owners: private company owned 70% by Petaluma Ltd with minority French and Australian viticultural interests
Chief winemaker: Matt Steel (Petaluma)
Year of foundation: 1988
Tonnes crushed on average each year: 80 (used for Smithbrook's own label)
Location: Pemberton
Area: 59.49 ha
Soils: 'karri' loam and 'marri' loam
Varieties planted: White—chardonnay, sauvignon blanc, semillon; Red—cabernet franc, cabernet sauvignon, merlot, petit verdot, pinot noir, shiraz
Leading wines: Smithbrook Chardonnay, Merlot, Pinot Noir, Cabernet Merlot
Notes: At the time of writing, Smithbrook was the region's second largest privately owned vineyard. It has a very strong quality-oriented proprietorship and chooses the best of its own considerable crop of grapes (about 500 tonnes) for wines produced under its own label. It won the SGIO (Western Australian) awards for the Pemberton region's best white and best red in

1997. The balance of fruit is sold only to other premium wine producers. Cellar door sales 7 days 10am–4pm excluding Christmas Day and Easter.

Smith Brook Farm (vineyard only) NR

Smith Brook Road, Pemberton, WA 6260
Ph 08 9772 3100

Owners: Vicky and Cliff Winfield
Year of foundation: 1992
Tonnes crushed on average each year: 30, increasing to 70 tonnes as the vineyard is fully planted and the vines come into full bearing
Location: Smith Brook
Area: 6 ha
Soils: 'karri' loam
Varieties planted: White—chardonnay; Red—merlot
Notes: Smith Brook Farm is a vineyard only and its grapes are sold to winemakers. There are no cellar door sales and no intention of making wine or having wine made.

Tantemaggie Wines (vineyard only) NR

Lot 1 Kemp Road, Pemberton, WA 6260
Ph 08 9776 1164

Owners: Pottinger family
Chief winemaker: none at the present time
Year of foundation: 1987
Tonnes crushed on average each year: at the moment all grapes are sold to Houghton
Location: Pemberton
Area: 20 ha
Soils: deep 'karri' loam
Varieties planted: White—chardonnay, sauvignon blanc, semillon, verdelho; Red—cabernet sauvignon
Leading wines: none at the present time
Notes: The Pottingers of Tantemaggie in recent vintages have sold all their grapes to

Houghtons. However, in the future, they may have wine made once more under the Tantemaggie label. Cellar door sales by appointment.

The Warren Vineyard **NR**

Conte Road, Pemberton, WA 6260
Ph/Fax 08 9776 1115

Owner: Anne Wandless
Chief winemaker: Andrew Forsell (contract)
Year of foundation: 1985
Tonnes crushed on average each year: 10
Location: Pemberton
Area: 1.5 ha
Soils: 'karri' loam
Varieties planted: White—none grown, but some white is made from purchased local fruit; Red—cabernet sauvignon, merlot
Leading wines: Warren Vineyard Cabernet Sauvignon, Merlot, Cabernet-Merlot
Notes: Anne Wandless owns and manages a typical, small, 'karri' loam vineyard close to the heart of Pemberton. It is non-irrigated and fertilised organically as she believes in maximum natural flavour. In the past, wine judges have agreed with her as she won the SGIO award for the best Pemberton red of 1991. Her wines are rarely seen outside the region but cellar door sales are available by appointment.

Treen Ridge Estate **NR**

Packer Road, Pemberton, WA 6260
Ph 08 9776 1131, Fax 08 9775 1176

Owners: Molly, Elizabeth and Barry Scotman
Chief winemakers: Andrew Mountford (reds, contract) and Blair Meiklejohn (whites, contract)
Year of foundation: 1992
Tonnes crushed on average each year: 4, rising to 8 as the vineyard matures and planting is completed
Location: Springfield
Area: 1.75 ha
Soils: sandy gravelly soils ('karri' loam)
Varieties planted: White—riesling, sauvignon blanc; Red—cabernet sauvignon, shiraz
Leading wine: Treen Ridge Shiraz
Notes: Treen Ridge has a very good north-easterly aspect, on 'karri' and 'marri' country between the Warren National Park and the Treen Forest. Cellar door sales facilities are available by appointment.

Woodsmoke Estate **NR**

Lot 2 Kemp Road, Pemberton, WA 6260
Ph/Fax 08 9776 0225

Owners: Rod and Carmel Liebech
Chief winemaker: Jane Brook Estate (contract)
Year of foundation: 1992
Tonnes crushed on average each year: 12, any greater quantities of fruit are sold to local winemakers
Location: Pemberton
Area: 2.25 ha
Soils: 'marri' and 'karri' loams
Varieties planted: White—sauvignon blanc, semillon; Red—cabernet franc, cabernet sauvignon
Leading wines: Woodsmoke Estate Classic Dry White, Cabernet Blend
Notes: Visits are by appointment and most sales take place through local licensed outlets.

WARREN VALLEY REGION (PROPOSED)

From a regional historical perspective, the Warren Valley region and the Pemberton region have much in common. Perhaps Pemberton has a slight claim to seniority in wine

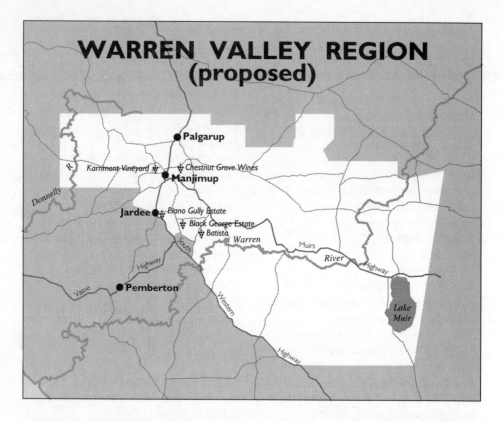

production but only by one vintage—1990 as opposed to 1991. Where they differ is primarily in soil type and climate and that after all is what regional identity is about.

Location: Manjimup latitude 34°14'S, longitude 116°09'E, about 255 km south-east of Perth
Elevation: 279 m with vineyards from 200–300 m
Topography and soils: Warren Valley is an undulating region which rises in altitude up to 300 m to the north of Manjimup. The principal type of soil is that which carried 'marri' trees ('marri' soils). The 'marri' soils are gravelly, lateritic sandy loams and gravelly loams. The gravel content of 'marri' soils is much prized because of its draining and soil-warming capabilities. Around Manjimup in warmer exposures, such soils are suitable for varieties such as cabernet sauvignon, but not for later-ripening varieties. There is also a second type of soil called 'karri' loam and the transition from 'marri' to 'karri' occurs south of Manjimup, midway to Pemberton.
Climate: Manjimup MJT 19.2°C, MAR na, HDD raw 1441, 1482 (cut-off and adjusted for latitude, daily temperature range and vine sites), AR 1055 mm (Oct–Apr 288 mm), RH 42% (3pm Jan), AI na, SH 7.2 (Gladstones). Though slightly warmer than Pemberton, Warren Valley can nevertheless be termed a cool temperate region with more than two-thirds of its annual rainfall occurring between May and September. Viticultural dangers occur largely from frost in the north of the region (Manjimup and north). Birds

present problems where native trees flower later than the ripening of early grape varieties.
Principal varieties: White—chardonnay, sauvignon blanc, verdelho; Red—cabernet sauvignon
Harvest time: (Manjimup) chardonnay early to mid-March, sauvignon blanc mid-March, pinot noir similar to chardonnay, cabernet sauvignon late April
Area: na
Principal wine styles: As with Pemberton it is too early to speculate about the major wine styles which will eventuate. In good sites cabernet sauvignon should ripen quite well, along with other 'Bordeaux' red varieties, though perhaps there should be a reservation about petit verdot. As for whites, chardonnay, sauvignon blanc and verdelho seem adequately suited to the region.

Batista NR

Franklin Road, Middlesex, WA 6260
Ph/Fax 08 9772 3530

Owners: Bob and Grace Peruch
Chief winemaker: contract
Year of foundation: 1993
Tonnes crushed on average each year: 6.5 but should increase as the vines come to maturity
Location: Middlesex
Area: 3.2 ha consisting of two vineyards at Middlesex (1 ha and 2.2 ha)
Soils: low yielding gravel and 'marri' red soils, well-drained with gravel and quartz texture
Varieties planted: White—none; Red—cabernet sauvignon, merlot, pinot noir, shiraz
Leading wines: Batista Pinot Noir, Sparkling
Notes: 1996 was Batista's first vintage for Pinot Noir and a five-star review by Huon Hooke, Mark Shields and Ralph Kyte-Powell in the *Sydney Morning Herald* and the Melbourne *Age* was the result. No cellar door sales.

Black George Estate NR

Black Georges Road, Middlesex, WA 6260
Ph 08 9772 3112, 08 9772 3569, Fax 08 9772 3102

Owners: Wilson family
Chief winemaker: Shelley Wilson
Year of foundation: 1991

Tonnes crushed on average each year: 35
Location: Middlesex
Area: 6.7 ha
Soils: deep gravelly loam over clay, well-drained
Varieties planted: White—chardonnay, sauvignon blanc, verdelho; Red—cabernet franc, merlot, pinot noir
Leading wines: Black George Estate Pinot Noir, Chardonnay, Sauvignon Blanc, Verdelho, Merlot
Notes: Like most wise men of the land, Doug Wilson has learnt not to rely on a single crop. Joy Wilson breeds alpacas. Though alpacas and vines may seem a curious mixture, the Warren Valley region certainly suits them both. Black George Vineyard is situated on a mixture of soils, part sandy gravel and part deep 'karri' loam, typical of the region which is so water-retentive that Doug Wilson does not irrigate. He feels it to be unnecessary with a rainfall of 1200 mm per year. He believes that 'if the vine is in balance and not stressed, then maximum flavour is achieved'. The Wilsons are a fully independent winemaking family, having a 250-tonne winery in the charge of Shelley Wilson, one of the increasing numbers of talented female Australian winemakers. Cellar door sales: each day 10am–4pm.

Bronze Wing Vineyard R7.5

Piano Gully Road, Middlesex, WA 6260
Ph 08 9296 4356

Owner: Westfield Wines
Chief winemaker: John Kosovich
Year of foundation: 1990
Tonnes crushed on average each year: 22 but expected to increase to 50 as vines come to full maturity
Location: Middlesex
Area: 5 ha
Soils: deep gravelly loam, 'jarrah-marri' country, well-drained over light gravelly clay
Varieties planted: Whites—chardonnay, verdelho; Reds—cabernet sauvignon, merlot, shiraz
Leading wines: Westfield Bronze Wing Chardonnay, Verdelho
Notes: Bronze Wing is a pretty spot on the north slope of a hill, overlooking Smith Brook. Its wines, made by John Kosovich in Perth, are excellent. The Chardonnay 1995 won gold medals in 1996 at the Royal Perth Wine Show and later at the Mount Barker Show, at which the author played a minor part in the judging. No local cellar door sales.

Chestnut Grove Wines R7

Perup Road, Manjimup, WA 6258
Ph 08 9772 4255, Fax 08 9772 4255

Owners: Kordic family
Chief winemaker: Alkoomi (contract)
Year of foundation: 1988
Tonnes crushed on average each year: 150
Location: Manjimup
Area: 16 ha
Soils: gravelly loam over clay and coffee rock, 'jarrah' country
Varieties planted: White—chardonnay, sauvignon blanc, verdelho; Red—cabernet sauvignon, merlot, pinot noir
Leading wines: Chestnut Grove Verdelho, Pinot Noir
Notes: Vic Kordic is very much a hands-on winegrower, inspecting his vineyard virtually every day. It seems that his attention to detail has benefited Chestnut Grove, which is not just

a pretty name but also a producer of chestnuts and olive oil. It is wine, however, which is establishing its national reputation, especially its Verdelho 1996 which gained a trophy and two gold medals in Western Australian wine shows. Cellar door sales by appointment only.

Constables (vineyard only) NR

Graphite Road West, Manjimup, WA 6258
Ph 08 9772 1375

Owners: Constable family
Chief winemaker: none
Year of foundation: 1987
Tonnes crushed on average each year: 150 (all grapes are presently sold to Houghton)
Location: Manjimup
Area: 12 ha
Soils: red gravelly loam over a clay base and in parts over a deep loam 'jarrah-marri' country
Varieties planted: White—chardonnay, riesling, sauvignon blanc; Red—cabernet franc, cabernet sauvignon, pinot noir
Leading wines: none
Notes: At the present time, Constables is purely a grower for Houghton. There are no plans for the reappearance of the Constables' label and no cellar door sales.

Karrimont Vineyard NR

Yanmah Road, West Manjimup, WA 6258
Ph/Fax 08 9772 1301

Owners: Nicholas family
Chief winemakers: John Wade and Vasse Felix (contract)
Year of foundation: 1987
Tonnes crushed on average each year: 40 (balance of fruit produced is sold to other winemakers)
Location: West Manjimup
Area: 30 ha
Soils: red gravelly loam, 'marri-jarrah' country

Varieties planted: White—chardonnay, sauvignon blanc, semillon; Red—cabernet franc, cabernet sauvignon, merlot, meunier, pinot noir, sangiovese
Leading wines: Yanmah Ridge Pinot Noir, Cabernet Merlot, Sauvignon Blanc, Chardonnay
Notes: Karrimont is a medium to large vineyard which both sells fruit to Western Australian winemakers and markets its wine under the Yanmah Ridge label. No residual herbicides or chemical insecticides are used. Cellar door sales: ring for times.

Piano Gully Estate **NR**

Piano Gully Road, Manjimup, WA 6258
Ph 08 9772 3140, Fax 08 9316 0336

Owner: Pearlbush Holdings P/L
Chief winemaker: contract
Year of foundation: 1986
Tonnes crushed on average each year: 50
Location: Middlesex
Area: 7 ha
Soils: gravelly loam with some pockets of clay
Varieties planted: White—chardonnay, verdelho; Red—cabernet sauvignon, pinot noir, shiraz
Leading wines: Piano Gully Chardonnay, Pinot Noir, Cabernet Sauvignon
Notes: With its vines now 10 years old, the Piano Gully vineyard is coming of age and will soon strike the right key. Visits are presently by

appointment, though it is planned to re-open cellar door sales in the next two years.

Sinclair Wines **NR**

Glenorin Springs Vineyard, Graphite Road, Glenorin, WA 6258 (close to One Tree Bridge)
Ph 08 9772 1406, Fax 08 9421 1191

Owners: John Healy and Darelle Sinclair
Chief winemaker: Stephen Bullied (Laurin Brook, contract)
Year of foundation: 1994
Tonnes crushed on average each year: 2, increasing to 40 as the vineyard is fully planted and the vines mature
Location: Glenorin
Area: 4 ha
Soils: 'karri' loam with 25–50% of gravel over clay
Varieties planted: White—chardonnay, sauvignon blanc; Red—cabernet sauvignon
Leading wine: Sinclair of Glenorin Cabernet Sauvignon
Notes: At 300 m in altitude and 1200 mm of rain annually, Glenorin Springs may seem a forbidding place for a vineyard, but the rain falls mainly in winter and supplies the natural springs with abundant water of great quality for irrigation. It is early days for Glenorin but a cellar door facility will eventuate within the next few years.

BLACKWOOD VALLEY REGION

The Blackwood Valley region has followed a familiar Australian rural path: exploration in the 1830s and 1840s, settlement a decade later, grazing and wool production in the later nineteenth century and then timber milling, which still continues in a small way. The area is also known for its development of subterranean clover at Dwalganup in the 1930s. Orcharding was also widespread in Boyup Brook about this time, but receded in the 1960s due to the salination of the Blackwood River and to poor returns. This area remains a rich mixed farming district but again poor economic returns have obliged some farmers to diversify by planting vineyards. Again there

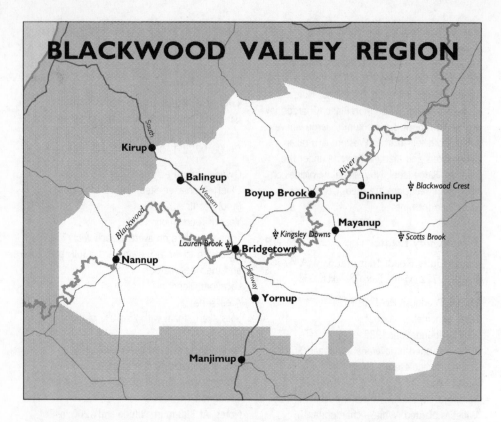

are problems due to the salinity of the Blackwood River, so local farmers use surface run-off water, collected in contour banks and dams for this purpose.

The urban centre of the region is Bridgetown, about 30 km west of Boyup Brook. It has a slightly higher rainfall than Boyup Brook, but a similar mixed farming economy. Orcharding still survives here in places as does local tin mining. About 50 km to the west of Bridgetown is Nannup, another mixed farming and grazing community where there are several grapegrowers and a thriving timber milling industry.

The wine history of the region is very recent, dating from 1978 when local farmer Max Fairbrass felt the region might be suitable because of table grapes grown years before by his grandfather. Max planted a 3-hectare vineyard of riesling, semillon, sauvignon blanc, cabernet sauvignon and shiraz. He was followed in 1987 by Brian and Kerry Walker at Scotts Brook.

Today the region comprises about 200 hectares of vineyard, yielding only about 200 tonnes but this is to be expected as many of the plantings occurred in 1995 and later. By the year 2000, the region should be producing about 1000 tonnes, further projections showing about 2000 tonnes by the year 2005.

Location: Bridgetown latitude 33°57'S, longitude 116°07'E, about 212 km south-south-east of Perth

Elevation: Bridgetown 154 m, but the region as a whole varies between 100 m (Nannup) and 340 m (parts of Boyup Brook)

Topography and soils: Most of the area is part of the Darling Plateau Systems, consisting of narrow plateau remnants and moderately incised valleys. Soils here are gravelly on the divides with yellow soils and red earths on valley slopes. Around Bridgetown and part of Nannup are deeply incised valleys with red and yellow earths, rocky outcrops on slopes and narrow alluvial terraces.

Climate: Bridgetown MJT 20.6°C, MAR na, HDD raw 1578, 1492 (cut-off and adjusted for latitude, daily temperature range and vine sites), AR 856 mm (Oct–Apr 219 mm), RH 36%, AI na, SH 7.9 (Gladstones). The Blackwood Valley region has dry summer months and a high winter rainfall. Temperatures are not excessive and it can be called a cool region.

Within the region, rainfall becomes greater as one approaches the coast, the area around Boyup Brook receiving 600–700 mm per annum, Bridgetown 800–900 mm and Nannup 1000–1100 mm. In the Bridgetown–Kirup locality, suitable vine sites (good gravelly loamy soils and good potential for water catchment) do exist but in the past the region has been downgraded by some writers because of an extreme risk of spring frosts due to low humidity, wide temperature variability and poor air drainage.

Max Fairbrass, the third generation of his family in the region, whose Blackwood Crest vineyard is near Boyup Brook some way to the north-east of Bridgetown, remembers many more frosts in his youth and feels that the region is becoming warmer. He has recently backed that judgment by planting more vineyard area. Boyup Brook, higher and drier than Bridgetown with possibly better air drainage, is proving a popular grape-growing area, but even here frost remains a risk and certainly should be taken into account if a vineyard site is being selected. Further west around Nannup, both climatic and soil conditions appear similar to the south-western part of the Geographe region and this area also should be quite suitable for viticulture.

Principal varieties: chardonnay, cabernet sauvignon, shiraz

Harvest time: chardonnay late February to early March, shiraz mid-March, cabernet sauvignon late March to early April

Total area: approx. 200 ha

Principal wine styles: It is too soon for any pronouncement, but medium to full-bodied reds made from cabernet sauvignon and shiraz are likely to be prominent

Blackwood Crest   **NR**

Chambers Road, Boyup Brook, WA 6244
Ph/Fax 08 9767 3029

Owners: Max and Roslynne Fairbrass
Chief winemaker: Max Fairbrass
Year of foundation: 1976
Tonnes crushed on average each year: 35
Location: Boyup Brook

Area: 8 ha (includes new plantings)
Soils: loamy gravelly soils, typical red gum 'marri' country
Varieties planted: White—chardonnay, riesling, sauvignon blanc, semillon; Red—cabernet sauvignon, shiraz
Leading wine: Blackwood Crest Shiraz
Notes: Max Fairbrass is the pioneer of the

region. He feels that the area is 'red' country and shiraz is a very good variety for the region, but he has not neglected whites. Cellar door sales: 10am–5pm each day.

Kingsley Downs NR

Dalmore Road, Winnijup, WA 6255
Ph 08 9761 7512, Fax 08 9761 7532

Owners: C and E Shedley
Chief winemaker: Chris Shedley
Year of foundation: 1987
Tonnes crushed on average each year: 12
(2 of which are used for own label)
Location: Winnijup
Area: 3 ha and growing
Soils: gravelly sandy loam over light clay and clayey loam over light clay
Varieties planted: White—chardonnay, sauvignon blanc, taminga; Red—cabernet franc, cabernet sauvignon, shiraz
Leading wine: Shedley's Cabernet Sauvignon
Notes: Chris Shedley is typical of the many hundreds of small Australian winegrowers who have been gripped by grape fever in the late twentieth century. His vineyard is growing each year by half a hectare and one day it will be a fulltime occupation. Sales by mail order and personal contact. No cellar door sales.

Lauren Brook NR

Eedle Terrace, Bridgetown, WA 6255
Ph 08 9761 2676, Fax 08 9761 1879

Owners: RS and LA Bullied
Chief winemaker: Stephen Bullied
Year of foundation: 1993
Tonnes crushed on average each year: 15 (in addition to estate-grown chardonnay, fruit is purchased from three local growers)
Location: Bridgetown
Area: 1 ha

Soils: deep well-structured red loam over clay
Varieties planted: White—chardonnay; Red—none
Leading wines: Lauren Brook Shiraz, Riesling, Cabernet Sauvignon, Bridgetown Blend (a Chardonnay-Semillon)
Notes: Lauren Brook is the only winery in Bridgetown, though with the pace of vineyard development in the region generally, it may not remain so for long. Cellar door sales: weekdays 11am–4pm, weekends 11am–5pm.

Scotts Brook NR

Scotts Brook Road, Boyup Brook, WA 6244
Ph 08 9765 3014, 08 9765 3021, Fax 08 9765 3015

Owners: Brian and Kerry Walker, Ian and Lorraine Robinson
Chief winemaker: contract, Mike Davies (consultant)
Year of foundation: 1987
Tonnes crushed on average each year: 40 but growing as recent plantings come into bearing (15 tonnes are used for Scotts Brook own labels)
Location: Boyup Brook
Area: 17.5 ha (including 1997 plantings of 4 ha)
Soils: gravelly loam over clay
Varieties planted: White—chardonnay, riesling, sauvignon blanc, semillon; Red—cabernet sauvignon, pinot noir, shiraz
Leading wines: Scotts Brook Cabernet Sauvignon, Chardonnay
Notes: Now a veteran compared with the ages of other vineyards in the region, Scotts Brook has won silver and bronze medals for its Cabernet Sauvignon at regional shows. Cellar door sales: weekends or by appointment.

CENTRAL WESTERN AUSTRALIA ZONE

This is a large area of country with few vineyards as yet. It seems 'continental' in nature with hot summers and cold winters. It contains no wine region at present.

Hotham Valley Estate R7.5

South Wandering Road, Wandering, WA 6308
Ph 08 9884 1525, Fax 08 9884 1079

Owners: a group of Perth investors
Chief winemaker: James Pennington
Year of foundation: 1987
Tonnes crushed on average each year: 70
Location: Wandering
Area: 12 ha
Soils: gravelly loam over clay
Varieties planted: White—chardonnay, chenin blanc, riesling, semillon; Red—cabernet franc, cabernet sauvignon, merlot
Leading wines: Hotham Estate Semillon, Chenin Blanc, Cabernet-Merlot
Notes: With 24 awards to its credit in recent years, Hotham Valley is a consistent performer at major Western Australian wine shows. No cellar door sales.

Stratherne Vale Estate NR

Campbell St, Cuballing, WA 6312
Ph 08 9881 2148, Fax 08 9881 3129

Owners: Gordon and Janette Suckling
Chief winemaker: James Pennington (contract)
Year of foundation: 1980
Tonnes crushed on average each year: 2
Location: Cuballing
Area: 1.6 ha
Soils: a light red, sandy, clayey loam
Varieties planted: White—none; Red—cabernet sauvignon, merlot, shiraz

Leading wine: Stratherne Vale Red (a blend of the red varieties mentioned above)
Notes: A very small local vineyard with sales only to local bottle shops. No cellar door sales.

Wandering Brook Estate ❦ NR

Wandering North Road, Wandering, WA 6308
Ph/Fax 08 9884 1064

Owners: Laurie and Margaret White
Chief winemaker: Paul Radikovich
Year of foundation: 1989
Tonnes crushed on average each year: 50, of which 20 are used for the Wandering Brook label
Location: Wandering
Area: 12 ha
Soils: gravel and coarse rock all over clay sloping down to heavy red and grey loam
Varieties planted: White—chardonnay, chenin blanc, verdelho; Red—cabernet sauvignon, merlot
Leading wines: Wandering Brook Verdelho, Unwooded Chardonnay, Chardonnay, Cabernet Sauvignon
Notes: Wandering Brook is establishing a good reputation at local wine shows, achieving gold and silver for its whites at the 1997 Perth Regions Wine Show. Cellar door sales: weekends 10am–6pm, weekdays by appointment, open lunches and dinners at weekends by appointment.

GREATER PERTH ZONE

This zone is the cradle of Western Australian viticulture, comprising the Swan Districts wine region, renowned for its fortifieds and rich white wines, and also the much newer and higher proposed region of Perth Hills.

Baldivis Estate R6.5

River Road, Serpentine, WA 6171
Ph 08 9525 2066, Fax 08 9525 2411

Owner: Kailis Consolidated Pty Ltd
Chief winemaker: Marcus Ansems
Year of foundation: 1982
Tonnes crushed on average each year: 140
Location: Serpentine
Area: 12 ha
Soils: typical 'tuart' country over a 'coffee' rock and limestone base
Varieties planted: White—chardonnay, sauvignon blanc, semillon; Red—cabernet sauvignon, merlot
Leading wines: Baldivis Estate Chardonnay, Unwooded Chardonnay, Cabernet-Merlot
Notes: Typical 'tuart' wines, light, fragrant, easy-drinking, lacking 'stuffing'. Cellar door sales: weekdays 10am–4pm, weekends and public holidays 11am–5pm.

Peel Estate R7

Fletcher Road, Baldivis, WA 6210
Ph 08 9524 1221, Fax 08 9524 1625

Owner/chief winemaker: Will Nairn
Year of foundation: 1974
Tonnes crushed on average each year: 130
Location: Baldivis
Area: 14.4 ha
Soils: 'tuart' country, typical deep free-draining sand over a limestone base
Varieties planted: White—chardonnay, chenin blanc, semillon, verdelho; Red—cabernet franc, cabernet sauvignon, merlot, shiraz, zinfandel
Leading wines: Peel Estate Wood Matured Chenin Blanc, Shiraz
Notes: Peel Estate is well known for its soft and spicy oak-matured Chenin Blanc and generously flavoured reds. Cellar door sales: 7 days 10am–5pm.

SWAN DISTRICTS REGION

Settlement of the Swan River colony took place in 1829. From the very first years of settlement, the alluvial flats of the Swan River district were found to be suitable for cereal crops and by 1833 over 500 acres were in cultivation to wheat, barley, oats and maize. In 1830 the townsite of Guildford at the junction of the Swan and Helena Rivers was established. Crops grown on the alluvial soil were carted to Guildford and transported by barge along the Swan to Perth and Fremantle.

From that time also there was a great interest in the vine, with records of plantings existing as early as 1834 and a wine cellar being dug even earlier by Thomas Waters. Two of the Swan Valley land grants made about that time, Houghton and Sandalford, are today household names in Western Australian viticulture. A large proportion of

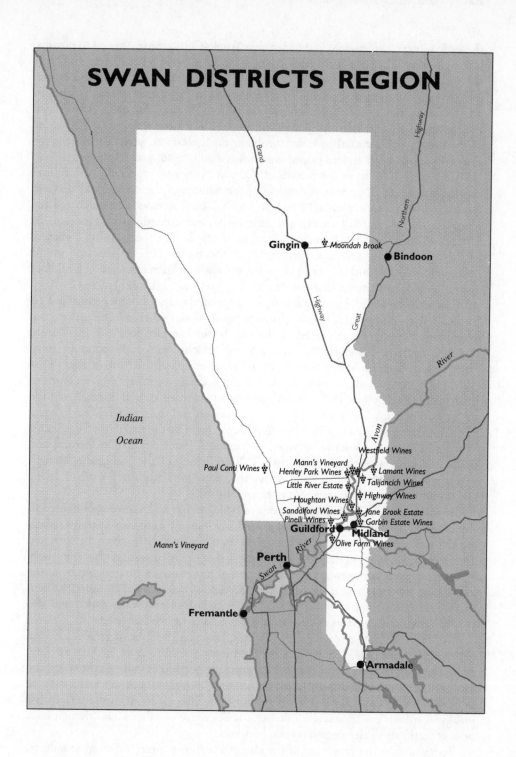

SWAN DISTRICTS REGION

Brand

Highway

Northern

Gingin ✾ *Moondah Brook*

Bindoon

Highway

Great

River

Avon

Indian

Ocean

Westfield Wines

Mann's Vineyard
Henley Park Wines ✾✾✾ ✾ *Lamont Wines*

Paul Conti Wines ✾

Little River Estate ✾ ✾ *Talijancich Wines*

✾ *Highway Wines*

Houghton Wines ✾

Sandalford Wines ✾ *Jane Brook Estate*
Pinelli Wines ✾ ✾ *Garbin Estate Wines*

Guildford **Midland**

✾ *Olive Farm Wines*

Mann's Vineyard

Perth ●

Swan *River*

Fremantle ●

Armadale ●

the early settlers were middle and upper class Anglo-Celtic gentry unused to physical labour, as were other owners of large tracts of land who were retired Army and Navy officers. The result was a substantial shortage of labour in the Swan River colony and so, in 1850, the penal system, never employed in the colony of South Australia and hardly tolerated in Victoria, was introduced into Western Australia. All Western Australian public buildings, roads and bridges after that time and until the cessation of the system were erected by convict labour. Such convicts were frequently given tickets-of-leave and therefore gained employment quite readily as labourers.

Though by 1860 there are records of 400 acres of vines, producing 90 000 litres of wine and nearly 20 tonnes of dried fruit, the founder of the commercial Western Australian wine industry must be said to be Dr John Ferguson who purchased the Houghton Estate in 1859, erecting a wine cellar and expanding the vineyard. By 1885, the York railway had been completed, indirectly causing the eclipse of Guildford as the major trading and transport centre of the Swan. This was because of the decision to site the southern terminus of the railway five kilometres east of Guildford at what is today the major business centre of the region—Midland Junction.

How sparsely would Australia have been populated were it not for goldrushes! As in the eastern colonies of Victoria and New South Wales 40 years earlier, there was an explosion of population caused by the rush to the 'eastern' goldfields of Western Australia in the 1880s and 1890s. It was a rush which came at an opportune time, for it caused Western Australia to avoid the worst effects of the bank crashes of the early 1890s in the eastern colonies. As the fields declined, many 'diggers' returned to the countryside closer to Perth with money to purchase land. The result was the subdivision of many larger estates in the Swan region and the creation of many small farms, including vineyards. This was a trend accelerated by the end of the First World War and the need to settle returned servicemen. Immigration from central and southern Europe also increased in the 1920s and many of the immigrants brought with them viticultural skills. From about this time good markets for table, drying and, to a lesser extent, wine grapes were established.

By the late 1930s over 2400 hectares of table, drying and wine grapes existed in the Swan Valley, about half of them owned by southern European migrants. Many are still run by their descendants. Though vineyards were chiefly grown for table and drying grapes, the wine industry also thrived. Important names at this time were Houghton, which commenced the production of its famous 'White Burgundy' in the late 1930s, Valencia and Swanville. The area under vine peaked in the 1940s and thereafter declined due to uncertainties in the dried fruit and wine market and also to urban pressures, but this decline now appears to have been arrested.

Until the 1980s, the Swan Valley area, its climate greatly favouring the production of fortified wines, was dotted with small wineries mostly owned by Yugoslav and Italian migrant families who made basic fortified wine, sold in bulk to customers who brought their own containers. But with the swing in public taste to fresher styles of table wine, bulk sales of fortified are becoming more difficult and the wineries formerly making fortifieds are themselves offering a wider range of table wines, though local sales of fortifieds in this region remain buoyant.

Today, due to the proximity of the city of Perth, the Swan Valley wine industry has limited opportunity for expansion, which has swung from the east to the north, Moondah Brook at Gin Gin. In addition there are vineyards at Bindoon and Chittering, though due to their altitude, these areas may become part of the proposed wine region of Perth Hills. The region as proposed falls into three sub-areas: the Valley floor (the area north from Guildford); Moondah Brook and Lennards Brook; and Wanneroo and the northern beaches.

Location: Guildford latitude 31°53'S, longitude 116°01'E, about 15 km north-east of Perth

Elevation: 8 m with most Valley plantings less than 60 m above sea-level

Topography and soils: The Swan Districts region is relatively flat to slightly undulating with several distinct types of soils. In its northern coastal strip (around Wanneroo) there is the typical 'tuart' country (deep free-draining sands over limestone). To the east as the Darling Scarp is approached there is the drainage basin of the Swan and here, on its western perimeter, the Valley is flat with coastal sands grading to deep reddish sandy loams forming the river terraces. These young alluvial soils are quite suitable for viticulture. Fringing these soils are grey-brown sands overlying clays, while between this area and the gravelly sands adjacent to the Scarp, there are poorly drained soils much less suited to viticulture.

Climate: (1) Guildford MJT 24.1°C, MAR na, HDD raw 2396, 1826 (adjusted for latitude and daily temperature range, but not for vine sites), AR 865 mm (Oct–Apr 220 mm), RH 40% (3pm Jan), AI na, SH 9.2 (Gladstones).

The Swan Valley is a very hot area, tending to favour the production of fortified wines and drying grapes, especially currants. It is cooled in summer generally from noon onwards by a south-west sea breeze, famous in cricketing circles as the Fremantle Doctor, and as the Valley extends to the north-east it is naturally favoured by this breeze. However, rich full-bodied whites and reds can be made, but they generally lack the freshness and fruit qualities of cooler areas. If such grapes are not stressed during ripening, they make up in body and softness what they lack in fruit freshness. If stressed, the reds become porty and jammy and generally lack structure. The whites, generally more successful, are made from verdelho, chenin blanc and chardonnay. So the Swan Valley vigneron, if intent on making finer styles of table wines, generally hopes for a cooler than average vintage.

In the northern part of the region around Gin Gin (Moondah Brook and Lennards Brook), the vineyard elevations are slightly higher, thus compensating in heat factors for the higher latitude. The Fremantle Doctor has a very beneficial effect here, too. As exemplified by the Houghton Moondah Brook table wines, the fruit grown there has always proved to be of very high quality.

(2) Wanneroo (Perth Obs) MJT 23.5°C, MAR na, HDD raw 2264, 1815 (adj for lat and daily temp range but not for vine sites), AR 883 mm (Oct–Apr 176 mm), RH 43% (3pm Jan), AI na, SH 9.2 (G).

This is the coastal strip of the Swan Districts region. Its predominant soil is 'tuart', deep sand over limestone, a frequently occurring soil type from Yanchep (north of Wanneroo) south as far as Bunbury and Busselton. It is arguable that on the basis of this soil type there should be a Western Australian 'South West Coastal' region, but it would be disparate in location and its climate would not be uniform. During its growing season, Wanneroo would seem to be fractionally cooler than other parts of Swan Districts, being favoured by strong south-west sea breezes. From my own experience of Paul Conti's Shiraz reds, its styles are lighter and softer, and this may result from the combination of lighter soils and slightly cooler climate.

In the Swan Districts region water for irrigation presents difficulties. Traditionally water has been sourced from bores as the Swan River was tidal and saline as far as Upper Swan. Shallow bores (less than 100 m in depth) have become saline in recent years and access to deeper reserves is tightly regulated due to urban demand. Most of the traditional Swan Valley vineyards are dry-grown, but growers with access to the Leederville aquifer (deeper than 100 m) enjoy good quality water which is rather high in iron content.

In the north of the region around Gin Gin, high quality water is available from Moondah Brook and is sufficient to irrigate over 90 ha of vines, whereas on the coast water can be sourced from shallow bores (less than 100 m in depth), but because of pressure from urbanisation, many vineyards are dry-grown.

Harvest time: chardonnay and verdelho mid-February, chenin blanc and shiraz late February, cabernet sauvignon first week of March

Principal varieties: In its youth chenin blanc shows appley, citrusy and tropical characters and is the leading variety of the Swan Districts region, dominating the plantings here. In this hot climate, whether on its own or in a blend, it produces rich and luscious wine which responds well to bottle age (such as Houghton White Burgundy, of which chenin was traditionally a part) and is often not at its best until 5–7 years old. It may be wooded or unwooded.

Verdelho, when vinified as a table wine, displays sherbety aromas and flavours when young. It is normally not oaked as it is considered to be an aromatic variety. With bottle age it becomes more complex, displaying honeysuckle and tropical characters. It can also be used as a dessert wine, as it commonly was until about 1970.

Chardonnay is as successful in the Swan Districts as in any other hot area of Australia, producing typically peachy aromas and flavours which are sometimes a little 'hot'.

Area: 360 ha (Swan Shire 1996)

Major wine styles: See principal varieties (above). Historically one style stands out above all others of the region and that is Houghton White Burgundy, a full-bodied white blend usually blended from 50% chenin blanc, 15–20% chardonnay, 15% muscadelle and smaller percentages of semillon and verdelho.

Garbin Estate Wines   **NR**

209 Toodyay Road, Middle Swan,
WA 6056
Ph/Fax 08 9274 1747

Owners: Garbin family
Chief winemaker: Peter Garbin

Year of foundation: 1956
Tonnes crushed on average each year: 20,
expanding to 100 by the year 2000
Locations: Middle Swan and Gin Gin
Area: 2 ha but a new 3 ha vineyard is being
developed on a 20 ha property at Gin Gin

Soils: Middle Swan sandy clay, Gin Gin red loam with intermixed gravel
Varieties planted: (Middle Swan) White— chenin blanc, verdelho; Red—cabernet sauvignon, merlot, shiraz. (Gin Gin) White— chardonnay, semillon; Red—none yet
Leading wines: Garbin Estate Shiraz, Chardonnay
Notes: This family winery is now in its second generation of ownership with a commitment to move from the old Swan practice of bulk winemaking to become a quality boutique producer. It all seems to be working quite smoothly with trophies and awards being gained at the Swan Valley Show. Cellar door sales: Mon–Sat 10am–5.30pm, Sun noon–5.30pm.

Henley Park Wines **NR**

149 Swan Street, West Swan, WA 6055
Ph 08 9296 4328, Fax 08 9296 4313

Owners: Claus Petersen and Malaysian interests
Chief winemaker: Claus Petersen
Year of foundation: 1935
Tonnes crushed on average each year: 70
Location: Henley Brook
Area: 4.4 ha
Soils: alluvial red clays
Varieties planted: White—chardonnay, chenin blanc, muscat gordo blanco, semillon; Red— cabernet sauvignon, merlot, pinot noir, shiraz
Leading wines: Henley Park Classic White (a chardonnay-chenin blend), Sparkling Rose (made by the champagne method)
Notes: This is a consistent winner of minor awards and the occasional gold at Western Australian wine shows. Cellar door sales: Tues–Sun 10am–5pm. There is also a cafe open Fri, Sat and Sun and public holidays.

Highway Wines **NR**

Great Northern Highway, Herne Hill, WA 6056
Ph 08 9296 4354

Owners: Bakranich family
Chief winemaker: Tony Bakranich
Year of foundation: 1954
Tonnes crushed on average each year: 40
Location: Herne Hill
Area: 10 ha
Soils: rich loam
Varieties planted: White—chenin blanc, muscat of alexandria, pedro semillon; Red—cabernet sauvignon, grenache, shiraz
Leading wine: Highway Wines Port
Notes: This traditional Swan Valley winery specialises in fortified wines which still enjoy a great local following. Cellar door sales: Mon–Sat 8.30am–6pm.

Houghton Wines **R9**

Dale Road, Middle Swan, WA 6056
Ph 08 9274 5100, Fax 08 9274 5372

Owner: BRL Hardy Ltd
Chief winemaker: Larry Cherubino
Year of foundation: 1836
Tonnes crushed on average each year: 700 and rising (from the company's Middle Swan vineyards)
Location: Middle Swan
Area: 44 ha
Soils: sand (called locally 'Herne Hill sand') about 20 cm deep over clay
Varieties planted: White—chardonnay, chenin blanc, pedro ximines, sauvignon blanc, semillon, verdelho; Red—none
Leading wines: Houghton
Notes: The largest winery in the west, Houghton is the production centre for all of BRL Hardy's many Western Australian grapes, whether originating in the Swan, Gin Gin or the cool south-western regions of Mount Barker, Margaret River, Pemberton or the Warren Valley. Its leading white is Houghton White Burgundy, once locally grown though scarcely so any longer. In fact, most of the Houghton wines produced are multi-area blends from Western Australia, unless

otherwise specifically indicated. Cellar door sales: each day except Christmas Day and Easter 10am–5pm.

Jane Brook Estate R7

229 Toodyay Road, Middle Swan, WA 6056
Ph 08 9274 1432, Fax 08 9274 1211

Owners: David and Beverley Atkinson
Chief winemaker: Lyndon Crockett
Year of foundation: 1972
Tonnes crushed on average each year: 200
Location: Middle Swan
Area: 12 ha
Soils: alluvial sandy gravelly clay
Varieties planted: White—chardonnay, chenin blanc, sauvignon blanc, verdelho;
Red—cabernet sauvignon, merlot, shiraz
Leading wines: Jane Brook Estate Wood Aged Chenin Blanc, Elizabeth Jane Methode Champenoise Chardonnay, Shiraz
Notes: Beverley Atkinson is proud of Jane Brook's Methode Champenoise Chardonnay, which was the most highly pointed sparkling wine at the 1997 Sheraton Awards, and its Shiraz which was awarded four stars in *Winestate*'s top 100. Cellar door sales: 7 days noon–5pm and casual al fresco lunches on the terrace.

Lamont Wines NR

Bisdee Road, Millendon, WA 6056
Ph 08 9296 4485, Fax 08 9296 1663

Owner: Corin Lamont
Chief winemaker: Mark Warren
Year of foundation: 1978
Tonnes crushed on average each year: 90 (in addition to the vineyard production, fruit is purchased from local growers)
Location: Millendon
Area: 5 ha
Soils: sandy loams to gravelly loams
Varieties planted: White—muscadelle, navera,

verdelho; Red—cabernet sauvignon, shiraz
Leading wines: Lamont Verdelho, Chenin Blanc, Chardonnay, Cabernet-Shiraz
Notes: This is a winery of consistently good standards, winner of the trophy for the Best Small Winemaker (WA) under 200-tonne crush at the 1997 Mount Barker Wine Show and the 1997 SGIO Award for Lamont Chenin Blanc. Cellar door sales: Wed–Sun 10am–4pm.

Little River Estate NR

Cnr West Swan and Forest Roads, Henley Brook, WA 6055
Ph 08 9296 4462, Fax 08 9296 1922

Owners: Bruno and Jan de Tastes
Chief winemaker: Bruno de Tastes
Year of foundation: 1934 (as Glenalwyn Wines)
Tonnes crushed on average each year: 45
Location: Henley Brook
Area: 5 ha
Soils: loam
Varieties planted: White—chardonnay, viognier;
Red—shiraz
Leading wines: Little River Estate Shiraz, Viognier
Notes: Cellar door sales, 7 days 10am–5pm.

Mann's Vineyard NR

105 Memorial Avenue, Baskerville, WA 6056
Ph/Fax 08 9296 4348

Owners: Dorham and Sally Mann
Chief winemaker: Dorham Mann
Year of foundation: 1988
Tonnes crushed on average each year: 9
Location: Baskerville
Area: 3 ha
Soils: red alluvial soil on a high river terrace
Varieties planted: White—none; Red—cabernet sauvignon
Leading wine: Mann (a sparkling cabernet sauvignon made by the Champagne method)
Notes: Located on a high bank with scenic

views of the Valley, the Mann cuverie is owned by former Sandalford winemaker and expert adviser to the WA industry Dorham Mann. It makes just one wine—a sparkling cabernet sauvignon. Cellar door sales: weekends 10am–5pm, otherwise by appointment.

Moondah Brook (vineyard only)   R8.5

7 Constable Street, Gin Gin, WA 6503

Owner: BRL Hardy Ltd
Chief winemaker: Larry Cherubino
Year of foundation: 1968
Tonnes produced on average each year: 1000 but will increase to 1500 as new plantings come into bearing
Location: Gin Gin
Area: 133.3 ha
Soils: deep sands, 'Gin Gin' sands
Varieties planted: White—chardonnay, chenin blanc, muscadelle, riesling, verdelho; Red—cabernet sauvignon
Leading wines: Moondah Brook Chenin Blanc, Verdelho, Chardonnay, Cabernet Sauvignon
Notes: Made at Houghton by former winemaker Paul Lapsley from the extensive Gin Gin vineyard, Moondah Brook is one of Western Australia's most reliable wine labels. These days its wines are sometimes blended with wines from other Houghton vineyards in the west, but quality remains very high. No local cellar door sales.

Olive Farm Wines   R6.5

77 South Eastern Highway, South Guildford, WA 6055
Ph 08 9277 2989, Fax 08 9279 4372

Owner/chief winemaker: Ian Yurisich
Year of foundation: 1829
Tonnes crushed on average each year: 50
Location: South Guildford (winery), Upper Swan (vineyard)
Area: 10 ha

Soils: deep alluvial loam on a clay base
Varieties planted: White—chardonnay, chenin blanc, gewurztraminer, sauvignon blanc, semillon, verdelho; Red—cabernet sauvignon, pinot noir, merlot, shiraz
Leading wines: Olive Farm Chardonnay, Cabernet-Shiraz-Merlot
Notes: Though it has not been continuously used as such, Olive Farm can justly claim to be the oldest wine cellar still in use in Australia. Cellar door sales: Mon–Fri 10am–5.30pm, weekends 11am–3pm, closed Wed.

Paul Conti Wines   R7.5

529 Wanneroo Road, Woodvale, WA 6026
Ph 08 9409 9160, Fax 08 9309 1634

Owner/chief winemaker: Paul Conti
Year of foundation: 1948
Tonnes crushed on average each year: 123
Location: (vineyards) Woodvale, Mariginiup, Carabooda
Area: 18 ha
Soils: 'tuart' country, deep free-draining quite fertile sand over limestone with similar soils on all three vineyards
Varieties planted: White—chardonnay, chenin blanc, sauvignon blanc; Red—cabernet sauvignon, grenache, muscat, pinot noir, shiraz
Leading wines: Paul Conti Mariginiup Shiraz, Chenin Blanc, Chardonnay, Cabernet Sauvignon
Notes: Paul Conti is one of the top makers of this area which, as noted above, is quite different in its soils to the rest of the Swan region. Except for some of the larger, better-resourced wineries, his wines have more finesse and style than most of their colleagues in the Swan, yet age well over 3–5 years. It is noteworthy also that, in the 1970s, he made some of the earliest wines from the Mount Barker sub-region. Cellar door sales: Mon–Sat 9.30am–5.30pm, Sun by appointment.

Pinelli Wines NR

30 Bennett St, Caversham, WA 6055
Ph 08 9279 6818, Fax 08 9377 4259

Owners: Pinelli family
Chief winemaker: Robert Pinelli
Year of foundation: 1979
Tonnes crushed on average each year: 150
Locations: Caversham and Middle Swan
Area: 2.8 ha (Caversham), 5.2 ha (Middle
Swan)
Soils: swan loam and alluvial red clay
Varieties planted: White—chenin blanc,
chardonnay; Red—cabernet sauvignon, shiraz
Leading wines: Pinelli Chardonnay, Chenin
Blanc, Cabernet Sauvignon
Notes: Pinelli is another Swan winemaker
making the transition from bulk wines to
specialised table wines and, by its show results,
making an excellent job of it. At the Royal
Perth Wine Show, Pinelli has won one gold,
three silvers and 15 bronzes in several show
outings. Cellar door sales: 7 days 10am–5pm.

Sandalford Wines R7.5

West Swan Road, Caversham, WA 6055
Ph 08 9274 5922, Fax 08 9274 2154

Owners: Peter and Debra Prendiville
Chief winemaker: Bill Crappsley
Year of foundation: 1840
Tonnes crushed on average each year: 100
from Caversham vineyard, but many more are
obtained from the Margaret River and Mount
Barker vineyards and also purchased from
growers
Location: Caversham
Area: 15 ha
Soils: alluvial and grey clay over white clay
Varieties planted: White—chenin blanc,
semillon, verdelho; Red—cabernet sauvignon,
shiraz
Leading wines: Sandalford Sandalera (a
fortified dessert wine), Caversham Chenin-
Verdelho, Caversham Cabernet-Shiraz (fruit

from Caversham accounts for about 60% of
the Caversham range)
Notes: Sandalford is one of Western Australia's
older and larger vineyards, founded by the Roe
family in 1840 and owned by it for many
years. These days, besides its Caversham
Vineyard, it has vineyards in Margaret River
and Mount Barker, crushing hundreds of
tonnes of fruit each vintage. Cellar door sales:
daily 10am–5pm, closed Christmas Day, Good
Friday and Anzac Day (am).

Talijancich Wines NR

26 Hyem Road, Herne Hill, WA 6056
Ph 08 9296 4289, Fax 08 9296 1762

Owners: James and Hilda Talijancich
Chief winemaker: James Talijancich
Year of foundation: 1932
Tonnes crushed on average each year: 150
(includes fruit purchased from outside growers)
Location: Herne Hill
Area: 6 ha
Soils: sandy gravel on a clay base
Varieties planted: White—muscadelle, semillon,
verdelho; Red—shiraz
Leading wines: Talijancich Julian James White
Liqueur (a blend of muscadelle, verdelho and
semillon), Julian James Red Liqueur (basically
shiraz with small quantities of grenache and
cabernet), Voices Dry White (a premium blend
of chardonnay, chenin and semillon),
Grenache, Shiraz
Notes: Over the years Talijancich has built up a
deserved reputation for the production of high
quality fortified wines. Cellar door sales:
Sun–Fri 11am–5pm, closed Sat.

Westfield Wines R8

180 Memorial Ave, Baskerville,
WA 6056
Ph/Fax 08 9296 4356

Owner/chief winemaker: John Kosovich
Year of foundation: 1922

Tonnes crushed on average each year: 80, including Bronze Wing
Location: Baskerville and Warren Valley, see also Bronze Wing (Warren Valley)
Area: 5.6 ha (Baskerville) and 5.2 ha (Bronze Wing)
Soils: (Baskerville) alluvial sandy gravelly clay
Varieties planted: White—chardonnay, chenin blanc, riesling, semillon, verdelho;
Red—cabernet sauvignon, merlot, shiraz
Leading wines: Westfield Chardonnay, Verdelho, Cabernet Sauvignon, Merlot, Liqueur Muscat
Notes: Westfield Wines is a consistent producer of wines of quality. At the Perth Wine Show it has twice (1996 and 1997) been most successful exhibitor in the 'under 300 tonnes produced' category. It also produces Chardonnays of complexity and style as well as that Swan Valley speciality, Liqueur Muscat.
Cellar door sales: 7 days 10am–4pm.

PERTH HILLS REGION (PROPOSED)

At the time of writing, Perth Hills as originally proposed did not have sufficient 'critical mass' to qualify as a wine region. However, it was suggested that two important viticultural areas, Bindoon and Chittering Valley be included as a northern part of the region. They are also part of the Darling Scarp with not dissimilar climates, but to the north of the region as originally proposed.

The main centres of the southern part of the region are Kalamunda and Mundaring. The area now called Kalamunda was first settled in 1839 when Benjamin Robbins began farming nearby. Timber-getting from the local jarrah forests also became a thriving industry later in the nineteenth century and during the first half of the twentieth, but the town itself was not founded until the year of Federation, 1901. About two years later, during the construction of the Mundaring Reservoir on the Helena River to supply water to Kalgoorlie 600 km away, the town of Mundaring was also established. In addition to timber-getting, early settlers noticed the fertility of the region's valleys and lower slopes and the abundance of water and so, in the early twentieth century, a fruit and vegetable growing industry thrived. The end of the First World War also saw returned soldiers settled on smallholdings and they too mostly turned to horticulture.

The first vineyard and winery in the southern part of the region was established in the 1880s and produced wine for almost 60 years until the winery was burnt down in 1945. The original Darlington Vineyard gave its name to a railway siding which ultimately became a town. There were also vines planted at Kalamunda at the turn of the century.

The modern era of viticulture in the region began in 1969 with the foundation of the Woodthorpe Vineyard near Parkerville. The vineyard is planted on 'marri' country and, now over a quarter of a century old, is the veteran vineyard of the Perth Hills. Woodhenge Vineyard in the Bickley Valley followed, being planted in 1974. At the present time there are more than 17 vineyards planted to wine grapes in the southern part of Perth Hills.

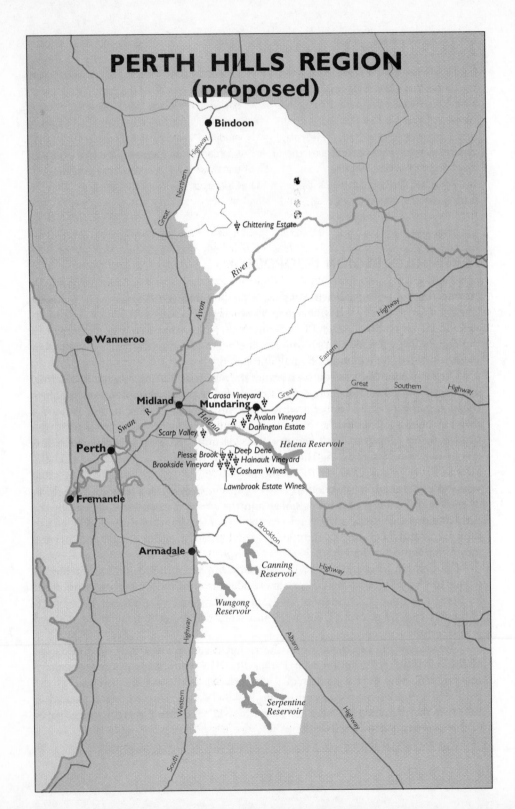

PERTH HILLS REGION
(proposed)

Bindoon

Chittering Estate

River

Avon

Wanneroo

Midland

Carosa Vineyard

Mundaring

Avalon Vineyard
Darlington Estate

Scarp Valley

Helena R

Helena Reservoir

Swan R

Perth

Piesse Brook   Deep Dene
Brookside Vineyard   Hainault Vineyard
          Cosham Wines

Lawnbrook Estate Wines

Fremantle

Great Northern Highway

Eastern Highway

Great   Great   Southern   Highway

Armadale

Brookton

Canning
Reservoir

Highway

Wungong
Reservoir

Albany

Serpentine
Reservoir

Highway

Western Highway

South

Location: Kalamunda latitude 31°59'S, longitude 116°03'E about 30 km east of Perth
Elevation: 100 m (western boundary of the region) to 405 m, with vineyard sites
located between 150 and 400 m in the southern part of the region, while in the
northern part (Bindoon) vineyards are situated between 100 and 200 m in altitude
Topography and soils: The region forms a strip of undulating country between the
coastal plain and the low rainfall wheat belt of Western Australia. Briefly it can be
described as the northern and central parts of the Darling Scarp. Natural vegetation
is jarrah and red gum hardwood forest. Vineyard soils fall into two main groups. On
hilltops and upper slopes, there are gravels with medium to light loam content,
whereas the valleys consist of mostly loams and alluvial soils. On the lower slopes,
both types are present. All soils overlie white granitic quartz clays at depths from
half a metre to three metres.

The natural fertility of these soils is low and needs to be assisted by artificial
fertiliser. However, where soils have previously been planted to orchards, which were
usually heavily fertilised, such soils are quite fertile. Overall, because of the underlying
clay subsoil, soils tend to retain good moisture levels throughout the growing season,
thus reducing but not eliminating completely the need for irrigation at that time.
Climate: Kalamunda MJT 23.1°C, MAR na, HDD raw 2175, 1772 (cut-off and
adjusted for latitude and daily temperature range but not for vine sites), AR 1069 mm
(Oct–Apr 220 mm), RH 45%, AI na, SH 9.2 (Gladstones). Other climatic detail:
Hainault Vineyard (Bickley) MJanT 22°C, MJulyT 8°C, MAR 14°C (taken for 10
years during the 1980s). The climate of the Perth Hills is typically Mediterranean
(cool wet winters and hot dry summers). Within the southern part of the region,
however, there is significant variation in microclimate. Within deep or elevated
valleys, sub-zero temperatures (frosts) are commonplace in winter and spring and,
because of its elevation, temperatures throughout the year are lower than in the
adjoining hot coastal plain. Nevertheless it must be classified as a hot area. Irrigation
is from dams and bores on individual properties. Hungry birds can also present
problems when grapes ripen before the native gums flower.
Harvest time: chardonnay last week of February, shiraz last week of February, cabernet
sauvignon second week of March.
Principal varieties: cabernet sauvignon, shiraz, chardonnay, pinot noir
Area: 75 ha (not including Bindoon and Chittering)
Principal wine styles: too early to be dogmatic but soft medium to full-bodied reds
made from merlot, shiraz and cabernet sauvignon appear to be most successful.

Avalon Vineyard

1605 Bailey Road, Glen Forrest,
WA 6071
Ph 08 9298 8049

Owners: David and Catherine Brown
Chief winemaker: Lyndon Crockett (contract)
Year of foundation: 1986

Tonnes produced on average each year: 8, of
which half are used for Avalon's own labels
Location: Glen Forrest
Area: 2 ha
Soils: gravel and loam on a south-facing slope
Varieties planted: White—chardonnay,
semillon; Red—cabernet sauvignon

Leading wines: Avalon Vineyard Cabernet Sauvignon, Chardonnay-Semillon
Notes: This is a small family vineyard with cellar door sales by appointment.

Brookside Vineyard **NR**

6 Loaring Road, Bickley, WA 6076
Ph 08 9291 8705, Fax 08 9291 5316

Owners: Lorna and Lionel Penketh
Chief winemaker: Jane Brook Estate (contract)
Year of foundation: 1984
Tonnes crushed on average each year: 3.5 but this is increasing as plantings made in 1995 come into bearing. About half the grapes produced are used for Brookside's own labels.
Location: Bickley
Area: 0.5 ha
Soils: gravelly loam with some clay
Varieties planted: White—chardonnay; Red—cabernet sauvignon
Leading wines: Brookside Chardonnay, Cabernet Sauvignon
Notes: This is a small family-run Perth Hills vineyard with cellar door sales by appointment.

Carosa Vineyard **NR**

310 Houston Street, Mount Helena, WA 6082
Ph/Fax 08 9572 1603, Fax 08 9572 1604

Owners: Jim and Carole Elson
Chief winemaker: Jim Elson
Year of foundation: 1984
Tonnes crushed on average each year: 4
Location: Carosa
Area: 2 ha but not yet fully bearing
Soils: deep sandy loam over clay, sandy loams over soft 'coffee' rock
Varieties planted: White—chardonnay, riesling, semillon; Red—cabernet sauvignon, merlot, pinot noir
Leading wines: Carosa Cabernet Merlot, Chardonnay
Notes: A small vineyard and winery to which

former Seppelt winemaker Jim Elson is devoting his retirement. Cellar door sales: weekends and public holidays 9am–5pm.

Chittering Estate **R6.5**

Chittering Valley Road, Lower Chittering, WA 6084
Ph 08 9274 7100, Fax 08 9274 2154

Owners: LC Development and Jendami Pty Ltd
Chief winemaker: contract
Year of foundation: 1982
Tonnes crushed on average each year: 150
Location: Lower Chittering
Area: 12 ha
Soils: gravelly loams of the Darling Scarp, well drained and quite fertile
Varieties planted: White—chardonnay, sauvignon blanc, semillon; Red—cabernet sauvignon, merlot
Leading wines: Chittering Estate Cabernet-Merlot, Chardonnay, Semillon-Sauvignon Blanc
Notes: This winery is noted for an austere Chardonnay and a more generously flavoured Semillon-Sauvignon Blanc. It changed hands in 1997, but the wine styles will presumably remain the same. Cellar door sales: weekends and public holidays 11am–4.30pm April–December. A light lunch menu is available.

Cosham Wines **NR**

101 Union Road, Carmel, WA 6076
Ph 08 9293 5424, Fax 08 9293 5062

Owners: Rod, Maxinne and Anthony Sclanders
Chief winemaker: Jane Brook (contract)
Year of foundation: 1989
Tonnes crushed on average each year: 6 but will double in the next two vintages as new plantings come into bearing
Location: Carmel
Area: 2 ha
Soils: gravelly loam on quite a steep slope, close-planted vines, running east–west
Varieties planted: White—chardonnay;

Red—cabernet franc, cabernet sauvignon, merlot, petit verdot, pinot noir, shiraz
Leading wine: Cosham Wines Cabernet-Merlot
Notes: This small family vineyard's wines are not often shown, but a bronze award at the Perth Hills Show was a pleasing result for the 1996 Cabernet-Merlot. No cellar door sales.

Darlington Estate **NR**

Lot 39 Nelson Road, Darlington, WA 6070
Ph 08 9299 6268, Fax 08 9299 7017

Owners: Balt, Francesca and Caspar van der Meer
Chief winemaker: Caspar van der Meer
Year of foundation: 1983
Tonnes crushed on average each year: 30
Location: Darlington and Parkerville
Area: 10 ha (Darlington 8 ha and Parkerville 2 ha)
Soils: gravelly loamy soil
Varieties planted: White—chardonnay, chenin blanc, sauvignon blanc, semillon; Red—cabernet franc, cabernet sauvignon, merlot, shiraz
Leading wines: Darlington Estate Cabernet Sauvignon-Merlot, Chardonnay, Sonata Sauvignon Blanc
Notes: Darlington Estate is now one of the veterans of the Perth Hills and has enjoyed great show success over the years. Cellar door sales: Thurs–Sun noon–5pm. There is a restaurant open between the same hours and for dinner Fri–Sat from 7pm.

Deep Dene **NR**

27 Glenisla Road, Bickley, WA 6076
Ph/Fax 08 9293 8339

Owner: Deep Dene Pty Ltd
Chief winemaker: Hainault Vineyard (contract)
Year of foundation: 1994
Tonnes crushed on average each year: 50
Location: Bickley

Area: 4 ha
Soils: gravelly loam on a steep slope
Varieties planted: White—none; Red—pinot noir, shiraz
Leading wines: Deep Dene Brut (a sparkling wine made from pinot noir), Pinot Noir, Shiraz
Notes: After many years at Hainault Vineyard for Perth Hills veteran, Peter Fimmel, Deep Dene is a new challenge for him and his fellow shareholders. Its priority is sparkling wine and it aims to produce 4000 cases per year. Cellar door sales by appointment.

Hainault Vineyard **NR**

255 Walnut Road, Bickley, WA 6076
Ph 08 9328 8011, Fax 08 9328 6895

Owners: Bill and Vicki Mackey
Chief winemaker: Celine Rousseau
Year of foundation: 1978
Tonnes crushed on average each year: 35
Location: Bickley
Area: 7 ha
Soils: vineyard on both sides of a small valley which is gravelly on top of its slope and loamy at the bottom over a white clay base
Varieties planted: White—chardonnay, gewurztraminer, semillon; Red—cabernet franc, cabernet sauvignon, merlot, pinot noir, shiraz
Leading wines: Hainault Semillon, Merlot
Notes: Hainault is an infrequent exhibitor at the Perth Hills Show, winning silver and bronze awards. Cellar door sales: weekends and public holidays 10am–5pm, otherwise by appointment.

Lawnbrook Estate Wines **NR**

Lot 101 Loaring Road, Bickley, WA 6076
Ph/Fax 08 9291 8425

Owners: Wiebe and Judi Tieleman
Chief winemaker: Jim Elson (contract)
Year of foundation: 1984
Tonnes crushed on average each year: 5

Location: Bickley
Area: 1 ha
Soils: heavy valley bottom loam
Varieties planted: White—chardonnay, semillon; Red—merlot, pinot noir, shiraz
Leading wines: Lawnbrook Estate Merlot, Pinot Noir, Semillon, Chardonnay (both unwooded)
Notes: This small vineyard includes a family-run restaurant, The Packing Shed, which is open Friday, Saturday, Sunday and public holidays for lunch and functions. Cellar door sales: 10am–5pm.

Piesse Brook NR

226 Aldersyde Road, Bickley, WA 6076
Ph 08 9293 3309

Owners: Dianne Bray, Ray and Lee Boyanich
Chief winemakers: Dianne Bray, Ray and Lee Boyanich, Mike Davies (consultant)
Year of foundation: 1974
Tonnes crushed on average each year: 28
Location: Bickley
Area: 3.2 ha
Soils: former orchard land with a variety of soils, gravelly clay loam on the slope and rich red loam on the flat

Varieties planted: White—chardonnay; Red—cabernet sauvignon, merlot, shiraz
Leading wine: Piesse Brook Shiraz
Notes: Piesse Brook Shiraz is a regular gold medal winner at local wine shows. Cellar door sales: Sat 1pm–5pm, Sun and public holidays 10am–5pm except February–March when sales are by appointment.

Scarp Valley NR

6 Robertson Road, Gooseberry Hill, WA 6076
Ph 08 9454 5748

Owners: Bob and Doris Duncan
Chief winemaker: Celine Rousseau (contract)
Year of foundation: 1978
Tonnes crushed on average each year: 0.5
Location: Gooseberry Hill
Area: 0.1 ha
Soils: granitic soils, trickle irrigation
Varieties planted: White—none; Red—shiraz
Leading wine: Scarp Valley Hermitage
Notes: This is a minute family-operated vineyard with no cellar door sales.

PART V

NEW SOUTH WALES

NEW SOUTH WALES WINE REGIONS

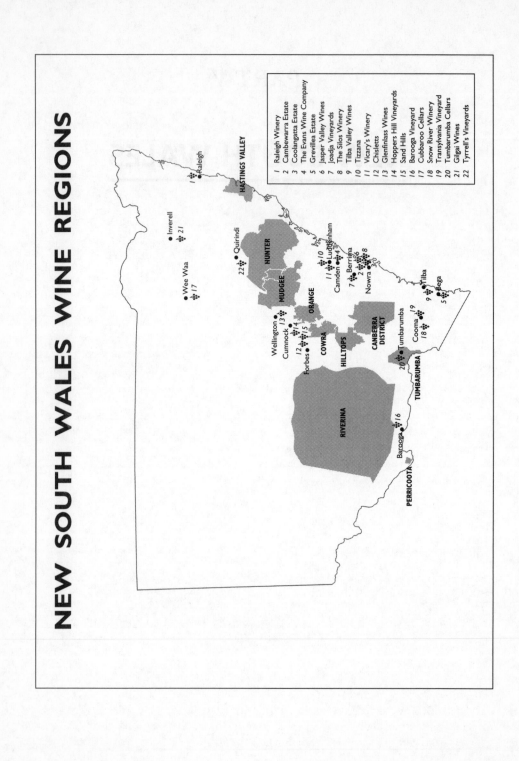

1 Raleigh Winery
2 Cambewarra Estate
3 Coolangatta Estate
4 The Evans Wine Company
5 Grevillea Estate
6 Jasper Valley Wines
7 Joadja Vineyards
8 The Silos Winery
9 Tilba Valley Wines
10 Tizzana
11 Vicary's Winery
12 Chisletts
13 Glenfinlass Wines
14 Hoppers Hill Vineyards
15 Sand Hills
16 Barooga Vineyard
17 Cubbaroo Cellars
18 Snow River Winery
19 Transylvania Vineyard
20 Tumbarumba Cellars
21 Gilgai Wines
22 Tyrrell's Vineyards

HASTINGS VALLEY

Raleigh 1

Inverell
21

Quirindi

HUNTER

Wee Waa
17

MUDGEE

ORANGE

22

Ludgenham
10
Camden 11
Berrima
7 2
Nowra 3
8

Tilba
Bega
9 5

Wellington
Cumnock 13
COWRA
12 14
Forbes 15

HILLTOPS

CANBERRA DISTRICT

Tumbarumba
Cooma 19
18

20

RIVERINA

TUMBARUMBA

Barooga 16

PERRICOOTA

❧ BIG RIVERS ZONE

This is a very large portion of New South Wales, stretching westwards from the Lachlan River at Forbes to the South Australian border near Cockburn, south-west from Forbes to the Murray River near Jingellic, and north-west along the Murray River to its junction with the South Australian border.

It is dry and hot and would be very arid were it not for the four big rivers, the Murray, the Darling, the Murrumbidgee and the Lachlan and their associated irrigation schemes. The zone includes four wine regions, Murray–Darling (see Victoria), Swan Hill (see Victoria), Riverina and Perricoota.

Barooga Vineyard (Vineyard only)

Barooga, NSW 3644

Owner: Southcorp Wines
Chief winemaker: Ian McKenzie
Year of foundation: 1921
Tonnes crushed on average each year: not disclosed but estimated at 3000
Location: Barooga in southern New South Wales across the Murray from Cobram in Victoria
Area: 293.5 ha consisting of two vineyards, Tarn Pirr 240 ha and Windarra 53.5 ha, the latter recently planted and not bearing at time of writing. There are plans for yet more expansion

Soils: variable, deep sand to clay sand, fairly typical alluvial terrace soils
Varieties planted: White—chardonnay, chenin blanc, semillon; Red—cabernet sauvignon, merlot, pinot noir, shiraz
Leading wines: various premium and semi-premium wines mostly in the Seppelt ranges
Notes: Though its cultivar composition obviously changes from time to time to reflect market conditions, Barooga has always been an important vineyard in the Seppelt scheme of things. These days of course it is chardonnay which is the kingpin as a contributor to both still and sparkling wine. Many years ago it was first planted to fortified and distilling varieties. There are no local cellar door sales.

PERRICOOTA REGION

The wine region of Perricoota is centred on Moama in New South Wales, immediately across the Murray River from the larger and better-known town of Echuca in Victoria. Its name dates from 1840 when former convict James Malden, one of the region's first squatters, named his property Perricoota. His rival Henry Hopwood, also a former convict, was one of the first squatters on what was to become the Victorian side of the river, founding Echuca and later planting one of the first vineyards in the area in 1858. By 1860–1870, the larger 'stations' on the New South Wales side of the river began to be subdivided and smaller farm holdings became the norm. Though grazing and wool growing remained a major use for these lands, crops such as wheat were successfully cultivated. To transport such products to market, the riverboat trade began to grow and Echuca at this time became the largest inland port in Australia.

Hopwood's vineyard in due course became the centre of an Echuca wine business, which flourished for a few years until his death in 1868. A further vineyard venture at Kanyapella 30 km east of Echuca also thrived briefly but, for lack of permanent irrigation, it failed because of recurrent droughts. In modern times the vinous history of the general Echuca area began in 1972 when Dr Peter Tisdall planted at Picola to the east of Echuca and purchased an old dairy in Echuca which he subsequently converted into a winery in 1978. The venture, under the supervision of John Ellis as its first winemaker, proceeded well through the 1980s but struck difficulties during the early 1990s and was sold ultimately to Mildara Blass who closed it in 1997.

The modern story of Perricoota began in 1993 and at the time of writing there are 19 growers, but no wineries in the region. Present vineyard area is 240 ha, but this is expected to increase to 480 ha by the year 2000.

Location: Moama latitude 36°8'S, longitude 144°50'E about 200 km north-north-west of Melbourne
Elevation: 94 m
Topography and soils: A typical Australian inland riverine landscape of flat terrain and remnants of river red gum forests. Its soils are generally red clay loams of good texture and fair to good moisture-holding capacity. Phosphorus levels are low, but those of potassium and sulfur high. Soil pH is moderately acidic (5.6), tending alkaline at depth. The soils of the region respond well to humus build-up and moderately deep chisel tillage to overcome hard pans caused by shallow ploughing in the past. Effects detrimental to productivity can be remedied by applications of gypsum, animal manure and nitrogenous fertilisers.
Climate: Echuca (Aerodrome) MJT 22.9°C, MAR 17.15°C, HDD raw 2006, AR 432.2 mm (Oct–Apr 222 mm), RH 50% (9am Jan), 28% (3pm Jan), AI na, SH na. (Moama) MJT 22.5°C, MAR na, HDD na, AR 476 mm (Oct–Apr na), RH na, AI na, SH na. A generally hot area but cooler than Murray-Darling and Swan Hill regions to the north-west. Frosts and equinoctial winds can cause problems during spring.
Harvest time: chardonnay late February early March, shiraz mid-March, cabernet sauvignon late March to early April.
Principal varieties: White—chardonnay; Red—cabernet sauvignon, merlot, shiraz
Total area: (1998) 240 ha predicted to double by the year 2000
Principal wine styles: too early to predict but there will probably be white and red table wines of good quality
Wineries and vineyards: there are as yet no local wineries, although the former Echuca winery of Tisdall (formerly owned by Mildara Blass) was recently sold and one grower, St Anne's, was contemplating construction of a winery before the year 2000.

RIVERINA REGION

The Riverina wine region incorporates the Murrumbidgee Irrigation Area and is the second largest wine-producing region in Australia and by far the largest in New South Wales. It was discovered in 1817 by the explorer John Oxley, who succinctly described it as 'a country, which for bareness and desolation has no equal'. Its early settlement was by squatters and pastoralists who soon had reason to dispute Oxley's pessimistic conclusion, for it produced good quality wool and excellent grain. It became so popular among pastoralists that by 1848 there was scarcely any land left unsettled along the Lachlan and Murrumbidgee Rivers. As an agricultural area, it received a further fillip from the Victorian and New South Wales goldrushes of the next decade, as much of its meat and wheat went to feed hungry diggers to the east and the south. The name Riverina, derived from the the adjective 'riverine', came into use as early as 1857. After the rushes, many thousands of sheep and cattle were grazed on the country adjacent to the rivers and the saltbush of the hinterland and the region became solidly prosperous. Grazing today remains an important industry in the general region.

The Riverina's first small irrigation experiment, doubtless inspired by the successes of the Chaffey brothers ten years before in Victoria and South Australia, occurred in 1899 when Samuel McCaughey established North Yanko Station on the Murrumbidgee near Yanko. His aim was to drought-proof family grazing properties and he established an extensive channel and pumping system for this purpose. He later strongly supported official irrigation schemes, which had their beginning in 1908. By July 1912, the first official scheme was open. The region's first vines were planted at Hanwood in the following year by the legendary 'JJ' McWilliam, who had purchased one of the first blocks (although irrigation had not reached it at the time of planting and he was obliged to have the vines watered by hand). Such was the enthusiasm for irrigated land that, by the outbreak of the First World War in August of the following year, some 622 farms covering 9700 ha were in operation. In 1917 McWilliam's Hanwood winery was erected.

The cessation of the war saw an expansion of the Irrigation Scheme, a rush of soldier settlement and in addition the first of the European immigrant families. There were of course more wineries, beginning with Penfolds in 1919. In 1924, Vittorio de Bortoli arrived and purchased land near Bilbul, erecting his winery in 1928. In 1930, Rossetto followed suit. However, not everything was rosy. Inexperience in irrigation procedures, the Great Depression, collapsing prices and subsequent financial failures during the 1930s caused many difficulties here as in other parts of Australia between growers and winemakers.

In 1933 the NSW Wine Grapes Marketing Board was set up. It continues its work at the present time. In the years prior to the Second World War the wine industry recovered, fortified wine exports increased and there was somewhat of a return to the prosperous days of the 1920s. It was in this period (1939) that Miranda opened its winery. The war, however, though it all but prevented wine export, was no death-blow to the wine industry. There were two armies, ours and the American, in training in Australia. Both had customary soldiers' thirsts and, though the majority preferred beer, wine certainly filled the bill in its absence.

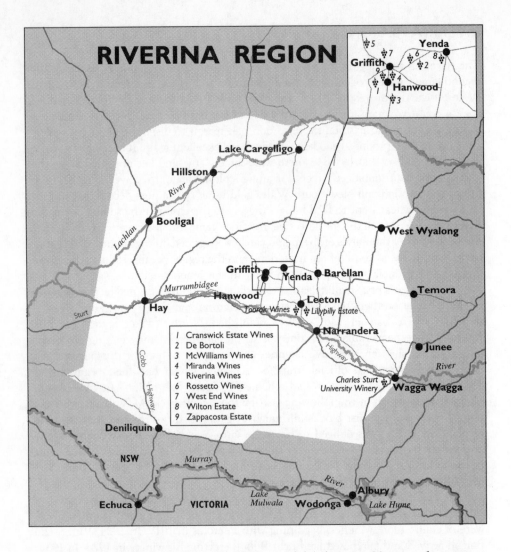

After the end of the Second World War and for the next 30 years, there was a stream of Italian immigration to the region and several of its wine companies date their foundation from this time—West End in 1945, Toorak Wines in 1964, Riverina and Casella both in 1969. In the 1960s the region also saw the development of the wine engineering company A&G Enterprises, which developed the world famous Potter Fermenter. In 1977 there was also a major advance in oenological and viticultural education, when the Riverina College of Advanced Education (today the Charles Sturt University) set up Australia's second wine school at Wagga Wagga. At this time also, there was a significant change in the nature of the varietal composition of the region's vineyards, a swing away from fortified and distilling varieties to premium table wine cultivars, especially white.

Today, as well as wine grapes, the Region is an important producer of grain, rice, vegetables and fruit crops. Its area under vine totals about 10 000 hectares, only 70% of which is currently bearing. Though its chief vineyards are centred on Leeton and Griffith, other irrigated areas throughout the region are experiencing a viticultural surge. There are vineyards at Wagga Wagga to the south-east, Jerilderie and Coleambally to the south and Hay and Hillston to the west. In addition, other vineyards are being established at Deniliquin, Narrandera, Darlington Point and Lake Cargelligo. In 1997, its wine grape production was over 115 000 tonnes. As well as viticulture, emigration has left its cultural imprint on the region. About 25% of the population of the area is either Italian or of Italian descent.

Location: Griffith latitude 34°10'S, longitude 146°2'E. Centred on the city of Griffith, the Riverina wine region is located on the south-western plains of New South Wales, about 650 km south-west of Sydney

Elevation: Winegrowing areas within the region vary from 90 to 230 m above sea-level. Important centres are: Griffith 136 m, Leeton 140 m, Hay 94 m, Hillston 123 m and Wagga 221 m

Topography and soils: The south-western plains of New South Wales are alluvial, resulting from the actions of ancient streams, emanating from the Great Dividing Range and bringing with them remnant soils, clays and gravels from that range. The Riverina region is a generally flat area of land. Its soils are principally red-brown earths with a loamy surface horizon 10–35 cm deep above a reddish-brown clay containing lime at a depth of 70 cm. Most of these red-brown earth deposits have subsequently been elevated above the general plain level and are found around lower hill slopes and river ridges. They are generally free-draining and many contain limestone rubble.

Land to the east, south and west of Griffith is generally flat containing red-brown earths varying from duplex soils in the horticultural areas to heavy cracking clays on the flood plains. To the north-west there are patches of Mallee (high calcium) soils.

Some soils are subject to waterlogging and, where this occurs, so does salinity in areas of impeded drainage, which causes salts to accumulate in the topsoil. Such soils can be reclaimed by redesigning farm drainage in conjunction with land-forming and tile-drainage.

Climate: Griffith (CSIRO) MJT 23.8°C, MAR 15.3°C, HDD raw (Sept–March) 2071, AR 409 mm, RH 55% (9am av Oct–Mar), 34.1% (3pm av Oct–Mar). Cf MJT 23.8°C, MAR 15.3°C, HDD raw 2201, AR 409 mm (Oct–Mar 197 mm), RH 51% (9am Jan), AI 506 mm, SH 9.3 (D&S). Leeton MJT 24.6°C, MAR na, HDD raw (Sept–Mar) 2162, AR 430 mm, RH 54.3% (9am av Oct–Mar), 34.6% (3pm av Oct–Mar). Hay MJT 25.1°C, MAR na, HDD raw (Sept–March) 2302, AR 365 mm, RH 53% (9am av Oct–Mar), 31.4% (3pm av Oct–Mar). Hillston MJT 25.6°C, MAR na, HDD raw (Sept–March) 2404, AR 361 mm, RH 50.7% (9am av Oct–Mar), 31.3% (av Oct–Mar). Wagga MJT 23.7°C, HDD raw (Sept–Mar)1890, AR 570 mm, RH 59.6% (av Oct–Mar), 37.3% (av Oct–Mar).

The region, as characterised by its high mean January temperatures, is very hot. Its annual rainfall is low but is spread evenly throughout the year. With the onset of autumn, temperatures cool and light showers occur, causing mists and an increase in relative humidity, ideal conditions for the spread of botrytis cinerea (noble rot).

Needless to say, irrigation is essential for the survival and growth of vineyards within the region. Good quality water for this purpose is drawn from the Murrumbidgee River at Berembed Weir 40 km east of Narrandera. It is directed through the main irrigation canal to a system of secondary channels, which reticulate low salinity water to about 3000 farms in the region entirely by gravity. A similar irrigation scheme operates in the Coleambally area, while grapegrowers in the Hillston and Hay districts pump directly from the Lachlan and Murrumbidgee Rivers. Traditionally, flood and furrow irrigation was used in the vineyards, though more recently environmental concerns have seen a move to undervine and drip irrigation, especially in recently planted vineyards. About one-fifth of all irrigation is now by drip.

Across the region, viticultural practices are generally uniform. Vines are trained high on a single or double foliage wire. Row width is 3.5 m with vines 2–3 m apart, resulting in a planting density of 1200 to 1500 vines per hectare. The region is phylloxera-free but prone to nematode infestation with the result that most new growers now take the precaution of planting on resistant rootstock. About a third of the region is mechanically pruned and the remainder hand-pruned to two bud spurs, though doubtless the mechanisation will increase as the region grows. The regime of quality water reliably supplied, long hours of sunshine, better clones and selection of virus-free planting material have ensured increasing quantities of adequately ripened grapes, which these days are mechanically harvested, often in the cool of the night, to preserve quality further.

Viticultural problems are few, though unusually high rainfall during the growing season may cause outbreaks of downy mildew. As mentioned, natural climatic conditions often favour the development of noble rot among semillon grapes. This is generally encouraged after the picking of white and red varieties for dry winemaking. *Harvest time*: chardonnay late February, semillon (dry style) late February to early March, merlot and shiraz mid March, cabernet sauvignon late March, semillon (botrytis affected) April

Principal varieties: (in order of quantity produced over 3000 tonnes, 1997 vintage) White—semillon, chardonnay, trebbiano, colombard, muscat gordo blanco; Red—shiraz, cabernet sauvignon

Total area: 10 000 ha (1997)

Principal wine styles: Botrytised Semillons of superb quality, fit to match the best in the world, and fortified wines of very good quality (more rarely these days because of depressed market conditions for such wines). With the advent of responsible, controlled drip irrigation and consequent higher fruit quality, there has also been a tremendous improvement in the last few years in the standards of red winemaking, especially in Cabernet Sauvignon and Merlot. Otherwise the region makes average to good quality varietal table wines likely to be found among cheap to medium priced bottles, mostly of a style suitable and recommended for current drinking.

Casella Wines NR

Farm 1471, Wakely Road, Yenda,
NSW 2681
Ph 02 6968 1346, Fax 02 6968 1196

Owners: Casella family
Chief winemaker: Alan Kennett
Year of foundation: 1969
Tonnes crushed on average each year: 10 000,
of which 300 tonnes are used for Casella's
own labels
Location: Yenda
Area: 220 ha
Soils: red-brown earths
Varieties planted: White—caverdella,
chardonnay, colombard, gewurztraminer,
marsanne, sauvignon blanc, semillon;
Red—cabernet sauvignon, merlot, shiraz
Leading wines: Carramar Estate Chardonnay,
Semillon-Sauvignon Blanc, Sauvignon Blanc,
Shiraz-Cabernet, Shiraz, Cabernet Sauvignon,
Botrytis Semillon
Notes: Casella was formerly a producer of bulk
wines but is now making the transition to
bottled varietals and blends, intended initially
for the markets of the eastern seaboard and
for export. The caverdella variety is unique to
Casella, but perhaps DNA testing will one day
show its true colours. No cellar door sales.

Charles Sturt University Winery 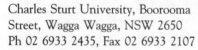 R9

Charles Sturt University, Boorooma
Street, Wagga Wagga, NSW 2650
Ph 02 6933 2435, Fax 02 6933 2107

Owner: Charles Sturt University
Chief winemaker: Kirsten Munro
Year of foundation: 1977
Tonnes crushed on average each year: 1300,
about 200 of which are used for Charles Sturt
University labels
Location: (vineyards) Wagga Wagga
Area: 15 ha (a further 6 ha were planted
during 1998)
Soils: basically loamy clay

Varieties planted: White—chardonnay,
gewurztraminer, muscadelle, muscat gordo
blanco, palomino, pinot gris, riesling, sauvignon
blanc, semillon, trebbiano, viognier; Red—
barbera, cabernet franc, cabernet sauvignon,
dolcetto, merlot, nebbiolo, pinot noir, shiraz,
tinta cao, touriga
Leading wines: Charles Sturt Reserve Cabernet
Sauvignon, Shiraz, Reserve Cowra Chardonnay
Notes: As is to be expected, this vineyard
contains a whole catechism of cultivars and, in
the modern way, Charles Sturt University
Winery has become fully commercial, its sales
expanding from about 3000 cases in 1991 to
17 000 during 1998. Its wines are blends
mainly from New South Wales sources, chiefly
Cowra, Hilltops, the Tumbarumba area and its
own vineyard. Its standards are high, especially
in Chardonnay and, for the future of Australian
wine, they need to be. It has won many
trophies, gold medals and other awards for all
its wines since its inception. Cellar door sales:
7 days 10am–4pm.

Cranswick Estate Wines R6

Walla Avenue, Griffith, NSW 2680
Ph 02 6962 4133, Fax 02 6962 2888

Owner: Cranswick Estate Wines Pty Ltd
Chief winemaker: Andrew Schulz and Ian
Hongell
Year of foundation: 1931
Tonnes crushed on average each year: 1500
from the company's own vineyards (about
10 000 tonnes crushed overall for the various
labels of the group)
Location: Griffith
Area: 145.9 ha
Soils: red-brown earths
Varieties planted: White—chardonnay,
colombard, gewurztraminer, marsanne,
semillon; Red—cabernet sauvignon, merlot,
ruby cabernet, shiraz
Leading wines: Cocoparra Vineyard

Chardonnay, Marsanne, Semillon, Cabernet Sauvignon, Shiraz
Notes: A highly successful, predominantly export-oriented winemaking enterprise has resulted from the executive 'buy-out' several years ago of the Cinzano interests in this property by Graham Cranswick Smith. Wines are light-bodied and chiefly of current drinking quality. Cellar door sales: 7 days 10am–4pm.

De Bortoli **R10**

De Bortoli Road, Bilbul, NSW 2680
Ph 02 6964 9444, Fax 02 6964 9400

Owners: De Bortoli family
Chief winemaker: Darren De Bortoli
Year of foundation: 1928
Tonnes crushed on average each year: 40 000 (includes fruit purchased from growers) all used for the company's own labels
Locations: Bilbul and Nericon
Area: 300 ha
Soils: clay ranging through to sandy loam
Varieties planted: White—chardonnay, colombard, muscat of Alexandria, semillon; Red—cabernet sauvignon, merlot, pinot noir, shiraz
Leading wines: De Bortoli Noble One Botrytis Semillon, Deen de Bortoli Chardonnay, Sauvignon Blanc, Cabernet Sauvignon, Shiraz, Durif, Premium Fortified wines
Notes: As well as a high quality location in the Yarra Valley, De Bortoli now has an international reputation for its aptly named Noble One, made entirely at Bilbul. The rating is given purely in relation to the Noble One, though the Griffith table wines are usually good value current drinking. Cellar door sales: Mon–Sat 9am–5pm, Sun 9am–4pm.

Lillypilly Estate **R8**

Farm 16, Lillypilly Road, Leeton, NSW 2705
Ph 02 6953 4069, Fax 02 6953 4980

Owner: P & A Fiumara and Sons Pty Ltd
Chief winemaker: Robert Fiumara
Year of foundation: 1982
Tonnes crushed on average each year: 150, all of which are used for the company's own labels
Location: Leeton
Area: 17 ha
Soils: red-brown earths
Varieties planted: White—chardonnay, gewurztraminer, muscat of Alexandria, riesling, sauvignon blanc, semillon; Red—cabernet sauvignon, shiraz
Leading wines: Lillypilly Estate Tramillon (a blend of gewurztraminer and semillon), Noble Muscat of Alexandria, Noble Riesling
Notes: This small almost 'boutique' producer by Riverina standards, has built up an excellent reputation for quality over the years, first with its Tramillon blend and more recently with a range of 'noble' (botrytised) whites. Cellar door sales: Mon–Sat 10am–5.30pm, Sun by appointment.

McWilliam's Wines **R10**

(i) Winery Road, Hanwood, NSW 2680
Ph 02 6963 0001, Fax 02 6963 0002

Owner: McWilliam's Wines Pty Ltd
Chief winemaker: Jim Brayne
Year of foundation: 1912
Tonnes crushed on average each year: 12 000, including fruit purchased from growers, but will increase substantially in the next two years
Location: Hanwood
Area: 300 ha expanding to 500 ha by 2000
Soils: Red-brown earths
Varieties planted: White—chardonnay, gewurztraminer, riesling, sauvignon blanc, semillon; Red—cabernet sauvignon, merlot, pinot noir, shiraz
Leading wines: McWilliam's Hanwood range, JJ McWilliam range, Inheritance range, fortifieds
Notes: This was the first winery in the region

erected in 1917 and is now the producer of many millions of litres of Riverina wine and in addition the wines of Barwang in the Hilltops region. The wine ranges (Hanwood and Inheritance) produced from local grapes are good standard whites and reds, usually quite suitable for current drinking. Hanwood's superior products are its botrytised Semillons and old Fortifieds, especially Muscat and Sherries. Cellar door sales from the distinctive Big Barrel: Mon–Sat 9am–5.30pm, Sun 10am–4pm.

(ii) Doug McWilliam Road, Yenda, NSW 2681 (winery only)
Ph 02 6968 1001, Fax 02 6968 1312

Owner: McWilliam's Wines Pty Ltd
Chief winemakers: Doug McWilliam and Jim Brayne
Year of foundation: 1922
Tonnes crushed on average each year: 3000
Leading wines: see McWilliam's Hanwood
Notes: The Yenda winery is a production facility only. There are no cellar door sales.

Mildara Blass (vineyard only) **NR**
Whitton, NSW 2680

Owner: Mildara Blass Ltd
Year of foundation: 1995
Tonnes produced on average each year: 1800
Location: Whitton
Area: 94 ha
Soils: red-brown earths
Varieties planted: White—chardonnay, chenin blanc, colombard, semillon; Red—pinot noir, ruby cabernet, shiraz
Leading wines: all the white grapes from this vineyard are sold within the industry, the reds only being used for Mildara Blass' more price-conscious ranges of wines
Notes: This is not a vineyard presently shining brightly in the Mildara firmament. There are no local cellar door sales.

Miranda Wines (winery only) **R9**
57 Jondaryan Avenue, Griffith, NSW 2680
Ph 02 6962 4033, Fax 02 6962 6944

Owner: Miranda Wines Pty Ltd
Chief winemaker: Doug Wilson
Year of foundation: 1939
Tonnes crushed on average each year: 13 000, all sourced from local growers
Location: Griffith
Leading wines: Miranda Golden Botrytis, Chardonnay, Mirrool Creek range
Notes: In common with other Riverina winemakers, Miranda has expanded recently into other regions and it too produces marvellous botrytised Semillons, winning trophies for the best sweet wine at the Adelaide Wine Show and Rutherglen Show in 1997. Its Mirrool Creek Chardonnay is also a wine of excellent quality in its price bracket. Cellar door sales: 7 days 9am–5pm.

Riverina Wines **R7.5**
Farm 1305 Hillston Road, Thargobang via Griffith, NSW 2680
Ph 02 6962 4122, Fax 02 6962 4628

Owner: Riverina Wines Pty Ltd
Chief winemaker: Sam Trimboli
Year of foundation: 1969
Tonnes crushed on average each year: 25 000, about 3000 of which are used for Riverina Wines' own labels
Locations: Thargobang and Yenda
Area: 1002.8 ha
Soils: red-brown earths
Varieties planted: (Ballingal 1) White—none; Red—barbera (9 ha), merlot (19.9 ha), ruby cabernet (7.9 ha), shiraz (8.6 ha), total 46.4 ha all fully bearing. (Ballingal 2 and 3) White—chardonnay (17.1 ha), gewurztraminer (4.1 ha), sauvignon blanc (11.3 ha), semillon (29.2 ha); Red—pinot noir (14.5 ha), total 76.2 ha all fully bearing. (Ballingal 4) White—none; Red—

cabernet sauvignon (68.4 ha) not yet fully bearing. (Ballingal 5) White—chardonnay (61.5 ha), chenin blanc (3.6 ha), verdelho (38.4 ha); Red—none, total 103.5 ha not yet fully bearing. (Ballingal 6) White—chardonnay (76.3 ha), semillon (23.5 ha); Red—none, total 99.8 ha not yet fully bearing. (Stephen Vale [Yenda]) White—chardonnay (23.8 ha), gewurztraminer (23.5 ha), marsanne (12.1 ha), semillon (38.9 ha), verdelho (71.5 ha); Red—cabernet sauvignon (95.3 ha), merlot (190.1 ha), pinot noir (22.3 ha), ruby cabernet (47.7 ha), shiraz (83.3 ha), total 608.5 ha not yet fully bearing

Leading wines: Warburn Estate range, Ballingal Estate range

Notes: These two very large, modern vineyards employ the ultimate in high-tech equipment to ensure maximum quality production while balancing this with environmental considerations. Drip irrigation, soil moisture monitoring, recycling of all drainage water and the use of soft, non-drifting pesticides are all important steps in this direction. Riverina Wines produces and sells many millions of litres of wine to the industry but its own bottled wines are tremendously successful among the cheaper ranges, the Ballingal Chardonnays and Merlots especially, as its show results prove. Harvest Trophy winner for Cabernet Sauvignon 1996 at National Wine Show 1997. Cellar door sales: 7 days 9am–5.30pm.

Rossetto Wines R7

Farm 576 Rossetto Road, Beelbangera, NSW 2680
Ph 02 6963 5214, Fax 02 6963 5542

Owner: Mrs Bianca Rossetto
Chief winemaker: Eddy Rossi
Year of foundation: 1930
Tonnes crushed on average each year: 10 000, about half of which is used for Rossetto's own labels
Location: Beelbangera

Area: 11 ha
Soils: red-brown earths
Varieties planted: White—chardonnay, semillon; Red—muscat hamburg, pinot noir, shiraz
Leading wines: Rossetto Mitchell Brooke Limited Release range
Notes: Like other Riverina winemakers, Rossetto is looking to some extent outside the Riverina in its search for finer styles of table wine. However, it is not buying vineyards for this purpose, only fruit. What we have seen is the introduction of the Mitchell Brooke Limited Release range with fruit from Langhorne Creek and Eden Valley and in its Varietal range a South Australian Sauvignon Blanc and also a Watervale Riesling. Yet its wines made from Riverina fruit are of a very good standard and regularly win show awards, especially the fortifieds, the Botrytised Semillons and quite often its Family Reserve Cabernet Merlot. Cellar door sales: Mon–Sat 8.30am–5.30pm.

Toorak Wines NR

Toorak Road, Leeton, NSW 2705
Ph 02 6953 2333, Fax 02 6953 4454

Owners: Frank and Vincent Bruno and family
Chief winemaker: Robert Bruno
Year of foundation: 1965
Tonnes crushed on average each year: 4500
Location: Leeton
Area: 60 ha
Soils: grey and red loam
Varieties planted: White—chardonnay, colombard, semillon; Red—cabernet sauvignon, shiraz
Leading wines: Toorak Wines Shiraz, Cabernet Sauvignon, Semillon-Chardonnay
Notes: Years ago this was a traditional Riverina producer of bulk wines, but it is now placing greater emphasis on table wines. Cellar door sales Mon–Sat 9am–5pm.

West End Wines R7.5

Braynes Road, Griffith, NSW 2680
Ph 02 6964 1506, Fax 02 6962 1673

Owner: William Calabria
Chief winemakers: William Calabria and
James Ceccato
Year of foundation: 1945
Tonnes crushed on average each year: 1500
Location: Griffith
Area: 51 ha
Soils: red-brown earths
Varieties planted: White—chardonnay,
semillon; Red—cabernet sauvignon, merlot,
shiraz
Leading wines: West End 3 Bridges Cabernet
Sauvignon
Notes: This winery and vineyard is showing
remarkable improvement over recent years
especially in its reds, as its 1996 3 Bridges
Cabernet Sauvignon has proved by winning a
top gold, two other golds, two silvers and a
Highly Commended award at various wine
shows since 1996. Its Merlot is also very good.
Cellar door sales: Mon–Fri 9–5, Sat 9am–3pm,
closed Sunday.

Wickham Hill (winery only) NR

22 Jensen Road, Griffith, NSW 2680
Ph 02 6962 2605, Fax 02 6962 7121

Owner: Orlando Wyndham
Chief winemaker: Phil Laffer
Year of foundation: 1972
Tonnes crushed on average each year: 8500,
all supplied by growers
Leading wines: part of Jacobs Creek range
(semillon and shiraz)
Notes: Wickham Hill's role has been changed.
What used to be the home of the Coolibah
range of cask wines now produces superior
semillon and shiraz wines for blending into the
Jacobs Creek range. Such wines occasionally
even find their way in small quantities into
Orlando wines of loftier standard than Jacobs
Creek. There are no cellar door sales.

Wilton Estate (winery only) R7

Whitton Stock Route, Yenda,
NSW 2681
Ph 02 6968 1303, Fax 02 6968 1328

Owner: R Graham Holdings Pty Ltd
Chief winemaker: Ralph Graham
Year of foundation: 1976 (as St Peters Estate)
Tonnes crushed on average each year: 3000, of
which 1000 are used for Wilton Estate labels
Location: no vineyards are owned, all fruit
being purchased from growers
Leading wines: Wilton Estate Cabernet-Merlot,
Cabernet Sauvignon, Chardonnay, Semillon,
Botrytised Semillon
Notes: A Riverina winery with an excellent
reputation for its table wines, especially its
Botrytised Semillon, and also for its
Chardonnay. Cellar door sales: Mon–Fri
9am–5pm, closed weekends.

Zappacosta Estate NR

Farm 161 Hanwood Road, Hanwood,
NSW 2680
Ph/Fax 02 6963 0278

Owners: Dino and Judy Zappacosta
Chief winemaker: Dino Zappacosta,
Brian Edwards (consultant)
Year of foundation: 1996
Tonnes crushed on average each year: 500,
about 100 of which are used for Zappacosta
labels
Location: Hanwood
Area: 20 ha
Soils: red-brown earths
Varieties planted: White—gewurztraminer,
riesling, semillon, trebbiano; Red—shiraz
Leading wines: Zappacosta Bin 18 Shiraz
Notes: Dino Zappacosta purchased the former
Franco's Winery recently. As a grower in the
region, he knows it well and intends to raise
the winery crush to 5000 tonnes in the near
future. Cellar door sales: 7 days 8am–5pm.

❧ Semillon

Semillon, so the marketers say, has become extremely hard to sell. It is supposedly 'boring' and without distinctive personality. To counter this perception of ennui, semillon is blended with chardonnay or sauvignon blanc and a plethora of ordinary 'commercial' wines result, or perhaps it even appears a month after vintage as a 'Nouveau'. However, it is a comment that should be taken seriously, since the measure of a grape-type's popularity among winemakers is directly proportional to its popularity among the wine-buying public and a supposed decline in popularity could be extremely serious for many parts of winegrowing Australia. Yet it may only be a measure of the times, when all varietal wines have to be instantly appealing to all sorts of palates. So perhaps the marketers should be ignored and the wine-buying public left to learn the virtue of patience and make its own judgment according to its own natural good sense.

In some respects, semillon is more versatile than chardonnay. It also can be made dry, without the use of oak or with the use of oak. It can be barrel-fermented, it can be malolactically fermented, it can be barrel-matured or simply left for a while in stainless steel and then bottled early. Importantly, though, when affected by botrytis cinerea (noble rot) it can be made sweet, producing a wine as luscious and complex as any made from riesling with much more appeal than, say, botrytised Chardonnay. Semillon does have personality and when young it can be as vibrant and alive as Sauvignon Blanc and often indistinguishable from it in herbaceousness. It is all a question of region and the imprint that any particular region, its growing conditions and style of viticulture make on semillon.

In moderately warm regions, such as Margaret River, semillon ripens mid-season and can assume grassy, tangy, sauvignon-like characters, as a natural function of its growing conditions. Its vines produce lots of foliage, creating shaded green berries and, in turn, methoxypyrazines (grassy, vegetative, capsicum-like characters) in the fruit. Here makers such as Moss Wood have tamed the naturally grassy characters of the region by the use of Scott-Henry trellising (which opens out the canopy thus reducing its density), by trimming and then leaf-plucking semillon as necessary and ripening the fruit to 13° Be. Such wine is then matured in stainless steel though 'batonage' (oak slats) are sometimes used during fermentation. This way, Keith Mugford of Moss Wood tries to mitigate the 'green' characters of Semillon, though he concedes that there is always a 'modicum' in Margaret River Semillon. The green vegetative style of semillon still appears occasionally on its own, though most makers in that region prefer to blend it with sauvignon blanc.

In warmer regions such as the Hunter Valley, it ripens early mid-season, has lemony, vanillan-lanolin (not derived from American oak) aromas and tends to neutrality (but not boredom) in flavour. It is here that the winemaker may seek to add further complexity to the wine by malolactic fermentation and/or barrel-ferment and maturity in American oak, unless—and here again the Hunter Valley region is an example—Semillon has a reputation for maturing well in bottle.

With age, the young tangy styles of Semillon assume cooked vegetative characters which are extremely unpleasant after about four years and so should be drunk while young and fresh. American oaked Semillons at any age usually reveal strong vanillan aromas and flavours that can be initially attractive unless the wood is overdone on palate. They do not always mature with great harmony, the oak often becoming dominant and the ripe semillon fruit becoming 'fat'. The non-oaked styles of the Hunter usually grow in lemon-toast complexity in bottle, often for a decade or more, and it is on this very distinctive character that the reputation of the Hunter as a Semillon producer is based.

Why do Hunter Semillons mature so distinctively? Possibly it is a function of the comparative lack of vigour and lower yield which semillon has on the rather poor sandy creek flats where it is mostly grown (its canopies are comparatively thin compared with Margaret River) and its growing climate, though quite hot, never seems as sunny or as dry as say Margaret River in summer. There is often a high humidity and even a slight cloud cover, which often halts semillon-ripening at about 11° Be and frequently the ripening phase thereafter does not seem to restart. Such fruit is fermented slightly oxidatively with low sulfurs, the result being a wine with lemony-strawy aromas and a neutral palate with minimal grassy characters, even sometimes with a minute amount of residual sugar, upon which the wine may 'live' during an extended bottle maturation. History has amply demonstrated that such styles may improve in bottle for up to 15 years and in some cases (as witness the Karl Stockhausen's Lindemans Semillon styles of 1970) even longer. Perhaps today, the wine-drinking public is just not patient enough.

CENTRAL RANGES ZONE

Containing some of the higher and therefore cooler vineyard sites in New South Wales, this is an area of great interest, extending as it does from Lithgow just to the west of the Blue Mountains to Forbes on the Lachlan River. The zone encompasses the wine regions of Mudgee, Orange and Cowra.

Chisletts NR

Wandary Lane, Forbes, NSW 2871
Ph 02 6852 3983

Owners: Chislett family
Chief winemakers: Frank and Les Chislett
Year of foundation: 1886
Tonnes crushed on average each year: 20
Location: Forbes
Area: 5.6 ha
Soils: grey river loam and sand
Varieties planted: White—doradillo, muscat gordo blanco, palomino, riesling, semillon, trebbiano; Red—cabernet sauvignon, pinot noir, red frontignac, shiraz
Leading wines: Fortifieds
Notes: This traditional winery specialises in fortifieds which are well suited to this very warm area of New South Wales. Cellar door sales: Mon–Sat 9am–5.30pm, Sun 1pm–5pm.

Glenfinlass Wines NR

Elysian Farm, Parkes Road, Wellington, NSW 2820 (about 8km south of the town)
Ph 02 6845 2221, 02 6845 2011, Fax 02 6845 3329

Owners: Brian and Myrea Holmes
Chief winemaker: Brian Holmes
Year of foundation: 1968
Tonnes crushed on average each year: 8, all used for Glenfinlass labels
Location: Wellington
Area: 2.5 ha

Soils: chiefly old alluvial soils of limestone origins
Varieties planted: White—sauvignon blanc; Red—cabernet sauvignon, shiraz
Leading wines: Glenfinlass Shiraz, Cabernet Sauvignon, Hill Vineyard (a red blend of Shiraz and Cabernet)
Notes: This is an old established vineyard with cellar door sales: Sat 9am–5pm or by appointment.

Hoppers Hill Vineyards NR

Googodery Road, Cumnock, NSW 2867
Ph 02 6367 7270

Owners: Bob and Pat Gilmour
Chief winemaker: Bob Gilmour
Year of foundation: 1978
Tonnes crushed on average each year: 7
Location: Cumnock
Area: 2.6 ha
Soils: The vineyard has heavy clay soils and is situated on a westerly slope with good air drainage. It is not irrigated
Varieties planted: White—sauvignon blanc; Red—cabernet franc, merlot
Leading wines: Hoppers Hill Cabernet Franc-Merlot
Notes: Bob Gilmour is a Pomerol and St Emilion enthusiast, hence the choice of red grape varieties for his vineyard. In addition his wines are made without added sulphur. Cellar door sales by appointment only.

Sand Hills

Sand Hills Road, Forbes, NSW 2871
(about 6 km east of Forbes)
Ph 02 6852 1437, Fax 02 6852 4401

Owner: John Saleh
Chief winemaker: Jill Lindsay, Woodonga Hill
(contract)
Year of foundation: 1920
Tonnes crushed on average each year: 10
Location: Forbes
Area: 3.6 ha
Soils: sand to sandy clay

Varieties planted: White—chardonnay,
colombard, semillon; Red—cabernet sauvignon,
mataro, merlot, pinot noir, shiraz
Leading wines: Sand Hills Chardonnay, Classic
Dry White (a Colombard-Semillon blend),
Shiraz Cabernet, Shiraz
Notes: Once Sand Hills had a definite emphasis
on fortifieds. These days, in accord with
modern market conditions, the emphasis is
very definitely on table wines which regularly
win bronze awards. Cellar door sales:
Mon–Sat 9am–5pm, Sun 12 noon–5pm.

COWRA REGION

Within a few years of the crossing of the Blue Mountains in 1813, large tracts of central New South Wales had been explored. In 1815 George Evans discovered the Lachlan River near its junction with the Belubela. Three years later, John Oxley and Allan Cunningham also came that way. In the late 1820s, they were followed by the inevitable squatters searching for grazing land and so, like much of the rest of the Central Ranges zone of New South Wales, the early history of Cowra is pastoral. The town which had its beginnings in the 1840s derives its name from the Aboriginal word *coura* meaning 'rocks', a reference to a ford across the Lachlan close to the town. Later in the nineteenth century, dairying became common and cereal crops such as wheat and barley were also planted. Indeed one of the earliest buildings in the town is the old Mill dating from 1861, now used as a cellar door outlet and restaurant by Windowrie. Orchards and undoubtedly vineyards were also a feature of the district.

In the New South Wales agricultural census of 1879, Cowra is shown as producing 3000 gallons (13 500 litres) of wine and, in 1893 in the *Cowra Free Press*, reference is made to a vineyard planted on James Ousby's farm 'with four kinds of wine grapes, Red Hermitage and Tokay being the principal varieties', and the wine made from these varieties being 'pronounced excellent'.

The modern history of the Cowra vine begins in 1972 when, in a bid for agricultural diversification, Allan Mitchell planted a small experimental vineyard on his property on the banks of the Lachlan, downstream of Cowra. In the same year a larger project was planned by an American company on slopes adjacent to the river south of the town. This was purchased by Sydney-based businessman Tony Gray and planting commenced in 1973. By 1975, a total of 36 ha, mostly of the 'new' chardonnay variety, had been planted. The region first came to prominence in winemaking terms in the late 1970s when eminent winemaker and now Australia's leading vigneron, Brian Croser, made his first Petaluma Chardonnays (1977–79) from

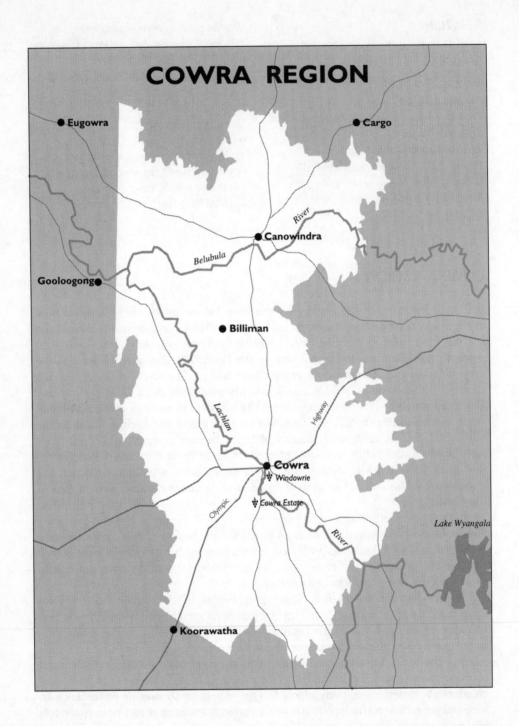

COWRA REGION

Eugowra

Cargo

River

Canowindra

Belubula

Gooloogong

Billiman

Lachlan

Highway

Cowra
Windowrie

Cowra Estate

Olympic

River

Lake Wyangala

Koorawatha

Cowra fruit while he was senior lecturer-winemaker at the Charles Sturt University at Wagga. In 1981 the initial Tony Gray vineyard was sold to Rothbury Estate, which began making what proved to be a very successful series of Cowra Chardonnays.

Later in the 1980s, a second vigorous phase of vine-planting ensued when, in 1987, near the village of Billimari north-west of the town, the Windowrie vineyard was commenced. The following year, the 'Cooraminta' vineyard of 220 ha was developed by Orlando-Wyndham, 5 km upstream of Cowra. Today, these two areas to the south and the north-west of the town are the centres of vinegrowing in the region, which supports over 900 ha of wine grapes. Despite this, there are no fully-equipped wineries in the region, although there is one crushing plant.

Location: Cowra latitude 33°50'S, longitude 148°41'E, about 230 km due west of Sydney

Elevation: 300 m. The region has an upper contour boundary of 400 m altitude, which conforms to the catchment area of the upper Lachlan. Most vineyards in the region are presently planted on undulating terrain between 250 and 350 metres in altitude.

Topography and soils: The valley of the Lachlan is filled with a deep alluvium varying in depth from 40 m near Cowra to 70 m just outside the Wine Region near Gooloogong. This consists of interbedded clays, sands, silts and gravels. The Belubela Valley similarly has alluvium but only as deep as 24 m. Within the Lachlan Valley, river terraces occur along the river on both banks. The Valley's western edge is defined by a sandstone ridge, while its eastern side is bounded by a series of gently undulating to rolling hills of Cowra granodiorite and, to the near north of Billimari, Canowindra porphyry. To the north-east of Canowindra, on the regional boundary, there are outcrops of limestone, the landscape there consisting of undulating hills with occasional steep slopes.

Generally the soils of the Cowra vineyards consist of siliceous sands on the crests of slopes, red podsols on the mid slopes and red-brown earths on the lower slopes. The red podsols are moderately permeable with moderate fertility and neutral pH. The red-brown earths are stable, well-drained soils with moderate permeability but low fertility.

Around Canowindra, there are non-calcic brown soils on the upper slopes with yellow and brown solodics in natural drainage lines. These soils are moderately permeable with limited drainage in the subsoil and are of low fertility.

From the south of the region (north of Koorawatha) through Morongla and north to Billimari, there is gently undulating country. The soils here are non-calcic brown soils on the hill crests with yellow podsols and yellow solodics on the middle and lower slopes. Such soils have moderate permeability, low fertility and are moderately erodible with poor drainage in the yellow solodics.

On the flood plains of the Lachlan and Belubela Rivers, the river terraces are comprised of non-calcic brown soils and red-brown earths, while the river flats consist of alluvial loams. Both soils are moderately to highly permeable and of low erodibility. The contrast is in fertility, the terrace soils having low to moderate fertility, the alluvial loams being highly fertile.

Climate: MJT 24.4°C, MAR na, HDD raw 2152, 1672 (cut-off and adjusted for latitude, daily temperature range and vine sites), AR 612 mm (Oct–Apr 361 mm), RH 34% (3pm Jan), AI na, SH 9.5 (Gladstones). (Other readings—local) MTWM (Jan) 23.25°C, MAR 15.65, HDD raw 2212, AR 615 mm (Oct–Apr 363 mm), RH 38% (Oct–Apr average 3pm), AI 248 mm, SH 9.5. Cowra is a hot region, its MJT and raw HDD being comparable with those of Riverina to the west. On this basis, the region would seem to be well suited to full-bodied table wines and indeed fortified styles should these ever recover market favour. Its Chardonnay can only be described as full-bodied, generous in flavour and suitable for early consumption (6 months to 2 years from vintage) in normal years. Its table wine reds chiefly made from cabernet sauvignon and merlot have similar characteristics to its Chardonnay. Nearly 60% of its annual rainfall falls during the growing season and the usual spray precautions against mildews should be taken. It is also prone to frosts during September, when early and mid-season varieties are at budburst. As in the Orange region, great care should be taken with site selection to ensure free air drainage.

All vineyards within the region are irrigated. The entire region is within the Lachlan Catchment Area and both the Lachlan and Belubela Rivers are regulated streams within this catchment area. Rights to irrigate from these are held by owners of adjoining lands on either 'low' or 'high' security allocations. The former are reduced by some percentage in some seasons, perhaps even down to nothing if the storage dams are low in spring, while the latter are reduced only to 70% in the driest of circumstances. Obviously for vinegrowing purposes high security allocations are preferred to low.

The waters of the Lachlan and its tributary, the Abercrombie, are stored by the Wyangala Dam which has a capacity of 1.25 million megalitres, about half of which is available to irrigators in times of full allocation, while the waters of the Belubela are held by the Carcoar Dam, much smaller in capacity at 23 000 megalitres for irrigation purposes. However, many irrigators here also have access to underground aquifers via bores.

At the present time the total allocation available for irrigators on both rivers is limited by the Murray-Darling system cap, set at 1993–94 usage levels on the Lachlan itself. There is an embargo on the issue of new licences though trade in existing licences is permitted within the Lachlan system, allowing adequate allocation of water to meet viticultural needs.

The quality of water from both rivers and from underground bores extracted within a few kilometres of these rivers is generally excellent.

Harvest time: chardonnay first week of March, cabernet sauvignon first week of April
Principal varieties: White—chardonnay; Red—no varieties yet appear to be outstanding, though merlot shows promise
Total area: 900 ha
Principal Wine Styles: Chardonnay

Cowra Estate (vineyard only) R6.5

Boorowa Road, Cowra, NSW 2794
Ph/Fax 02 6342 1136

Owner: John Geber
Chief winemaker: Simon Gilbert (contract)
Year of foundation: 1973
Tonnes produced on average each year: 1200
Location: Cowra
Area: 73 ha
Soils: red podsolic soils
Varieties planted: White—chardonnay,
gewurztraminer, riesling, sauvignon blanc;
Red—cabernet franc, cabernet sauvignon,
merlot, pinot noir
Leading wines: Cowra Estate Chardonnay,
Merlot, Cabernets
Notes: This is Cowra's oldest established
vineyard and is responsible conjointly with
Rothbury Estate for the Chardonnay reputation
of the region. Cellar door sales: Tues–Sun
10am–4pm. The Quarry Cellars restaurant is
open for lunch 12–2pm Tues–Sun and for
dinner Thurs–Sat from 7pm.

Richmond Grove (vineyard only) R7

Reids Flat Road, Cowra, NSW 2794

Owner: Simeon Wines Ltd
Chief winemaker: Phil Laffer
Year of foundation: 1989
Tonnes crushed on average each year: 4000
Location: Cowra
Area: 315 ha
Soils: alluvial sandy loams on river flats, red
podsolics on slopes
Varieties planted: White—chardonnay,
sauvignon blanc, semillon, verdelho; Red—
cabernet franc, cabernet sauvignon, malbec,
merlot, pinot noir, ruby cabernet, shiraz
Leading wines: part of Wyndham Estate Bin 555
Shiraz, part of Bin 444 Cabernet Sauvignon,
Richmond Grove Cowra Chardonnay, Verdelho,
part of Jacobs Creek reds
Notes: This is the former Orlando Wyndham

vineyard, sold to Simeon Wines in 1994 but
still managed by Orlando Wyndham. All the
fruit is purchased by Orlando Wyndham and
conitinues to form an important part of the
wines mentioned. No local cellar door sales.

Rothbury Estate (vineyard only) R7

Boorowa Road, Cowra, NSW 2794

Owner: Mildara Blass
Chief winemaker: Adam Eggins
Year of foundation: (Cowra Vineyard) 1973
Tonnes crushed on average each year: 400
Location: Cowra
Area: 47 ha
Soils: sandy loams over clay
Varieties planted: White—chardonnay,
sauvignon blanc; Red—none
Leading wines: Rothbury Estate Cowra
Chardonnay
Notes: This is the home of a ready drinking,
generously flavoured Chardonnay which placed
Cowra firmly on the wine map. No local cellar
door sales.

Windowrie NR

Windowrie Road, Canowindra,
NSW 2804
Ph 02 6344 3264, Fax 02 6344 3227

Owners: O'Dea family
Chief winemakers: Charles Sturt University,
Brokenwood, Arrowfield (all contract)
Year of foundation: 1987
Tonnes produced on average each year: 600
and rising (of which about 25 are crushed for
Windowrie's own labels)
Location: Canowindra
Area: 48 ha
Soils: sedimentary, a red loam (about 0.75 m
deep) overlying a red clay loam over red clay
Varieties planted: White—chardonnay,
sauvignon blanc, semillon; Red—cabernet
franc, cabernet sauvignon, merlot, pinot noir,
shiraz

Leading wines: Windowrie Chardonnay, Cabernet

Notes: Windowrie Vineyard consists of three vineyards, all managed by Windowrie Viticultural Services. These are Windowrie Estate (as above), Kelvin Grove and Troopers, all freehold title totalling in area about 200 ha. Windowrie itself owns 48 ha and the balance, in blocks ranging fron 3.2 ha to 8.4 ha, is owned by various investors and groups. Cellar door sales available from the Mill Wine and Function Centre, Vaux Street, Cowra.

MUDGEE REGION

The region's first settlers, George and Henry Cox, reached Mudgee in February 1822. It was obvious from the first that its inhabitants intended that their settlement should have a decent start in life, as the early town planner, Robert Hoddle, was engaged to design the layout of the 'town' in 1823. (He used a grid pattern that he was obviously fond of, for he used a similar plan for Melbourne 14 years later.) Official municipal status was slower in arrival, the 'village' being officially gazetted in 1838 and not until 1860 did it officially become a 'town'. Until that time it had been the centre of a predominantly pastoral neighbourhood (though Adam Roth, an early German settler, had planted vines on his property, Craigmoor, in the 1850s). A great spurt of growth occurred with the discovery of gold at nearby Gulgong and all around Mudgee in the 1860s and 1870s, when the area's population soared to over 20 000. After this bout of gold fever, it was its flat fertile pastures, not gold, that continued to be Mudgee's mainstay. Perhaps Mudgee's outstanding citizen, though he was scarcely known at the time he lived there, was the poet Henry Lawson. Time makes hearts and memories grow fonder and Lawson is of blessed memory in modern Mudgee.

In the 1840s New South Wales was extremely short of skilled agricultural labour. Sir William Macarthur (son of the notorious John), one of Australia's most famous vignerons of the middle of the nineteenth century, convinced the New South Wales and British governments that this shortage could be remedied by importing indentured agricultural labourers from Europe. A number of German labourers applied and were allotted to various settlers. Once their period of service had expired they were free either to stay or return to Germany. Most stayed. Adam Roth was such a man who, in the 1850s, after service with Macarthur, found his way to Mudgee and began wine production in 1858. Roth and his large family remained in the area (indeed by 1880 there were 13 wineries, six of which were operated by Roth and his sons) and other German emigrants were attracted to it with the result that, for the next 30 years, the Mudgee area became the largest German settlement in Australia outside the Barossa Valley. However, what was a thriving Mudgee wine industry by 1890 was seriously affected by the bank crashes in the eastern Australian colonies two to three years later. Mudgee's wineries never quite recovered and by the mid-1960s there were only two wineries, Jack Roth at Craigmoor and Alf Kurtz.

The red wine boom and the town's relatively short distance from Sydney gave added impetus to the minute Mudgee wine industry at this time. New capital flowed to the region from wine-interested professionals from Sydney. New vineyards were planted and new wineries erected in this 'nest in the hills'. Important at that time

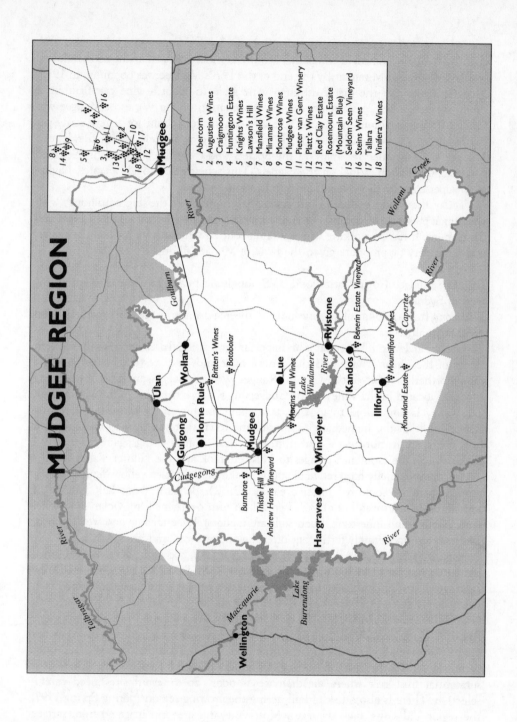

MUDGEE REGION

1	Abercorn
2	Augustine Wines
3	Craigmoor
4	Huntington Estate
5	Knights Wines
6	Lawson's Hill
7	Mansfield Wines
8	Miramar Wines
9	Montrose Wines
10	Mudgee Wines
11	Pieter van Gent Winery
12	Platt's Wines
13	Red Clay Estate
14	Rosemount Estate (Mountain Blue)
15	Seldom Seen Vineyard
16	Steins Wines
17	Tallara
18	Vinifera Wines

Mudgee

Britten's Wines
Botobolar

Ulan
Wollar
Home Rule
Guigong
Mudgee
Cudgegong
Bumbrae
Thistle Hill
Andrew Harris Vineyard

Lue
Martins Hill Wines
Lake Windamere
River
Windeyer
Hargraves

Rylstone
Kandos
Benerin Estate Vineyard
Illford
Mountifford Wines
Knowland Estate

Goulburn River
Wollemi Creek
Capertee River

Wellington
Maccquarie
Lake Burrendong
River

Talbragar River

and of continuing importance are the Roberts' family winery at Huntington and, slightly later, the Transfield company's Montrose winery. Another who soon followed was Ian MacRae at Miramar. By the end of the 1970s Mudgee was booming. In 1978, Mudgee was one of the first Australian wine areas to adopt a wine certification of origin scheme, when the Society for the Appellation of the Wines of Mudgee was formed. It was a voluntary system whereby winemakers could for a few cents per bottle apply to have their wines (made from grapes grown solely within the defined Mudgee area) awarded the mark of the Society and carry the entitlement 'Certified Mudgee Appellation Wine' on their labels. This scheme no longer operates, having been superseded by the Geographical Indications system.

Today the Mudgee area has attracted the attention of the 'big battalions', with the major presence of Orlando Wyndham and to a lesser extent Mildara Blass and Rosemount. It has 14 working wineries and about 26 vineyards with cellar door sales, and a meadery (appropriate given the fame of Mudgee's honey).

Location: Mudgee (town) latitude 32°35'S, longitude 149°35'E, about 261 km north-west of Sydney
Elevation: (town) 454m. The vineyards of the region are located between 470 and 1080 m in altitude.
Topography and soils: The region is an important transitional area between the western slopes of the Great Divide and the central tablelands and western plains. It is the most northerly region of the Central Ranges Wine Zone, its principal town being Mudgee (located in the valley of the Cudgegong River, a tributary of the Macquarie). The valley is dominated to its east, south and south-west by the Great Dividing Range, while in the immediate vicinity of the town there are low to medium-sized hills to its north, north-west and north-east, the country rising again on the road back through the Goulburn Ranges to Muswellbrook and the Hunter Valley.

Its soils are chiefly hard red duplex (Dr 2) and hard mottled yellow duplex (Dy 3), though there are some red massive earths (Gn 2). Beneath about half a metre of topsoil, there is a subsoil of clay and gravel, in turn overlying Ordovician sandstone, slate, phyllite and limestone. Such soils are moderately permeable and well drained. They are also moderately fertile but often low in nitrogen and phosphorus.
Climate: MJT 22.9°C, MAR 15°C, HDD raw 2055, AR 668 mm (Oct–Mar 361 mm), RH 63% (9am Jan), AI 303 mm, SH 8 (D&S). Cf MJT 23.3°C, MAR na, HDD raw 2085, 1617 (cut-off and adjusted for latitude, daily temperature range and vine sites), AR 667 mm (Oct–Apr 405 mm), RH 42% (3pm Jan), AI na, SH 9.1 (Gladstones). Local MJT 23.25°C, MAR 15.4°C, HDD raw 2075, AR 669 mm (Oct–Apr 405 mm), RH 63% (9am Jan), 39% (3pm Jan), AI na, SH na. The warm climate favours the production of full-bodied reds and whites and would favour fortifieds, market conditions permitting. Like the rest of the regions in the Central Ranges zone, there is a substantial frost risk where air drainage is poor. So vineyard sites need careful selection. There is also a risk of hail during the growing season (during Spring 1997, the region did suffer such damage). Most vineyards are drip irrigated from surface dams, collected from rainwater run-off and from bores. There is also some availability from the Cudgegong River.

Harvest time: generally late February to early April, in paricular chardonnay in late February, shiraz and semillon first to second week of March, cabernet sauvignon late March to early April

Principal varieties: White—chardonnay, semillon; Red—shiraz, cabernet sauvignon, merlot

Total area: (1997) circa 1580 ha (821 ha bearing, 759 ha non-bearing)

Principal wine styles: Ripe full-bodied reds, especially Shiraz, which cellar well over 4–5 years and sometimes longer. Comparisons are odious, but there is a slight similarity to the reds of Clare in South Australia which is at a similar altitude and only a degree of latitude further south.

Abercorn NR

Cassilis Road, Mudgee, NSW 2850
Ph 02 6373 3106, Fax 02 6373 3108

Owners: Timothy and Constance Stevens
Chief winemaker: John Baruzzi (contract)
Year of foundation: 1972
Tonnes crushed on average each year: 75, about half of which are used for Abercorn's labels
Location: Mudgee
Area: 8 ha
Soils: sand over clay
Varieties planted: White—chardonnay, sauvignon, semillon; Red—cabernet sauvignon, shiraz
Leading wines: Abercorn Mudgee Chardonnay, Cabernet Sauvignon, Shiraz
Notes: Timothy and Constance Stevens intend that Abercorn's wines be of premium quality. The vineyard is one planted by Craigmoor and is now quite mature. The winemaking in John Baruzzi's hands will be skilled and appropriate, with Francois Freres barriques for the Chardonnay and a mixture of French and American oak for the Shiraz. There are presently no cellar door sales, though it is anticipated that they will commence in 1999.

Andrew Harris Vineyards R8.5

Sydney Road, Mudgee, NSW 2850
Ph 02 6373 1213, Fax 02 6373 1296

Owners: Andrew and Debbie Harris
Chief winemaker: Adrian Lockhart, Simon Gilbert (consultant)
Year of foundation: 1991
Tonnes crushed on average each year: 800, of which about 100 are used for Andrew Harris labels
Location: Mudgee
Area: 90 ha
Soils: red to brown loam over gravelly clay
Varieties planted: White—chardonnay, riesling, sauvignon blanc, semillon, verdelho; Red—cabernet sauvignon, merlot, shiraz
Leading wines: Andrew Harris The Vision (a Shiraz and Cabernet Sauvignon blend), Reserve Cabernet Sauvignon, Reserve Shiraz, Reserve Chardonnay, Premium Cabernet Sauvignon, Premium Shiraz, Premium Chardonnay
Notes: There are no 'ordinary' wines in the Andrew Harris Vineyards ranges, only The Vision, Reserve and Premium. Substantial investment in its vineyard and winery (erected in time for 1997 vintage) has ensured that the enterprise is off to an exciting start. Its wine show record at the Sydney and Mudgee Wine Shows is impressive and certainly wine quality is excellent. As might be envisaged from this region, the reds, in particular The Vision, have enjoyed spectacular success under Simon Gilbert's stewardship and his supervisory role will continue. No cellar door sales until 2001.

Augustine Wines R7

George Campbell Drive, Mudgee,
NSW 2850
Ph 02 6372 3880, Fax 02 6372 2977

Owner: Mildara Blass Ltd (lessee)
Chief winemaker: Adam Eggins
Year of foundation: 1918
Tonnes crushed on average each year: 620
Location: Mudgee
Area: 55 ha
Soils: brown sandy loam over clay subsoils,
fertile, friable and well-drained
Varieties planted: White—chardonnay,
gewurztraminer, semillon; Red—aleatico,
cabernet sauvignon, merlot, pinot noir, shiraz
Leading wines: Rothbury regional labels
including Mudgee Shiraz and Mudgee
Cabernet Merlot
Notes: Augustine is one of the veteran
vineyards of Mudgee, having been founded by
Dr Fiaschi in 1918. These days its grapes form
part of the Rothbury regional range of wines.
Cellar door sales: Fri–Tues 10am–4pm.

Benerin Estate Vineyard NR

27 Rodgers Street, Kandos, NSW 2848
Ph 02 6379 4406, Fax 02 6379 4996

Owners: Richard and Rachel Trounson
Chief winemaker: Pieter van Gent (contract)
Year of foundation: 1995
Tonnes crushed on average each year: 10,
increasing to 20 as its vines mature and come
into bearing
Location: Kandos
Area: 4 ha
Soils: brown loam over limestone and clay
Varieties planted: White—chardonnay;
Red—cabernet sauvignon, merlot, sangiovese,
shiraz
Leading wines: Benerin Estate Wells Parish
Chardonnay, Cabernet Sauvignon
Notes: A new winegrowing and winemaking
venture high in the hills near Kandos, once

famous for its cement works. On other parts of
their lands, Richard and his father Barry are
contracted growers for Southcorp, but Richard
is establishing Benerin Estate as a vehicle for
his own label. Cellar door sales anticipated in
1999.

Botobolar NR

Botobolar Lane, Mudgee, NSW 2850
Ph 02 6373 3840, Fax 02 6373 3789

Owners: Kevin and Trina Karstrom
Chief winemaker: Kevin Karstrom
Year of foundation: 1971
Tonnes crushed on average each year: 100, all
of which are used for the Botobolar labels
Location: Mudgee
Area: 23 ha
Soils: yellow podsolic heavy clay loam
Varieties planted: White—chardonnay,
crouchen, gewurztraminer, marsanne, riesling
Red—cabernet sauvignon, mourvedre, pinot
noir, shiraz
Leading wines: Botobolar Cabernet-Shiraz-
Mourvedre, Shiraz, Cabernet, Chardonnay,
Marsanne, Preservative-free Red (made of Pinot
Noir), Preservative-free White (Crouchen)
Notes: Botobolar is a member of the National
Association of Sustainable Agriculture Australia
and as such is an organic vineyard. There are
two preservative-free wines and others
conventionally made. Cellar door sales:
Mon–Sat 10am–5pm, Sun 10am–3pm.

Britten's Wines NR

Stoney Creek Road, Cooyal, NSW 2850
Ph 02 6373 5320

Owners: Stephen, Barrie, Eileen and Jane
Britten
Chief winemaker: contract
Year of foundation: 1984
Tonnes crushed on average each year: 25,
about half of which are used for Britten's
Wines own labels

Location: Cooyal
Area: 8 ha
Soils: red loam with a clay base
Varieties planted: White—chardonnay, riesling, semillon; Red—cabernet sauvignon, merlot
Leading wines: Britten's Wines Cabernet-Merlot, Chardonnay, Semillon
Notes: Britten's does not mature its wines in oak which means that many show judges would find them atypical. However, this does not matter so much with Semillon, which is their wine, enjoying most show success, latterly with a bronze medal at the Mudgee Show. Cellar door sales: weekends and public holidays, Sat 10am–5pm Sun 9am–3pm.

Burnbrae NR

Hargraves Road, Mudgee, NSW 2850
Ph 02 6373 3504, Fax 02 6373 3601

Owner/chief winemaker: Alan Cox
Year of foundation: 1970
Tonnes crushed on average each year: 20, aiming at 100+ by 2000
Location: Mudgee
Area: 18 ha subject to revitalisation
Soils: sandy loam and basalt, rather acid
Varieties planted: White—chardonnay, muscat gordo blanco, riesling, semillon; Red—cabernet sauvignon, merlot, black muscat, shiraz
Leading wines: Burnbrae Cabernet Sauvignon
Notes: Burnbrae was recently purchased by Alan Cox and the vineyard is being rehabilitated. Its fortifieds had a good reputation. Cellar door sales: 9am–4pm every day except Tuesdays.

Craigmoor R7.5

Craigmoor Road, Mudgee, NSW 2850
Ph 02 6372 2208, Fax 02 6372 3883

Owner: Orlando Wyndham
Chief winemaker: Robert Paul
Year of foundation: 1858
Tonnes produced on average each year: 800

Location: Mudgee
Area: 70 ha
Soils: reddish ironstone with some clay loam
Varieties planted: White—chardonnay, sauvignon blanc; Red—cabernet sauvignon, merlot, pinot noir, shiraz
Leading wines: Craigmoor Shiraz, Cabernet Sauvignon, Chardonnay
Notes: Craigmoor is where Mudgee wine began with Adam Roth in the 1850s, a family dynasty that ended with the death in 1969 of Adam's grandson, Jack, who was an excellent winemaker. (In 1966, I well remember tasting a gold medal winning 1963 Shiraz made by Jack.) It entered a troubled period from then until its acquisition by Wyndham Estate in the 1980s. These days Craigmoor has ceased to be a working winery, housing instead a wine museum and a restaurant. Cellar door sales: Mon–Sat 10am–4.30pm, Sun and public holidays 10am–4pm.

Huntington Estate R9

Cassilis Road, Mudgee, NSW 2850
Ph 02 6373 3825, Fax 02 6373 3730

Owners: Bob and Wendy Roberts
Chief winemaker: Susie Roberts
Year of foundation: 1969
Tonnes crushed on average each year: 300, of which 280 are used for Huntington Estate labels
Location: Mudgee
Area: 42 ha
Soils: varied soils but chiefly red to sandy clay loams over clay and limestone
Varieties planted: White—chardonnay, semillon; Red—cabernet sauvignon, merlot, pinot noir, shiraz
Leading wines: Huntington Estate Shiraz, Cabernet Sauvignon, Cabernet-Merlot, Semillon
Notes: Except for Craigmoor and Mudgee Wines, Huntington is the oldest winery in the region and it has created an envied reputation, not only for its wines but also for its

marvellous Music Festival. Over the years, it has specialised in full-bodied reds (in fact that is how many of them, together with the denoting variety/ies, were classified in earlier times) and these are invariably some of the best of the region. Its Shiraz is usually the longest lived and always worth cellaring for several years, though the reds are always released with some bottle age and at very reasonable prices. Cellar door sales: Mon–Fri 9am–5pm, Sat 10am–5pm, Sun 10am–3pm.

Knights Vines **NR**

Henry Lawson Drive, Eurunderee
NSW 2850
Ph 02 6373 3954, Fax 02 6373 3750

Owners: Peter and Maria Knights
Chief winemaker: Peter Knights
Year of foundation: 1971 (vineyard),
1991 (winery)
Tonnes crushed on average each year: 23
Location: Eurunderee
Area: 5 ha
Soils: red-grey clay loam on a clay base
Varieties planted: White—muscat gordo blanco, riesling, sauvignon blanc, semillon; Red—merlot, muscat hamburgh, shiraz
Leading wines: Eurunderee Flats Shiraz, Merlin Rouge (light red), Knight Vines Round Table Tawny Port
Notes: A regular winner of awards for fortifieds at the Mudgee Show including a recent gold for Muscat. Cellar door sales: Sun–Fri 10am–4pm, Sat 9am–5pm.

Knowland Estate **NR**

Mount Vincent Road, Running Stream,
NSW 2850
Ph 02 6358 8420, Fax 02 9923 1462

Owner: Peter R Knowland and Associates Pty Ltd
Chief winemaker: Peter Knowland
Year of foundation: 1990

Tonnes crushed on average each year: 10, expanding to 40 as the vines come to maturity
Location: Running Stream
Area: 4 ha
Soils: basalt
Varieties planted: White—gewurztraminer, sauvignon blanc; Red—cabernet sauvignon, cabernet franc, merlot, pinot noir
Leading wines: Knowland Estate Pinot Noir, Sauvignon Blanc
Notes: Peter Knowland feels that he has found the best spot in New South Wales for pinot noir and sauvignon blanc; that is, when he found out how to get his vines to take up phosphorus. Now all is going well and the vineyard, one of the highest in New South Wales at 1080 m, is proceeding to full production. A winemaker of experience, Peter feels that his Sauvignon Blanc (now in its third year of production) is the best Australian example he's tasted, in fact rivalling the better ones of Marlborough. His Pinot Noir also holds great excitement for him. Cellar door sales by appointment.

Lawson's Hill **NR**

Henry Lawson Drive, Eurunderee
NSW 2850
Ph 02 6373 3953, Fax 02 6373 3948

Owners: Jose and June Grace
Chief winemaker: contract
Year of foundation: 1985
Tonnes crushed on average each year: 50
Location: Eurunderee
Area: 8.5 ha
Soils: clayey loams to red basalt on a clay base
Varieties planted: White—chardonnay, sauvignon blanc, verdelho; Red—cabernet sauvignon, malbec, merlot, pinot noir
Leading wines: Lawson's Hill Merlot, Cabernet Sauvignon
Notes: This was Henry Lawson's childhood home and is now a not-so-small family vineyard. Jose Grace finds that his Merlot is

proving very popular. Cellar door sales: 7 days
9.30am–5pm.

Lowe Family Wines R8

Tinja Road, Mudgee, NSW 2850
Ph 015 298 294, no fax

Owners/winemakers: David Lowe and Jane
Wilson
Year of foundation: 1974 (vineyard), 1999
(winery)
Tonnes crushed on average each year: 200
Location: Mudgee
Area: 1 ha (Maitland), 13.6 ha (Mudgee)
Soils: (Mudgee) red basalt over quartzy red clay
over limestone
Varieties planted: (Mudgee) White—
chardonnay; Red—barbera, merlot, sangiovese,
shiraz. (Hunter) Red—merlot
Leading wines: Lowe Family Semillon,
Chardonnay, Orange Red (a cabernet
sauvignon, cabernet franc merlot blend),
Merlot (Hunter-Mudgee), Shiraz (Hunter)
Notes: Another new winery for Mudgee with
its fruit sourced from old established vineyards
by Hunter veteran David Lowe, who won two
trophies for whites at the 1998 Hunter Valley
Wine Show. Cellar door sales only by
appointment.

Mansfield Wines NR

Eurunderee Road, Mudgee, NSW 2850
Ph 02 6373 3871, Fax 02 6373 3708

Owners: Peter Mansfield and Ian McLellan
Chief winemaker: Bob Heslop
Year of foundation: 1976
Tonnes crushed on average each year: 50
Location: Mudgee
Area: 6.8 ha
Soils: red basalt over clay
Varieties planted: White—chardonnay,
sauvignon blanc, white frontignac;
Red—cabernet sauvignon, merlot
Leading wines: Mansfield Golden Gully

(a sauvignon blanc-dominant blend),
Chardonnay, Cabernet-Merlot
Notes: This long-established winemaker shows
occasionally at the Mudgee Wine Show,
winning silvers and bronzes. Cellar door sales:
Mon–Sat 9am–5pm, Sun 10am–5pm.

Martins Hill Wines NR

Sydney Road, Mudgee, NSW 2850
(16 km south of Mudgee)
Ph/Fax 02 8373 1248

Owners: Michael Sweeney and Jan Kenworthy
Chief winemaker: (contract)
Year of foundation: 1985
Tonnes crushed on average each year: 12, but
expected to reach 20
Location: Martins Hill
Area: 2 ha
Soils: Silurian aged acid volcanic
Varieties planted: White—sauvignon blanc;
Red—cabernet sauvignon, pinot noir, shiraz
Leading wines: Martins Hill Sauvignon Blanc,
Pinot Noir (light red style)
Notes: Martins Hill is an organically grown
vineyard and typical of the enthusiastic revival
of winegrowing in the Central Ranges of New
South Wales. The Sauvignon Blanc 1996 was
awarded a bronze at the local show. Cellar
door sales: none. Sales by mail order.

Miramar Wines R8.5

Henry Lawson Drive, Mudgee,
NSW 2850
Ph 02 6373 3874, Fax 02 6373 3854

Owner/chief winemaker: Ian MacRae
Year of foundation: 1977
Tonnes crushed on average each year: 120
Location: Mudgee
Area: 25 ha
Soils: variable clay loams over deep friable clays
Varieties planted: White—chardonnay, riesling,
sauvignon blanc, semillon; Red—cabernet
sauvignon, pinot noir, shiraz

Leading wines: Miramar Shiraz, Chardonnay, Semillon, Cabernet Sauvignon, Method Champenoise Sparkling
Notes: Ian MacRae is one of the veterans of Mudgee winemaking and the winner of many trophies at the Mudgee Show. His wines are certainly worth a detour. Cellar door sales: 7 days 9am–5pm.

Montrose Wines R8.5

Henry Lawson Drive, Mudgee, NSW 2850
Ph 02 6373 3883, Fax 02 6373 3795

Owner: Orlando Wyndham
Chief winemaker: Robert Paul
Year of foundation: 1974
Tonnes crushed on average each year: 1000 from Mudgee, but other fruit from the Hunter Valley and Cowra is also vinified here
Location: Mudgee
Area: 110 ha consisting of two vineyards, Montrose (50 ha) and Oakfield (60 ha)
Soils: clay loam varying to reddish ironstone on tops of hills
Varieties planted: (Montrose) White—chardonnay, gewurztraminer, riesling, sauvignon blanc, semillon; Red—cabernet sauvignon, pinot noir, shiraz. (Oakfield) White—riesling, semillon, verdelho, white frontignac; Red—barbera cabernet franc, cabernet sauvignon, chambourcin, nebbielo, sangiovese, shiraz
Leading wines: Montrose Cabernet Sauvignon, Shiraz, Unwooded Chardonnay, Barbera, Sangiovese. Wine from Montrose also forms part of the Wyndham Estate reds Bin 444 and 555, as well as part of the Poets Corner range.
Notes: Montrose, originally erected by the owners of the Transfield engineering group, is the biggest winery in Mudgee and now the headquarters of winemaking for Orlando Wyndham in New South Wales. It is notable chiefly for its excellent reds. Cellar door sales: Mon–Fri 9am–4pm, Sun 10am–4pm. Closed Sat.

Mountilford Winery NR

2 km off the Sydney Road, at Ilford
50 km south of Mudgee
Ph/Fax 02 6358 8544

Owners: Helen and Don Cumming
Chief winemaker: Don Cumming
Year of foundation: 1976
Tonnes crushed on average each year: 12
Location: Ilford
Area: 5 ha
Soils: loam and shale over grey clay
Varieties planted: White—gewurztraminer, pinot gris, riesling, sylvaner; Red—cabernet sauvignon, shiraz
Leading wines: Mountilford Pinot Gris, Riesling, Cabernet Sauvignon, Shiraz
Notes: At 950 m altitude, Mountilford is a long-established family vineyard and one of the highest vineyards before Orange, where there are several higher. Cellar door sales: 7 days 10am–4pm.

Mudgee Wines NR

280 Henry Lawson Drive, Mudgee, NSW 2850
Ph 02 6372 2258

Owner/chief winemaker: Jennifer Meek
Year of foundation: 1963
Tonnes crushed on average each year: 5
Location: Mudgee
Area: 5 ha
Soils: clay on limestone
Varieties planted: White—chardonnay, gewurztraminer, riesling, trebbiano; Red—black muscat, cabernet sauvignon, pinot noir, shiraz
Leading wines: Mudgee Wines Riesling, Chardonnay
Notes: This long-established, organically cultivated vineyard produces preservative-free wines made on their own yeasts. Cellar door sales: Thurs–Mon 10am–5pm, Tues–Wed by

appointment, open 7 days during school holidays.

Pieter van Gent Winery NR

Black Springs Road, Mudgee, NSW 2850
Ph 02 6373 3807, Fax 02 6373 3910

Owners: Pieter and Sheila van Gent
Chief winemaker: Pieter van Gent
Year of foundation: 1978
Tonnes crushed on average each year: 150
Location: Mudgee
Area: 15.2 ha (3.2 ha not bearing)
Soils: clayey loam
Varieties planted: White—chardonnay, muller-thurgau, muscat gordo blanco, semillon, verdelho, white frontignac; Red—cabernet sauvignon, merlot, red frontignac, shiraz
Leading wines: Pieter van Gent Sundance Soft Red (a blend of red frontignac, cabernet sauvignon and shiraz), Chardonnay, Cabernet Sauvignon
Notes: A regular winner of trophies at the Mudgee Show for fortifieds. Cellar door sales: Mon–Sat 9am–5pm, Sun 11am–4pm.

Platt's Wines NR

cnr Cassilis Road and Henry Lawson Drive, Mudgee, NSW 2850
Ph 02 6372 7041, Fax 02 6372 7043

Owners: Barry and Marina Platt
Chief winemaker: Barry Platt
Year of foundation: 1983
Tonnes crushed on average each year: 190, of which 100 tonnes are used for Barry Platt's own labels
Location: (vineyard) Gulgong
Area: 24 ha
Soils: red basalt above a shaley clay
Varieties planted: White—chardonnay, gewurztraminer, semillon; Red—cabernet sauvignon
Leading wines: Platt's Wines Cabernet Sauvignon, Barrel Fermented Chardonnay

Notes: Platt's Wines is now located in the newly restored Fairview Winery, originally built in 1895 by a son of Adam Roth. Cellar door sales: 7 days 9am–5pm. There is also a cafe and a guesthouse with three bedrooms.

Red Clay Estate NR

269 Henry Lawson Drive, Mudgee, NSW 2850
Ph/Fax 02 6372 4596

Owner/chief winemaker: Kenneth W Heslop
Year of foundation: 1988 (vineyard), 1997 (winery)
Tonnes crushed on average each year: 10, all of which are used for Red Clay labels
Location: Mudgee
Area: 2.5 ha
Soils: heavy red to brown clay
Varieties planted: White—chardonnay, sauvignon blanc, white frontignac; Red—cabernet sauvignon, merlot, shiraz
Leading wines: Red Clay Cabernet-Merlot, Rose (of pinot noir), Chardonnay, Sauvignon Blanc
Notes: This is a very new winery and vineyard with cellar door sales: Fri–Mon 10am–5pm.

Rosemount Estate (vineyards only) R8

Henry Lawson Drive, Mudgee, NSW 2850

Owner: Rosemount Estate
Chief winemaker: Philip Shaw
There are two Rosemount vineyards in Mudgee, both located on Henry Lawson Drive.

(i) Mountain Blue
Year of foundation: 1953
Tonnes produced on average each year: not disclosed but estimated at 430
Area: 85 ha
Soils: red-brown loam, clays, over red clay subsoil

Varieties planted: White—none; Red—cabernet sauvignon, shiraz
Leading wines: Mountain Blue range

(ii) Hill of Gold
Year of foundation: 1973
Tonnes produced on average each year: not disclosed but estimated at 400
Area: 40 ha
Soils: red-brown loam, clays, over red clay subsoil; on hill patches quartz and slate subsoils
Varieties planted: White—chardonnay, sauvignon blanc; Red—cabernet franc, cabernet sauvignon, merlot, pinot noir, shiraz, zinfandel
Leading wines: Mountain Blue range
Notes: Contributors to the Mountain Blue range. No local cellar door sales.

Seldom Seen Vineyard R7
Craigmoor Road, Mudgee, NSW 2850
Ph 02 6372 4482, Fax 02 6372 1055

Owner: Seldom Seen Vineyard Pty Ltd (vineyard leased)
Chief winemaker: Barry Platt
Year of foundation: 1987
Tonnes crushed on average each year: 110, of which about 60 tonnes are used for Seldom Seen's labels
Location: Mudgee
Area: 17.8 ha
Soils: red-brown basalt to a depth of half a metre over a gravelly clay subsoil
Varieties planted: White—chardonnay, gewurztraminer, semillon; Red—none
Leading wines: Seldom Seen Barrel Fermented Chardonnay, Wooded Semillon, Unwooded Chardonnay, Unwooded Semillon
Notes: Seldom Seen is a prolific winner of gold, silver and bronze show awards at the Mudgee Wine Show and other shows, mostly in Museum classes.

Steins Wines NR
Pipeclay Lane, Mudgee, NSW 2850
Ph 02 6373 3991, Fax 02 6373 3709

Owner/chief winemaker: Robert Stein and Greg Barnes
Year of foundation: 1976
Tonnes crushed on average each year: 60
Location: Mudgee
Area: 8 ha
Soils: brown-grey loam with a clay subsoil
Varieties planted: White—chardonnay, gewurztraminer, riesling, semillon; Red—black muscat, cabernet sauvignon, shiraz
Leading wines: Stein's Chardonnay, Shiraz
Notes: Steins is a very successful exhibitor at the Mudgee Show in 1997 with 16 awards from 20 entries including a gold for 1996 Shiraz. Cellar door sales: 7 days 10am–4.30pm.

Tallara NR
Lawson Farm, Edgell Lane, off Cassilis Road, Mudgee, NSW 2850
Ph 02 6372 2408, Fax 02 6372 6924

Owner: Tinobah Pty Ltd
Chief winemaker: Simon Gilbert (contract)
Year of foundation: 1973
Tonnes crushed on average each year: 300, of which about 50 are used for Tallara's own labels
Location: Mudgee
Area: 55 ha (including new plantings made in 1997)
Soils: browny-red loams
Varieties planted: White—chardonnay, semillon; Red—cabernet sauvignon, merlot, shiraz
Leading wines: Tallara Cabernet Sauvignon, Shiraz
Notes: This long-established grower uses a small part of its own grapes for its own labels. Cellar door sales by appointment.

Thistle Hill R8

McDonalds Road, Mudgee, NSW 2850
Ph 02 6373 3546, Fax 02 6373 3540

Owners: David and Lesley Robertson
Chief winemaker: David Robertson
Year of foundation: 1976
Tonnes crushed on average each year: 40
Location: Mudgee
Area: 11 ha
Soils: basalt over ironstone 0.6 m deep,
permeable to about 4 m and some red clay
subsoil
Varieties planted: White—chardonnay, riesling;
Red—cabernet sauvignon, pinot noir
Leading wines: Thistle Hill Cabernet Sauvignon
Notes: Renowned over the years for its
Cabernet Sauvignon, Thistle Hill also makes
excellent Chardonnay. Cellar door sales: 7 days
9am–5pm. There are also picnic and barbecue
facilities and a 3-bedroom cottage for rental.

Vinifera Wines

194 Henry Lawson Drive, Mudgee,
NSW 2850
Ph 02 6372 2461, Fax 02 6372 6617

Owners: Tony and Debbie McKendry
Chief winemaker: Stephen Dodd (contract)
Year of foundation: 1994
Tonnes crushed on average each year: 10,
increasing to 20
Location: Mudgee
Area: 7.2 ha
Soils: red duplex and yellow clay
Varieties planted: White chardonnay, semillon;
Red—cabernet sauvignon, tempranillo
Leading wines: Vinifera Tempranillo
Notes: Vinifera Wines is a very new vineyard
(not irrigated as yet) into only its second
vintage at time of writing. The Spanish red
variety tempranillo is a definite point of
interest. No cellar door sales as yet.

ORANGE REGION

It is common knowledge now among vignerons that if you wish to grow cool-climate grapes, you either seek a high latitude or a high altitude. That may explain the popularity of southern Victoria and Tasmania on the one hand and places like Stanthorpe and Orange on the other. Other pieces of pragma are pome and stone fruit—if they grow well and ripen slowly, then grapes often follow their example. Most of the areas mentioned have grown apples and peaches extremely well and it is not their fault if they are now being supplanted there by growers seeking better returns from the wine grape.

Orange was named in 1828 by Major Mitchell, Surveyor-General of New South Wales, after Prince William of Orange (did the House of Orange ever use any other Christian name? This one was a rather loose cannon who had fought in the Peninsular War). It had been discovered by another famous Surveyor-General of New South Wales, John Oxley, in 1820 and was proclaimed a village in 1846. Like much of central New South Wales and Victoria, it enjoyed a goldrush in 1851 and thereafter grew rapidly, settling down into solid agricultural prosperity for the rest of the century. In the present century, it has been a thriving horticultural centre and table grapes were once an important product. Orange was also on the shortlist for consideration as our Federal capital, but was rejected because of a shortage of water (a problem that still plagues the inhabitants of Orange and its surrounds, but more of this later).

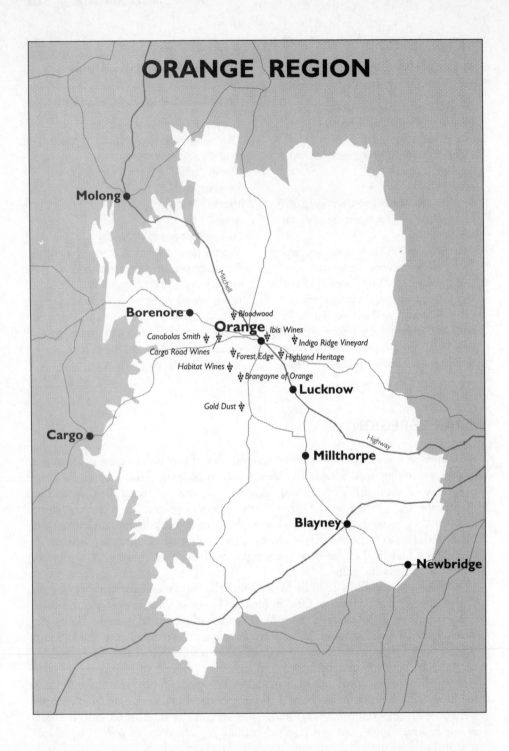

ORANGE REGION

Molong

Mitchell

Borenore

Bloodwood

Orange   *Ibis Wines*

Canobolas Smith   *Indigo Ridge Vineyard*

Cargo Road Wines   *Highland Heritage*

Forest Edge

Habitat Wines

Brangayne of Orange

Lucknow

Gold Dust

Cargo

Highway

Millthorpe

Blayney

Newbridge

Today, Orange remains a leading grower of horticultural products (apples, pears, peaches, cherries, plums and nectarines). The table grapes have declined in importance and today their place is being taken by wine grapes. Other products are beef, lamb and wool. Gold also remains on the agenda with the opening of Australia's largest open-cut goldmine at Cadia.

The wine history of the region began as recently as the early 1980s, but nearby Molong had been the subject of trial plantings by the late Graham Gregory on behalf of the New South Wales Department of Agriculture more than 30 years before. The pioneers of the region were the Doyles of Bloodwood, the Swansons of Cargo Road Wines and Highland Heritage Estate. In 1988 Philip Shaw of Rosemount Estate also developed a major vineyard. By 1995, there were 150 hectares of vines, but this area has since been virtually tripled by the establishment of the Little Boomey Vineyard of 277 hectares. By 1996 the vineyard area of the region was over 570 hectares with only about 75 hectares of bearing vines. These yielded some 700 tonnes in 1996, most of which were vinified in the Hunter Valley.

Location: latitude 33°19'S, longitude 149°03'E, about 270 km west-north-west of Sydney
Elevation: 922 m with vineyards ranging in altitude from 600 m to 1100 m
Topography and soils: The region is hilly and undulating, a relatively young uplifted topography caused by the volcanic activity of Mount Canobolas, its dominant feature. Indeed this extinct volcano might well be in John Gladstones' words 'a projecting or isolated' hill, a factor which—together with, say, excellent air drainage—may prove its vineyards to be 'the very best'. Basalt rock is common in the area of the mountain, which also shows limestone outcrops from 600 m altitude. Such outcrops underlie much of the country of higher elevation. The region is also the source of tributary streams to the Lachlan and Macquarie Rivers, which run west into the Murray-Darling system.

There are four main soil types used for viticulture in the region as follows. Kraznozems are deep, well-drained clay soils derived from tertiary basalt material. These are located adjacent to Mount Canobolas and extend for a radius of about 10 km and even further towards Millthorpe. These soils, usually found at higher elevations overlying limestone, are quite fertile and promote strong vine vigour. Red earths/red-brown earths are older, gradational soils of red-brown clay loam over redder light clays. Such soils are slightly acid, well-drained and of medium to high fertility. Red podsols/brown podsols are duplex soils of red-brown to brown loam over medium to heavy clay. These soils are generally shallower, are of lower fertility and only moderate vigour. They are also slightly acid in nature. *Terra rossa*, though rarer in the region, are present in isolated areas in its west and lie above hard limestone outcrops. They have a more neutral pH, are well-drained and are excellent for viticulture, provided that water is available.
Climate: MJT 19.45°C, HDD (Oct–Apr) 1254, MAR 14.35°C, AR 916 mm (Oct–Apr 483 mm), RH (9am Jan), 62% (3pm Jan 44%). AI 103 mm, SH (av Oct–April) 8.8 (Orange Agricultural Research and Veterinary Centre, 1976–1996). It is tempting as a generality to declare Orange a cool region and so it is—between 900 and 1100 m

in altitude—but as altitude decreases so the region becomes warmer, the MJT becoming 20.5°C at 600 m.

Orange might be viewed as a viticultural 'layer-cake', with varieties favouring warmer climes at, say, 500–600 m, cultivars preferring slightly cooler conditions at 700–800 m and so on, as one ascends, to varieties such as pinot noir on the very top layer and presumably chardonnay of differing styles being produced at each level. This notion is, of course, fanciful but Orange certainly does seem to have a capacity for climatic and therefore varietal versatility within its boundaries. Altitude, however, poses its own problems—low relative humidity and low concentration of carbon dioxide.

Its annual rainfall, varying within the region from 750 to 915 mm (more than half of which falls during the October–April growing season) is generous enough and needs to be, for the Orange region lies within the Murray-Darling basin of New South Wales and there has been an embargo in force since July 1995 on the issuing of irrigation licences within this area. Irrigation where permitted is from dams and bores in existence before the embargo. Thus, unless there were pre-existing dams or bores, young vineyards planted after that date have been obliged to rely on natural rainfall, a dependence which in times of drought can be most detrimental to their development. At the time of writing, the New South Wales government was moving with snail-like celerity in respect of the issue, though the Orange Region Vignerons Association has submitted a proposal to it to create a model for procedures for the use of water resources within the high country.

The region has a frost risk during spring and again from mid to late autumn, so great care should be taken in the selection of vineyard sites by ensuring that such sites have good air drainage and do not face south, thereby avoiding the chill factors of cold southerly or south-westerly winds. Strong easterly winds during summer sometimes cause canopy roll and problems with flowering. The very presence of a mountain such as Mount Canobolas of about 1400 m in altitude ensures that Orange weather changes quickly with snow and sleet a possibility virtually at any time of the year. Hail is also possible in certain areas. Powdery mildew can be a problem, but is controlled by systemic spraying early in the season and later by sulfur.

Harvest time: this varies with altitude. Chardonnay at 850 m late March, at 900 m mid April, at 960 m early May. Cabernet Sauvignon at 850 m second to third week of April, at 900 m third week of April, at 960 m early May.

Principal varieties: (August 1996) White—chardonnay (198 ha), sauvignon blanc (27 ha), riesling and others (2 ha); Red—cabernet sauvignon (130 ha), shiraz (128 ha), merlot (55 ha), pinot noir (18 ha), cabernet franc and others (9 ha)

Total area: (August 1996) 567 ha

Principal wine styles: From the varieties planted and my tastings to date, Orange is undoubtedly a region of light to medium-bodied fruit-driven whites of style and elegance and medium- to full-bodied reds which are fruit-dominant and well balanced. Orange Chardonnay and Orange Cabernet will be wines of national importance in the next twenty years.

Bantry Grove Farms (vineyard only)

 NR

Newbridge, NSW 2795
Ph 02 6368 1036, Fax 02 6368 1116

Owners: Terrey and Barbie Johnson
Chief winemaker: no wines commercially made
Year of foundation: 1990
Tonnes produced on average each year: 40, increasing to about 200 when all vines are in full bearing
Location: Newbridge (at the southernmost tip of region) 960 m
Area: 15 ha
Soils: deep old basaltic, red clay loam of moderate vigour
Varieties planted: White—chardonnay, sauvignon blanc; Red—cabernet sauvignon, merlot, pinot noir
Leading wines: none commercially made
Notes: Terrey and Barbie Johnson are perfectly content as grapegrowers and have no plans for a Bantry Farms label. At 900 m and at the southernmost tip of the region, Bantry Grove Farms has the latest cabernet vintage of the region.

Bloodwood

 R7.5

4 Griffin Road, Orange, NSW 2800
Ph 02 6362 5631, Fax 02 6361 1173

Owners: Stephen and Rhonda Doyle
Chief winemaker: Stephen Doyle, Jon Reynolds (contract)
Year of foundation: 1982
Tonnes crushed on average each year: 75
Location: Orange
Area: 10 ha
Soils: friable, red, gravelly, loamy topsoil, tending to be acid
Varieties planted: White—chardonnay (clones P58, I10v5 and I10v3), riesling; Red—cabernet franc, cabernet sauvignon, merlot (clone D3v14), malbec, petit verdot, pinot noir clone MV6), shiraz

Leading wines: Bloodwood Chardonnay, Cabernet Sauvignon
Notes: Stephen Doyle is the veteran grower/maker of the region, making several riesling 'ice' wines during his career from fruit picked late in June and on one occasion in July. Though Bloodwood varies in altitude from 840–870 m in altitude, he reports that frost during the growing season is rare provided good site selection has been made in the first place. Cellar door sales by appointment. There are also from time to time special wine release dinners.

Brangayne of Orange

 NR

49 Pinnacle Road, Orange, NSW 2800
Ph 02 6365 3229, Fax 02 6365 3170

Owner: Brangayne Pty Ltd
Chief winemaker: Simon Gilbert (contract)
Year of foundation: 1994
Tonnes crushed on average each year: vineyard yet to come into full bearing, but about 300 tonnes are anticipated
Location: Orange
Area: 26 ha
Soils: volcanic loam
Varieties planted: White—chardonnay, sauvignon blanc; Red—cabernet sauvignon, merlot, pinot noir, shiraz
Leading wines: Brangayne of Orange Chardonnay
Notes: There are two vineyards here, one high, the other higher. Like the rest of Orange, they both have extremely cool climate conditions. I am told they both give good colour and good flavour. No cellar door sales. Mail order only.

Canobolas Smith

 R8

Boree Lane, off Cargo Road, Orange, NSW 2800
Ph/fax 02 6365 6113

Owners: Murray and Toni Smith
Chief winemaker: Murray Smith

Year of foundation: 1986
Tonnes crushed on average each year: 45, of which 25 are used for Canobolas Smith labels
Location: Orange
Area: 8 ha including 2 ha of recent plantings not yet in bearing
Soils: kraznozem, volcanic basalt
Varieties planted: White—chardonnay, semillon; Red—pinot noir, cabernet sauvignon, cabernet franc, merlot, shiraz
Leading wines: Canobolas Smith Chardonnay, Alchemy (a red blend of the best barrels of reds other than pinot noir), Pinot Noir
Notes: From his purposely unirrigated vineyard at 800 m in altitude, Murray Smith produces some of the leading wines of the Orange region, handcrafted wines such as the recent Chardonnay which won a trophy at the Canberra Regional Wine Show. Murray is a minimalist, that is minimal use of herbicides and no insecticides at all. Cellar door sales: weekends and public holidays 11am–5pm.

Cargo Road Wines NR

Cargo Road, Fernlidster, Orange, NSW 2800 (12 km from Orange on the Cargo Road)
Ph/Fax 02 6365 6100

Owner: James Sweetapple
Chief winemakers: James Sweetapple, Rob Crawford (contract)
Year of foundation: 1983
Tonnes crushed on average each year: 17, but will increase to 40 when new plantings come into full bearing
Location: Orange
Area: 8 ha including 5 ha of new plantings
Soils: deep red volcanic soils
Varieties planted: White—sauvignon blanc, riesling, traminer; Red—cabernet sauvignon, merlot, zinfandel
Leading wines: Cargo Wines Floral (a blend of traminer and riesling), Cabernet-Merlot, Zinfandel

Notes: Founded by the Swansons in the early 1980s, and recently purchased by James Sweetapple, Cargo Road Wines at 860 m altitude has magnificent views. The vineyard is unirrigated with 3 hectares of established vines. Cellar door sales by appointment.

Forest Edge NR

'Merindah', Old Canobolas Road, Nashdale, NSW 2800
Ph 02 6365 3434, Fax 02 6362 6202

Owner/chief winemaker: Rob Crawford
Tonnes produced on average each year: 50 (about 2 tonnes used for Forest Edge labels)
Location: Nashdale
Area: 7 ha
Soils: deep basaltic loam
Varieties planted: White—chardonnay, sauvignon blanc; Red—cabernet franc, cabernet sauvignon, merlot, pinot noir
Leading wines: Forest Edge Sauvignon Blanc
Notes: At the present time most of Rob Crawford's fruit finds its way to the Hunter Valley. But that will change once Forest Edge comes into full production and a bigger winery is available. Cellar door sales by appointment only.

Gold Dust R7

South Park, Millthorpe, NSW 2798
Ph 02 6366 5168, Fax 02 6361 9165

Owners: John and Jacqui Corrie
Chief winemaker: Simon Gilbert (contract)
Year of foundation: 1992
Tonnes crushed on average each year: vineyard not yet fully bearing but anticipated to be 50
Location: Forest Reef
Area: 5 ha
Soils: kraznozems
Varieties planted: White—chardonnay, riesling; Red—cabernet sauvignon, merlot
Leading wines: Gold Dust Riesling
Notes: Gold Dust is located in the foothills of

Mount Canobolas and, at 900 m in altitude, it has a lofty location similar to most other Orange vineyards. The vineyard is frost-free and well drained. The vineyard's first wine was a riesling, good enough at its first showing to win a bronze medal in Perth. Cellar door sales by appointment.

Habitat Wines NR

Old Canobolas Road, Orange, NSW 2800, (13 km south-west of Orange)
Ph 02 6365 3294

Owner: Susan Sanders
Chief winemakers: Phil Stevenson/Charles Sturt University, Kirsten Munro (contract)
Year of foundation: 1989
Tonnes crushed on average each year: 6, of which 2 are retained for Susan Sanders' own label
Location: Orange
Area: 2 ha
Soils: deep basaltic loam
Varieties planted: White—sauvignon blanc, pinot gris; Red—merlot, pinot noir
Leading wine: Ibis Habitat Pinot Noir
Notes: At 1100 m altitude on the slopes of Mount Canobolas, this vineyard must be one of the highest in Australia. I am informed that its Pinot Noir bears a good resemblance in colour, nose and palate to those of Southern Victoria, which proves only that in New South Wales pinot noir might need to be grown at similar altitudes to produce recognisably good Pinot and that, in winter, it may occasionally be necessary to wear skis to complete the pruning. No cellar door sales yet.

Highland Heritage

Mitchell Highway, Orange, NSW 2800
Ph 02 6361 3612, Fax 02 6362 6183

Owner: D'Aquino brothers
Chief winemaker: John Hordern (contract)
Year of foundation: 1985

Tonnes crushed on average each year: 40
Location: Orange
Area: 14 ha (including new plantings)
Soils: granite loam
Varieties planted: White—chardonnay, riesling, sauvignon blanc; Red—merlot, pinot noir, shiraz
Leading wines: Highland Heritage Estate Sauvignon Blanc, Chardonnay
Notes: At nearly 900 m altitude, Highland Heritage is one of the older established Orange estates. It exhibits both locally and abroad. It is a consistent award winner with its Sauvignon Blanc and its Chardonnay won a gold medal at the Royal Melbourne Wine Show in 1997. Cellar door sales: Sat–Sun in summer 9.30am–5pm. At other times of year, every day 9am–3pm except Christmas Day and Good Friday. There is also a restaurant.

Ibis Wines NR

Kearneys Drive, Orange, NSW 2800
Ph 02 6362 3257, Fax 02 6361 2256

Owner/chief winemaker: Philip Stevenson
Year of foundation: 1988
Tonnes crushed on average each year: 10
Location: Orange
Area: 1 ha
Soils: red and yellow podsols over heavy clay
Varieties planted: White—chardonnay, riesling; Red—cabernet franc, cabernet sauvignon, pinot noir
Leading wines: Ibis Wines Cabernet Sauvignon
Notes: Philip Stevenson is another of Orange's mountaineer-vignerons. His vineyard is a kilometre in altitude. Such a rarefied atmosphere obviously does his vines no harm, for he regularly exhibits at Cowra Show and receives bronze medals. Cellar door sales: Sat–Sun noon–5pm, at other times by appointment.

Indigo Ridge Vineyard NR

Icely Road, Orange, NSW 2800
Ph/Fax 02 6362 1851

Owners: Paul Bridge and Trish McPherson
Chief winemaker: Jon Reynolds (contract)
Year of foundation: 1995
Tonnes crushed on average each year: 40
tonnes anticipated by 2000
Location: Orange
Area: 4 ha
Soils: Red volcanic earth
Varieties planted: White—sauvignon blanc;
Red—cabernet sauvignon
Leading wines: first commercial vintage is
1998, but there will be two wines only—
Sauvignon Blanc and Cabernet Sauvignon
Notes: Paul Bridge was one of the architects of
the Orange Region Geographical Indication. His
first crop of any substance was picked in 1998.
Jon Reynolds is a winemaker of several years'
experience of Orange vintages. No cellar door
facilities as yet.

Little Boomey Vineyard (vineyard only) NR

Little Boomey, near Molong,
NSW 2866
(18 km north-east of Molong)

Owners: Central Highlands Management Ltd
on behalf of several syndicates of investors
Years of foundation: 1995–96
Tonnes produced on average each year: the
vineyards are not yet in full bearing
Location: Little Boomey
Area: 490 ha
Soils: of volcanic origin, basaltic shaley soils to
heavy basalt soils
Varieties planted: White—chardonnay,
marsanne, riesling, sauvignon blanc, semillon,
verdelho; Red—cabernet sauvignon, merlot,
shiraz
Leading wines: no wine has yet been produced
Notes: This is a huge vineyard or series of

vineyards, especially for an area so
comparatively untried as Orange. It is capable
of producing many thousands of tonnes and
obviously needs purchasing clients of large
winemaking capacity, such as Southcorp
Wines.

Canobolas Vineyard (vineyard only) R8

Forbes Road, Orange, NSW 2800
(10 km west of Orange opposite Mount
Canobolas)

Owners: Philip Shaw and the Oatley family
Year of foundation: 1989
Tonnes produced on average each year: 300
Location: Borenore
Area: 100 ha of which 25 are currently bearing
Soils: limestone basalt shaley, wind blown soils
Varieties planted: White—chardonnay; Red—
cabernet sauvignon, pinot noir, merlot, shiraz
Leading wines: Rosemount 'Orange' range
Notes: This is the source of Rosemount's
exciting Orange Cabernet and Orange
Chardonnay, good wines that will be much
more readily available once the recently
enlarged vineyard comes into bearing. There
are no local cellar door sales.

Three Brothers Vineyard (vineyard only) NR

Spring Terrace Road, Spring Terrace near
Millthorpe, NSW 2798
Ph 02 6366 5117

Owners: Chris and Kathryn Bourke
Chief winemaker: not yet appointed
Year of foundation: 1992
Tonnes crushed on average each year: 10
Location: Millthorpe
Area: 2 ha
Soils: kraznozems
Varieties planted: White—none;
Red—cabernet sauvignon, shiraz

Leading wines: no wines yet commercially available

Notes: The Three Brothers Vineyard has a fairly low profile at the present time. All fruit is sold to Charles Sturt University at Wagga, where it probably contributes to some multiregional blend. Though the time will arrive when Chris Bourke will make his own wine, it is not yet. No cellar door sales.

❦ HUNTER VALLEY ZONE

This is a wine zone, only slightly larger than its component wine region—Hunter.

HUNTER REGION

Hunter Valley or Hunter? Except for the Newcastle metropolitan area and some coastal strips, wine zone and wine region seem identical, yet the logic of it lies in the boundaries of the Hunter catchment area. As yet, there is only one sub-region, Broke Fordwich (which for its uniqueness among the rest of the Hunter relies on its more fertile soils and its slightly warmer climate), though it is inevitable that more will come into existence sooner rather than later. As to what the sub-regions will be, logic, geographic separation, the concentration of wineries and vineyards, soil types and common usage might postulate simply Lower and Upper, as in the Medoc. It has been suggested, however, that old parish names such as Pokolbin and Rothbury or districts such as Lovedale and Mount View might be used. Certainly Pokolbin is one of Australia's best-known wine names.

The Hunter is Australia's oldest viticultural area, yet its principal city, Newcastle, had its origins because of coal deposits, noticed by Lieutenant Shortland in 1797. In 1804, it became both a convict depot for recalcitrants and a coal mine. A decade later, agricultural development began on the fertile alluvial flats of the Lower Hunter Valley to the west of Newcastle and, by 1832, there were about 6 hectares of vineyards on the river flats north and west of present-day Maitland. They were shared among ten settlers and it is not exactly known who was first to plant, though an educated guess might lead us to James Kelman, the brother-in-law of James Busby, Australia's apostle of viticulture. Famous names of this period included George Wyndham, James King and, a little later, Dr Henry Lindeman. The winegrowers soon divorced themselves from other agricultural interests, especially the pastoralists, and soon became quite skilful in political lobbying, pressing their cause for the immigration of skilled labour with local and British authorities. By 1847, the Hunter Valley Vineyard Association was set up. Settlement of the Pokolbin region in the southern part of the Lower Hunter commenced in the mid-1850s as ancestors of wine families prominent today, such as Tyrrell and Drayton, planted their first vineyards.

To the north-west, settlement of the Upper Hunter began in the 1820s and its first vineyard, the original 'Rosemount', was established in 1864 by Carl Brecht, a German shepherd, a demeaning description of a man with great winemaking talent.

Following the bank crashes of the 1890s, however, the region became economically depressed until coal was once more discovered in the first decade of the twentieth century near present-day Cessnock. Such depression was not to leave the Hunter wine industry for 70 years. The industry disappeared altogether in the Upper Hunter and gradually slid into virtual oblivion in the Lower, despite the efforts of the immortal winemaker Maurice O'Shea. By 1956, vineyard area had declined to 489

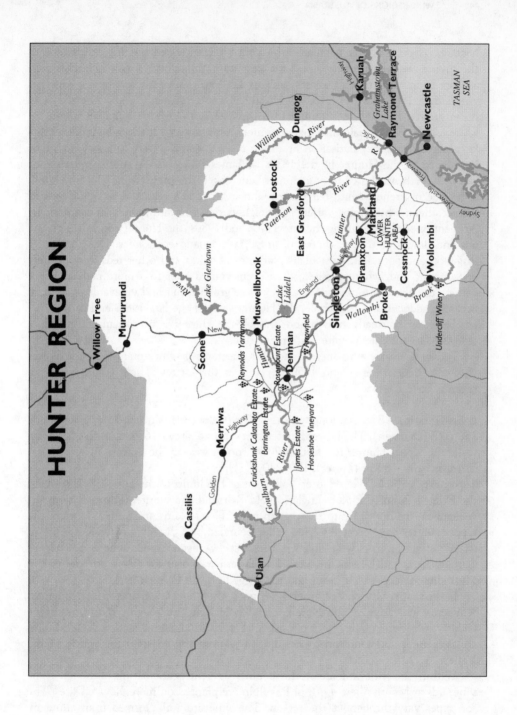

HUNTER REGION

Karuah

Grahamstown Lake

Raymond Terrace

Newcastle

TASMAN SEA

Dungog

Williams

River

Lostock

River

Paterson

East Gresford

River

Maitland

LOWER HUNTER AREA

Hunter

Branxton

Cessnock

Wollombi

Muswellbrook

Lake Glenbawn

Lake Liddell

Singleton

Broke

Underdiff Winery

Brook

Willow Tree

Murrurundi

River

Scone

New

Rosemount Estate

Reynolds Yarraman

Hunter

Denman

Arrowfield

Wollombi

Merriwa

Highway

Cruickshank Calatoota Estate

Barrington Estate

River

James Estate

Horseshoe Vineyard

Cassilis

Golden

Goulburn

Ulan

hectares. A decade later popular enthusiasm for Hunter red was increasing, due to the culture change wrought by post-war migration, the efforts of wine publicists such as Len Evans and to enthusiasts such as Dr Max Lake, whose Hunter cabernet vineyard in 1963 was the first new Hunter planting for many years. The red wine boom arrived in 1968, continuing into the 1970s, though changing its colour to white, much to the chagrin of many Hunter shiraz growers. It was a boom due in its later stages to the popularisation of a then obscure grape variety called chardonnay, introduced to the Hunter in the 1830s by James Busby. Its Australian renaissance can be directly attributed to one Hunter winemaker, the irrepressible Murray Tyrrell, a devotee of French white burgundies who instinctively felt, and was later proved correct, that a 'white pinot' variety in a neighbouring vineyard was in fact chardonnay. As mentioned above, during the late 1970s and 1980s, the Hunter continued on the ups and downs of the big-dipper of grape fashion and economics. Due to lack of irrigation and poor soil, most of its plantings of shiraz and other reds were entirely uneconomic and, where possible, these were grafted over to a more popular white variety, usually chardonnay. If not, they were grubbed out and vineyards once more became paddocks. On the whole, the Hunter story of the late 1980s and early 1990s has been one of steady growth and, though the Hunter is no viticultural paradise, reports of its early demise are quite premature.

Today, there are 48 wineries and 1900 hectares of vines planted in the Lower Hunter with 9 wineries and 1050 hectares in the Upper. There is also one sub-region, Broke Fordwich.

Location: latitude 32°60'S, longitude 151°20'E (Cessnock), latitude 32°20'S longitude 150°60'E (Denman). The Lower Hunter vineyards are about 165 km north of Sydney, while the Upper Hunter is a further 70 km north-west of the Lower.
Elevation: 100–180 m (Lower), 120–240 m (Upper)
Topography and soils: The Hunter Valley sits at the limits of three geological systems, the Sydney Basin, the New England Fold Belt and the Hunter Thrust System. Its geology can be divided into three main parts. Flood plains and valley slopes of the Upper Hunter have created a wide valley bounded by a dissected plateau of resistant triassic strata in the west and on the east by rugged mountainous country of Carboniferous and Devonian strata. The eastern wall of the valley south and east of Muswellbrook consists of lower and less rugged hills of Permian strata.

In the south of the Valley, around Cessnock, there are Devonian and Carboniferous sediments indicative of the New England Fold Belt and rough Triassic sandstone country, while the Valley floor consists of Permian sediments, made of shales, tuffs, conglomerates and sandstone, extending west from the coast to the centre of the Valley.

Within the vineyard areas, the country is gently undulating, although some vineyards at Mount View south of Pokolbin are planted on more elevated sites. The soil types vary throughout the region. The vineyard soils, formed from alluvium, include brown clays and black earths, red podzols and lateritic podzols, formed on old river terraces, non-calcic brown soils and yellow solodic soils, generally found in drainage channels. In the lower Hunter, vineyard soils vary from friable red duplex to deep friable loams, while the soils of Upper Hunter vineyards are well drained, moderately fertile, black silty loams and red duplex soils, moderately acid to alkaline and also well drained.

Climate: Cessnock MJT 22.7°C, MAR 12.8°C, HDD raw 2070, AR 740 mm (Oct–Apr 530 mm), RH 58% (9am Jan), AI na, SH 7.3 (D&S). Cf MJT 23.8°C, MAR na, HDD raw 2327, 1812 (cut-off and adjusted for latitude, daily temperature range and vine sites), AR 746 mm, (Oct–Apr 493 mm), RH 47% (3pm Jan), AI na, SH 7.8 (G). Jerry's Plains MJT 23.6°C, MAR na, HDD 2358, AR 635 mm (Oct–Apr 423 mm), RH 47% (9am Jan), AI na, SH 8.2 (G). Cf Scone MJT 24.6°C, MAR na, HDD raw 2380, 1772 (cut-off and adjusted for latitude and daily temperature range but not vine sites), AR 634 mm (Oct–Apr 419 mm), RH 40% (3pm Jan), AI na, SH 8.5 (Gladstones). Muswellbrook MJT 22.3°C, MAR 12.7°C, HDD 2170, AR 620 mm (Oct–Apr 400 mm), RH 75% (9am Jan), AI na, SH 7.5 (HV Vineyard Assn). This warm to hot region is often described as a sub-humid climatic zone, its summers being typically hot and humid with a high cloud cover, especially noticeable in the Lower Hunter. Rain, sometimes very heavy, is common just before and during harvest and a 'good year' is generally characterised by a dry summer. Average annual rainfall (Cessnock 740 mm) decreases as one moves away from the coast (Muswellbrook 620 mm). The region is generally frost-free during the growing season and birds do not constitute a major problem. Chief disease factors are downy mildew for which a spray program commences in mid-Spring and, during wet to very wet years, bunch rot. Hail also occurs during the spring and summer months. The heat of the Hunter Valley during the ripening season is often tempered by the light afternoon cloud cover, mentioned above. This factor— when accompanied by the fact that the ratio of growing season sunshine hours as opposed to the total of effective day degrees is low—explains why the Hunter produces soft, medium- to full-bodied whites and reds and cannot grow satisfactory fortified styles as compared with areas like the Swan though the raw HDDs are very similar (Cessnock av daily SH 7.3, Guildford av daily SH 9.2).

Drip irrigation is commonly employed in the region, though water resources in the Lower Hunter are generally restricted to farm storage dams and occasional bores, while properties in the Upper Hunter adjacent to rivers have access to a good supply of quality water. Here, too, farm storage dams are important.

Harvest time: The region's normally high temperatures generally result in an early, comparatively uniform and short vintage period, commencing in late January for cultivars such as gewurztraminer and pinot noir and finishing in early March for varieties like cabernet sauvignon.

Principal varieties: Though varietal fashion often decrees the planting of certain grape varieties, the Hunter's most suitable grape varieties have long been settled. These are semillon and shiraz. Of the rest, only chardonnay, as responsive to skilful winemaking in warm areas as it is in cool, has made the grade. Pinot noir in this region makes an ordinary dry red except in very special years and cabernet sauvignon exhibits only average fruit characters and is very reliant on wood for any complexity. Sauvignon blanc produces quite fat and soft wines without the vibrant varietal life of cooler areas, while riesling rarely achieves the concentrated lime citrus characters so sought-after by makers and consumers alike. Perhaps only merlot needs further consideration.

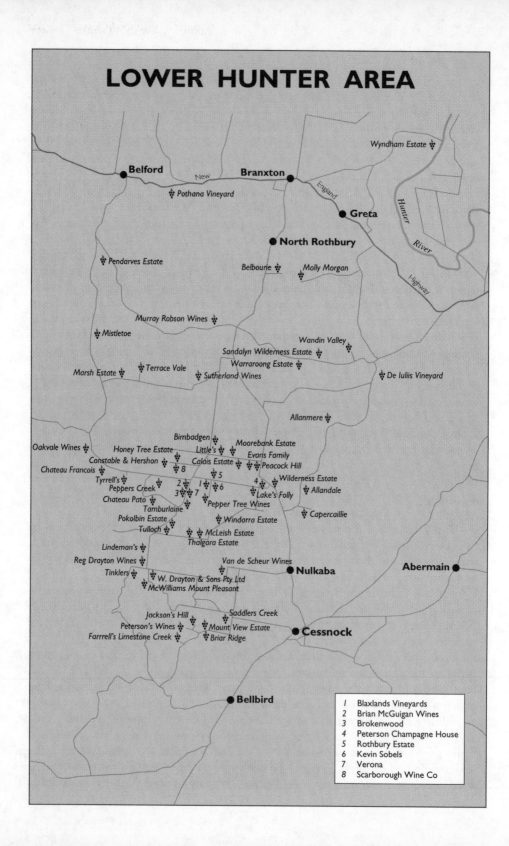

LOWER HUNTER AREA

Wyndham Estate ⚘

● **Belford**   New   ● **Branxton**   England

⚘ Pothana Vineyard   ● **Greta**

Hunter

● **North Rothbury**   River

⚘ Pendarves Estate   Belbourie ⚘   Molly Morgan ⚘   Highway

Murray Robson Wines ⚘

⚘ Mistletoe   Wandin Valley ⚘

Sandalyn Wilderness Estate ⚘
Warraroong Estate ⚘
Marsh Estate ⚘   ⚘ Terrace Vale   ⚘ Sutherland Wines   ⚘ De Iuliis Vineyard

Allanmere ⚘

Bimbadgen ⚘   Moorebank Estate ⚘
Oakvale Wines ⚘   Honey Tree Estate   Little's ⚘   Evans Family ⚘
Constable & Hershon ⚘   ⚘ 8   Calais Estate ⚘   ⚘⚘ Peacock Hill
Chateau Francois ⚘   ⚘ 5
Tyrrell's ⚘   ⚘ 2 ⚘ 1   4 ⚘   ⚘ Wilderness Estate
Peppers Creek ⚘   ⚘ 6   ⚘ Allandale
Chateau Pato ⚘   3 ⚘⚘ 7   ⚘ Lake's Folly
Tamburlaine ⚘   Pepper Tree Wines ⚘
Pokolbin Estate ⚘   ⚘ Capercaillie
Tulloch ⚘   ⚘ Windarra Estate
⚘ McLeish Estate
Thalgara Estate ⚘
Lindeman's ⚘
Reg Drayton Wines ⚘   Van de Scheur Wines ⚘
Tinklers ⚘   ● **Nulkaba**   **Abermain** ●
⚘ W. Drayton & Sons Pty Ltd
⚘ McWilliams Mount Pleasant

Jackson's Hill ⚘   Saddlers Creek ⚘
Peterson's Wines ⚘   ⚘ Mount View Estate
Farrrell's Limestone Creek ⚘   ⚘ Briar Ridge   ● **Cessnock**

● **Bellbird**

1	Blaxlands Vineyards
2	Brian McGuigan Wines
3	Brokenwood
4	Peterson Champagne House
5	Rothbury Estate
6	Kevin Sobels
7	Verona
8	Scarborough Wine Co

The Semillon of the Lower Hunter is one of the world's unique wines, often starting life as a comparatively low-alcohol neutral white (sometimes as low as 10.5% Alc v/v) and then with 5–10 years cellar age developing magnificent toasty characters on nose and palate, while retaining sufficient acidity still to be lively in the mouth. Shiraz, too, from good years in the Lower Hunter displays soft berry flavours when young which become more savoury with increasing bottle age and after 5–10 years in bottle exhibit definite regional characters of earth and leather, complex traits which make a very rewarding bottle. Chardonnay, however, reacts similarly in the Hunter to any other warm Australian area. Subject to rare exceptional years, it can be drunk at 6–9 months of age and should not be kept longer than three years from vintage. Otherwise that rich nutty flavour becomes flabby and oxidised.

Total area: 1900 ha (Lower Hunter), 1050 ha (Upper Hunter)

Adams Peak NR

Adams Peak Road, Broke, NSW 2330
Ph 02 6579 1179

Owner: Nick Micos
Chief winemaker: Neil McGuigan (contract)
Year of foundation: 1989
Tonnes produced on average each year: 7
Location: Broke
Area: 0.8 ha
Soils: basalt, loam
Varieties planted: White—chardonnay, semillon; Red—cabernet sauvignon, shiraz
Leading wines: Adams Peak Chardonnay-Semillon, Cabernet-Shiraz
Notes: A very small family vineyard situated on basaltic soil on the Fordwich Sill. Both white and red have recently won bronze medals at the Hunter Valley Wine Show at Singleton. No cellar door sales.

Allandale R7.5

Lovedale Road, Pokolbin via Maitland, NSW 2321
Ph 02 4990 4526, Fax 02 4990 1714

Owner: Villa Villetri Wines Pty Ltd
Chief winemaker: Bill Sneddon
Year of foundation: 1978
Tonnes crushed on average each year: 225
Location: Lovedale

Area: 7 ha
Soils: sandy loam over clay
Varieties planted: White—chardonnay, semillon; Red—pinot noir
Leading wines: Allandale Chardonnay
Notes: Allandale is a low-profile winery but by no means an unknown boutique. It specialises in Chardonnay, which is usually of the generously drinkable Hunter mould. It grows less than 20% of its fruit requirements and, like many Hunter wineries of its size, has spread its intake of fruit to encompass areas other than the Hunter Valley. In Allandale's case, fruit is sourced also from Mudgee and the Hilltops districts. Cellar door sales: Mon–Sat 9am–5pm.

Allanmere R7.5

Lovedale Road, Lovedale, NSW 2320
Ph 02 4930 7387, Fax 02 4930 7900

Owners: Greg Silkman, Gary Reed, Craig Brown-Thomas, Stephen Allen
Chief winemakers: Gary Reed and Greg Silkman
Year of foundation: 1985
Tonnes crushed on average each year: 20
Location: Lovedale
Area: 10 ha
Soils: loam about 40 cm over clay

Varieties planted: White—chardonnay;
Red—none
Leading wine: Allanmere Durham Chardonnay
Notes: Allanmere is a successful Hunter
boutique established by Dr Newton Potter,
who sold recently to the present owners, two
of whom, Greg Silkman and Gary Reed, are
experienced Hunter winemakers. As a
consequence, quality should remain high.
Cellar door sales: 7 days 10am–5pm.

Arrowfield   R7

Denman Road, Jerry's Plains, NSW 2330
Ph 02 6576 4041, Fax 02 6576 4144

Owners: Hokuriko Coca-Cola Bottlers Co and
Peter Helene
Chief winemaker: Don Buchanan
Year of foundation: 1969
Tonnes crushed on average each year: (from
Arrowfield's own Hunter Vineyard) 620,
balance from other sources including Cowra,
Barossa and McLaren Vale about 1800 tonnes
Location: Jerry's Plains
Area: 65 ha
Soils: coarse chocolate brown sandy loam
interspersed with clay, deep and free-draining
but not fertile
Varieties planted: White—chardonnay,
sauvignon blanc, semillon; Red—cabernet
sauvignon, merlot, pinot noir, shiraz
Leading wines: Arrowfield Show Reserve range
(which includes Chardonnay, Cabernet
Sauvignon, Shiraz and Semillon)
Notes: Arrowfield was prophetically named, as
it was destined to undergo the 'slings and
arrows of outrageous fortune' in its very first
decade. It narrowly missed the Hunter red
boom of the 1960s and early 1970s, then was
faced with the white boom of the mid-1970s,
having virtually an entirely red vineyard. It also
suffered from the poor economics of Hunter
winegrowing at that time and soon entire
vineyards of shiraz were being top-grafted if
possible, or uprooted if not. Since then quite a

few changes of ownership have occurred, but
its winemaking has been consistent and
dedicated to quality, which is maintained to
the present time. Its Show Reserve range of
wines is often very impressive, as it has chosen
to buy select parcels of fruit from other
regions. Cellar door sales: 7 days 10am–5pm.
Restaurant open for lunch Wed–Sun.

Barrington Estate   R7

Yarraman Road, Wybong, NSW 2333
Ph 02 6547 8118, Fax 02 6547 8039

Owners: Gary and Karen Blom
Chief winemaker: contract
Year of foundation: 1960
Tonnes crushed on average each year: 450
Location: Wybong
Area: 70 ha (with a further 60 ha planned
before the turn of the century)
Soils: light sandy loam, heavy black loam, red
podsols
Varieties planted: White—chardonnay,
semillon; Red—cabernet sauvignon, merlot,
shiraz
Leading wines: Yarraman Road Chardonnay,
Cabernet Shiraz
Notes: Since 1994, the Blom family have
owned what was once Penfolds Dalwood
Estate at Wybong, which was sold by that
company in 1978 to Rosemount Estate. The
early history of Wybong Estate, which at its
zenith comprised about 180 ha of vineyard,
was unfortunate. There was little, if any,
irrigation and many grape varieties were
planted on unsuitable soils. Despite the quality
of some of the early wines from Wybong, for
Penfolds, it turned out to be an economic
disaster. Though irrigation was installed in the
early 1970s, it was then necessary to graft over
many red varieties to white to meet the white
wine boom of the mid-1970s. These economic
shocks at Wybong were perhaps the major
reason for their decision to leave the Hunter
Valley in 1978 after a presence there of

70 years. It fell to the succeeding owner, Rosemount, to rectify the Wybong Estate and to make effective use of the large winery on the site, which they did until 1992 when it became a storage facility. Cellar door sales by appointment only.

Belbourie Wines **R5**

Branxton Road, Rothbury, NSW 2321
Ph 02 4938 1556

Owner: Roberts family
Winemaker: Bob Davies
Year of foundation: 1964
Tonnes crushed on average each year: 10
Location: Rothbury
Area: 2 ha
Soils: sandy loam and ironstone gravel
Varieties planted: White—semillon; Red—none
Leading wines: Belbourie Belah, Barramundi (both made from semillon), Bunyan Shiraz
Notes: This old-established vineyard is now in its second generation of Roberts' family ownership. Cellar door sales: weekends and holidays to 6pm.

Beyond Broke Vineyard **NR**

Cobcroft Road, Broke, NSW 2330
(opp Hill of Hope Winery)
Ph/Fax 02 4362 1702

Owners: Robert and Terry Kennedy
Chief winemaker: Andrew Margan (contract)
Year of foundation: 1996
Tonnes crushed on average each year: 85 and increasing
Location: Broke
Area: 22.8 ha
Soils: basalt volcanic red to chocolate clays
Varieties planted: White—chardonnay, semillon, verdelho; Red—none
Leading wines: Beyond Broke Chardonnay, Semillon, Verdelho
Notes: In 1996 the Kennedy family purchased an older vineyard, originally established about

1980, and are in the process of restoring it. Their first vintage was 1997. There are no cellar door sales at the present time.

Bimbadgen Estate **NR**

Lot 21 McDonalds Road, Pokolbin, NSW 2320
Ph 02 4998 7585, Fax 02 4998 7732

Owner: Mulpha Pty Ltd
Chief winemaker: Kees Van de Scheur
Year of foundation: 1972 (as Bimbadgen since 1996)
Tonnes crushed on average each year: 375
Location: Pokolbin
Area: 44 ha
Soils: loam over clay, un-fertile
Varieties planted: White—chardonnay, semillon; Red—cabernet sauvignon
Leading wines: Bimbadgen Shiraz, Chardonnay, Cabernet Sauvignon, Semillon
Notes: Bimbadgen is yet another incarnation of the McPherson winery erected in 1972, which has passed through three proprietorships between times. It is now Bimbadgen—may fortune shine upon it! Cellar door sales: Mon–Fri 9.30am–4.30pm, weekends and public holidays 10am–5pm.

Blaxlands Vineyards **NR**

Broke Road, Pokolbin, NSW 2320
Ph 02 4998 7550, Fax 02 4998 7802

Owner: Chris Barnes
Chief winemaker: Trevor Drayton (contract) in consultation with Chris Barnes
Year of foundation: 1976
Tonnes crushed on average each year: 7
Location: Pokolbin
Area: 2.5 ha
Soils: deep red cracking clays over clay subsoil
Varieties planted: White—chardonnay, semillon; Red—none
Leading wines: Blaxlands Chardonnay, Chardonnay Semillon

Notes: A small producer as both vineyard area and crush suggest, Blaxlands makes full-bodied whites which are available at Blaxlands Restaurant and Wines Sales, close to the vineyard, at usual cellar door hours.

Brian McGuigan Wines R6.5

Cnr McDonalds and Broke Roads,
Pokolbin, NSW 2320
Ph 02 4998 7400, Fax 02 4998 7401

Owner: Brian McGuigan Wines Ltd
Chief winemaker: Peter Hall
Year of foundation: 1992
Tonnes crushed on average each year: 4000
Location: (Lower Hunter) Pokolbin—Hunter Ridge 32 ha, winery block 3 ha. (Central Hunter Valley) Broke Fordwich—Spring Mountain 42 ha, Saxonvale 72 ha, Yellowrock 17.2 ha. (Upper Hunter) Richmond Grove 112 ha, Hollydeen 40 ha, Denman 56 ha
Area: 374.2 ha
Soils: (Lower Hunter) Hunter Ridge—red podsols, sandy loam and yellow clay; Winery Block— red podsols over clay. (Broke Fordwich) Saxonvale—deep red loam, alluvial sand; Spring Mountain—chiefly sandy loam; Yellowrock—fertile sandy loam. (Upper Hunter) Denman—rich black alluvial loam; Hollydeen— brown alluvials, red podsols; Richmond Grove—sandy loam.
Varieties planted: White—chardonnay, semillon, verdelho; Red—cabernet sauvignon, merlot, shiraz
Leading wines: Brian McGuigan Wines currently has several ranges of wines: the export range at the cheaper end of the market as exemplified by wines such as First Harvest Semillon Chardonnay (in origin chiefly from South East Australia); the Bin range such as Bin 2000 Hermitage (from South Australia); and the Personal Reserve and Shareholders' range consisting of wines such as McGuigan Brothers Personal Reserve Chardonnay. There is also a Hermitage Road range, named after the former

Orlando-Wyndham Hermitage winery, recently repurchased from that company.
Notes: Is there life after Wyndham Estate? Certainly for Brian McGuigan. His namesake publicly listed company currently occupies the former Hungerford Hill winery and crushes about 4000 tonnes from extensive Hunter vineyards, although vineyard resources throughout Australia are much larger. The quality of the Personal Reserve and Shareholders' range is good, while the other ranges will appeal to the price-conscious.

Briar Ridge Vineyard R8

Mount View Road, Mount View via Cessnock, NSW 2325
Ph 02 4990 3670, Fax 02 4990 7802

Owners: John Davis and Neil McGuigan
Chief winemaker: Neil McGuigan
Year of foundation: 1972
Tonnes crushed on average each year: 250
Location: Mount View
Area: 50 ha
Soils: red loam over limestone
Varieties planted: White—chardonnay, sauvignon blanc, semillon, traminer, verdelho, viognier; Red—cabernet sauvignon, merlot, shiraz
Leading wines: Briar Ridge Stockhausen Semillon, Shiraz, Chairman's Chardonnay
Notes: Formerly one of the leading Hunter boutique wineries, belonging to Murray Robson as Squire Vineyard, then as the Robson Vineyard, Briar Ridge was purchased and renamed by John Davis in the late 1980s. Since then production and area have expanded substantially but quality has remained high. With Neil McGuigan joining the partnership in 1994 as winemaker, the reputation of Briar Ridge should only increase. Winemaker emeritus Karl Stockhausen, nationally renowned for the Hunter Semillons made by him for Lindemans, remains as consultant.

Brickman's Vineyard NR

Lot 28 Wollombi Road, Payne's Crossing, NSW 2330
Ph 02 4998 3358

Owners: Rodowicz family
Chief winemaker: (contract)
Year of foundation: 1994
Tonnes produced on average each year: 16
Location: Broke Fordwich
Area: 2.5 ha
Soils: sandy alluvial loam
Varieties planted: White—chardonnay, semillon; Red—muscat
Leading wines: Brickman Chardonnay, Brickman Semillon
Notes: Peter Rodowicz is the originator of the city vigneron franchise concept (owned by his company Loaa Pty Ltd, see entry on Van de Scheur Wines). There are no cellar door sales.

Broke Estate on Monkey Place Creek R6.5

Broke, NSW 2330
Ph 02 6572 4028, Fax 02 6572 1513

Owners: Bill and Bliss Ryan
Chief winemakers: Simon Gilbert Wine Services and Hill of Hope Winery (contract)
Year of foundation: 1988
Tonnes crushed on average each year: 260
Location: Broke
Area: 16 ha
Soils: sandy loam alluvial
Varieties planted: White—chardonnay, sauvignon blanc; Red—cabernet sauvignon, cabernet franc
Leading wines: Broke Estate Chardonnay, Cabernets
Notes: Bill Ryan is the grower of a very flavoursome Chardonnay and the Chairman of the Broke Fordwich Wine Company Pty Ltd, established to promote and sell the wines of the new Broke Fordwich sub-region. No cellar door sales

Broke Fordwich Wine Co Pty Ltd NR

Po Box 116, Broke, NSW 2330

Owners: This is a private company formed in 1997 by 21 winegrowers within the Broke Fordwich sub-region to promote and sell the wines of the sub-region.

Brokenwood Wines NR

McDonalds Road, Pokolbin, NSW 2320
Ph 02 4998 7559, Fax 02 4998 7893

Owner: Brokenwood Wines Pty Ltd
Chief winemaker: Iain Riggs
Year of foundation: 1970
Tonnes crushed on average each year: 1000
Location: Pokolbin
Area: 15.5 ha
Soils: dry loam over clay, known locally as Pokolbin red podsols
Varieties planted: White—chardonnay, semillon; Red—cabernet sauvignon, merlot, shiraz
Leading wines: Brokenwood Graveyard Shiraz, Hunter Valley Semillon
Notes: Brokenwood is the vineyard of which the author was one of three founding partners in 1970. It began to change from its 'hobby' status in 1975, when an adequate winery was built to accommodate what was hoped to be 20–30 tonnes of fruit. That hope was never fulfilled, at least not from the original Brokenwood vineyard. The change continued in 1978 when what was to be called the Graveyard Vineyard was purchased from the then large Hunter company, Hungerford Hill. The company was at that time very much concerned, along with many other Hunter producers, by the financial problems created by the poor economics of, and the poor public response to, Hunter Valley Shiraz. At Brokenwood, new partnership equity had been progressively introduced since the mid-1970s and with it came new enthusiasm from those

doctors, geologists, marine biologists and company executives who so willingly devoted their weekends to vineyard and winery activity. In 1982, a trickle of white wine was made and when Iain Riggs joined Brokenwood late in that year to supervise the construction of a 200-tonne winery and all wine production thereafter, Brokenwood ceased to be a hobby. Since then, wine production has increased substantially and Brokenwood wine horizons, never limited solely to the Hunter Valley, have expanded to become national. It is fair to say that national respect for Brokenwood now justifies those national horizons. Its wine portfolio concentrates on quality. From the Hunter there is Graveyard Shiraz, an estate wine totally restricted to its Graveyard Vineyard origin and not only to origin but to ultimate quality as well (in poor Hunter years—and they happen all too often—Graveyard Shiraz is declassified and does not appear). There is also Hunter Valley Semillon, iconoclastic in that, when young, it is fresh and lemony in aroma, avoiding the neutrality of many young Hunter Semillons, but, like the best of its breed, maturing well over 6–10 years to a nutty, honeyed excellence. Due to my ongoing involvement with Brokenwood, I have not rated it. Cellar door sales: every day 10am–5pm except Christmas and Good Friday.

Calais Estates **R6**

Palmers Lane, Pokolbin, NSW 2320
Ph 02 4998 7654, Fax 02 4998 7813

Owner/chief winemaker: Colin Peterson
Year of foundation: 1987 as Calais Estates, prior to that it was known as Wollundry
Tonnes crushed on average each year: 600
Location: Pokolbin
Area: 10 ha
Soils: volcanic soil on hills, light sandy loam over yellow clay
Varieties planted: White—chardonnay, semillon; Red—cabernet sauvignon, shiraz

Leading wines: Calais Estate Reserve Shiraz, Chardonnay, Cabernet Sauvignon
Notes: Colin Peterson is an experienced Hunter winemaker whose Chardonnays have an excellent show record. Cellar door sales: 9am–5pm each day except Sunday 10am–5pm.

Casuarina Vineyard (vineyard only) **NR**

Hermitage Road, Pokolbin, NSW 2320

Owner: Peter Meier
Year of foundation: 1970
Tonnes produced on average each year: 32
Location: Pokolbin
Area: 5 ha
Soils: sandy alluvial loams
Varieties planted: White—chardonnay, sauvignon blanc, semillon; Red—none
Leading wines: all grapes are sold
Notes: Casuarina Estate is owned by well-known Hunter food identity Peter Meier, who curiously enough appears to have resisted the temptation to sell his own wine through his Casuarina restaurant. There are no cellar door facilities.

Capercaillie **R7.5**

Londons Road, Lovedale, NSW 2325
Ph 02 4990 2904, Fax 02 4991 1886

Owners: Alasdair and Patricia Sutherland
Winemaker: Alasdair Sutherland
Year of foundation: 1975 (vineyard planted by former owner, Ben Dawson)
Tonnes crushed on average each year: 75
Location: Lovedale
Area: 5.6 ha
Soils: alluvial loam, red podsols
Varieties planted: White—chardonnay, gewurztraminer; Red—none
Leading wines: Capercaillie Chardonnay, Unoaked Chardonnay, Gewurztraminer Dessert Style
Notes: Old Hunter hand Alasdair Sutherland,

formerly chief winemaker of the now defunct Saxonvale Estate at Broke, is a well-respected and experienced professional. After some years out of the industry running a restaurant on the north coast of New South Wales, he returned to the Hunter, purchasing the former Dawson Vineyard in 1995. His expertise with chardonnay is renowned and he has decided to purchase all his red grapes and semillon. From local sources and the Hastings Valley come semillon, shiraz and chambourcin, while from the exciting Orange area and the premium Coonawarra region come the 'Bordeaux' brigade (cabernets sauvignon and franc and merlot). The results will be highly palatable. Cellar door sales: Mon–Sat 9am–5pm and Sun 10am–5pm.

Caprera Grove
(vineyard only) NR

697 Milbrodale Road, Broke, NSW 2330
Ph 02 6579 1344, Fax 02 6579 1355

Owners: Christopher and Belinda Elsmore
Chief winemaker: not yet appointed
Year of foundation: 1995
Tonnes crushed on average each year: none yet, but when the vineyard is wholly planted and the vines are in bearing, about 80 tonnes are anticipated
Location: Broke Fordwich
Area: 8 ha
Soils: sandy loam, alluvial over clay, podsols
Varieties planted: chardonnay only at time of writing, but semillon and more chardonnay will be added as well as shiraz
Leading wines: no wines yet made
Notes: Caprera Grove is quite small, but it amply illustrates the enthusiasm and enterprise of many Australians who wish to establish their own vineyards. If only James Busby could realise what he started. No cellar door sales at the present time as no wine will be available until the year 2000.

Catherine Vale Vineyard NR

Milbrodale Road, Bulga, NSW 2330
Ph/Fax 02 6579 1334

Owners: Bill and Wendy Lawson
Chief winemaker: Horseshoe Wines (contract)
Year of foundation: 1993
Tonnes crushed on average each year: 34 (1997 first vintage), but this may increase as the vines come into full bearing
Location: Bulga
Area: 4.2 ha
Soils: sandy loam over clay
Varieties planted: White—chardonnay, semillon; Red—none
Leading wines: Catherine Vale Chardonnay, Semillon
Notes: Catherine Vale is not only a totally different lifestyle, but a new and very busy occupation for retired schoolteachers Bill and Wendy Lawson. Like many new small vineyards throughout Australia, it is all their own work. First vintage was 1997 in this presently all white vineyard and cellar door facilities were opened in August that year. Cellar door sales: weekend and public holidays 10am–4pm, other times by appointment.

Chateau Francois R7

Broke Road, Pokolbin, NSW 2321
Ph 02 4998 7548, Fax 02 4998 7805

Owner/chief winemaker: Dr Don Francois
Year of foundation: 1969
Tonnes crushed on average each year: 9
Location: Pokolbin
Area: 2.4 ha
Soils: sandy, clayey soils
Varieties planted: White—semillon; Red—pinot noir, shiraz
Leading wines: Chateau Francois Shiraz Noir, Semillon
Notes: Don Francois is an old Hunter hand and his 'Chateau' perhaps the first of the mini-wine ventures of the first Hunter wine boom of the

late 1960s. Certainly it is the oldest survivor. It was designed originally as a one-man operation with assistance from friends at crucial times of the year. In the shadow of the Brokenback Range and protected from southerly weather, it is beautifully sited on a north-facing hill with extensive views over the Hunter Valley and the distant Barrington Tops. Despite winning many awards at wine shows over the years, Don has resisted what must have been a great temptation to expand. His Semillon is one of the more reliable traditionally made whites of the Valley and his red blend pleasantly soft and easy-drinking. Cellar door sales are available by appointment.

Chateau Pato **R7**

Thompson's Road, Pokolbin, NSW 2320
Ph 02 4998 7634

Owner: Helen Paterson
Chief winemaker: Nicholas Paterson
Year of foundation: 1980
Tonnes crushed on average each year: 6
Location: Pokolbin
Area: 2 ha
Soils: red volcanic loams, black loams
Varieties planted: White—chardonnay;
Red—pinot noir, shiraz
Leading wines: Chateau Pato Shiraz
Notes: Chateau Pato was founded by the late David Paterson, 'Pato' to his many friends. He was a very popular media personality and a great enthusiast for the Hunter and its wines. Chateau Pato Shiraz continues his memory. Cellar door sales by appointment.

Cockfighters Ghost *(vineyard only)* **R6**

Milbrodale Road, Broke, NSW 2330
Ph 02 9237 3413

Owner: David Clarke
Chief winemaker: Neil McGuigan (contract)
Year of foundation: unknown but believed to

be a soldier-settlement block originally planted about 1920
Tonnes crushed on average each year: 90
Location: Broke
Area: 10 ha
Soils: alluvial sandy loam
Varieties planted: White—chardonnay, semillon; Red—shiraz
Leading wines: Cockfighters Ghost Chardonnay, Semillon, Shiraz
Notes: Cockfighters Ghost is not a second label of Poole's Rock as is sometimes thought, but a stand-alone brand with its own supporting vineyard. Neil McGuigan makes the Chardonnay, Semillon and Shiraz while Phil Ryan does the Unwooded Chardonnay. Pinot Noir, made by John Wade and sourced from Pemberton and Mount Barker in Western Australia, is also available, as is a Hunter Verdelho. No cellar door sales.

Constable & Hershon Vineyards **R5**

1 Gillards Road, Pokolbin, NSW 2320
Ph/Fax 02 4998 7667

Owners: Constable and Hershon families
Chief winemaker: Neil McGuigan (contract)
Year of foundation: 1982
Tonnes crushed on average each year: 40
Location: Pokolbin
Area: 6.3 ha
Soils: red volcanic soils
Varieties planted: White—chardonnay;
Red—cabernet sauvignon, merlot
Leading wines: Constable & Hershon Chardonnay, Cabernet Merlot
Notes: This is a boutique vineyard set beside four gardens, one 'secret' and others of roses, herbs and sculptures. Cellar door sales: 7 days 10am–5pm and garden tours available.

Cruickshank Calatoota Estate R5

2656 Wybong Road, Wybong,
NSW 2333
Ph 02 6547 8149, Fax 02 6547 8144

Owner: John Cruickshank
Chief winemaker: Hartley Smithers
Year of foundation: 1974
Tonnes crushed on average each year: 100
Location: Wybong
Area: 10.2 ha
Soils: sandy loams graduating to heavy black
soil
Varieties planted: White—none; Red—cabernet
franc, cabernet sauvignon, shiraz
Leading wines: Cabernet Rose, Cabernet
Sauvignon Vat 1, Two Cabernets
Notes: Calatoota is the realised dream of John
Cruickshank and now one of the older estates
of the Upper Hunter. It relies entirely on its
own fruit and has always specialised in red
wine. Some years ago and much against the
trend of fashion, it added to its list a Cabernet
Rose which has since become very popular.
Cellar door sales: winter 7 days 9am–5pm,
summer 7 days 9am–6pm.

Cullingral Vineyard NR

Merriwa, NSW 2329 (on the Merriwa
River, 17 km south of the town)
Ph 02 9938 5166, Fax 02 9938 4786

Owners: Patricia and Michael Laurence
Chief winemaker: John Hordern (contract)
Year of foundation: 1986
Tonnes crushed on average each year: 8
Location: Merriwa, Upper Hunter
Area: 3 ha
Soils: sandy loam over clay and in parts over
sandy gravel
Varieties planted: White—semillon;
Red—shiraz
Leading wines: Cullingral Shiraz, Semillon
Notes: This is a small Upper Hunter vineyard
developed slowly in the dry-land tradition of

the Hunter region, irrigation being used only to
alleviate vine stress. After 10 years trialling
various clones, Michael Laurence feels
equipped to plant two more hectares. There
are no cellar door sales.

De Iuliis Vineyards NR

Lot 1 Lovedale Road, Keinbah,
NSW 2321
Ph 02 4930 7403, Fax 02 4968 8192

Owners: G and AM De Iuliis
Chief winemaker: David Hook (contract)
Year of foundation: 1990
Tonnes crushed on average each year: 100
Location: Keinbah
Area: 15 ha
Soils: heavy clay loam, acidic, some cracking
clays (Biscay)
Varieties planted: White—chardonnay,
semillon, verdelho; Red—merlot, shiraz
Leading wines: De Iuliis Chardonnay, Shiraz
Notes: The De Iuliis family is a recently
established Hunter grower and of good size,
retaining about 15 tonnes for their own label
and selling the rest. To date one silver and four
bronze medals have been awarded at various
Hunter Valley Wine Shows during the 1990s.
Tasting is by appointment only.

Reg Drayton Wines Pty Ltd NR

Cnr McDonalds and Pokolbin Mountain
Roads, Pokolbin, NSW 2320
Ph/Fax 02 4998 7523

Owner: Robyn Drayton
Chief winemakers: Andrew Spinaze and
Andrew Thomas (contract)
Year of foundation: 1989
Tonnes crushed on average each year: 80
Location: Pokolbin (two separate vineyards—
Pokolbin Hills, Lambkin Estate)
Area: 13.7 ha
Soils: (Pokolbin Hills) light alluvial loam;
(Lambkin) red basalt loam

Varieties planted: White—chardonnay, semillon, verdelho; Red—shiraz
Leading wines: Reg Drayton Lambkin Semillon, Pokolbin Hills Chardonnay, Pokolbin Hills Shiraz
Notes: Established by the late Reg Drayton in 1989 and now successfully carried on by Robyn Drayton, Reg Drayton Wines is a small- to medium-sized family winery specialising in typical Hunter whites and reds, which regularly win awards at the Hunter Valley and various capital city wine shows. Another speciality is the Port Crock. Cellar door sales: 7 days 10am–5pm.

W Drayton & Sons Pty Ltd R7

Bellevue Winery, Oakey Creek Road, Pokolbin, NSW 2320
Ph 02 4998 7513, Fax 02 4998 7743

Owners: Drayton family
Chief winemaker: Trevor Drayton
Year of foundation: 1853
Tonnes crushed on average each year: 1200
Location: Pokolbin (Bellevue and Oakey Creek)
Area: 100 ha
Soils: sandy alluvial loam over clay on Oakey Creek. Slightly heavier loam again over clay by the winery at Bellevue
Varieties planted: White—chardonnay, semillon, verdelho; Red—cabernet sauvignon, merlot, shiraz
Leading wines: Drayton Semillon, Chardonnay, Verdelho, William Shiraz
Notes: Drayton's (with Tyrrells) is one of the ancestral wineries of the Hunter Valley, its equally ancestral log press (long since retired) bearing mute testament to its seniority. It restricts its winemaking to Hunter fruit only and will celebrate its 150th anniversary in 2003. Of its wine range, its Chardonnay is often very good (its 1979 was excellent) and its Shiraz is of the traditional Hunter style. Cellar door sales: Mon–Fri 8am–5pm, weekends 10am–5pm.

Drew's Creek Wines NR

Lot 5 Wollombi Road, Broke, NSW 2330
Ph/Fax 02 6579 1062

Owners: Graeme Gibson and Jennifer Burns
Chief winemaker: David Lowe (contract)
Year of foundation: 1992
Tonnes crushed on average each year: 60
Location: Broke
Area: 5 ha
Soils: alluvial flat, mountain wash (rocky, pebbly) soils
Varieties planted: White—chardonnay; Red—merlot
Leading wines: Drew's Creek Chardonnay, Merlot
Notes: Graeme Gibson is an energetic lawyer-winegrower, who has been largely instrumental in creating and organising the Broke Fordwich sub-region of the Hunter. Yet Drew's Creek Wines, in its selection of grape varieties, has departed somewhat from Hunter tradition. There is not a semillon or shiraz vine anywhere in sight. However, as Hunter varieties go, merlot is very promising and chardonnay is always generously flavoured. Cellar door sales by appointment only.

Elysium Vineyard NR

Milbrodale Road, Broke, NSW 2330
Ph/Fax 02 9664 2368

Owner: Dr Victoria Foster
Chief winemaker: Tyrrells (contract)
Year of foundation: 1985
Tonnes produced on average each year: 9
Location: Broke
Area: 1 ha
Soils: sandy loam over gravel, alluvial
Varieties planted: White—verdelho; Red—none
Leading wine: Elysium Verdelho
Notes: A very small vineyard with a verdelho monoculture and a cottage which

accommodates from 2–14 persons. Cellar door sales available when there are no guests. Otherwise the wine is sold locally to the better restaurants of the region.

Evans Family R8

Lot 157 Palmers Lane, Pokolbin, NSW 2321
Ph 02 4998 7333, Fax 02 4998 7798

Owner: Len Evans Holdings Pty Ltd
Chief winemaker: Keith Tulloch (contract)
Year of foundation: 1976
Tonnes crushed on average each year: 30
Location: Pokolbin
Area: 7 ha
Soils: oxidised basalt on limestone, sandy clay soils
Varieties planted: White—chardonnay; Red—gamay, pinot noir
Leading wine: Evans Family Chardonnay
Notes: The winner of *Decanter*'s Wineman of the Year award in 1997, Len Evans is the larger than life character of Australian wine. His almost modest vineyard in the Hunter Valley testifies to his broader sphere of loyalty. He is no mere Hunter spokesman. He is a man of national concept, rather than local detail, very much preferring the big picture to the domestic miniature. Perhaps this is why the Evans Family Vineyard is not quite as well known as it should be. Its Chardonnay is always worthwhile seeking out for its consistently good quality in all years. Cellar door sales by appointment only.

Farrell's Limestone Creek Vineyard NR

Mount View Road, Mount View via Cessnock, NSW 2325
Ph 02 4991 2808, Fax 02 4991 3414

Owners: John and Camille Farrell
Chief winemaker: Neil McGuigan (contract)
Year of foundation: 1981

Tonnes crushed on average each year: 58
Location: Mount View
Area: 7.2 ha
Soils: red loam over limestone
Varieties planted: White—chardonnay, sauvignon blanc, semillon, verdelho; Red—cabernet sauvignon, merlot, pinot noir, shiraz
Leading wines: Limestone Creek Chardonnay, Semillon
Notes: This is a small family vineyard, beautifully sited on a hillside in the picturesque Mount View district. It has about a thousand cases of wine made each vintage for cellar door purposes and sells the rest of its fruit to wineries. It exhibits with some success in local wine shows. Cellar door sales: weekends and public holidays 10am–5pm.

Foate's Ridge NR

Lot 24 Fordwich Road, Broke, NSW 2330
Mail: PO Box 1749, Neutral Bay NSW 2089
Ph 02 6579 1284, Fax 02 9904 4196

Owner: Anthony JM Foate
Chief winemaker: Drayton's Family Wines (contract)
Year of foundation: 1991
Tonnes crushed on average each year: 75
Location: Broke
Area: 6 ha
Soils: chiefly light alluvial loam; the balance is deep red volcanic loam
Varieties planted: White—chardonnay, verdelho; Red—none
Leading wine: Foate's Ridge Chardonnay
Notes: Foate's Ridge is a vineyard only, selling its fruit to Drayton's Family Wines and receiving wine in return for sale under the Foate's Ridge label. The wine is available by mail order from Anthony Foate or from the Broke Village Store. There are no current cellar door sales

Fordwich Estate Vineyard NR

2 Fordwich Road, Fordwich via Broke,
NSW 2330
Ph/Fax 02 6579 1197

Owners: Warren and Julia Moore
Chief winemaker: Andrew Margan (contract)
Year of foundation: 1991
Tonnes crushed on average each year: 120
Location: Fordwich
Area: 10 ha
Soils: half red basalt, half sandy alluvial loam
Varieties planted: White—chardonnay,
verdelho; Red—cabernet sauvignon, merlot
Leading wines: Fordwich Estate, Chardonnay,
Verdelho, Cabernet Sauvignon, Merlot
Notes: Warren and Julia Moore sell most of
their crop to winemakers in the district,
retaining about 10% (800 cases) for their own
wine sales requirements. There are no cellar
door sales at present.

Glenguin Wine Company R7

River Oaks Vineyard
Lot 8 Milbrodale Road, Broke,
NSW 2330
Ph 02 6579 1011, Fax 02 6579 1009

Owners: Tedder family
Chief winemaker: Robin Tedder with the advice
of Andrew Caillard MW (wine is made at
Simon Gilbert's winery)
Year of foundation: 1988
Tonnes crushed on average each year: 135
Location: Broke
Area: 16 ha
Soils: deep red weathered basalt and pebbley
clay, overlain in parts by alluvial sandy loam
Varieties planted: White—chardonnay,
semillon; Red—shiraz
Leading wines: Glenguin Chardonnay,
Unwooded Chardonnay, Semillon
Notes: Glenguin has two labels, Glenguin for
the pick of the vintage and River Oaks for
some or all of the rest. Its first commercially

released wine was a very promising Semillon.
Doubtless, this will be the first of many
excellent whites. Its reds are awaited. Cellar
door sales presently by appointment.

Good Shepherd Vineyard (vineyard only) NR

Mount View Road, Mount View,
NSW 2325 (adjoining Briar Ridge)
Ph 02 4926 1211, Fax 02 4926 1193

Owners: Robert and Anne Foggo
Chief winemaker: no wine yet made
Year of foundation: 1996
Tonnes crushed on average each year:
none yet
Location: Mount View
Area: 3 ha
Soils: red volcanic clay over limestone
Varieties planted: White—none; Red—shiraz
Leading wines: for the future, Shiraz, but there
are no wines yet produced from this vineyard
Notes: It is early days for Mount View Ridge.
No cellar door sales.

Herlstone Vineyard (vineyard only) NR

Cnr Branxton Road and Palmers Lane,
Pokolbin, NSW 2321

Owner: Herlstone Vineyard Pty Ltd
Chief winemaker: none, the vineyard sells all
its fruit
Year of foundation: 1969
Tonnes crushed on average each year: 240
Location: Pokolbin
Area: 26 ha
Soils: brown red podsols over a limestone ridge
(top of hill), heavy clay at the bottom of the
slope
Varieties planted: White—semillon; Red—pinot
noir, merlot, shiraz
Leading wines: none, all fruit sold
Notes: Before being sold some years ago,
Herlstone was one of the jewels of the

Rothbury crown, producing delicate Semillons which were always a delight to drink.

Hill of Hope Winery   **R6.5**

Cobcroft Road, Broke, NSW 2330
Ph 02 6579 1161, Fax 02 6579 1373

Owner: Michael Hope
Chief winemaker: Andrew Margan
Year of foundation: 1995
Tonnes crushed on average each year: 170 (1997) but will increase as new plantings come into bearing, ultimately (by the year 2001) 685 tonnes are planned to be crushed
Location: There are three vineyards, Hope Estate at Milbrodale Road, Broke, a second around the winery and a third, Troon, at Whittingham near Singleton
Area: 68 ha (Hope Estate 30 ha, Winery 25 ha, Troon 13 ha)
Soils: (Hope Estate) alluvial sandy loam with spots of clay; (Winery) rich red basalt over clay; (Troon) alluvial sandy loam
Varieties planted: White—chardonnay, semillon; Red—cabernet sauvignon, merlot, pinot noir, shiraz
Leading wines: Hill of Hope Bin 1 Chardonnay (first made in 1996)
Notes: Hill of Hope is a reincarnation of the old Saxonvale winery and Michael Hope, a successful pharmacist with no particular wine background, is a man with a mission, and that is not only to create his own successful Hill of Hope brand, which will on present projected tonnages be producing over 50 000 cases of wine by the year 2001 but also to bring the Broke Fordwich sub-region into national and perhaps even international prominence.
Cellar door sales: 7 days 10am–4pm.

Hillside Vineyard
(Vineyard only)   **NR**

Lot 2 Marrowbone Road, Pokolbin, NSW 2320
Ph 02 4991 4370

Owners: EM and RJ Barnum
Chief winemaker: none
Year of foundation: 1979
Tonnes produced on average each year: 100
Location: Pokolbin
Area: 14 ha
Soils: red podsols, alluvial river loam and black basalt over slate and limestone
Varieties planted: White—chardonnay, traminer, verdelho; Red—cabernet sauvignon, merlot, shiraz
Leading wines: no wine is produced, all grapes are sold

Hollyclare Vineyard   **NR**

Milbrodale Road, Broke, NSW 2330
Ph 02 6579 1193, Fax 02 6579 1269

Owner: Ballingarry Holdings Pty Ltd (the Holdsworth family)
Chief winemaker: Tamburlaine (contract)
Year of foundation: 1989
Tonnes crushed on average each year: 20
Location: Broke
Area: 5 ha
Soils: sited on a slope, the vineyard soils vary from a deep sandy alluvial loam to a more shallow clay loam on the hillside
Varieties planted: White—chardonnay, semillon; Red—shiraz
Leading wine: Hollyclare Chardonnay
Notes: Situated in the fast-growing Broke area, Hollyclare is a small family-owned vineyard producing about 1500 cases of white and red wine per year. Cellar door sales: weekends 10am–5pm.

Honey Tree Estate Wines   **NR**

16 Gillards Road, Pokolbin, NSW 2320
Ph/Fax 02 4998 7693

Owners: David and Anne Leary
Chief winemaker: (contract)
Year of foundation: 1970
Tonnes crushed on average each year: 50

Location: Pokolbin
Area: 9 ha
Soils: clay
Varieties planted: White—clairette,
gewurztraminer, semillon; Red—cabernet
sauvignon, shiraz
Leading wines: Honey Tree Estate Clairette
Notes: Accommodation is available. Cellar door
sales: 7 days 10am–5pm.

Horseshoe Vineyard   R6.5

Horseshoe Road, Horseshoe Valley via
Denman, NSW 2328
Ph 02 6547 3528, Fax 02 6547 3548

Owner: Anthony Hordern & Sons Pty Ltd
Chief winemaker: John Hordern
Year of foundation: 1969
Tonnes crushed on average each year: 45
Location: Horseshoe Valley, Upper Hunter
Valley
Area: 10 ha
Soils: red earth over clay
Varieties planted: White—chardonnay,
semillon; Red—shiraz, zinfandel
Leading wines: Horseshoe Semillon, Horseshoe
Chardonnay
Notes: John Hordern began his winemaking
career with one advantage at least—mature
vines. His first vintage was in 1986 and since
then he has specialised in whites, semillon
particularly. As for reds, he holds out high
hopes for his new planting of zinfandel. Cellar
door sales: 10am–4pm weekends and public
holidays only, at other times by appointment.

Hungerford Hill   NR

Formerly an independent producer of Hunter
and Coonawarra wines, Hungerford Hill owned
its own winery and sales complex at the
Hungerford Village at the corner of Broke and
McDonalds Roads, Pokolbin. It was purchased
by Seppelt (then part of South Australian
Brewing) in the late 1980s for its Coonawarra

vineyards and its winery was later sold to Brian
McGuigan Wines Ltd. It now exists only as a
Southcorp brand for the marketing of regional
red and white wines of New South Wales
origin.

Inglewood Vineyard   R6.5

Yarrawa Road, Denman, NSW 2328
(about 1km south of the town)
Ph 02 6547 2556, Fax 02 6547 2546

Owner: Inglewood Vineyard Pty Ltd
Chief winemaker: Simon Gilbert (contract)
Year of foundation: 1988
Tonnes produced on average each year: 1400,
increasing to 2000 by the year 1999 when all
vines have been planted and are in bearing
Location: Denman, Upper Hunter
Area: 160 ha
Soils: alluvial sandy loam and red sandy clay
loam over sandstone
Varieties planted: White—chardonnay,
semillon, verdelho; Red—cabernet franc,
cabernet sauvignon, merlot, pinot noir, ruby
cabernet, shiraz
Leading wines: Inglewood Show Reserve range,
which includes Chardonnay, Semillon, Cabernet
Sauvignon and Shiraz
Notes: Inglewood is a large vineyard which sells
most of its fruit to an outside winery, while
retaining 15% for its own labels, Inglewood
Show Reserve and Two Rivers. No cellar door
sales at the present time, but large groups may
be catered for by appointment.

Jackson's Hill Vineyard   NR

Mount View Road, Mount View via
Cessnock, NSW 2325
Ph 02 4990 1273, Fax 02 4991 3233

Owners: Michael and Pamela Winbourne
Chief winemaker: Michael Winbourne
Year of foundation: 1984
Tonnes crushed on average each year: 18
Location: Mount View

Area: 2.5 ha
Soils: basaltic loam over limestone
Varieties planted: White—semillon; Red—
cabernet franc, cabernet sauvignon, merlot
Leading wines: Jackson's Hill Cabernet Franc,
Semillon, Late Harvest Botrytised Semillon
Notes: Jackson's Hill is spectacularly situated
above Cessnock on the scenic Mount View
Road. Cellar door sales: Thur–Mon 10am–5pm.

James Estate R5.5

Mudgee Road, Baerami via Denman,
NSW 2333
Ph 02 6547 5168, Fax 02 6547 5164

Owner: David James
Chief winemaker: Peter Orr
Year of foundation: 1971 (as Serenella), 1998
James Estate
Tonnes crushed on average each year: 150
Location: Baerami, Upper Hunter
Area: 30 ha
Soils: sandy loams over clay, red loams
Varieties planted: White—chardonnay, sylvaner;
Red—cabernet franc, cabernet sauvignon,
merlot, pinot noir, shiraz
Leading wines: James Estate Bin GCC
Chardonnay, Shiraz, Semillon, Verdelho, Merlot
Notes: This Upper Hunter estate was founded
by the late Giancarlo Cecchini in 1971 and its
winery was erected in 1990. It was sold by the
Cecchini Family in late 1997 to its present
owner. Cellar door sales: 7 days 10am–4.30pm.

Janannie Vineyard NR

Talga Road, Rothbury, NSW 2320
Ph 02 4930 7537

Owners: Ron and Margaret Keir
Chief winemaker: Ron Keir
Year of foundation: 1983
Tonnes crushed on average each year: 0.75
Location: Lovedale
Area: 0.8 ha
Soils: acidic clay

Varieties planted: White—chardonnay,
semillon; Red—cabernet sauvignon, pinot noir,
shiraz, touriga
Leading wines: Janannie Shiraz, Semillon
Notes: This is an extremely small non-irrigated
vineyard, which Ron Keir is happy to describe
as 'fun'. No cellar door sales.

Kindred's Lochleven Estate
(vineyard only) NR

McDonald's Road, Pokolbin, NSW 2320

Owners: EN Kindred, EN Kindred Pty Ltd and
Kindred's Lochleven Estate
Chief winemaker: none, wine is sometimes
made under contract, but not every year
Year of foundation: 1973
Tonnes produced on average each year: 210
Location: Pokolbin
Area: there are two vineyards, Homestead
20 ha, Lochleven 20 ha
Soils: (Homestead) red clay loam, well-drained;
(Lochleven) dark chocolate red loam over clay
Varieties planted: (Lochleven) White—
chardonnay, marsanne, semillon; Red—
cabernet sauvignon, pinot noir, shiraz.
(Homestead) White—chardonnay, semillon;
Red—shiraz
Leading wines: none
Notes: No cellar door sales.

Kurrajong Vineyard
(vineyard only) NR

Lot 4 Hermitage Road, Pokolbin,
NSW 2321
Ph 02 6574 7117

Owners: Joe and Lynda Jones
Chief winemaker: none yet
Year of foundation: 1992
Tonnes crushed on average each year:
about 50
Location: Belford
Area: 6 ha
Soils: black alluvial top soil over sandy loam
over clay over limestone

Varieties planted: White—semillon, verdelho;
Red—shiraz
Leading wines: Kurrajong Vineyard Verdelho
Notes: Kurrajong is one of the legion of small
vineyards that typify the winegrowing boom of
the late 1980s and early 1990s. The Joneses
hope to have cellar door sales within two
years. Their wine will be made by one of the
wineries in the region.

Lake's Folly R9

Broke Road, Pokolbin, NSW 2321
Ph 02 4998 7507, Fax 02 4998 7322

Owners: Lake family
Chief winemaker: Stephen Lake
Year of foundation: 1963
Tonnes crushed on average each year: 60
Location: Pokolbin
Area: 12 ha
Soils: volcanic red basalt over limestone on the
hill; sandy loam over clay on the creek flat
Varieties planted: White—chardonnay; Red—
cabernet sauvignon, merlot, petit verdot, shiraz
Leading wines: Lake's Folly Chardonnay,
Cabernets (a blend of cabernet sauvignon,
petit verdot, shiraz and merlot)
Notes: In 1963, Dr Max Lake, after leaving no
sod unturned in his search for good Hunter
Valley 'dirt' (never an easy task), decided on a
south-east facing block across the Broke Road
from McWilliam's famous Rose Hill vineyard.
The Folly, as his friends soon called it, was the
first new winery and vineyard established in
the Hunter Valley this century and remains
Australia's most famous boutique. It became,
as Max intended, instantly famous for its
Cabernet Sauvignon, a variety which is never
really favoured by Hunter Valley conditions.
Early Folly Cabernet Sauvignons had a certain
'Bordeaux' flair about them, possibly due to
new small oak with which most red consumers
of the time, including myself, had little
acquaintance, but some of them were criticised
for their disparity of fruit and oak. Whatever

the criticisms, just or unjust, the Folly Cabernet
Sauvignon (or Cabernets, as it has now
become) remains an Australian icon. The Folly
is now equally famous for its Chardonnay.
Cellar door sales: Mon–Sat 10am–4pm, closed
Sundays.

Latara (Vineyard only) NR

McDonalds Road, Pokolbin, NSW 2320
Ph 02 4998 7320

Owners: Latara Pty Ltd
Chief winemaker: no wine produced
commercially
Year of foundation: 1978
Tonnes produced on average each year: 35
Location: Pokolbin
Area: 5 ha
Soils: sandy alluvial soils
Varieties planted: White—chardonnay,
semillon; Red—shiraz
Leading wines: no wine produced
Notes: Latara is a vineyard only, but is notable
for its quite remarkable semillon. Brokenwood,
its chief purchaser, thinks so, Latara semillon
being the basis of Brokenwood Semillon since
its inception in 1983. No cellar door sales.

Lindemans Hunter River Winery R9

McDonalds Road, Pokolbin, NSW 2320
Ph 02 4998 7501, Fax 02 4998 7682

Owner: Southcorp Wines
Chief winemaker: Patrick Auld
Year of foundation: 1870
Tonnes crushed on average each year: not
disclosed but estimated at 150
Location: Pokolbin
Area: 31.7 ha (Ben Ean and Steven Vineyards)
Soils: (Ben Ean) red fertile loamy soils; (Steven)
dark brown clay loams over shaley limestone
Varieties planted: White—semillon; Red—shiraz
Leading wines: Lindemans Hunter River range,
Semillon, Chardonnay, individual vineyard

releases such as Steven Hermitage and more rarely these days older Classic Release wines
Notes: Lindeman and the Hunter Valley is one of the historic wine associations of Australia. The company was founded by Dr Lindeman at Cawarra near Gresford in the Hunter Valley in 1843 and has had a continuous presence in the Valley since that time. The move to Pokolbin took place about 1912 when the Lindeman family purchased the Ben Ean vineyard from John McDonald who had established it in 1870. It is renowned for its Semillon whites, which often age magnificently and its soft-palated welcoming Shiraz reds, which also mature extremely well. Cellar door sales: Mon–Fri 9am–4.30pm, other days 10am–4.30pm.

Little's Winery R5.5

Lot 3 Palmers Lane, Pokolbin,
NSW 2320
Ph 02 4998 7626, Fax 02 4998 7867

Owners: Little and Kindred families
Chief winemaker: Ian Little
Year of foundation: 1983
Tonnes crushed on average each year: 90
Location: Pokolbin
Area: 21 ha (two vineyards 16.5 ha and 4.5 ha)
Soils: red podsols over clay becoming sandier as the vineyard proceeds down hill
Varieties planted: White—chardonnay, semillon; Red—pinot noir, shiraz
Leading wines: Little's Black Label Chardonnay, Semillon, Shiraz
Notes: A small family-operated winery. Cellar door sales: 7 days 10am–4.30pm.

Lowe Family Wine Company NR

9 Paterson Road, Bolwarra, NSW 2320
Ph 02 4930 0233

Owners: David Lowe and Jane Wilson
Chief winemakers: David Lowe (white), Jane Wilson (red)

Year of foundation: 1996
Tonnes crushed on average each year: 160
Locations: Maitland and Mudgee
Area: 1 ha (Maitland) and 13.6 ha (Mudgee)
Soils: clay over sandstone, sand in parts
Varieties planted: (Mudgee) White—chardonnay; (Mudgee and Maitland) Red—merlot
Leading wines: Lowe Family, Unwooded Semillon, Unwooded Chardonnay, Chardonnay, Merlot, Orange Red (a blend of cabernet sauvignon, cabernet franc and merlot)
Notes: Independence for one-time Rothbury winemaker David Lowe and his wife Jane, who use their considerable talents on Hunter, Mudgee and Orange fruit. No cellar door sales.

Majors Estate (vineyard only) NR

Majors Lane, Keinbah, NSW 2321
Ph 02 4930 7328, Fax 02 9522 9355

Owners: Allan and Rosemary McMillan
Chief winemaker: Alasdair Sutherland (contract)
Year of foundation: 1988
Tonnes crushed on average each year: 50, but increasing to 100 by the year 2000 as newly planted vines come into bearing
Location: Keinbah, Lovedale
Area: 14 ha
Soils: chocolate loam and red podsols
Varieties planted: White—chardonnay, semillon; Red—chambourcin, shiraz
Leading wines: Majors Estate Chardonnay
Notes: This is a growing vineyard with an olive grove of 3 hectares and wines that are not yet produced each vintage. No cellar door sales at present.

Maluna Vineyard (vineyard only) NR

Maxwell's Road, Pokolbin, NSW 2320

Owner: Dr Don Maxwell
Chief winemaker: no wines are made
Year of foundation: 1971

Tonnes produced on average each year: 120
Location: Pokolbin
Area: 18 ha
Soils: Red podsolic and alluvial sandy soils
Varieties planted: White—chardonnay,
semillon; Red—malbec, pinot noir, shiraz
Leading wines: none
Notes: Don Maxwell is one of the many wine-
interested doctors, who was forced to choose
one career or the other. He quotes the example
of the first wine made off his vineyard which
won a gold, three silvers and a bronze award in
its short show career. Despite this, he decided
his vocation was medicine, not winemaking, but
he does retain a great enthusiasm for growing
grapes on a historic Hunter site, formerly owned
by a member of the Wilkinson family. There are
no cellar door facilities.

Margan Family Winemakers   R6.5

'Ceres Hill', Milbrodale Road, Broke,
NSW 2330
Ph/Fax 02 6579 1246

Owners: Andrew and Lisa Margan
Chief winemaker: Andrew Margan
Year of foundation: 1991
Tonnes crushed on average each year: 30, but
will increase as younger vines come into
bearing
Location: Broke
Area: 9.6 ha
Soils: sandy alluvial loams to red volcanic basalt
over sand
Varieties planted: White—chardonnay,
semillon; Red—cabernet sauvignon, shiraz
Leading wines: Margan Family, Hunter Valley
Shiraz, Hunter Valley Chardonnay, Hunter
Valley Semillon
Notes: Andrew Margan worked for Tyrrells as a
winemaker for some years before establishing
his Ceres Hill vineyard. His first vintage was in
1997. He also purchases grapes from other
local vineyards. No cellar door sales at this
stage.

Marsh Estate   R7

Deasey's Road, Pokolbin, NSW 2321
Ph 02 4998 7587, Fax 02 4998 7884

Owner/Chief winemaker: Peter Marsh
Year of foundation: 1978
Tonnes crushed on average each year: 100
Location: Pokolbin
Area: 21 ha
Soils: red volcanic loam on the hillside, sandy
soils on the creek flat and a mixture of both in
between
Varieties planted: White—chardonnay,
semillon; Red—cabernet sauvignon, merlot,
shiraz
Leading wines: Marsh Estate Chardonnay,
Marsh Estate Sauternes
Notes: Since 1978, former pharmacist Peter
Marsh has built a true wine estate in every
sense of the word. It uses only its own
(unirrigated) fruit and all wine is made there,
including a luscious botrytised Semillon which
Peter, traditionally, calls Sauternes. There is also
a Sparkling Chardonnay. Cellar door sales:
7 days, weekdays 10am–4.30pm, weekends
10am–5pm.

McLeish Estate   NR

Lot 3 De Beyers Road, Pokolbin,
NSW 2320
Ph 02 4998 7754

Owners: Bob and Maryanne McLeish
Chief winemakers: David Hook (Chardonnay,
contract) and Iain Riggs (Semillon, contract)
Year of foundation: 1992
Tonnes crushed on avearge each year: 28
Location: Pokolbin
Area: 4 ha
Soils: red podsols over clay
Varieties planted: White—chardonnay,
semillon; Red—none
Leading wines: McLeish Estate Chardonnay,
Semillon
Notes: A small estate producing the white

mainstays of the Hunter, Semillon and Chardonnay. The Semillon 96 gained a silver medal at the Hunter Valley Small Winemakers Show at Maitland in 1996. Cellar door sales: 7 days 10am–5pm from 1998.

McWilliam's Mount Pleasant R9

Marrowbone Road, Pokolbin, NSW 2321
Ph 02 4998 7505, Fax 02 4998 7761

Owner: McWilliam's Wines Pty Ltd
Chief winemaker: Phillip Ryan
Year of foundation: 1880
Tonnes crushed on average each year: 700
Location: Vineyards at three locations (Mount Pleasant, Lovedale, Rosehill)
Area: 125 ha
Soils: (Mount Pleasant) dark brown basaltic loam over limestone; (Lovedale) grey alluvial sandy loam and light clay; (Rosehill) red basaltic loam over limestone
Varieties planted: White—chardonnay, montils, semillon, verdelho; Red—cabernet franc, cabernet sauvignon, merlot, pinot noir, shiraz
Leading wines: Mount Pleasant, Elizabeth, Lovedale Semillon, Rosehill Shiraz, Maurice O'Shea Chardonnay, Shiraz. There are also special Museum releases of Elizabeth from time to time
Notes: Mount Pleasant carries on a marvellous Hunter tradition. Founded in 1880, it was owned in the 1920s and 1930s by that doyen of the Hunter Valley, the much revered Maurice O'Shea. He sold a half-share in the winery and vineyard to its present owners, the McWilliam family, in 1932, but retained his winemaking and managerial position. During the 1940s and until his death in 1956, he made some legendary reds, which are still spoken of in awe. McWilliam's is the last of the Hunter wineries to release a mature semillon, 'Elizabeth', at 5 years of age. Facilities include restaurant, barbecue/picnic area, winery tours 11am–2pm. Cellar door sales: 7 days 10am–4.30pm.

Milbrovale Estate NR

Milbrodale Road, Broke, NSW 2330
Ph 02 6579 1381, Fax 02 6579 1008

Owners: Owens family
Chief winemaker: Simon Gilbert (contract)
Year of foundation: 1996
Tonnes crushed on average each year: vineyard not yet in bearing, but anticipated to be 350 tonnes
Location: Broke
Area: 30 ha
Soils: alluvial sandy loam, red in colour
Varieties planted: White—chardonnay, semillon, verdelho; Red—shiraz
Leading wines: none yet
Notes: It is early days for Milbrovale Estate. Cellar door sales will be established in 1999.

Mistletoe Vineyard R7

Lot 1 Hermitage Road, Pokolbin, NSW 2321
Ph 02 4998 7770, Fax 02 4998 7792

Owners: Ken and Gwen Sloan
Chief winemaker: John Reynolds (contract)
Year of foundation: 1989
Tonnes crushed on average each year: 20
Location: Pokolbin
Area: 4 ha
Soils: podsols, medium to heavy clay
Varieties planted: White—chardonnay, semillon; Red—shiraz
Leading wines: Mistletoe Chardonnay, Shiraz, Semillon in traditional non-wooded style
Notes: The wines are very much in the modern yet traditional mode of the Hunter: a barrel-fermented Chardonnay, a traditional non-wooded Semillon and a full-flavoured Shiraz. The vineyard was previously part of the now-defunct Hermitage Estate, but it has more august ancestry than that, its name going back to the turn of the century as part of the old Mistletoe Farm. Cellar door sales: Thurs–Tues

11am–6pm. Two accommodation units are available for rental.

Molly Morgan Vineyard R6.5

Talga Road, Allandale, NSW 2321
Ph 02 4930 7695, Fax 02 9221 4168

Owner: A syndicate of Sydney businessmen
Chief winemaker: (contract)
Year of foundation: 1984
Tonnes crushed on average each year: 55
Location: Lovedale
Area: 10 ha
Soils: sandy loam over clay
Varieties planted: White—chardonnay, riesling, semillon; Red—shiraz
Leading wines: Molly Morgan Vineyard Joe's Block Semillon, Shiraz
Notes: There are spectacular south-west views to the Brokenback Range and a single vineyard medal-winning Semillon from Joe's Block.
Cellar door sales: 10am–5pm weekends and public holidays, other times by appointment only.

Moorebank Estate R6

Palmers Lane, Pokolbin, NSW 2320
Ph 02 4998 7610, Fax 02 4998 7367

Owners: Debra Moore and Ian Burgess
Chief winemakers: Iain Riggs (Brokenwood), Gary Reed (Calais), both by contract
Year of foundation: 1977
Tonnes crushed on average each year: 30
Location: Pokolbin
Area: 5 ha
Soils: cracking clays on the top of the hill with sandy alluvial loam on the creek flat
Varieties planted: White—chardonnay, gewurztraminer, semillon; Red—merlot
Leading wines: Moorebank Traditional Hunter Semillon, Barrel Fermented Chardonnay, Merlot
Notes: One of the prides of Moorebank is its 130-year-old ironbark press, these days in retirement as no wine is made on site. Its

Chardonnay and Semillon are very reliable and its 100% Merlot is quite a rare red among the more usual Shiraz of the Lower Hunter Valley. Cellar door sales: Fri–Mon 10am–4pm, otherwise by appointment.

Mount Eyre Vineyards (vineyard only) NR

Wollombi Road, Broke, NSW 2330
(about 1 km past Broke on the Singleton Road)
Ph/Fax 02 6579 1087

Owners: Robert and Eugenie Gillies
Chief winemakers: Simon Gilbert and Andrew Margan (contract)
Year of foundation: 1971
Tonnes crushed on average each year: 120, but expected to increase to 250 as vineyard planting is completed and the vines come into full bearing
Location: Broke
Area: 20 ha
Soils: alluvial sandy loam to loamy clay
Varieties planted: White—chardonnay, semillon; Red—cabernet franc, cabernet sauvignon, shiraz
Leading wines: no wines yet produced
Notes: Robert and Eugenie Gillies are recent vignerons having purchased Mount Eyre only in 1996, so it is quite understandable that their plans for the future are not yet settled. At present, there is no wine produced under the Mount Eyre label and there are no cellar door facilities.

Mount View Estate R7

Mount View Road, Mount View via Cessnock, NSW 2325
Ph 02 4990 3307, Fax 02 4991 1289

Owner: HW Tulloch (Mount View Wines) Pty Ltd
Chief winemaker: Keith Tulloch
Year of foundation: 1971

Tonnes crushed on average each year: 45
Location: Mount View
Area: 6 ha
Soils: deep red cracking clay over powdery
limestone, well-drained
Varieties planted: White—chardonnay,
semillon, verdelho; Red—cabernet sauvignon,
merlot, pinot noir, shiraz
Leading wines: Mount View Chardonnay,
Verdelho, Shiraz, Cabernet Sauvignon
Notes: Mount View is a well-established and
successful small producer with a solid record in
the Hunter Valley Wine Show. Cellar Door
sales: weekdays 10am–4pm, weekends and
public holidays 10am–5pm.

Murray Robson Wines R6

'Bellona', Old North Road, Rothbury,
NSW 2335
Ph 02 4938 3577, Fax 02 4938 3411

Owners: Lynley and Murray Robson
Chief winemaker: Murray Robson
Year of foundation: 1995
Tonnes crushed on average each year: 50
Location: Rothbury
Area: 4.5 ha
Soils: a hillside vineyard divided into three soils;
sandy soils over shale over clay on the creek
flat, a darker loam over friable clay in the
middle of the hill and at the top, a dark brown
loam over friable clay and some ironstone
Varieties planted: White—chardonnay,
semillon, traminer; Red—cabernet sauvignon,
merlot, muscat, pinot noir, shiraz
Leading wines: Murray Robson, Chardonnay,
Shiraz, Semillon, Cabernet Sauvignon
Notes: Murray Robson, with 25 years of Hunter
winemaking experience, is a veteran of the
region. 'Bellona' is his third essay into Hunter
winemaking, after Robson Vineyard at Mount
View and Murray Robson Wines at Halls Road,
Pokolbin. Murray hopes it is a case of third
time lucky. Cellar door is open, as Murray says,
'all day, every day.'

Oakvale Wines R6

Broke Road, Pokolbin, NSW 2320
Ph 02 4998 7520

Owners: Barry and Jan Shields
Chief winemaker: Barry Shields
Year of foundation: 1893 as Elliott's (under its
present ownership, since 1983).
Tonnes crushed on average each year: 150
Location: Pokolbin
Area: 13 ha
Soils: sandy alluvial soils over a light clay base
Varieties planted: White—chardonnay;
Red—shiraz. Hunter semillon and cabernet
sauvignon, and cabernet sauvignon from
Orange are also purchased
Leading wines: Peach Tree Unwooded
Chardonnay, Peach Tree Semillon, Peppercorn
Special Reserve Shiraz
Notes: Not only doctors but solicitors too can
retire to make wine. Barry and Jan Shields left
a busy legal life to lead an even busier vinous
one. To satisfy the palate, Barry Shields has a
range of bottle-aged whites and reds. To
satisfy the mind, he also has a good collection
of wine books, available for purchase. Cellar
door sales: 9am–5pm every day.

PJ O'Loughlin Vineyard NR

Lot 43 Milbrodale Road, Broke,
NSW 2330
Ph/Fax 02 6579 1339

Owners: PJ and M O'Loughlin
Chief winemaker: Simon Gilbert (contract)
Year of foundation: 1993
Tonnes produced/crushed on average each
year: 30
Location: Broke
Area: 5 ha
Soils: alluvial sandy loam
Varieties planted: White—chardonnay;
Red—none
Leading Wine: O'Loughlin Milbrodale Road
Vineyard Chardonnay (wooded and unwooded)

Notes: The O'Loughlin Vineyard had a great start to its viticultural career, its Unwooded Chardonnay 1996 winning gold at Cowra, silver at Melbourne and bronze at the Hunter Valley and Brisbane shows, an award repeated at Brisbane by its oaked Chardonnay. Like others in the region, they were disappointed by an inclement 1997 vintage. No cellar door sales.

Parrot Stump Farm (vineyard only) NR

Lot 4 Talga Road, Lovedale, NSW
Ph 02 9235 3947, Fax 02 9221 4168

Owner: Geoff Petty
Chief winemaker: none, no wine is made as all grapes are sold
Year of foundation: 1998
Tonnes produced on average each year: the vineyard is yet to come into full bearing
Location: Lovedale
Area: 4.4 ha
Soils: sandy loam over clay
Varieties planted: White—chardonnay; Red—shiraz
Leading wines: no wines will be produced
Notes: Accommodation available for weekend or mid-week booking.

Peacock Hill NR

Cnr Branxton Road and Palmers Lane, Pokolbin, NSW 2320
Ph/Fax 02 4998 7661

Owners: George Tsiros and Silvi Laumets
Chief winemaker: David Lowe (contract)
Year of foundation: 1968
Tonnes crushed on average each year: 20
Location: Pokolbin
Area: 7 ha
Soils: brown or red podsols on a limestone ridge
Varieties planted: White—chardonnay; Red—cabernet sauvignon, merlot, shiraz

Leading wines: Peacock Hill, Shiraz, Cabernet
Notes: This is an established vineyard with its oldest vines now fully mature and subjected to minimal use of chemicals. All vines are pruned by hand and all fruit is hand-picked. Cellar door sales: Fri–Mon 9am–5pm, at other times by appointment.

Pendarves Estate R7

Lots 10–12 Old North Road, Belford, NSW 2335
Ph 02 6574 7222, Fax 02 9970 6152

Owners: Philip and Belinda Jill Norrie
Chief winemaker: Tamburlaine (contract)
Year of foundation: 1986
Tonnes crushed on average each year: 133
Location: Belford
Area: 20 ha
Soils: clay on limestone
Varieties planted: White—chardonnay, sauvignon blanc, verdelho; Red—chambourcin, malbec, merlot, meunier, pinot noir, shiraz
Leading wines: Pendarves Verdelho, Pendarves Chardonnay
Notes: Philip Norrie is a busy medical practitioner, author and protagonist for the therapeutic qualities of wine, when consumed in moderation. His Pendarves vineyard sits atop the Belford Dome (a local outcrop of limestone beneath a clayey topsoil). The area has long been famous in Hunter wine lore. Near here was James Busby's Kirkton property, managed by his brother-in-law William Kelman who, 160 years ago, grew some of the first Hunter vines and made some of the earliest Hunter wine. In the middle of this century, Elliott's Semillons, also from Belford, became famous. It is an area which may, in due course, become a sub-region of Hunter. Cellar door sales: weekdays by appointment, weekends 11am–5pm.

Peppers Creek Winery R6

Cnr Ekerts and Broke Roads, Pokolbin,
NSW 2321
Ph 02 4998 7532, Fax 02 4998 7531

Owners: Peter and Pamela Ireland
Chief winemaker: Peter Ireland
Year of foundation: 1987
Tonnes crushed on average each year: 8
Location: Pokolbin
Area: 1 ha
Soils: poor clay soil
Varieties planted: White—none; Red—merlot
Leading wines: Peppers Creek Chardonnay,
Merlot
Notes: Peppers Creek is a family-run business
offering wines made on the premises, antiques
and accommodation. Its Merlot is full-flavoured
and well made. Cellar door sales: Wed–Sun
10am–4pm.

Pepper Tree Wines R8.5

Halls Road, Pokolbin, NSW 2320
(winery)
Audrey Wilkinson Vineyard, Oakdale,
De Beyers Road, Pokolbin (vineyard)
Ph 02 4998 7539, Fax 02 4998 7746

Owner: Pepper Tree Wines Pty Ltd
Chief winemaker: Chris Cameron
Year of foundation: 1993
Tonnes crushed on average each year: 550
Locations: Pokolbin (Halls Road and Audrey
Wikinson), Coonawarra
Area: 28 ha (Pokolbin), 10 ha (Coonawarra)
Soils: red volcanic loam over limestone, black
alluvial
Varieties planted: (Halls Road) White—
chardonnay; Red—cabernet sauvignon, merlot,
pinot noir, shiraz. (Audrey Wilkinson) White—
chardonnay, semillon, traminer, verdelho;
Red—cabernet sauvignon, malbec, merlot,
shiraz. (Coonawarra) White—chardonnay;
Red—cabernet franc, cabernet sauvignon,
merlot

Leading wines: Pepper Tree Reserve range,
Chardonnay, Semillon, Verdelho, Cabernet
Sauvignon, Classics (cabernet blend), Malbec,
Merlot, Shiraz
Notes: Pepper Tree is a recent quality addition to
the ever-growing ranks of Hunter wineries. Its
crush in excess of 500 tonnes and its vineyard
locations take it well and truly out of the
boutique class and into the realm of a small
commercial winery. Its Reserve Chardonnay and
Cabernet Sauvignon are usually excellent. It
intends to restore the historic Audrey Wilkinson
winery at Oakdale in the near future. Cellar door
sales: weekdays 9am–5pm, weekends and
public holidays 9.30am–5pm, closed Christmas
Day and Good Friday.

Peterson Champagne House NR

Cnr Branxton and Broke Roads,
Pokolbin, NSW 2321
Ph 02 4998 7881, Fax 02 4998 7882

Owner: Peterson Champagne House Ltd
Chief winemaker: Gary Reed
Year of foundation: 1995
Tonnes crushed on average each year: 150
(including fruit purchased from the cool high-
altitude Orange district of NSW)
Location: Pokolbin
Area: 8 ha
Soils: podsolic soils over clay
Varieties planted: White—chardonnay;
Red—none
Leading wines: (all sparkling) Semillon Pinot
Noir, Chardonnay Pinot Noir Meunier,
Chardonnay Pinot, Chardonnay (100%),
Semillon (100%), Shiraz
Notes: The Hunter Valley is not noted for its
sparkling wine, but with care and attention to
detail, winemakers can certainly produce a
more than satisfactory sparkling wine. Peterson
House has half a million bottles on tirage, with
base wines made partially from fruit purchased
from vineyards in the exciting Orange district.
Cellar door sales: 7 days 9am–5pm.

Peterson's Wines R8

Mount View Road, Mount View,
NSW 2325
Ph 02 4990 1704, Fax 02 4991 1344

Owners: Peterson family
Chief winemaker: Gary Reed
Year of foundation: 1971
Tonnes crushed on average each year: 1000
Location: Mount View
Area: 22 ha
Soils: red volcanic loam over limestone
Varieties planted: White—chardonnay,
semillon; Red—cabernet sauvignon, malbec,
merlot, pinot noir, shiraz
Leading wines: Peterson's Chardonnay,
Semillon, Shiraz, Cabernet Sauvignon
Notes: Petersons are renowned for their Hunter
Chardonnays, the paragon of which was the
1986. It went on in 1987 to win the Qantas
Cup (an Australia–USA wine challenge). They
are rarely less than very good. Cellar door
sales: Mon–Sat 9am–5pm, Sun 10am–5pm.

Pokolbin Estate Vineyard NR

McDonalds Road, Pokolbin, NSW 2321
Ph 02 4998 7524, Fax 02 4998 7765

Owners: Richard Friend and John Hindman
Chief winemakers: Neil McGuigan (contract),
Trevor Drayton (contract)
Year of foundation: 1980
Tonnes crushed on average each year: 45
Location: Pokolbin
Area: 20 ha
Soils: poor clay soil, graduating to grey sandy
soils over clay on the creek flat
Varieties planted: White—riesling, semillon;
Red—shiraz
Leading wines: Pokolbin Estate Semillon, Shiraz
Notes: This established Hunter vineyard sells
most of its fruit each year and has part made
into wine by its purchasing winemakers. It is
well known for its selection of older wines, not
only from its own vineyard, but from other

local producers. Cellar door sales: each day
10am–6pm.

Poole's Rock Vineyard R7.5

Wollombi Road, Broke, NSW 2330
Ph 02 6579 1251, Fax 02 6579 1277

Owner: David Clarke
Chief winemaker: Phil Ryan (contract)
Year of foundation: 1988
Tonnes crushed on average each year: 60
Location: Broke
Area: 5 ha
Soils: deep sandy alluvial loam
Varieties planted: White—chardonnay;
Red—none
Leading wines: Poole's Rock Chardonnay
Notes: Poole's Rock, the Hunter estate of
Sydney banker, David Clarke, is a monoculture,
based entirely on chardonnay. When young it
is usually an elegant, if rather light, style

Pothana Vineyard R6.5

'Carramar', Pothana Lane, Belford,
NSW 2335
Ph 02 6574 7164, Fax 02 6574 7209

Owners: WC, JM and DW Hook
Chief winemaker: David Hook
Year of foundation: 1983
Tonnes crushed on average each year: 60
Location: Belford
Area: 8 ha
Soils: part sandy loam, part clay and shale
Varieties planted: White—chardonnay,
semillon; Red—pinot noir, shiraz
Leading wines: Pothana Chardonnay, Shiraz
Notes: This boutique winery produces soft,
full-flavoured Chardonnays and Shiraz reds in
typical Hunter style. Tasting by appointment.

Reynolds Yarraman R8.5

Yarraman Road, Wybong, NSW 2333
Ph 02 6547 8127, Fax 02 6547 8023

Owners: Jon and Jane Reynolds
Chief winemaker: Jon Reynolds
Year of foundation: 1967
Tonnes crushed on average each year: 300
Location: Wybong
Area: 18 ha
Soils: Higher western slope, sandy loam with
sandstone outcrops; central flat, fine loam over
red sand; river flat, deep rich dark alluvial loam
Varieties planted: White—chardonnay,
semillon, traminer; Red—merlot, shiraz
Leading wines: Reynolds Chardonnay, Semillon,
Shiraz, Orange Chardonnay, Cabernet
Sauvignon
Notes: Jon Reynolds is a winemaker of 25
years' experience throughout Australia, though
chiefly in Western Australia and the Hunter
Valley. He purchased his Wybong vineyard in
1989 and has greatly improved the wines,
more recently extending the range with
excellent cabernet sauvignon and chardonnay
from the Orange area of New South Wales.
These are made at Wybong and sold under the
Reynolds Orange label.

Rosemount Estate R9.5

Hunter Valley Winery, Rosemount Road,
Denman, NSW 2328
Ph 02 6549 6400, Fax 02 6549 6499

Owner: Rosemount Estates Pty Ltd
Chief winemaker: Philip Shaw
Year of foundation: 1969
Tonnes crushed on average each year: not
disclosed, but estimated at 5000
Location: Vineyards in the Hunter Valley,
Denman (attached to winery), Giant's Creek
(Sandy Hollow), Yarrawa and Roxburgh
(Muswellbrook)
Area: (Hunter vineyards) not disclosed, but
estimated at 400 ha (see also Langhorne
Creek, Mudgee, Orange, McLaren Vale and
Coonawarra regions)
Soils: (Giant's Creek) weathered sandstone over
pebbly grey clay; (Yarrawa) alluvial gravel over

brown clay; (Denman) alluvial river bed;
(Roxburgh) terra rossa over broken limestone
Varieties planted: White—(Roxburgh)
chardonnay, semillon; (Giant's Creek)
chardonnay, semillon; (Yarrawa) sauvignon
blanc; (Denman) chardonnay, gewurztraminer,
semillon; Red—none
Leading wines: Roxburgh Chardonnay, Giant's
Creek Chardonnay, Balmoral Shiraz
Notes: Rosemount Estate is one of the success
stories of Australian winemaking. An Upper
Hunter grower, it pioneered the renaissance of
winemaking in that area in the early 1970s. It
surmounted the difficulties of the mid-1970s
by anticipating the white wine boom (its Rhine
Riesling and Traminer-Rieslings introduced
many Australians to white wine) and was
prominent in the development and promotion
of the ensuing surge of Australian chardonnay
(introducing at least one New South Wales
politician to it). Since then it has become a
national winemaking company, expanding its
vineyard interests in New South Wales to
Mudgee and Orange and then to South
Australia, where it now has vineyards in
McLaren Vale, Langhorne Creek and
Coonawarra. Its Hunter whites (such as
Roxburgh Chardonnay) have always
commanded more respect than its reds, but
red wines from other regions such as its
Balmoral Shiraz and Coonawarra Reserve
Cabernet are worthy of the highest respect,
while its blended reds show great consistency.
Cellar door sales: Mon–Sat 10am–4pm, Sun
(summer) 10am–4pm, (winter) noon–4pm.

Rothbury Estate R7.5

Broke Road, Pokolbin, NSW 2320
Ph 02 4998 7555, Fax 02 4998 7870

Owner: Mildara Blass Ltd
Chief winemaker: Adam Eggins
Year of foundation: 1968
Tonnes crushed on average each year: 1037

Location: Pokolbin (Brokenback and Pokolbin vineyards), Denman, Cowra
Area: Pokolbin 249 ha, Denman 284 ha (see also Cowra)
Soils: (Brokenback) red sandy loam to brown sand; (Pokolbin) shallow clay over shaley clay; (Denman) heavy black alluvial soil, red friable loams quite deep
Varieties planted: White—chardonnay, sauvignon blanc; Red—cabernet sauvignon, merlot, pinot noir, shiraz
Leading wines: Rothbury Estate Reserve Shiraz, Hunter Valley Chardonnay, Cowra Chardonnay
Notes: Rothbury has been part of the Mildara Blass (Fosters Brewing) group since 1996 and, despite the leading wines noted above, almost certainly some repositioning of certain brands is taking place at the time of writing. One of the strange paradoxes of the Rothbury saga is that, having been one of the great protagonists of the variety in the 1970s and producing some excellent Semillons during that decade, it did not have one bearing semillon vine on its Hunter vineyards at the time of takeover. Such is fashion. Cellar door sales: 7 days 9.30am–4.30pm.

Ryan Estate Vineyard (vineyard only) NR

Marrowbone Road, Pokolbin, NSW 2321
ph 02 4990 2401

Owners Phillip and Sylvia Ryan
Chief winemaker: presently all grapes are sold
Year of foundation: 1988
Tonnes crushed on average each year: 36
Location: Pokolbin
Area: 6 ha
Soils: brown clay soils over brown-red clay
Varieties planted: White—chardonnay, semillon; Red—merlot, shiraz
Leading wines: none as yet
Notes: Ryan Estate is intended as a retirement occupation for McWilliam's Hunter winemaker Phillip Ryan. In the meantime, it helps to pay

its way by the sale of its fruit to McWilliam's Wines. No cellar door sales.

Saddlers Creek Winery R6.5

Marrowbone Road, Pokolbin, NSW 2320
Ph 02 4991 1770, 02 4991 2482

Owner: Saddlers Creek Pokolbin Pty Ltd
Chief winemaker: John Johnstone
Year of foundation: 1990
Tonnes crushed on average each year: 80
Location: Pokolbin (winery)
Area: no vineyard owned, the winery sources its fruit by contract purchases from an Upper Hunter grower
Leading wines: Blue Grass Cabernet Sauvignon, Marrowbone Chardonnay, Equus Shiraz
Notes: This is a boutique winery making full-flavoured Shiraz and Cabernet reds. Cellar door sales: 7 days 9am–5pm.

Sandalyn Wilderness Estate NR

Wilderness Road, Rothbury, NSW 2321
Ph/Fax 02 4930 7611

Owner: WL and SE Whaling
Chief winemaker: contract
Year of foundation: 1988
Tonnes crushed on average each year: 40
Location: Rothbury
Area: 6.5 ha
Soils: red-brown loam over friable clay
Varieties planted: White—chardonnay, semillon, verdelho; Red—pinot noir, shiraz
Leading wines: Sandalyn Wilderness Pinot Noir
Notes: Cellar door sales: 7 days 10am–5pm.

Scarborough Wine Co R9

Gillards Road, Pokolbin, NSW 2320
Ph 02 4998 7563, Fax 02 4998 7786

Owners: Ian and Merralea Scarborough
Chief winemaker: Ian Scarborough
Year of foundation: 1985
Tonnes produced each year on average: 100,

though about 50 tonnes of purchased fruit are also crushed
Location: Pokolbin
Area: 10 ha
Soils: red volcanic loam over limestone
Varieties planted: White—chardonnay; Red—pinot noir
Leading wines: Scarborough Chardonnay
Notes: Ian Scarborough is a specialist Chardonnay maker, and an excellent one at that. His preference is for an elegant 'Chablis' style lighter than the usual full-flavoured Hunter. He makes his whites to age well and, so that his consumers can appreciate his winemaking objectives, he does not usually release them until they are two years old.
Cellar door sales: 7 days 9am–5pm.

Sentry Rock Vineyard (vineyard only) NR

Fordwich, Bulga, NSW 2330
Ph 02 6579 1076

Owner: John Tulloch
Chief winemaker: none
Year of foundation: 1919
Tonnes produced on average each year: 150
Location: Fordwich
Area: 27 ha
Soils: sandy loam
Varieties planted: White—chardonnay, semillon, verdelho; Red—none
Leading wines: none produced
Notes: On this estate there are still two of the original soldier settlement blocks established after the First World War and a few of the original vines. No cellar door sales.

Kevin Sobels Wines R5

Broke and Halls Road, Pokolbin, NSW 2320
Ph 02 4998 7766, Fax 02 4998 7475

Owner: Kevin Sobels Pty Ltd
Chief winemaker: Kevin Sobels

Year of foundation: 1992
Tonnes crushed on average each year: 75
Location: Pokolbin
Area: 10 ha
Soils: shallow sandy soils over clay (Pokolbin red podsols)
Varieties planted: White—chardonnay, gewurztraminer, semillon; Red—pinot noir, shiraz
Leading wines: Kevin Sobels Sparkling Burgundy (made from pinot noir), Chardonnay, Semillon, Shiraz
Notes: Kevin Sobels, another Hunter 'veteran', is now making wine at his third Hunter venue, after Queldinburg in Muswellbrook and the Old McPherson Winery in McDonalds Road.
Cellar door sales: 7 days. As Kevin says, 'if the lights are on and the doors are open, so are we!'.

Somerset Vineyard (vineyard only) NR

Oakey Creek Road, Pokolbin, NSW 2320
Ph 02 4998 7526

Owner: Ivan T Howard
Chief winemaker: none
Year of foundation: 1965
Tonnes produced on average each year: 160
Location: Pokolbin
Area: 29.5 ha
Soils: red limestone soils over limestone, lighter sandy loam over yellow clay
Varieties planted: White—chardonnay, semillon, verdelho; Red—shiraz
Leading wines: no wines produced, all grapes are sold
Notes: Somerset is one of the older established Pokolbin vineyards. There are no cellar door sales, but its grapes have formed part of some excellent Hunter wines.

Sunnybrook (see Hill of Hope)

Sutherland Wines R6

Deasey Road, Pokolbin, NSW 2320
Ph 02 4998 7650, Fax 02 4998 7603

Owners: Sutherland family
Chief winemaker: Neil Sutherland; assistant
winemaker Nicholas Sutherland
Year of foundation: 1979
Tonnes crushed on average each year: 100
Location: Pokolbin
Area: 22 ha
Soils: red clay
Varieties planted: White—chardonnay, chenin
blanc, semillon; Red—cabernet sauvignon,
pinot noir, shiraz
Leading wines: Sutherland Chenin Blanc,
Semillon, Shiraz, Cabernet Sauvignon
Notes: Sutherland Wines has become virtually a
specialist in chenin blanc and in sparkling
wines. There is a white table wine and a
Chenin Cremant. There is also a Pinot-
Chardonnay sparkling white. They win medals
regularly at the Hunter Small Winemakers
Show at Maitland. Cellar door sales: 7 days
10am–5pm.

Tamburlaine R7.5

McDonalds Road, Pokolbin, NSW 2321
Ph 02 4998 7570, Fax 02 4998 7763

Owner: Landos Pty Ltd
Chief winemaker: Mark Davidson
Year of foundation: 1966
Tonnes crushed on average each year: 500
Location: Pokolbin
Area: 30 ha
Soils: shallow clay loam over clay
Varieties planted: White—chardonnay,
muscadelle, semillon, verdelho; Red—cabernet
sauvignon, merlot, pinot noir, shiraz
Leading wines: Chapel Dry Red, Chapel Reserve
Chardonnay
Notes: Tamburlaine is yet another vineyard
founded by a doctor, Lance Allen, who sold it
in 1985. Since then, Mark Davidson has made

Tamburlaine one of the Hunter's leading
smaller labels (these days not so small as it
crushes 230 tonnes for its own label). Cellar
door sales: 7 days 9.30am–5pm.

Terrace Vale R7

Deasy's Road, Pokolbin, NSW 2321
Ph 02 4998 7517, Fax 02 4998 7814

Owner: Terrace Vale Wines Pty Ltd
Chief winemaker: Alain Leprince
Year of foundation: 1971
Tonnes crushed on average each year: 180
Location: Pokolbin
Area: 37 ha
Soils: sandy loam on flat over sandstone and
clay rising to old podsolic soils over clay
Varieties planted: White—chardonnay,
sauvignon blanc, semillon, traminer; Red—
cabernet sauvignon, merlot, pinot noir, shiraz
Leading wines: Terrace Vale Chardonnay Bin 2,
Semillon Bin 1A, Cabernet Sauvignon Bin 7
Notes: This is one of the older established
boutique wineries of the Hunter Valley with a
good reputation for its Chardonnays. I well
remember its 1979. Cellar door sales: 7 days
10am–5pm.

Thalgara Estate R7

De Beyers Road, Pokolbin, NSW 2320
Ph 02 4998 7717, Fax 02 4998 7774

Owner/chief winemaker: Steve Lamb
Year of foundation: 1987
Tonnes crushed on average each year: 50
Location: Pokolbin
Area: 8 ha
Soils: red podsols over clay, and smaller areas
of limestone
Varieties planted: White—chardonnay,
semillon; Red—shiraz
Leading wines: Thalgara Show Reserve
Chardonnay, Shiraz
Notes: Steve Lamb and Thalgara continue to
do what they know best—Chardonnay and

Shiraz of flavour and quality. They do very well at local shows and occasionally at higher levels such as the National Show in Canberra. Cellar door sales: 7 days 10am–5pm.

Tinklers NR

Pokolbin Mountains Road, Pokolbin, NSW 2320
Ph 02 4998 7435, Fax 02 4998 7529

Owners: Tinkler family
Chief winemaker: Ian Tinkler
Year of foundation: 1970
Tonnes produced on average each year: 300, of which 10 are used for the Tinkler label
Location: Pokolbin
Area: 30 ha
Soils: red basalt over limestone varying to heavier black soils and sandy loams over clay and limestone
Varieties planted: White—chardonnay, semillon, verdelho; Red—cabernet franc, cabernet sauvignon, merlot, muscat hamburgh, pinot noir, shiraz
Leading wines: Tinklers Semillon, Shiraz, Verdelho, Chardonnay
Notes: The Tinklers carry on a mixed farm. Besides the wines, there are table grapes, fruit and vegetables, all in season. Cellar door sales: 7 days 10am–5pm.

Tinonee Vineyard NR

Milbrodale Road, Broke, NSW 2330
Ph 02 6579 1308, Fax 02 6579 1308

Owners: Ian and Cherry Craig
Chief winemaker: Andrew Margan (contract)
Year of foundation: 1997
Tonnes crushed on average each year: 60, of which about 25 are used for the Tinonee label
Location: Broke
Area: 8 ha
Soils: red volcanic basalt and sandy loam
Varieties planted: White—chardonnay, verdelho; Red—durif, merlot, shiraz

Leading wines: Tinonee Chardonnay, Verdelho, Shiraz, Durif
Notes: The Broke Fordwich area is expanding rapidly. Ian and Cherry Craig are the first to plant durif in the Hunter. In dry, hot years of which there are all too few, it should thrive. Cellar door sales: 7 days 10am–4pm.

Tintilla Wines NR

Lot 32 Hermitage Road, Pokolbin, NSW 2320
Ph 0411 214 478, Fax 02 9736 6894

Owners: Robert and Mary Lusby and family
Chief winemaker: Jon Reynolds (contract)
Year of foundation: 1993
Tonnes crushed on average each year: 1998 was first vintage, 50 tonnes anticipated by 1999
Location: Pokolbin
Area: 10 ha
Soils: red clay on limestone (part of the Belfarm Dome), alluvial sandy soils
Varieties planted: White—semillon; Red—cabernet sauvignon, merlot, sangiovese, shiraz
Leading wines: Tintilla Shiraz, Sangiovese
Notes: Tintilla is another young Hunter vineyard with high hopes for the future. Interestingly, the Lusby family is one of the first in the Hunter to plant sangiovese, the red grape of Tuscany and Chianti. The Italian connection is further strengthened by an olive grove, producing fruit for pickling and for oil. No cellar door sales as yet.

Tower Estate NR

Broke Road, Pokolbin, NSW 2320

Owner: a syndicate of businessmen
Chief winemaker: Dan Dineen
Year of foundation: 1998
Tonnes crushed on average each year: 150
Location: Pokolbin
Area: 4 ha
Soils: red sandy loam over clay

Varieties planted: White—chardonnay
Leading wine: Tower Estate Chardonnay
Notes: A very recent venture formed by Hunter identities Len Evans and Brian McGuigan, which aims to become a superior boutique winery, sourcing quality fruit from premium Australian areas and selling all its products at cellar door or by mail order. Cellar door sales: 7 days from early 1999; hours not decided at time of writing.

Traminer Park Vineyard NR

341 Wollombi Road, Broke, NSW 2330
Ph 02 6379 1201, Fax 02 6579 1244

Owner: Traminer Pty Ltd (the Boland family)
Chief winemaker: Andrew Margan (contract)
Year of foundation: 1969
Tonnes crushed on average each year: 25, about 10 of which are used for Traminer Park's own label requirements
Location: Broke
Area: 4.8 ha (together with 2.4 ha in the course of planting)
Soils: Mountain washy loamy sand
Varieties planted: White—chardonnay (Penfolds 1958 clone), gewurztraminer; Red—merlot (D3 V14 clone)
Leading wines: Traminer Park Chardonnay, Merlot
Notes: Cellar door sales: Sat noon–4pm.

Troon Vineyard (see Hill of Hope)

JY Tulloch & Son Pty Ltd R7.5

Glen Elgin, De Beyers Road, Pokolbin, NSW 2320
Ph 02 4998 7580, Fax 02 4998 7682

Owner: Southcorp Wines
Chief winemaker: Pat Auld
Year of foundation: purchased 1895
Tonnes crushed on average each year: not disclosed, but estimated at 50

Location: Pokolbin
Area: 8.8 ha
Soils: red volcanic loam over friable clay
Varieties planted: White—chardonnay; Red—shiraz
Leading wines: Tulloch Verdelho, Unoaked Chardonnay, Hector of Glen Elgin (Shiraz), Cabernets
Notes: Tulloch was once a family-owned vineyard and in the 1960s perhaps the most prestigious name in the Hunter Valley. Alas, that is long gone. After the Tulloch family sold Glen Elgin in 1966, it went through many hands and at times was promoted as a national brand. Under Southcorp ownership, it is again solely a Hunter brand and at the present time is Hunter winemaking headquarters for Lindemans, Tullochs and the Hungerford Hill brand. Cellar door sales: Mon–Fri 9am–4.30pm, other days 10am–4.30pm.

Tyrrells Vineyards Pty Ltd R9

Ashmans, Broke Road, Pokolbin, NSW 2321
Ph 02 4993 7000, Fax 02 4998 7723

Owner: Tyrrells Vineyards Pty Ltd
Chief winemaker: Andrew Spinaze
Year of foundation: 1858
Tonnes crushed on average each year: 3200
Locations: Pokolbin, Scone, Quirindi (NSW); Heathcote (Vic); McLaren Vale and Coonawarra (SA)
Area: 149.5 ha (Pokolbin), 100.7 ha (Scone), 15.4 ha (Heathcote). See also McLaren Vale, Northern Slopes and Limestone Coast (345.2 ha in all).
Soils: (Pokolbin) light sandy alluvial soil, red clay over chocolate loam over limestone; (Scone) light sandy soil, some gravel
Varieties planted: White—blanquette, chardonnay, chenin blanc, pedro ximenes, riesling, sauvignon blanc, semillon, traminer, trebbiano; Red—cabernet franc, cabernet

sauvignon, grenache, merlot, petit verdot, pinot noir

Leading wines: Tyrrell's Vat 1 Semillon, Vat 47 Chardonnay, Vat 9 Shiraz, Vat 6 Pinot Noir

Notes: A lover of Burgundy-style, both white and red, Murray Tyrrell has, in his lifetime, seen and presided over Tyrrells expansion from a small family-owned Pokolbin winery to a national winemaking undertaking. In the 1970s, he was responsible for the burgeoning popularity of chardonnay, making his first white from that variety in the inauspicious Hunter vintage of 1971. This tiny beginning led to the chardonnay boom of the 1980s and 1990s. The white wines of Australia have never been the same since the famous Vat 47 Chardonnay of 1973. Even though the Hunter Valley climate rarely favours that variety, he has espoused pinot noir also with hardly less success, his 1976 wine winning an international award at the Gault-Millau Wine Olympics in 1979. In the pursuit of quality and complexity, Tyrrells have, in the 1990s, expanded into Victoria and South Australia. Doubtless growth will continue. Cellar door sales: Mon–Sat 8am–5pm, closed Sundays.

Undercliff Winery **NR**

Yango Creek Road, Wollombi, NSW 2325
Ph/Fax 02 4998 3322

Owners: James and Janet Luxton
Chief winemaker: James and Janet Luxton
Year of foundation: 1994
Tonnes crushed on average each year: 16
Location: Wollombi, Hunter
Area: 2 ha
Soils: sandy loam over clay
Varieties planted: White—semillon; Red—shiraz
Leading wines: Undercliff Winery Semillon, Shiraz
Notes: This small Hunter winery in the south of the region has hand-made wines and the added attraction of an etching gallery run by one of Australia's leading etchers, Janet Luxton. Open Sat–Sun and public holidays 10am–4pm. At other times by appointment only.

Van de Scheur Wines **NR**

Lot 2, O'Connors Lane, Pokolbin NSW 2321
Ph/Fax 02 4998 7789, Fax 02 4998 7847

Owner/chief winemaker: Kees Van de Scheur
Year of foundation: 1994
Tonnes crushed on average each year: 30
Location: Pokolbin
Area: 4 ha
Soils: red friable loams over limestone
Varieties planted: White—chardonnay, semillon; Red—cabernet sauvignon, shiraz
Leading wines: Van de Scheur Chardonnay, Shiraz
Notes: Kees van de Scheur is a man of experience in all facets of Hunter Valley wine. With his wife Helen he has hit on a new approach to wine marketing—let the clients loose in the winery. Indeed let them go the whole hog. Plant, prune, pick, assist with vintage and then experience the moment of truth, making their own wine. His City Vignerons form winemaking teams and do just that. Their wines are assessed in a competition held after vintage. The program invites his clients to become members and put their own names on panels of vines. So a City Vigneron may be very busy or just do nothing. There is no direct cost, just an undertaking to buy two cases of wine a year. There are of course Chardonnay, Semillon, Shiraz and Cabernet Sauvignon wines made by Kees himself. Cellar door sales: 7 days 10am–5pm.

Verona Vineyard **NR**

McDonalds Road, Pokolbin, NSW 2320
Ph 02 4998 7668, Fax 02 4998 7430

Owner: Yore family
Chief winemaker: Simon Gilbert (contract)

Year of foundation: 1972
Tonnes crushed on average each year: 300
Location: Muswellbrook and Pokolbin (there is also a vineyard at Condobolin on the Lachlan River)
Area: Muswellbrook 22 ha, Pokolbin 5 ha
Soils: (Pokolbin) clay loam over clay; (Muswellbrook) alluvial loam
Varieties planted: White—chardonnay, sauvignon blanc, semillon; Red—shiraz
Leading wines: Verona Chardonnay
Notes: After producing a large number of wines in the 1970s and 1980s, Verona these days virtually confines itself to chardonnay, with pecan nuts as a diversification. Cellar door sales: 7 days 10am–5pm.

Wandin Valley Estate R7.5

Wilderness Road, Rothbury, NSW 2321
Ph 02 4930 7317, Fax 02 4930 7814

Owners: James and Philippa Davern
Chief winemaker: Geoff Broadfield
Year of foundation: 1973 as Millstone Vineyard, 1991 as Wandin Valley Estate
Tonnes crushed on average each year: 120
Location: Lovedale
Area: 8.4 ha
Soils: red volcanic clay, loamy black soils
Varieties planted: White—chardonnay; Red—cabernet sauvignon, ruby cabernet, shiraz
Leading wines: Wandin Valley Estate Chardonnay, Cabernet Sauvignon
Notes: James Davern has enjoyed a double helping of success, as owner of an extremely successful Hunter winery (120 show medals since 1991) and in his alter ego as television producer. Geoff Broadfield understands Hunter chardonnay very well and regularly produces gold-medal winning wines from that variety. Wandin Valley has 'Tuscan villas set amongst the vines', a village cricket ground with a traditional English pavilion, and cellar door sales: 7 days 10am–5pm.

Warraroong Estate (formerly Fraser Vineyard) NR

Wilderness Road, Rothbury, NSW, 2321
Ph 02 4930 7594, Fax 02 4930 7199

Owners: an Australian couple resident overseas who do not wish their names disclosed
Chief winemaker: Adam Rees with consultant
Year of foundation: 1986
Tonnes crushed on average each year: 20
Location: Rothbury
Area: 6 ha
Soils: sandy over clay, loam over clay
Varieties planted: White—chardonnay, sauvignon blanc, semillon, chenin blanc; Red—malbec, shiraz
Leading wines: Warraroong Estate Malbec, Shiraz
Notes: At the time of writing, the Fraser Vineyard had just been sold and little detail of the incoming purchasers, their names, their wine intentions or even the new name of the property were available. However, there is accommodation and cellar door sales: 7 days 10am–5pm.

Wattlebrook Vineyard (vineyard only) NR

Fordwich Road, Broke, NSW 2330

Owner: Peter McLellan
Chief winemaker: no wine presently made
Year of foundation: 1994
Tonnes crushed on average each year: anticipated to be 400 when the vineyard is fully planted and in full bearing
Location: Broke
Area: 32 ha
Soils: red basalt and sandy loams
Varieties planted: White—chardonnay, semillon, verdelho; Red—cabernet sauvignon, shiraz
Leading wines: none produced
Notes: Wattlebrook is located on the fertile Fordwich sill. It sells all its grapes to a local

winery. Its second industry is lavender, which is also flourishing. There are no cellar door or lavender sales.

Wilderness Estate R7

Branxton Road, Pokolbin, NSW 2320
Ph 02 4998 7755, Fax 02 4998 7750

Owners: Joe Lesnik and John Baruzzi
Chief winemaker: John Baruzzi
Year of foundation: 1996
Tonnes crushed on average each year: 300
Location: Pokolbin
Area: 23 ha (a vineyard of 18 ha on Wilderness Road is also leased)
Soils: sandy gravelly soils, well drained
Varieties planted: White—chardonnay, semillon, traminer, verdelho; Red—cabernet sauvignon, merlot, pinot noir, shiraz
Leading wines: Wilderness Estate Chardonnay, Semillon, Cabernet-Merlot, Shiraz
Notes: Wilderness Estate is a very new Hunter identity, a partnership of the winemaking and marketing talents of former Orlando-Wyndham chief winemaker John Baruzzi and the vineyard and winery resources of Hunter veteran Joe Lesnik. There will be two labels—Wilderness Estate and Black Creek. Cellar door sales: 7 days 9am–5pm.

Windarra Estate NR

De Beyers Road, Pokolbin, NSW 2320
Ph/fax 02 4998 7648

Owners: Max and Brigite Andresen
Chief winemaker: Thomas Young (contract)
Year of foundation: 1981 (vineyard), 1985 (winery)
Tonnes crushed on average each year: 25
Location: Pokolbin
Area: 6 ha
Soils: old red clay
Varieties planted: White—chardonnay, semillon; Red—muscat, shiraz
Leading wines: Windarra Tawny Port

Notes: Max Andresen is a potter who has a thriving business making port crocks. Naturally his leading wine is a tawny style. Cellar door sales: Tues–Sun 10am–4.30pm.

Windsor's Edge Vineyard (vineyard only) NR

McDonalds Road, Pokolbin, NSW 2321
Ph/Fax 02 4998 7737

Owners: Tim and Jessie Windsor
Chief winemaker: no grapes are available yet, but Simon Gilbert will be requested to make the wine
Year of foundation: 1996
Tonnes crushed on average each year: none yet, first vintage 1998
Location: Pokolbin
Area: 2.1 ha planted 1996, 2 ha planted 1997, 2.6 ha planted in 1998 (6.6 ha in all)
Soils: loam or red clay, sandy loam on yellow clay refined and loam over white clay, brown loam
Varieties planted: White—chardonnay, semillon; Red—chambouran, shiraz, graciano, tempranillo and tinta cao anticipated at some time in the future
Leading wines: none yet
Notes: The Windsors have a property of 52 ha at the Black Creek end of McDonalds Road. It is the site of the old Picnic Racetrack. At the time of writing, Tim Windsor was completing a viticulture degree at Charles Sturt University and, among such more established Hunter varieties as semillon and shiraz, feels that the Spaniards graciano and tempranillo are worth a gamble. No cellar door sales as yet.

Wyndham Estate (Dalwood) NR

Dalwood Road, Dalwood, NSW 2335
Ph 02 4938 3444, Fax 02 4938 3422

Owner: Wyndham Estate Pty Ltd
Chief winemaker: Robert Paul
Year of foundation: 1971 (by Brian McGuigan), 1828 (by George Wyndham)

Tonnes crushed on average each year: 60
Location: Dalwood
Area: 30 ha
Soils: alluvial sandy loams
Varieties planted: White—blanquette, chardonnay, semillon; Red—cabernet sauvignon, shiraz
Notes: The cradle of Australian winemaking, this estate was founded by George Wyndham in 1828 and vines were certainly being grown there by 1832. It continued as a leading Hunter Valley vineyard for the next 60 years until it fell on hard times in the 1890s, a fact which caused a correspondent of the *Maitland Mercury* to lament that 'the departed glory of Dalwood is a thing to be deplored'. In the early twentieth century, it was purchased by Penfolds, who remained there over 60 years, before moving to Dalwood Estate in the upper Hunter Valley. Then in 1970, the property was sold to the McGuigan family and soon after became Wyndham Estate. During the 1970s and 1980s, it grew rapidly until taken over by Orlando in 1990. Under the tutelage of Brian McGuigan, its wines became very consistent and keenly priced but were never outstanding, a policy which continues to the present time. On a smaller scale, however, policies are changing. After being closed for some years as an operating winery, Dalwood now specialises in small batches of the traditional wine specialities of the Lower Hunter Valley, shiraz and semillon. Cellar door sales: weekdays 9.30am–5pm, weekends 10am–4pm.

Brian McGuigan Wines (Pokolbin) R6.5

Mistletoe Farm Road, Pokolbin, NSW 2320
Ph 02 4998 7521, Fax 02 4998 7796

Owner: Brian McGuigan Wines Ltd
Year of foundation: 1971
Tonnes crushed on average each year: 500
Location: Pokolbin
Area: 100 ha
Soils: darkbrown loam over clay and lighter sandy soils
Varieties planted: White—semillon; Red—merlot
Leading wines: see prior Brian McGuigan Wines entry
Notes: Hermitage Estate, a product of the Hunter wine boom of the 1960s, established its vineyard and winery on land that had known vines as Mistletoe Farm in the early twentieth century. By 1974 Hermitage was cash-strapped, friendless and in receivership and was acquired by Wyndham Estate in 1978. For some years until 1997, the former Hermitage winery was used as the Hunter production headquarters of Orlando Wyndham. From mid-1997, the majority of Hunter production moved to the Montrose winery at Mudgee, leaving only Dalwood with a small capacity as its only operating winery in the Hunter. It seems ironic that Brian McGuigan Wines Ltd has now repurchased the old Hermitage winery. Cellar door sales: 7 days 10–5pm.

Broke Fordwich Sub-region

The first thirty years of the sub-region's history are identical to those of the Hunter region. However, in 1820, following John Howe's explorations north of Windsor, the areas south and west of present-day Singleton saw its first settlers along the Upper Hunter and Goulburn Rivers. An early settler in the sub-region was John Blaxland, brother of Gregory, who had been born in Fordwich, Kent, and arrived in Sydney in 1805 on the suggestion, it is said, of Sir Joseph Banks. Blaxland had been granted over 2000 ha of land, mostly in the Broke area. Fordwich Homestead, from which Blaxland pursued his pastoral interests, was built in 1829 and was also allowed to be

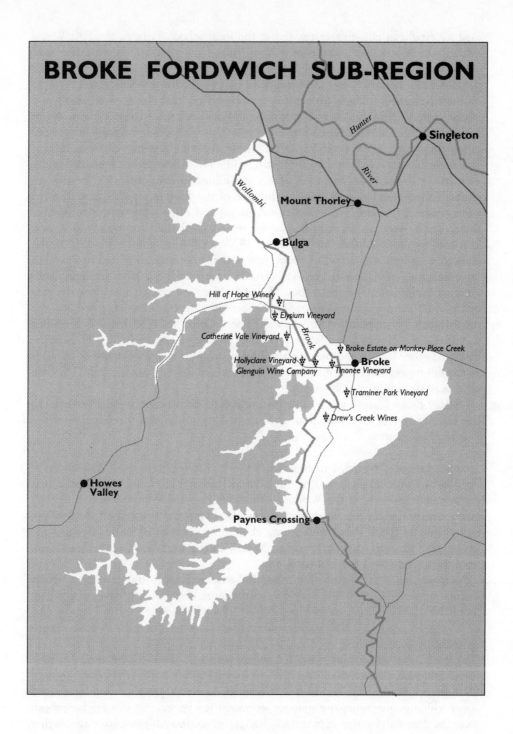

BROKE FORDWICH SUB-REGION

Singleton

Hunter

River

Mount Thorley

Wollombi

Bulga

Hill of Hope Winery

Elysium Vineyard

Catherine Vale Vineyard

Brook

Broke Estate on Monkey Place Creek

Hollyclare Vineyard

Glenguin Wine Company

Broke

Tinonee Vineyard

Traminer Park Vineyard

Drew's Creek Wines

Howes Valley

Paynes Crossing

used for Anglican church services and as the local school. Prior to the First World War, the area was used mostly for grazing, though by 1910 the larger estates had begun to be subdivided. After that war, the area became subject to the Fordwich Soldiers Settlement Scheme and vines were first planted in the sub-region by some of those returned soldiers from 1920 on. However, the blocks were small and uneconomic. When the Great Depression of 1929 decimated the wine industry in the early 1930s, the vine blocks were sold mostly to Tullochs, who had commenced purchasing them as early as 1922. The last of the vine-growing soldier-settlers of Fordwich sold his block to the Elliott family in 1940. These blocks remained under vine and in the ownership of the Tulloch and Elliott families until 1965 in the case of the Tullochs and slightly later in the case of the Elliotts. By this time, the red wine boom of the late 1960s was in full swing and other vineyards were planted there. There were no wineries in the sub-region until the Saxonvale winery and vineyards were established in the early 1970s. All fruit from Fordwich, as the grapegrowing area was called in those days, was previously transported to Pokolbin for vinification. Yet, despite the skill of its early winemakers, Mark Cashmore and Alasdair Sutherland, and the success of its Chardonnays, the company encountered financial difficulties throughout its short history and its assets finally passed into the ownership of Wyndham Estate. Its winery was closed in 1988 but was reopened recently as the Hill of Hope Winery, making its first vintage there in 1997. During this time other large companies such as Lindemans also planted extensive vineyards in the sub-region and McWilliam's also had plans for substantial vineyards. They too have moved on from the sub-region.

Today Broke Fordwich is a sub-region of reborn enthusiasm paying little heed to the reverses of the past. May that enthusiasm be justified and the mistakes of the past not be repeated.

Location: latitude 32°46'S, longitude 151°5'E. The sub-region is about 20 km west of Pokolbin in what might be called the Central Hunter Valley and is defined as part of the catchment area of the Wollombi Brook, falling within the Shire of Singleton below the 200 m contour line. It is of irregular shape and situated on the left and right banks of the Brook, commencing about 15 km south of Broke. It abuts the Brook, as it flows north-west for about 35 km, ending near Warkworth about 5 km from its juncture with the Hunter River.

Topography and soils: Apart from the Brokenback Range, the terrain is gently undulating with vineyard sites varying in altitude from virtually sea-level to nowhere more than 200 m. Most of its vineyards are planted on sandy loam, loam or clay loam of good depth. Such soils are moderately acid, permeable and well drained with moderate to high fertility.

Climate: It is an undeniably warm sub-region with MJT 23.75°C. Its annual rainfall is 647 mm with about two-thirds of this (428 mm) falling during the growing season (October to April). Like the Lower Hunter, it enjoys the ameliorating light cloud cover which accompanies the summer afternoon sea breeze, but this sea breeze can often be blocked by the Brokenback Range, which possibly explains the higher summer temperatures. As in the Lower Hunter, heavy rain at vintage causing direct damage to fruit and consequent attacks of bunch rot (botrytis) can create problems both as regards quantity and quality. Spraying for downy mildew is necessary from October to February. There is also a danger of hail during spring and summer.

Other than by natural rainfall, most vines in the sub-region are watered by drip irrigation, either by water taken directly from Wollombi Brook or from storage dams filled from the Brook. Water may also be taken from under the bed of the Brook by spear points. Bore water of good quality is also used, but water bores require a licence from the New South Wales Government.

Harvest time: Vintage is generally about two weeks later than the Lower Hunter for corresponding varieties (i.e. from mid-February to late March).

One of the distinguishing factors of Broke Fordwich viticulture as opposed to Lower Hunter viticulture generally is that about 90% of the vineyards in the sub-region are of a Scott-Henry type and most of the remainder rely on vertical shoot positioning for canopy management. Also because of the extra vigour of the vines caused by the greater fertility of the sub-region's soils, rows are generally planted further apart than in other areas of the Hunter region. An average vineyard spacing would be 3-metre row width with vines 1.8 m apart. Production is also greater with yields about double those of the Lower Hunter.

Now all of this might lead a casual observer to conclude that Broke Fordwich is just another sub-region devoted to producing maximum quantity at the expense of quality. This is not the case, provided that the vines are not overcropped and the crop carried can ripen properly. It has been contended that the Chardonnays of the Broke Fordwich sub-region have a particular sub-regional melony flavour mainly because of the fertility of the soil, while Chardonnays from the Lower Hunter have a peachy character mainly because of the less fertile nature of the soil. Such statements must be treated with caution and are unfortunate because soil fertility or infertility in itself has little to do with flavour production. The development of flavourants (i.e. pigments, flavours and aromas) is the product of the vine's ripeness, metabolism and climatic factors. Warmth and soil structure (e.g. soil warmth and drainage) are much more relevant. This is not to say that a skilled palate might not notice some flavour or aromatic differences between Broke and Pokolbin Chardonnays, but they would certainly not be due to soil fertility or lack of it.

It has also been contended that in Semillon, the Broke Fordwich sub-region produces lemony citrus characters as opposed to the Semillon of the Lower Hunter which shows more of a lanolin or soapy character. Lemony citrus characters in semillon are of course not peculiar to Broke Fordwich. They exist in most other warm areas, such as the Barossa Valley, Clare and certainly the Lower Hunter. Again this cannot be the product of soil fertility or lack of it. Flavour production, and therefore differences between areas, is more the product of the vine's ripeness metabolism which in turn is due to climate and factors other than soil fertility.

In regard to red wines and in particular cabernet sauvignon, it is also argued that the Broke Fordwich sub-region produces intense flavour and colour in this variety. This argument may be based on the 1993 vintage, a very abnormal year for the Hunter Valley and one of very late ripening for most varieties including cabernet sauvignon. Such relatively cool, late-ripening and dry years rarely occur in the Hunter Valley. I have noticed, however, in over 30 years of tasting Hunter Cabernet Sauvignon that cool, dry, rather late-ripening Hunter years certainly show cabernet sauvignon picked off relatively young vines at its varietal best (*viz* Lake's Folly Cabernet Sauvignon 1967, Brokenwood Cabernet Sauvignon 1975). Yet cool, dry years are very much the exception there. Wet, humid years (e.g. 1971, 1978, 1984, 1988, 1989) and hot drought years (1977, 1981, 1991) are predominant. When Hunter cabernet sauvignon vines become older (about 6–7 years of age), they seem to lose the innate vibrant berry character of the variety and become much more regional and leathery in nature. All of this goes to show that shiraz in most years is a much more suitable variety for the Hunter Valley as a whole than cabernet sauvignon.

The Broke Fordwich sub-region now encompasses 607 hectares of vineyard, which produces approximately 3250 tonnes of grapes. Its chief white grape varieties are (in tonnages from 1997 vintage), chardonnay (1305), semillon (560), verdelho (145) and traminer (100) and in reds, cabernet sauvignon (575), shiraz (130) and merlot (110). Shiraz surely deserves to be more popular.

Vineyards and wineries located within the Broke Fordwich sub-region are: Adams Peak, Bacchus Fine Wines, Beyond Broke Vineyard, Broke Estate on Monkey Creek, Catherine Vale, Drews Creek Wines, Elysium Vineyard, Esslemont Estate, Foates Ridge Wines, Fordwich Estate, Glenguin Wines, Hill of Hope Winery, Hollyclare Vineyard, Howards Way Vineyard, Milbrodale Vineyard (O'Loughlin), Margan Family Vineyard, Mount Eyre Vineyards, Payne's Crossing Vineyard, Peschar Family Vineyard, Poole's Rock Vineyard, Tinonee Vineyard and Traminer Park Vineyard. Most have been detailed above. Others, despite several attempts, proved impossible to contact.

❧ SOUTH COAST ZONE

This is a long and narrow strip of land commencing on the central coast of New South Wales and proceeding south along the coastline to the Victorian border. The zone extends west as far as the Blue Mountains, includes the Sydney Metropolitan area, the old wine area of Camden, the Southern Highlands, the Shoalhaven Valley and the Bega Valley. Its southern parts seem more favoured for viticulture due principally to drier climates and less humidity.

No wine regions have yet been formed within its boundaries, but there are several small vineyard areas.

Climate: Bega MJT 20.7°C, MAR na, HDD raw 1817, 1630 (cut-off and adjusted for latitude, daily temperature range and vine sites), AR 871 mm (Oct–Apr 547 mm), AI na, SH 7.9 (Gladstones).

Cambewarra Estate **NR**

520 Illaroo Road, Cambewarra,
NSW 2540
Ph/Fax 02 4446 0170

Owners: Geoffrey and Louise Cole
Chief winemaker: Mark Davidson (contract)
Year of foundation: 1991
Tonnes crushed on average each year: 25
Location: Cambewarra
Area: 4.8 ha
Soils: alluvial topsoil, clay subsoil
Varieties planted: White—chardonnay, verdelho; Red—cabernet sauvignon, chambourcin
Leading wines: Cambewarra Estate Verdelho, Chardonnay, Cabernet Sauvignon, Chambourcin
Notes: A great deal of show success has come Cambewarra's way recently. A gold medal was won at the 1997 Cowra Show for Cabernet Sauvignon 1996 and a trophy for the same wine at the 1998 Sydney Show; a high silver also for a wooded Chardonnay; finally a gold for Chambourcin, which is sometimes an unlovely variety, at the recent Yass Show. All of this points to a bright future for Cambewarra. Cellar door sales: weekends

10am–5pm and public holidays and school holidays.

Coolangatta Estate **NR**

Coolangatta Village, 1335 Bolong Road, Shoalhaven Heads, NSW 2535
Ph 02 4448 7131 Fax 02 4448 7997

Owner: Bishop family
Chief winemaker: Tyrrells (contract)
Year of foundation: 1988
Tonnes produced on average each year: 55, all of which are used for Coolangatta Estate labels
Location: Shoalhaven Heads
Area: 7 ha
Soils: upper slopes brown loam over a shale base; lower slopes well-drained sandy loam
Varieties planted: White—chardonnay, sauvignon blanc, semillon, verdelho; Red—cabernet sauvignon, chambourcin, merlot, shiraz
Leading wines: Coolangatta Estate Alexander Berry Chardonnay, Verdelho, Semillon, Chambourcin, Cabernet-Shiraz
Notes: This is a restoration of an original convict-built settlement dating from 1822 and

one of the first settlements on the South Coast of New South Wales. Its originators were Alexander Berry and Edward Wollstonecraft, early Sydney merchants who gave their names to several parts of Sydney's lower North Shore and were among that area's first settlers also. The 1991 Alexander Berry Chardonnay won a gold medal and trophy at the 1997 National Show and must certainly have matured well. Cellar door sales: 10am–4pm daily. There is also a restaurant.

The Evans Wine Co NR

Camden Estate, Macarthur Road, Camden, NSW 2570

Owner: Greg Penman, lessee Evans Wine Co
Chief winemaker: contract
Year of foundation: 1980
Tonnes produced on average each year: 200
Location: Camden
Area: 18 ha
Soils: alluvial grey loam
Varieties planted: White—chardonnay;
Red—none
Leading wine: Camden Chardonnay
Notes: This is a mature vineyard formerly owned by Norman Hanckel and for a few years leased by Rothbury Estate. Its soil is rich alluvial loam many metres deep. It adjoins the Nepean River and is not far from the original Camden Park Vineyard planted during John Macarthur's time and made famous by his son Sir William. No cellar door sales.

Grevillea Estate NR

Buckajo Road, Bega, NSW 2550
Ph 02 6492 3006, Fax 02 6492 5330

Owner/chief winemaker: Nicola Collins
Year of foundation: 1980
Tonnes crushed on average each year: 58, all of which are used for Grevillea Estate's own labels
Location: Bega

Area: 6.4 ha
Soils: almost half and half granite soils and decomposed shale
Varieties planted: White—chardonnay, gewurztraminer, riesling, sauvignon blanc; Red—cabernet sauvignon, merlot
Leading wines: Grevillea Estate Chardonnay, Merlot, Cabernet Sauvignon
Notes: Grevillea Estate is a working vineyard within a working dairy farm. All its wines are estate-grown, made, matured, bottled and labelled. In addition to cellar door sales, hours for which are 9am–5pm daily, there is a restaurant located in an 1860s milking hall open from Sun–Fri noon–2pm and other tourist activities, including wetlands walks and viewing the milking.

Jasper Valley Wines NR

152 Croziers Road, Berry, NSW 2535
Ph/Fax 02 4464 1596

Owners: Jasper Valley Wines Pty Ltd
Chief winemaker: Chris Niccol (contract)
Year of foundation: 1976
Tonnes crushed on average each year: not disclosed
Location: Berry
Area: 3 ha
Soils: basalt with shale subsoil
Varieties planted: White—chardonnay, gewurztraminer, riesling, semillon; Red—cabernet sauvignon, shiraz
Leading wines: Jasper Valley Chardonnay, Traminer Riesling, Shiraz, Cabernet Sauvignon, Fortifieds
Notes: This is a tourist oriented winery in a well-known tourist area of the New South Wales South Coast. Cellar door sales: Mon–Sat 9am–5.30pm, Sun 10am–5pm.

Joadja Vineyards NR

Cnr Greenhills and Joadja Roads,
Berrima, NSW 2577
Ph/Fax 02 4878 5236

Owners: Kim Moginie and Frances Moginie
Chief winemaker: Kim Moginie
Year of foundation: 1983
Tonnes crushed on average each year: 35,
most of which are used for Joadja Vineyards'
own labels
Location: Berrima
Area: 7 ha
Soils: rich basalt soils
Varieties planted: White—chardonnay,
sauvignon blanc; Red—cabernet sauvignon,
malbec
Leading wines: Joadja Vineyards regional
varietal wines (see varieties)
Notes: The winery is located in the wet, cool
Southern Highlands area south-west of Sydney,
which now has many new small vineyards,
which are yet to be proved. Cellar door sales:
7 days 10am–5pm.

The Silos Winery NR

Princes Highway, Jaspers Brush, NSW
2535 (about 6.4 km south of Berry)
Ph 02 4448 6082, Fax 02 4448 6246

Owners/chief winemakers: Kate Khoury and
Gaynor Sims
Year of foundation: 1985
Tonnes crushed on average each year: 16, all
of which are used for The Silos labels
Location: Jaspers Brush
Area: 4 ha
Soils: a mix of clay and shale
Varieties planted: White—chardonnay,
sauvignon blanc, semillon; Red—cabernet
sauvignon, malbec, merlot, shiraz
Leading wines: The Silos Merlot, Semillon
Notes: Located in a century-old dairy, The Silos
is a popular landmark in a well-known tourist
area of the South Coast of New South Wales.

The varietal wines grown on the property are
hand-made except for the Traminer-Riesling,
the Fortifieds and Sparkling. The makers,
though self-taught, have attended several
winemaking courses and are professional in
their winemaking approach. Cellar door sales:
Wed–Mon 10am–5pm, closed Tuesdays, open
7 days during school holidays. There is also a
restaurant and accommodation.

Tilba Valley Wines NR

Glen Eden Vineyard, Old Highway,
Tilba, NSW 2546
Ph 02 4473 7308

Owner/chief winemaker: Barry Field
Year of foundation: 1978
Tonnes crushed on average each year: 25
Location: Tilba
Area: 6.5 ha
Soils: clayey shale on top of decomposed
granite and quartz
Varieties planted: White—chardonnay,
gewurztraminer, riesling, semillon;
Red—cabernet sauvignon, shiraz
Leading wines: Tilba Valley Chardonnay,
Traminer-Riesling
Notes: A small family winery. Cellar door sales:
Mon–Sat 10am–5pm, Sun 11am–5pm.

Tizzana NR

518 Tizzana Road, Ebenezer, NSW 2756
Ph 02 4579 1150, Fax 02 4679 1216

Owner/chief winemaker: Peter Auld
Year of foundation: 1887
Tonnes crushed on average each year: 5
Location: Ebenezer
Area: 2 ha
Soils: light sandy loams, pH just a little acid
Varieties planted: White—none; Red—aleatico,
cabernet sauvignon, black muscat, shiraz
Leading wines: Tizzana Rosso di Tizzana (a light
dry red), and a wide range of Fortifieds
Notes: Dr Thomas Fiaschi was an Italian-
Australian surgeon who practised for many

years in Australia, always extolling the medical benefits of wine. Tizzana was Dr Fiaschi's original winery, erected in 1887. Cellar door sales: weekends and public holidays noon–6pm, otherwise by appointment.

Vicary's Winery NR

Northern Road, Luddenham, NSW 2745
Ph 02 4773 4161, Fax 02 4773 4411

Owner/chief winemaker: Chris Niccol
Year of foundation: 1923
Tonnes crushed on average each year: 10 from the home vineyard, but 150 overall (including purchased fruit)
Location: Luddenham
Area: 5 ha
Soils: heavy clay
Varieties planted: White—chardonnay, gewurztraminer; Red—none
Leading wine: Vicary's Chardonnay
Notes: Chris Niccol shows his wines at the Hunter and Cowra Shows and over the last decade has won a commendable number of medals (5 trophies and 100 medals). A few years ago, Vicary's might have been termed one of the few remaining wineries in a Sydney region succumbing everywhere to suburbia, but a compelling interest in winegrowing and winemaking is making its presence felt once more in the Sydney area, which will have its own status as a wine region in the not too distant future. Cellar door sales: Mon–Fri 9am–5pm, weekends 11.30am–5pm.

❧ SOUTHERN NEW SOUTH WALES ZONE

A generally elevated zone extending from the southern boundary of the Central Ranges Zone (Cowra) to the Murray River at Jingellic. It is generally a cool area and includes the wine regions of Canberra District, and Hilltops and the proposed region of Tumbarumba.

Snowy River Winery NR

Rockwell Road, Berridale, NSW 2628
Ph 02 6456 5041, Fax 02 6456 5005

Owner: Manfred Plumecke
Chief winemaker: Charles Sturt University, Wagga (contract)
Year of foundation: 1984
Tonnes crushed on average each year: 27
Location: Berridale
Area: 3.2 ha
Soils: decomposed granite, very thin topsoil
Varieties planted: White—muller thurgau, riesling, siegerrebe, sylvaner; Reds—none
Leading wines: Snowy River Riesling, Noble Riesling, Muller Thurgau-Sylvaner (blend)
Notes: Located on the banks of the Snowy River, the vineyard is irrigated by pumping from that river. It is otherwise a very cool area where reds will not ripen. Cellar door sales: 7 days 10am–5pm.

Transylvania Vineyard NR

Monaro Highway, Cooma, NSW 2630
(15 km north of the town)
Ph 02 6452 4374, Fax 02 6452 6281

Owners: Peter and Maria Culici
Chief winemaker: Peter Culici
Year of foundation: 1988
Tonnes crushed on average each year: 25
Location: Monaro plains north of Cooma
Area: 14 ha
Soils: part is red loamy topsoil, part granitic; the vineyard is irrigated from sweet bore water
Varieties planted: White—chardonnay, muscadelle, sauvignon blanc; Red—cabernet sauvignon, merlot, pinot noir
Leading wines: Transylvania Chardonnay, Cabernet Sauvignon-Merlot, Pinot Noir, Muscat.
Notes: I have driven along the Monaro Highway for 40 years and never expected to see a vineyard here, but most expectations prove ill-founded and this was just another one. This vineyard is very high at 860 m and would see snow several times a year. Its vines are very interesting too, with a rather cold aspect, planted facing west away from the morning sun. The reason is that, in its first few minutes of rising, the sun causes great damage to plants facing it which have been frosted during the night and very early morning. So the Transylvanian vines have extra time to adjust to any frost effect with the result that such damage may not be as severe. Nevertheless, its immediate environment is extremely cool and the vineyard soils may not warm as quickly as with an eastern or north-eastern aspect. Still, there are different approaches in viticulture as in most things. I am informed that its cabernet sauvignon can reach 14° Be in potential alcohol. Cellar door sales: 9am–5pm daily.

CANBERRA DISTRICT REGION

As a winegrowing region, Canberra District is a creature of government, centred on and named after Australia's capital, though more than half of it is located outside the capital's boundaries, in New South Wales to its north-west, north, north-east and east. Many of its vignerons have worked for the Federal government and its agencies during their professional lives. It is not a large vine area. Recent estimates still place its size at no more than 100 ha, but it does have the benefit, for its market purposes, of a growing city of 300 000 souls, many of whom are Federal government employees, within a forty-five minute drive of any of the winery sites.

As a winegrowing area it dates only from the early 1970s, though there is evidence that, about 130 years ago, there were wineries in the Yass district of New South Wales in the north of the present region, the last of these closing in the early years of the twentieth century. Today, there are numerous wineries in the region, the principal winegrowing sites being close to the villages of Bungendore, Hall and Murrumbateman.

Location: latitude 35°20'S, longitude 149°10'E, the region is around Canberra and about 280 km south-west of Sydney

Elevation: 500–800 m

Topography and soils: The region consists of four basic rock groups, Ordovician isoclinally folded sediments, acid volcanic rocks, granite and Devonian sandstone. Its north-west section, the vineyards around Murrumbateman and Wallaroo, is undulating country with open flat valleys of porphyry-derived soils. East of the Yass River, the terrain rises to the 'Cullarin Horst', a dissected plateau on sedimentary rocks. Here are located some of the higher altitude vineyards of the region. The country continues to rise in the east of the region. Around Lark Hill, above Bungendore, the soils are clayey loam on shale. Separate soil information is given below in respect of individual vineyard sites.

Climate: Canberra Airport MJT 20.1°C, MAR na, HDD raw 1405 (Kirk), AR 633 mm (Airport), RH 46% (3pm), yearly average (Kirk). Cf MJT 20.4°C, MAR na, HDD raw 1504, 1514 (cut-off and adjusted for latitude, daily temperature range and vine sites), AR 651 mm (Oct–Apr 417 mm), RH 35% (3pm Jan), AI na, SH 8.3. Canberra District is a dry area and drip irrigation from surface dams and bores is necessary to prevent vine stress as relative humidity is low and consequently its evaporation rate is quite high. It has a mild rather than extremely cool climate, yet should suit varieties such as pinot noir, except in very warm years, and is certainly too cool in most years for late ripening Mediterranean varieties such as grenache and mourvedre. As for those cultivars in between (the majority), it is quite satisfactory.

Climatic hazards include spring frosts (as are common through most of the Central and Southern Tablelands and the Monaro district of New South Wales), though such frosts are often not widespread in the Canberra District, but limited as usual to sites of poor air drainage. Birds are also a danger, but netting is an effective countermeasure.

Harvest time: late March (traminer, pinot noir, chardonnay) to early May (cabernet sauvignon)

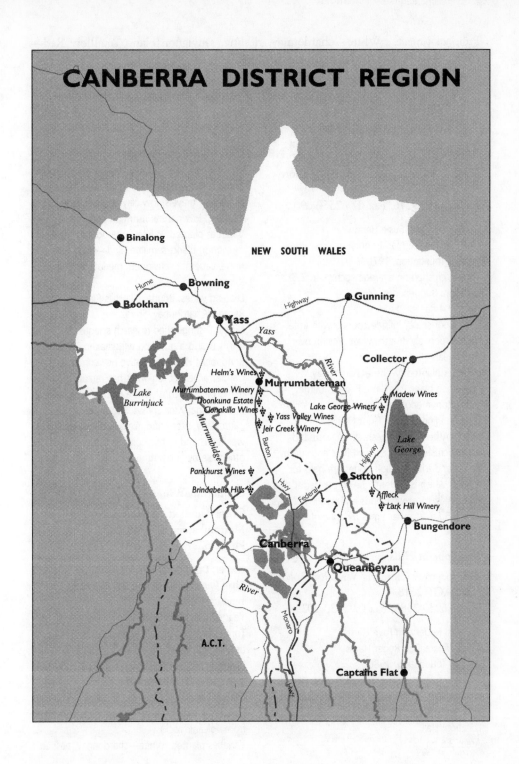

CANBERRA DISTRICT REGION

Binalong

NEW SOUTH WALES

Hume

Bowning

Bookham

Gunning

Highway

Yass

Yass

River

Collector

Helm's Wines

Murrumbateman

Madew Wines

Murrumbateman Winery

Doonkuna Estate

Lake George Winery

Lake
Burrinjuck

Clonakilla Wines

Yass Valley Wines

Jeir Creek Winery

Barton

Lake
George

Murrumbidgee

Highway

Pankhurst Wines

Hwy

Sutton

Brindabella Hills

Federal

Affleck

Lark Hill Winery

Canberra

Bungendore

River

Queanbeyan

Monaro

A.C.T.

Hwy

Captains Flat

Principal varieties: White—chardonnay, riesling, sauvignon blanc, semillon; Red—cabernet sauvignon, merlot, pinot noir, shiraz
Total area: 100 ha
Principal wine styles: Cabernet-Merlot, Shiraz, Sauvignon Blanc, Chardonnay, Pinot Noir, Riesling, Semillon

Affleck NR

RMB 244 Gundaroo Road, Bungendore, NSW 2621
Ph 02 6236 9276, Fax 02 6236 9090

Owners: Ian and Susie Hendry
Chief winemaker: Ian Hendry
Year of foundation: 1976
Tonnes crushed on average each year: 2.5
Location: Bungendore
Area: 2.4 ha
Soils: poor shaley hillside country with little topsoil, possibly due to water erosion over many years
Varieties planted: White—chardonnay, sauvignon blanc, semillon; Red—cabernet sauvignon, merlot, muscat, pinot noir, shiraz
Leading wine: Affleck Pinot Noir
Notes: Affleck is a very small vineyard and winery crushing only its own fruit and run by family and friends. High hopes are held for merlot, which is currently being planted. Cellar door sales: most weekends and public holidays 10am–5pm, at other times by appointment.

Brindabella Hills R8

4 Woodgrove Close via Wallaroo Road, Hall, ACT 2618
Ph 02 6230 2583, Fax 02 5230 2023

Owners: Roger and Faye Harris
Chief winemaker: Roger Harris
Year of foundation: 1986
Tonnes crushed on average each year: 48, of which about 35 are used for the Brindabella Hills labels
Location: Hall
Area: 3.5 ha

Soils: red and orange duplex soils (Dr and Dy); sandy loams over gravelly clay on decomposed granite; colluvial silty clay loam over coarse sands and gravels; low clay content, free draining; low natural nutrition and pH
Varieties planted: White—chardonnay, riesling, sauvignon blanc, semillon; Red—cabernet franc, cabernet sauvignon, merlot, pinot noir, shiraz
Leading wines: Brindabella Hills Riesling, Reserve Chardonnay, Shiraz
Notes: Distinguished research scientist Dr Roger Harris is also a qualified winemaker. Though Brindabella Hills is a relative newcomer to the Canberra District region, it has rapidly made its mark, being a consistent award winner in local and regional wine shows. Its whites are particularly interesting. Cellar door sales: weekends and public holidays 10am–5pm, otherwise by appointment.

Clonakilla Wines R8

Crisps Lane off Gundaroo Road, Murrumbateman, NSW 2582
Ph 02 6227 5877, Fax 02 6251 1938

Owner: Dr John TO Kirk
Chief winemakers: John TO Kirk and Timothy P Kirk
Year of foundation: 1971
Tonnes crushed on average each year: 18, rising to 30 when new plantings come into bearing
Location: Murrumbateman
Area: 3 ha
Soils: red kandosol (a sandy clay loam derived from volcanic rock)
Varieties planted: White—chardonnay, riesling,

sauvignon blanc, semillon, viognier;
Red—brown muscat, cabernet franc, cabernet
sauvignon, merlot, pinot noir, shiraz
Leading wines: Clonakilla Shiraz, Cabernet-
Merlot
Notes: Dr John Kirk is a pioneer of the
Canberra District region, making his first
vintage there in 1976. He has also carried out
considerable local climatic research and feels
that the region has climatic similarities to
Bordeaux. Clonakilla has established an
excellent reputation for its reds. His Shiraz in
particular with a touch of viognier (a la Côte
Rotie) is quite impressive and different from
the usual run of Australian warm area Shiraz.
Cellar door sales: 7 days 11am–5pm except
Christmas Day and Good Friday.

Doonkuna Estate   R7

Barton Highway, Murrumbateman,
NSW 2582
Ph/Fax 02 6227 5085

Owners: Barry and Maureen Moran
Chief winemaker: Malcolm Burdett
Year of foundation: 1973
Tonnes crushed on average each year: 29
Location: Murrumbateman
Area: 3.4 ha
Soils: black humus on a clay base
Varieties planted: White—chardonnay, riesling,
sauvignon blanc; Red—cabernet sauvignon,
pinot noir, shiraz
Leading wines: Doonkuna Estate Riesling,
Chardonnay, Cabernet Sauvignon, Sauvignon
Blanc, Pinot Noir, Shiraz
Notes: Established in 1973, Doonkuna is one of
the veterans of the Canberra wine region. It is
a consistent medal winner at local wine shows.
Cellar door sales: Sun–Thurs noon–4pm.

Helm's Wines   R7

Butts Road, Murrumbateman, NSW 2582
Ph/Fax 02 6227 5953

Owners: Ken and Judith Helm
Chief winemaker: Ken Helm (consultant Gerry
Sissingh)
Year of foundation: 1973
Tonnes crushed on average each year: 100
Location: Murrumbateman
Area: 3 ha (contract growers are currently
developing a further 15 ha of vineyard, which
commenced bearing in 1998 vintage)
Soils: good alluvial soils varying to poor quartzy
hillside soils over white pipe-clay subsoil
Varieties planted: White—chardonnay,
muller-thurgau, riesling; Red—cabernet franc,
cabernet sauvignon, merlot
Leading wines: Helm Wines Cabernet Merlot,
Cabernet Sauvignon, Unoaked Chardonnay
Notes: A former CSIRO researcher, Ken Helm is
one of the pioneers of the Canberra region,
making his twenty-first vintage in 1997. Cellar
door sales: each day except Tuesdays and
Wednesdays, 11am–5pm.

Jeir Creek Winery   NR

Gooda Creek Road, Murrumbateman,
NSW 2582
Ph 02 6227 5999, Fax 02 6227 5900

Owners: Rob and Kay Howell
Chief winemaker: Rob Howell
Year of foundation: 1984
Tonnes crushed on average each year: 60,
increasing to 100 by the year 2000
Location: Murrumbateman
Area: 8.5 ha
Soils: quartz porphyry (decomposed granite)
based
Varieties planted: White—chardonnay, riesling,
sauvignon blanc; Red—cabernet sauvignon,
merlot, muscat de frontignan, pinot noir, shiraz
Leading wines: Jeir Creek Cabernet Merlot,
Sauvignon Blanc, Chardonnay, Riesling
Notes: A small- to medium-sized family-owned
winery. Cellar door sales: Fri–Sun and public
holidays 10am–5pm.

Lake George Winery **NR**

Federal Highway, Collector, NSW 2581
Ph/Fax 02 4848 0039

Owner/chief winemaker: Dr Edgar Riek OAM
Year of foundation: 1971
Tonnes crushed on average each year: 16,
about 9 of which are used for Lake George
Winery labels
Location: Lake George
Area: 3.5 ha
Soils: complex soils generally in three groups,
the dominant soil being a fan outwash from
the metamorphosis of the Cullarin escarpment,
the others being a shingle shoreline terrace of
the lake consisting of the same material and
finally a small area of sub-marginal swamp
behind the shoreline terraces. Dr Riek finds the
shingle especially interesting with regard to
pinot noir
Varieties planted: White—chardonnay, pinot
gris, semillon, viognier; Red—cabernet
sauvignon, merlot, pinot noir
Leading wines: Lake George Pinot Noir,
Chardonnay, Merlot, Sauternes, Sherries,
Muscat
Notes: Dr Edgar Riek is one of the pioneers of
viticulture in the Canberra District and was also
a moving spirit in the foundation of the
National Wine Show. The fortifieds made
originate from North East Victoria. No cellar
door sales.

Lark Hill Winery **R9**

RMB 281 Gundaroo Road, Bungendore,
NSW 2621
Ph/Fax 02 6238 1393

Owners: Dave and Sue Carpenter
Chief winemaker: Sue Carpenter
Year of foundation:1978
Tonnes crushed on average each year: 100
(including some contract winemaking)
Location: Bungendore
Area: 5 ha

Soils: poor shallow clayey soils over shale and
slate rock
Varieties planted: White—chardonnay, riesling,
sauvignon blanc; Red—cabernet sauvignon,
merlot, pinot noir
Leading wines: Lark Hill Chardonnay, Riesling,
Sauvignon Blanc-Semillon, Pinot Noir,
Cabernet-Merlot, Methode Champenoise
Notes: At 860 m in altitude, Lark Hill sits on a
cool hilltop north of Bungendore, exposed
somewhat to the elements. David Carpenter
believes that Lark Hill's own degree-day
summation is far cooler than most of the
region, which sits at between 500 and 600 m
in altitude. As a consequence, vintage is in
May for all varieties, except for the April
picking of pinot noir and chardonnay used for
sparkling wine base. Lark Hill has always made
excellent reds, especially Cabernet-Merlot, but
it was thought that the region was not
generally suited to pinot noir. Recently,
however, its 1996 Pinot Noir received a gold
medal at the 1997 Sydney Wine Show and
turned such conventional thought on its ear.
Cellar door sales: 7 days 10am–5pm.

Madew Wines **R6.5**

'Westering', Federal Highway, Lake
George, NSW 2581
Ph 02 4848 0026

Owners: David Madew Snr, David and Romilly
Madew
Chief winemaker: David Madew
Year of foundation: 1994
Tonnes crushed on average each year: 45 and
rising as new vines come into full bearing
Location: Lake George
Area: 8 ha
Soils: gravel wave banks of Lake George over
clay base and also black soil over clay
Varieties planted: White—chardonnay, pinot
gris, riesling; Red—cabernet sauvignon, merlot,
pinot noir, shiraz

Leading wines: Madew Riesling, Merlot, Shiraz-Cabernet, Pinot Noir
Notes: Formerly Westering vineyard, Madew was purchased by the Madew family about 4 years ago and is presently undergoing a period of rapid expansion. Benefitting from the warming influence of the nearby lake, it enjoys magnificent views across it to the distant hills beyond. David's Riesling is my pick of his wines. Cellar door sales: Thurs–Sun noon–6pm.

Murrumbateman Winery   NR

Barton Highway, Murrumbateman, NSW 2582 (3 km south of the village)
Ph 02 6227 5584, Fax 02 6227 5987

Owners: Michael Marriman, Reg Shaw, Bill Carson and Duncan Leslie
Chief winemaker: Duncan Leslie
Year of foundation: 1972
Tonnes crushed on average each year: 30
Location: Murrumbateman
Area: 2.52 ha
Soils: fine clay soils on a pipe-clay and granite base
Varieties planted: White—chardonnay, sauvignon blanc; Red—cabernet sauvignon, shiraz
Leading wines: Murrumbateman Winery Sauvignon Blanc, Cabernet-Merlot
Notes: This was one of the first Canberra region wineries to be established. A fully licensed restaurant is available. Cellar door sales: 10am–5pm daily.

Pankhurst Wines   R8

Old Woodgrove, Woodgrove Close, Hall, NSW 2618
Ph/Fax 02 6230 2592

Owners: Christine and Alan Pankhurst
Chief winemaker: Sue Carpenter (contract)
Year of foundation: 1986

Tonnes crushed on average each year: not disclosed, but estimated at 25
Location: Hall
Area: 2.8 ha
Soils: weathered granite soils of good depth, which retain moisture well
Varieties planted: White—chardonnay, sauvignon blanc, semillon; Red—cabernet sauvignon, merlot, pinot noir
Leading wines: Pankhurst Cabernet Merlot, Pinot Noir, Chardonnay
Notes: A very promising vineyard, which utilises only its own fruit for its wines. It has been a consistent winner of bronze medals at many wine shows, and there has been an encouraging number of silvers and a gold for Pinot Noir at Cowra in 1997. Cellar door sales by appointment.

Yass Valley Wines   NR

Crisps Lane, Murrumbateman, NSW 2582
Ph/Fax 02 6227 5592

Owners: Mick Withers and Anne Hillier
Chief winemaker: Mick Withers
Year of foundation: 1979
Tonnes crushed on average each year: 10
Location: Murrumbateman
Area: 1.8 ha
Soils: heavy clay loams with a thin sandy A horizon, tending to be boron-deficient, sometimes zinc-deficient and very acidic
Varieties planted: White—riesling, semillon, traminer, verdelho; Red—aleatico, barbera, merlot, shiraz
Leading wines: Yass Valley Riesling, Cabernet Sauvignon-Merlot, Traminer, Shiraz
Notes: This is a mature vineyard as regards its riesling and traminer plantings which were made in 1979. Cellar door sales: weekdays by appointment, weekends and public holidays 11am–5pm.

HILLTOPS REGION

The region was first settled in the 1820s after Hamilton Hume's exploration of the Yass district in 1821 had opened it up for squatting. However, as squatting was illegal until 1830, there are no records of settlements or settlers until that year. The first settlements within the region were near the present-day towns of Boorowa, Harden and Young. Its population was greatly increased in 1856 by a local epidemic of mid-nineteenth century gold fever, a contagion which in 1861 provoked the inter-racial riots between Chinese and European diggers at Lambing Flat (present-day Young). Inevitably the luckier diggers bought land within the region to graze sheep and cattle.

However, the age of closer settlement was at hand and the passing of the NSW Lands Act of 1861, which provided for smaller blocks, led to more intensive farming. The arrival of the railway in 1877 was also of great assistance to an area which was, by that time, primarily agricultural. By the 1890s, orcharding had commenced in the region and first-quality crops of apples, pears, quinces, grapes and cherries were consigned to the Sydney markets. Orcharding continued to expand after WWI and the region was still more closely settled by returning soldiers after the passing of the Soldier Settlement Acts. Today the Young area is still famous for its cherries.

The region dates its wine history from 1860 with the arrival at the 'Three Mile Rush' of Nichole Jasprizza, a Croatian from Dalmatia. Like the wisest of those who rushed to the goldfields, Jasprizza did not intend to mine but to supply the miners with food and beverages by growing fruit and vegetables and making wine. He settled on a property near Young known as Summer Hill. He evidently prospered, for 20 years later he sponsored the immigration of three of his nephews, Tony, Valdo and Andrew Cunich, who brought with them—as was the fashion of emigrants from winegrowing countries—vine cuttings. In this case, it was a muscat type, known as snowy muscat from Yanyana in Dalmatia. Grapes were planted in three locations, Jasprizza's Summer Hill property, opposite Summer Hill on the Old Monteagle Road and at Cherry Grove on the Boorowa Road near Young. Some of the original vines exist today. The orchard and vineyard plantings of Jasprizza and his nephews continued to expand until the early years of the twentieth century and reached 240 hectares in extent. Grapegrowing continued until the 1940s when it began to be unprofitable due to labour shortages and increasing costs. In 1960 the old vineyards, by that time neglected, were grubbed out and more profitable cherries and stone fruit planted in their place.

Yet vineyards did not depart the district for long. In 1969, Peter Robertson of 'Barwang', perhaps with the intention of 'diversifying'—a popular rural concept in those days—but probably inspired by the report of the late Graham Gregory recommending the region for viticulture—planted an eight-acre vineyard on his property, having propagated cuttings obtained from McWilliam's at Griffith. He chose cabernet sauvignon, shiraz, riesling and semillon. His intention was to sell the fruit to McWilliam's. But fate in an unusual form stepped in—the fruit fly. Robertson's first vintage, in 1974, coincided with an outbreak of fruit fly in the district and quarantine restrictions prevented its sale to Griffith. Nor was he any luckier in attempting to sell his fruit in the Hunter Valley. So in six weeks, he set up a winery

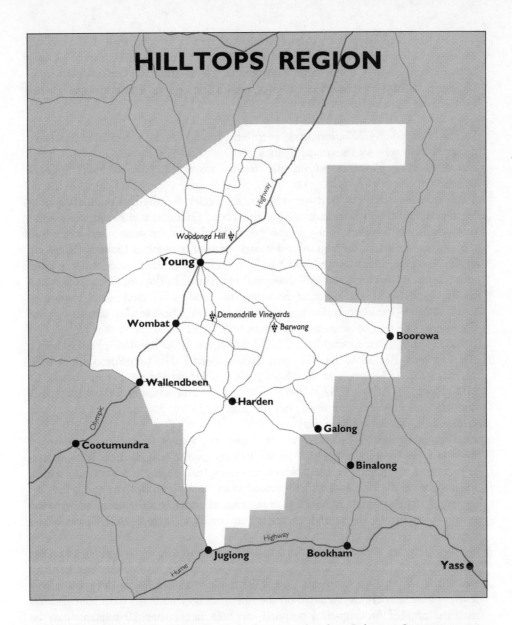

HILLTOPS REGION

and made his first vintage. Beginner's luck or not, his first Cabernet Sauvignon won a silver medal at the National Wine Show in Canberra. He continued winemaking at Barwang until 1988 when he sold the property to McWilliam's. Meanwhile, others had been following in Robertson's footsteps. In 1973, the Moppity Park vineyard was established, followed in 1979 by Hercynia Vineyard (now Demondrille Vineyards) and Nioka Ridge (since renamed Barwang Ridge). It was also about this time that Cartobe Vineyard (now called Castle's Creek) was planted. To complete the list, Woodonga Hill was established in 1986.

Though there have been grapes within the region for well over 100 years, its name is much more recent, being devised in 1983 by Andrew Birks, then a lecturer in wine science at Charles Sturt University. Today there are two wineries and 10 vineyards of more than 5 ha in area within the region. There are many more vineyards of less extent.

Location: latitude 34°20'S, longitude 148°18'E (Young), 34°34'S, 148°21'E (Harden), about 360 km west-south-west of Sydney

Elevation: most plantings within the region are within the altitude range of 450–600 m

Topography and soils: As its name suggests, the region is hilly and undulating. It is located around the formation known as the Young Granites, which run in a north–south direction between Young in the north, Harden in the centre and Jugiong in the extreme south of the region and stretch eastwards as far as Galong. There are small areas of Aeolian (wind-blown) soils around Young and Harden but the chief soils found in these areas are red duplex and red earths. In the east of the region and on its boundaries to the north of Boorowa are found rather sandy soils, formed by the Wyangala Granites found in this part of the region. These tend to salinity because they were once part of an ancient seashore.

Climate: Young (Post Office) MJT 22.6°C, MAR na, HDD raw 1847, MAR 15.9°C, AR 653 mm, RH 33%, AI 147 mm, SH na (local). Harden (Post Office) MJT 23.7°C, HDD 1931 (raw), MAR 15.6°C, AR na, RH na, AI na, SH na (local). Cf MJT 22.9°C, MAR na, HDD 1847, 1609 (cut-off and adjusted for latitude, daily temperature range and vine sites), AR 657 mm (Oct–Apr 359 mm), RH 33%, (3pm Jan), AI na, SH 9.6 (Gladstones).

Young's altitude is 440 m. The raw degree day figures (taken in the centre of town in a brick courtyard) almost certainly overstate the true position. Its vine sites are higher and therefore cooler. Notwithstanding this, Young is a very sunny area. In sunlight hours, Young with 2041 is second in New South Wales only to Griffith according to Gladstones. About 55% of the annual rainfall occurs during the growing season (Oct–April), the rainfall increasing in the more rugged easterly parts of the region.

Vineyards are commonly drip-irrigated from private dams or bores, but of course there are restrictions on the use of irrigation within the Murray–Darling basin of which the Hilltops Region forms part. Such restrictions confine water use to 1994 levels. These restrictions are based on the rules that no dam larger than 10 megalitres may be installed for irrigation purposes, no area larger than 10 hectares may be irrigated from such a dam, and dams may not be installed on a designated water course. What constitutes a designated water course is decided by officers of the NSW Land and Water Resources Department. Further, no new licences are presently being issued for the use of water from water courses. There have also been instances of restrictions on the use of bore water within the Lachlan River basin. The standard of bore water used for drip irrigation should also be checked regularly, but is usually of sound quality, especially if taken from higher areas.

Water apart, there are no real problems in the Hilltops Region except birds, which are effectively deterred by electronic means. Mildews and botrytis can be controlled by the usual spray methods and frost presents no difficulties if the vineyard sites have been chosen on slopes and ridges with good air drainage.

Harvest time: Chardonnay is harvested at the end of March and early April, riesling early April, and sauvignon blanc and semillon at the end of March. Pinot noir is picked at the end of March, shiraz and merlot mid-April, and cabernet sauvignon at the end of April.

Principal varieties: White—chardonnay, sauvignon blanc, semillon, traminer; Red—cabernet sauvignon, merlot, shiraz

Total area: na

Principal wine styles: It is really early days to determine the definitive wine styles of the Hilltops Region. The Cabernet Sauvignon and Shiraz reds of Barwang, which are full-bodied, moderately but not overtly fruity and well balanced by sufficient tannin and acid, are presently the benchmark reds of the region, which will become noteworthy for such reds in the future. Hilltops would also suit fortified wines, should these ever return to market favour, and perhaps also finer styles of sweet botrytised whites, though I doubt whether it will ever achieve the lusciousness of areas such as Griffith.

Barwang **R9**

Barwang Road, Barwang Via Harden
NSW 2587

Owner: McWilliam's Wines Pty Ltd
Chief winemaker: Jim Brayne
Year of foundation: 1969
Tonnes crushed on average each year: 800
Location: Barwang, Harden
Area: 100 ha
Varieties planted: White—chardonnay, riesling, sauvignon blanc, semillon; Red—cabernet sauvignon, merlot, pinot noir, shiraz
Leading wines: McWilliam's Barwang Chardonnay, Shiraz, Cabernet Sauvignon
Soils: decomposed reddish granite soils on a clay base
Notes: The first and biggest producer in the Region, Barwang was founded in 1969 by the late Peter Robertson who sold it in 1988 to McWilliam's. Its wines are typical of the firm but full-flavoured styles of the region and are produced expertly at Griffith by Jim Brayne. There is a winery on site, but it is used only for crushing purposes. There are no local cellar door sales.

Demondrille Vineyards **NR**

Prunevale Road, Prunevale via Harden
NSW 2587
Ph 02 6384 4272, Fax 02 6384 4292

Owners: Pam Gillespie and Robert Provan
Chief winemakers: Pam Gillespie, Gerry Sissingh (consultant), Kirsten Munro (contract)
Year of foundation: 1979
Tonnes crushed on average each year: 25
Location Prunevale
Area: 9.1 ha including 3.6 ha non-bearing
Soils: red sandy loam over clay aeolian
Varieties planted: White—chardonnay, riesling, sauvignon blanc, semillon, traminer; Red—cabernet sauvignon, merlot, pinot noir, shiraz
Leading wines: Demondrille Vineyards Tin Shed Riesling, Stan Dessert Wine (a blend of aleatico, traminer, frontignac, semillon), Purgatory (a pinot noir rose), The Dove Sauvignon Blanc-Semillon, The Raven Shiraz, Black Rose Cabernet-Merlot, Bloodline Pinot Noir
Notes: Demondrille has an eclectic selection of labels and wines, designed by Pam Gillespie not only to match food but to win trophies as

well. Such is the case with The Dove, which won a trophy for best Sauvignon Blanc-Semillon at the Canberra Regional Wine Show. Cellar door sales: weekends 10.30am–5pm or by appointment. Luncheon by appointment.

Woodonga Hill **NR**

Cowra Road, Young, NSW 2594
Ph/Fax 02 6382 2972

Owner: Woodonga Hill Pty Ltd
Chief winemaker: Jill Lindsay
Year of foundation: 1978
Tonnes crushed on average each year: 55
Location: Young

Area: 10 ha
Soils: Burrengong series 1,2,3 deep red soils with a clay base
Varieties planted: White—chardonnay, gewurztraminer, riesling, sauvignon blanc, semillon; Red—cabernet franc, cabernet sauvignon, gamay, meunier, shiraz, touriga
Leading wines: Woodonga Hill Riesling, Cabernet Sauvignon
Notes: Woodonga Hill shows regularly at local shows, particularly Canberra Regional, Cowra and Rutherglen. Its Cabernet and Shiraz Reds are consistent winners of silver and bronze awards. Cellar door sales: 7 days 9am–5pm.

TUMBARUMBA REGION (PROPOSED)

This proposed region is centred upon the Tumbarumba and Tooma districts of the western Snowy Mountains area of New South Wales. These areas, together with Batlow to the north, have historically been successful apple-growing locations.

Grape growing within the proposed region was pioneered by Frank Minutello and Ian Cowell some 15–20 years ago and today there are 28 vineyards in the region. In 1997, plantings of wine grape varieties extended over an area of 309 ha with chardonnay and pinot noir accounting for over three-quarters of the plantings. Details are as follows: chardonnay 154 ha, pinot noir 87 ha, cabernet sauvignon 25 ha, sauvignon blanc 14 ha, meunier 11.5 ha, shiraz 10.8 ha, merlot 5.85 ha and several other varieties ripening early to mid-season. Southcorp Wines is the dominant end user of the grapes produced chiefly for sparkling wine base and for early ripening table wines. Current labels utilising wines from the region are Hungerford Hill Tumbarumba Sauvignon Blanc and Tumbarumba Chardonnay, George Martin Pinot Noir and Black Range Sparkling. Climatic details are sparse but Tumbarumba is quite cool with a mean January temperature of 19°C. There is also one local cellar door outlet, Tumbarumba Cellars.

❦ NORTHERN RIVERS ZONE

This zone is constituted by the north coastal area of New South Wales, extending from the coast just to the north of Newcastle to the Queensland border, and westwards to the Great Divide. It is generally warm, wet and humid and because of these features, it is not particularly suited to viticulture. However, the wines of the proposed Hastings River wine region have been quite successful, especially the Chardonnays.

Raleigh Winery **NR**

Queen Street, Raleigh, NSW 2454
Ph 02 6655 4388

Owners: Neil and Lavinia Dingle
Chief winemaker: Lavinia Dingle (makes the wines at Cassegrain in Port Macquarie)
Year of foundation: 1982
Tonnes crushed on average each year: 9
Location: Raleigh
Area: 1.5 ha
Soils: the vineyard is situated on an alluvial flood plain, which is nevertheless quite well-drained

Varieties planted: White—gewurztraminer, riesling, semillon; Red—cabernet franc, pinot noir, shiraz
Leading wines: Raleigh Semillon-Chardonnay, Pinot Noir Rouge (a rose style), Shiraz-Merlot-Cabernet, Gewurztraminer-Riesling, Ruby Port
Notes: A small vineyard in what might be otherwise termed banana country. However the wines are shown regularly and have won three bronze medals at the Royal Hobart Show.
Cellar door sales: 7 days 10am–5pm, closed Christmas and Good Friday.

HASTINGS VALLEY REGION (PROPOSED)

Situated at the mouth of the Hastings River, the urban centre of the proposed region is Port Macquarie, which was established as a penal settlement in 1821. The area's first vines are believed to have been planted as early as 1837 by Henry Fancourt White, a Colonial Assistant Surveyor. From that time and until the 1890s, viticulture, probably using a mixture of vitis vinifera and hybrid varieties, prospered in the region and by 1890 there were 33 wineries and vineyards. Shortly thereafter, bank crashes shook all the colonial economies of eastern Australia, and the Hastings River wine industry wound down, to disappear entirely between the First and Second World Wars. A small number of vineyards, however, persisted until about 1950, their produce being used for fresh fruit and jam-making. The modern era of Hastings Valley winemaking began in 1980 when John Cassegrain planted his first vineyard.

Location: latitude 31°30'S, longitude 152°53'E, 400 km north north-east of Sydney
Elevation: most vineyards are situated within 15 km of the coast and planting elevations vary between 10 and 50 m in altitude

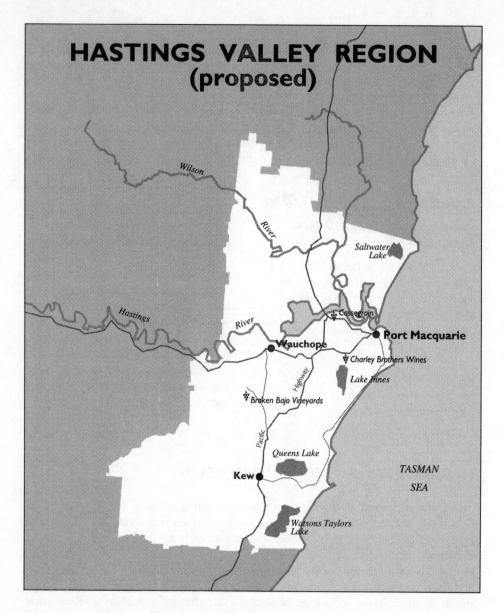

HASTINGS VALLEY REGION
(proposed)

Topography and soils: The region slopes gently upwards from the coast towards the west. Its soils vary from areas of deep red kraznozems and alluvial red soils to red podsolics on the tops of coastal ridges and yellow podsols at the bottom of such ridges. As the soil type changes, so do drainage capacities. The kraznozems and alluvial soils have excellent drainage, while the red podsols drain reasonably well. The poorest of all in drainage are the yellow podsols, which require careful attention in this respect.

Climate: Port Macquarie MJT 21.9°C, MAR 8.45°C, HDD (Sept–Feb raw) 1695, AR 1515 mm (Sept–Feb 740.3 mm), RH 77.8% (9am Jan). The Hastings Valley has a very warm and humid maritime climate. Even allowing for the fact that its vintage usually commences late in January and is complete about five weeks later, almost half of its annual rainfall occurs during the growing season. Prevailing breezes in summer are north-easterly, cooling the vineyards in the afternoon and evening but also increasing humidity. Due to the frequency of rain during the growing season, the vineyards within the region are generally not irrigated but strict attention therefore must be paid to anti-fungal sprays.

Harvest time: one of the earliest regions in Australia generally commencing vintage in late January and finishing in early March

Principal varieties: White—chardonnay (39.97 ha), semillon (22.91 ha), sauvignon blanc (7.34 ha), verdelho (5.73 ha); Red—chambourcin (51.94 ha), pinot noir (22.45 ha), cabernet sauvignon (18.28 ha), cabernet franc (14.9 ha), shiraz (12.9 ha), merlot (6.75 ha). It is to be noted that chambourcin is a vinifera hybrid, which shows great resistance to moulds.

Total area: (1998) bearing 210 ha, non-bearing 8.1 ha

Principal wine styles: Cassegrain is the largest winery in the region and by its recent show results must be judged the success of the region's wines. In its whites, Chardonnay has enjoyed reasonable success, mostly at a show standard of silver and bronze medals, but with the occasional gold, while Semillon has also won a modicum of similar medals. In the reds, Cabernet Merlot blends have performed almost as well as Chardonnay. Chambourcin and Shiraz also have won bronze awards. As a general rule the Region's reds are medium-bodied with good vinosity and style.

Broken Bago Vineyards NR

Bago Road, Wauchope, NSW 2446
Ph 02 6585 7128, Fax 02 6585 7099

Owners: Jim and Kay Mobbs
Chief winemaker: John Cassegrain (contract)
Year of foundation: 1985
Tonnes crushed on average each year: 100, about a quarter of which is used for Broken Bago labels
Location: Wauchope
Area: 14 ha
Soils: red alluvial soils from kraznozem, well structured and well drained, fertile and of 3 m in depth
Varieties planted: White—chardonnay, verdelho; Red—cabernet sauvignon, chambourcin, pinot noir

Leading wines: Broken Bago Chambourcin, Sparkling Chambourcin
Notes: A recent cellar door sales business (opened Jan 1996) specialising in the grape variety chambourcin, which tolerates the high humidity of the New South Wales North Coast. I have not tasted the wines. Cellar door sales: daily 11am–5pm.

Cassegrain R7.5

Pacific Highway, Port Macquarie, NSW 2444
Ph 02 6583 7777, Fax 02 6584 0354

Owners: John and Eva Cassegrain
Chief winemaker: John Cassegrain
Year of foundation: 1980
Tonnes crushed on average each year: 800, of

which about 550 are crushed for Cassegrain's own labels
Location: Port Macquarie
Area: 180 ha
Soils: kraznozems, red and yellow podsols
Varieties planted: White—chardonnay, colombard, gewurztraminer, sauvignon blanc, semillon, trebbiano, verdelho; Red—cabernet franc, cabernet sauvignon, chambourcin, malbec, merlot, pinot noir, shiraz
Leading wines: Cassegrain Semillon, Chardonnay, Chambourcin
Notes: Cassegrain is the region's largest grower and winery by far. Its founder, John Cassegrain, has been innovative in pioneering 'clos' farming, a French concept whereby many small adjoining yet separately-owned farms grow the same crop yet are managed and run as one large farm. Some of his vineyards are also bio-dynamic (organic) and have a grade A certification from the Bio-Dynamic Research Institute of Australia. In an often warm and humid coastal region, Cassegrain wines are of a consistent quality, regularly winning silver and bronze awards and more occasionally golds at capital city and regional wineshows. Cellar door sales: 7 days 9am–5pm. There is also a restaurant.

Charley Brothers Wines **NR**
The Ruins Way, Port Macquarie, NSW 2444
Ph 02 6581 1332, Fax 02 6581 0391

Owner: Charley Brothers Pty Ltd
Chief winemaker: John Cassegrain (contract)
Year of foundation: 1988
Tonnes crushed on average each year: 50, about 20 of which are used for Charley Brothers' labels
Location: Port Macquarie
Area: 10.5 ha
Soils: kraznozems, well-drained deep red-brown friable clay loam and yellow grey podsolics
Varieties planted: White—chardonnay, semillon; Red—cabernet sauvignon, merlot, pinot noir, shiraz
Leading wines: Charley Brothers Shiraz, Chardonnay, Pinot Noir
Notes: Inneslake, the property on which the vineyard is situated, saw vines in the 1840s and other types of fruit in the years since. In 1988, Bob and Jim Charley, influenced by the Cassegrain family, decided to replant to vines. Though the wines are no longer shown, there were early successes in the form of bronze and silver medals at the Hunter Valley Wine Show in the early 1990s. I have not tasted the wines, but they are certain to be well made under John Cassegrain's direction. Cellar door sales: Mon–Fri 2.30pm–4.30pm, weekends and public holidays 10am–5pm.

❦ NORTHERN SLOPES ZONE

A large area stretching from the north of Central Ranges Wine Zone and the Hunter Valley Wine Zone to the Queensland border. Its south-eastern boundary is the escarpment of the Liverpool Ranges. Its western boundary is generally the Newell Highway, running as far north as the Queensland border at Goondiwindi and then along the border as far east as Kyogle. It includes all the New South Wales territory south of the Granite Belt in Queensland, which seems already to be overflowing with vines into the Tenterfield and Glen Innes areas of New South Wales. Perhaps in the future, a cross-border region may result. Other areas such as Armidale might well prove suitable as vineyard sites, but frosts may present ongoing problems.

Gilgai Wines NR

Tingha Road, Gilgai, NSW 2360
Ph 02 6723 1204, Fax 02 6722 2876

Owner/chief winemaker: Keith Whish
Year of foundation: 1968
Tonnes crushed on average each year: 20
(about 3 of which are used for Gilgai's own labels)
Location: Gilgai near Inverell
Area: 5.5 ha
Soils: old decomposed red laterite
Varieties planted: White—sauvignon blanc, semillon, riesling, trebbiano; Red—cabernet sauvignon, grenache, malbec, mataro, pinot noir, shiraz
Leading wines: Gilgai Shiraz-Malbec, Ports
Notes: An old established vineyard owned and run by Dr Keith Whish. Cellar door sales: Mon–Sat 10am–6pm, Sun 12 noon–6pm.

Tyrrells Vineyards (vineyard only)

Quirindi

Owner: Tyrrells Vineyards
Chief winemaker: Andrew Spinaze
Year of foundation: 1987
Tonnes crushed on average each year: not disclosed, but estimated at 200
Location: Quirindi
Area: 24.5 ha
Soils: red clay loam
Varieties planted: White—chardonnay; Red—cabernet sauvignon
Leading wines: Tyrrells Old Winery range
Notes: This vineyard is historic in that it was Tyrrells first purchase outside the Hunter Valley. Since then there have been several more. There are no local cellar door sales.

❦ WESTERN PLAINS ZONE

An extensive area of western and north-western New South Wales. The Forbes area is where three wine zones meet: Western Plains (to the north-west), Big Rivers (to the south-west) and Central Ranges (to the east). The Lachlan River west of Forbes forms the boundary between Big Rivers and Western Plains, while the Newell Highway and the Parkes–Cootamundra Railway Line the border between the Central Ranges and the other two. There are no wine regions within the Western Plains Zone.

Cubbaroo Cellars

Burren Junction Road, Wee Waa,
NSW 2388
Ph 02 6796 1741, Fax 02 6796 1751

Owner: Ron Radford
Chief winemaker: contract
Year of foundation: 1967
Tonnes crushed on average each year: 300
Location: Wee Waa
Area: 32 ha

Soils: alluvial loam
Varieties planted: White—none;
Red—cabernet sauvignon, shiraz
Leading wines: Cubbaroo Cellars Shiraz, Cabernet Sauvignon, Port
Notes: A long established vineyard near Wee Waa which has in the past won awards for its reds at capital city wineshows and plans to show again. Cellar door sales: 7 days 10am–10pm.

PART VI

QUEENSLAND AND
NORTHERN TERRITORY

QUEENSLAND AND NORTHERN TERRITORY WINE ZONES

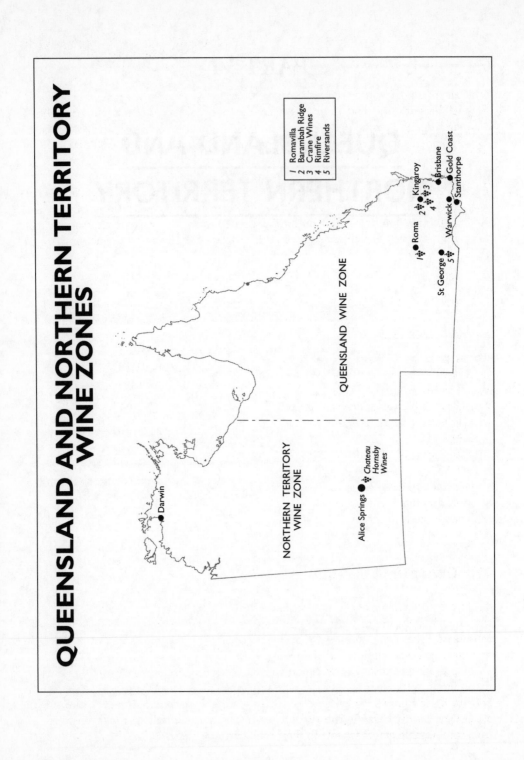

1 Romavilla
2 Barambah Ridge
3 Crane Wines
4 Rimfire
5 Riversands

QUEENSLAND WINE ZONE

Kingaroy
Brisbane
Gold Coast
Stanthorpe
Roma
Warwick
St George

NORTHERN TERRITORY WINE ZONE

Chateau Hornsby Wines
Alice Springs

Darwin

It is fair to say that Queenland's wine history began when a 23-year-old Cornishman, Samuel Bassett, who had during his peregrinations worked for his uncle at East Maitland in the Hunter Valley, planted a few hundred vines near Roma in central Queensland in 1863. From this small beginning in a most unlikely and arid spot, Bassett's venture thrived. By 1900, Romavilla, as the estate was called, extended to 180 hectares. Most of the wine was fortified and this favoured contemporary market trends, although white and red table wines appear to have been offered and irrigation was introduced. Bassett even sent his son William to learn winemaking from Leo Buring. Bassett family ownership continued until 1973, the wine styles remaining largely unchanged. The winery still exists today, though production is much smaller.

Romavilla

Northern Road, Roma, Qld 4455
(just north of the town)
Ph/Fax 07 4622 1822

Owners: David and Joy Wall
Chief winemakers: David and Richard Wall
Year of foundation: 1863
Tonnes crushed on average each year: 20
Location: Roma, Central Queensland
Area: 8 ha
Soils: sandy loams on the edge of the flood plain of the Bungil Creek
Varieties planted: White—chenin blanc, crouchen, muscat blanc, riesling, syrian; Red—muscat hamburg, shiraz

Leading wines: (table wines) Romavilla Chenin Blanc, Riesling-Muscat Blanc, Shiraz; (fortifieds) Romavilla Madeira, Very Old Liqueur Muscat, Very Old Tawny Port, Amontillado Sherry
Notes: The oldest winery in Queensland and, in about 1890, one of Australia's largest vineyards. Wisely, it still concentrates on the wine styles it has known for the last 130 years, fortifieds, which entirely suit the area's hot climate and consistently win silver and bronze awards at Queensland and other regional shows. Cellar door sales: weekdays 8am–5pm, Sat 9am–12noon and 2pm–4pm, closed Sundays.

THE GRANITE BELT AREA

There are no wine regions in Queensland—yet! The first is not far off and it will be the Granite Belt, high in the Great Divide and centred around Stanthorpe in the south-east. Like many other vine sites in Australia, it began as an area of orchards and table grapes, established in the main by Italian migrants and their descendants.

A possible precursor of the area's wine industry was the involvement of a local parish priest of Italian origin, Fr David, who planted a few vines in the late 1870s and possibly made his own wine for sacramental use. It is more certain, however, that the area's wine history began in the 1920s when local farmers of Italian origin made wine from surplus table grapes for sale to their cane-cutting compatriots in the north.

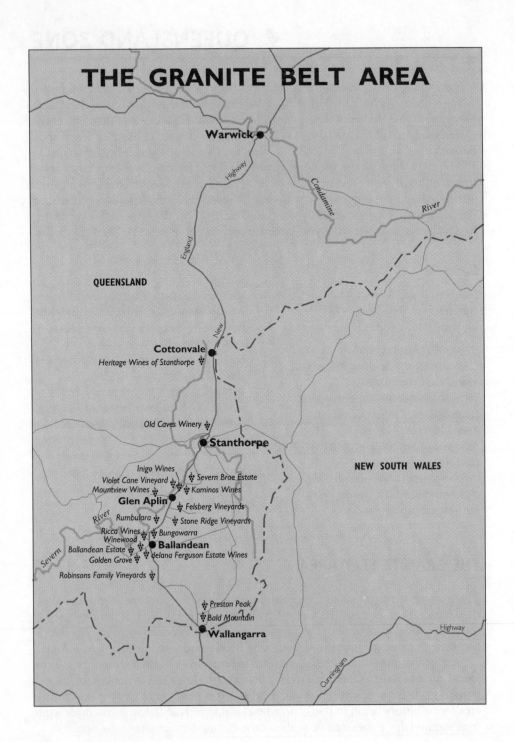

THE GRANITE BELT AREA

Warwick

Highway

Condamine

River

England

QUEENSLAND

New

Cottonvale
Heritage Wines of Stanthorpe

Old Caves Winery

Stanthorpe

NEW SOUTH WALES

Inigo Wines
Violet Cane Vineyard
Mountview Wines   *Severn Brae Estate*
                                 Kominos Wines
Glen Aplin
                    Felsberg Vineyards
River   *Rumbulara*
                    Stone Ridge Vineyards
Ricca Wines   *Bungawarra*
Winewood
Severn   *Ballandean Estate*   **Ballandean**
         Golden Grove   *delana Ferguson Estate Wines*

Robinsons Family Vineyards

                    Preston Peak
                    Bald Mountain
Wallangarra

Cunningham

Highway

So for nearly 40 years Stanthorpe winemaking remained wedded to the table grape until, in the mid-1960s, the increasing enthusiasm for red wine throughout Australia heightened local interest. In 1965, the modern wine history of the Granite Belt commenced when the first hectare of shiraz was planted by the Ricca Family. In 1969, Toowoomba solicitor John Robinson and his wife Heather began to establish the Robinson Family Vineyard, followed in 1970 by Angelo Puglisi at Sundown Valley Vineyards (later to become Ballandean Estate) where in 1974 Angelo made the first 'winegrape' wine of the district, a Shiraz. A spate of vineyards, wineries and replantings followed in the 1970s. Biltmore Cellars (later to be called Mount Magnus), the largest of the table grape wineries, was replanted partially with winegrapes in 1972. Rumbalara was begun in 1974. Bungawarra (originally a 'table grape' winery established in the 1920s) was refurbished and converted to wine grapes about the same time. Komino's was founded in 1976 and Winewood in 1979. Vineyard development continued in the 1980s with Stone Ridge in 1981 and Bald Mountain in 1987.

Today, most wine varieties are grown in the Granite Belt, though wine continues to be made from table grapes chiefly for bulk sale to local markets.

Location: Stanthorpe, latitude 28°40', longitude 151°56'E, about 185 km south-west of Brisbane on the NSW border
Altitude: Stanthorpe 810 m with vineyards between 750 and 900 m
Topography and soils: A mountainous and undulating terrain, befitting one of the higher parts of the Great Divide, stretching in a generally south-westerly direction from Applethorpe through Stanthorpe to Ballandean and then south-easterly to Wallangarra on the NSW border. Similar undulating country, soils and climate extend to Tenterfield, a few kilometres inside NSW, so any future region should encompass this area also. Its main soils are almost uniform throughout the district and, as the area's name suggests, consist of decomposed granite. They are well-drained and easily cultivated. Northcote describes them as 'Uc2.21 (bleached sands)' and 'Dy 5.41 (sandy mottled yellow duplex)', whose moisture-retention may be satisfactory for vineyards if they are reasonably shallow and found above a clayey subsolum. If they are deep, their free-draining attributes can lead to vine stress in times of drought. They usually tend to be acid. The Dy5 soils are often lacking in the nutrient elements phosphorus and nitrogen, while Uc2 soils are deficient in phosphorus, very low in potassium and calcium and low in nitrogen.
Climate: MJT 20.5, MAR 13.1°C, HDD raw 1703, AR 795 mm (Oct–Mar 503 mm), RH 69% (9am Jan), AI 9 mm, SH 8.1 (Dry & Smart), MJT 21.6 (G), HDD raw 1887 1670 (cut off and adjusted for latitude and daily temperature range but not for vine sites), AR 760 mm (Oct–April 519 mm), RH 49% (3pm Jan), AI na, SH 8.4 (Gladstones). The Granite Belt is an area of high elevation, but unlike other Australian areas of like altitudes, is obviously quite warm and wet during the growing season, as 68% of its rain falls at that time. This, of course, increases relative humidity and reduces drought stress but increases the risk of mildews and rots. The differences between the MJTs quoted by Gladstones and Dry & Smart can only be explained because of different weather stations, the degree days only being similar because of

Gladstones' cut-off at 19°C. Without this, Stanthorpe has a considerably warmer HDD of 1872.

The area is frost-prone in certain parts during the growing season—one winegrower reporting 40 instances of temperatures between -1° and -12°C during one growing season—and it is subsequently necessary to install spray irrigation to combat frosts and, further, to resort to late pruning during October as another preventative measure. Careful site selection is therefore necessary. Birds may also be a problem in some years, but not if native flowering trees are available before the grapes are ripe.

Principal varieties: White—chardonnay, semillon; Red—cabernet sauvignon, merlot, shiraz

Harvest time: chardonnay late February, semillon mid-March, shiraz mid-March, cabernet sauvignon late March

Principal wine styles: In red styles, the area seems to favour varieties with softer, less tannic palates. Shiraz is arguably the leading variety of the area, although merlot also shows promise. In whites, semillon can present problems in wet vintages due to bunch rot.

Total area: c200 ha.

Bald Mountain R7.5

Cnr Old Wallangarra Road and Hickling Lane, Wallangarra, Qld 4383
Ph 07 4684 3186, Fax 07 4684 3433

Owners: Denis and Jackie Parsons
Chief winemaker: Simon Gilbert (contract)
Year of foundation: 1985
Tonnes crushed on average each year: 70
Location: Wallangarra
Area: 7 ha
Soils: granite-derived gravel about 3 m deep, free-draining
Varieties planted: White—chardonnay, sauvignon blanc; Red—cabernet sauvignon, shiraz
Leading wines: Bald Mountain Shiraz-Cabernet, Shiraz
Notes: Bald Mountain was attacked by spring frosts in 1986 and 1987, but Denis Parsons persisted when others might have given the site up as unsuitable. He has not had a spring frost since. Whether this proves the efficacy of persistence or the infrequency of Bald Mountain frosts I don't know, but I do know that Bald Mountain has had an excellent wine show record in the past decade. The whites are good, but the reds in particular are of an excellent standard. Cellar door sales: 7 days 10am–5pm.

Ballandean Estate R7

Sundown Road, Ballandean, Qld 4382
Ph 07 4684 1226, Fax 07 4684 1288

Owners: Angelo and Mary Puglisi
Chief winemakers: Mark Ravenscroft and Angelo Puglisi
Year of foundation: 1970
Tonnes crushed on average each year: 275, about 200 of which are used for Ballandean's own labels
Location: Ballandean
Area: 30 ha
Soils: shallow decomposed granite, not fertile and in need of careful management
Varieties planted: White—chardonnay, sauvignon blanc, semillon, sylvaner, white muscat; Red—cabernet sauvignon, malbec, merlot, shiraz
Leading wines: Ballandean Estate Shiraz,

Semillon, Sylvaner (a late harvest dessert style)
Notes: Angelo Puglisi made the region's first
winegrape red in 1974 and both he and the
region have come a long way since, so far in
fact that Ballandean was most successful
exhibitor in the 1997 National Small
Winemakers Show. Wine quality is consistently
good. Cellar door sales: 7 days 9am–5pm.

Bungawarra NR

Bents Road, Ballandean, Qld 4382
Ph/Fax 07 4684 1128

Owner: Jeff Harden
Chief winemaker: Bruce Humphery-Smith
(contract)
Year of foundation: 1973
Tonnes crushed on average each year: 20
Location: Ballandean
Area: 5.5 ha
Soils: a heavy sandy granitic loam, deep and
well-drained
Varieties planted: White—chardonnay,
gewurztraminer, semillon; Red—cabernet
sauvignon, malbec, muscat hamburgh, shiraz
Leading wines: Bungawarra Foundation
(unwooded) Chardonnay, Paragon (a shiraz
cabernet blend), Traminer, Liqueur Muscat
Notes: A vineyard which is now mature on
typical Ballandean crushed granite soils. Cellar
door sales: 7 days 10.30am–4.30pm.

denlana Ferguson Estate Wines NR

Sundown Road, Ballandean, Qld 4382
Ph 07 4684 1263

Owner/chief winemaker: Dennis Ferguson
Year of foundation: 1995
Tonnes crushed on average each year: 8
Location: Ballandean
Area: 1.4 ha
Soils: granite based soils
Varieties planted: White—chardonnay;
Red—cabernet sauvignon, shiraz

Leading wines: denlana Unwooded
Chardonnay, Cabernet Sauvignon
Notes: Dennis Ferguson has achieved a lot in a
short time, winning two major Queensland
awards for successive Cabernet Sauvignons.
Cellar door sales: 10am–5pm daily, except
Wednesday.

Felsberg Vineyards NR

Townsends Road, Glen Aplin, Qld 4381
Ph 07 4683 4332, Fax 07 4683 4377

Owner/chief winemaker: Otto Haag
Year of foundation: 1983
Tonnes crushed on average each year: 30
Location: Glen Aplin
Area: 8 ha (1 ha coming into bearing)
Soils: granitic, sandy loams free-draining but
slightly acidic
Varieties planted: White—chardonnay,
gewurztraminer, riesling; Red—cabernet
sauvignon, merlot, shiraz
Leading wines: Felsberg Cabernet Sauvignon,
Merlot, Chardonnay
Notes: Felsberg has only shown its wines in the
last five years but has achieved satisfactory
silvers and bronzes at wineshows such as the
National Small Winemakers at Stanthorpe and
Cowra. Cellar door sales: 7 days 9am–5pm.

Golden Grove NR

Sundown Road, Ballandean, Qld 4382
Ph 07 4684 1291, Fax 07 4684 1247

Owners: Sam and Grace Costanzo
Chief winemaker: Sam Costanzo and
consultants
Year of foundation: 1958
Tonnes crushed on average each year: 60, and
growing
Location: Ballandean
Area: 8 ha, not all bearing
Soils: decomposed granite and traprock loam,
drip irrigation from Accommodation Creek
Varieties planted: White—chardonnay,

sauvignon blanc, semillon, white muscat;
Red—cabernet sauvignon, merlot, muscat
hamburgh, shiraz
Leading wines: Golden Grove Estate Shiraz,
'Muscadeen' (a locally popular white made
from white muscat grown at Ballandean)
Notes: Golden Grove Estate tells a typical
Ballandean story. A family orchard and table
grape vineyard established over 50 years ago
which has gradually changed to wine grapes.
The only table grapes still grown are muscat
hamburgh and white muscat and both, when
vinified, have a popular local appeal. Cellar
door sales: 7 days 8am–6pm.

Heritage Wines of Stanthorpe NR

Granite Belt Drive, formerly New
England Highway, Cottonvale, Qld 4375
Ph 07 4685 2197, Fax 07 4685 2112

Owners: Bryce and Paddy Kassulke
Chief winemaker: Jim Barnes
Year of foundation: 1992
Tonnes crushed on average each year: 50
Location: Cottonvale
Area: 4 ha, but growing to 12 ha by 2000
Soils: decomposed granite
Varieties planted: White—chardonnay,
sauvignon blanc; Red—cabernet sauvignon,
merlot, shiraz
Leading wines: Heritage Wines of Stanthorpe
Chardonnay, Shiraz
Notes: Heritage has only recently been showing
its wines but its reds have performed creditably
winning silvers and bronzes. Cellar door sales:
7 days 9am–5pm; there are barbecue facilities.

Inigo Wines NR

Lot 2 New England Highway,
Glen Aplin, Qld 4380
Ph 07 4683 4382, Fax 07 4683 4208

Owner: Dr Janis Carter
Chief winemaker: Bernard Carter
Year of foundation: 1994

Tonnes crushed on average each year: 2
tonnes anticipated for 1998, but will increase
substantially when all vineyard is planted and
in bearing
Location: Glen Aplin
Area: 9 ha in all consisting of two vineyards,
4ha owned by Bernard Carter and 5 ha by
Janis
Soils: granite loam
Varieties planted: White—chardonnay, riesling,
sauvignon blanc, semillon, verdelho;
Red—barbera, cabernet sauvignon, malbec,
merlot, pinot noir, shiraz, zinfandel
Leading wine: Inigo Merlot
Notes: A new involvement for Dr Janis Carter
and her husband, Bernard, who hope to
produce 100 tonnes when the vineyards come
into full bearing. I have not tasted the wine.
No cellar door sales yet.

Kominos Wines R7

New England Highway Severnlea,
Qld 4352
Ph 07 4683 4311, Fax 07 4683 4291

Owners: Tony, Stephen and Penelope Comino
Chief winemaker: Tony Comino
Year of foundation: 1976
Tonnes crushed on average each year: 75
Location: Severnlea
Area: 12 ha (including 4 ha of new plantings)
Soils: shallow granite soils
Varieties planted: White—chardonnay, chenin
blanc, riesling, sauvignon blanc, semillon;
Red—cabernet franc, cabernet sauvignon,
merlot, shiraz
Leading wines: Kominos Shiraz, Cabernet
Sauvignon, Chardonnay
Notes: A consistent medal winner in interstate
wine shows. At last count, Tony Comino
reckoned 85 medals in 10 years. Wine quality
is high. Cellar door sales: 7 days 9am–5pm.

Mountview Wines NR

Mount Stirling Road, Glen Aplin,
Qld 4381
Ph 07 4683 4316, Fax 07 4683 4111

Owners: David and Linda Price
Chief winemaker: David Price
Year of foundation: 1990
Tonnes crushed on average each year: 20
Location: Glen Aplin
Area: 2 ha
Soils: crushed granite
Varieties planted: White—chardonnay,
sauvignon blanc, semillon; Red—cabernet
sauvignon, merlot, shiraz
Leading wines: Mountview Shiraz, Cabernet-
Merlot, Cerise (a sweet red)
Notes: Both red wines are consistent award
winners, the Mountview Shiraz gaining the title
of Best Queensland Red at the Sheraton
Brisbane *Courier Mail* Queensland Wine
Awards for the years 1994–96. Cellar door
sales: Sat–Wed 9am–5pm, except Sun
10am-4pm, open public and school holidays.

Old Caves Winery NR

New England Highway, Stanthorpe,
Qld 4380
Ph 07 4681 1494, Fax 07 4681 2722

Owners: David and Shirley Zanatta
Chief winemaker: David Zanatta
Year of foundation: 1980
Tonnes crushed on average each year: 25
Location: Stanthorpe
Area: 2ha not yet in bearing, currently fruit is
purchased from growers
Soils: sandy decomposed granite on clay
Varieties planted: White—chardonnay,
sauvignon blanc; Red—cabernet sauvignon,
shiraz
Leading wines: Old Caves Classic White
(a semillon sauvignon blanc blend), Shiraz,
Tawny Port
Notes: A small winery and tourist oriented

business owned by the Zanatta family, who are
delighted by the silver medal for Classic White
won at the National Small Winemakers Show
in 1997. Cellar door sales: 7 days 10am–5pm.
There is also a cafe open at weekends and
functions are catered for by arrangement.

Preston Peak NR

Old Wallangarra Road, Wyberba,
Wallangarra, Qld 4383
Ph 07 4684 3480, Fax 07 4684 3154

Owners: Ashley Smith and Kym Thumpkin
Chief winemaker: Philippa Hambleton
Year of foundation: 1994
Tonnes crushed on average each year: 45, but
will increase to 120 as new plantings come
into bearing
Locations: Wyberba (Granite Belt) and Preston
(near Toowoomba)
Area: 7 ha (Preston 1.3 ha and Wyberba
5.7 ha)
Soils: At 860 m in altitude, the Wyberba
vineyard has typical free-draining granite-
derived soils.The Preston vineyard is terraced
on a steep rocky east-facing slope and lower in
altitude at 640 m.
Varieties planted: White—chardonnay,
sauvignon blanc, viognier, white muscat; Red—
cabernet sauvignon, merlot, nebbiolo, shiraz
Leading wines: Preston Peak Code Flag White
(a blend of sauvignon blanc, chardonnay and
semillon), Shiraz
Notes: Ashley Smith is pleased with his reds
and has grafted some established semillon to
cabernet. He is pleased with his show results
also, having won several capital city show
medals for his Shiraz. Cellar door sales:
Saturday 9am–4pm, Sunday (long weekends
only) same times.

Ricca Wines NR

Ricca Road, Ballandean, Qld 4382
Ph 07 4684 1235, Fax 07 4681 3883

Owner/chief winemaker: Joe Ricca
Year of foundation: 1960
Tonnes crushed on average each year: 36
Location: Ballandean
Area: 8 ha
Soils: decomposed granite loam, well-drained, varying into dark loam
Varieties planted: White—italia, riesling, semillon, sultana, waltham cross, white muscat; Red—cabernet sauvignon, muscat hamburgh, purple cornichon, shiraz
Leading wines: bulk wines sold to a local clientele. As Joe Ricca says, he is just about the last seller of bulk wines in Queensland.
Notes: Joe Ricca carries on a Granite Belt tradition of using table grapes for winemaking. Both table grapes and wine grapes are used and blended into styles which have a local popularity. Cellar door sales: 8.30am–5pm.

Robinsons Family Vineyards R7.5

Curtin Road, Lyra, Ballandean, Qld 4382
Ph 07 4684 1216, Fax 07 4639 2718

Owners: John and Heather Robinson
Chief winemaker: Rod MacPherson
Year of foundation: 1969
Tonnes crushed on average each year: 50
Location: Ballandean
Area: 14 ha (there are two separate vineyards, Lyra and Ballandean)
Soils: infertile,shallow duplex soils, granite derived sandy loams
Varieties planted: White—chardonnay, gewurztraminer, sauvignon blanc, semillon; Red—cabernet sauvignon, merlot, pinot noir, shiraz
Leading wines: Robinson Family Vineyards Shiraz, Vintage Brut
Notes: While his vineyards are not generous bearers, John Robinson believes quality makes up for quantity and that the shallow duplex granite derived soils and a hillside site are important factors in shiraz quality in Ballandean. He is very pleased also with

his Vintage Brut. Cellar door sales: 7 days 9am–5pm.

Rumbulara NR

Fletcher Road, Fletcher, Qld 4381
Ph 07 4684 1206, Fax 07 4683 4335

Owner: Rumbulara Vineyards Pty Ltd
Chief winemaker: Robert Gray
Year of foundation: 1974
Tonnes crushed on average each year: 50
Location: Fletcher
Area: 8 ha
Soils: decomposed granite soils
Varieties planted: White—riesling, semillon; Red—cabernet sauvignon, merlot muscat, pinot noir, shiraz
Leading wines: Rumbulara Vineyards Semillon, Cabernet Sauvignon, Liqueur Muscat
Notes: At the time of writing this property was for sale and I have not recently tasted the wines. Cellar door sales: 7 days 9am–5pm.

Severn Brae Estate NR

Lot 2 Back Creek Road, Severnlea, Qld 4352
Ph 07 4683 5292, Fax 07 3391 3821

Owner/chief winemaker: Bruce Humphery-Smith
Year of foundation: 1987
Tonnes crushed on average each year: 8
Location: Severnlea
Area: 6 ha, three of which are not yet bearing
Soils: coarse particled granite with a pan-layer at 1.5 m
Varieties planted: White—chardonnay; Red—merlot, sangiovese, shiraz
Leading wines: Severn Brae Chardonnay, Shiraz
Notes: Severn Brae Shiraz has proved its mettle at recent Sheraton Brisbane Courier Mail Wine Awards, winning the award for best Queensland Red in 1996 and 1997. Cellar door sales: 10am–5pm weekends and public holidays.

Stone Ridge Vineyards **R7.5**
Limberlost Road, Glen Aplin, Qld 4381
Ph 07 4683 4211, Fax 07 4681 3445

Owners: Jim Lawrie and Anne Kennedy
Chief winemaker: Jim Lawrie
Year of foundation: 1981
Tonnes crushed on average each year: 20
Location: Glen Aplin
Area: 2 ha
Soils: decomposed granite, free-draining
Varieties planted: White—chardonnay,
semillon; Red—cabernet franc, cabernet
sauvignon, malbec, merlot, petit verdot, shiraz
Leading wines: Stone Ridge Shiraz,
Chardonnay, Malbec
Notes: Jim Lawrie has built up a solid
reputation for his reds, especially his Shiraz. His
Chardonnay is good, too, as is his Malbec,
which these days has the benefit of the other
'Bordeaux' varieties listed above. Cellar door
sales: 7 days 10am–5pm.

Violet Cane Vineyard **NR**
13 Wallace Court, Glen Aplin,
Qld 4381
Ph/Fax 07 4683 4251

Owners: Adam Chapman and Greg Anderson
Chief winemaker: Adam Chapman
Year of foundation: 1994
Tonnes crushed on average each year: 2
Location: Glen Aplin
Area: 0.8 ha
Soils: decomposed granite soil over a clay
subsoil

Varieties planted: White—viognier;
Red—merlot
Leading wines: Violet Cane Merlot
Notes: Adam Chapman is a busy winemaker
now working in the Burnett Valley. Violet Cane
Vineyard is tiny, but certainly not a hobby.
Cellar door sales: Fri–Sun 9am–4pm.

Winewood **NR**
Sundown Road, Ballandean,
Qld 4382
Ph/Fax 07 4684 1187

Owners: Ian and Jeanette Davis
Chief winemaker: Ian Davis
Year of foundation: 1985
Tonnes crushed on average each year: 15
Location: Ballandean
Area: 5 ha, including 2 ha of new plantings
Soils: sandy granite soils, typically free-draining
but varying in depth
Varieties planted: White—chardonnay,
marsanne; Red—cabernet franc, cabernet
sauvignon, merlot, shiraz
Leading wines: Winewood Marsanne,
Chardonnay-Marsanne, Mackenzies Run
(a blend of the cabernets and merlot),
Shiraz-Marsanne
Notes: Ian Davis is pleased with his reds and is
moving to add more Rhone varieties, such as
grenache, to his vineyard. It is interesting to
note his blending of shiraz and marsanne.
Cellar door sales: 9am–5pm weekends and
school holidays.

BURNETT VALLEY

North of Toowoomba and about 2½ hours' drive north-west of Brisbane at an altitude
of 400–500 metres is the Burnett Valley. Its urban centre is Kingaroy, famous for its
peanuts. As a winegrowing area, the Burnett Valley is very much at the experimental
stage and seems likely to be to be a warm, wet and humid site, especially during the

growing season. However, early vintages (there have been three) have been promising enough, with chardonnay showing its usual tolerance of virtually any conditions and shiraz also appearing to be quite at home there.

Barambah Ridge

79 Goschnicks Road, Redgate via Murgan, Qld 4605
Ph 07 4168 4766, Fax 07 4168 4770

Owner: South Burnett Wines Ltd
Chief winemaker: Bruce Humphery-Smith
Year of foundation: 1995
Tonnes crushed on average each year: 180, of which 150 are used for Burambah Ridge's own labels
Location: Redgate, Burnett Valley
Area: 6.85 ha
Soils: grey-brown loam over clay
Varieties planted: White—chardonnay, semillon; Red—cabernet sauvignon, shiraz
Leading wines: Barambah Ridge Chardonnay (unwooded)
Notes: The Burnett Valley has in a very short time become very significant in Queensland wine production terms and so far its 'oldest' producer has a very good record, its 1997 Unwooded Chardonnay winning the gold medal and Trophy for the Best Queensland White Wine at the *Courier Mail* Sheraton Queensland Wine awards in 1997. Cellar door sales: 7 days 10am–5pm.

Crane Wines

Kingaroy, Qld 4610 (about 10 km from town in the South Burnett Valley)
Ph/Fax 07 4162 7647

Owners: John and Sue Crane
Chief winemaker: John Crane
Year of foundation: 1992
Tonnes crushed on average each year: 5
Location: Kingaroy
Area: 3 ha
Soils: fertile free-draining red scrub soils over basalt
Varieties planted: White—chardonnay, riesling, sauvignon blanc, semillon; Red—cabernet sauvignon, merlot, pinot noir, shiraz
Leading wines: Crane's Shiraz, Semillon, Sauvignon Blanc
Notes: I have no knowledge of the wines. Cellar door sales: daily 9am–4pm, closed Wednesdays and Thursdays.

OTHER LOCALITIES

Rimfire

via Bismarck St, Maclagan, Qld 4352
Ph 07 4692 1129, Fax 07 4692 1260

Owners: Connellan family
Chief winemaker: Tony Connellan
Year of foundation: 1992
Tonnes crushed on average each year: 60
Location: Maclagan, Bunya Mountains, north of Toowoomba
Area: 8ha
Soils: brown basalt loam
Varieties planted: White—chardonnay, colombard, marsanne, taminga, verdelho; Red—cabernet franc, ruby cabernet, shiraz, tarrango

Leading wines: Rimfire Estate Chardonnay, Verdelho

Notes: Rimfire has been a very successful diversification for the Connellan Family. Show results to date have been impressive and include a gold medal for its Chardonnay and the Trophy as Champion Dry White Table Wine at the National Small Winemakers Show in Stanthorpe. Cellar door sales: 7 days 10am–5pm.

Riversands Vineyards NR

St George, Qld 4487
Ph 1800 357 622, 07 4625 3643,
Fax 07 4625 5043

Owners: Alison and David Blacket
Chief winemaker: Mark Ravenscroft
(Ballandean Estate, contract)

Year of foundation: 1990 (winegrapes)
Tonnes produced on average each year: 30, (for Riversands label purposes)
Location: St George, south-west Queensland
Area: 4 ha
Soils: sandy loam
Varieties planted: White—chardonnay, sauvignon blanc, semillon, white muscat; Red—merlot, shiraz
Leading wines: Riversands Sauvignon Blanc, Sweet Reds
Notes: Riversands is a mixed table grape and wine grape vineyard located in the hot dry south-western Queensland area. About one quarter of the vineyard is devoted to winegrapes. Cellar door sales: 7 days 8am–6pm.

❦ NORTHERN TERRITORY ZONE

The Northern Territory is an unlikely area for viticulture, being hot and arid in its southern parts, and hot and humid in its tropical north. However, wine is made, though whether winemaking will ever be more than a tourist diversion, is hard to say.

Chateau Hornsby Wines NR

Petrick Road, Alice Springs, NT 0870
(10 km south-east of the town)
Ph 08 8955 5133, Fax 08 8955 5532

Owner: Denis Hornsby
Chief winemaker: Gordon Cook
Year of foundation: 1974
Tonnes crushed on average each year: 15
Location: Alice Springs
Area: 3.5 ha
Soils: coarse red sand high in iron oxide and, Denis Hornsby adds, 'not much else'. Irrigation, which of course is necessary, comes from a bore 100 metres deep. The water is high in calcium and carbonates but 'is suitable for the job'.
Varieties planted: White—chardonnay, riesling, semillon; Red—cabernet sauvignon, shiraz
Leading wines: Chateau Hornsby Early Red (Shiraz), Shiraz
Notes: Australia's furthest winery from anywhere! Cellar door sales: 7 days 11am–4pm. There is also a restaurant.

✿ GLOSSARY

Baume (Be): a measure of sugar in grape juice, or unfermented sugar in fermenting musts or dessert or table wine

Biscay: a self-mulching, dark-coloured, cracking clay

Cytokinins: plant hormones formed in growing root tips. They ascend via the xylem system to upper plant parts and have two major functions: a) to promote cell multiplication in newly differentiating tissues; and b) to attract sugar and other nutrients to where they are in greatest concentration. Adequate cytokinins promote bud-burst, lateral branching, the development of leaves and fruiting structures and fruit-set. Cytokinin production and its transmission from the roots are encouraged by ample sunshine and leaf exposure and consequent ample sugar to the roots, as well as by a warm, well-aerated root environment.

Dr: red duplex (a soil classification)

Dy: yellow duplex (a soil classification)

Geographical Indication: the places of origin of Australian wine (i.e. the wine zones, regions and sub-regions)

Gibberellin: a plant hormone causing growth of its stem

Gout de Terroir: a French term meaning literally 'the taste of the earth'. The distinctive taste given to certain wines by the vineyard soils in which they are grown, for example, the characteristic flinty taste of French Chablis or older Hunter River Shiraz.

Hedging: the training of vines into a hedge by removing excessive foliage to aid aeration, sunlight penetration and ripening

Hotspots: areas of excessively hot fermentation within fermenting grape musts, especially applicable to pinot noir

Hundred: in South Australia, a part of a local government district, originally an administrative division of an English county, equivalent to a 'parish' in other Australian states

Leaf-plucking: the hand plucking of leaves from around bunches of grapes to aid ripening

Lyre: a trellising system shaped like a 'U' whereby vine-shoots are trained upwards between two pairs of foliage wires so that the fruiting zone of the vine is basal and the canopy walls are inclined slightly outwards

Must: the mixture of grape juice, skins and seeds that emerges from a grape crusher, which later becomes wine after fermentation

New World: winemaking countries outside Europe

Phylloxera: the vine louse, an aphid that eats the roots of vitis vinifera vines, ultimately causing their demise. It has proved resistant to all means of eradication and the only means of control is by replanting vitis vinifera cultivars on phylloxera-resistant root-stocks.

Pigeage: a French term describing the Burgundian practice of foot-stamping the must of pinor noir to even out its fermenting temperature by removing hot-spots. A practice now commonly used in the New World for the production of superior Pinot Noir.

Scott-Henry: a trellising system originally developed in Oregon, USA named after its developers and further refined by Dr Richard Smart. It utilises two fruiting wires, one at 1 metre in height and the other at 1.15 metres. The shoots on the upper wire are trained upwards between two pairs of foliage wires and those on the bottom wire downwards generally using one foliage wire.

Traditional expression: a term describing how or when the wine is made, for example, Botrytis, late harvest, bottle-fermented

Veraison: the change of colour of grapes as they ripen, especially noticeable in red varieties, but occurring equally in whites

Vertical shoot positioning (VSP): a trellising system designed to train shoots into a narrow vertical canopy, increasingly common in cooler vineyard areas of Australia

❦ BIBLIOGRAPHY

Busby, James *A Treatise on the Culture of the Vine*, R. Howe Government Printer, Sydney, 1825 (as reprinted by David Ell Press, Sydney, 1979)

Coombe, B and Dry, P (eds) *Viticulture* vol. 1, Winetitles, Adelaide, 1988

Dunstan, D *Better Than Pommard*, Australian Scholarly Publishing and Museum of Victoria, Melbourne, 1994

Gladstones, J *Viticulture and Environment*, Winetitles, Adelaide, 1992

Jacqueline, L and Poulain, R *Wines and Vineyards of France*, Paul Hamlyn, London, 1962

Niewwenhuis, J *A Preliminary Assessment of Soil Groups for Wine Grape Production in the Ovens Valley*, Wangaratta Regional Development Corp, 1993

Smart, RE and Dry, P *Viticulture* vol. 2, Winetitles, Adelaide, 1988

Ward, E *Vineyards of Victoria*, 1862 (reprinted by Sullivans Cove, nd)

❦ ACKNOWLEDGEMENTS

In the preparation of this book, I acknowledge and have been extremely grateful for the cooperation of the many vignerons and winemakers who have given unstintingly of their time to respond to my letters, faxes and phone queries concerning their vineyards, wineries and winemaking. However, I would especially like to thank Ernie Sullivan, the secretary of the Geographical Indications Committee, for his generous assistance concerning applications made for regional and sub-regional status.

✿ INDEX OF WINERIES, CELLAR-DOOR SALES FACILITIES AND VINEYARDS

❧ WINE TASTING NOTES

❦ WINE TASTING NOTES

❦ WINE TASTING NOTES

❦ WINE TASTING NOTES

❧ WINE TASTING NOTES

❦ WINE TASTING NOTES

❧ WINE TASTING NOTES

❧ WINE TASTING NOTES